SHAKESPEARE SURVEY

SHAKESPEARE SURVEY

AN ANNUAL SURVEY OF
SHAKESPEARE STUDIES AND PRODUCTION

59

Editing Shakespeare

EDITED BY

PETER HOLLAND

CAMBRIDGE
UNIVERSITY PRESS

CAMBRIDGE UNIVERSITY PRESS
Cambridge, New York, Melbourne, Madrid, Cape Town, Singapore, São Paulo

Cambridge University Press
The Edinburgh Building, Cambridge CB2 2RU, UK

Published in the United States of America by Cambridge University Press, New York

www.cambridge.org
Information on this title: www.cambridge.org/9780521868389

© Cambridge University Press 2006

First published 2006

Printed in the United Kingdom at the University Press, Cambridge

A catalogue record for this publication is available from the British Library

ISBN 13   978 0 521 86838 9 hardback
ISBN 10   0 521 86838 6 hardback

EDITOR'S NOTE

Volume 60, on 'Theatres for Shakespeare', will be at press by the time this volume appears. The theme of Volume 61 will be 'Shakespeare, Sound and Screen'.

Submissions should be addressed to the Editor at The Shakespeare Institute, Church Street, Stratford-upon-Avon, Warwickshire cv37 6hp, to arrive at the latest by 1 September 2007 for Volume 61. Pressures on space are heavy and priority is given to articles related to the theme of a particular volume. Please send a copy you do not wish to be returned. Submissions may also be made via e-mail attachment to pholland@nd.edu. All articles submitted are read by the Editor and at least one member of the Advisory Board, whose indispensable assistance the Editor gratefully acknowledges.

Unless otherwise indicated, Shakespeare quotations and references are keyed to *The Complete Works*, ed. Stanley Wells, Gary Taylor *et al.* (Oxford, 1986).

Review copies should be addressed to the Editor as above. In attempting to survey the ever-increasing bulk of Shakespeare publications our reviewers inevitably have to exercise some selection. We are pleased to receive offprints of articles which help to draw our reviewers' attention to relevant material.

P. D. H.

CONTRIBUTORS

CHRISTIE CARSON, *Royal Holloway, University of London*
BRANDON S. CENTERWALL, *University of Washington*
ALAN C. DESSEN, *University of North Carolina, Chapel Hill*
CARY DIPIETRO, *University of Toronto at Mississauga*
MICHAEL DOBSON, *Birkbeck, University of London*
BALZ ENGLER, *University of Basel*
LYNN FOREST-HILL, *University of Southampton*
SUZANNE GOSSETT, *Loyola University, Chicago*
RONALD GRAY, *Emmanuel College, University of Cambridge*
ANDREW GURR, *University of Reading*
JONATHAN HOLMES, *Royal Holloway, University of London*
MACDONALD P. JACKSON, *University of Auckland*
JOHN JOWETT, *The Shakespeare Institute, University of Birmingham*
BERNICE W. KLIMAN, *Nassau Community College, State University of New York*
TOM LOCKWOOD, *University of Birmingham*
RUTH MORSE, *Université Paris 7, Denis-Diderot*
JÚLIA PARAIZS, *Central European University, Budapest*
PATRICIA PARKER, *Stanford University*
EDWARD PECHTER, *Concordia University*
ERIC RASMUSSEN, *University of Nevada, Reno*
JEANNE ADDISON ROBERTS, *American University, Washington*
TOM ROONEY, *Central European University, Budapest*
ELIZABETH SCHAFER, *Royal Holloway, University of London*
JAMES SHAW, *The Shakespeare Institute, University of Birmingham*
EMMA SMITH, *Hertford College, University of Oxford*
MICHAEL TAYLOR, *University of New Brunswick*
RONALD A. TUMELSON II, *University of Alabama*
STANLEY WELLS, *The Shakespeare Birthplace Trust*

CONTENTS

CONTENTS

ILLUSTRATIONS

LIST OF ILLUSTRATIONS

EDITING SHAKESPEARE'S PLAYS IN THE TWENTIETH CENTURY

JOHN JOWETT

A BRIEF HISTORY

Shakespeare editing in the twentieth century involves a history of practice, and a history of ideas about the text. The present article will deal with each in turn, recognizing the problematic relation between them. Both were grounded in the work of the New Bibliography, a movement that would determine the direction of Shakespeare textual studies and editing for most of the century. As will become evident, the New Bibliography had lost much of its erstwhile prestige and authority by the end of the century, though the editorial methods it advocated had been subject to development rather than outright rejection. Its inheritance to the twenty-first century currently remains subject to negotiation.

A. W. Pollard's close intellectual companionship with W. W. Greg and R. B. McKerrow formed the first keystone to the movement.[1] Pollard's follower John Dover Wilson soon joined the three. The New Bibliography may be characterized by its mix of commitment to scientific rigour in investigating every aspect of a text's transmission and a sometimes credulous optimism in its project of finding the techniques to identify and eliminate the errors accrued through that process. From its beginnings as a small clique centred on Trinity College, Cambridge it expanded to establish an editorial orthodoxy and to place textual issues firmly on the curriculum for the study of Shakespeare. By the mid-century it had developed beyond its original concern with Shakespeare and early modern literature to offer a set of editorial principles that it aimed to apply to all canonical works.

Especially in the early years, the achievements of the New Bibliography were monumental. McKerrow's edition of Thomas Nashe, Pollard and G. R. Redgrave's *Short-Title Catalogue*, Greg's *Bibliography of the English Printed Drama*, his studies of the Stationers' Company and of dramatic manuscripts, his general editorship of the Malone Society Reprints series, and later Charlton Hinman's exhaustive study of the printing and proof-correcting of the 1623 First Folio, the Norton facsimile of the first Folio, Marvin Spevack's Concordance, and Peter Blayney's ground-breaking investigation of the printing of the First Quarto (Q1) of *King Lear* are only some of the more conspicuous examples.[2] All of these supplied material that provided

---

[1] F. P. Wilson, 'Sir Walter Wilson Greg', *Proceedings of the British Academy*, 45 (1959), 307–34.

[2] Thomas Nashe, *Works*, ed. Ronald B. McKerrow, 5 vols. (London, 1904–10); A. W. Pollard and G. R. Redgrave, *A Short-Title Catalogue of Books Printed in England, Scotland, and Ireland, and of English Books Printed Abroad, 1475–1640* (London, 1950); W. W. Greg, *A Bibliography of the English Printed Drama to the Restoration*, 4 vols. (London, 1939–59); Greg, *A Companion to Arber: Being a Calendar of Documents in Edward Arber's 'Transcript of the Registers of the Company of Stationers of London, 1554–1640', With Text and Calendar of Supplementary Documents* (Oxford, 1967); Greg, ed., *Dramatic Documents from the Elizabethan Playhouse: Stage Plots, Actors' Parts, Prompt Books*, 2 vols. (Oxford, 1931); Charlton Hinman, ed., *The First Folio of Shakespeare: The Norton Facsimile* (London, New York, Sydney, and Toronto, 1968); Marvin Spevack, *A Complete and Systematic Concordance to the Works of Shakespeare*, 9 vols.

foundations essential to the textual study of Shakespeare, establishing an invaluable if intimidating edifice of knowledge and resource to confront the aspiring editor.

In contrast, the difficulty in achieving a Shakespeare edition that would meet the criterion of scholarly rigour demanded by the New Bibliography may be measured by the slow progress in the first half of the century towards producing the flagship Oxford complete works. The edition was mooted as early as 1904 and set up under the editorship of R. B. McKerrow in 1929, who died in 1940 leaving the project substantially incomplete; limited further progress was made by his successor Alice Walker. Over the course of the century old-spelling editions of the works of Nashe, Ben Jonson, Thomas Dekker, Christopher Marlowe, Francis Beaumont and John Fletcher, George Chapman, and John Webster were all to appear, and some of these remain the standard editions today. But the *desideratum* of an old-spelling complete works of Shakespeare was realised only in the little-known and belated old-spelling version of an editorial project strongly associated with modernization, the revived Oxford Shakespeare of 1986.[3]

The Arden Shakespeare, initiated at the very end of the nineteenth century with the publication of Edward Dowden's 1899 edition of *Hamlet*, predated the New Bibliographers' turn to original spellings. The delays entailed in producing an edition of the complete works were avoided by this and other series that published one play per volume over a period of time. Arden volumes appeared regularly over thirty years, under the general editorship of W. J. Craig and, later, R. H. Case.[4] They provided generous commentaries written to meet the needs of the growing body of university and advanced school students.

The earliest major series properly initiated in the new century was the Cambridge University Press New Shakespeare, prepared under the editorship of John Dover Wilson and, in its early years, Arthur Quiller-Couch.[5] It followed the Arden model of adopting modern spelling. The first three volumes appeared in 1921. From the outset, the main burden

of the practical editing fell on the shoulders of Wilson, who undertook to apply the thinking of the New Bibliography to the text of Shakespeare. His *Manuscript of Shakespeare's 'Hamlet'* was perhaps the most influential and far-going attempt to study printed editions as indirect and imperfect evidence for the manuscript Shakespeare originally wrote.[6] As an editor, Wilson was inclined to push quasi-scientific speculation informed by inferences about palaeography to its limit, and so to establish a basis for freer emendation than was characteristic of the century's editorial work.

Another distinctive trait of the New Shakespeare was its presentation of stage directions. In the nineteenth century it had become common to find editorial additions to stage directions marked off in square brackets. Wilson turned the procedure on its head: rather than mark off editorial additions, he placed wording from the original texts in quotation marks. The effect was to create, amidst the rigours of New Bibliographical procedure, a place for substantial and significant editorial text in the stage directions that was not differentiated from the text of the quarto or Folio copy. Wilson's practice was to use this space very freely, writing stage directions that sometimes assumed the proscenium arch and sometimes adopted a style of depiction more appropriate to a novel: '*An open place in Rome, before the Capitol, beside the entrance to which there stands the monument of the Andronici. Through a window opening on to the balcony of an upper chamber in the Capitol may be seen the Senate in session.*'[7]

(Hildesheim, 1968–80); Peter W. M. Blayney, *The Texts of 'King Lear' and their Origins*, Vol. 1, *Nicholas Okes and the First Quarto* (Cambridge, 1982).

3 William Shakespeare, *Complete Works*, Original Spelling Edition, gen. ed. Stanley Wells and Gary Taylor (Oxford, 1986).
4 Andrew Murphy, *Shakespeare in Print: A History and Chronology of Shakespeare Publishing* (Cambridge, 2003), p. 207.
5 Wilson was later assisted by J. C. Maxwell, G. I. Duthie and Alice Walker.
6 John Dover Wilson, *The Manuscript of Shakespeare's 'Hamlet' and the Problems of its Transmission*, 2 vols. (Cambridge, 1934).
7 Cited in Wells, *Re-editing Shakespeare for the Modern Reader* (Oxford, 1984), p. 84, with the laconic comment 'Not too easily, I should have thought'.

With the exception of Wilson's treatment of stage directions, the Arden and New Shakespeares influenced many subsequent series, some of them still in progress, some of them by design more or less scholarly than others, some prepared by one or two editors and others by a large team. They include the second Arden series (1951–82), Pelican (1957–67), Signet (1963–8), New Penguin (1967–), Oxford (1982–), New Cambridge (1984–), Folger (1992–), and third Arden (1995–). All were in modern spelling and punctuation.

Meanwhile, the decades of the early-to-mid century brought in a number of significant modernised editions of the complete works. W. J. Craig supplemented his work on the Arden series with a complete edition for Oxford University Press in 1911–12. George Lyman Kittredge's 1936 edition for Ginn in Boston endured to be reissued in 1944 as the Viking Portable Shakespeare, which itself was reissued by Penguin in 1977. Two major complete works appeared in 1951; they were edited by Hardin Craig for the American publisher Scott, Foreman and Company, and by Peter Alexander for Collins in Glasgow. The latter remains in print. Hardin Craig's edition became the basis for David Bevington's revision of 1973, which was in turn revised for the Bantam Shakespeare (individual plays and groups of plays, 1988), and for new editions of the complete works under Bevington's sole name (1980, 1992, 1997).

The Craig–Bevington dominance was successfully challenged by G. Blakemore Evans's conservative Riverside for Houghton Mifflin in 1974, which in North America became probably the most widely favoured complete works. A decade later, the Oxford Shakespeare, under the general editorship of Stanley Wells and Gary Taylor, established itself as the most innovative edition of the century, offering two separate versions of *King Lear*, and risking what some users felt to be eccentric choices such as its restoration of the original name Oldcastle for the more familiar Falstaff in *1 Henry IV*. The Oxford Shakespeare also stood out for its endorsement of the theatrical dimension of the text, which, as will be seen below, entailed a favourable disposition towards Folio texts that

were thought to be related to theatre playbooks, along with a generous provision of editorial stage directions to clarify the action. With some limited but crucial alterations, including a reversion to Falstaff, the Oxford text was used for the American Norton edition (1997), which gained currency as an alternative to the staid and dependable Riverside for its combination of Oxford textual adventurism and the critically chic introductions of Stephen Greenblatt and his colleagues.

Despite the pragmatic defeat of the old-spelling ideal, the disparity between the treatment of Shakespeare and of his contemporaries kept the issue visible and subject to periodic debate.[8] The Riverside edition resisted the full logic of modernisation. Evans offered 'basically a modern-spelling text', but 'an attempt has been made to preserve a selection of Elizabethan spelling forms that reflect, or may reflect, a distinctive contemporary pronunciation'.[9] Examples include *haberdepois*, *fift*, *wrack*, *bankrout*, *fadom* and *vild*. When Stanley Wells revitalised the defunct Oxford Shakespeare he rejected compromise and, for the first time in editorial history, gave serious attention to the principles and practice of establishing a consistent and thorough-going approach to modernization. He argued that modernization was defensible as the preferred treatment and no mere commercial or populist second-best solution.[10] The practical guidance he offered on the subject became a standard point of reference for editors working for other projects.

The Oxford Shakespeare was, as a project, unusual in that it issued both a complete works (in old and modern spelling) and a fully and separately edited series. It brought together the heavily annotated series, such as the Arden and Cambridge, with the plain-text complete works, exemplified in

---

8 The disparity was more evident in collected works than individual editions, where series of drama such as the Revels, New Mermaid, and Regents Renaissance were modelled on the modernized Shakespeare edition.

9 G. Blakemore Evans, ed., *The Riverside Shakespeare* (Boston and New York, 1974), p. 39.

10 Stanley Wells, *Modernizing Shakespeare's Spelling*, with Gary Taylor, *Three Studies in the Text of Henry V* (Oxford, 1979); Wells, *Re-Editing Shakespeare*.

the Alexander text. All these editions were issued by British publishers. In contrast, series such as the Penguin, Pelican and Signet offered annotation on a scale sufficiently contained for them to be brought together as an edition of the complete works. The annotated complete works and slim-line series was more characteristic of American publishers.

If the critical, modernized edition dominated the publishing history of Shakespeare, it was supplemented by less widely circulated editions in less standard formats. The century inherited the New Variorum series, which was revived under the management of the Modern Languages Association and still slowly continues in its gargantuan project of collocating a record of all significant textual variants and commentary. Though the text for the New Variorum is a diplomatic transcript of the First Folio text, this form of editing has not elsewhere been widely favoured. Apologists for the modernized critical edition have long urged that a photofacsimile should be used as a supplement for the purposes of those whose needs are not well served by modernisation and other aspects of editing. Indeed photography, the symptomatic technology of the age of mechanical reproduction, was fully embraced by the New Bibliography. Greg himself made key manuscript materials available in his *Dramatic Documents from the Elizabethan Playhouse* and initiated the Oxford Shakespeare Quartos series of facsimiles. Folio facsimiles were prepared by Sidney Lee (1902), Helge Kökeritz and Charles Tyler Prouty (1955), and Charlton Hinman (1968). The last, founded on Hinman's exhaustive study of the Folger Shakespeare Library's large collection of Folio copies, represented a marked advance on its predecessors. It has been both praised and criticized for presenting a reproduction of the Folio in a form that probably never existed, in which all the pages stand in their corrected state.

Alongside this uneasy rapprochement between movable, emendable text and immutable image of text came, towards the end of the century, an increased awareness of alternative versions and differing possible treatments of them. As computers began to be serviceable in the production of

print editions by way of word processing, collation, concordancing, statistical analysis, text databases, and image storage, they began also to present the possibility of an alternative to the printed edition itself. That alternative could draw on and foster the newly heightened awareness of textuality and textual instability. The most obvious potential of an electronic edition is to offer a hyper-inclusive compendium of all that matters. In practice, in the electronic editions as they began to be planned at the end of the century, design, structure and selectivity became as crucial as in a print edition – though all three criteria were reconstructed in terms tailored to the new medium. It had been recognized that such editions should be produced to high standards of editing. The Internet Shakespeare Editions, the prime example of its kind to have emerged by the end of the century, sets out its general aim 'to make available scholarly editions of high quality in a format native to the medium of the Internet'.[11] The series guidelines require a modernized and edited readers' text as the key point of reference, but nevertheless the theoretical issues surrounding the foundations of the text may be less critical in a more permissive electronic environment where there is no single text. The extent to which scholarly electronic editions will transform Shakespeare study remains to be seen, but at the end of the twentieth century its role remained, at most, supplementary to the print edition.

CANON AND COLLABORATION

The account of Shakespeare editions has so far begged important questions about the constitution of 'Shakespeare' as the object of editing. What did Shakespeare write? How are those works to be ordered, and what story does the ordering of them tell? How significant are the works of doubtful authorship? To what extent did Shakespeare collaborate with other dramatists? These are the pragmatic questions. In recent decades the question of attribution has been pursued with vigour, and yet in

---

[11] 'Internet Shakespeare Editions: Aims and Structure', accessed from the project's online homepage at http://ise.uvic.ca/.

uneasy relationship with what has sometimes been called collaboration theory, which has questioned the basic premise of the solitary, autonomous and sovereign author on *a priori* grounds.

Yet for much of the twentieth century the questions just listed played a minor part in their presentation. In 1908 Tucker Brooke edited a collection of *The Shakespeare Apocrypha* which lumped together plays now thought to be probably Shakespeare collaborations, such as *Two Noble Kinsmen* and *Edward III*, with plays with virtually no credible claim to be even partly Shakespearian, such as *Sir John Oldcastle*. Brooke argued against the likelihood of any of the plays in his collection being actually Shakespearian, with the exception of what we now know as the 'Hand D' section of *Sir Thomas More*.[12] For most of the century, the plays Brooke gathered together would remain safely excluded from the canon as it was edited.

The New Bibliographers combined recognition of the theoretical possibility of collaboration with minimisation of the extent to which it applied to Shakespeare. The key moment came in 1924, when E. K. Chambers delivered a withering attack on 'The Disintegration of Shakespeare'.[13] The disintegrators in question were the throng of critics who had made an intellectual hobby of identifying in the canonical works the hands of other dramatists. Considering the irresponsibly impressionistic approach of the school that Chambers attacked, his admonitions were timely. But they drove the question of Shakespeare as a collaborator into the shadow for half a century. S. Schoenbaum's insistence on rigour in attribution study reinforced the view of Shakespeare as a non-collaborator for another generation.[14] The 1951 Alexander complete works is typical of the representation of the canon as it stood at mid century. Alexander followed the content and order of the Folio, adding one play, *Pericles*, which is now understood to be a collaboration with George Wilkins, and the non-dramatic poems. An appendix included a transcript of the Hand D passage in *Sir Thomas More*.

Despite some false starts such as the attribution of 'A Funeral Elegy' to Shakespeare,[15] despite the strictures of collaboration theorists who have

misleadingly insisted on an inevitable association between attribution scholarship and the post-Enlightenment ideology of the solitary author,[16] and in contrast with areas of textual study discussed below in which the past two decades have seen increasing scepticism, in the past twenty years attribution study has developed increasingly sophisticated techniques that have led to a more precise understanding of what and how Shakespeare wrote. The Oxford Shakespeare was the first complete works to advance the provocative claims that Shakespeare probably collaborated with Thomas Middleton on *Timon of Athens*, that Middleton adapted *Measure for Measure* as well as *Macbeth*,[17] and that Shakespeare wrote less than half of *1 Henry VI*.[18] Since 1986, Shakespeare's complete authorship of *Titus Andronicus* has been widely rejected in view of the impressive cogency of the case for George Peele's hand in the play.[19] Of *Edward III*,

---

[12] 'It seems improbable, then, for many reasons, that Shakespeare had an interest in the original construction of any of the doubtful plays': C. F. Tucker Brooke, ed., *The Shakespeare Apocrypha: Being a Collection of Fourteen Plays which have been Ascribed to Shakespeare* (Oxford, 1908), p. xii. Brooke's collection included *Arden of Faversham*, *Edward III* and *Two Noble Kinsmen*, but not *Pericles*, which he accepted as Shakespearian.

[13] E. K. Chambers, 'The Disintegration of Shakespeare', British Academy Annual Shakespeare Lecture 1924, in Lascelles Abercrombie *et al.*, *Aspects of Shakespeare* (Oxford, 1933), pp. 23–48.

[14] S. Schoenbaum, *Shakespeare and Others* (Washington, DC, 1984).

[15] The poem was printed in the Norton and revised Riverside and Bevington editions, all issued in 1997. The attribution to Shakespeare is decisively refuted in Brian Vickers, *Counterfeiting Shakespeare: Evidence, Authorship, and John Ford's Funerall Elegye* (Cambridge, 2002).

[16] See especially Jeffrey Masten, *Textual Intercourse: Collaboration, Authorship, and Sexualities in Renaissance Drama* (Cambridge, 1997).

[17] As argued in Gary Taylor and John Jowett, *Shakespeare Reshaped, 1603–1623* (Oxford, 1993).

[18] As elaborated in Gary Taylor, 'Shakespeare and Others: The Authorship of *1 Henry VI*', *Medieval and Renaissance Drama in England* 7 (1995), 145–205.

[19] The arguments for Peele's hand are digested and developed in Brian Vickers, *Shakespeare, Co-author: A Historical Study of Five Collaborative Plays* (Oxford, 2002).

the Oxford editors wrote, 'if we had attempted a thorough reinvestigation of candidates for inclusion in the early dramatic canon', it would have begun with that play (*Textual Companion*, p. 137). The play was subsequently published in the New Cambridge series,[20] and is included as a collaboration in the 2005 Second Edition of the Oxford *Complete Works*. Recent work, as yet unpublished, suggests that *Arden of Faversham* may be at least partly by Shakespeare.[21] We can now see that the catalogue of plays written in collaboration is longer than is usually recognized (and may yet grow longer still); it includes *Edward III*, *1 Henry VI*, *Titus Andronicus*, *Sir Thomas More*, *Timon of Athens*, *Pericles*, *Henry VIII*, *Two Noble Kinsmen*, the lost play *Cardenio*, and perhaps *Arden of Faversham*.[22] *Sir Thomas More* was recognized for most of the century as a play in which Shakespeare collaborated on the revision. It was rarely printed in full in Shakespeare editions,[23] but the case for doing so increased as the picture filled out of Shakespeare's other collaborative work. Attribution scholarship was and is redefining what is meant by 'Shakespeare' in ways that affect both editorial theory and the wider critical imagination.

LOCALIZING BADNESS

Just as, in the earlier twentieth century, plays were divided firmly between the canonical and the Apocryphal, with little acceptance of the intermediate concept of collaboration, so texts were divided between the camps of good and bad. In both respects, the work of the later century sought to replace these dichotomies.

The intellectual background to the century's editorial work on Shakespeare was determined by the publications of Pollard on the classification of texts.[24] Previous textual critics had developed some sense that the quartos varied in character, and indeed the suggestion that the First Quartos of *Hamlet* and *Romeo and Juliet* might derive from memorial reconstruction by actors goes back to Tycho Mommsen in 1857. The work of P. A. Daniel anticipated later developments by confirming a number of individual quartos as particularly corrupt. Pollard transformed the field of study

by generating an overall hypothesis as to textual origins.

Pollard's most crucial intervention came in the chapter in his *Shakespeare Folios and Quartos* headed 'The Good and Bad Quartos' (pp. 64–80). Investigating the regulation of entitlement to publication as evidenced in the Stationers' Register, he noted a high level of correspondence between textual 'goodness' and regular, authorised publication. One criterion of textual virtue was the implied verdict of the Folio editors in accepting printed copy; Pollard also took into account the quality of the text on its own terms. The criterion for authorized publication was regular entry in the Stationers' Register. As Greg later summarized,

> The novel feature in Pollard's argument was the demonstration that the issue of each of these five 'bad' quartos was in some way peculiar: *Romeo and Juliet* and *Henry V* were not entered in the Stationers' Register at all; *Hamlet* and *Pericles* were published by stationers other than those who had made the entrance; *The Merry Wives of Windsor* was entered by one stationer and transferred to another the same day.[25]

Pollard interpreted the 'conditional' entry in the Stationers' Register of 1598 prohibiting the printing of *Merchant of Venice* without licence from the

---

[20] *King Edward III*, ed. Giorgio Melchiori (Cambridge, 1998).

[21] I am grateful to MacD. P. Jackson for sending me a copy of his persuasive paper 'Shakespeare and the Quarrel Scene in *Arden of Faversham*' (forthcoming) in advance of publication.

[22] For overviews, see MacD. P. Jackson, *Studies in Attribution: Middleton and Shakespeare* (Salzburg, 1979); Gary Taylor, 'The Canon and Chronology of Shakespeare's Plays', in Stanley Wells and Taylor, with John Jowett and William Montgomery, *William Shakespeare: A Textual Companion* (Oxford, 1987; subsequently *Textual Companion*), pp. 69–144; Jonathan Hope, *The Authorship of Shakespeare's Plays* (Cambridge, 1994); Richard Proudfoot, *Shakespeare: Text, Stage, and Canon* (London, 2001); and Brian Vickers, *Co-Author*.

[23] An exception is Harold Jenkins's text in Charles Jasper Sisson's edition of the *Complete Works* (London, 1954).

[24] Alfred W. Pollard, *Shakespeare Folios and Quartos: A Study in the Bibliography of Shakespeare's Plays 1594–1685* (London, 1909); *Shakespeare's Fight with the Pirates and the Problems of the Transmission of his Text* (Cambridge, 1920).

[25] W. W. Greg, *The Editorial Problem in Shakespeare* (Oxford, 1942; revised edn, 1954), p. 10.

Lord Chamberlain, and the puzzling orders of 1600 whereby four Shakespeare plays were entered as 'to be staied', as the Chamberlain's Men's mainly successful attempts to block unauthorized publication (pp. 66–7). They indicated, therefore, that Shakespeare and his company were doing battle with 'pirates' who sought to steal their plays and publish them surreptitiously. Pollard shifted the taxonomy of the text of Shakespeare, which had been suspicious of the quartos as a whole, by disclosing that the majority of quartos were free of this taint of badness. Corruption could be limited to the texts that were irregularly printed and were later rejected by the Folio editors.

Pollard had worked in close collaboration with W. W. Greg. In his preface he confessed, 'In some sections of this study Mr Greg and I have been fellow-hunters, communicating our results to each other at every stage' (p. vi). Greg was to publish both his own note on the *Hamlet* quartos and an old-spelling edition of *Merry Wives* in 1910.[26] Where Pollard's book had focused on the publishing context, Greg's edition of *Merry Wives* was a ground-breaking and detailed textual study in which he identified the actor of the Host of the Garter as the person who had reported and assembled the quarto text. Greg's work in turn stimulated a number of other detailed studies published in the early decades of the century in which the case for memorial transmission was developed in relation to individual quarto texts. Thus Q1 *Hamlet*, *Henry V*, and *Romeo and Juliet* were identified as 'bad' quartos, as were the first editions of *2 Henry VI* and *3 Henry VI*.[27] Critics who saw *The Taming of the Shrew* as first issued under the title *The Taming of A Shrew* placed *A Shrew* under the same general heading, though *A Shrew* was more usually regarded as an independent non-Shakespearian version rather than a memorial reconstruction.[28] *Pericles* also joined the group of 'bad' quartos, despite being recognised as a text that was complicated yet further by the issue of joint authorship.[29]

The significance of memorial reconstruction was two-fold. First, it enabled the affected texts to be labelled as 'bad' (though the nature of that badness

could never quite be declared homogeneous) and assigned a marginal position in the editing of the plays in question. Second, it sustained the narrative of piracy by aligning the irregular circumstances of publication noted by Pollard with an activity on the part of actors that could readily be interpreted as theft. But by 1942, when Greg published *The Editorial Problem in Shakespeare*, this apparently strong convergence of textual analysis and book history had begun to look vulnerable. Greg pointed out the limits of the evidence of the Stationers' Register:

absence of registration is not in itself evidence of piracy nor always accompanied by textual corruption; nor is simultaneous entrance and transfer proof of dishonest dealing . . . On the other hand, some pieces that were quite regularly entered prove to have thoroughly bad texts.[30]

The suspected texts now included the quartos of *King Lear* and *Richard III*. Both had been regularly entered in the Register and, though subjected to heavy annotation, were to be accepted as the foundations for the Folio texts. But both had nevertheless now emerged as 'presumably piratical and surreptitious' (p. 13).

A problem Greg recognized as early as his study of *Merry Wives* was that the effects of bad reporting

---

[26] W. W. Greg, 'The *Hamlet* Quartos, 1603, 1604', *MLR* 5 (1910), 196–7; Greg, ed., *Shakespeare's 'Merry Wives of Windsor' 1602* (London, 1906).

[27] George Ian Duthie, *The 'Bad' Quarto of 'Hamlet': A Critical Study* (Cambridge, 1941); Alfred Hart, *Stolne and Surreptitious Copies* (Melbourne, 1942); Harry Reno Hoppe, *The Bad Quarto of 'Romeo and Juliet'* (Ithaca, 1948); Peter Alexander, 'II *Henry VI* and the Copy for *The Contention* (1594)', *TLS*, 9 October 1924, 629–30; Alexander, '*3 Henry VI* and *Richard Duke of York*', *TLS*, 13 November 1924, 730.

[28] Peter Alexander, 'The *Taming of a Shrew*', *TLS*, 16 September 1926, 614.

[29] Greg, *Editorial Problem*, pp. 72–6. In this chapter I retain the term '"bad" Quartos', both apologetically in the absence of a more satisfactory label and unapologetically as an historical designation.

[30] Greg, *Editorial Problem*, pp. 11–12. On the significance of entry in the Stationers' Register, see also Peter W. M. Blayney, 'The Publication of Playbooks', in *A New History of Early English Drama*, ed. John D. Cox and David Scott Kastan (New York, 1997), 383–422.

cannot always be distinguished from those of adaptation. Shortening of a text, for instance, can be an effect of adaptation rather than bad memory. The instability of the boundary between the effects of memory and the effects of adaptation persistently plagued accounts of the 'bad' quartos, as did the difficulty in making all the textual data conform to any detailed fleshing-out of the hypothesis. But Greg and others were nevertheless able to argue persuasively that if textual shortening is produced not by cutting but by rough, unShakespearian, and sometimes garbled paraphrase, and if the metricality of verse is sometimes severely damaged in the process, it is hard to see how a redactor working from a manuscript could produce such a text, and an effect of the limitations of memory is evidently manifested.

In the mid twentieth century this hypothesis of memorial reconstruction was tested against alternative postulates. A number of critics suggested that the affected quartos were put together from shorthand scripts taken by members of the theatre audience. This view is now generally discounted on the basis that early modern shorthand systems were inadequate to the task.[31] Another explanation is that they represent early authorial versions that were later filled out to become the plays we know from the longer quartos and Folio.[32] This view did not gain wide acceptance, not least on account of features of language and metre, some of them quantifiable, that have been shown to lie outside the range of Shakespeare's style at any point in his writing.[33] Moreover, the early draft hypothesis acutely conflicts with the signs of theatrical adaptation that numerous critics have observed as marking these as late texts in the process of transmission.

Towards the end of the century Kathleen O. Irace was able to confirm, for some texts more clearly than others, that the suspected reconstructions show a pattern of varying correspondence with their longer counterparts first noted by Greg.[34] She produced a statistical analysis showing that where the actor was on stage, his part was relatively well transmitted, and the parts of other actors were transmitted with intermediate reliability; the

least accurate parts of the text were those where the actor or actors were offstage. The demonstration was more convincing for some texts than others. *Merry Wives* was a particularly clear example. Here the hypothesis of memorial reconstruction was immensely strengthened, for it is hard to think of any alternative way to account for the phenomenon.

The spirit of the 1990s was, however, hostile to the New Bibliography, to its polarization of 'good' and 'bad', and to its optimistic drive to make the convoluted transmission of the text knowable. Paul Werstine's sharp, cynical critiques set the tone, and proclaimed, unignorably, that the days of the New Bibliography were over.[35] Memorial reconstruction became a key instance in the crisis in theory and methodology, as the point where the work of the New Bibliographers was least empirical and so the Achilles' heel of the whole movement.

Where Werstine addressed the historical evolution of editorial theory, Laurie E. Maguire investigated the texts themselves, taking on board non-Shakespearian examples as well as the Shakespearian 'bad' quartos.[36] By excluding the standard analytic method of comparing the suspect text with its longer counterpart, and by carefully investigating the demonstrable effects of memory on textual transmission rather than making assumptions about it, Maguire established a more rigorous and

---

[31] Duthie, *The 'Bad' Quarto of 'Hamlet'*, pp. 12–18.
[32] Hardin Craig, *A New Look at Shakespeare's Quartos* (Stanford, 1961). The view is espoused in numerous articles by Steven Urkowitz.
[33] Gary Taylor, in *Textual Companion*, pp. 84–6.
[34] Kathleen O. Irace, *Reforming the 'Bad' Quartos: Performance and Provenance of Six Shakespearean First Editions* (Cranbury, London, and Mississauga, 1994).
[35] See especially 'McKerrow's "Suggestion" and Twentieth-Century Shakespeare Textual Criticism', *Renaissance Drama*, n.s. 19 (1988), 149–73; 'Narratives about Printed Shakespeare Texts: "Foul Papers" and "Bad" Quartos', *Shakespeare Quarterly*, 41 (1990), 65–86; 'A Century of "Bad" Shakespeare Quartos', *Shakespeare Quarterly*, 50 (1999), 310–33; 'Post-Theory Problems in Shakespeare Editing', *Yearbook of English Studies*, 29 (1999), 103–17.
[36] Laurie E. Maguire, *Shakespearean Suspect Texts: The 'Bad' Quartos and their Contexts* (Cambridge, 1996).

narrowed approach to the question than other investigators. She did not allow herself, for instance, to explore the kind of analysis conducted at the same time by Irace. It is perhaps not surprising that their conclusions differed. Maguire found very few probable or possible cases of memorial reconstruction – though, given her self-imposed limitations and the scepticism that characterised the period, it is significant that *Merry Wives* still emerged as a 'probable' memorial reconstruction (p. 286), and Q1 *Hamlet* as a 'possible' one (p. 256). If her work offered a strong critique of memorial reconstruction as a general explanation for the 'bad' Quarto, the hypothesis survives her rigorous approach at least in vestigial form.

The 'bad' quartos were emerging in the 1990s as distinctive more by virtue of adaptation than corruption. Every text was opened up for study and potential or actual performance without prejudice as a version in its own right.[37] As the century closed, the present writer's edition of *Richard III* and Stanley Wells's *King Lear* for the Oxford series took the erstwhile 'doubtful' quartos as the primary text of choice.[38] But even in this environment memorial reconstruction could not be banished. It continued to offer a compelling if problematic and partial explanation for a number of texts displaying distinctly unShakespearian features that had not been adequately explained by other theories.

AUTHOR AND THEATRE

In Greg's consolidation of New Bibliographical thought in 1942, Pollard's explanation of the 'good' quartos was also looking as unsatisfactory as his account of the 'bad'. Pollard had developed his earlier work on the text of Shakespeare in the Sanders lectures given at Cambridge University in 1915. Reading at face value Shakespeare's co-actors John Heminges and Henry Condell's claim in the preliminaries to the First Folio that 'wee haue scarse receiued from him a blot on his papers' at face value, he had argued that the manuscripts that became the printers' copy for F were Shakespeare's original drafts (*Fight*, p. 60). These had probably been submitted for licence to the Master of the Revels

and adapted for use in the theatre as a promptbook (pp. 63–4). The same explanation was extended to the 'good' quartos. The players would be prepared to surrender their promptbook to the printers for a few weeks for 'the superior convenience of a printed prompt-copy' (p. 66).

Greg forcefully questioned several of Pollard's premises. Here the manuscript of *Sir Thomas More* became significant. A 1923 collection of essays edited by Pollard with major contributions from Greg advanced the case that Hand D was Shakespeare's.[39] Hand D's writing habits did not correspond with the account given by the Folio editors of Shakespeare's blot-free papers. 'Recent criticism', Greg notes, 'is inclined to discount their statement' (*Editorial Problem*, p. 29). Ironically, Pollard's project on *Sir Thomas More* had undermined his earlier work on the quartos.

Greg went on to draw a distinction, based on his study of other surviving dramatic manuscripts of the period, between 'foul papers' and 'fair copy'. This latter might be prepared by either the dramatist (or one of them in a collaboration) or a professional scribe. For Greg, the signs of textual cleanness combined with annotation for theatrical use are typical of Folio plays printed from manuscript, or with reference to manuscript. The 'good' quartos, in contrast, display features that suggest Shakespeare's rough draft, or 'foul papers', such as difficulties resulting from hasty handwriting, undeleted first sketches of a phrase or passage that stood alongside its replacement, misplaced interlinear or marginal insertions, inconsistent forms and abbreviations of speech-prefix, and imaginatively descriptive but theatrically redundant wording in stage directions. When the company relinquished a manuscript

---

37 As witnessed by the New Cambridge Early Quartos series, and readings of 'bad' quartos such as in Leah Marcus, *Unediting the Renaissance: Shakespeare, Marlowe, Milton* (London, 1996).

38 *The Tragedy of King Richard III*, ed. John Jowett (Oxford, 2000); *The History of King Lear*, ed. Stanley Wells (Oxford, 2000).

39 Alfred W. Pollard, ed., *Shakespeare's Hand in the Play of Sir Thomas More, with the Text of the Ill May Day Scenes* (Cambridge, 1923).

for publication during Shakespeare's lifetime, they would have retained the licensed promptbook and sent the back-up document instead (*Editorial Problem*, p. 33, p. 107).

Greg's account of 'foul papers' split up Pollard's large group of reliable texts, differentiating between the typical 'good' quarto and typical Folio texts. It posited a correspondence, first suggested by McKerrow, between signs of inconsistency and irregularity found in the 'good' quartos such as *Love's Labour's Lost*, Q2 *Romeo and Juliet*, *Merchant of Venice*, *1 Henry IV*, and *Much Ado* with similar signs in manuscript authorial drafts.[40] This enabled Greg to claim that, despite the difficulties in Pollard's argument, the grounds for optimism as regards the 'good' quartos were actually stronger than he had realized, as they were especially close to an authorial draft (*Editorial Problem*, pp. 95–7).

The term 'foul papers' was borrowed from its use to describe various kinds of rough draft in the early modern period and elevated to mean the dramatist's complete draft as a standard category in the description of dramatic manuscripts. Greg's difficulty was that no extant manuscript fully conforms to the description. Nevertheless, it is self-evident that any 'fair copy' had an antecedent of some form, that any transcript is a copy of something else. The passages written by the dramatists identified as Henry Chettle, Thomas Heywood, Shakespeare and Thomas Dekker in *Sir Thomas More* and the entirety of a manuscript such as *The Captives* correspond in many ways with Greg's description of foul papers – except insofar as some of them have been lightly annotated by a theatrical scribe, the *Sir Thomas More*, additions do not make up a complete draft, and Greg himself commented that *The Captives* does not show much authorial alteration (*Folio*, p. 108).

These exceptions proved concerning to more recent critics such as Werstine who have demanded that early modern play production must fall within processes that generate fixed categories of manuscript if the analysis of Greg and others is to have any utility. Greg himself indeed sought to classify play texts, yet he consistently showed awareness of the limits of categorization and recognized

that each individual text displayed unique characteristics that were likely to place it in ambiguous relationship with the category to which it putatively belonged. In addition to the theatre-oriented manuscripts, Greg recognized another type, the 'literary' transcript prepared for a private reader such as a patron. He referred to dramatic manuscripts (specifically those used as Folio copy) as 'a misty mid region of Weir, a land of shadowy shapes and melting outlines, where not even the most patient inquiry and the most penetrating analysis can hope to arrive at any but tentative and proximate conclusions'.[41] This statement reflects his awareness of the diversity of feature in the extant dramatic manuscripts, as well as the complexities of transmission to print.

Mistiness notwithstanding, for Greg the foul papers and the transcript of them that became the promptbook were the two key documents in the composition and preparation of the play for the theatre. Both would normally be held by the theatre company. In Fredson Bowers's influential development of Greg's work the number of categories swelled to thirteen. Bowers both extended and codified the diversity that was already acknowledged in, and yet partly occluded by, Greg's simpler system made up of the binaries foul and fair, theatrical and literary, authorial and scribal.[42] As Bowers pointed out, in Robert Dabourne's letter to Philip Henslowe in which he refers to 'the foule sheet', Dabourne indicates that the company would pay him only for 'ye fayr' that he was copying out when Henslowe's man called on him (p. 15). If the foul papers would often not have been accepted by the company, this would partly explain why the survival of 'foul papers' is so rare. At the risk of assuming a wasteful use of resource in multiple

---

[40] R. B. McKerrow, 'The Elizabethan Printer and Dramatic Manuscripts', *Library*, IV, 12 (1931–2), 253–75; McKerrow, 'A Suggestion Regarding Shakespeare's Manuscripts', *Review of English Studies*, 11 (1935), 459–65.

[41] W. W. Greg, *The Shakespeare First Folio: Its Bibliographical and Textual History* (Oxford, 1955), p. 103.

[42] Fredson Bowers, *On Editing Shakespeare and the Elizabethan Dramatists* (Philadelphia, 1955), pp. 11–12.

transcription, Bowers suggests that there might have been a common expectation that the dramatist should deliver a fair copy in his own hand, and that this fair copy might itself have been transcribed. In this case the fair copy can be described as an intermediate manuscript.[43] Bowers points out the editorial implication. If the company's spare manuscript was at least sometimes an author's fair copy rather than foul papers, the editorial treatment of those texts may have been too liberal. Editors had assumed that the printer's copy would have been full of illegible readings, interlineations, side-notes and the like, and emended accordingly, but these features would not be expected to the same degree in the kind of copy Bowers postulates (pp. 19–20).

The Oxford Shakespeare editors considered it clear enough that texts such as Q2 *Romeo and Juliet*, Q1 *2 Henry IV*, and even a text Bowers had proposed as 'intermediate', Q2 *Hamlet*, displayed exactly the range of features to be expected of foul papers. But other 'good' quartos did not: for instance Q1 *Merchant of Venice* is described as 'Holograph (fair copy), or perhaps a scribal transcript of it', and *1 Henry IV* as a 'scribal transcript of authorial papers' (*Textual Companion*, pp. 145–6). Similarly, Folio *All's Well That Ends Well* is accounted 'Holograph (foul paper)', with the qualification that 'The foul papers may have been annotated by a book-keeper' (*Textual Companion*, p. 147). The terminology developed by Pollard and Greg remains in place but, in the spirit of Greg in his more permissive aspect, there is no expectation that texts will conform neatly to a fixed model.

In view of the Oxford Shakespeare's emphasis on the text as performed in the theatre, work on the surviving but non-Shakespearian dramatic manuscripts by William Long and others has a key role to play, and no doubt will develop further. Long's study of the anonymous manuscript play *Woodstock*, for instance, shows the limited but cumulative annotation of the script for a series of stagings, and Long notes the reluctance to delete earlier but superseded annotations.[44] This picture resonates well with the evidence in Folio texts that earlier playbooks were annotated for later revivals,

both suggesting that full transcription was a costly exercise that would be avoided except when necessary. Taylor refined the earlier work of W. T. Jewkes on act divisions, to confirm that in printed texts they relate to performance at the indoors Blackfriars theatre, where breaks were needed to replace the candles.[45] In the case of plays written before the King's Men occupied the Blackfriars, the presence of act divisions in a Folio text shows that the play was printed with influence from a theatrical manuscript in use after 1608. Examples include *A Midsummer Night's Dream*, *Measure for Measure*, *Richard II*, and *King John*. The expurgation of profanity can be analysed to comparable effect. It may be demonstrable as in the case of *Richard II*, where the Quarto can be compared, or merely inferrable as in the case of *Measure for Measure*, where there is no earlier edition. In either case, it reflects modification of a text written before profanity was outlawed by the 1606 Act to Restrain Abuses of Players, and so adds to the presence of act divisions as a sign of a promptbook in later use.[46]

The understanding that most of the Folio texts were related to theatrical manuscripts remained in place throughout the century. Progress was steadily made in identifying the nature of the copy: the edition used for quarto copy, and the nature of the intermixing of quarto and manuscript copy in plays.[47] Knowledge of the involvement of scribes in supplying copy was advanced by Trevor Howard-Hill's work identifying Ralph Crane as the copyist behind *The Tempest*, *Two Gentlemen of Verona*, *Merry Wives*, *Measure for Measure*, and *The Comedy of Errors*.[48] E. A. J. Honigmann showed

---

[43] Bowers, 'The Copy for Shakespeare's *Julius Caesar*', *South Atlantic Bulletin*, 43 (1978), 23–36. For a critique, see *Textual Companion*, p. 387.

[44] '"A bed / for woodstock": A Warning for the Unwary', *Medieval and Renaissance Drama in England* 2 (1985), 91–118.

[45] In Taylor and Jowett, *Shakespeare Reshaped*, pp. 3–50.

[46] Taylor and Jowett, pp. 51–106.

[47] The fullest study is J. K. Walton, *The Quarto Copy for the First Folio of Shakespeare* (Dublin, 1971), though substantial further work has been done on a number of plays.

[48] T. H. Howard-Hill, *Ralph Crane and Some Shakespeare First Folio Comedies* (Charlottesville, 1972).

that Crane's hand probably also lay behind Folio *Othello*.[49] Scribal features were also identified in plays printed from evidently clean copy that had previously often been assumed to be holograph, both in quarto (*1 Henry IV*) and Folio (*Anthony and Cleopatra, Coriolanus*).[50]

Yet one important conclusion reached in the work surrounding the Oxford Shakespeare was that the licensed promptbook was not itself released to supply direct copy for the Folio compositors. Either a play was printed more or less directly from quarto (as with *Romeo and Juliet*), or readings were annotated from playbook to quarto (as with *Midsummer Night's Dream, Richard II*, and many other plays), or a pre-theatrical manuscript in Shakespeare's hand was used (as with *The Comedy of Errors* and *Henry V*), or the playbook was transcribed (as in the case with the Crane transcripts).[51] Accordingly, a premise of Pollard's argument remained valid at the end of the century. That is to say, if none of Shakespeare's plays was printed directly from the licensed promptbook, the printed texts fall into two broad categories, pre-theatrical and post-theatrical. They roughly correspond with Pollard's good and bad. But these are broad categories indeed: the pre-theatrical might include authorial rough drafts, authorial fair copies, and manuscripts lightly annotated in anticipation of a new transcript; the post-theatrical covers scribal transcripts as well as later theatrical adaptations and reconstructions.

The single point of fixity in this description is not as stable as it might appear. As already noted, a promptbook or (to adopt the term favoured by Long)[52] a playbook might be in use over a number of years, and synchronically present a diachronic process of adaptation to new and different conditions of staging. Such a manuscript does not represent the play as first performed, nor does it usually represent the play as last performed under the sanction or influence of the dramatist. Does a critical editor need to strip away, not only the veil of print, but also the veil of posthumous adaptation? Such questions arise with some immediacy in the case of *Measure for Measure* and *Macbeth*, both of which survive only in Folio texts thought to be adapted for the stage after Shakespeare's death.

The attraction of the Oxford Shakespeare's emphasis on the document there referred to as the promptbook as the key theoretical point of reference lies in a convergence of different forms of non-exclusive authority upon that document. These may be summarised as the dramatist, the company itself (as agents of a collective form of 'publication' on the stage), and the licensing Master of the Revels (as source of official sanction of the state). Yet this convergence on this document is not straightforward. The permissive or active engagement of the author is facilitated in Shakespeare's case by his special position as both dramatist and sharer. As for the endorsements that follow, it was Greg who had articulated the two criteria for a 'promptbook' as the theatre book-keeper's annotations which lead towards the management of stage actions and the Master of the Revels' licence. A critical difficulty is that a number of Greg's promptbooks do not hold a licence.[53] The exact status of the unlicensed playbook is therefore uncertain and problematises the assumption of a single document.

Some critics towards the end of the century found that the lack of exact fit between the theorised models mapping the territory and the materials to which they apply indicated that the misty land of Weir was unexplorable. For Werstine, the absence of a pure example of foul papers and doubts as to the historical evidence for memorial reconstruction dealt fatal blows to the edifice Pollard and Greg had built up. Addressing McKerrow's 'Suggestion', Werstine pointed to the survival in extant promptbooks of features that had been thought typical of foul papers. At a cursory reading Werstine here and elsewhere may seem to be saying

---

49 E. A. J. Honigmann, *The Texts of 'Othello' and Authorial Revision* (London, 1996).

50 See *Textual Companion*, pp. 329–40, 549, 593.

51 Taylor and Jowett, *Shakespeare Reshaped*, especially pp. 237–43.

52 Long, 'A bed'. But see Tiffany Stern, 'Behind, the Arras: The Prompter's Place in the Shakespearean Theatre', *Theatre Notebook* 55 (2001), 110–18.

53 For a summary, see Greg, *Folio*, pp. 162–3.

that the New Bibliographers were wrong on all counts. His arguments do not sustain such a conclusion, and possibly were not intended to do so. They succeed in advancing the subtler proposition that there are no stable points of reference upon which to plot a categorisation that can be applied to the lost copy for printed plays. His conclusion that the New Bibliography presents 'narratives' rather than knowledge is well taken in the limited sense that applies to all reconstruction. Indeed, Werstine's advocacy of a shift in textual study from grand narrative to local case-study, as has happened in the academic discipline of history, perhaps offers the best indication of how his work transforms the field.

COPY TEXT AND VERSIONS

The ground reviewed in the previous two sections concerns the knowledge, and the conceptualisation of knowledge, on which critical editorial practice is founded, and is specific, almost entirely, to Shakespeare and early modern drama. I turn now to questions that are grounded in general editorial theory, though with very particular application to Shakespeare.

Though Bowers was about to enlarge its agenda, at the middle of the century Anglo-American critical editing was still grounded firmly in and around Shakespeare study. Greg's 'Rationale of Copy-Text' was a key statement that continues to be influential.[54] It was founded on the distinction between 'substantive' and 'accidental' aspects of the text, the 'substantives' being the words as signifiers and the 'accidentals' being spelling, punctuation, abbreviated speech-prefixes, and other features of layout.[55] The distinction in itself was not new, and indeed is based on a distinction made in compositors' treatment of copy as early as in the account of Joseph Moxon in 1683–4.[56] Greg's innovation was to declare that editors should treat accidentals and substantives in some circumstances differently. He accepted McKerrow's strictures on the impossibility of restoring Shakespeare's spelling and punctuation, but urged nevertheless, on purely pragmatic grounds, that the copy text should be selected on the basis of having the lowest level of scribal and compositorial interference with the accidentals, so being in this respect closest to Shakespeare's own practices. If, however, this principle were extended to the substantives it would result in a 'slavish' adherence to the copy text. Choice of copy-text for accidentals is a mere 'necessity' (p. 26). Despite his commitment to the old-spelling edition, Greg is almost disdainful towards the features of accidence. The essence of editing lies in establishing the substantives.

Greg's aim was to liberate the editor from the 'tyranny of copy text' ('Rationale', p. 26). The immediate intent of the article was to provide a principled basis for adopting, for instance, justifiable Folio readings where a quarto was the copy text. The procedure Greg advocated sharpened the distinction between the edition's basis in the copy text as a document and its aspiration to recover the text that Shakespeare wrote, rejecting the former in favour of the latter. This gave the editor a freer hand in detecting and emending error in the copy, and so opened up a more eclectic approach to editing. The editing of substantives 'belongs to the general theory of textual criticism and lies altogether beyond the narrow principle of the copy-text'.[57]

The fullest impact of the separation of accidentals from substantives is reserved for works where authors revised their own work. McKerrow had noted that in the case of an 'ancestral' series of editions where an author had marked up a copy of a printing with corrections and revisions for the next edition, the first edition would be closest to the author's manuscript as regards 'spelling and punctuation, neither of which would matter if the text were to be used as the basis of a

---

[54] W. W. Greg, 'The Rationale of Copy-Text', *Studies in Bibliography*, 3 (1950–1), 19–36.

[55] The accidentals are in fact often not void of signification.

[56] Joseph Moxon, *Mechanick Exercises on the Whole Art of Printing (1683–4)*, ed. Herbert Davis and Harry Carter (Oxford, 1958).

[57] 'Rationale', p. 26. Greg had previously addressed the identification and correction of error in *Principles of Emendation in Shakespeare* (London: British Academy, 1928).

modern-spelling edition'; an old-spelling editor would need to accept this as copy-text and introduce into it such later readings as were deemed to be authorial (*Prolegomena*, p. 18). The aim was to reach 'the nearest approach to our ideal of an author's fair copy of his work in its final state'. To achieve this, McKerrow argued that an editor should address not the individual variant in the revised reprint but the whole set: 'we must accept *all* the alterations of that edition, saving any which seem obvious blunders or misprints'. Greg preferred in principle to examine each reading in its own right.

In both critics' formulations the work is considered to go through one or more stages of authorial evolutions which improve the text but that do not give rise to separate versions at the level of either theory or practice, as McKerrow's reference to the fixed ideal indicates. Moreover – and this is why Greg's formulation is, for Shakespeare, more permissive – the New Bibliographers did not think of Shakespeare as a revising author. They had a strong orientation towards the binaries of good and bad, not only as regards texts, but also as regards individual readings. Part of the intractability they found in plays such as *Hamlet*, *Lear* and *Othello* was that the two main substantive texts did not readily yield to a hierarchy of good and bad.[58]

Revision entails an image of Shakespeare the author as a writer who is dissatisfied with his first attempt rather than a natural genius, and an image of the text as subject to instability and even indeterminacy. Yet the theory of Shakespeare as a reviser begins with a simple observation about the fixed material objects, the quarto and Folio texts of his plays. If two texts differ, those differences can be framed in terms of questions about textual production rather than deformation. Here, questions of Shakespeare's relationship with the theatre companies to which he belonged become pressing. How can Shakespeare the author be dissociated from companies that included Shakespeare the actor? If the Folio texts often relate to playbooks, on what basis are they as alienable from the editorial process? And finally, given the provenance of such texts, how else, other than in terms of authorial revision,

are coherent variations in structure and verbal detail to be explained?

These questions began to be pursued with diligence and energy in work on *King Lear* that led to the Oxford Shakespeare, in a series of investigations that revitalized textual study in a way scarcely seen since the early work of Greg and Pollard.[59] The work of these scholars, revisionist in two senses of the word, turned round the New Bibliographers' presumption in favour of the pre-theatrical text. In the particular case of *King Lear*, they drew on Peter Blayney's investigation of the printing of the Quarto which led to the conclusion that this text was badly printed from a manuscript that was likely to be authorial, and so was not a 'doubtful' quarto or memorially transmitted text.[60] If, as in Thomas Clayton's study of the opening scene of *Lear*, individual verbal variants had significant literary and theatrical import, if they contributed to an overall and connected strategy of revision, if as such they related to cuts and additions, then the variants in question could scarcely be other than of an authorial complexion.[61] The minor and 'indifferent' variants inevitably resist critical investigation in such terms, but the further the argument for revision could be extended, the more it made sense to treat the 'indifferent' variants in the same way as the more fully characterised authorial variants, much in the spirit of McKerrow's discussion of a text's variants as a cohort or class, while remaining alert to the inevitable presence of errors of transmission in any text.

Such thinking underlay the Oxford Shakespeare presentation of two separate texts, printed under the Quarto and Folio titles of *The History of*

---

[58] See McKerrow, *Prolegomena*, p. 13.

[59] Michael J. Warren, 'Quarto and Folio *King Lear* and the Interpretation of Albany and Edgar', in *Shakespeare, Pattern of Excelling Nature*, ed. David Bevington and Jay L. Halio (Newark and London, 1978), pp. 95–107; Gary Taylor and Michael Warren, eds., *The Division of the Kingdoms: Shakespeare's Two Versions of 'King Lear'* (Oxford, 1983).

[60] For Blayney, see n. 2.

[61] Thomas Clayton, '"Is this the promis'd end?": Revision in the Role of the King', in Taylor and Warren, eds., *Division*, pp. 121–41.

King Lear and *The Tragedy of King Lear*. But the Oxford editors found this play quantitatively rather than qualitatively different from other Shakespeare texts. Authorial revision was seen to account for major changes in a number of plays – in particular *Hamlet*, *Troilus* and *Othello* – and for more localized variants in many other plays. In these cases the Oxford edition printed only one text, because, although there were good reasons for envisaging two separate versions, the more limited extent of variation made it impractical to offer two texts. Latterly the general editors regretted supplying only one text of *Hamlet*.[62]

Revision theory as it applies to Shakespeare shares something with the theory of memorial reconstruction. In most accounts, neither offers a complete explanation in itself. Both usually take on the adjunct of theatrical adaptation. If in the case of 'bad' quartos it had proven difficult to disentangle the corrupting effect of poor memory from the reconstitutive effect of adaptation, much the same proved true of the authorial and theatrical variant in, for instance, *King Lear*, or the cuts in Folio *Hamlet*. Despite the predominance of authorial revision in the Oxford account of the play, the editors recognized that in the revised plays generally it was possible that changes such as deletions and alterations to stage directions may not have been directly effected by Shakespeare. In their thinking the dramatist wrote for the play to be performed, and the company's alterations would fulfil his intention to bring this about. There was therefore a wide difference between changes that were made by the theatre companies to which Shakespeare belonged and the undertakings of the reconstructors, even if they were actors. Authorial authority devolved onto theatrical changes to the text in some circumstances, but not all. This represented a radical change from earlier criticism, where the actors were almost always represented as agents of corruption. Stanley Wells in particular had brought onto the scene of editing a view of Shakespeare as a man of the theatre, and in the General Introduction to the *Textual Companion* Gary Taylor took this idea into rapprochement with Jerome McGann's writings on the socialization of the text.[63] Whereas

McKerrow had defined the ideal state of the text as the author's fair copy before it had been altered in the theatre (*Prolegomena*, p. 6), for Wells and Taylor the integrity of the play derives from authorially sanctioned theatre practice as well as direct authorial inscription.[64]

The Oxford Shakespeare treatment of *King Lear* found widespread assent in that there have been few attempts to reject the presence of authorial revision; indeed all subsequent editions (except reprints) have taken revision into account. The textual landscape had changed decisively. For instance, in the case of a textual variant editors now had to consider not simply which reading was correct, but whether the variant represents either two alternative valid readings or one valid reading alongside one error. Editing in this environment is unstable. Some critics have expressed opposition to the extent to which the revision hypothesis colonized the textual variant in *Lear* and other plays. Passages have been re-examined to show that other causes of variation, such as censorship, scribal confusion or compositorial space-saving, might be serious or arguably better local alternatives.[65]

---

[62] Stanley Wells and Gary Taylor, 'The Oxford Shakespeare Re-Viewed by the General Editors', *Analytic and Enumerative Bibliography*, n.s. 4 (1990), 6–20.

[63] *Textual Companion*, p. 34; p. 63, n. 34; citing Jerome J. McGann's influential *A Critique of Modern Textual Criticism* (Chicago, 1983).

[64] *Textual Companion*, p. 64, n. 53, citing James Thorpe, 'The Aesthetics of Textual Criticism', *PMLA*, 80 (1965), 465–82: the 'integrity of the work of art' derives from 'those intentions which are the author's, *together with those others of which he approves or in which he acquiesces*'. See also T. H. Howard-Hill, 'Modern Textual Theories and the Editing of Plays', *The Library*, VI, 11 (1989), 89–115.

[65] Ann R. Meyer, 'Shakespeare's Art and the Texts of *King Lear*', *Studies in Bibliography* 47 (1994), 128–46; R. A.Foakes, 'French Leave, or Lear and the King of France', *Shakespeare Survey 49* (Cambridge, 1996), pp. 217–23; Foakes, ed., *King Lear* (Walton-on-Thames, 1997); Richard Knowles, 'Revision Awry in Folio *Lear* 3.1', *Shakespeare Quarterly*, 46 (1995), 32–46; Robert Clare, '"Who is it that can tell me who I am?": The Theory of Authorial Revision between the Quarto and Folio Texts of *King Lear*', *The Library*, VI, 17 (1995), 34–59; Paul Hammond, 'James I's Homosexuality and the Revision

These criticisms sometimes aim to suggest either that the revision hypothesis has been exaggerated or that the causation cannot be decided. The most detailed argument along the former lines has addressed not *King Lear* but *Othello*. In 1965, E. A. J. Honigmann wrote a pioneering study entitled *The Stability of Shakespeare's Text*.[66] This suggested, among other things, that some of the textual variants in Shakespeare are best explained as authorial second thoughts. Naturally, the revisionists of the 1980s saw Honigmann's work as an important precursor of their own. There was, however, a significant difference in approach. Honigmann was committed to putting in action Greg's advice to analyse every variant in the light of a thorough investigation of every cause of textual variation. In the case of *Othello*, he found many, as became vividly clear in his 1996 response to the revisionists.[67] As a critique of the revision hypothesis, Honigmann's later study has two main points. First, he particularizes the agents of transmission, most notably by identifying the scribe behind the Folio text as Crane. This is persuasive textual scholarship, though our independent knowledge of Crane's work suggests that he cannot be held responsible for the major verbal variants. Second, Honigmann identifies both Folio and Quarto texts as independent derivatives. As a consequence, passages found only in the Folio are diagnosed not as additions to the Folio but inept theatrical cuts in the Quarto. Honigmann's reading of these large-scale structural variants, including the presence of the 'Willow Song' in Folio but not Quarto, admits no simple linear development from Quarto to Folio by way of authorial revision, as the Quarto is itself a degenerate text. Honigmann still admits the presence of authorial revision in a number of verbal variants, but his hypothesis denies the possibility of revision being a general explanation of the textual differences. Both texts are flawed witnesses to underlying authorial texts, and the differences between those texts are limited. In the case of 'indifferent' variants, the presumption is pushed away from the author and back towards non-authorial transmitters of the text.

In contrast, other critics found that the authorial bias of the revision hypothesis was beside the point, and so resisted the endeavour in the Oxford Shakespeare to correct error. Though similar in that it leads to multi-text presentations, the theoretical model of textual materialism summarised in the phrase 'particular textualizations' lies at some distance from the model of authorial revision. Revision attends to causes and the processes of making; textual materialism addresses only outcomes, specifically, in the case of Shakespeare, the surviving quartos and Folio. The 'Shakespearian Originals' series of the 1990s based itself on this approach, giving priority to the first printing of a play no matter what it was.[68] For instance Q1 *Henry V* is preferred over the Folio even though it is both more corrupt and later as a version of the play. This approach offers no basis on which to emend even the most palpable printer's error, as the 'textualization' and the 'version' are treated as the same thing.

ORIENTATIONS

The deconstructive interpretation of textual instability and revision theory stepped considerably beyond the attempt to identify the text of Shakespeare as the text of a particular printing. Jonathan Goldberg, for instance, declared that 'An examination of the textual properties of Shakespearian texts . . . will never produce a proper, selfsame Shakespearian text'; thus, he went on to say, in terms reminiscent of Walter Benjamin's account of the age of mechanical reproduction, 'we have no originals, only copies. The historicity of the text

---

of the Folio Text of *King Lear*', *Notes and Queries*, 242 (1997), 62–4.

66 E. A. J. Honigmann, *The Stability of Shakespeare's Text* (London, 1965).

67 See n. 49.

68 The phrase 'particular textualizations' is from Graham Holderness and Bryan Loughrey's general introduction, in, e.g., *The cronicle history of Henry the fift, With his battell fought at Agin Court in France. Togither with Auntient Pistoll*, ed. Holderness and Loughrey (Lanham, Maryland, 1993), p. 8.

means that there is no text itself'.[69] Goldberg shifts fast from the observation 'we have' to the declaration 'there is', as though what we don't have must be denied existence elsewhere, and hovers unstably between an observation about lost manuscripts and a hypothesis about the intrinsic nature of text as reinscription. But his observation chimes well with what textual critics were advising throughout the century: 'it is very doubtful whether, especially in the case of the earlier plays, there ever existed any written "final form"'; 'we cannot be certain of any close approach to the author's manuscript'; 'we cannot hope to achieve a certainly correct text, not so much on account of the uncertainties of transmission – though they are sometimes serious – as because the author may never have produced a definitive text for us to recover'; 'The written text of any such [theatrical] manuscript thus depended on an unwritten para-text which always accompanied it'; 'the perfection of permanence is unattainable if the text itself was never fixed'.[70] The point of difference lies in whether the Shakespearian textual condition allows any meaningful and coherent practice of editing.

By the end of the century it had become habitual to dismiss the New Bibliography.[71] To some critics, all that was left of it were ruins of a former age. Its aspiration to move away from the extant printed text in search of lost manuscripts was hopelessly idealist in its intellectual foundation. This idealism, combined with a naive positivism, led to binary categorizations that bore limited relation to the fluidity of textual production in the early modern theatre. The movement's dedication to recovering an authorial script isolated Shakespeare from the contingencies of theatre and his involvement in collaborative playwrighting. Its post-Romantic figuration of the author also diminished to the point of insignificance the possibility that Shakespeare revised his own works. Its technicalization of text now began to look like part of an outmoded masculinist culture that purveyed patriarchal attitudes and mystified its subjective judgements with the aura of science.[72] The death of the author proclaimed by Roland Barthes in 1968 seemed likely to lead to the death of the editor. Editing was in danger of retreating to being a mere pragmatics of an ousted ideology as well as a redundant technology. An 'unediting' movement led by the anarchically brilliant interventions of Randall McLeod pressed towards the view that editions should be abandoned in the classroom and replaced with photofacsimiles – an impractical suggestion for most purposes.[73]

It is a paradox that editing was probably revitalized by the intellectual stimulus of the new textualism and its engagement between textual study and the newer, theoretically inflected forms of literary study. The activity of editing became more self-conscious, more prepared to disclose its processes to the reader and to address text as a question of epistemology as much as philology. An editor was increasingly likely to be an emerging female scholar

---

[69] Jonathan Goldberg, 'Textual Properties', *Shakespeare Quarterly*, 37 (1986), 213–17, p. 214 and p. 217. See also Marion Trousdale, 'A Trip Through the Divided Kingdoms', *Shakespeare Quarterly*, 37 (1986), 218–23; and Margreta de Grazia and Peter Stallybrass, 'The Materiality of the Shakespearean Text', *Shakespeare Quarterly*, 44 (1993), 255–84. For a response to such approaches, see Ian Small, '"Why edit anything at all?": Textual Editing and Postmodernism: A Review Essay', *English Literature in Transition*, 38 (1995), 195–203.

[70] McKerrow, *Prolegomena*, p. 6 and p. 7; Greg, *Editorial Problem*, p. ix; *Textual Companion*, p. 2 and p. 18. But see, in contrast, Andrew Gurr, 'Maximal and Minimal Texts: Shakespeare v. The Globe', *Shakespeare Survey 52* (Cambridge, 1999), 68–87: 'My argument is, first, that the standard practice of the early companies did require them to possess an "ideal" text of their plays. It was not quite what modern editors seek to retrieve, but it was what the players themselves saw as their maximal version of the text' (p. 70).

[71] But see G. Thomas Tanselle, *Textual Criticism since Greg: A Chronicle, 1950–1985* (Charlottesville, 1987), for a stout defence of the New Bibliography.

[72] Valerie Wayne, 'The Sexual Politics of Textual Transmission', in *Textual Formations and Reformations*, ed. Laurie E. Maguire and Thomas L. Berger (Newark and London, 1998), 179–210; Maguire, *Suspect Texts*, pp. 26–32; Marcus, *Unediting*.

[73] The term 'unediting' was influentially established in Randall McLeod, 'UN *Editing* Shak-speare', *Sub-Stance*, 33–4 (1982), 26–55. MacLeod's introduction to his collection of essays *Crisis in Editing: Texts of the English Renaissance* (New York, 1994), pp. x–xi, typically suggests that his own paper on George Herbert's 'Easter Wings' seems to reveal that there is 'no role for future editions'.

trained in new historicism or feminism rather than an older male scholar trained in textual bibliography. There was a skills shortage in the more technical aspects of editing, but the newer practitioners were often effective in communicating the significance and fascination of textual issues to a wider readership as well as in adopting a fully current critical idiom.

If editing therefore continued with vigour, it did so notwithstanding the loss of confidence in some of its founding assumptions – not quite adrift, but certainly lacking some of its moorings. An unmet need had arisen for a textual criticism that embraced the more valuable insights of the 1980s and 1990s while offering a meaningful application to editorial practice. Peter Shillingsburg's work defined the different applications of editorial practice depending on the orientation of the editor to the text, the medium and the intended reader; in doing so it suggested the inevitability of editing.[74] The question most relevant to Shakespeare readers is not whether to edit, but how to edit.

For certain purposes a focus on the fixed printed artefact is all to the point. In the closing years of the twentieth century and after, scholars began to ask important questions about Shakespeare as a published author in his own lifetime and shortly after.[75] What authorial presentation is he given? Are the Folio preliminaries heartfelt testimonies, cultural negotiations or bookselling ploys?[76] Is it true that Shakespeare wrote plays without a view to print publication?[77] Which plays were in print, where were they sold, when, and in what possible combinations? Who read Shakespeare?[78] Yet these are specialized matters as compared with the huge range of work that falls under the twin heading of literary and theatrical study.

While accepting the need for responsibly edited texts, Barbara Mowat argued that the editor should defer not to the author but to the needs of the reader.[79] The limitation of this approach is that potentially it licenses the editor to act according to convenience rather than principle. It might be asked whether there is any real point where the reader is best served by a falsification of the author (whatever that might entail). As regards substantive readings, the answer is surely 'no'. Despite the quite considerable difficulties in determining and maintaining the boundary that sets them apart, accidentals are another matter.

As to that origin underlying the texts in books printed sometimes after Shakespeare's death, the sometimes converged and sometimes conflicting claims of author and theatre might be impossible to resolve. For an editor, theatrical authority will seem a vacuous term if it cannot discriminate between Q1 *Merry Wives*, Folio *Macbeth*, and a text printed, it would appear, with reference to a relatively unadapted playbook such as Folio *Julius Caesar*.[80] Moreover, at the end of the century some critics had tentatively returned to a view of Shakespeare as a poet. Lukas Erne has suggested that the typically long Shakespeare text is beyond the utility of theatre and has instead a literary aspiration. His views, though controversial, potentially destabilize the notion that Folio texts are close to the play as performed.[81] It remains to be seen what the implications might be for practical editing. But for editorial theory Erne's title *Shakespeare as Literary Dramatist* is indicative of a new emphasis at the beginning of the twenty-first century, one that pares back the theatrical dimension and asserts on new grounds the presence of Shakespeare the author in the field

---

[74] Peter Shillingsburg, *Scholarly Editing in the Computer Age* (Georgia, 1986; rev. edn, Ann Arbor, 1996).

[75] David Scott Kastan, *Shakespeare and the Book* (Cambridge, 2001).

[76] Margreta de Grazia, *Shakespeare Verbatim: The Reproduction of Authenticity and the 1790 Apparatus* (Oxford, 1991).

[77] Lukas Erne, *Shakespeare as a Literary Dramatist* (Cambridge, 2003).

[78] Heidi Brayman Hackel, '"Rowme" of its Own: Printed Drama in Early Libraries', in Cox and Kastan, eds., 113–30; Sasha Roberts, *Reading Shakespeare's Poems in Early Modern England* (Basingstoke and New York, 2003).

[79] Barbara Mowat, 'The Problem of Shakespeare's Text(s)', *Shakespeare Jahrbuch* 132(1996), 26–43.

[80] 'Relatively' as the play was written before 1608 but in the Folio text has act breaks.

[81] See also Gurr (n. 70).

of textual study. The recent upsurge in interest in Shakespeare's biography points in a similar direction. Nevertheless, any restatement of an authorial orientation would need to be conscious that the author as invoked by the editor is a construct rather than a given entity, and to be conditioned by awareness of the nature of Shakespearian textual production in all its complex uncertainty. This implies a strong sense of struggle between the stubborn contingency of physical materials and the aspirational endeavour of the editor, a struggle that resists any pat resolution.[82]

---

[82] I am grateful to James Purkis for generously detailed and astute comments on a draft of this chapter.

CRISIS IN EDITING?

EDWARD PECHTER

For the first time in fifty-four years, the editors of *Shakespeare Survey* have devoted an issue to 'Editing Shakespeare'. Perhaps they are motivated by a concern that has been gaining in currency since at least as early as 1988, when Randall McLeod chose 'Crisis in Editing' as the theme for the annual Conference on Editorial Problems at the University of Toronto.[1] *The Division of the Kingdoms* had appeared five years earlier and McLeod's own 'UN *Editing* Shak-speare' a year before that;[2] but 'Crisis in Editing' extended its claims beyond the special problems of the *Lear* text or any particular quarrel with received opinion to suggest that editing itself was in a critical condition.

This idea, in one form or another, has been in regular circulation ever since. In 1993, Margreta de Grazia and Peter Stallybrass, reflecting on the proliferation of *Lear* versions, foresaw 'a radical change indeed' not just in textual criticism but in all forms of Shakespearian practice. 'As a result of this multiplication, Shakespeare studies will never be the same.'[3] The editors of two recent collections on editorial matters claim we are in the midst of a transformation analogous to the sweeping institutional and conceptual revolutions – the new maps, the Reformation, print dissemination – of the Renaissance itself.[4] Implicit in these momentous re-enactments is the notion of a paradigm shift and, in the most recent *Cambridge Companion*, Barbara Mowat adopts this idea as the organizing principle for her analysis, concluding with a catalogue of the recently produced 'paradigm-threatening' critiques as a result of which 'hardly a "fact" supporting New Bibliographical assumptions remains standing'.[5]

Before accepting these claims, consider G. Thomas Tanselle's cautionary suggestions in a piece called 'Historicism and Critical Editing: 1979–85'. Devoting five pages to D. F. McKenzie's attempt in 'some of his recent work' to 'make authorship more a social than a private activity' and another eight pages to Jerome McGann's advocacy of 'social editing' as an antidote to the tendency in the Greg–Bowers tradition (as McGann sees it) 'to "suffocate textual studies" by limiting it to a narrow "psychological and biographical context"', Tanselle was fully aware of the intensity and magnitude of the attacks on New Bibliography; yet he is unpersuaded by the claims of 'some recent editors' that

---

For advice and suggestions, my thanks to Richard Abrams, Anthony Dawson, Patrick Finn, Alan Galey, E. A. J. Honigmann, Michael Neill, Ron Rosenbaum and the anonymous *Survey* reader, none of whom should be assumed to share the views of the piece.

1 Randall M Leod [sic], ed., *Crisis in Editing: Texts of the English Renaissance* (New York, 1994).
2 Gary Taylor and Michael Warren, eds., *The Division of the Kingdoms: Shakespeare's Two Versions of 'King Lear'* (Oxford, 1983); 'UN *Editing* Shak-speare', *Sub-Stance*, 33–4 (1982), 26–55.
3 'The Materiality of the Shakespearean Text', *Shakespeare Quarterly*, 44 (1993), 255–83; p. 255.
4 See Laurie Maguire and Thomas L. Berger, eds., *Textual Formations and Reformations* (Newark and London, 1998), p. 11 and p. 13; and Lukas Erne and Margaret Jane Kidnie, eds., *Textual Performances: The Modern Reproduction of Shakespeare's Drama* (Cambridge, 2004), p. 1.
5 Barbara A. Mowat, 'The Reproduction of Shakespeare's Texts', in Margreta de Grazia and Stanley Wells, eds., *The Cambridge Companion to Shakespeare* (Cambridge, 2001), pp. 13–29, p. 23 and p. 24.

'the field is at present in a state of crisis': 'the fact that different people hold different opinions about basic issues is not a sign of crisis; it points to the perennial situation in any challenging and lively field'.[6]

We don't have to agree with this opinion (Tanselle himself may no longer hold it); but how do we decide? how get to a position from which to determine whether the crisis in editing is real or just apparent? Leah Marcus begins a recent piece with the assertion that there 'has in recent years been a seismic shift in the way Shakespearian scholars view the early printed versions of the plays';[7] but unlike geological earthquakes, which produce an immediately evident rubble not just of 'supporting "facts"', cracks in the conceptual foundation can be determined only in retrospect.

For the time being, plausible guessing is about all we can hope for. My guess is that the crisis is real, and that in the differences between New Bibliographers and their most stringent critics – call them, for economy's sake, 'Newer Bibliographers' – more than the editing of Shakespeare is at stake. I take this dispute to be symptomatic of a crisis in 'Shakespeare studies' generally, as de Grazia and Stallybrass claim, even 'English studies' altogether, as Ann Thompson and Gordon McMullan suggest, introducing yet another recent collection on the topic.[8] Finally (though it belongs first), I should declare my belief that Newer Bibliography's challenges to editorial tradition have outlived their purpose. I write this piece in the probably quixotic hope that the critics producing these challenges will abandon their project for something more productive.

Let me begin with a test case, the differences between W. W. Greg, the protagonist in any story about editing Shakespeare, and Scott McMillin, one of the most compelling antagonists to New Bibliography in current work, concerning the provenance of Q1 *Othello*. In his 2001 edition for the Cambridge Early Quartos series, McMillin rejects 'the standard editorial position', established by Greg in *The Shakespeare First Folio* and adopted by almost all subsequent editors, that Q1 derives

from Shakespeare's foul papers.[9] As McMillin sees it, New Bibliographers have exaggerated the evidence for foul papers (vague stage directions and speech prefixes, idiosyncratic spelling and usages are less reliable indicators than have been thought) and underestimated 'signs of *other* textual origins in Q1', including 'signs of a prompt copy' (p. 4, McMillin's emphasis). McMillin's chief evidence for a prompt copy consists of the approximately 160 F lines not included in Q. Like E. A. J. Honigmann in his Arden 3 edition and its accompanying book on the *Othello* text,[10] McMillin sees these lines as cuts from rather than additions to an earlier text. But where Honigmann's conviction of a foul papers origin rests on a series of complicated inferences (authorial revisions, false starts, deletions sometimes missed by the scribe), McMillin thinks that 'the search for new signs of foul papers may have created more problems than it solves, for it calls upon fictions of competence and incompetence in the transmission of text to suit the changing needs of a hypothesis for which there is no documentary evidence in the first place' (p. 13).

Against this 'strained and unconvincing' account (p. 14), McMillin proposes a 'plain and obvious explanation of the 160 F lines which are missing in Q1', namely 'that Q1 proceeds from a theatre script which has been reduced for performance' (p. 13), specifically as a 'scribal copy taken from the dictation of actors who had memorized their

---

[6] *Textual Criticism since Greg: A Chronicle, 1950–1985* (Charlottesville, 1987), p. 122, p. 127 and p. 153. The piece originally appeared in *Studies in Bibliography*, 39 (1986), 1–46 and, like all *SB* material, is available on line at http://etext.lib.virginia.edu/bsuva/sb/.

[7] 'The Two Texts of *Othello* and Early Modern Constructions of Race', in Erne and Kidnie, *Textual Performances*, pp. 21–36, p. 21.

[8] *In Arden: Editing Shakespeare: Essays in Honour of Richard Proudfoot* (London, 2003), pp. xvi–xvii: 'the recent explosion of work' in 'editing and textual criticism' has 'moved' such matters 'from the periphery of English studies to the much-debated centre'.

[9] *The First Quarto of 'Othello'*, p. 4 (subsequent references interpolated parenthetically).

[10] *Othello* (Walton-on-Thames, 1997) and *The Texts of 'Othello' and Shakespearian Revision* (London and New York, 1996).

parts'. This hypothesis can account for a number of features in the text, but as McMillin concedes, in most cases 'other interpretations are possible for each of these kinds of textual phenomena' (p. 35). The foul papers hypothesis on the other side can also account for a number of features of the text and, though hardly self-evident, is more plausible than McMillin suggests.[11] The question then becomes whether the marginal increase in explanatory power — those relatively few variants hard to explain in any other way — justifies adopting a collective-dictation hypothesis, especially when the scenario required to imagine its realization turns out to include its own unlikely elements as well.

McMillin himself acknowledges one: 'I do not think scribes would have preferred working this way. They were trained to copy from manuscript, setting their own pace' (p. 43). But what of the actors' preferences? They were, we know, tremendously busy. 'With daily performances, each of a different play, actors had to learn or relearn their lines either during the day, or as soon as the day's performance ended. Naturally that had to be their priority. Situations existed in which plays no longer in repertory had to be revived, the actor being obliged to (re)learn a script for performance the following day.' Tiffany Stern, from whom I am quoting, concludes from this hectic schedule that 'with so little time to learn or relearn parts for performance, it is unlikely, in these instances, that there was any collective rehearsal at all'.[12] Collective dictation in the manner McMillin supposes seems even less likely; and while there would have been occasions — off season, during plague closures and between tours — when the actors were less rushed, even then the dictation scenario hardly seems to fit McMillin's description as 'an *economical* way of putting together a new prompt book' (p. 35, my emphasis). For if, as McMillin is surely right to say, Q1 *Othello* is not 'a "bad" Quarto' or pirated text but 'a prompt book legitimately prepared' (pp. 7–8), why didn't the actors take advantage of their in-house position to use an available old book as copy for the new? Loss may be hypothesized and is, in fact, documented in other instances, two of

which we will glance at in a moment: Beaumont and Fletcher's *Bonduca* and *A King and No King*. But in both these cases, a lost play book did not drive the company to the desperate expedient of actors dictating remembered performances: there was an earlier draft to fall back on. McMillin's scenario requires us to believe that the company lost *all the transcripts ever in its possession* — the author's first draft, the fair copy, the prompt books produced for previous revivals, even the copy licensed by the Master of the Revels — of one of the most popular plays of their resident playwright.[13] To this amazing

---

[11] The sorts of oddities Honigmann describes, sometimes in conjunction with double redactions, may be found across the canon – including *Romeo*, *Love's Labour's Lost*, *Caesar* and *Timon* – and have suggested a foul papers origin to others as well. See MacD. P. Jackson, 'The Transmission of Shakespeare's Text', in Stanley Wells, ed., *The Cambridge Companion to Shakespeare Studies* (Cambridge, 1986), pp. 163–85, p. 168; E. A. J. Honigmann, 'Shakespeare's Deletions and False Starts', *Review of English Studies*, 56 (2005), 37–48; and Anthony B. Dawson, 'The Imaginary Text, or the Curse of the Folio' in Barbara Hodgdon and W. B. Worthen, eds., *A Companion to Shakespeare and Performance* (Oxford, 2005), pp. 141–61.

[12] *Rehearsal from Shakespeare to Sheridan* (Oxford, 2000), pp. 56–7.

[13] McMillin speculates that the licensed copy was under review by the Master of the Revels while rehearsals were proceeding. 'The idea that the company would wait for the licensed prompt book to be returned from the Master . . . seems much too sedate a procedure for a busy commercial repertory company' (p. 43). But if the company expected a long delay, why didn't they put together a prompt book before submitting their evidently unique copy to the Master? Moreover, what evidence is there to believe that they *did* anticipate a long delay? In 1633, Sir Henry Herbert declared that 'All old plays ought to bee brought to the Master of the Revells, and have his allowance to them, for which he should have his fee.' But this was a new or more rigorously applied policy under a Master who had grown increasingly authoritarian as his tenure progressed. A few weeks after Herbert assumed the duties of the office in 1623, he authorized revivals for two plays previously reviewed by Sir George Buc on the basis evidently of nothing more than the verbal assurance that there were no profane performance additions or revisions. In one of these cases, he was even willing to overlook the loss of the originally licensed copy ('the allowed booke'), and in both cases, he waived his fee. These look like instances of a mere *pro forma* process with a quick turnaround. The time-consuming

carelessness, we must now add extraordinary good luck for, by all current accounts, the scribe who prepared the text for the Folio had access to an independent transcript for his copy[14]: what was incredibly lost is miraculously found.[15]

Such independent support as exists to justify the group dictation hypothesis emerges with McMillin's suggestion that Q1 *Othello* is based on a manuscript prepared for a private patron. The evidence for this, 'act divisions and "literary" stage directions' (p. 5), was noticed by Greg who, based on the scattered references to such copies and the dates for the few that have survived, came to the relatively circumscribed conclusion 'that at the time the copy for the First Folio was being got together a few private transcripts were already abroad'.[16] Greg's caution does not prevent him from anticipating McMillin's own view. In his summary conclusions, 'put dogmatically and stripped of qualification', Greg describes Q1 *Othello* as deriving 'from a private transcript of foul papers' (*First Folio*, p. 427). It is the 'foul papers' part that troubles McMillin, who objects that Greg, after bringing the private-transcript possibility 'fully into view', then 'sends it packing' with 'a neat turn of phrase' by which he attributes its preparation to 'the book-keeper', thereby managing to keep the transcription within at once the company's established holdings and sight of the author's draft (p. 5). McMillin is right to claim that 'the book-keeper' says more than Greg can know, but what does McMillin know that allows him to envisage a mode of production – actors dictating from remembered performances – effectively detached from the line of transmission back to the author?

The answer is, 'Humphrey Moseley's comment, in the preface to the Beaumont and Fletcher Folio of 1647, that the actors had made transcripts of the performance versions of some plays . . . : "When these Comedies and Tragedies were presented on the Stage, the Actours omitted some Scenes and Passages (with the Authour's consent) as occasion led them; and when private friends desir'd a Copy, they then (and justly too) transcribed what they Acted"' (p. 35). Moseley's comment might indeed be taken to describe actors dictating performances but, as H. R. Woudhuysen remarks, what the actors 'were transcribing is unclear: they may have been writing the plays out from memory or they may have been copying them from play-books'.[17] McMillin assumes a version of the first possibility, Greg the second and, since Moseley's words can be interpreted either way, we are left looking for signs in the existing record to decide which assumption is more plausible. McMillin can't point to any: 'no certain example of such a private theatrical transcript made by an actor – or deriving from him – has been identified'.[18] What have been identified, however, are private transcripts deriving from the author's draft or the book-keeper's book – Greg's assumption. Greg himself, in fact, transcribed the manuscript of *Bonduca* for the

process McMillin imagines for *Othello* would have occurred under an even more permissive regime than that of the early Herbert. See J. Q. Adams, ed., *The Dramatic Records of Sir Henry Herbert* (New Haven, 1917), pp. 20–1; Gerald Eades Bentley, *The Profession of Dramatist and Player in Shakespeare's Time* (Princeton, 1971), pp. 158–61; and N. W. Bawcutt, ed., *The Control and Censorship of Caroline Drama: the Records of Sir Henry Herbert, Master of the Revels 1623–73* (Oxford, 1996), p. 142 and pp. 182–3.

[14] See G. B. Evans, *et al.*, *The Riverside Shakespeare*, 2nd edn (Boston, 1997), p. 1288; and Stanley Wells and Gary Taylor, *et al.*, *William Shakespeare: A Textual Companion* (New York and London, 1997), p. 477.

[15] And the results turn out to be amazingly good – too good to be true. In the Introduction to his edition of *Othello* (Oxford, 2006), Michael Neill remarks that, even accepting the full-cast-dictation hypothesis, 'one might expect to find more numerous instances of apparent mishearing in an aurally constructed text' (p. 426). Neill suggests 'that the scribe might also have had access to a manuscript with which he could piece out the imperfections of what the actors dictated' (p. 427), but immediately concedes that 'If that were so, it is difficult to see why dictation would have been necessary in the first place.' He then hypothesizes that the scribe might have had access to the actors' written-out parts (p. 428), thereby loading an additional complication on to an interpretive structure already collapsing under the weight of its own too-much.

[16] *The Shakespeare First Folio: Its Bibliographical and Textual History* (Oxford, 1955), p. 154 (subsequent references interpolated parenthetically).

[17] *Sir Philip Sidney and the Circulation of Manuscripts, 1558–1640* (Oxford, 1996), p. 141.

[18] Woudhuysen, *Sir Philip Sidney*, p. 142.

Malone Society, 'evidently a copy of the play prepared for a private collector', in which the scribe,
faced with some missing scenes near the end of the
play, explains that '*the booke where [it] by it was first
Acted from is lost: and this hath beene transcrib'd from
the fowle papers of the Authors wch were found*'.[19] *Bonduca* is 'a private transcript of foul papers' – exactly
what Greg supposes for Q1 *Othello*.

That Greg's interpretation of Moseley corresponds with at least one piece of supporting
evidence doesn't prove him right.[20] Nor does
the absence of corroborating documents prove
McMillin wrong; the survival rate for Renaissance
playtexts and manuscripts is low, and a negative is
never provable anyway. But there is an additional
reason for scepticism about actor-derived transcripts as McMillin imagines them, and it comes
from Moseley himself. Like almost everyone working out of Moseley, McMillin quotes only a few
sentences, but look at the passage extended to
include a sentence before and after:

One thing I must answer before it bee objected; 'tis this:
When these *Comedies* and *Tragedies* were presented on
the Stage, the *Actours* omitted some Scenes and Passages
(with the *Authour's* consent) as occasion led them; and
when private friends desir'd a Copy, they then (and justly
too) transcribed what they *Acted*. But now you have both
All that was *Acted*, and all that was not; even the perfect
full Originalls without the least mutilation.[21]

As the context makes clear, Moseley's statement
about private copies is made in response to an anticipated objection to his claim that the 1647 Folio
is 'a *New Booke*'. Moseley makes the claim at the
very beginning of his 'Stationer to the Readers'
and hammers it home: although 'A *Collection of
Playes* is commonly but a *New Impression*' of previously published material, his book is limited to
those pieces never printed before. He grants that
some of his material may have circulated in private copies but insists, in the last bit quoted above,
that his versions are 'full Originalls' rather than
the performance abridgements he associates with
private copies, which allows him to reaffirm his
claim that the 1647 Folio is an authentically new
publication.

Quoted by themselves, the two sentences in the
middle of this passage can make Moseley sound like
a descriptive or enumerative bibliographer, disin-
terestedly surveying the field. But as the claims of
a book-seller trying to promote the virtues of an
expensive volume, the sentences signify in a different sense. They are more restricted; he is referring
not to a general category of text, only to instances
in which some of 'these plays', the ones included
in his Folio, might be said to have been published
before. There is one play in particular to which we
might think he is referring – *Bonduca*, which is in
fact included and (as we have seen) probably a private copy. The fit is not exact; the private copy is
not much shorter than the version Moseley prints,
and its omissions evidently not performance cuts.
But exact fits take us back to scientific bibliography,
and I doubt whether we should interpret Moseley's
words as so specifically targeted or as based on very
detailed knowledge. Rather, it looks as though he
has confused what we now recognize as one kind
of text, private patron copies, with another, bad
Quartos, in order to create a nonce-category that,
whether examples of it ever existed or not, serves
his rhetorical interests. I take it simply that, having heard *something* about what might be construed
as prior publication in the form of presentation

---

[19] (Oxford, 1951), pp. v, 90.

[20] There is, in fact, another very close example in Q1 *A King
and No King*, published in 1619 by Thomas Walkley, who
published Q1 *Othello* in 1622 and two other King's Men
productions between these dates, all four of these taken to
be an associated group. Walkley's dedication of *A King* to
Sir Thomas Neville pretty clearly identifies the Q1 copy as
a private patron manuscript, and the likely copy for that
manuscript, according to Robert Turner's textual analysis,
is 'the authors' final draft of the play rather than the company's promptbook' which, he offers reason to believe, was
lost. See Robert K. Turner, Jr, ed., *A King and No King*
(Lincoln, Nebraska, 1963), p. 2 and p. xxvii. Lee Bliss, who
has recently edited the play for the Revels Edition, accepts
Turner's views in all respects (Manchester, 2003), pp. 40–4.

[21] Arnold Glover, ed., *The Works of Francis Beaumont and John
Fletcher*, 10 vols. (Cambridge, 1905), vol. 1, p. xiii. Moseley's
full statement is also available in Greg's *Bibliography of the
English Printed Drama to the Restoration*, 4 vols. (Oxford, 1939–
59), vol. 3, p. 1233; and on EEBO.

copies, he adds to this whatever 'everyone knows' about the publication of abridged performance scripts, and thus pre-empts a charge of false advertising.[22]

Presumably he got some of his information from the actors. Moseley 'was on good terms' with them,[23] and he evidently intends to keep things that way. His parenthetical 'and justly too' gestures amiably in their direction in a way that tends to work against his main claim for the value of uncut authorial originals. In accommodating both actor- and author-generated texts and representing actors and authors as solicitous of each other's interests, Moseley ignores the substantial evidence of conflict so often emphasized in both contemporary and current accounts. (As McMillin wittily remarks, 'Heywood would have found Moseley's view of the author's co-operation a little too sunny' [p. 35], and think how Webster or, especially, Jonson might have reacted.) But if Moseley does not testify reliably to the whole truth and nothing but the truth about actor–author relations, he does not presume to that kind of authority; he just wants to keep everybody happy – authors, actors, book buyers on budgets, frail female readers, what have you[24]: the kind of self-projection we might expect from a soft-selling book publisher.

As with textual categories and author–actor relations, so with the process of textual transmission: Moseley is not an unimpeachable witness. In the amorphous good feeling with which the passage is suffused, 'transcribed what they *Acted*' should not be translated into a precise and disinterested description of what really happened. Like Heminges and Condell's reference to 'stolen and surreptitious copies', as David Scott Kastan interprets it, Moseley's preface 'enacts the classic "before and after" advertiser's strategy, and can hardly be taken as a definitive account of the early texts'.[25] If we are 'unclear' what Moseley was describing, he was probably unclear himself. But he doesn't really need to know what he is talking about; clarity and precision are not in his rhetorical interest – and, I am suggesting, inappropriate to his readers' expectations. Not that Moseley is deceptive; all the evidence suggests that he is a scrupulous and hon-

est book publisher; but a book publisher he is.[26] If there is deception here, it is not his but ours, misleading ourselves into taking blurb puffery for bibliography.

In the days before New Bibliography achieved prominence, Sidney Lee took Moseley's statement to describe how most Renaissance play manuscripts, including the texts in the Shakespeare Folio of 1623, got into print. Such an opinion seems outrageous now, but McMillin's declaration that 'My impression is that transcriptions of stage versions, mentioned by Moseley, reached print rather often' (p. 35) suggests we are still over-extending the range and over-defining the details of Moseley's reference. Nearly as much of a gap exists between what Moseley was writing about and what we take him to be writing about as between Borachio's 'seest thou not what a deformed thief this fashion is?' and the Watch's 'I know that Deformed'. An adjective is mistaken for a proper noun, giving parthenogenetic birth to a human being who is endowed with a history (''a has been a vile thief seven year') and precise social attributes ('a gentleman . . . 'a wears a lock'; *Much Ado*, 3.3). If this is what we've done with Moseley, the collective dictation scenario is purely an effect of discourse, and the reason we have found

---

[22] I am here following Peter M. W. Blayney's canny suggestion: 'Moseley is expecting someone to object (because "everyone knows") that plays were usually abridged for performance'. 'The Publication of Playbooks', in John D. Cox and David Scott Kastan, eds., *A New History of Early English Drama* (New York, 1997), pp. 383–422, p. 394.

[23] R. C. Bald, *Bibliographical Studies in the Beaumont & Fletcher Folio of 1647* (Oxford, 1937), p. 3.

[24] By restricting his volume to previously unpublished material, he has kept down both the price ('I would have none say, they pay twice for the same Booke') and the size (otherwise '*Ladies* and *Gentlewomen* would have found it scarce manageable').

[25] *Shakespeare and the Book* (Cambridge, 2001), p. 77.

[26] Compare Bald, *Bibliographical Studies*: 'an examination of the texts forming the bulk of the volume shows the extent to which Moseley's preface is to be relied upon, and vindicates his reputation for fair and just dealing *as a publisher*' (p. 114, my emphasis). Unlike Moseley, Heminges and Condell had evidently no commercial interest in their project, so there is even less reason to infer (as Kastan seems to do) any disingenuousness on their part.

no examples is that it never happened to begin with.[27]

How is it that Scott McMillin, though setting out to find a 'plain and obvious' alternative to New Bibliographical tradition, summons up his own 'fictions of competence and incompetence in the transmission of text' (lost books, a found book) 'to suit the changing needs of a hypothesis for which there is no documentary evidence in the first place' (the dictation scenario) and winds up producing a Rube Goldberg machine even more 'strained and unconvincing' than the one he seeks to displace? The convergence of such opposed critical trajectories seems surprising. The peculiar difficulties of the *Othello* text may be one factor – so intransigent that fundamentally different editors find themselves similarly sceptical about even their own accounts;[28] but in addition to this, and despite claims about seismic shifts, New and Newer Bibliographers occupy a fair amount of common and relatively stable ground. Both acknowledge elements of truth in each other's claims about authorial and non-authorial signs in the text. McMillin recognizes that foul papers exist *somewhere* in the background of QI; hence his comment on Othello's 'set [F "soft"] phrase of peace' that the Q reading is 'appropriate' because it coincides with 'other Shakespearian uses' (p. 65). And New Bibliographers don't believe that the foul papers *themselves* constituted the copy for Q. To expand on an earlier quotation: 'That foul papers lie behind QI, *probably at the remove of a scribal transcript*, is now the standard editorial position'; it was in fact Greg's who, along with most of his followers, would have found nothing to disagree with in McMillin's claim that the manuscript behind QI *Othello* is one 'on which Shakespeare may never have left a mark in his own hand' (p. 3).

The issue, then, comes down to how much mediation exists – how many transcriptions intervene – between the author's draft and the text we have, and this difference, though merely of degree, is hugely consequential. An abundance of mediation effectively disrupts the line of transmission; past a certain point, the multiplication of layers adds up to impenetrability, and there would be no getting back to an authorial origin. In McMillin's view, the goal of recovering authorial intention predisposes New Bibliographers to regard mediation as minimal. In developing this claim, McMillin builds on the work of Paul Werstine who, if it is true that 'hardly a "fact" supporting New Bibliographical assumptions remains standing', is entitled to a major share of the responsibility:

Paul Werstine has shown that a characteristic move in the logic of the New Bibliography is to frame textual problems according to the most economical line of transmission, from author (foul papers) to acting company (prompt book) to printing house. This economy creates a binary logic, with foul papers and prompt copy as the active terms. Left out of consideration . . . are other kinds of copy, such as transcripts made for private patrons, or transcripts made for later revivals of the play [which would] break the economical chain of agents.

(p. 6)

In other words, New Bibliographers refuse to countenance a proliferation of manuscripts because it would jeopardize their interpretive interests to do so, investing rather in those unlikely accounts that they wish to be true: 'optimistic enough to believe that an authentic Shakespearian *Othello* can be determined' (p. 2), they invent a foul-papers origin that turns Q 'into a repository of hope and desire' (p. 3). By 'offering the hope of knowing Shakespeare's first conception of the play', Honigmann represents the 'fullest and most imaginative version' of 'the New Bibliography working to catch sight of its desired objects, the imagined Shakespeare manuscripts' (p. 8).

---

[27] Some other discussions of patron copies and of Moseley: Harold Love, *Scribal Publication in Seventeenth-Century England* (Oxford, 1993), pp. 65–70; Richard Dutton, *Licensing, Censorship and Authorship in Early Modern England: Buggeswords* (Basingstoke, 2000), pp. 90–113; and Lukas Erne, *Shakespeare as Literary Dramatist* (Cambridge, 2003), p. 89.

[28] See Greg, *First Folio*, p. 370; Honigmann, *Texts of 'Othello'*, pp. 145–6; and Evans, *Riverside Shakespeare*, p. 1299. McMillin is no exception. 'I set this down', he says of his dictation scenario, 'more assertively than is perhaps warranted' (p. 35).

But what if New Bibliographical assumptions are basically right? Given the material lost from this period (we don't know how much – that's the problem) and the ambiguity of the evidence in what survives, we cannot determine whether the manuscripts in Shakespeare's milieu circulated in a relatively frugal or abundant economy. (The six *Game at Chess* manuscripts might suggest proliferation; but their survival, given the exceptional scandal and censorship surrounding Middleton's play, might suggest that frugal assumptions would fit better elsewhere.) And if abundance is no less a speculative assumption than economy, then everything McMillin says about New Bibliography can apply to his own project equally well. Maybe he finds the dictation scenario plausible because he wants to; proliferation caters to his interpretive interest, allowing him to deliver a knockdown blow to Greg and his followers, for 'If this practice went on often', as Woudhuysen says, 'its effect on theories about the copy-text for printed plays would be devastating'.[29] Much virtue in 'if'; although nothing corresponding to this practice 'has been identified' in any single instance, McMillin is undeterred from his 'impression' that this procedure occurred not just once but 'rather often'. If taking Heminge and Condell as 'a definitive account' is 'testimony to our desire for the authentic Shakespeare', then taking Moseley as definitive is testimony to our desire for the absence of the authentic Shakespeare.[30] This is the Newer Bibliography working to catch sight of its desired objects, manuscripts proliferating in such abundance that any putatively Shakespearian draft is bound to be lost in the shuffle.

Here, then, is yet another similarity: New and Newer Bibliography are both based on predisposition – assumptions or 'impressions' that cannot be verified with 'apodictic certainty'. In this respect, moreover, they resemble all other interpretive projects, ranging from the most complex to the most simple, and even to those apparently pre-interpretive perceptions which might seem to constitute a 'value-neutral' cognitive foundation from which to judge among contending interpretive claims. As D. F. McKenzie puts it, 'To observe at

all is to bestow meaning of some kind on the thing observed; to gather particular pieces of evidence is to seek those relevant to some preconceived notion of their utility'.[31] Like turtles, it's interpretation all the way down.[32]

Both New and Newer Bibliographers work more or less comfortably within this situation, making do with what they've got – 'circumstantial' rather than 'veridical evidence', say.[33] McMillin's disarmingly candid 'impression' implicitly concedes that his conclusions are impressed on inconclusive evidence or, more accurately, derived from the assumptions by which he determines 'precisely what counts as evidence and what does not, how data are to be constituted as evidence, and what implications are to be drawn . . . from the evidence thus constituted';[34] but he evidently finds

---

[29] *Sir Philip Sidney*, p. 141.

[30] Kastan, *Shakespeare and the Book*, p. 77.

[31] D. F. McKenzie, 'Printers of the Mind: Some Notes on Bibliographical Theories and Printing-House Practices', *Studies in Bibliography*, 22 (1969), 1–75, pp. 3–4.

[32] See Hayden White, *Metahistory: The Historical Imagination in Nineteenth-Century Europe* (Baltimore, 1973): 'there are no apodictically certain theoretical grounds on which one can legitimately claim an authority for any one of the [interpretive] modes over the others as being more "realistic"' (p. xii); and it is 'fruitless' to 'argue among contending conceptions of the historical process on cognitive grounds which purport to be value-neutral in essence' (p. 284). As Morse Peckham puts it in *Man's Rage for Chaos: Biology, Behavior, and the Arts* (Philadelphia, 1965): '*To perceive is to categorize a configuration* by ascribing to it the attributes of a conventionalized category . . . Sign perception is not a passive response to a stimulus but a dynamic interaction involving both sign and interpretation . . . Ultimately, to *perceive* is to *choose, will, intend*' (p. 90, Peckham's emphases).

[33] Michael D. Bristol's distinction in 'How Good Does Evidence Have to Be?', in Edward Pechter, ed., *Textual and Theatrical Shakespeare: Questions of Evidence* (Iowa City, 1996), pp. 22–43, pp. 23–9. See also Meredith Skura, 'Is There a Shakespeare after the *New* New Bibliography?', in R. B. Parker and S. P. Zitner, eds., *Elizabethan Theater: Essays in Honor of S. Schoenbaum* (Newark and London, 1996), pp. 169–83, pp. 171–2; and Anthony B. Dawson, 'Correct Impressions: Editing and Evidence in the Wake of Post-Modernism', in Thompson and McMullan, *In Arden*, pp. 31–47, p. 40.

[34] See White, *Metahistory*, p. 284.

this impression adequate as a foundation for his account. Greg often strikes a similar tone: 'plausible guessing is about all we can hope for' given 'the frequent ambiguity of the evidence', but 'we may yet reach conclusions of some interest' (*First Folio*, p. 175).

Greg's 'all we can hope for' confirms McMillin's claim about New Bibliographical motivations ('repository of hope and desire'), but is the presence of hope in an interpretive enterprise a bad thing? Its absence, after all, doesn't lead to better interpretation, or to any interpretation at all. (In Dante, abandoning hope means losing the benefit of the intellect and locates you in hell.) Hope is a necessary precondition for interpretive work, like its mate, 'desire', for if 'academic and scientific discourse is . . . as rooted in human desire as a love letter or a legal complaint',[35] then desire, while it may undermine some of our interpretive performances, must underlie all of them. As must the imagination. You'd think imagination is a good thing for a Shakespearian but, in McMillin's canny innuendo about solipsism, 'imaginative version' is code for 'wishful thinking'.[36] But if wishful thinking is a scandal, interpretation must be a scandal; based on assumptions and driven by values, interpretation is a kind of wishful thinking. Wishful thinking – motivated by hope, desire, and imagination – is the only kind of thinking we've got.

The antifoundationalist critics who have brought us here suggest where to go now. According to Hayden White, if we cannot distinguish between interpretive modes as more or less '"realistic"', the 'best grounds for choosing' become 'ultimately aesthetic or moral rather than epistemological'. In Richard Rorty's terminology, we transfer interest from correspondence, how well an interpretive mode mirrors 'what is really out there', to coherence and consequence, what it adds up to and where it's going.[37] The important matter is not that New and Newer Bibliography are based on assumptions and values (what mode isn't?), but that they are based on different assumptions and values, and it is on these differences that we ought to concentrate. We need to ask: 'why are New Bibliographers so

interested in authorial intention? why are Newer Bibliographers so averse to this interest? what do they offer as an alternative? and which interests seem better, morally or aesthetically or pragmatically, as the basis for critical practice?' These questions focus on deliberate motivation, as though New and Newer Bibliographers understood what they were doing; but since there is no reason to believe that editorial theorists are, any more than the rest of us, fully informed about the values underlying their work, the answers will depend as much on the origins, identity and consequences of critical practices as on the declared intentions of the practitioners themselves.

If we begin with New Bibliographical interest in authors, consider Greg's 'The Rationale of Copy-Text', probably his best-known piece, and one that reflects more or less directly on these matters of history, identity and direction. 'The Rationale' enters an ongoing debate whether New Bibliography is chiefly a scientific method providing, in Dover Wilson's words, 'a foundation of fact' for 'literary judgements' which 'are notoriously shifting as sand', or whether it is itself chiefly engaged with literary judgments, in which case, as Tanselle puts it, 'Editing is not a prerequisite to scholarly literary criticism; it is a part of that criticism.'[38] Greg

---

[35] George L. Dillon, *Contending Rhetorics: Writing in Academic Disciplines* (Bloomington, 1991), p. 2.

[36] 'Wishful thinking' is the third term in the distinction I borrowed from Bristol.

[37] White, *Metahistory*, p. xii; see also Rorty's *Philosophy and the Mirror of Nature* (Princeton, 1979), and Thomas S. Kuhn, *The Structure of Scientific Revolutions*, 2nd edn (Chicago, 1970), from whom the second quotation is taken (p. 206).

[38] Dover Wilson is quoted by F. P. Wilson, who adds a confirming sentence that 'The fact may be rock-like, but the interpretation a castle of sand built upon the rock.' See *Shakespeare and the New Bibliography*, revised and ed. Helen Gardner (Oxford, 1970), p. 112. For Tanselle see 'Textual Study and Literary Judgment', reprinted in *Textual Criticism and Scholarly Editing* (Charlottesville and London, 1990), pp. 325–37, p. 337. Fredson Bowers at different times argues both positions. In 'Hamlet's "sullied" or "solid" Flesh: A Bibliographical Case History', he dismisses the mere 'opinion' of 'literary argument', where 'little certainty can obtain', in favour of the 'mechanical evidence of bibliography' by which he 'can

comes down resoundingly on the latter side, supporting 'the discretion of an editor', whose 'liberty of judgment' he is centrally 'concerned to uphold'.[39] As Greg sees it, there is 'a definite limit to the field over which formal rules are applicable', and any 'editor who declines or is unable to exercise his judgement and falls back on some arbitrary canon, such as the authority of the copy-text, is in fact abdicating his editorial function' (p. 28).

Fredson Bowers, while granting 'it is all very well for Sir Walter to talk of the responsibility of the editor to back his own judgement', wonders whether 'The Rationale' has 'thrust us back into the eighteenth-century confusion' of undisciplined eclecticism. He finds reassurance in New Bibliography's 'essential difference' from the work of earlier editors, who treated Shakespearian materials like texts from antiquity, descending in various independent lines over the centuries in a way that disallows any glimpse of convergence in an authoritative point of origin. By contrast, the 'increased understanding of the bibliographical method' appropriate to Shakespearian texts allows New Bibliographers to locate authorial intentions at the start of relatively short lines of transmission, an advance that has 'altered the eclectic approach to editing to such a degree that there is scarcely a parallel between the current position and that of the past'.[40]

Greg would hardly disagree. He had contributed more than anyone to this 'increased understanding', according to which, as he put it, 'what really mattered was what sort of manuscripts they were that lay behind the earliest texts'.[41] But when Bowers claims that 'critical judgement must *expand from a logical basis* in bibliographical and linguistic fact', he locates method in a position of logical priority to critical judgement, and with this claim Greg was not prepared to go along.[42] In fact, 'The Rationale' has it just the other way round, investing in a 'frankly subjective procedure' (p. 31) as producing results

preferable to those achieved through following any mechanical rule. I am, no doubt, presupposing an editor of reasonable competence; but if an editor is really

incompetent, I doubt whether it much matters what procedure he adopts . . . And in any case, I consider that it would be disastrous to curb the liberty of competent editors in the hope of preventing fools from behaving after their kind. (p. 32)

Greg's divergence from Bowers's position is nowhere clearer than in his indebtedness to A. E. Housman's 'Application of Thought to Textual Criticism'. 'Knowledge is good, method is good', Housman concludes, 'but one thing beyond all others is necessary; and that is to have a head, not a pumpkin, on your shoulders, and brains, not pudding, in your head'.[43] 'The Rationale' appropriates not just Housman's argument but his tone. Fools 'behaving after their kind' captures Housman's 'devastating sarcasm' (p. 20) – Greg's sole appreciative reference to current authority in the piece.

---

now expose an error in criticism' and 'establish the text for an individual reading' ('sallied' is right). See *Shakespeare Survey 9* (Cambridge, 1956), pp. 44–8, p. 44 and p. 47. But in *On Editing Shakespeare* (Charlottesville, 1966), he maintains that 'the sole function of linguistic analysis and of textual bibliography, with all its mechanical aids, is to guide an editor's critical intelligence' (p. 178). For a fair-minded and knowledgeable review of New Bibliography's 'mixed signals' on this matter, see Laurie E. Maguire, *Shakespearean Suspect Texts, The 'Bad' Quartos and Their Contexts* (Cambridge, 1994), pp. 42–59, p. 42.

[39] *Studies in Bibliography*, 3 (1950–1), 19–36, p. 30 (subsequent references interpolated in parentheses).

[40] *On Editing Shakespeare*, pp. 82–3.

[41] It is only with this recognition, Greg remarks, that his work really took off. See his review of Bowers's *On Editing Shakespeare and the Elizabethan Dramatists* in *Shakespeare Quarterly*, 7 (1956), 101–4, p. 101.

[42] *On Editing Shakespeare*, p. 72. I have italicized the predicative metaphor, as I do in the following comparable passages: 'Although there can be no substitute for critical taste, criticism must have a bibliographical *basis*' (p. 83); 'critical and linguistic . . . criteria must operate *within the framework* of the general bibliographical conditions' (p. 94); 'The whole question *turns on the single point* of the assignment as much as possible by *non-literary means*, of degrees of authority for texts in whole or in part, this estimate thereupon being *used as a referent* for consistent assumptions on which eclectic editing can be *based*' (pp. 95–6).

[43] J. Diggle and F. R. D. Goodyear, eds., *The Classical Papers of A. E. Housman*, 3 vols. (Cambridge, 1972), vol. 3, pp. 1058–69, p. 1069.

And here, in Greg's identification with Housman, is where the question of identity, what New Bibliography is, metamorphoses into the historical question, where it comes from. Where Bowers emphasizes the 'essential difference' by which New Bibliographers have advanced beyond editors of classical texts, Greg makes common cause with a classical editor against the claims of his colleague McKerrow. Bowers celebrates radical innovation ('scarcely a parallel' with 'the past'), but Greg aligns himself with a critic who thunders against the self-congratulatory progressivism by which 'the most frivolous pretender has learnt to talk superciliously about "the old unscientific days"'.[44]

Greg has no intention of abandoning the methodological advance that allows him to identify foul-papers origins for early texts; but in 'The Rationale' he stands outside his practice in order to locate it within an extensive continuing history. And from the perspective of this *longue durée*, the question of textual provenance looks less like 'what really mattered' (Bowers's 'essential difference') than, in Freud's memorable phrase, 'the narcissism of minor differences'.[45] In an extraordinary achievement of self-detachment, having worked for years to establish the uniquely defining features of his practice, Greg now represents New Bibliography as not essentially new, just the latest instalment in an ongoing dialectical interplay between systematic method and critical taste.

Going on from when, exactly? Greg doesn't ask this question, but if we want to continue down the path to which 'The Rationale' points us, we come, pretty much everyone agrees, to Edmond Malone. As the 'greatest early editor of Shakespeare's works', Malone's 'dedication to discovering the facts of literary history through manuscripts and early editions laid the foundations for the scholar's code and the modern study of literature'.[46] Malone's *Historical Account of the English Stage* is almost unwaveringly focused on the primitives of a historicist agenda – names, dates, places and the authority by which they are established.[47] 'Facts', Peter Martin declares, 'not politics, drove his research'.[48] And yet, as Martin himself recognizes, Malone's supposedly self-sustained research depended on the support of extrinsic '[c]ultural and political circumstances', including 'the astonishing worship of Shakespeare as the national poet' during 'the second half of the eighteenth century' which by itself guaranteed that 'what he had to offer was especially valued'.[49] Jonathan Bate, reflecting on the diverse 'appropriators of Shakespeare' in Malone's

---

44 'The Application of Thought', p. 1069. 'The old unscientific days are everlasting' he adds; 'they are here and now; they are renewed perennially by the ear which takes formulas in, and the tongue which gives them out again, and the mind which meanwhile is empty of reflexion and stuffed with self-complacency.'

45 In 'The Taboo of Virginity' (1917), Freud argues that the special hostility we feel to those who closely resemble us derives from the threat they seem to represent to our egotistical sense of distinct individuality. See *The Standard Edition of the Complete Psychological Works of Sigmund Freud*, trans. James Strachey, 24 vols. (London, 1953–74), vol. 11, p. 199.

46 This is the blurb from Peter Martin, *Edmond Malone, Shakespearean Scholar: A Literary Biography* (Cambridge, 1995). Malone didn't invent professional literary study single-handedly and *ex nihilo*. For ways in which Capell anticipated Malone's innovations, see Alice Walker, 'Edward Capell and his Edition of *Shakespeare*', in Peter Alexander, ed., *Studies in Shakespeare: British Academy Lectures* (Oxford, 1964), pp. 132–48; Mowat, 'Reproduction of Shakespeare's Texts', pp. 15–18; and Martin, pp. 31–9, who also sees Dr Johnson as an important precursor. Peter Seary wants to take the story back even earlier, arguing in *Lewis Theobald and the Editing of Shakespeare* that, as 'the first to edit Shakespeare systematically', Theobald deserves to be called 'the founder of modern scholarship devoted to Renaissance English literature' (Oxford, 1990), p. vii and p. ix.

47 His rare deviations from the discourse of sober scholarship sound perfunctory. When he proclaims the right of English rather than Italian theatre to the 'honour' of being 'the most ancient in Europe', the value of defeating foreign competition is clearly secondary to establishing the factual coordinates of English theatrical origins. See Malone's *Poems and Plays of Shakspeare*, 10 vols. (London, 1790), vol. 1 Part 2, p. 3.

48 *Edmond Malone*, p. 136. Martin is commenting on Malone's insouciant response to a congratulatory letter from Edmund Burke, who believed the 1790 edition affirmed the civilizing power of tradition: if Burke 'wanted to equate his history of the stage with the history of the state, that was fine with Malone.' A copy of Burke's letter is prefixed to the *Historical Account* in James Boswell's 'Third Variorum' edition of *The Plays and Poems of William Shakspeare*, 21 vols. (London, 1821), vol. 3, pp. 3–4.

49 *Edmond Malone*, p. xvi.

time, remarks that the 'one premise shared by all' of them 'is that his plays matter, that they are to be valued – which is why they are worth appropriating', illustrating the point with 'some rousing words' from Hazlitt: 'People would not trouble their heads about Shakespear, if he had given them no pleasure, or cry him up to the skies, if he had not first raised them there. The world are not grateful *for nothing*.'[50] Malone doesn't cry Shakespeare up to the skies but doesn't have to; he focuses soberly on the facts, but the rhetoric is epideictic by default. His whole apparatus for retrieving an authentic Shakespeare is secured by the conviction, shared with his contemporaries, that the Shakespeare text merits all the attention he lavished on it.[51]

At this point, it might seem that we have wandered so far down the path pointed to by Greg's 'Rationale' as to lose contact altogether with the original territory. The bardolatrous 'premise' that produced late-eighteenth-century Shakespeare 'worship' opens an apparently unbridgeable gap between New Bibliography and its historical origins. New Bibliographers insistently repudiate the idea of an appreciation independent of a disciplined critical faculty. Even in the libertarian mood of 'The Rationale', Greg worries about a 'reliance on personal taste' (p. 28) and endorses editorial discretion only with a proviso: 'intrinsic merit' can determine readings 'so long as by "merit" we mean the likelihood of their being what the author wrote rather than their appeal to the individual taste of the editor'(p. 29). Tanselle puts this idea at the centre of his work, tirelessly reiterating that 'most basic distinction between editions in which the aim is historical – the . . . reconstruction of what the author intended – and those in which the editor's own personal preferences determine' critical action.[52]

This distinction, though, is not so easy to sustain as it may sound: can we really determine authorial intention independently of our own preferences? In their scientific moods, New Bibliographers sometimes identify authorial intention with textual properties, as though foul papers were themselves the final object of their interest[53]; but while autho-

rial intention may be 'implied' by or 'inferred' from textual properties, it is not embedded in them.[54] In MacDonald Jackson's words, the author is a 'hypothetical' rather than empirical category, what 'Shakespeare "would have" approved'.[55] According to Anthony Dawson, editors pursue 'an ideal', not 'what the author wrote', but 'what the author would have written had he had all his wits about him – a situation that could never quite be achieved in real life'.[56] As an imagined point of reference guiding editorial judgment, the author is 'always

---

[50] *Shakespearean Constitutions: Politics, Theatre, Criticism (1730–1830)* (Oxford, 1989), p. 9.

[51] Thomas Postlewait shrewdly remarks that Margreta de Grazia, in *Shakespeare Verbatim: The Reproduction of Authenticity and the 1790 Apparatus* (Oxford, 1991) does to Malone what she claims Malone does to Shakespeare – separates 'him from the specific aspects of his career and age, making him a singular, obsessive figure, basically enclosed within his campaign for authenticity'. See 'The Criteria for Evidence: Anecdotes in Shakespearean Biography, 1709–2000', in W. B. Worthen with Peter Holland, ed., *Theorizing Practice: Redefining Theatre History* (Basingstoke and New York, 2003), pp. 47–70, p. 63.

[52] See *Textual Criticism since Greg*, p. 102. Two more examples from the same source: 'critical' editing is 'an attempt to establish the author's own words' while 'creative' or 'aesthetic' editing aims to produce 'the artistically "best" text' based on 'subjective decisions reflecting only one's own tastes and inclinations' (p. 51). 'The issue turns on whether editorial judgement is conceived of as being directed toward establishing authorially intended readings or readings that appeal to the editor's own literary sensibility' (p. 99).

[53] This seems to be underlying Fredson Bowers's belief, originally expressed in 1954, that 'Some day' the 'final capstone' will 'be placed' on 'what may be called a definitive text of Shakespeare'; see *On Editing Shakespeare*, p. 100 and p. 101. Mowat ('Reproduction of Shakespeare's Text', p. 21) quotes some supremely confident claims dating from the late 1960s and early 1970s that editorial work is on the verge of possessing the 'ultimately authoritative' or 'fully definitive' Shakespearian text.

[54] For the 'implied author', see Wayne C. Booth, *The Rhetoric of Fiction* (Chicago, 1961). Fredson Bowers identifies the goal of editorial work as 'to approximate as nearly as possible an *inferential* authorial fair copy'; see 'Textual Criticism', in James E. Thorpe, ed., *The Aims and Methods of Scholarship in Modern Languages and Literatures* (New York, 1968), pp. 23–42, p. 26 (my emphasis).

[55] 'The Transmission of Shakespeare's Text', p. 166.

[56] 'The Imaginary Text', p. 141.

a fiction'.[57] When the author is Shakespeare – the agency imagined to produce those reading and theatrical experiences that generate the most durable and intense interpretive engagement – it might be called a supreme fiction. Any attempt to identify Shakespearian intention in this sense is bound to be based substantially on assumptions and values that reflect an 'editor's own personal preferences'.

Boswell the Younger, writing to support an emendation proposed by Warburton for a much-debated line in *Othello*, declares that 'a regulation which contains so much beauty' must be the invention of 'our great author' and not 'merely the refinement of a critic'.[58] The reverentially bardolatrous tone of 'our great author' is remote from the casual 'author [with] all his wits about him', but conceptually the two are hard to tell apart. Is New Bibliography no more than this – Bardolatry toned down? 'Toned down' is the wrong way to put it. What should be emphasized, rather, is New Bibliography's enrichment of earlier work. Greg and his followers may not be so sharply different as they claim from 'the undisciplined eclecticism' of 'editorial work before the present century';[59] but they achieved a vast increase in knowledge, leading to (or perhaps from) some remarkable conceptual breakthroughs and an extraordinarily productive method for dealing with the early texts. All this may not have brought us to Shakespeare's intention as in itself it really is (no critical practice can claim that), but it has added immeasurably to the intellectual sophistication of what we do and the complexity of the institutional systems within which we do it. Yet one thing remains unchanged from Malone's time, driving the enterprise as much for New Bibliographers as for Shakespearians around 1800: the 'premise' that Shakespeare's plays are *something*, engaging our interest first as 'matters of concern' and only then as 'matters of fact';[60] and that taking part in the long history of reflection about them – whether in critical editions, commentary, or theatrical production – is a good thing.

So much for New Bibliography's interest in the author, now to the repudiation of that interest

on the other side. Newer Bibliographers have no shortage of arguments why an author-centered editorial practice is bad. It is unhistorical (Shakespeare didn't write for publication, authorial status as we know it didn't exist in the Renaissance), antitheatrical (performance is a collective enterprise, the playwright has only a small part), and politically objectionable (cultural production is identified with an elite notion of the gifted individual). The concepts of history, theatre and politics underwriting these claims may be tendentious and devoid of content – or so I have argued elsewhere[61]–but their widespread persistence suggests they are nourished by deeper convictions. Once again, I am interested in underlying assumptions and values, and Paul Werstine's critique of Greg and his followers, undertaken in an array of strongly argued

57 I am reversing Walter J. Ong's eminently reversible claim that 'The Writer's Audience Is Always a Fiction', *PMLA*, 90 (1975), 9–21.
58 *Plays and Poems*, vol. 9, p. 465. The line, 'Put out the light, and then put out the light' (5.2.7), provoked comment and emendations by Rowe, Pope, Theobald, Fielding, Dr Johnson, Capell, Malone and many others. Furness reproduces much of the debate, which carried on to his own time (and in fact continues until at least as recently as Ridley's Arden 2 edition). See *The New Variorum Othello* (Philadelphia, 1886), pp. 294–6.
59 Tanselle, *Textual Criticism and Scholarly Editing*, p. 329. See also Jackson, 'The Transmission of Shakespeare's Text': 'Until this century, editors tended to choose solely according to literary-dramatic criteria, as they perceived them' (p. 167).
60 See Bruno Latour, 'Why Has Critique Run out of Steam? From Matters of Fact to Matters of Concern', *Critical Inquiry*, 30 (2004), 224–48.
61 See 'Making Love to Our Employment; or, the Immateriality of Arguments about the Materiality of the Shakespearean Text', *Textual Practice*, 11 (1997), 51–68; 'Literary and Cultural Texts: Why Shakespeare Studies should not be Peaceful', in Graham Bradshaw, Angus Fletcher and John Mucciolo, eds., *The Shakespearean International Yearbook, Volume III* (Aldershot, 2003), pp. 103–14; and 'What's Wrong With Literature?', *Textual Practice*, 17 (2003), 205–26. This is not to disagree with the claims of McGann and many others that author-based criticism often limits commentary to a suffocatingly narrow 'psychological and biographical context' (see p. 20); but to say that many of the performances in a particular mode are disappointing does not discredit the mode itself (Sidney's argument in the *Defence*).

essays published during the last twenty or so years, is the place to look.

McMillin's 'economy' and 'binary logic' fairly characterize Werstine's main point: New Bibliography is founded on the reduction of complex materials into a single axis of difference, as when, in *Shakespeare's Folios and Quartos* (1909), A. W. Pollard 'divides all the quartos into just two classes, labelling them the "good" and the "bad"'. Despite its 'nearly absurd simplicity' compared with the 'large and multiple differences' among the quartos themselves, 'the binarism and rigidity of his original distinction' has, Werstine claims, been perpetuated.[62] Seven years later, he tells the same story with a new protagonist: Greg 'reduces a dispersed heterogeneity of manuscripts' into a 'binary system', with the '"promptbook"' serving 'as the opposite of "fowle papers"'; and again 'editors and scholars' who 'labor under the influence of Greg's theory . . . continue to evade the complexity exhibited in the range and diversity of the extant manuscripts'.[63] To reductionism Werstine adds the charge of idealism: the categories constituting New Bibliographical binaries 'are hypothetical constructs that have yet to be empirically validated': 'no documentary evidence' survives for the category Greg 'designated "foul papers"' ('Narratives', p. 81), and his 'stipulations of tidiness' as the defining features of promptbooks 'are merely ideal and were rarely, if ever, in force for theatrical manuscripts' ('Plays', p. 485).

But Greg himself acknowledges all this. It 'would be a great mistake', he says about promptbooks, not 'to suppose' that 'a good deal of untidiness' was typically 'tolerated';[64] and if we lack evidence for foul papers, this is not just because of 'the uncertainties of transmission' but 'because the author may never have produced a definitive text for us to recover'.[65] Both concessions are reiterated in *The Shakespeare First Folio* during Greg's attempt, moving from general commentary to detailed discussion, to lay out his overall method. Just after his remark about 'plausible guessing' (quoted p. 28 above), he twice cautions that any identification of authorial or theatrical origins can proceed only by 'ignoring the possibility' of interference between categories

unlikely to be independent of each other. Moreover, the passage emphatically concludes, 'it must be remembered that foul papers and prompt-books do not exhaust the possibilities regarding the copy from which the texts were printed' (p. 175).

Such acknowledgements identify foul papers and promptbook as heuristic rather than empirical categories. Their binarism is not meant as a comprehensive description of the more diversely nuanced materials Greg understands to be out there, but as an interpretive strategy, serving to organize the field for the kind of analysis he deems appropriate. In making these admissions, Greg displays none of the embarrassment Werstine evidently thinks he should. I 'will show', he declares as if exposing methodological impropriety, that 'Greg's theory is logically *a priori* . . . to any survey of the manuscripts' ('Plays', p. 481); but logical priority is in the nature of theory. 'Despite the highly rational integrity of Greg's narrative', Werstine observes, 'it in fact exceeds the documentary evidence' ('Plays', p. 488); but without doing so, it would cease to count as explanation. If we are to blame 'Greg's haste to produce a general rational theory' for driving him to devise an interpretive system 'chronologically prior to his own limited survey' of the manuscripts, how much more empirical-inductive surveying would be enough? Given the inadequacy of the material, too much irresolvable uncertainty about the too few surviving manuscripts, 'an objective survey of the extant dramatic manuscripts' will

---

[62] 'Narratives About Printed Shakespeare Texts: "Foul Papers" and "Bad" Quartos', *Shakespeare Quarterly*, 41 (1990), 65–86, p. 65 (subsequent references interpolated parenthetically).

[63] 'Plays in Manuscript', in Cox and Kastan, *A New History*, pp. 481–97, p. 482, p. 489 and p. 482 (subsequent references interpolated parenthetically).

[64] Quoted from the *Dramatic Documents from the Elizabethan Playhouses* by Maguire, *Shakespearean Suspect Texts*, p. 44.

[65] Quoted by Joseph Loewenstein from *The Editorial Problem in Shakespeare* in 'Authentic Reproductions: The Material Origins of the New Bibliography', in Maguire and Berger, *Textual Formations*, pp. 23–44, p. 36. Loewenstein, to whom I am much indebted, remarks that, 'When we casually attribute a monological, idealized, and stipulative attitude to textuality to prepostmodern critics, we should not suppose ourselves to be referring to Greg' (p. 39).

not by itself – that is, without evidence-exceeding hypotheses from which to proceed deductively – get us any closer to interpretive conclusions ('Plays', p. 481). Even the richest database and all the time in the world would never let us reach the threshold Werstine evidently requires for, as D. F. McKenzie maintains, 'no finite number of observations can ever justify a generalization'.[66] The consequence of following Werstine's program is to situate interpretive practice on a path going nowhere.

The critique of New Bibliographical economy and binarism arrives at the same dead end. All interpretation begins with an economizing action – establishing a field of inquiry within a larger, potentially infinite mass of phenomena. Interpretation is inherently reductive in a descriptive sense; to say that Greg 'reduces a dispersed heterogeneity' merely identifies Greg's interpretive practice *as* an interpretive practice. (From a more sympathetic perspective, it might be called selective or even creative in its capacity to invent hypotheses that bestow meaning.) Binarism is the most stringent form of economy, reduction squeezed into *reductio ad absurdum*, but its 'absurd simplicity' is just what makes it useful and even necessary. Binaries constitute the elemental foundation of existence and consciousness. In the beginning, a series of divisions – between light and darkness, waters under and above the firmament, etc. – formed the intention, content and consequence of God's creative word. Given the 'antithetical' or differential nature of language, all thought continues perforce to be generated within the structure of binary logic.[67] Without binary logic the operating system crashes; nothing would be left.

From this angle, it is no surprise that Werstine's critique of New Bibliographical binaries is itself binary-dependent. Greg's interest in foul papers 'is the product not of reason but of desire' ('Narratives', p. 75); in a version of this doublet thirteen years later, Werstine directs us to 'what we can know, rather than feel' about a foul-papers provenance.[68] Reason-knowledge vs. desire-feeling: despite claims 'to open up a space in textual criticism between the "good"/"bad" axis', the space

turns out to be enclosed within a good/bad axis that is no less a 'rigidified hierarchy' than the one it displaces ('Narratives', p. 83). The issue, then, is not the presence of binaries (they are ubiquitous) but their nature and value, the uses they serve and the judgments we make about them. I don't share Werstine's judgement in rejecting affect any more than I did McMillin's in dismissing hope and desire, and the reasons need no reiteration here; but in the case of the most important of the binaries sustaining Werstine's critique, the aesthetic vs. the historical, some more expansive reflection is in order.

Disputing the claim that 'Hand D' in the *More* manuscript is Shakespeare's, Werstine declares that 'authorship is an aesthetic, rather than a historical category'.[69] In a discussion of the *Hamlet* texts, he dismisses any evaluation of the Q2/F variants as based on 'purely aesthetic patterns' that 'can have no claim to historicity', adding that to 'claim that such patterns must originate with Shakespeare is to abolish the distinction between history and aesthetics'.[70] In both passages, the aesthetic is linked with the author, defined as a 'single agent' ('Narratives', p. 86) whose coherent and conscious intention produces a 'single "meaning"' realized immediately in an 'aesthetic design' whose 'self-evident' and 'unassailable integrity' requires us to acknowledge ourselves 'in the presence of Shakespeare's true art' ('Textual Mystery', p. 16 and p. 24). As a description of some mediocre current practice, this is amusing and beneficial, but as an account of the aesthetic it is deeply misleading. The aesthetic, as originating in Enlightenment and Romantic thought, locates

---

[66] 'Printers of the Mind', p. 3.

[67] For 'antithetical', see Freud's 1910 paper, 'The Antithetical Meaning of Primal Words', in *The Standard Edition*, vol. 11, pp. 155–61.

[68] 'Housmania: Episodes in Twentieth-century "Critical" Editing of Shakespeare', in Erne and Kidnie, *Textual Performances*, pp. 49–62, p. 57.

[69] 'Close Contrivers: Nameless Collaborators in Early Modern London Plays', in C. E. McGee and A. L. Magnusson, eds., *The Elizabethan Theatre XV* (Toronto, 2002), pp. 3–19, p. 17.

[70] 'The Textual Mystery of *Hamlet*', *Shakespeare Quarterly*, 39 (1988), 1–26, p. 24 (subsequent references interpolated parenthetically).

itself not in authorial agency or textual properties, but in 'the constitution of a perceiving subject'.[71] Werstine's characterization is thus not historical, but it serves his rhetorical purpose, which is precisely to make history – or an idea of history – seem good. The aesthetic functions within his argument as a risible impossibility against which 'the historical' emerges on the back side of the binary as both accessible and worthy of respect.

But what is it, exactly, that emerges? According to Werstine, 'history is histories, multiple narratives' to account for the state of early printed texts which were, after all, 'open to penetration and alteration not only by Shakespeare himself and by his fellow actors but also by multiple theatrical and extra-theatrical' agents ('Narratives', p. 85 and p. 86). With Foucault, he rejects the idea that the various contingent materials of history should be made to reveal any '"timeless and essential secret"' but for '"the secret that they have no essence or that their essence was fabricated in a piecemeal fashion from alien forms"' ('Textual Mystery', p. 26). He appropriates Nietzsche's claim '"that the actual causes of a thing's origin and its eventual uses, the manner of its incorporation into a system of purposes, are worlds apart; that everything that exists, no matter what its origin, is periodically reinterpreted . . . [omitting 'by those in power'] in terms of fresh intentions"'.[72]

As a card-carrying antifoundationalist, I am not about to quarrel with any of this, but the question remains where it leads. For Foucault, a sense of the constructedness of history serves to shift the interpretive question from production, 'who is speaking' the text, to the more interesting and useful questions of reception, 'Where has it been used, how can it circulate, and who can appropriate it?'[73] Without this shift, we are left with nothing more than the futility of pursuing inaccessible and uninteresting kinds of knowledge. The elision of 'by those in power' from the Nietzsche passage entails the same kind of diminution into negative critique. Nietzsche identifies a gap between origin and use not just to describe an epistemological problem, but to offer an opening for philosophical *übermenschen*, 'those in power', to energize the interpretive will. Werstine seems to have assimilated the deconstructive aspects of antifoundationalism but ignores the 'edifying' consequences by which it encourages the construction of new meanings.[74]

His own system, rather, seems to discourage meaning. He urges us to replace 'Greg's *a priori* theory' about theatrical manuscripts with 'an *a posteriori* conclusion that respects their variety and disuniformity' ('Plays', p. 495). But since there is no way to sort out the textual markings deposited by the many diverse agents who may have 'penetrated and altered' them, this respect leaves us with nothing to say. As Werstine puts it, if the theory can 'be recognized as only an undemonstrable hypothesis, then we can stop pretending . . . we know

---

[71] See John Guillory, *Cultural Capital: The Problem of Literary Canon Formation* (Chicago, 1993), p. 275. For Hazlitt, the value of Shakespearian drama is 'absolutely independent of . . . the author'; and for Emerson, Shakespeare is 'out of the category of eminent authors . . . and only just within the possibility of authorship'. See P. P. Howe, ed., *The Complete Works of William Hazlitt*, 21 vols. (London, 1930–4), vol. 5, p. 50; and Richard Poirier, ed., *Ralph Waldo Emerson* (Oxford, 1990), p. 339.

[72] 'Touring and the Construction of Shakespeare Textual Criticism', in Maguire and Berger, *Textual Formations*, p. 45–66, p. 59.

[73] Michel Foucault, 'What is an Author?', in Josué V. Harari, ed., *Textual Strategies: Perspectives in Post-Structuralist Criticism* (Ithaca, 1979), pp. 141–60, p. 160. This shift returns the aesthetic to its origin in the 'perceiving subject' and restores it to its historical dimension in another sense as well – as interpretive history ('*rezeption-esthetik*' or '*nachleben*'). Werstine's claim that the interpretive history of *Hamlet*, inscribed throughout centuries of commentary, performance and critical editing, 'can have no claim to historicity' is like Andrew Gurr's contention that the chief impediment to recovering historical origins – the earliest performances of Shakespeare's plays, and Shakespeare's own preference (as Gurr assumes it) for performance rather than publication – is the 'inheritance we live with, centuries of concern for edited texts that give the play in its most full form'. See 'Maximal and Minimal Texts: Shakespeare v. the Globe', *Shakespeare Survey 52* (Cambridge, 1999), pp. 68–88, p. 68. In contrast, see Anthony B. Dawson's compelling arguments for New Bibliography as 'in the full sense of the term, an *historical* endeavour' ('The Imaginary Text', p. 141).

[74] For 'edification', see Rorty, *Philosophy*, pp. 357–72.

what we see';[75] or again, anyone who 'examines the extant manuscripts themselves instead of relying on Greg' will be 'confronted with the radical indeterminacy of identifying what kind of manuscript may lie behind a printed dramatic text' ('Plays', p. 492). It is reasonable to urge editors 'to be more skeptical about their claims to know the origins' of texts;[76] but since Plato, scepticism has served as a means to beget desire, and with the repudiation of desire among Newer Bibliographers scepticism dwindles into a terminal nescience. Hermeneutic abstinence in the face of the 'irreducible historical messiness of the actual manuscripts' is claimed as a way 'to engage the fierce particularities of the extant manuscripts' each of which 'can then be appreciated in its uniqueness as the matrix of a variety of possible scholarly narratives about the inscription of early English drama' ('Plays', p. 482, p. 492 and pp. 494–5). But since every text constructed by this method turns out to be yet one more product of an identically unknowable multiplicity of possible agents, the result is not fierce particularity but undifferentiated sameness. This is what Stephen Greenblatt has called the 'slime of history',[77] an amorphous viscosity with whose otherness it would be impossible to engage even if we wanted to.

And the practical consequences of all this? In 'What is an Editor?', Stephen Orgel understatedly acknowledges that his editorial work 'hasn't done much to take into account' his own (pioneering and hugely influential) contributions to the Newer Bibliography and then reflects on 'requirements' that 'are not really reconcilable'.[78] According to R. A. Foakes, a disconnection characterizes much 'of the explosion of writing about textual criticism and about editing in recent years' in that 'many of those publishing advice or admonitions to editors have never edited a work themselves', and their counsel seems 'to have no bearing' on the 'practical work' involved.[79] Orgel and Foakes imply that current editorial theory is not just irrelevant but hostile to editorial practice. The suggestion is made explicit by Anthony Dawson, who argues that without authorial intention or some compa-

rable sense of 'the immaterial idea . . . behind the textual manifestations', it 'would be impossible to edit at all', and by Giorgio Melchiori, for whom Newer Bibliographers have 'created an all-inclusive and all-purpose negative narrative intended to nullify all narratives by their predecessors', and to leave editors 'in a kind of limbo, not knowing what to present to readers and performers as an authentic text of a play'.[80]

This conclusion, that the Newer Bibliography is designed to terminate editorial practice, needs qualification. When Randall McLeod asserts that 'photography has killed editing' and asks 'what rationale can there be for editing?', he is not claiming that all editing is purposeless, only 'that *critical* editions suck'.[81] As he sees it, in fact, the same technology that has killed critical editing gives birth to new editorial possibilities in the form of '*photo*facsimiles' that let us 'present the authoritative texts very much as they appeared to Shakespeare's contemporaries', thereby eliminating 'the pervasive

---

[75] 'A Century of "Bad" Shakespeare Quartos', *Shakespeare Quarterly*, 50 (1999), 310–33, p. 330.

[76] See '"The Cause of This Defect": *Hamlet*'s Editors', in Arthur F. Kinney, ed., *'Hamlet': New Critical Essays* (New York and London, 2002), pp. 115–33, p. 116.

[77] 'Shakespeare and the Exorcists', in Gregory S. Jay and David L. Miller, eds., *After Strange Texts: The Role of Theory in the Study of Literature* (Birmingham, Alabama, 1985), pp. 101–23, p. 101.

[78] *The Authentic Shakespeare and Other Problems of the Early Modern Stage* (New York and London, 2002), pp. 15–20, p. 16 and p. 17

[79] 'Shakespeare Editing and Textual Theory: A Rough Guide', *Huntington Library Quarterly*, 60 (1999), 425–42, p. 425.

[80] See Anthony B. Dawson, 'Correct Impressions', in Thompson and McMullan, *In Arden*, pp. 31–47, p. 42; and Melchiori, 'The Continuing Importance of New Bibliography', in Thompson and McMullan, *In Arden*, pp. 17–30, p. 19 and p. 24. As Foakes remarks, 'However strenuously theorists try to discredit the notion of intention . . . editors in practice continue to find the idea of the author necessary' ('Shakespeare Editing', p. 434). For a more discreet version of the point, see Robert Weimann, *Author's Pen and Actor's Voice: Playing and Writing in Shakespeare's Theatre* (Cambridge, 2000), p. 41.

[81] See 'from *Tranceformations in the Text of "Orlando Furioso"*', *Library Chronicle of the University of Texas at Austin*, 20 (1990), 62–86, p. 72 and p. 76 (McLeod's emphasis).

bias of the pre-photographic age of transmission and of the tradition of editorial and compositorial middlemen it fostered'.[82] Werstine's death-of-editing claims are similarly restricted. It is the '"critical" editing of Shakespeare', he specifies, that 'has had its day'; and for him too its demise heralds 'a new beginning': once having 'rightly abandoned' the 'goal of establishing the text of a metaphysical "work" that transcends its evidently imperfect printed states', editors may now 'strive for the humanly possible goal of editing one or more of the early printed texts, without claiming to locate either author or work in relation to these printed versions'.[83] Werstine is probably thinking of diplomatic transcriptions rather than '*photo*facsimiles', but the fundamental consistency of his programme with McLeod's should be clear enough.

To claim that Newer Bibliography is designed to terminate *only* critical editing, however, drastically underestimates the consequences of the programme. If critical editing is a subset of the larger category of editing itself, so is editing itself – as 'not a prerequisite to scholarly literary criticism' but 'a part of that criticism' – an element within a larger enterprise. Like Greg in 'The Rationale', Tanselle believes that the interpretive judgement required to produce a critical edition is effectively identical to the interpretive judgement exercised in critical commentary. But if critical editing and critical commentary are different aspects of the same project, then the un-editing program has un-interpreting consequences as well. Eliminate the 'bias' of 'middlemen', 'abandon' all mediating efforts to relate texts to an author or work or any other 'immaterial idea', and it won't be just a form of editing but 'Shakespeare studies' and 'literary studies' altogether (to recall the claims from which we started) that will disappear. As Meredith Skura puts it, the 'quite remarkable power' of the Newer Bibliography's program, extending beyond 'the editorial process' to include 'us noneditors' as well, produces a situation in which 'there is no way of going about our business at all'.[84]

By now, the full implications of Newer Bibliography's departure from tradition should be clear: its aversion to the author and to critical editing

represents the conviction – 'premise' – that Shakespeare is not worth troubling our heads about, and that the long history of interpreting, editing and performing Shakespearian texts ought to be abandoned. Given the evident flourishing of all these enterprises at present, I must be exaggerating the situation, and I want to conclude with some moderating concessions. For one thing, 'Newer Bibliography' is an abstraction, no more of 'a clearly defined programme at a particular moment in time' than was the New Bibliography,[85] and it includes critics who do not share the un-editing programme I have described here.[86] Besides, to return to my earlier point that editorial theorists enjoy no more sovereign self-knowledge than the rest of us, even the most unremitting of Newer Bibliographers seem reluctant to live with the consequences of their own programme.[87] And finally,

---

[82] 'UN *Editing* Shak-speare', p. 37 and p. 38.

[83] 'Housmania', in Erne and Kidnie, *Textual Performances*, p. 58, p. 58, p. 60 and p. 59.

[84] 'Is There a Shakespeare?', in Parker and Zitner, *Elizabethan Theater*, p. 172.

[85] See E. A. J. Honigmann, 'The New Bibliography and its Critics', in Erne and Kidnie, *Textual Performances*, pp. 77–93, p. 77.

[86] Michael Warren, one of the earliest and most influential interrogators of New Bibliography, seeks not just to expose 'the pervasive bias' of editorial tradition but to replace it with an enriched sense of meaning in the original texts; he does re- rather than un-editing. For a characteristically scintillating recent example, see 'The Perception of Error: the Editing and the Performance of the Opening of *Coriolanus*', in Erne and Kidnie, *Textual Performances*, pp. 127–42.

[87] The wonderful Folger editions Werstine has produced with Barbara Mowat illustrate the inconsistencies I am talking about. He claims that the Folger *Othello* 'is an edition, not of the "work", but of the Folio printing of *Othello*, and therefore' not 'a "critical" one'; but as Michael Neill points out, Werstine and Mowat 'chose to use F as the basis for their New Folger edition on the grounds that it is "the more accurate" of the two' early texts, just as any unregenerate critical editor would. According to Werstine, the Folger *Lear* breaks with the 'intellectual tyranny' of critical editions but, as Foakes points out, it is basically indistinguishable from his own Arden 3 edition, or even Furness's 1880 Variorum. Like Jerome McGann, 'one of the most incisive and articulate theorizers of post-Bowers bibliography', whose 'beautifully edited Byron looks, after all, very much like everyone

I don't want to overestimate the reach of Newer Bibliography. Despite claims that 'Editing has suddenly become . . . a hot topic (arguably *the* hot topic in Shakespeare studies)', most Shakespearians probably pay no more attention now to the Newer Bibliography than they did to the New in the days of its hegemony – just enough to work up an adequate response should the topic come up at a dinner party or a doctoral oral.[88]

It remains true, nonetheless, that Newer Bibliography resonates strongly with views held among a wide range of Shakespearians for whom 'unediting' and 'New Bibliographical binarism' are not household phrases, and that a significant constituency of Shakespearians in and out of Newer Bibliography, all across the ranks up to the most influential senior scholars, are arguing positions that seem to repudiate the interpretive modes that have sustained us going back at least to the time of Hazlitt and Malone. This noteworthy development invites explanation, and I have some Bright Ideas for linking the spirit of denial in current work to the particular circumstances of our professional life; but ideas, bright or otherwise, may be irrelevant to a transformation for which explanation is neither necessary nor, frankly, possible. Change happens – that's it,

that's all. Like living organisms, cultural practices exhaust themselves and die, or metamorphose into different forms. Whether this is happening now – a *bona fide* paradigm shift, an authentic crisis in editing – is, as I said at the beginning, too early for us to know for sure. If it is, if we are no longer sustained by the pleasure and value Hazlitt claimed as the self-evident consequence of engaging with Shakespeare's plays, then I think the situation of Shakespeare studies may be desperate. On the other hand, I cannot imagine I would have worked up this piece if I altogether lacked hope. There is always hope, quixotic though it may be – hope, desire and imagination.

---

else's Byron', Werstine seems to be beset with contrariety of desire. For this material, see Werstine, 'Housmania', in Erne and Kidnie, *Textual Performances*, p. 59; Neill, *Othello*, p. 433; Foakes, 'Shakespeare Editing', p. 442; and Orgel, 'What is an Editor?', p. 16.

[88] The quotation, from David Scott Kastan's *Shakespeare After Theory* (New York and London, 1999), p. 59 (Kastan's emphasis), is echoed by Erne and Kidnie according to whom 'editing and textual studies have become hot topics that attract ever-increasing attention – even in *The New Yorker*' (*Textual Performances*, p. 1), and by Thompson and McMullan (see note 8).

ON BEING A GENERAL EDITOR

STANLEY WELLS

The Editor has asked me to write about being a General Editor of Shakespeare, a function which I have fulfilled – and continue to fulfil – both for Penguin Books and for Oxford University Press and to which I have devoted a significant portion of my life. I could write an entire autobiography centring on the subject, but that would not be welcome here. So let me set down some thoughts relating to the various tasks that the General Editor has to perform, and to the qualities that he (please read 'or she' throughout) needs to bring to them. And let me attempt to illustrate these from my experiences over not much less than half a century in which much of my time has been devoted to this practice. I shall confine myself largely to the general editing of a multi-volume edition rather than of the Complete Works, which is a subject in itself. And I shall not concern myself at all with the general editing of a monograph series such as the Oxford Shakespeare Topics, on which I have worked happily with Peter Holland since its inception.

The first and perhaps most important task of a General Editor is to lay down the principles to which he and his publisher wish his edition to conform. The publisher's wishes are vital. Editions have to be financed, and it is the publisher who provides the financial backing. This does not mean that an edition needs to be driven by commercial considerations alone. Shakespeare can be a status symbol. Publishing houses may feel that their lists are incomplete if they do not include an edition of his works. They – by which one has to mean a number of individuals within the publishing house who are responsible for its policy – may even acknowledge a duty to provide the scholarly community with editions which fulfil their needs but are unlikely to make a profit. This is especially likely to be true of scholarly publishing houses, though I have yet to encounter a publisher who was oblivious to financial considerations.

The first edition with which I was associated was the New Penguin. If I seem to give disproportionate space to it, that is because, although its General Editor was T. J. B. Spencer, I worked very closely with and for him from its inception, and in the process formed many of the ideas that I was later to apply both to the Oxford Complete Works and to the multi-volume Oxford Shakespeare. I edited three plays for the New Penguin and was credited as its Associate Editor. After Spencer died, in 1988, I succeeded him as *de facto* editor of the ongoing New Penguin edition, though my employment by Oxford University Press meant that this was not publicly acknowledged. Then in 2005 I was officially credited as General Editor of what is now called the Penguin Shakespeare in undertaking a major revision, with Paul Edmondson as my co-supervisory editor.

The impetus for the Penguin edition came from within the publishing house itself. It may well have been driven partly by a recognition of the high public interest in Shakespeare evinced by the celebrations in 1964 for the four-hundredth anniversary of his birth. Terence (or T. J. B., as we used to write in those more formal days) Spencer had fairly recently taken over from Allardyce Nicoll as Director of the

University of Birmingham's Shakespeare Institute, which at that time had premises in both Birmingham and Stratford-upon-Avon. One of Penguin's executives, Charles Clark, approached Spencer to discuss the inauguration under his General Editorship of a new edition of the Complete Works which would conform to the image presented by that publishing house, an image which may be summed up as appealing to the 'general reader'. The politics of publishing, and the nature of editions already on the market, inevitably formed a background to the project. All the existing British editions dated from before the war – a landmark of psychological if not of logical significance. Penguin itself had on its books an edition prepared entirely by G. B. Harrison which had appeared from 1937 to 1959. It offers a chronology followed by very brief introductory essays on Shakespeare himself, the Elizabethan theatre, and the play; this amounts in total, to take *As You Like It* as an example, to no more than a dozen pages. The text is followed by idiosyncratic notes and a straightforward glossary. Based eccentrically on the First Folio, whose punctuation it generally and illogically retains while modernizing spelling, and offering relatively little help to the reader, it already seemed out of date, and I should suppose it was not selling well.

At this time two British editions with high scholarly ambitions were on the market. Cambridge University Press offered the New Shakespeare – commonly referred to then as the new, or New, Cambridge Shakespeare – which had started publication as long ago as 1921, under the General Editorship of Arthur Quiller-Couch – who dropped out in 1931 after contributing the introductions to fourteen comedies – and John Dover Wilson. In 1964 it was struggling towards completion, which it achieved belatedly in 1966 with the publication of the now half-blind but eternally sprightly Wilson's edition of the Sonnets, the Introduction originally printed independently as a mischievous riposte to A. L. Rowse's views on the biographical aspects of the poems. Though its volumes were printed in paperback the series was too recondite, and its earlier volumes were by now too old-fashioned both textually and critically, for it to compete seriously

in the mass market to which Penguin aspired – and which indeed it had largely created.

To some extent the Cambridge series had been overtaken by the ongoing Arden edition – what we now know as Arden 2, begun in 1951, originally as a revision of its first series, dating as far back as 1899 – which at that time was under the General Editorship of 'the Harolds' – Harold Jenkins and Harold Brooks. It was somewhat in the doldrums, and it too was forbidding in its academicism.

Moreover, competition on the paperback market, which Penguin sought to dominate, had appeared from overseas. The Pelican, under the General Editorship of the highly respected senior scholar Alfred Harbage (born in 1901), had started to appear in 1956 and was drawing close to completion, which it achieved in 1967. A little more recent was the Signet, which began to appear in 1963 under the direction of Sylvan Barnet, a good scholar with less of an independent reputation, though the fact that his paperback edition was completed within five years suggests that he was enviably efficient as a General Editor. Both the Pelican and the Signet editions differentiated themselves from the Cambridge and Arden series in clearly seeking to attract a popular market. The Pelican is unambitious in scope, offering a few pages on Shakespeare and his Stage and a very brief section on 'The Texts of His Plays' written by the General Editor, a short Introduction – roughly 2,000 words – to the play by the volume editor, and simple glossarial notes printed on the same page as the text. Harbage recruited a distinguished team of contributors but asked little of them, even though they included some of the best textual scholars of the time, some of them veterans, others at an early stage in their careers. Among them were Fredson Bowers, G. Blakemore Evans (later to edit the Riverside edition), George Walton Williams, M. A. Schaaber, Charles T. Prouty and Charlton Hinman. In the Preface, written when the Pelican editions came to be printed together, with revisions, as a single hardback volume in 1969, Harbage notes that 'Leaders in bibliographical study in this country have edited the more difficult texts, and have generously lent their counsel in the case of the less difficult ones.'[1] This series, like others before and after it, apparently evolved as it progressed; Harbage remarks that 'At first no textual apparatus was supplied, but after the early volumes of the edition had appeared, it seemed advisable to include an essential minimum.'[2] I wonder if this was done in an attempt to keep up with the competition offered by the Signet series. Other editors selected by Harbage included scholars who were best known as theatre historians, such as Gerald Eades Bentley, Bernard Beckerman and Richard Hosley; others were primarily critics: Northrop Frye, for instance, undertook *The Tempest*, Maynard Mack *Antony and Cleopatra*, and Harry Levin *Coriolanus*, all relatively straightforward texts. Only Harbage himself, with *Macbeth*, *Henry V*, and the textually difficult *King Lear* and *Love's Labour's Lost*, undertook more than one text – a case of the General Editor coming to the rescue: 'My original intention was to edit only *Macbeth* in addition to serving as factotum. *King Lear* and *Love's Labor's Lost* were edited by me after the persons whom I first asked to do so declined, and *Henry V*, so that its original editor could include the play in his own series.'[3] There are two women on the list, Josephine Waters Bennett (*Much Ado About Nothing*), and Madeleine Doran (*A Midsummer Night's Dream*), who had published important textual studies of *King Lear* and *Henry VI*.

The Signet, no doubt conscious of the competition, offers more: a series of Prefatory Remarks common to each volume and written by the General Editor, briefly supplying biographical information, a chronology, a short essay on 'Shakespeare's Theater', and an equally brief essay on 'The Texts of Shakespeare', the whole amounting to about fourteen pages, common to each volume. This is followed by a critical–cum–scholarly Introduction considerably more substantial than those in the Pelican edition, normally written by the volume editor. The text of the work follows, its lines numbered in fives; very brief explanatory notes, almost entirely lexical and historical, with a few referring to the staging of the play, are printed at the foot of the page. These are signalled, innovatively and, as it turned out, somewhat controversially, by bubbles

in the text itself. At the back of the book comes a brief textual note, simply describing the textual situation relating to the individual work, followed by a straightforward list of departures from the substantive text or texts. Then comes an essay on the work's sources, followed by extracts from, e. g., Plutarch, Cinthio, and Holinshed. The most innovative feature of the edition is its inclusion of a few selected extracts from criticism of the work, and the volumes are rounded off by a selection of 'Suggested References' – a brief bibliography. Clearly the series appears pretty comprehensive in catering for the needs of student readers, and it seems to have succeeded well in its competition with the Pelican. It drew upon a more international team of contributors, and it seems fair to say that Barnet laid more emphasis on critical than on textual expertise. Most of his editors, like Harbage's, were from America – they include Daniel Seltzer, Alvin Kernan, Mark Eccles, Bertrand Evans, Norman Holland and Edward Hubler, with Barnet himself for *Titus Andronicus* – but also the British Frank Kermode, Kenneth Muir, John Russell Brown and Barbara Everett (the only woman except for the British-born Barbara Rosen who shared responsibility for *Julius Caesar* with her American husband William Rosen), the Germans Wolfgang Clemen (whose edition of *A Midsummer Night's Dream* was, I am told, 'ghosted' by Dieter Mehl) and Ernest Schanzer, and the Indian S. Nagarajan.

These American editions are not textually ambitious; indeed, it is a remarkable fact that (if we except the New Variorum edition, started in 1871 and still far from complete, and which in any case is by definition rather a compendium of existing scholarship than in itself innovative) there has never been a multi-volume American edition of Shakespeare with textual and overall scholarly aspirations comparable to those offered by British publishers.

At this time, so far as I understand it, Pelican books of America and Penguin Books of England

---

[1] Alfred Harbage, ed., *William Shakespeare: The Complete Works* (New York, 1969), p. ix.

[2] Harbage, p. ix.

[3] Harbage, p. x.

stood in a semi-autonomous relationship to each other. In his Preface, Harbage wrote that 'In 1953 Mr H. F. Paroissien, who had founded in Baltimore the American subsidiary of Penguin Books Ltd, invited me to edit a series corresponding to *The Penguin* [i. e. the Harrison] *Shakespeare*, which could not be distributed in this country [i. e. America] owing to contractual agreements. Since there were at the time, incredible as it may now seem, only a few of Shakespeare's plays available in soft cover, a complete edition would obviously serve a useful purpose. However, it seemed to me that its value would be greatly enhanced if it represented a collaborative effort among American scholars rather than my personal enterprise. I was asked to draw up a plan, and presented this to Sir Allen Lane and his directors in London in 1954.'[4] In 1964, then, Penguin could both import books originating from its sister company in America and also embargo the sale of those books in England if they were seen as competing with their native products. (Later, for instance, they imported the Pelican *Hamlet* as a stopgap until their own edition appeared.) Additional background information to Clark's approach to Spencer is provided by the Oxford DNB entry, written by John C. Ross, on G. B. Harrison, who had also edited the plays for the American publisher Harcourt Brace: 'When Penguin wished to extend sales of its Shakespeares to the United States, he could not agree to this, as he felt that this would violate the spirit of his contract with Harcourt. Penguin, therefore, embarked on a new series of editions by separate editors, to which American publication would not be a barrier.' This may be a bit disingenuous: when the New Penguin edition first appeared it was not sold in the States because of the existence of the Pelican edition.

The Signet editions were on sale in England. Both business acumen and national pride favoured the inauguration of a new series.

Most of those present at the meeting in Stratford were themselves experienced editors, such as Kenneth Muir and R. A. Foakes. At this point in my career I had edited Robert Greene's *Perimides the Blacksmith* and *Pandosto* for my PhD thesis, sub-

mitted in 1962. My work, supervised by Norman Sanders, was intended, along with other texts prepared by members of the Institute, to form part of a complete Oxford edition of Greene's works with I. A. Shapiro and Johnstone Parr as its General Editors. It never saw the light of day, though a number of theses on the shelves of the Institute library bear witness to the effort that a number of young scholars put into it. (In fact my thesis was eventually published in poorly reproduced photographic form by Garland, in 1988.) Also in 1964 I produced an edition of a substantial selection from the writings of Thomas Nashe as the first volume of the now defunct Stratford-upon-Avon Library, edited by John Russell Brown and Bernard Harris and published by Edward Arnold. So I was present at the meeting both as a junior lecturer working closely with and for Spencer and also by virtue of my interest in editorial work.

At this stage of the enterprise the aim was to discuss the general lines along which a new edition might be organized. One very basic decision facing a General Editor is what titles to include. Some of Shakespeare's works sell far worse than others and, over the years, it has become clear that once an edition has established its reputation, the quality of individual volumes does not necessarily correlate with their sales. We could not reasonably expect, for example, *Titus Andronicus*, *King John*, or the Henry VI plays to sell as well as more popular plays such as *Hamlet*, *Macbeth* and *Romeo and Juliet*. We wanted an edition which could be called complete, but even this leaves certain options open. Adventurously, it was decided (possibly later) to include the collaborative *The Two Noble Kinsmen* (though at that stage no one would have considered including *Edward III*), and to publish *The Rape of Lucrece* in one volume and *Venus and Adonis* and other poems in another. In the end, partly because of poor sales of *Lucrece*, along with the death of its editor, it was eventually replaced by a volume which included all the poems except the Sonnets and *A Lover's Complaint*.

---

[4] Harbage, p. ix.

One of the most contentious issues was whether explanatory notes should be printed at the foot of the page, as in the most strongly competitive editions, or at the back of the book, as in Harrison and Dover Wilson. Students, some people argued, preferred notes to be available for easy reference at the foot of the page, as in the Arden, the Pelican and the Signet. Others, perhaps remembering Dr Johnson's injunctions both that notes 'are a necessary evil' and that 'the mind is refrigerated by interruption',[5] favoured a clean page, with notes at the back. It was, I believe, Charles Clark, speaking on behalf of Penguin, who cast the die in favour of continuing Harrison's practice. To my mind this decision has much to do with the success of the series. For one thing, it differentiates the Penguin edition from most of those with which it has had to compete over close on forty years. (The Dover Wilson Cambridge also had a clean – and beautifully designed – page.) Certainly some readers studying the text may find it convenient to be able to glance down to the foot of the page to resolve a difficulty. But a clean page offers several advantages. It permits uninterrupted reading. It is easier for actors to use, both because it allows more text to the page and because it leaves more room for scribbling in the margins – a factor which may appeal to students too. And perhaps best of all, the fact that the editor does not feel constrained by lack of space permits a more relaxed and literate style of annotation, obviating the temptation to use uncivilized abbreviations of the 'cf. Tr. & Cr. v.3.41' variety. (Nevertheless, when, in 2002, Penguin reprinted *Hamlet*, in a larger format and without its textual apparatus, in a 'Great Books' series, the notes appeared at the foot of the page. This was the publisher's decision. It has not sold particularly well.)

As I remember it, Clark said that he liked to think that a buyer travelling from London to Stratford to see a play could read the text in a train on his way there and the introduction on the way back. This raised the question of whether the customary essay on the play might be printed as an Afterword (as was the practice in editions of some classic texts at the time) rather than at the beginning, but we settled for the traditional ordering of the contents.

We spent hours discussing whether to signal the presence of notes and, if so, how. Some favoured the use of an asterisk in the text. Signet's bubbles – abhorrent to me (though as very much the junior participant I kept my opinions largely to myself) – had their supporters. Eventually we opted for elegant simplicity: to number the text in tens – some favoured fives – and allow readers to do their own counting.

We also had to decide what to do about textual issues. Wishing the editions to have full scholarly respectability we felt that textual notes were needed, but that if they were to be of any value they should be presented with more concern for the understanding of the non-specialist reader than in the Arden edition. Editors were not expected to undertake original textual investigations but were free to do so if they wished; some of them did, and their editions make fresh contributions to the editorial tradition. We wished to disembarrass the Introductions of over-technical material, particularly disliking the way in which Arden editors customarily opened their Introductions with off-putting sections baldly headed 'The Text' and 'The Date of the Play'. As a consequence we decided to print a discussion of textual issues, written as accessibly as the editor could manage, along with lists of collations, at the back. This relates to the printing of the text as well as to the inclusion of free-standing textual notes. Should we, for example, use typographical devices, such as square brackets, in the text to signal that stage directions were altered from, or added to, those of the original editions? The consensus was that we should prefer to keep the text as free from algebraical signs as possible, and to this end we decided to present conservatively edited stage directions in the text while listing original directions among the textual notes so that an interested reader could identify changes.

There is also the matter of changes to the text itself. The second Arden series has what Tom Berger has memorably called the 'band of terror'

---

[5] From the Preface (1765), in *Johnson on Shakespeare*, ed. Arthur Sherbo (New Haven, 1968), The Yale Edition vol. 7, p. 111.

of collations forming a barrier reef at the foot of the page between the text and the notes. We preferred to record textual changes in lists at the back, dividing them up in a way that facilitated easy reference: so for example Spencer's edition of *Hamlet* has seven separate lists; the first records departures from its copy text, the Second Quarto, deriving from the Folio; the second (with only two entries), gives readings deriving from the First (1603) Quarto (Spencer adventurously printed the passage from Hamlet's advice to the Players which 'gives examples of the silly "character" jests of the comic actors'). Next comes a list of emendations to Q2, followed by a collation of the stage directions which gives them first as they appear in the edition, then in their original form 'along with the more interesting F directions not accepted in this edition'; then a list of 'the variant readings and forms of words more commonly found in other editions' (i.e. rejected emendations); and finally a list of 'the more important passages found in Q2 but omitted in F'. This setting out of textual material exemplifies Spencer's wish to present the reader with all the material necessary to a scholarly understanding of the text's complexities with the greatest possible lucidity.

Some of the decisions I have already mentioned relate to aspects of design. The appearance of the page is only partly the province of the designer. For the Penguin we worked with the eminent typographer Hans Schmoller (who by one of history's accidents is held to merit an entry in Oxford DNB denied to Spencer). He was aware of the need, for example, to use a type-face narrow enough to avoid as far as possible the turn-over of lines of verse. But some aspects of design relate to scholarly issues and must concern the General Editor. At the time we were designing the Penguin edition scholars were emphasizing Shakespeare's practical involvement with the theatres of his time with missionary zeal; and some members of the Shakespeare Institute, most notably John Russell Brown, were, with the encouragement of Allardyce Nicoll, leaders of this movement. Increasing awareness of the non-representational nature of the stages of Shakespeare's time led to significant shifts in the

presentation of the text. It was still common for editors to follow their eighteenth-century forebears in supplying directions for scenic location: thus Kenneth Muir's Arden 2 *King Lear* places Act 1 Scene 3 in 'A Room in the Duke of Albany's Palace' and the following scene in 'A Hall in the Same'. And in J. M. Nosworthy's *Cymbeline* (at the time of writing still the current Arden edition) the long final scene is said to take place 'In Cymbeline's Tent', which must have got pretty crowded by the end of the play. To abandon this practice, while allowing editors to mention the fictional location of scenes in their notes where it seemed helpful to do so, was a purely editorial decision, but some non-substantive matters involve the designer as well as the editor. An important one goes as far back as those who prepared copy for the First Folio, or who gave instructions for the way in which it was prepared, in adapting playhouse manuscripts and early Quarto texts of Shakespeare in a manner that was probably influenced by Ben Jonson's practice in some of his Quartos and in his own Folio, by importing literary modes of presentation influenced by classical texts, especially by dividing the plays into acts and scenes against both the printing and the theatrical practice of Shakespeare's time – none of the Quartos printed in his lifetime has any such divisions. The typography as well as the wording of Arden and the Signet editions was essentially readerly in its emphasis on breaks, each act starting on a fresh page and headed in large centred capitals: 'ACT II', then on a new line 'SCENE I.' The largely inauthentic scene divisions are similarly prominent, with particularly unfortunate effect in for instance the Arden *Antony and Cleopatra*, where Act 3 has thirteen scenes and Act 4 fifteen, some of them only a few lines long. For the Penguin we sought to try to replicate for the reader the sense of continuous performance by minimizing the size of act and scene indicators, and by printing them in the margin. There would of course be a case for eliminating act divisions, at least for most of the play, as Robert Smallwood and I were to do in the Revels edition of Thomas Dekker's *The Shoemaker's Holiday* of 1979, and as was later done for certain texts in the Oxford Complete Works;

elimination of scene divisions too would approach still further to authenticity, but was discounted because it would make it impossible for the reader to use standard works of reference.

Other matters, too, were discussed: we wondered, for example, whether to follow Signet's example in printing extracts from critics, but Spencer particularly opposed this, believing that they inevitably gave the impression of a spurious orthodoxy, privileging certain views over others. It was decided instead to include a survey of writings about each work under the heading of Further Reading. We also considered including stage histories, but it was thought more appropriate to encourage editors to make critical use of such material in their introductions, which, with a recommended length of between 10,000 and 12,000 words, were to be more substantial and wide-ranging in scope than those in competing series.

Our deliberations on these and other matters led eventually to the two most important of all tasks for a General Editor: the preparation of a set of Editorial Procedures designed to inform individual editors as they go about their work, and the choice of editors themselves. I had been made especially aware of the need for the former in writing my thesis. Students working on the proposed Greene edition were asked to contribute to the compilation of a set of rules for overall guidance of editors. This was fine, but in the meantime we were also supposed actually to complete editions in order to win our degrees, which meant that we had to make up many of the rules for ourselves as we worked. Our frustration with the General Editors was great. The Procedures for the New Penguin edition resulted partly from the decisions made at the initial meeting, which were later refined and amplified by Spencer with some input from me as a result of my reading of the scripts as they came in. A major contribution came from the Penguin copy-editor, Judith Wardman, in the process of preparing the first batch of texts submitted for publication. Her meticulous eye for detail and passion for consistency contributed immeasurably to the professionalism of the edition. As a result we were able eventually to offer editors a 35-page document

which formed I suspect the most detailed set of guidelines thus far prepared for a Shakespeare edition.[6] In subject matter it ranges from the length and scope of the Introduction through such matters as abbreviations for the titles of plays to minutiae such as the use of round brackets (forbidden in the text) and of semi-colons.

It is, of course, one thing to offer, another to receive. To persuade editors actually to absorb and act upon the advice they are given – especially if, as is likely to happen, they have already edited for a series with different procedures and so think they know already how it should be done – is not always easy. We expected editors to type their own texts from original editions, but there were cases where it became apparent to me, as I read through their typescripts when they were first submitted, that they had followed the all-too-common practice of marking up an already existing text and then having that typed.

Even with the precedent of the New Penguin edition behind me, when in 1978 I took up my position as General Editor of an Oxford Shakespeare I felt impelled to spend the first few months of my employment in the preparation of a new set of Editorial Procedures. I was especially concerned with the problems of modernizing spelling and other aspects of presentation, including capitalization, italicization, and so on. Up to that date no extended theoretical discussion of this issue had appeared in print. In many earlier editions it had been left to the haphazard practices of the printers – as indeed it appears to have been in the printing houses of Shakespeare's time.

---

[6] In 1959 Fredson Bowers wrote that 'The guidance that single editors of recent Elizabethan series have received from general editorial instructions both in England and America has certainly been insufficient.' 'Principle and Practice in the Editing of Early Dramatic Texts', in *Textual and Literary Criticism* (Cambridge, 1959), p. 180. Harbage's Pelican edition had started to appear three years earlier, though Bowers's contribution, *The Merry Wives of Windsor*, dates from 1963. (R. B. McKerrow's *Prolegomena for the Oxford Shakespeare* of 1939 is of course invaluable, but is rather an account of his own practice in the texts he prepared for his proposed edition than a set of guidelines for other editors.)

During the 1950s, particularly, there had been a tendency to conservatism, resulting in the preservation in some Arden editions of forms such as 'murther', 'burthen', and 'mo'. I was particularly impelled to action by my irritation with the practice in the Riverside edition of incorporating what its editor, G. Blakemore Evans, called 'a selection of Elizabethan spelling forms that reflect, or may reflect, a distinctive contemporary pronunciation'.[7] I remember saying, somewhat pompously, when I first saw this edition on Spencer's desk that it represented 'a retrograde step in Shakespeare editing'. He agreed. It had the practical disadvantage of calling for many more glosses than normal, most of them serving no purpose beyond reassuring readers that the weird spellings they saw before them were not ghastly errors. So for example 'A single opening of Riverside's *2 Henry IV* includes *kinreds*: kindreds, *idlely*: idly, *heckfers*: heifers, *Saint Albons*: St Albans, and *chevalry*: chivalry.'[8] But more importantly it created a spurious impression of an equivalence between scholarship and antiquarianism. In writing the first section of my Editorial Procedures, concerned with the spelling, I had the help and encouragement of Helen Gardner and the language scholar Norman Davis, both of whom were sympathetic with my aims. But not all linguists were even aware of the problems. I remember speaking to a distinguished Professor of English Language in the University who, on hearing I was working on a modern-spelling edition, said disdainfully that people might as well be reading Agatha Christie. When I asked him what edition he himself used, he replied that it was the Globe (which of course is modernized). That part of my Editorial Procedures which deals with spelling was published in 1979 as *Modernizing Shakespeare's Spelling, with three Studies in the text of Henry V*, the latter by Gary Taylor, early fruits of our joint work on the Oxford Complete Works.

When it comes to choosing individual editors for a multi-volume series, a General Editor needs to think long and hard about the qualities he should be seeking. Some are common to any kind of edition – and for that matter, any kind of scholarly publication. One of them, obviously but impor-

tantly, is reliability. The efficient completion of a series is dependent upon the General Editor's selection of editors who can respect deadlines and, if they know they are not going to be able to meet them, can be honest and realistic in their estimates of when they may be able to do so. This also means that the General Editor, in fairness to colleagues and to his publishers, must sometimes know when to be ruthless in cancelling contracts. If the editor has not so far done much work it should be easy – there are even scholars whom I have suspected of signing a contract so that they can state on their cv that they 'are editing' a work for Oxford University Press rather than having any serious intention of doing so. But to cut off a scholar who has put a great deal of effort into an edition while being unable, for whatever reason – psychological or practical – to complete it is a grave responsibility and I am conscious of not always having fulfilled it. Several editors chosen for both the New Penguin and the Oxford series fell by the wayside, for one reason or another, and had to be replaced, with consequent delays; others have taken far longer to complete their task than they – and I, and the publishers – had estimated. The New Penguin still lacked one play – *Cymbeline* – until the fully revised edition began to appear, in 2005.

Another quality that should, but cannot always, be taken for granted is accuracy. No one is perfect, but editorial work is more dependent on the capacity to get things right than many other sorts of literary endeavour. A General Editor who appoints a slapdash editor is making a rod for his own back. There are scholars whose reputations have been saved, or even made for them, by their copy-editors.

Not all series require the full gamut of skills that may be associated with the editorial function. The Cambridge Shakespeare in Production series, for example, permits the use of an already

---

[7] G. Blakemore Evans, ed., *The Riverside Shakespeare* (Boston, 1974), p. 39.
[8] Stanley Wells and Gary Taylor, *Modernizing Shakespeare's Spelling with three Studies in the Text of Henry V* (Oxford, 1979), p. 5.

existing text and expects the editor to concentrate on supplying information derived from theatre history. Editions intended for schools require specialized kinds of pedagogical apparatus, and those intended for a non-Anglophone readership make special demands. The projected readership of the Penguin edition called for what we might call good generalists – versatile scholars with no axe to grind, and with a flair for writing for what the Procedures call 'a wide public of general readers and of students'. 'The scholarship of the New Penguin Shakespeare', say the Procedures, 'should be immaculate, but this edition is not intended as a rival to the new Arden.' This did not preclude the appointment of editors, such as Harold Oliver, G. K. Hunter, Kenneth Muir, R. A. Foakes, A. R. Humphreys and E. A. J. Honigmann who had already edited for Arden, but it also opened the way for younger or less experienced scholars with little or no experience of editing, and for others who had made their reputation primarily as critics, such as Anne Righter/Barton (*The Tempest*), Barbara Everett (*All's Well That Ends Well*), R. L. Smallwood (*King John*), and myself (*A Midsummer Night's Dream*, *Richard II*, and *The Comedy of Errors*). G. R. Hibbard, who initially had little experience of editing, was to become a wonderful stalwart of the series, and later did work of equal excellence for the Oxford. Spencer himself contributed an exemplary edition of *Romeo and Juliet* to the first batch to be published; I remember Richard Hosley, who had edited the play for Yale in 1954, picking up an early copy and saying that Spencer 'had got all the hard bits right.' The relative amplitude of its annotation encouraged later contributors to write fuller notes than we had thought were expected.

The Oxford edition, on the other hand, was indeed intended to rival the Arden. In establishing its editorial principles I was much influenced by my work on the Penguin, but also – perhaps excessively – by the Arden itself. Like the New Penguin, the Oxford edition (now available in the World's Classics series, though its earlier paperback volumes did not appear under this label) aims at a high degree of accessibility while offering a more

thorough covering of scholarly issues than the New Penguin. Like Arden 2 it prints both notes and collation lines on the page. I wish I had had the simple but excellent idea, later adopted in Arden 3, of printing the collation lines under, not above, the explanatory notes. In selecting contributors I have been reluctant to appoint anyone who lacked serious bibliographical training and previous editorial experience, and in at least one case I have regretted having done so. An ideal editor – if such a paragon exists – will command many different skills. For the most comprehensive kinds of edition he/she needs to be, at least, a bibliographer (in the full range of senses that the word encompasses), a lexicographer, a theatre historian, a cultural and social historian, a literary critic, and a prose stylist. It might seem that one way of coping with the need for such a multiplicity of qualifications would be to encourage collaboration between scholars who between them encompass a wider range of skills than each individually commands. I have worked in this way myself, with Robert Smallwood on the Revels *The Shoemaker's Holiday* and with Roger Warren on the Oxford *Twelfth Night*. And sometimes a General Editor has to step in when necessity prevails: when Spencer died leaving his Penguin *Hamlet* incomplete, I wrote the notes for several scenes, wrote and compiled the textual material, commissioned Anne Barton to write an Introduction, and saw the edition through the press. Nevertheless in general, collaboration on editions is a policy of which I am wary. I think that in a fully integrated edition one and the same person will have worked through all the problems of the text, explained them in the notes, and applied his or her full knowledge of the play in writing the introduction. Especially I believe that the textual editor should be responsible for the explanatory notes. I felt this strongly when, in editing the text of *The Shoemaker's Holiday*, I found that Bowers, in his old-spelling edition, for which he did not have to write explanatory notes, had left unemended readings which I was sure he would have wished to alter if he had had to explain what they meant.

Also in question is the degree to which the General Editor should be an acknowledged collaborator. Although I have been graciously willing to accept tributes to my patience, generosity, and so on in Prefaces, the spectacle of Harold Brooks tip-toeing through the footnotes of the Arden made me resolve to keep myself out of the notes, and with few exceptions I have held to this. I was especially conscious of the need to hold back in acting as General Editor for plays of which I had myself prepared the texts for the Oxford Complete Works. In *As You Like It*, for example, I had modernized Arden to Ardenne; Alan Brissenden disagreed with me and, although I may have tried a bit of gentle persuasion, I did not impose my opinion on him. There are many other cases where I should have edited the texts differently if I had been doing them myself, and some instances where I felt a pang of regret that the editor did not accept my ideas; and I still wish I had argued rather harder than I did to dissuade Michael Neill, in his excellent edition of *Antony and Cleopatra*, from spelling the hero's name as Anthony – a source of much confusion thereafter. But there would have been no point in having a separate edition if it had merely replicated and repackaged the texts of the Complete Works. There is, as I constantly but with little success try to persuade publishers to acknowledge, no such thing as a definitive edition.

Having said this, however, it is necessary also to say that the General Editor does have a real contribution to make to the editions for which he is responsible. This comes mainly on delivery of copy. It has been my practice to read carefully through the introductory and annotative material, looking for error, making spot checks and asking for thorough checking if this reveals an above average susceptibility to error, suggesting additional (or fewer) annotations, and seeking compression of phrasing so that the notes do not take over the page. This can be laborious. I once spent three weeks over Christmas boiling down an over-zealous editor's prose. Often I have asked for changes ranging from minor rephrasing to major restructuring of Introductions. But the amount of additional work that the editor can realistically be expected to undertake is limited.

There are times when I have observed with a sigh that an editor, having failed, for example, to observe the proposed word limits, has written a monograph rather than an Introduction, but not had the heart to wield the blue pencil too drastically. Above all, at this stage I check the text and collations against the copy-text, looking not only for error, but also for points at which the editor has failed to observe the conventions of this particular edition. I may feel a need to suggest, for instance, different modernization of spelling and punctuation, additional or rephrased stage directions, even new emendations. Eventually the package goes back to the editor with a request for correction and revision. If the incidence of error is high I may ask for more work to be done, but ultimately the editor has to accept responsibility for what appears over his or her name. It is always a comfort to know that the full script will be scrutinized by a copy-editor, and the Oxford edition has benefited greatly from the work in this capacity of, especially, Christine Buckley. The need to insert accurate line numbers in Introduction and notes causes us to have the text set in type and corrected first – getting line numbers right is not always easy – and I aim to read it at this stage, and then to read all the ancillary material in first proof, but when the edition is at page proof stage I generally content myself with an overall scrutiny, trying for example to make sure that notes are placed as closely as possible to the text to which they refer. Of course there are other little details to attend to, like illustrations and captions and the jacket copy and the blurb and publicity. Sadly, reviews are liable to be scarce after the first batch of editions has appeared, but *Shakespeare Survey* does its bit in telling us where we have gone wrong and even, sometimes, in patting us on the back.

The task of a General Editor has its trials and tribulations, but it has its rewards, too, as the row of books grows along the shelves and one envisages the possibility of living to see it complete – so long as no one adds yet another title to the canon.

ALTERING THE LETTER OF *TWELFTH NIGHT*: 'SOME ARE BORN GREAT' AND THE MISSING SIGNATURE

PATRICIA PARKER

Some are become great, some atcheeues greatnesse, and some haue greatnesse thrust vppon em . . .

First Folio

We are all aware of passages from Shakespeare where the editorially emended text has become not only what is familiar but possibly also what is preferred or even beloved. One of the most famous and frequently cited is Theobald's 'a babled of green fields' in the scene of Falstaff's death in *Henry V*, a 'babbled' that in modern editions replaces the Folio's 'a Table of greene fields' and the potential sexual allusion to backgammon and its 'green fields' that has recently been argued for these lines.[1] What I want to consider here is a much less well-known case of editorial reconstruction, though of an equally familiar text – the letter of the Letter Scene in *Twelfth Night*, in which the famous formula starting with 'some are born great' appears nowhere in any of the Folio texts and the familiar 'Fortunate-Unhappy' signature does not appear until the eighteenth century, when it was created by Capell, and accorded its own separate line by Malone, the form in which we usually see it in modern editions.[2]

My reason for foregrounding these influential emendations is that in the course of preparing a new Norton Critical Edition of *Twelfth Night*, I have found that the fact that neither of these appears in the Folio texts of the play came as a surprise not only to me but to other experienced Shakespearians. What I want, then, to do in what follows is to trace the historical process of their editorial creation, and to open up for discussion other possibilities for considering the Folio texts themselves, as well as ways of making the process of historical production more visible to readers.

Here, then, are the Folio versions from the Letter Scene itself, starting with the 1623 First Folio and the 1632 Second Folio. The

I wish to thank those who encouraged or engaged with me in this work, in addition to the audiences to which I presented it: Tom Berger, Alan Dessen, Lukas Erne, Andrew Gurr, Jonathan Hope, M. J. Kidnie, Bernice Kliman, the late Scott McMillin, Randall McLeod, Lois Potter, Eric Rasmussen, Sanford Robbins, Michael Warren and Paul Werstine.

[1] See Duncan Salkeld, 'Falstaff's Nose', *Notes and Queries*, September 2004, 284–5, which in its sense that the Folio needs to be taken seriously here joins Hilda Hulme's earlier investigations in 'Falstaff's Death: Shakespeare or Theobald?', *Notes and Queries*, July 1956, 283–87, and *Explorations in Shakespeare's Language* (London, 1962), pp. 136–7.

[2] Following Capell's '*The fortunate-unhappy*', modern editions routinely print either 'The Fortunate-Unhappy' (retaining Capell's hyphen) or 'The Fortunate Unhappy' on a separate line (as in Malone) and make 'Daylight' Malvolio's first word in response to the letter. Unless otherwise noted, quotations from Shakespeare throughout are to *The Riverside Shakespeare*, ed. G. Blakemore Evans (Boston, 1974). In some quotations it is necessary to modernize the Folio versions, but all passages quoted from are reproduced in facsimile here.

Mal. M,O,A,I. This simulation is not as the former: and yet to crush this a little, it would bow to mee, for euery one of these Letters are in my name. Soft, here followes prose : *If this fall into thy hand, reuolue.* In my stars I am aboue thee, but be not affraid of greatnesse : Some are become great, some atcheeues greatnesse, and some haue greatnesse thrust vppon em. Thy fates open theyr hands, let thy blood and spirit embrace them, and to invre thy selfe to what thou art like to be : cast thy humble slough, and appeare fresh. Be opposite with a kinsman, surly with seruants : Let thy tongue tang arguments of state ; put thy selfe into the tricke of singularitie. Shee thus aduises thee, that sighes for thee. Remember who commended thy yellow stockings, and wish'd to see thee euer crosse garter'd : I say remember, goe too, thou art made if thou desir'st to be so : If not, let me see thee a steward still, the fellow of seruants, and not woorthie to touch Fortunes fingers Farewell. Shee that would alter seruices with thee, the fortunate vnhappy daylight and champian discouers not more : This is open, I will bee proud, I will reade politicke Authours, I will baffle Sir *Toby,* I will wash off grosse acquaintance, I wilbe point deuise, the very man. I do not now foole my selfe, to let imagination iade mee ; for euery reason excites to this, that my Lady loues me. She did commend my yellow stockings of late, shee did praise my legge being crosse-garter'd, and in this she manifests her selfe to my loue, & with a kinde of iniunction driues mee to these habites of her liking. I thanke my starres, I am happy : I will bee strange, stout, in yellow stockings, and crosse Garter'd,

even with the swiftnesse of putting on. Ioue, and my starres be praised. Heere is yet a postscript. *Thou canst not choose but know who I am. If thou entertainst my loue, let it appeare in thy smiling, thy smiles become thee well. Therefore in my presence still smile, deere my sweet, I prethee.* Ioue I thanke thee, I will smile, I will doe every thing that thou wilt have me. *Exit.*

(First Folio, 1623)

Mal. M.O.A.I. This simulation is not as the former : and yet to crush this a little, it would bow to me, for every one of these Letters are in my name. Soft, here followes prose : *If this fall into thy hand, revolue.* In my Starres I am above thee, but be not affraid of greatnesse : Some are become great, some atcheeve greatnesse, and some have greatnesse thrust upon em. Thy fates open their hands, let thy blood and spirit embrace them, and to inure thy selfe to what thou art like to be : cast thy humble slough, and appeare fresh. Be opposite with a kinsman, surly with servants : Let thy tongue tang arguments of State ; put thy selfe into the tricke of singularity. Shee thus advises thee, that sighes for thee. Remember who commended thy yellow stockings, and wish'd to see thee ever crosse garter'd : I say remember, goe too, thou art made if thou desir'st to be so : If not, let me see thee a steward still, the fellow of servants, and not worthy to touch Fortunes fingers Farwe'l. Shee that would alter services with thee, the fortunate unhappy daylight and champian discovers not more : This is open, I will be proud, I will reade politicke Authors, I will baffle Sir *Toby,* I will wash off grosse acquaintance, I willbe point devise, the very man. I doe now foole my selfe, to let imagination iade me ; for every reason excites to this, that my Lady loves me. She did commend my yellow stockings of late, she did praise my legge being crosse-garter'd, and in this she manifests her selfe to my love, and with a kind of injunction drives me to these habits of her liking. I thanke my starres, I am happy : I will be strange, stout, in yellow stocking, and crosse garter'd

(Second Folio, 1632)

Second Folio makes several historically influential changes to the letter – including its change of F1's 'atcheeues greatnesse' (a subject-verb combination common elsewhere in Shakespeare) to 'atcheeve greatnesse', a grammatical change that simultaneously renders it consonant with the later citations from the letter by Malvolio (3.4) and the Clown Feste (5.1).[3] Notably, however, F2 did *not* change 'Some are become great' to 'born great' to make it fit with Malvolio's citation in Act 3, even though it did make the change from 'atcheeuues' to 'atcheeve' in the very same line. The Third and Fourth Folios complicated the formula we now know as 'Some are born great, some achieve greatness, and some have greatness thrust upon 'em' still further by changing 'thrust' to 'put'.[4]

[3] In relation to the kind of subject–verb pairing represented by F1's 'some atcheeues', see Jonathan Hope, *Shakespeare's Grammar* (London, 2003), pp. 161–2.

[4] F4 actually has '*some are become great, some atchieue greatness, and some, and some haue greattness put upon them*' (a 'them' that also corresponds to the 'them' used by Malvolio in Act 3). F3 also introduced new problems, such as 'bow me' for 'bow to me' in Malvolio's introductory lines to his reading of the letter.

Here is the Third Folio:

> *Mal. M. O. A. I.* This fimulation is not as the former: and yet to crufh this a little; it would bow me, for every one of thefe Letters are in my name. Soft, here followes profe : *If this fall into thy hand, revolve. In my Stars I am above thee, but be not afraid of greatneß : Some are become great, fome atchieve greatneß, and fome have greatneß put upon em. Thy fates upon their hands, let thy bloud and fpirit embrace them, and to inure thy felf to what thou art like to be: caft thy humble flough, and appear fresh. Be oppofite with a kinfman, furly with fervants : Let thy tongue tang arguments of State ; put thy felf into the trick of fingularity. She thus advifes thee, that fighes for thee. Remember who commended thy yellow ftockings, and wifh'd to fee thee ever croß garter'd : I fay remember, go too, thou art made, if thou defir'ft to be fo : If not, let me fee thee a fteward ftill, the fellow of fervants ; and not worthy to touch Fortunes fingers : Farewell. She that would alter fervices with thee, the fortunate unhappy daylight and champion difcovers not more : This is open, I will be proud, I will read politick Authours, I will baffle Sir Toby, I will wafh off groffe acquaintance, I will be point devife, the very man. I do now foole my felfe, to let*

And the Fourth Folio:

> *Mal. M. O. A. I.* This fimulation is not as the former ; and yet to crufh this a little, it would bow me, for every one of thefe Letters are in my name. Soft, here followes profe : *If this fall into thy hand, revolve. In my Stars I am above thee, but be not afraid of greatneß ; fome are become great, fome atchieve greatneß, and fome, and fome have greatneß put upon them. Thy fates upon their hands, thy blood and fpirit embrace them, and to inure thy felf to what thou art like to be ; caft thy humble flough, and*

But once again, neither altered 'are become great' to 'born great'. There is, therefore, no version of these famous lines that is identical in *any* of the scenes in which they appear in the Folio versions of the play, since Feste's final citation of the letter in Act 5 has (in the modernized version of this anomalous iteration) 'some have greatness *thrown* upon them'.

In the Letter Scene itself, the 'some are become great' wording remains unchanged from F1 through F4, despite the other alterations to which these lines are subjected. 'Become great' rather than the long-standing editorial 'born great' (usually ascribed to

Rowe) is so unfamiliar to us that it may provoke an immediate resistance. But our resistance may itself be a symptom of what Barbara Mowat has observed of the impact of Rowe in particular, including the way in which his versions 'laid a heavy early eighteenth century hand on the way Shakespeare is still perceived on the page', and of 'how very difficult it is for editors, even today, to shake off that hand and consider afresh what the Folio and Quarto editors, compilers, and compositors left us'.[5]

I am not interested in getting back to an 'authentic' Shakespearian version – a will o' the wisp that work on these earliest versions has long taught us to resist. But what I would like to do is to take up Mowat's challenge to try to consider afresh the more unfamiliar early versions, and instead of advocating any particular solution, to make both these texts and the historical process of their editorial reconstruction more visible, so that readers can engage with the problems themselves.

We might begin by reflecting on the fact that in none of the early Folios – or in either of the two seventeenth-century promptbooks we have for *Twelfth Night* – does the familiar 'born great' appear in the Letter Scene itself.[6] As Peter Holland suggests, with understated irony, in his introduction to

[5] Barbara A. Mowat, 'Nicholas Rowe and the Twentieth-Century Text', in *Shakespeare and Cultural Traditions*, ed. Tetsuo Kishi, Roger Pringle and Stanley Wells (London, 1994), pp. 314–22, p. 320. See also Andrew Murphy's comments on Rowe in 'Texts and Textualities: a Shakespearian History', in *The Renaissance Text: Theory, Editing, Textuality*, ed. Andrew Murphy (Manchester, 2000), p. 199: 'Rowe's edition seeks to systematize the text, reducing its pluralistic codes to uniformity by, for example, standardizing character names and locations and imposing consistency in act and scene divisions.'

[6] See G. Blakemore Evans, ed., *Shakespearean Prompt-Books of the Seventeenth Century* (Charlottesville, 1960–), vol. 8, pp. 59–69, on the copy of F3 used as a Smock Alley promptbook (and dated by him as sometime between 1674 and 1685) and the 'Folger Second Folio *Twelfth Night* PB of uncertain date and possibly earlier than the Smock Alley *Twelfth Night*' (Evans, p. 61). Evans notes (p. 68) in relation to the former that 'Hand I' (identified as a seventeenth-century hand) makes 'only one certainly identifiable textual change' to 4.2, in contrast to 'Hand II' an 'intrusive eighteenth-century hand' that 'substitutes emendations proposed by Rowe through Hanmer'. Neither of these seventeenth-century promptbooks makes

Rowe's 1709 edition, what we are quoting when we iterate the now culturally familiar formula is not the letter but Malvolio's version of it, cross-gartered before Olivia, in Act 3.[7] It is thus Malvolio – that avowed crusher of 'letters' so that they might 'bow' to him – who is the authority for what became historically the long-standing editorial version of the formula itself.

All four Folio versions of Malvolio's own cross-gartered delivery are consistent in progressing through the now-familiar sequence, from 'some are born great' to 'some achieve greatness' to 'some have greatness thrust upon them'.[8] We tend to assume that Malvolio is quoting directly from the letter here, though in the Folios no such graphically determinative markers appear, including in the opening line of the entire sequence (which FI prints as 'Be not afraid of greatnesse: 'twas well writ'). Modern editors routinely add quotation marks around each of the phrases assumed to be a direct quotation from the letter – from 'Be not afraid of greatness' and 'Some are born great' to 'And some have greatness thrust upon them.' And most add dashes, so that 'Some are born great –' and 'Some achieve greatness –' are seen as fragments of a continuous quotation that comes to an end with 'thrust upon them'.

To the assumption, however, that Malvolio is directly or faithfully quoting from the letter in this scene and thus authorizing both quotation marks and the retroactive rewriting of the letter itself, this scene in Act 3 adds its own complicating variations. The lines that proceed from 'born' to 'thrust' are remarkably the same in all four Folio versions (whose printing of the lines in the Letter Scene diverge so strikingly from one another.) But when Malvolio goes on in this same scene in Act 3 to recall other parts of the letter, the situation is less clear. Once again, modern editors put quotation marks around the phrases that Malvolio seems to be directly quoting, but in at least one famous textual instance, not even F2's generally accepted 'correction' renders an absolutely faithful or identical citation of the letter itself – though it appears in quotation marks in modern editions. And even though Malvolio refers in this scene to

what 'concurs directly with the letter' (3.4.65–6), he goes on to describe other supposed directions that have no certain referents in the letter of the letter itself, claiming that it 'sets down the manner how: as a sad face, a reverend carriage, a slow tongue, in the habit of some sir of note, and so forth' (3.4.71–4), when it is unclear, for example, what 'a sad face' might be citing, since the postscript explicitly counsels him to appear 'smiling' (2.5.176).

With regard to the specifically textual crux in this scene, F2 changes FI's 'let thy tongue langer with arguments of state' to 'let thy tongue tang with arguments of state', a reading that is continued in Ff3–4. Hanmer (1743 and 1745) therefore altered the letter itself to read 'tang with', so as to make it fit exactly with Malvolio's cross-gartered citation of it in Act 3, while Capell (1767–8) standardized the anomaly in the opposite direction, changing 'tang with' to 'tang' in 3.4 to make it correspond exactly with the wording of the letter in Act 2, a change also adopted by the Arden2 editors of the play.[9] The New Cambridge editor, by contrast, prints F2's 'tang with' and provides a note that explains F2's 'correction' as a standardizing of the line with the wording of the letter from which Malvolio is

---

changes to the lines from 2.5, 3.4 and 5.1 under consideration here or to the ending of the letter discussed below.

7   Peter Holland, Introduction to *The Works of Mr William Shakespear, edited by Nicholas Rowe, 1709* (London, 1999), pp. vii–xxx, p. viii.

8   There are only very minor changes in spelling ('borne' in FI and F2; 'born' in Ff3–4; 'greatness' and 'Greatness' in F4 vs 'greatnesse' in FI–3; 'sayst' in FI–2 vs. 'say'st' in Ff3–4). All four Folio texts here also have 'thrust upon them' rather than the Letter Scene's 'thrust vppon em' (FI), 'thrust upon em' (F2) or '*put upon em*' (F3) or '*put upon them*' (F4).

9   See p. 459 of Hanmer's 1743 edition and p. 465 of his 1745 edition; and p. 55 of Capell. Arden2 editors Lothian and Craik follow Capell in changing F2's 'tang with' to 'tang' to make this phrase in 3.4 correspond exactly to its counterpart in 2.5, adding the following note: '**tang**] Turner notes that *OED*'s only example of 'tang with' is this line; he therefore concludes that 'tang' should be the reading here, as at [2.5].150, and conjectures that the compositor either carried over the 'with' from his previous line (which contains the word twice) or introduced it in the attempt to make better sense in conjunction with the word which he misread as 'langer'.'

presumed to be quoting; but argues against the Arden2 standardization, remarking that 'Some editors delete the following preposition though there is no reason to do so.'[10] But even while printing F2's divergent 'tang with', the New Cambridge editor (like other modern editors who print 'tang with' rather than the 'tang' of the Letter Scene itself) still continues to surround Malvolio's words here with the quotation marks that suggest that Malvolio's rendition of the letter is identical with it.

Wells and Warren, the play's Oxford World's Classics editors, like Arden2, follow Capell in bringing Malvolio's citation into line with the letter of the letter in Act 2 (by printing 'tang' instead of 'tang with' in these lines from Act 3). But they then, contradictorily, offer a note that questions not only the necessity of doing so but whether it is even necessary to assume that Malvolio's citations from the letter are accurate (a perception that might similarly be applied to his 'Some are born great' were it not so naturalized as the authoritative version of the letter):

F reads 'langer with'; F2 corrects this to '*tang* with'; Capell in turn emends to *tang*, omitting 'with' to bring it in line with the original letter (2.5.141). This is not absolutely essential, since not all quotations from the letter in the play are accurate.[11]

Wells and Warren's reminder here that it is 'not absolutely essential' to make Malvolio's 3.4 version identical with the letter in Act 2, 'since not all quotations from the letter in the play are accurate' recalls most strikingly the Clown's later rendering of greatness as not 'thrust' but 'thrown'. But in a scene in which neither this textual crux nor Malvolio's rendering of the letter's prescriptions on the 'manner how' concurs exactly with the letter he reads out loud in Act 2, might it be time to ask if a similar caveat should be extended to the automatic editorial replacement of the Folios' unanimous 'become' with 'born'?

One of the puzzles that might be put before readers – if the change of the letter from 'become' to 'born' is not simply to be naturalized or rendered historically invisible – is how to explain the divergence between the letter in the Letter Scene and

Malvolio's cross-gartered citation of it in Act 3, if not as a textual 'error' that needs to be 'corrected'. In the conversations and presentations to audiences in which I have been involved since beginning work on my own edition of *Twelfth Night*, various character-based motivations have been suggested, in addition to the possibility that it may be an accidental misremembering, or one of the kinds of inconsistencies familiar from other Shakespeare texts. These have included that Malvolio's 'Some are born great' (when spoken directly before his mistress) might be a compliment to Olivia as a reminder of her high birth. But in a Shakespeare corpus where internal consistency is frequently absent (though often supplied through editorial improvement), such a character-based motivation may itself be importing historically later norms through which to read the difference here. Editors of *Twelfth Night*, remarking on Feste's divergent 'thrown', note not only that the Clown was not present at the original onstage reading from the letter in Act 2 or Malvolio's recalling of it in Act 3 (an absence which, once again, suggests a characterological basis for his misquotation) but also that such variation from a 'letter' occurs elsewhere in Shakespeare, even when the onstage reader is in both cases the same. The Arden2 editors Lothian and Craik (though like all editors after Rowe, they rewrite the letter to fit with Malvolio's 'born'), provide, for example, the following gloss to Feste's 'thrown': that it is 'probably not a mistake but Shakespeare's own casual variation.'[12] Their reference to Staunton in this note evokes a strain

---

[10] *Twelfth Night or What You Will*, ed. Elizabeth Story Donno (Cambridge, 1985), p. 110.

[11] See *Twelfth Night, Or What You Will*, ed. Roger Warren and Stanley Wells (Oxford, 1994), p. 172; and *William Shakespeare: The Complete Works*, ed. Stanley Wells, Gary Taylor, John Jowett, and William Montgomery (Oxford, 1986), p. 796, which also prints Capell's emended 'tang' rather than F2's 'tang with' for Malvolio's lines in 3.4.

[12] See *Twelfth Night*, ed. J. M. Lothian and T. W. Craik (London, 1975), pp. 151–2. See also Stephen Booth's comments on Feste's anomalous 'thrown' and the question of whether it is 'all one', in relation to a play and a canon where 'There is no reason to expect Shakespeare to quote himself faithfully',

of nineteenth-century commentary recorded more fully in the Furness Variorum, which cites first Dyce (ed. 1) questioning whether 'thrown' is 'an oversight of the author? or an error of the scribe or printer?' and then goes on to cite the responses of both Staunton (1859) and Wright (1885):

STAUNTON   We believe it to be neither one nor the other, but a purposed variation common to Shakespeare in cases of repetition, possibly from his knowing, by professional experience, the difficulty of quoting with perfect accuracy. – W. A. WRIGHT   It is more likely that Shakespeare was quite indifferent in the matter, for in *All's Well*, [5.3.]313, where Helena reads from a written letter, she varies from the same document as given in [3.2].

The parallel with *All's Well* – also cited by the Arden editors – is one in which Helena is presented as the reader of the letter in both scenes, but the 'text' of the letter is in each iteration markedly different:

Helena Look on this letter, madam; here's my passport: [*Reads*] *When thou canst get the ring upon my finger, which never shall come off, and show me a child begotten of thy body that I am father to, then call me husband; but in such a 'then' I write a 'never'.*

(3.2)

HELENA   O my good lord, when I was like this maid
I found you wondrous kind. This is your ring,
And, look you, here's your letter. This it says:
When from my finger you can get this ring
And is by me with child, & c. This is done;
Will you be mine now you are doubly won?

(5.3)[13]

Here – in a way that is *not* standardized into congruence by modern editors, who routinely mark off these lines in Act 5 as a quotation – the letter is allowed to differ from itself, even though the lines are delivered on stage by the same reader or speaker.[14]

Even more tellingly within *Twelfth Night* itself, the Clown's speech in Act 5 goes on to recall other lines from his own onstage encounters with Malvolio in Acts 1 and 4, which are marked by quotation marks in modern editions but differ from

their 'originals'. The lines of the Clown that the Arden editors themselves register contradictorily as quotations while relegating the divergence from their originals to commentary notes are 'By the Lord, fool, I am not mad' and 'Madam, why laugh you at such a barren rascal, and you smile not, he's gagged?' (5.1.372–3 and 373–5). Neither fits exactly what Feste might be presumed to be quoting here – Malvolio's 'I am not mad, Sir Thopas' (4.2.40) and Malvolio's 'I marvel your ladyship takes delight in such a barren rascal . . . Look you now, he's out of his guard already; unless you laugh and minister occasion to him, he is gagged' (1.5.81–6).[15]

In other words, even when the character 'quoting' from an earlier scene was present in it – as with

---

since 'characters misquote all the way through the canon', in *Precious Nonsense* (Berkeley, 1998), p. 180.

[13] I am quoting here from the Arden2 edition of *All's Well That Ends Well*, ed. G. K. Hunter (London, 1959), 3.2.55–9 and 5.3.303–8, because it uses italics for the lines in 5.3 to suggest that they are a quotation, whereas the Folios do not use italics for these Act 5 lines, though they do have italics for the lines of the letter read in Act 3. Other modern editions similarly put these lines in Act 5 in quotation marks.

[14] This letter has not escaped grammatical correction. G. K. Hunter's Arden2 edition keeps the Folios' 'is' in 'is by me with child' – a subject–verb alignment that would likewise argue for printing the Folio's text as 'some achieves greatness' in the Letter Scene. In the case of *All's Well*, Oxford World's Classics editor Susan Snyder changes the Folio's 'is' to Rowe's 'are by me with child' and notes that [Gary] 'Taylor speculates that F's *is* might have come about through Shakespeare's forgetting whether the original challenge appeared in Helen's letter or the Countess's, so that the second person quotation slips into the third person, and that the following *& c* suggests his intention, not carried out, to check the wording.' The reference is to *William Shakespeare: A Textual Companion* by Stanley Wells and Gary Taylor (Oxford, 1987), p. 499, where Taylor insists that 'is' here is an error that 'needs to be corrected', even if it is 'authorial'.

[15] All of the quotations here are from the Arden2 edition of Lothian and Craik, which puts these lines in quotation marks but then adds a note on the former that '"By the Lord" is nowhere used by Malvolio in [4.2]' and another note that the lines from 'Madam' to 'gagged' are 'a fairly close paraphrase of 1.5.81–6, but again not a precise reproduction of these lines.' In the case of the former, it is not even clear that the example I give here – 'I am not mad, Sir Thopas' – is the closest candidate from the Act 4 scene.

the case of the Clown's anything-but-literal renderings here – or when the text of a letter is cited by the same character who read it in an earlier scene (as with Helena in *All's Well*), consistency is not the result, however reliable the reporter or reader is expected to be. In the case of Malvolio, editors routinely comment that even the text of the letter in Act 2 – rendered in the Arden edition as 'Remember, who commended thy yellow stockings, and wished to see thee ever cross-gartered' – is contradicted within the scene itself by Maria's 'he will come to her in yellow stockings, and 'tis a colour she abhors, and cross-gartered, a fashion she detests' (2.5.198 – 200).[16] As the accompanying Arden note suggests (p. 70), Malvolio's 'fancy' may here be working against any memory he might plausibly have – at least on the evidence of Maria's reporting. Why, then, did *Malvolio*'s version of 'Some are born great, some achieve greatness, and some have greatness thrust upon them' become the reliable and authoritative version, basis for the retroactive rewriting of the letter itself?

For modern readers unfamiliar with the more alien-sounding locutions of Elizabethan English, part of the attraction of the formula uttered in the Folios by Malvolio alone is that it appears, in contrast to 'Some are *become* great', to offer a clear contrast between a presumed reference to Olivia (as one 'born great') and her steward as one who might 'achieve greatness' or here find greatness 'thrust' upon him. This was my own reaction when I first encountered the four Folios' 'Some are become great' rather than the familiar 'born'. But, as Jonathan Hope, Arden3 language consultant and author of *Shakespeare's Grammar*, pointed out to me, 'Some are become great' is a familiar seventeenth-century locution (as its persistence through the Folios suggests) – parallel in the Shakespeare corpus to a line such as 'it joys me / To see you are become so penitent' in *Richard III* (1.2.207–8); and it is clearly distinct from 'some achieve greatness' since 'some are become great' would have meant in the period 'Some have (already) become great', distinguishing it from those for whom greatness might still be achieved.[17] 'Some are become great, some achieve (or as in F1 "achieves") greatness, and

some have greatness thrust upon 'em' would thus not only reflect the 'become' of all four Folio texts of the Letter Scene but would answer the objection that 'born' is needed to correct a Folio error because it would be the only way of differentiating the first two parts of this famous sequence.

In one of the public contexts in which I have presented the Folio texts and their difference from the familiar formula – the 2005 Annual Shakespeare Lecture at the CUNY Graduate Center – a member of the academic audience subsequently wrote to me that 'there might be a good reason why Olivia (actually Maria) might wish to write "some are become great" rather than "some are born great". Olivia was born noble and wealthy but her ability to fall in love with and marry whom she pleases regardless of status (Malvolio in the joke letter, Cesario / Sebastian in the event) depended not on her birth but on the fact that she had become a free woman, a feme sole as the lawyers put it, owing to the death of her father and her brother.' He went on to note that 'This might be important to Olivia, but Malvolio, quoting the letter from memory in 3.4, might well distort the words because his own focus is not on her autonomy but on the difference in status between them – for him what is important is that she was "born great" and he was not.'

Whatever any particular interpreter might make of the reason for the Folios' 'become great', this response made me realize that only when we foreground such often-forgotten early texts – and approach them in a way that does not immediately assume that they are in need of correction – can such a discussion even begin. Pausing over the potential implications of the Folios'

---

[16] As Alan Dessen has reminded me, omitting these Malvolio-uttered lines (to remove a perceived contradiction between Malvolio's memory and Maria's reporting) has become a standard move in recent productions.

[17] John Andrews's Everyman edition, it might be noted here, produces a text that is neither the Folios nor the familiar editorial version, by unnecessarily printing 'Some become Great' (rather than 'Some are become great') and adding a note to explain 'become Great' as 'grow "Great" simply by virtue of who they are' (p. 94). See *Twelfth Night*, ed. John F. Andrews (London, 1991), p. 94.

'become' rather than 'born' might also return us to the importance more generally within the play of *becoming* great – not just in relation to Olivia's case, or what has been thrust upon *her*, but in relation to the multiple trajectories of upward mobility within it. The Folios' 'some are become great' simultaneously challenges the familiar sense that we know what or who is designated by each of the contrasts in this famous series, even as it refuses to accord one sole position to Olivia herself.

In a larger sense, using the Folio rather than the emended editorial text of the letter's phrasing would at the same time mean that no single instance of this line from this enigmatic letter in *Twelfth Night* is ever identical with itself – something suggestive for a play filled with misquotations and errors, and a plot of identity and non-identity complicated by its brother–sister twins. In a play in which other letters or expected quotations are variously distorted – as in Toby's decision to deliver Andrew's letter not literally but differently 'by word of mouth' (3.4.191) – and a zanily literalistic mode of faithful delivery is comically parodied when Feste the 'fool' delivers the letter of Malvolio the 'madman' in Act 5, can we claim with any confidence that Malvolio's citation of the letter from the Letter Scene must necessarily constitute the faithful (or identical) delivery that editorial tradition has made so familiar?

How did it become so familiar? Most scholarly editions cite the late-seventeenth-century Douai manuscript as the first to change 'become' to 'born' in 2.5 (it also changes Feste's 'thrown' to 'thrust').[18] But what is striking about the process of eighteenth-century editorial standardizing of this famous phrase is that it does *not* spring fully formed from Rowe's 1709 edition, which prints '*born Great*' but then continues the line as '*some atchieve Greatness, and some have Greatness put upon them*', reproducing Ff3 – 4's 'put' rather than 'thrust'.[19] In Rowe 1, in other words, no single version of this line within the play is identical. It was not until Rowe's 1714 edition (or Rowe 3) that the full-fledged formula appeared within the letter itself – as '*some are born Great, some atchieve Greatness, and some have Greatness thrust upon them*'. But though it standardizes the formula in the letter itself – with momentous consequences for all subsequent editions – Rowe's 1714 edition does not standardize the letter's 'tang Arguments of State' with Malvolio's 'tang with' in Act 3 or change Feste's 'thrown'.

Rowe's 1714 altering of the letter to fit with Malvolio's 'born great' sequence in Act 3 did indeed have a momentous impact on all subsequent editors. Pope repeats it in his editions of 1723 and 1728 and all editors after 1714 follow suit, even when they retain the anomaly of Feste's 'thrown' and even when other Rowe emendations are ultimately rejected.[20] Theobald – taking the process of

---

[18] On the Douai ms. associated with the English Roman Catholic foundations at Douai and thought to have been prepared for 'some kind of theatrical production, most probably of an amateur nature' (Evans, p. 165), see G. Blakemore Evans, 'The Douai Manuscript – Six Shakespearean Transcripts (1694–5)', *Philological Quarterly*, 41 (1962), 158–72; and Ann-Marie Hedbäck, 'The Douai Manuscript Reexamined', *PBSA*, 73 (1979), 1–18, which does not, however, discuss examples from *Twelfth Night*. As Evans notes (p. 167), Douai's changes (in addition to anticipating Rowe's change in 2.5 to 'born' and Theobald's change of Feste's 'thrust' to 'thrown') include 'back trip' (for 'backtrick' in 1.3), 'an ass, I doubt not' (of which Evans comments this 'MS destroys the pun'), and 'alwaies cross-gartered' for Ff's 'euer cross-garter'd' in both 3.4 and the Letter Scene in 2.5.

[19] See p. 850 of *The Works of Mr. William Shakespeare, edited by Nicholas Rowe, 1709*, vol. II (London, 1999). Rowe's phrasing here is actually closest to F3's '*some atchieve greatness, and some have greatness put upon em*' rather than F4's '*some atchieve greatness, and some, and some have greattness put upon them*', though it is generally assumed that he is following F4 and he prints F4's 'them' rather than 'em.' The lines may be simply Rowe's correction of F4's ('*some, and some*') repetition here. Rowe's 1709 edition also corrects Ff3–4's 'bow me' to 'bow to me' (as in F1–2).

[20] Rowe (1709 and 1714) follows F4 (and all Folios after F1) in deleting the 'not' from the First Folio's 'I do not now foole my selfe' – a reading that continued in Pope (1723 and 1728) but was ultimately replaced by Theobald (1733) and Hanmer (1743) who, like Warburton (1747), Capell (1767–8) and Steevens (1773) print 'not.' Rowe's 1714 edition, unlike his 1709 edition, also changes the Folios' consistent 'are' in 'every one of these Letters are in my name' (F1) to 'is' – an emended text that also appears in Pope (1723; 1728), Hanmer (1743; 1745), Theobald (1733; 1740; 1752), Warburton (1747–8); Johnson (1765), Steevens (1773; 1778) and Rann (1787).

standardization still further – even changes Feste's 'thrown' to 'thrust', producing a text in which all three iterations of this line from *Twelfth Night* are (indeed) identical with each other. Theobald's change of Act 5's 'thrown' to 'thrust' actually persisted for a time – appearing in Hanmer (1743 and 1745), Warburton (1747), and Dr Johnson (1765). It was only with Capell (1767–8) that Feste's 'thrown' was restored. But even after Capell, Bell's acting edition (1774) has Feste say 'thrust', like Theobald making all three iterations the same.²¹

Other eighteenth-century attempts to make the letter and Malvolio's citation from (or memory of) it identical engage, as we have seen, the anomalous 'tang with' and 'tang', as if no detail were too small or insignificant to be overlooked by the standardizing impulse. Even though all of these attempts at standardization (including Theobald's elimination of the anomalous 'thrown') did not last, they stand as a record of the drive to make the letter uniform – the same motive cited by later editors for Rowe's influential 'born.'²²

Rowe's 1714 '*some are born Great, some atchieve Greatness, and some have Greatness thrust upon them*' altered the letter for all subsequent editions, effacing the Folios' 'some are become great' by making all three terms of this famous sequence consistent with Malvolio's rendition in Act 2. By the time of Malone's epoch-making 1790 edition, the formula had long since become secure. What is curious in Malone, however, is that even as he prints the by-then familiar formula, his note to its appearance in the letter in Act 2 adds: 'This necessary emendation was made by Mr Rowe. It is justified by a subsequent passage in which the clown recites from memory the words of this letter' – a justification not through Malvolio but through the Clown whose final recitation is strikingly not identical with the formula, even though it does have 'born'. And this inconsistent gloss from Malone is iterated in subsequent Variorum editions, even as they too print the Clown's anomalous 'thrown'.

If the letter, finally, is not 'all one' even in these eighteenth-century editions, which entertained but finally rejected Theobald's attempt to make all three citations congruent, might we then revisit the question of 'Some are *become* great?' And might our resistance to this possibility be influenced by the fact that the Malvolio formula has become not only familiar but beloved?

fortunate unhappy daylight and champian discovers not more . . .   (First Folio)

I want to move now to the other striking editorial emendation to the letter. The words used as an epigraph here (with minor variations in spelling) appear in a sequence in all four Folio texts of the letter in *Twelfth Night*. How, then, did we end up with 'The Fortunate Unhappy' signature that appears on a separate line in modern editions? The First Folio (like the Second) fails to provide italics, so it is not clear where the letter ends and Malvolio's reaction

---

But Capell (1767–8), Malone (1790), and the 1793 Variorum print Ff's 'are.'

²¹ Steevens (1773 and 1778), Rann (1787), Malone (1790) and the Variorum edition of 1793 join Capell in restoring the Folios' 'thrown' for Feste's final recall of the letter in Act 5.

²² In *Twelfe Night, or, What You Will*, edited by Horace Howard Furness (Philadelphia, 1901), p. 172, Furness comments, for example, '*are become great*] This phrase is afterward quoted twice, once by Malvolio, in his interview with Olivia ([3.4.]44), and again by the Clown, in the last scene ([5.1.]390); and in both cases it is given 'some are born great.' ROWE, accordingly, for the sake of uniformity, changed 'become' to *born* in the present passage, and therein has been uniformly followed by succeeding editors.'

In 1903 – in an edition of the play that was part of a series of one-volume Folio-based Shakespeare editions produced by these two female editors, whose glosses are rarely quoted by modern editors – Charlotte Porter and Helen A. Clarke add a note to the 'are become' of the Folio text that suggests that conformity between it and Malvolio's recitation in Act 3 may not be essential: '*become great*: Rowe's change to born great makes this passage conform with its repetition, [3.4].44 and [5.1].390. Possibly Shakespeare improved unconsciously on his first phrase.' See p. 138 of *Twelfe Night, Or What You Will by William Shakespeare*, edited by Charlotte Porter and Helen A. Clarke (New York, 1903).

Modern editors, however, frequently justify printing Rowe's 'born' in the letter scene for the sake of consistency with Malvolio's version in Act 3. Lothian and Craik, for example, comment on their choice of 'born' in the Letter Scene over the Folio's 'are become' that 'Rowe's emendation is proved correct by [3.4].30 and [5.1].369', even though they print Feste's anomalous 'thrown' in Act 5.

begins. 'This is open, I will bee proud, I will reade pollticke Authours' (F1, and the same in the other three Folios with minor differences in spelling) is clearly spoken by Malvolio, but the intervening words that follow 'Farewell' are up for grabs. One possible reading, given the First Folio's comma (rather than full stop) after 'Farewell', would be to read the entire syntactical sequence that follows from it as an enigmatic circumlocution where a clear signature might be expected, so that the First Folio letter would come to a (modernized) end with: 'Farewell, she that would alter services with thee, that fortunate unhappy daylight and champian discovers not more.'

This would make the entire phrase ('that fortunate unhappy daylight and champian discovers not more') follow syntactically from and further define the enigmatic 'She' (in apposition to it).[23] It would also view the colon the First Folio places after 'more' as marking the end of the letter and the beginning of Malvolio's reaction to it – as colons do in some earlier lines from the letter in this scene: '*To the unknowne belou'd, this, and my good Wishes*: Her very Phrases' (TLN 1104–5); *I may command, where I adore*: Why shee may command me' (TLN 1124–5). In this reading of F1's ambiguous text, Malvolio's first lines would thus be what follows from its colon here: 'This is open, I will bee proud', a reading of F1 suggested by its placing of a comma rather than a full stop after 'Farewell.' The Second Folio, by contrast, puts a full stop after 'Farwell', so that its slightly altered 'Shee that would alter services with thee, the fortunate unhappy daylight and champian discovers not more' (which substitutes 'the' for F1's 'tht' but also concludes with a colon) could *either* be the end of the letter – with Malvolio's 'This is open' as his first reaction – *or* the first words spoken by Malvolio himself. This latter option is the one taken in F3 and F4, where the letter comes to a clear (and now italicized) end on '*Farewell*' and Malvolio's first words in response are 'She that would alter services with thee, the fortunate unhappy daylight and champion discovers not more: This is open, I will be proud' (Ff3 – 4).

To trace the shifting fortunes of the letter's ending through its eighteenth-century editions is to see Capell's eventual creation of 'the fortunate-unhappy' as a signature as part of a historical process of grappling both with the question of where the letter should end and with the paradoxical formulation of the 'fortunate unhappy' itself. Both F3 and F4, as already noted, end the italicized letter on the closing word '*Farewell*', following it with F2's full stop rather than F1's comma – so that 'She that would alter services with thee, the fortunate unhappy daylight and champion discovers not more' (Ff3 – 4) become Malvolio's first words in response.[24] But Rowe's first (1709) edition makes the momentous decision to extend the italics so that the letter ends '*Farewel. She that would alter Services with thee.*' Rowe thus not only extends the letter but changes the Fourth Folio's comma after 'thee' to a full stop, making '*She that would alter services with thee*' into a kind of periphrastic signature, after *Farewel*. He then removes the oxymoron or paradox in 'fortunate vnhappy' completely by changing it to the following sentence, as Malvolio's new first words: 'The fortunate and happy Day-light and Champian discovers not more: This is open . . .' Rowe's 1714 edition does the same.

Pope – in both 1723 and 1728 – alters 'discovers not more' to 'discovers no more' (in a fashion that lasted through several other editions) but otherwise follows Rowe, once again ending the italicized letter with '*Farewel. She that would alter services with thee*' and removing the paradoxical 'fortunate vnhappy' by beginning Malvolio's response with 'The fortunate and happy day-light and champian discovers no more: this is open.' Theobald (in both 1733 and 1740) adds a comma in '*She, that would alter services with thee*', as if establishing a more definitive signatory 'She', but otherwise follows suit (including

---

[23] In this sense it might suggest that nothing could be (enigmatically) more clear, a sense that would fit with paradoxical formulations elsewhere in *Twelfth Night*, including 'lustrous as ebony' in 4.2, as well as the postscript that begins '*Thou canst not choose but know who I am.*' In another reading of the syntax, it might be construed as following from 'thee' (or Malvolio himself).

[24] F3 and F4 also add a colon after 'fingers' so that the text reads '*not worthy to touch Fortune's fingers: Farewell. She . . .*'

printing 'fortunate and happy' instead of 'fortunate unhappy').

Several other changes happen on the way to Capell's signature solution. Hanmer (1743) makes yet another change to the end-point of the italicized letter – printing '*Farewel. She that would alter services with thee the fortunate and happy*', thus turning 'fortunate and happy' into a compound describing Malvolio himself, whose reaction to the letter then begins with 'Day-light and champian discover no more' (an adjustment of 'discovers' to 'discover'), a reading repeated in Hanmer 2 (1745). Warburton (1747), similarly, ends the letter with '*Farewel. She, that would alter services with thee, the fortunate and happy*', treating 'Day-light and champian discovers no more' as Malvolio's first words; and then adds a note that would appear in subsequent editions, commenting on this correction of the punctuation or pointing of editions prior to this extension of the letter to 'the fortunate and happy' as its proper end:

with thee. The fortunate and happy day-light and champian discovers no more:] Wrong pointed: We should read, – *with thee, the fortunate and happy. Day-light and champian discover no more:* i.e. Broad day and an open country cannot make things plainer.

Johnson (1765) – who reproduces Warburton's note – prints '*Farewel. She, that would alter services with thee, the fortunate and happy*' as the end of the letter, and 'Day-light and champian discovers no more' as Malvolio's first words. Hanmer, Warburton, and Johnson, in other words, all extend the italicized letter to end with '*the fortunate and happy*'. The stage was thus set by 1767 for Capell's solution, which keeps the capitalized 'Day-light' as Malvolio's first word but transforms '*The fortunate-unhappy*' into a definitive signature:

M A L. M, O, A, I; – This simulation is not as the former: and yet, to crush this a little, it would bow to me, for every one of these letters are in my name. Soft; here follows prose.

[*reads*].

If this fall into thy hand, revolve. In my stars I am above thee; but be not afraid of greatness: Some are born great, some achieve greatness, and some have greatness thrust upon them: thy fates open their hands; let thy blood and spirit embrace them. And, to inure thyself to what thou art like to be, cast thy humble slough, and appear fresh: be opposite with a kinsman, surly with servants: let thy tongue tang arguments of state; put thyself into the trick of singularity: She thus advises thee, that sighs for thee. Remember who commended thy yellow stockings; and wish'd to see thee ever cross-garter'd: I say, remember. Go to: thou art made, if thou desir'st to be so; if not, let me see thee a steward still, the fellow of servants, and not worthy to touch fortune's fingers. Farewel. She that would alter services with thee, The fortunate-unhappy.* Day-light, and champian, discovers not more: this is open. I will be proud, I will read politick authors, I will baffle sir *Toby*, I will wash off gross acquaintance, I will be point-devise the very man . . . [25]

Capell's own *Notes and Various Readings to Shakespeare* (1779) detail what he terms the 'corruption' introduced by Rowe and other editors (indicated here, because he does not cite them by name):

The gross corruption below it was heal'd by the first modern out of p. 54, where the words are repeated: But this service of his [i.e. Rowe] is overbalanc'd by a corruption introduc'd by himself at 41, 13. that runs through all his succeeders, reading – "*fortunate* and *happy;*" and, thus alter'd, the words are made by him and two successors [Pope, Theobald] epithets to *day-light* and *champian*, their letter ending at "*thee:*" the other two moderns [Hanmer, Warburton] do indeed continue the letter to the end of '*unhappy*', but write and point it in this fashion, – *She that would alter services with thee, the fortunate and happy*; by which junction the epithets' application in them will be to Malvolio: and all these blunders rose out of the first printer's negligence; who gives no part of the letter in Italicks except the seven first words of it, and has no point whatever after *unhappy*: – "*The fortunate-unhappy*" is Olivia's subscription, implying – fortunate in her possessions, but unhappy in love; and is of excellent quaintness, suited to the epistle: which (to touch of that by the by) has such pointing from moderns, that their most favourer can never say 'twas conceiv'd by them.[26]

---

[25] *Mr William Shakespeare his Comedies, Histories, and Tragedies*, ed. Edward Capell (1767), vol. 4, pp. 40–1.
[26] *Notes and Various Readings to Shakespeare*, by Edward Capell (1779–80), vol. 2, part 4, pp. 147–8.

Capell's newly crafted signature became the model for subsequent editions, which likewise follow him in making 'Daylight and champian discovers not more' into Malvolio's first words.[27] Steevens (1773) ends the letter with '*Farewel. She, that would alter services with thee, the fortunate-unhappy*', and even adds an inaccurate comment that 'The Folio, which is the only ancient copy of this play, reads, *the fortunate-unhappy*, and so I have printed it. The *fortunate-unhappy* seems to be the subscription of the letter.' Steevens (1778) and Rann (1787) capitalize '*The fortunate-unhappy*' as if to demarcate it as a signature even more from its closing flourish ('*She, that would alter services with thee*'). And then, finally, Malone (1790) moves it to a separate line, producing the fully-separated signature we still see in modern editions:

Go to; thou art made, if thou desirest to be so; if not, let me see thee a steward still, the fellow of servants, and not worthy to touch fortune's fingers. Farewel. She, that would alter services with thee,

The fortunate-unhappy.

Day-light and champian discovers not more: this is open. I will be proud, I will read politick authors . . .[28]

Malone's creation of a full-blown signature on its own separate line – repeated in the 1793 Variorum and through subsequent editions – thus produced the fully separated signature that we and our students now see as the standard form of the letter in all modern editions (with Capell's hyphen or without it).

Furness's Variorum, while printing the First Folio text, writes approvingly of Capell's innovation:

HANMER was the first to perceive, that the letter ended with 'vnhappy' and that 'daylight' is the beginning of Malvolio's comment; but like all the editors from ROWE to JOHNSON, he vitiated his text, by reading 'fortunate and happy'. CAPELL was the first to perceive that 'The fortunate vnhappy' is the subscription.

But he soon after rejects another Capell innovation as going too far to 'improve' Shakespeare, remarking – of the Folio lines where Malvolio comments

'euery reason excites to this, that my Lady loues me' and 'a kinde of iniunction driues mee to these habites of her liking' – that Capell 'conjectured that we should here read: 'for *very* reason' and 'with a kind of injunction',' conjectures that 'are good, but somewhat too much in the way of improving Shakespeare' (p. 176). As with Rowe's sense-altering change of 'Thou canst not choose but know who I am' to 'choose to know' or Theobald-through-Johnson's altering of Feste's 'thrown' to thrust' – might it be time to reconsider the editorial improvement of Capell and Malone's editorially generated signature? Or to puzzle out the Folio's 'Shee that would alter seruices with thee, tht fortunate vnhappy daylight and champian discouers not more' without assuming that it needs to be carved up as it was in the eighteenth century into part letter, part signature, and part Malvolio's response? And are there ways of making the issue *visible* as a textual puzzle, rather than simply and automatically reproducing Capell's 'improvement'?

Making the Folio versions visible (as they are, say, in the facsimile versions here) would also enable a reader to puzzle out why editors might perceive a need to separate 'fortunate vnhappy' from 'daylight' (in the phrase that ultimately became, by the time of Capell and Malone, so distinctly separated as a signature) and provoke debate about whether compositorial spacing should be counted or discounted here. It might be argued, for example, that the space in FI between 'vnhappy' and 'daylight' calls out for the insertion of a full stop and the conversion of 'daylight' into the capitalized 'Daylight and champian discovers not more' that we find in modern editions as Malvolio's first words. But the First Folio also has a space between 'my' and 'yellow' in 'She did commend my yellow stockings', where there is no conceivable need for inserted punctuation. So irregular compositorial spacing in

---

[27] Bell's 1774 edition still prints '*Farewel. She that would alter services with thee, the fortunate and happy*', but other editions after the date of Capell's 1767–8 edition follow him in printing his signature in some form.

[28] *The Plays and Poems of William Shakespeare*, ed. Edmond Malone (1790), vol. 4.

a passage of prose (which occurs elsewhere in *different* places in all four Folios) may not justify such a momentous change as the eighteenth-century carving up of the entire syntactical unit to produce a signature for the letter.

There is also the question of whether this enigmatic letter requires a signature at all, either in general or to make it more consonant with the other two letters that appear in this play – Andrew's formal challenge to Cesario read out in Act 3 (which ends with '*Thy friend as thou usest him, & thy sworne enemie*, Andrew Ague-cheeke') and Malvolio's letter in Act 5 (which ends with *The madly us'd Malvolio*).[29] The letter found by Malvolio and 'crushed' a little to signify his own intended name is already different in having no clear or unequivocal addressee, in contrast to the 'Youth' of Andrew's later letter or the 'Madam' of Malvolio's aggrieved epistle in Act 5. Since in that respect it already departs from the clarity of those salutations, might it have no clear signature either? Might it end instead simply with 'Farewell' (as Ff3–4 appear to read the full stop F2 places after 'Farwell') or with the enigmatic and periphrastic locution of F1's 'Shee that would alter seruices with thee, tht fortunate vnhappy daylight and champian discouers not more' – a circumlocution that simultaneously obscures and suggests that the writer's identity is open to view? The letter is itself an enigma to be read – or crushed – concealing its writer while at the same time starting its (teasing) postscript with '*Thou canst not choose but know who I am*' (F1). The absence of the normally expected signature may be precisely appropriate, rendering its riddle as 'lustrous as ebony' or as 'transparent as barricadoes' (4.2.36–8), to adopt the paradoxical formulation famous from Feste's own encounter with this crusher of letters in Act 4, or the paradoxical 'fortunate unhappy daylight' itself.

There is also, finally, the issue of whether reference to formal epistolary style in the period would even be the last word on whether Capell's (or any other) signature for this letter needs to be provided – or the assumption that the text would be in error without it. Here, a striking instance

within the Shakespeare corpus itself suggests that contemporary epistolary conventions may not be the decisive or exclusive reference here. In the 1600 Quarto of *The Merchant of Venice*, what one commentator calls a 'disembodied letter' arrives to inform Bassanio that 'my ships have all miscarried, my Creditors growe cruel' but does not bear any signature.[30] If that letter is not supplied with its missing signature by editors of that play, perhaps our understanding of the conventions of epistolary style (which could themselves be famously irregular in the period) needs more dramatic, and Shakespearian, adjustment. Finally, it might be objected that in the case of the letter in the Letter Scene, an editorially-created signature may be necessary because the letter has a 'postscript'. But do we have the evidence we would need to muster that a postscript would *require* a signature, particularly in a Shakespearian context in which letters themselves fail to follow any necessarily consistent form? And might the beginning of the postscript with '*Thou canst not choose but know who I am*' even be suggesting that this construing (or crushing) should be possible even without a signature, coyly continuing the combination of claimed openness and enigma from the letter itself?

Once again, my posing of these questions is to open a fresh consideration of the issues, rather than to close them down with the automatic or traditional editorial decision. The challenge I have as an

---

[29] The quotations here are from F1, but the other three Folios are essentially the same (with only a few minor differences in spelling). In the case of both letters, the Folios also mark the difference graphically (through the use of italics in one or the other) between the signature and the letter. Modern editions frequently put the signatures on a separate line.

[30] On this 'disembodied letter' in the 1600 Quarto of *The Merchant of Venice* – to which editors give no signature though they routinely supply its missing speech prefix by having it read by Portia – see Howard Marchitello, '(Dis)embodied Letters and *The Merchant of Venice*: Writing, Editing, History', *ELH* 62 (1995), 237–65 (esp. 243–4), who also cites the differential closural forms of Hamlet's letter to Claudius in the Q2 and F texts of that play, and Jonathan Goldberg's discussion of them in relation to the problematics of the signature more generally, in 'Hamlet's Hand', *Shakespeare Quarterly*, 39 (1988), 307–27, esp. 324–6.

editor of *Twelfth Night* is – as with all editions – the question of what to print on the page. But given that it is in this case a 'Critical Edition' and that such an edition would necessarily bring into the classroom the kind of criticism that has called into question the editorial changes that produced the texts our students read, foregrounding the problem as an issue for discussion may be the best way for readers to see the textual puzzles themselves and the historical process through which the standardized texts were produced. It has been suggested to me, for example, that reproducing the four Folio texts of the letter and the major reconstructions they underwent during the eighteenth century would be a way of making it possible for readers of the edition to chart the changes by which the familiar version was historically produced – as a more visible alternative to the fragmentary shorthand of collation notes in the scholarly 'band of terror' or the effacing of the historical process altogether in most classroom-oriented editions. This would be possible quite easily over just a few layout pages and would fit with other parts of the edition, which will be foregrounding textual issues as well as gender, performance and other issues in the criticism it reprints – including the timing of Malvolio's cross-gartered entry (a Folio stage direction traditionally moved by editors) discussed by Alan Dessen and Laurie Osborne's examination of the difference between the Folio text ('Alas, O frailtie is the cause, not wee, / For such as we are made, if such we be') and the standard text encountered in modern editions, which follow Rann in erasing the considerable virtue in F's 'if', in lines where the

Folio's 'O frailtie' rather than F2's generally adopted 'our frailtie' simultaneously complicates the question of (assumed) gender.[31]

One of the advantages of such a layout – as the basis for a teaching exercise that would foreground rather than obscure the process of historical production – would be to enable more advanced students to engage directly in the difficult process of coming to decisions and all students and readers to see how much of what they read in modern editions was created long after Shakespeare's death, including through the Folio texts themselves. Setting this famously enigmatic letter before the reader – without closing it down through the already established means – might also provide a way of demonstrating to students and others how much of the text is still open to interpretation even at the most basic level. Perhaps then – whether we find this process exhilarating, or unsettling, or both – we might truly say that fortunate unhappy daylight and champian discovers not more.

---

[31] The Criticism excerpts referred to here are from Dessen's *Recovering Shakespeare's Theatrical Vocabulary* (Cambridge, 1995), pp. 23–4; and Laurie Osborne's 'Editing Frailty in *Twelfth Night*: "Where lies your Text?"', in *Reading Readings: Essays on Shakespearean Editing in the Eighteenth Century*, ed. Joanna Gondris (London, 1998), pp. 209–23. I also want to express my gratitude here to Bradley Ryner, who experimented in an undergraduate setting with a number of the textual issues with which I have been working in the course of preparing this edition; and Jonathan Hope, who experimented at a more advanced level with the issues raised in this chapter, in a class of graduates specializing in Renaissance literature.

'A THOUSAND SHYLOCKS': ORSON WELLES AND *THE MERCHANT OF VENICE*

TOM ROONEY

Today Orson Welles (1915–85) is known to most in the Shakespeare community for his work on the New York stage in the 1930s, primarily the 'voodoo' *Macbeth* (1936) and 'fascist' *Julius Caesar* (1937), and for his film adaptations of *Macbeth* (1948), *Othello* (1952) and *Chimes at Midnight* (1965). Less well known is that at the very outset of his career Welles co-edited three Shakespeare plays with Roger Hill, his former prep school headmaster at the Todd School in Woodstock, Illinois. *Everybody's Shakespeare* was published by Todd Press in 1934, and included modern spelling versions of *The Merchant of Venice*, *Twelfth Night* and *Julius Caesar*. These first appeared in individual editions, but later they were collected and published as one book. The primary audience was high school and college students, and the editorial apparatus was designed to get them not to study the plays but rather 'Read them. *Enjoy them.* Act them.'[1] To this end Hill cut the texts, Welles created nearly 500 drawings to illustrate the plays, they wrote detailed stage directions together, and each penned introductory essays (Hill on the life and the editorial tradition; Welles on staging the plays). It was a true work of collaboration, and produced at a time when Welles was still in his teens.

While over the years Welles's stage and film work has been the subject of much scholarship, these 'performances' on the page have not received nearly enough attention.[2] Simon Callow argues that 'Welles's sense of theatre, the wit and point of his drawing, and the articulate enthusiasm of his approach makes *Everybody's Shakespeare* one of the outstanding achievements of his entire output'

(p. 185). His editorial work on *The Merchant of Venice* especially deserves wider recognition today because, apart from a few minutes of film shot years later, this is the only evidence we have of Welles engaging with the play.[3]

EVERYBODY'S SHAKESPEARE

The title page of the 1934 Todd Press edition announces its editorial intentions right away: EVERYBODY'S SHAKESPEARE/THREE PLAYS/EDITED FOR READING AND ARRANGED FOR STAGING. This is a Shakespeare edition to be read for pleasure, and used as a guide to putting on the

---

[1] *Everybody's Shakespeare* introductory essay: 'Advice To Students: On Studying Shakespeare's Plays', p. 3. There are four separately paginated sections in the 1934 edition. The first section (pp. 3–28) includes a group of six introductory essays. The other three sections are made up of the plays themselves. To further complicate matters, however, each play has its own introductory material too. Thus the unusual citation style used here.

[2] Two notable exceptions are Simon Callow, *Orson Welles: The Road to Xanadu* (New York, 1995) and Michael Anderegg, *Orson Welles, Shakespeare and Popular Culture* (New York, 1999). Callow provides the best overview of the project among the many biographies. Anderegg is more interested in the socio-historical significance of the work, and how it relates to Welles's Shakespearian films. Reading both inspired me to pursue the editorial angle further.

[3] In the 1960s Welles attempted to film *The Merchant of Venice*. All that survives are a few minutes of footage. As these are only fragments, however, they will not be discussed here. The footage is included in the documentary film *Orson Welles: One Man Band*, and is available on the Criterion Collection DVD of *F for Fake* (2005).

plays, not as a tool for critically analysing them. For the editors, studying the plays should only come after they had been read over and over again, and had been staged; the time for the 'literary dissecting table' was only 'after the music sings in your heart and their characters are part of your intimate acquaintanceship'.[4] It should be noted that this performance-centred approach to Shakespeare was years ahead of its time. Hill and Welles were among the first educators to encourage this kind of thinking in the classroom; despite this, however, their contribution has gone unrecognized in the field.[5]

How did Hill and Welles help students? Not by providing glosses, as most editors do. The opening scene of *The Merchant of Venice* is a good example of how the teacher and his former student approached the text:

ACT I
Scene I
VENICE – A Street

Some producers have opened the play with music, peopling the stage with peddlars [sic] and vendors of sweets and folk of every degree walking up and down in pursuit of their business, a colorful and interesting picture of Venetian street life in the age of Shakespeare. With the entrance of Antonio and his friends the crowd melts away and the play is permitted to begin. For most productions a simple setting is the best. It needn't take up much of the space on the stage nor need be elaborately pictorial. Center and side entrances seem to be called for and a piece center, a bench or steps or something to sit on. (Sketches here are suggestions.)

As the play opens Antonio, a prosperous merchant, a dignified, quite well-dressed gentleman of middle-age, enters chatting with friends of his, two gentlemen of Venice: Salarino and Salanio. They come downstage and pause; talking–

ANTONIO In sooth, I know not why I am so sad:
It wearies me–You say it wearies *you*;
But how I caught it, found it, or came by it,
What stuff 'tis made of, whereof it is born,
I am to learn. (*Sighs*)
And such a want-wit sadness makes of me,
That I have much ado to know myself.
SALARINO (*Wisely*) Your mind is tossing on the ocean.
SALANIO (*Nodding*) Believe me, sir, had *I* such venture
  forth,

The better part of my affections would
Be with my hopes abroad. I know Antonio
Is sad to think upon his merchandise.
ANTONIO Believe me, no. I thank my fortune for it,
My ventures are not in one bottom trusted,
Nor to one place . . .

(*Everybody's Shakespeare: The Merchant of Venice*, p. 5)

Note how heavily the two editors have intervened: their detailed scene introduction, cuts and conflations in the text, and parenthetical and italicized stage directions are all quite startling. These decisions are radical, but are typical for all three plays in the edition. Most scenes have as lengthy and detailed a Shavian introduction as shown here. For example, the one for Act I Scene 3 is over 220 words long. It begins 'VENICE – A Public Place/*Usually Before Shylocks' House*':

There are countless arrangements for this scene, but many of the most successful have employed these elements: A little square with a fountain or a well in the center, to one side Shylock's house, or part of it showing the door, and a window above, the wall of another house across from it; and running across the back a canal with other buildings visible behind. Also, if possible, because it has been found tremendously effective in stage business, a bridge. Shylock, instead of entering after the curtain has risen, might be "discovered" either at his door or at the top of this bridge.

Several cuts and conflations in the text have also been made. The most notable is in the first scene of the play, where the opening 70 lines have been reduced to 35, eliminating much of the discussion of Antonio's ships. The other major textual revision was to combine the two scenes involving Morocco into one. In the 1970s Welles articulated the reasons behind these changes to an interviewer:

The text was cut so as to leave only a minimum of things that wouldn't be understood. Because it seems to me that the first thing to do for a student at school is to make him

---

4 *Everybody's Shakespeare*: 'Advice To Students', p. 3.
5 For example, Charles Frey credits J. L. Styan with introducing 'the play way' in the early 1970s ('Teaching Shakespeare in America', *Shakespeare Quarterly*, 35 (1984), 541–59).

love Shakespeare, not to make him hate it. He can learn to love Shakespeare by staging it himself in simplified form. This edition was designed to allow a student to get into costume and perform. I thought that if he could do this, he wouldn't be afraid to read the complete texts of Shakespeare as he grew up, or to see more refined productions.[6]

The italicized inflections to indicate a character's state of mind are also ubiquitous: Shylock at times speaks *doubtfully*, *emphatically*, and *deliberately*, while Portia does so *ruefully*, *determinedly*, and *gravely*; Morocco is described as *self-important*, Bassanio *dazed*, and Old Gobbo *bewildered*; while Nerissa acts *seriously*, Launcelot Gobbo *pompously*, Gratiano *glibly* and Antonio – of course – *sadly*. It would take a Herculean effort to catalogue all the words used in the text to describe how the characters behave and, while at times they can be somewhat obvious, they do help readers 'hear' the play.

Of course the most striking editorial feature of *Everybody's Shakespeare* is pictorial: Welles created more than 490 drawings to help readers 'see' the three plays. Most pages include at least two or three illustrations. These include renderings of stage settings, all proscenium-based, with some influenced by the work of early twentieth-century designers such as Craig. A few are even copied from real productions. There are over 92 of these stage pictures in all, 39 of them in *The Merchant of Venice*. Competing stage pictures often appear in groups of three or four at the start of a scene as well, so no one conception dominates the play. These drawings are effective not only because they are diverse, but because they are 'modern', that is, firmly rooted in the proscenium stage tradition. Contemporary readers could engage with the play on theatrical terms they were familiar with. Today's editors of Shakespeare could learn something from Welles and Hill; rather than reproducing poorly composed or badly cropped promotional photos of the modern stage productions they discuss in their introductions, they might instead include some renderings of scenes by the designers of these productions.[7]

The rest of the drawings Welles made are of the characters: individual, pair and group portraits, and sometimes a strip of drawings illustrating stage busi-

ness. In his introductory essay 'On Staging Shakespeare and on Shakespeare's Stage,' Welles describes the philosophy behind these pictures:

In illustrating I have drawn you a lot of Shylocks but not nearly enough. There are a thousand Shylocks: grim patriarchs, loving fathers, cunning Orientals, and even comics with big noses. And this goes for Malvolio and Marc Antony, Brutus and Sir Toby Belch . . . and all the rest of these characters . . . You can draw them, and what's more important, play them, exactly as you wish. I have simply made pictures of the best known and most important versions of these people. But it's up to you.[8]

One of the most endearing drawings Welles created was a small illustration for the introduction, in which a long line of Shylocks stretch out to the horizon; they appear to be waiting to audition for a part in *Everybody's Shakepeare*.[9] More than thirty Shylocks appear in the text itself, including reproductions of illustrations of famous actors in the role such as Charles Macklin, Charles Macready, Edwin Forrest and Henry Irving. There are also many impressionistic drawings of the character, for example talking with Bassanio, standing alone before a Venetian bridge, and confronting Antonio as he is led off to jail by two guards. The first is a 'close-up' of the two men from the waist up, their austere features clearly visible. In the second, Shylock is just a tiny figure dwarfed by a proscenium stage set of the Rialto. The third is composed of quick line drawings; no features on any of the faces are

---

[6] Richard Marienstras, 'Orson Welles: Shakespeare, Welles and Moles', in *Orson Welles Interviews*, ed. Mark Estrin (Jackson, 2002), p. 157.

[7] The speculative drawings in the Cambridge editions of how scenes may have been staged at the Globe Theatre, while interesting, are wrong-headed, because no readers will have ever seen a play there. Few will even have made it to the restored version in London. The majority, however, will have seen Shakespeare in a modern playhouse.

[8] *Everybody's Shakespeare* introductory essay: 'On Staging Shakespeare and on Shakespeare's Stage: A Chapter by Orson Welles', p. 27.

[9] The Welles estate did not respond to repeated requests for permission to reproduce this and other illustrations. This is a pity, for readers should have an opportunity to see the work as well as read about it.

discernible, but Shylock's squared shoulders and Antonio's crooked stance say as much as 'I'll have my bond' and 'I pray thee, hear me speak'.

The effect these multiple Shylocks have on the reader is indeed to leave the character open to interpretation. However, these depictions often contrast sharply with how Shylock comes across in the text itself:

Out of the bearded face cut with hard wrinkles, peer glinting black eyes, surprisingly keen. One knotted hand grasps his stick, the other works slowly at his side, the fingers rubbing together meditatively as though counting money . . . His bearing is stately; his manner proud, even in the presence of Christians. But behind this austerity we detect the passion Shylock strives to keep hidden; a consuming, almost insane loathing for his rival Antonio.

(introduction to Act 1 Scene 3)

As mentioned above, lines of dialogue often appear with italicized adjectives and adverbs describing a character's mood:

SHYLOCK (*Reciting with exasperating monotony*)
Three thousand ducats for three months, (*Straightening; very quietly*) and Antonio bound –
BASSANIO (*Impatiently*) Your answer to that.
SHYLOCK (*Doubtfully*) Antonio is a good man –
BASSANIO (*Testily*) Have you heard any imputation to the contrary?
SHYLOCK (*Quickly*) Oh, no, no, no, no, (*Smirking*) My manner in saying he is a good man is to have you understand me that he is sufficient.

In the introduction to *The Merchant of Venice*, Welles or Hill (it is not clear) writes that they had to be 'somewhat dogmatic' when it came to textual characterization, in order to avoid confusing or boring the reader.[10] Thus the Shylock in the text is not as sympathetically 'drawn' as the many Shylocks who appear beside him on the page.

THE MERCURY SHAKESPEARE AND THE MERCURY TEXT RECORDS

In 1938, following Welles's stage success in New York, Todd Press republished the collected edition of *Everybody's Shakespeare* with one major change: the credit on the title page was switched from 'Roger Hill and Orson Welles' to 'Orson Welles and Roger Hill'. No doubt this was due to the growing fame of the wunderkind director. That same year the publisher Harper and Brothers bought the rights to the book and started to publish them individually again, this time as *The Mercury Shakespeare*; these were designed to be used in conjunction with 78 rpm recordings of Welles and his Mercury Theatre colleagues performing the plays in a studio, produced by Columbia Records. The importance of *The Mercury Text Records* in the field of Shakespearian recordings was significant, as these were the first (almost) full-length performances issued. Previously only short extracts from the plays had been available on record, performed by the likes of John Barrymore, John Gielgud and Ellen Terry.[11]

For *The Mercury Shakespeare*, the editors kept all the introductory essays intact, but re-edited the plays themselves. Now that actors were interpreting the words on record, there was no need for such italicized directions as *warmly*, *austerely*, and *placidly*; all were removed, along with many of the lengthier scene introductions. Some of the drawings were also cut, others had captions removed, and a few were repositioned in the text. The revised opening of *The Merchant of Venice* in 1938 began:

Stage business set in this manner (behind vertical lines) is in addition to that recorded phonographically on Mercury Text Records. On these records the cast acts the entire [sic] play and Orson Welles, as narrator, adds the descriptive matter enclosed in parenthesis.

ACT I
Scene I
VENICE – A Street
(*Enter Antonio, Salarino, and Salanio*)

Some producers have opened the play with music, peopling the stage with peddlars [sic] and vendors of sweets walking up and down in pursuit of their business, a colorful and interesting picture of Venetian street life in the age of Shakespeare. With

---

[10] *Everybody's Shakespeare: The Merchant of Venice*, p. 3.
[11] In 1941 a *Mercury Shakespeare* text and recording of *Macbeth* was released.

the entrance of Antonio and his friends the crowd melts away
and the play is permitted to begin.

ANTONIO In sooth, I know not why I am so sad:
It wearies me—You say it wearies you;
But how I caught it, found it, or came by it,
What stuff 'tis made of, whereof it is born,
I am to learn.
And such a want-wit sadness makes of me,
That I have much ado to know myself.
SALARINO Your mind is tossing on the ocean.
SALANIO Believe me, sir, had I such venture forth, The
   better part of my affections would
Be with my hopes abroad. I know Antonio
Is sad to think upon his merchandise.
   (*The Mercury Shakespeare: The Merchant of Venice*, p. 3)

A profound change in editorial strategy is evident from the opening direction: the accompanying records have become the primary focus. *Everybody's Shakespeare* was explicitly designed to get students to actively access the plays, but *The Mercury Shakespeare* calls for more passive participation. Now students are to follow along as Welles and his colleagues perform the play. No one (it seems) is expected simply to read this version.

The problem with this change in editorial policy is clear when listening to Welles and company while reading the text. While many of the performances hold up well after nearly seventy years – Brenda Forbes as Portia and Norman Lloyd as Launcelot Gobbo are particularly fine – Welles himself disappoints as both Shylock and Morocco. As usual, his deep sonorous voice is used to full effect in both roles, but he seems to lack direction, often taking long pauses in the most inappropriate places. This is downright exasperating when following along in the text, because the reader sees just how much he is overindulging here. Had the two editors accurately reproduced the performance on the page, Shylock's aside in Act 1 Scene 3 would have looked like this:

How like a fawning *(pause)* Publican he looks! *(pause)*
I hate him *(pause)* for he is a Christian. *(pause)*
But more for that *(pause)* in low simplicity
He lends out money gratis *(pause)* and brings down
The rate of usance here with us in Venice. *(pause)*

If I catch him once upon the hip, *(pause)*
I will feed fat the ancient grudge I bear him.

All the other actors play the text; Welles, alas, plays the method actor.

He also plays the narrator, breathlessly reading stage directions throughout. Harry Thorton Moore, in an a 1940 overview of Shakespeare on record, was critical of this approach:

His 'master of ceremonies' tendency . . . is particularly distressing when he describes, in stage directions, actions of the characters he is himself playing, such as the Prince of Morocco and Shylock. The interference with Shylock is most destructive at the play's climax – in the middle of a passionate speech, Shylock stops to describe himself as standing over Antonio with an upraised knife . . . And it may be that this double burden of being actor-régisseur . . . contributes towards making Shylock an artificial reading.[12]

To the thousand Shylocks on the pages of *Everybody's Shakespeare* then can be added another from the recording of *The Mercury Shakespeare*: an artificial one.

RECEPTION AND AFTERLIFE

Welles's disappointing performance as Shylock is in marked contrast to his outstanding success as Shakespearian editor: both *Everybody's Shakespeare* and *The Mercury Shakespeare* were admired, and remained popular, for many years. *The Chicago American* and *The New York Herald Tribune* reviewed them favourably, as did the writers of an internal newsletter for the New York City Board of Education.[13] Harry Thorton Moore tempered his criticism of Welles the actor by endorsing Welles the pedagogue, arguing 'That the Mercury albums are good for schoolroom use is self-evident: Shakespeare is made entertaining as well as self-instructive, and the hatred so many children

---

[12] Harry Thorton Moore, 'Shakespeare on Records', *Theatre Arts*, 24 (June 1940), 450–4.
[13] The two newspaper reviews are quoted in Frank Brady, *Citizen Welles: A Biography of Orson Welles* (New York, 1989). The newsletter is discussed in Anderegg, 55.

early acquire from blundering teachers in the subject may be greatly minimized if these recordings are given widespread use.'[14] And a 1940 survey of secondary school teachers found that the recordings were indeed popular with students; one instructor was quoted as saying 'All types of scenes and speeches seemed to be sharpened and rendered much more vital and realistic . . . by the playing of the records.'[15]

By 1942 *Time* magazine was reporting that over 100,000 copies had been sold.[16] While the source for this may have been Welles himself, a master at self-promotion, there is no doubt the works continued to sell. In the 1950s the plays were re-issued with $33\frac{1}{3}$ rpm recordings by McGraw Hill, and in this form they remained on sale until the 1960s. Today the recordings are once more available on cd, but without the accompanying *Mercury Shakespeare* texts.[17] In the case of *The Merchant of Venice*, then, only one of Welles's Shylocks has survived.

In her biography of Orson Welles, Barbara Leaming writes about her 1983 meeting with the then eighty-eight year-old Roger Hill. Although Welles himself was sixty-nine at the time, Leaming describes how his old headmaster was still looking out for 'his beloved protégé'.

I witness this when, from his immense hoard of Wellesiana, intact since Todd (crumbly photos and cryptic copies of Orson's letters and diaries) [he] gingerly extracts a rare old edition of *Everybody's Shakespeare*, which he presses upon me in hopes that I know an agent or publisher who might be interested in reissuing it. No need to mention any of this to Orson, he informs me – but if we succeed perhaps it will bring Orson a little extra cash, which, his mentor says ruefully, he could use just now.[18]

No reissue ever appeared. Welles died two years later; Hill lived on another few years. And copies of *Everybody's Shakespeare* are even rarer today than when Leaming met Hill.

Perhaps the reason so little work has been done on *Everybody's Shakespeare* and *The Mercury*

Shakespeare over the years is because both have long been out of print, and in recent years only a few scholars – Welles scholars – have even seen them. It is highly unlikely a general reader will stumble across a copy of the *Mercury Shakespeare* edition of *The Merchant of Venice* next to an Arden or Oxford edition on the shelf in a second-hand bookshop. And while today many of the individual editions can be bought at a moderate price, a collected edition is quite expensive indeed; most sell for hundreds, if not thousands, of dollars. During the research for this article, after much searching, I was able to track down a decent copy of the 1938 Todd Press reprint for a (somewhat) reasonable price. I believe it was worth every penny, but like Hill I think a wider audience deserves to see *Everybody's Shakespeare* too, especially in Britain, where for too long Welles's contribution has been misrepresented and/or disparaged.[19] Were more people in the Shakespeare community to see the 'thousand Shylocks' he created for *The Merchant of Venice*, they would see another side of the actor/director/magician/showman: Orson Welles, co-editor.

---

[14] Moore, 454.

[15] In Anderegg, 54–5.

[16] 'Orson's Alma Mater,' *Time*, 9 March 1942, p. 50.

[17] These are produced by Pearl Plays and Poets, a division of Pavilion Records Ltd. For this article, their 1998 version of *The Merchant of Venice* (GEMS 0029) was used.

[18] Barbara Leaming, *Orson Welles* (New York, 1985), p. 95.

[19] For an example of the former, see the too brief entry on Welles in the recent *Oxford Companion*; it makes no mention of *Everybody's Shakespeare*. 'Orson Welles' in *The Oxford Companion to Shakespeare*, ed. Michael Dobson and Stanley Wells (Oxford, 2001), p. 517. A good example of the latter is David Daniell's one-paragraph dismissal of the Mercury Theatre stage production of *Julius Caesar* in his introduction to the latest Arden edition of the play. In the space of just a few sentences he calls it 'a distant version of the play', complains that 'it could hardly be called Shakespeare', and lumps it together with 'other similar mangled versions', *Julius Caesar*, ed. David Daniell (London, 2002), pp. 110–11.

THE DATE AND AUTHORSHIP OF HAND D'S CONTRIBUTION TO *SIR THOMAS MORE*: EVIDENCE FROM 'LITERATURE ONLINE'

MacDONALD P. JACKSON

The famous three pages added by 'Hand D' to the multi-authored manuscript play *Sir Thomas More* have been accepted as Shakespeare's by recent editors of his complete works.[1] But scepticism about the attribution is still expressed by prominent scholars, and a new study by Ward E. Y. Elliott and Robert J. Valenza, in which the disputed material is subjected to their 'silver bullet' methods of computer-aided testing, concludes that the probabilities are solidly against Shakespeare's authorship.[2] Elsewhere I have attempted to rebut their arguments.[3] Here I adduce some fresh evidence in favour of the majority view.

The approach to be reported on took advantage of the availability of the Chadwyck-Healey 'Literature Online' electronic database, which includes searchable texts of virtually all extant early modern English drama.[4] For much of the twentieth century, scholars attempting to establish the authorship of anonymous plays of Shakespeare's age, or to apportion shares in collaborative ones, relied on citing verbal parallels between a doubtful work and the writings of some favoured candidate. The main problem with this methodology was that it permitted only one outcome – the display of a certain number of similarities in phrasing, deemed 'significant' by the compiler, but difficult for any uncommitted judge to assess. Ostensibly impressive evidence of this kind could be collected in support of mutually exclusive theories. The implicit assumption was always that only common authorship could explain the quantity and quality of the parallels listed, but since different investigators, employing the same method, reached opposing

[1] *William Shakespeare: The Complete Works*, gen. eds. Stanley Wells and Gary Taylor (Oxford, 1986); the revised Oxford *Complete Works* (2005) includes the whole of *Sir Thomas More*, though without accepting Shakespeare's authorship of more than the pages of Hand D (Addition II.D) and More's soliloquy (Addition III) in scribal hand C; *The Riverside Shakespeare*, ed. G. Blakemore Evans (Boston, 1974; 2nd edn, 1997); The Norton Shakespeare, gen. ed. Stephen Greenblatt (New York, 1997). My line references are to the Riverside edition. The basic facts about *Sir Thomas More* are set forth in Stanley Wells and Gary Taylor, with John Jowett and William Montgomery, *William Shakespeare: A Textual Companion* (Oxford, 1987), pp. 24–5. A key volume is *Shakespeare and 'Sir Thomas More': Essays on the Play and its Shakespearian Interest*, ed. T. H. Howard-Hill (Cambridge, 1989), which is a sequel to Alfred W. Pollard, ed., and others, *Shakespeare's Hand in 'The Play of Sir Thomas More'* (Cambridge, 1923). Indispensable is W. W. Greg's Malone Society transcript of the British Library manuscript (MS Harley 7368), *The Book of Sir Thomas More* (Oxford, 1911; repr. with supplement by Harold Jenkins, 1961). Brian Vickers summarizes the case for Shakespeare in *Shakespeare Co-Author: A Historical Study of Five Collaborative Plays* (Oxford, 2002), pp. 35–43.

[2] Ward E. Y. Elliott and Robert J. Valenza, 'Two Tough Nuts to Crack: Did Shakespeare Write the "Shakespeare" Portions of *Sir Thomas More* and *Edward III*?', forthcoming in *Shakespeare Yearbook*. Prominent among those sceptical of the attribution to Shakespeare have been Michael L. Hays, 'Shakespeare's Hand in *Sir Thomas More*: Some Aspects of the Paleographic Argument', *Shakespeare Studies*, 8 (1975), 241–53; Paul Ramsey, 'Shakespeare and *Sir Thomas More* Revisited: or, A Mounty on the Trail', *Papers of the Bibliographical Society of America*, 70 (1976), 333–46, and 'The Literary Evidence for Shakespeare as Hand D in the Manuscript Play *Sir Thomas More*: A Re-re-consideration', *The Upstart Crow*, 11 (1991), 131–55; Carol Chillington, 'Playwrights at Work: Henslowe's, not Shakespeare's, *Book of Sir Thomas More*', *English Literary Renaissance*, 10 (1980), 439–79; Arthur F. Kinney, 'Text,

conclusions, the assumption must often have been unjustified.

A systematic, electronically aided search for phrases and collocations that a doubtful text shares with five or fewer plays of a given period can, in contrast, yield results susceptible of evaluation. The investigator need have no theory whatsoever, and if he or she does have one, it may or may not be supported by the findings. The old procedure was designed to demonstrate a prior belief, eluding refutation. The focus was solely on resemblances between a disputed text and the works of a single claimant. But when searching is comprehensive, proceeding according to pre-set rules, playwrights A, B, C, D, . . . and Z have equal opportunities to emerge as the writer whose idiolect has most in common with that of the play, scene, or passage under investigation. In fact most authors do repeat themselves in ways that distinguish their writing from others'. When the technique of 'Literature Online' searching is applied to work of known authorship, it yields the correct result, and it has repeatedly confirmed attributions made on independent but substantial grounds.[5]

It can also help answer questions of chronology. The date at which Hand D made his addition to *Sir Thomas More* remains in dispute. The editors of the Oxford Shakespeare settle on 1603–4, while the Revels editors, Vittorio Gabrieli and Giorgi Melchiori, think that all the Additions were made 'not later than 1594'.[6] Numbers of links in rare phrases and collocations tend to be highest between closely contemporaneous plays: frequency of linkages and chronological proximity are strongly correlated, irrespective of authorship. Evidently a changing linguistic climate affected what was said on stage.

The text of Hand D's scene was therefore entered phrase by phrase, collocation by collocation, and even content word by content word into the 'Literature Online' search boxes and all links with five or fewer plays first performed within the period 1590–1610 were recorded.[7] A slight relaxation of the rule of thumb for rarity was allowed when links with at least four out of six plays, or at least five out of seven were with a single author. Not to have

allowed this adjustment would have excluded some clear authorial indicators, though it slightly favours playwrights prolific during the defined period. In any case, analyses can be conducted with and without these few exceptional items. The techniques of 'Literature Online' searching have been described elsewhere.[8] The sharing of a rare single word is insufficient to create a link, unless it is a hyphenated compound or is supported by striking similarities of imagery or thought. Since texts are in original spelling, all possible spellings of a word must be tried. Truncation and any-letter symbols can facilitate this process. Familiarity with early modern quartos and manuscripts is essential, though the *Oxford English Dictionary* provides guidance. Modifications to the database have made it

---

Context, and Authorship of *The Booke of Sir Thomas Moore*', in *Pilgrimage for Love: Essays in Early Modern Literature in Honor of Josephine A. Roberts*, ed. Sigrid King (Tempe, Arizona, 1999; Medieval and Renaissance Texts and Studies, 213), pp. 133–60; Paul Werstine, 'Shakespeare, *More* or Less: A. W. Pollard and Twentieth-Century Shakespeare Editing', *Florilegium*, 16 (1999), 125–45. E. A. J. Honigmann responds to Werstine in his excellent 'Shakespeare, *Sir Thomas More* and Asylum Seekers', *Shakespeare Survey 57* (Cambridge, 2004), pp. 225–35.

3 MacD. P. Jackson, 'Is "Hand D" of *Sir Thomas More* Shakespeare's? Thomas Bayes and the Elliott-Valenza Authorship Tests', forthcoming.

4 The website, available to subscribing institutions, is <http://lion.chadwyck.co.uk>.

5 MacDonald P. Jackson, *Defining Shakespeare: 'Pericles' as Test Case* (Oxford, 2003), pp. 190–217. Articles employing it are: MacD. P. Jackson, 'Late Webster and his Collaborators: How Many Playwrights Wrote *A Cure for a Cuckold*', *Papers of the Bibliographical Society of America*, 95 (2001), 295–313; 'Determining Authorship: A New Technique', *Research Opportunities in Renaissance Drama*, 41 (2002), 1–14; 'A Lover's Complaint Revisited', *Shakespeare Studies*, 32 (2004), 267–94; 'John Webster, James Shirley, and the Melbourne Manuscript', forthcoming in *Medieval and Renaissance Drama in England*; Gary Taylor, 'Middleton and Rowley – and Heywood: The Old Law and New Attribution Technologies', *Papers of the Bibliographical Society of America*, 96 (2002), 165–217.

6 *Textual Companion*, pp. 124–5; Vittorio Gabrieli and Giorgio Melchiori (eds.), *Sir Thomas More* (Manchester, 1990), p. 27. On the same page they say that topical allusions point to 1593–4.

7 The 'Advanced Search' in 'Literature Online' allows one to set 'first performed' limits.

8 Most fully in Jackson, *Defining Shakespeare*, pp. 193–203.

unnecessary to worry about differences in old and modern conventions in the use of u/v and i/j, when a 'help' slot is activated.

Data collected in this way are listed below. The line reference is to the Riverside Shakespeare's modernized text of Hand D of *Sir Thomas More*. Phrases and collocations from other plays are given in my own *ad hoc* modernization of the 'Literature Online' originals. Dates are those of the Oxford *Textual Companion* for Shakespeare and *Annals of English Drama* for other dramatists, and these two reference works have served as the main authorities for naming authors.[9] Some attributions are doubtful; these will be discussed if relevant to the final analysis of the data. Phrases are identical in wording (once modernized) in Hand D's pages and the other plays cited, unless a variation is listed. Even if a locution is marginally better matched by one or more plays than by others, all items qualifying as 'rare' are included.

Peace, hear (1): Chettle, Dekker, and Haughton, *Patient Grissil* (1600); Sharpham, *Cupid's Whirligig* (1607).

a Harry groat (1–2): 'King Harry groats': Dekker and Webster, *Westward Ho* (1604).

alevenpence (2): Shakespeare, *Love's Labour's Lost* (1594–5).

nine shillings (2): Beaumont and Fletcher, *The Woman Hater* (1606); Chettle, Day (and Haughton), *The Blind Beggar of Bednal Green* (1600).

nine shillings a bushel (2–3): 'four shillings a bushel': Anon., *A Knack to Know a Knave* (1592).

beef at four nobles a stone (3): 'a stone of beef': Sharpham, *Cupid's Whirligig* (1607); 'four nobles': Anon., *Every Woman in Her Humour* (1607); Sharpham, *The Fleer* (1606).

come to that pass (4): Anon., *The Return from Parnassus* (1600); 'come to this pass': Middleton, *A Trick to Catch the Old One* (1605); 'brought you to that pass': Anon. 'W. S.', *Thomas Lord Cromwell* (1600); 'brought him to this pass': Shakespeare, *King Lear* (1605–6); 'brought a woman to this pass': Chapman, *Monsieur D'Olive* (1605).

eat more (5): Drayton, Hathway, Munday, and Wilson, *Sir John Oldcastle* (1599).

a halfpenny loaf (7): Lyly, *Mother Bombie* (1591); 'halfpenny loaves': *2 Henry VI* (1591).

is merely (8): Chapman, *Monsieur D'Olive* (1605); Greville, *Alaham* (1600); Shakespeare, *Othello* (1603–4); Chapman, *Caesar and Pompey* (1605).

to the undoing of (8): Daborne, *A Christian Turned Turk* (1610); 'the undoing of': Jonson, *Every Man out of His Humour* (1599); Samuel Rowley, *When You See Me You Know Me* (1604).

'tis enough to (10): Chapman, *The Blind Beggar of Alexandria* (1596); Day, *The Isle of Gulls* (1606).

the mercy of the King (17): 'the sovereign mercy of the King': Shakespeare, *Richard II* (1595).

have us upon th' hip (18): 'upon the hip': Shakespeare, *The Merchant of Venice* (1596–7); 'have thee on the hip': Shakespeare, *The Merchant of Venice* (1596–7); 'have our Michael Cassio on the hip': Shakespeare, *Othello* (1603–4); 'have him on the hip': Fletcher, *The Noble Gentleman* (1606); 'ha' him on the hip': Marston, *The Dutch Courtesan* (1605); 'had you on the hip': Marston, *The Dutch Courtesan* (1605).

the King's mercy (19): Chapman, *Byron's Tragedy* (1608).

show no mercy (19): 'showest no mercy': Beaumont, *The Knight of the Burning Pestle* (1607).

How say you now (22): Anon. 'W. S.', *Thomas Lord Cromwell* (1600), Anon., *A Warning for Fair Women* (1599); Marlowe, *Doctor Faustus* (1592); Shakespeare, *As You Like It* (1599–1600); Shakespeare, *The Comedy of Errors* (1594).

---

9 Alfred Harbage, rev. S. Schoenbaum, and S. Wagonheim, *Annals of English Drama 975–1700* (London and New York, 1989). I have also consulted the chronological table in *The Cambridge Companion to English Renaissance Drama*, ed. A. R. Braunmuller and Michael Hattaway (Cambridge, 1990, repr. 1997), pp. 419–46.

Hold, in the King's name hold! (26): Drayton, Hathway, Munday, and Wilson, *Sir John Old-castle* (1599).

Friends, masters, countrymen . . . let's hear him (27–30): 'let us hear him. / Friends, Romans, countrymen': Shakespeare, *Julius Caesar* (1599).

Peace ho (28): Anon., *Timon* (1602); Shakespeare, *As You Like It* (1599–1600); Shakespeare, *Coriolanus* (1608) twice; Shakespeare, *Julius Caesar* (1599) five times; Shakespeare, *Measure for Measure* (1603); Shakespeare, *The Merchant of Venice* (1596–7); Shakespeare, *Romeo and Juliet* (1595). In the Quarto (1600) of *The Merchant of Venice* the same spelling as in Hand D ('how' for 'ho') is used.

I charge you keep the peace (28): Beaumont and Fletcher, *Love's Cure* (1606); Dekker and Middleton, *1 Honest Whore* (1604). Only these two exact parallels are included, because there are as many as six less exact.

let's hear him (30, 42): Chapman, *May Day* (1602); Dekker and Webster, *Northward Ho* (1605); Heywood, *How a Man May Choose* (1602); Jonson, *Sejanus* (1603); Shakespeare, *Antony and Cleopatra* (1606).

Peace, I say (35): Beaumont and Fletcher, *The Coxcomb* (1609); Haughton, *Grim the Collier* (1600); Shakespeare, *Antony and Cleopatra* (1606); Shakespeare, *As You Like It* (1599–1600); Shakespeare, *Coriolanus* (1608); Shakespeare, *The Merry Wives of Windsor* (1597–8) twice; Shakespeare, *Twelfth Night* (1601).

peace! Are you men of wisdom or what are you? (35–6): 'peace! / My masters are you mad, or what are you?': Shakespeare, *Twelfth Night* (1601), the only example of 'or what are you'.

no, no, no, no, no (38): Dekker, *Blurt Master Constable* (1601); Heywood, *The Rape of Lucrece* (1607); Shakespeare, *Antony and Cleopatra* (1606); Shakespeare, *Coriolanus* (1608); there are also cases of four successive 'no's in three Shakespeare plays and four non-Shakespeare plays, and of six in two non-Shakespeare plays.

Whiles they (39): Anon., *The Pilgrimage to Parnassus* (1599); Brandon, *Octavia* (1591);

Haughton, *Englishmen for My Money* (1598); Shakespeare and others, *1 Henry VI* (1592); Shakespeare, *Julius Caesar* (1599).

bear down (40): Chapman, Jonson, and Marston, *Eastward Ho* (1605); Daniel, *Cleopatra* (1593); Jonson, *Sejanus* (1603).

Shall we hear (41): Shakespeare, *Coriolanus* (1608); Shakespeare, *Cymbeline* (1610); Shakespeare, *Much Ado About Nothing* (1598); Shakespeare, *Othello* (1603–4); Shakespeare, *Richard III* (1592–3); Anon., *The True Tragedy of Richard III* (1591).

'A keeps (42): Sharpham, *Cupid's Whirligig* (1607).

'a made (42): Shakespeare, *Henry V* (1598–9); Barry, *Ram Alley* (1608); Day, William Rowley, and Wilkins, *The Travels of the Three English Brothers* (1607).

Even by the rule (46): Shakespeare, *Julius Caesar* (1599).

among yourselves (46): Middleton, *Your Five Gallants* (1607) twice; Anon. 'W. S.', *Locrine* (1594).

peace, silence (50): Shakespeare, *Julius Caesar* (1599), the only instance without an appellation or other word intervening between the two.

Good masters (57): Shakespeare, *Cymbeline* (1610); Shakespeare, *Othello* (1603–4); Shakespeare, *The Winter's Tale* (1609); Tomkis, *Lingua* (1607).

Ay, by th' mass (58): Middleton, *The Phoenix* (1604); Chapman, Jonson, and Marston, *Eastward Ho* (1605); 'Ay, by the mass': Dekker, *The Shoemakers' Holiday* (1599).

a good house-keeper (58): 'a good old house-keeper': Jonson, *Poetaster* (1601).

I thank your good worship for (58–9): 'I thank your good worship': Middleton, *The Phoenix* (1604); 'We do thank your good worship for' (twice): Percy, *The Cuckqueans and Cuckolds Errants*; 'I do thank your very good worship for': Percy, *The Cuckqeans and Cuckolds Errants* (1601). These are the closest parallels, with Percy's including 'for' and Middleton's beginning 'I thank'.

cry upon (61): Anon., *Soliman and Perseda* (1592); 'cry upon't': Shakespeare, *Twelfth Night* (1601); less exact instances of 'crying on' are common.

not one of you (62): Anon., *The Weakest Goeth to the Wall* (1600); Shakespeare, *The Winter's Tale* (1609).

such fellows (63): Dekker, *Blurt Master Constable* (1601); Heywood, *How a Man May Choose* (1602); William Rowley, *A Shoemaker, a Gentleman* (1608); Tomkis, *Lingua* (1607).

That could have (64): Anon., *Charlemagne* (1604); Fletcher, *The Noble Gentleman* (1606); Shakespeare (and Peele), *Titus Andronicus* (1592).

grown up (65): Day, *The Isle of Gulls* (1606).

bloody times (66): Shakespeare, *3 Henry VI* (1591).

brought you to (of a physical or mental state, not a literal location) (67): Anon. 'W. S.', *Thomas Lord Cromwell* (1600); Heywood, *Fortune by Land or Sea* (1609); Shakespeare, *Measure for Measure* (1603); Shakespeare, *Troilus and Cressida* (1602). The examples of 'brought to this pass' in *Cromwell* and *Lear*, under the entry at line 6, have been excluded.

to the state of men (meaning 'adulthood') (67): 'to man's estate', Shakespeare, *Twelfth Night* (1601); there are several examples of 'the state of (a) man' in the plays of Shakespeare and other playwrights, but not with reference to attaining an adult age.

which cannot choose but (70): Haughton, *Grim the Collier* (1600); Shakespeare, *1 Henry IV* (1596–7); 'cannot choose but' (without 'which') is relatively common.

much advantage (as a verb) (71): Heywood, *The Four Prentices of London* (1594).

the majesty of England (73): Anon. 'W. S.', *Thomas Lord Cromwell* (1600); Anon., *Nobody and Somebody* (1605); 'the . . . majesty of England': Dekker and Webster, *Sir Thomas Wyatt* (1602); Shakespeare, *King John* (1596).

Imagine that you see (74): 'imagine that I see': Anon., *Look About You* (1599), the only examples of 'imagine that . . . see'.

Their babies at their backs, with their poor luggage (75): 'Come, bring your luggage nobly on your back': Shakespeare, *1 Henry IV* (1596–7), the only collocations of 'luggage' with 'back(s)', and in *1 Henry IV* what is carried is human, like the babies in *More*.

for transportation (76): Day, *The Isle of Gulls* (1606); Heywood, *2 Edward IV* (1599) twice.

Not one of you (83): Anon., *The Weakest Goeth to the Wall* (1600); Shakespeare, *The Winter's Tale* (1609).

fancies wrought (84): 'fancy wrought': Beaumont, *The Woman Hater* (1606); Jonson, *The Case Is Altered* (1597).

men like ravenous fishes Would feed on one another (86–7): 'makes 'em like fishes one devour another': Middleton, *The Puritan* (1606); 'ravenous fishes' (likened to devouring men): Chettle, *Hoffman* (1602); 'would feed on one another' (of men): Shakespeare, *Coriolanus* (1608); 'rav'nous fishes' appears in a Shakespeare scene of *Henry VIII* (1.2.79), which falls outside the 1590–1600 period.

Before God, that's as true as the gospel (88): 'By God, is true as 'pistle and gospel': Chettle, Dekker, and Haughton, *Patient Grissil* (1600).

let's mark him (89): 'let us mark what he doth': Warner, *Menaechmi* (1592).

if you will mark (91): Shakespeare, *As You Like It* (1599–1600).

'tis a sin (93): Marston, *The Dutch Courtesan* (1605).

did forewarn us (94): 'forewarning us', Chapman, *Caesar and Pompey* (1605); an instance of 'forewarned us' in *Woodstock* has been ignored, since the date is in dispute, though it is probably 1606–1608.

in arms 'gainst (95): Greene, *Selimus* (1592) three times; Anon. 'W. S.', *Locrine* (1594).

Marry, God forbid that! (96): 'Marry, God forbid': Anon., *Leir* (1590); Anon., *Alphonsus Emperor of Germany* (1594); Field, *A Woman is a Weathercock* (1609); 'God forbid that' (where 'that' is demonstrative pronoun, not a relative): Shakespeare, *3 Henry VI* (1591).

Nay, certainly (97): Shakespeare, *As You Like It* (1599–1600); Shakespeare, *Antony and Cleopatra* (1606).

For to the King ('for' meaning 'because') (98): Dekker, *Satiromastix* (1601).

God hath . . . lent (98): 'God had lent': Anon., *Leir* (1590); 'if God have lent': Shakespeare, *All's Well That Ends Well* (1604–5); 'God had lent': Shakespeare, *Romeo and Juliet* (1595).

Of dread, of justice (in connection with sovereignty) (99): 'Justice, dread Sovereign': Drayton, Hathway, Munday, and Wilson, *Sir John Oldcastle* (1599); 'justice, my dread Leige': Anon., *Lust's Dominion* (1600).

power and command (as a noun doublet) (99): 'your power and your command': Shakespeare, *Othello* (1603–4); 'command And power': Mason, *The Turk* (1607).

his figure (102): Shakespeare, *Troilus and Cressida* (1602); Shakespeare, *King John* (1596).

throne and sword (103): 'sword and . . . throne': Heywood, *The Rape of Lucrece* (1607).

a god on earth (104): Day, William Rowley, and Wilkins, *The Travels of the Three English Brothers* (1607); Heywood, *1 The Fair Maid of the West* (1604); Heywood, *The Golden Age* (1610); Shakespeare, *Richard II* (1595).

Rising 'gainst . . . rise 'gainst (of insurrection against God's appointed deputy, the sovereign) (105–6): 'rebel rout That thus do rise 'gainst their anointed king': Anon., *Jack Straw* (1591).

In doing this (107): Shakespeare, *Cymbeline* (1610).

Wash your foul minds with tears (108): 'speaking of her foulness, Washed it with tears': Shakespeare, *Much Ado About Nothing* (1598); 'when I wash my brain and it grow fouler': Shakespeare, *Antony and Cleopatra*. Washing with tears is common, but these are the only passages that share three elements with *More*: foulness, washing, and with tears; or washing, mind or brain, and foulness.

against the peace (109): Anon., *A Warning for Fair Women* (1599); Shakespeare, *2 Henry IV* (1597–8).

unreverent knees (110): 'unreverent shoulders': Shakespeare, *Richard II* (1595), the only examples of 'unreverent' qualifying a part of the body.

kneel to be forgiven (111): 'kneel And ask forgiveness': Anon., *Leir* (1590); 'forgive these lover's faults, That kneeling': Anon., *The Taming of a Shrew* (1592); 'I'll kneel to thee. Forgive me': Chettle and Munday, *The Death of Robert Earl of Huntingdon* (1598); 'I'll kneel down And ask of thee forgiveness': Shakespeare, *King Lear* (1605–6).

rebel captain (114): 'captains of this rebel rout': Anon., *Jack Straw* (1591).

When there is no (118): Anon., *The Birth of Hercules* (1604); Shakespeare, *Much Ado About Nothing* (1598).

lead . . . in lyam To slip him like a hound (121–2): 'slipped me like his greyhound': Shakespeare, *The Taming of the Shrew* (1590–1); 'like a . . . greyhound in the leash To let him slip': Shakespeare, *Coriolanus* (1608).

the majesty of law (121): 'The majesty and power of law': Shakespeare, *2 Henry IV* (1597–8).

like a hound (122): Porter, *Two Angry Women of Abingdon* (1598); Shakespeare, *Othello* (1603–4).

say now the King . . . Should (in the sense 'suppose now . . . ') (122–4): 'Say now the vinter's wife Should': Barry, *Ram Alley* (1608); 'Say now that I should': Jonson, *Sejanus* (1603).

come too short (123): 'comes too short': Shakespeare, *All's Well That Ends Well* (1604–5); Shakespeare, *Antony and Cleopatra* (1606); Shakespeare, *King Lear* (1605–6) twice; Shakespeare, *Much Ado About Nothing* (1598).

so much . . . As but to (124–5): 'So much as but to': Shakespeare, *Cymbeline* (1610); Heywood, *The Rape of Lucrece* (1607).

great trespass (124): Jonson, *Every Man in His Humour* (1598).

but to banish (125): Daborne, *A Christian Turned Turk* (1610).

give you harbor (128): 'give me . . . harbour': Shakespeare, *Measure for Measure* (1603).

adheres to (129): 'adhere to': Marston, *Antonio's Revenge* (1600).

you must needs be (130): Heywood, *If You Know Not Me* (1604); Shakespeare, *Henry V* (1598–9); Wilson, *The Cobbler's Prophecy* (1590).

Whet their . . . knives (134): 'whet their knives': Beaumont and Fletcher, *The Woman Hater* (1606); 'whet the knife': Anon., *Arden of Faversham* (1591); 'whet your knives': Dekker and Webster, *Sir Thomas Wyatt* (1602); 'whet thy knife': Shakespeare, *The Merchant of Venice* (1596–7); 'whet'st a knife': Shakespeare, *Richard III* (1592–3).

Spurn you like dogs (135): 'spurned . . . as a dog': Anon., *Alphonsus Emperor of Germany* (1594); 'a dog whom I'll scarce spurn': Dekker, *2 Honest Whore* (1605); 'spurn me like a dog': Heywood, *A Woman Killed with Kindness* (1603); 'Away, unpeacable dog, or I'll spurn thee hence': Shakespeare and Middleton, *Timon of Athens* (1605); 'spurn like dogs': Wilkins, *The Miseries of Enforced Marriage* (1606).

like as if (135): Chapman, *A Humorous Day's Mirth* (1597).

your comforts (137): Chapman, *Caesar and Pompey* (1605); Chapman, *Byron's Tragedy* (1608); Dekker, *The Whore of Babylon* (1606); Jonson, *Epicoene* (1609).

To be thus us'd (139): Brandon, *Octavia* (1591); 'be thus used': Beaumont and Fletcher, *The Woman Hater* (1606).

Faith, 'a says true (141): ''a says true': Day, *Law Tricks* (1604); 'he says true, i'faith': Middleton, *A Mad World My Masters* (1606); 'he says true too, i'faith': Middleton, *The Phoenix* (1604); 'My faith, he says true': Warner, *Menaechmi* (1592).

procure our pardon (143): 'procure her pardon': Anon., *A Warning for Fair Women* (1599); 'procure his pardon': Beaumont and Fletcher, *The Woman Hater* (1606); Heywood, *1 Edward*

IV (1599); 'procure a pardon': Heywood, *1 Edward IV* (1599).

Submit you to (144): Shakespeare, *Coriolanus* (1608).

their mediation to (145): 'mediation to': Anon., *The Return from Parnassus* (1600); 'their mediation': Shakespeare, *Antony and Cleopatra* (1606).

Give up yourself to (146): 'give up yourself . . . to': Jonson, *Sejanus* (1603); Shakespeare, *Antony and Cleopatra* (1606).

mercy may be found (147): 'mercy . . . was found': Beaumont and Fletcher, *The Maid's Tragedy* (1610); 'found such mercy': Heywood, *2 Edward IV* (1599).

mercy . . . if you so seek it (147): 'seek for mercy': Marlowe, *Edward II* (1592).

if you so (followed by a verb) (147): Anon., *The Weakest Goeth to the Wall* (1600); Middleton, *A Yorkshire Tragedy* (1606); Middleton, *The Phoenix* (1604); Percy, *The Cuckqueans and Cuckolds Errants* (1601).

No doubt some pertinent items have been overlooked, perhaps through their use of unforeseen spellings. But all plays have been treated on the same terms, and the patterns that emerge are so clear that even a very much larger margin of error than seems to me remotely possible could not account for them. Many of the above locutions are utterly nondescript, but they are sufficiently rare to be used in only five or fewer of the extant plays first performed within the two decades 1590–1610, and analysis reveals a marked association with authorship and chronology. When those chronological limits are set, the 'Literature Online' searches turn up a few links with plays that fall outside them, according to *Annals of English Drama*. These have been disregarded, as have links to other parts of *Sir Thomas More* itself. Altogether, some 225 extant plays belong to the period, and almost half of them have at least one link to Hand D's pages. These include thirty of the thirty-five Shakespeare plays of the period and ninety-eight of the remaining 190. Fifteen plays have four or more links as shown in the table.

Shakespeare	*Julius Caesar*	1599	9
Shakespeare	*Antony and Cleopatra*	1606	8
Shakespeare	*Coriolanus*	1608	8
Shakespeare	*Othello*	1603–4	6
Shakespeare	*As You Like It*	1599–1600	5
Beaumont and Fletcher	*The Woman Hater*	1606	5
Percy	*The Cuckqueans*	1601	4
Shakespeare	*Cymbeline*	1610	4
Shakespeare	*King Lear*	1605–6	4
Shakespeare	*The Merchant of Venice*	1596–7	4
Shakespeare	*Much Ado About Nothing*	1598	4
Middleton	*The Phoenix*	1604	4
Jonson	*Sejanus*	1603	4
Anon. 'W. S.'	*Thomas Lord Cromwell*	1600	4
Shakespeare	*Twelfth Night*	1601	4

Not only do five Shakespeare plays head the list, but Shakespeare remains the dominant presence in its lower half, five of the nine plays with four links being his. Percy's *The Cuckqueans* makes the top fourteen through its three variations on 'I thank your good worship for.' Admittedly, *Julius Caesar*'s repetitions of 'Peace ho' (which occurs five times in the play) are responsible for its high place on the list, but it would still be ranked fourth equal if this call were to be counted only once. All five of the non-Shakespeare plays with four or more links are by different authors. The links with Shakespeare are remarkably varied. Some were noted in R. W. Chambers's classic study of sequences of thought, mostly pertaining to the threat of disorder, that were shared by Hand D's pages and plays by Shakespeare.[10] The present 'Literature Online' study confirms the significance of Chambers's parallels, even at the verbal level: parallels with Shakespeare far outnumber parallels with other dramatists.

Chambers connected Hand D's scene to mob scenes in *2 Henry VI*, *Julius Caesar* and *Coriolanus*, to

Ulysses's picture of anarchy in *Troilus and Cressida*, and to Albany's of humanity preying upon itself in *King Lear*. But the inventory of links also uncovers an interesting association with purely comic disorder – the drunken commotion of Sir Toby, Feste and Sir Andrew Aguecheek in *Twelfth Night*. In *Sir Thomas More*, Shrewsbury addresses the rabble, 'My masters' (29), and calls, 'Peace, I say, peace! Are you men of wisdom or what are you?' (35–6), but two lines later they are yelling 'no, no, no, no, no'. In *Twelfth Night*, Maria has no sooner urged the revellers to be quieter, 'For the love o' God, peace!', than Malvolio intervenes with 'My masters, are you mad? Or what are you?' (2.3.85–6); Feste's chorus to the song, 'O no, no, no, no' follows shortly afterwards (112), while 'Peace, I say' is used by Sir Toby as the pranksters eavesdrop on Malvolio in the box-tree scenes (2.5.34). The whole 'Literature Online' database – Poetry, Drama, and Prose – affords no parallel that is anything like as close. The only two instances of 'Are you . . . or what are you?' are straightforward requests for information in John Leigh's comedy *Kensington Gardens* (1720) and Sir Walter Scott's novel *Quentin Durward* (1823), whereas in both *Sir Thomas More* and *Twelfth Night* the speaker, trying to control those disturbing the peace, asks a rhetorical question implying that they have taken leave of their senses. Clearly, either Shakespeare's *Twelfth Night* was echoed by an

---

10 R. W. Chambers, 'Shakespeare and the Play of *More*', in *Man's Unconquerable Mind* (London, 1939, repr. 1952), pp. 204–49; this is the final and fullest version of his essay. John Jowett has pointed out to me two links between Hand D's scene and Shakespeare that, although not qualifying for inclusion in my inventory of phrases and collocations, are nevertheless striking. Hand D's word 'hurly' (113), as distinct from the compound 'hurly-burly', is found in no other play from the English public theatre except *The Taming of the Shrew* (1590–1), *King John* (1596), and *2 Henry IV* (1597–8), twice in the spelling 'hurley'. Ouside Hand D there is only one example of 'charter'd' (138) in the period: in *Henry V* (1598–9). 'The elements' are chartered in Hand D's pages, 'the air' in *Henry V*, but whereas 'charter'd' means 'licensed' in *Henry V*, the air being 'a charter'd libertine' (1.1.48), free to rove and dally, in Hand D's 'charter'd unto them' it means rather 'reserved for their use'. I am grateful to Dr Jowett for helpful comments on the draft of this article.

unknown Hand D, or an unknown Hand D was echoed by Shakespeare, or Hand D and Shakespeare are one and the same man. Since *Twelfth Night* first reached print in the Shakespeare First Folio of 1623 and *Sir Thomas More* seems never to have been staged, identity of authorship would be the most probable explanation of this unique parallel, even if there were no other evidence pointing to the same conclusion.

The results also indicate a seventeenth-century date of composition for Hand D's scene. The Shakespeare plays with the most links all belong to the period 1596–1610, and the non-Shakespeare plays to 1600–6.

It is necessary, however, to consider the three cases where a phrase occurring in more than five plays has been recorded because of the concentration of instances in the work of a single playwright, who in each case happens to be Shakespeare. 'Peace ho' (28) occurs eleven times in six Shakespeare plays, and only once outside Shakespeare – in the anonymous play *Timon*, which bears some relation to Shakespeare and Middleton's *Timon of Athens*: which was written first is uncertain.[11] 'Peace, I say' (35) occurs six times in five Shakespeare plays and once in each of two plays by other dramatists. 'Shall we hear' (41) is found in five Shakespeare plays and in only one other, the anonymous *True Tragedy of Richard III*, a possible minor source for Shakespeare's *Richard III*. It would, I think, be unreasonable to disallow these links, which seem highly evidential. They would disqualify themselves on a strict 'five or fewer plays' rule only by being *too* Shakespearian, and the riders to the rule were established in advance, before searching began, in the light of earlier experience with the 'Literature Online' technique. Even so, omitting every one of these links would still leave *Antony and Cleopatra* with the greatest number of links, and six Shakespeare plays, along with five non-Shakespeare plays, having four or more links to Hand D's scene.[12]

Moreover, if we comb through the inventory of shared locutions and extract those that link Hand D's scene to a single play, or to two or more plays by a single author, we find twenty-six links with the thirty-five Shakespeare plays and twenty-three

with all the rest, 190 of them in all. Fifteen of the links are to a single Shakespeare play, three are to two Shakespeare plays, and one is to four Shakespeare plays, with one of those four affording two instances of the relevant phrase. There are four of these especially rare phrases or collocations in *Julius Caesar* and two in each of *Antony and Cleopatra*, *As You Like It*, *Coriolanus*, *Richard II*, *Twelfth Night*, and two non-Shakespeare plays that include episodes of civil unrest: *Jack Straw* and *Sir John Oldcastle*. So the rarer the locutions, the stronger the association with Shakespeare becomes. And of course none of the extra-rare Hand D links – with a single playwright of 1590–1610, and in all but four cases a single play – was admitted through the extension to the simple strict criterion of rarity. The results strongly support the identification of Hand D with Shakespeare, and cannot easily be explained away. The systematic nature of the searching, giving equal opportunities to all dramatists of the period to appear as leading authorial candidate, answers Ramsey's astute objection to the case built up for Shakespeare that 'when eager and shrewd observers seek in a wide field for likenesses, some unlikely looking resemblances are apt to appear'.[13]

Thirteen plays have three rare phrases or collocations in common with Hand D's scene: Chapman, *Caesar and Pompey* (1605); Sharpham, *Cupid's Whirligig* (1607); Marston, *The Dutch Courtesan* (1605); Heywood, *2 Edward IV* (1599); Day, *The Isle of Gulls* (1606); Anon, *Leir* (1590); Shakespeare,

---

[11] M. C. Bradbrook, in 'Blackfriars: The Pageant of *Timon of Athens*', a chapter of her *Shakespeare the Craftsman* (London, 1969), pp. 144–67, proposed that the anonymous *Timon* comedy at certain points burlesqued the Shakespeare–Middleton play. James C. Bulman, 'The Date and Production of *Timon* Reconsidered', *Shakespeare Survey 27* (Cambridge, 1974), pp. 111–27, argued that the comedy was a source for *Timon of Athens*. John Jowett agrees with him in his edition, *The Life of Timon of Athens* (Oxford, 2004), p. 20.

[12] The tallies would be: *Antony and Cleopatra* 7, *Othello* and *The Woman Hater* 5, and *Coriolanus*, *Cymbeline*, *Julius Caesar*, *King Lear*, *The Cuckqueans*, *The Phoenix*, *Sejanus*, and *Thomas Lord Cromwell* all 4.

[13] Ramsey, 'Shakespeare and *Sir Thomas More* Revisited', p. 339. Werstine, 'Shakespeare, *More* or Less', implicitly makes the same point throughout.

Measure for Measure (1603); Heywood, *The Rape of Lucrece* (1607); Shakespeare, *Richard II* (1596); Drayton, Hathway, Munday, Wilson, *Sir John Oldcastle* (1599); Anon, *A Warning for Fair Women* (1599); Anon, *The Weakest Goeth to the Wall* (1600); and Shakespeare, *The Winter's Tale* (1609). Only two playwrights are represented more than once in that list: Shakespeare three times and Heywood twice. Heywood's authorship of the anonymously published *Edward IV* has been widely accepted but is far from certain. More importantly, only two plays are earlier than 1599: the anonymous old *Leir*, which Shakespeare echoed in *King Lear*, and his own *Richard II* (1596).

Analysing links in terms of individual plays and their dates overcomes the twin difficulties that some playwrights were much more prolific within the period than others and that the numbers of surviving plays written and performed for the first time varied considerably from year to year, with the second of the two pertinent decades producing more than the first. A comparison between Hand D links to Shakespeare's first seventeen plays, from *The Two Gentlemen of Verona* (1590–1) to *2 Henry IV* (1597–8), and Hand D links to his next eighteen, from *Much Ado About Nothing* (1598) to *Cymbeline* (1610), is unaffected by fluctuations in productivity:

1590/1–1597/8	17 plays	27 links	1.59 per play
1598–1610	18 plays	65 links	3.61 per play

Calculating the links with non-Shakespeare plays in relation to the numbers first performed within two nine-year periods is fraught with uncertainties but reveals a similar pattern:[14]

1590–1598	51 plays	32 links	0.63 per play
1599–1607	109 plays	120 links	1.10 per play

The three-year period with the highest proportion of links per non-Shakespearian play is 1605–7 and the single year with the highest proportion is 1600, which is interesting in view of the fact that the three Shakespeare plays with the most links are *Julius Caesar* (1599), *Antony and Cleopatra* (1606), and *Coriolanus* (1608), the last two being separated only by the collaborative *Pericles* in the Oxford chronology. But genre doubtless influences such results, and all that we can infer with confidence is that Hand D is Shakespeare and that he made his contribution to *Sir Thomas More* in the seventeenth century.[15] The Oxford *Textual Companion* dating of 1603–4 is obviously much nearer the mark than Gabrieli and Mechiori's Revels Plays dating of 1593–4. Textual scholars can continue to study Hand D's pages in the confidence that they are his autograph draft of *Sir Thomas More*'s best scene as he was composing it and committing it to paper, at the height of his playwriting career.

---

[14] I have derived counts of plays first performed in each year from the chronological table in *The Cambridge Companion to English Renaissance Drama*, which is based on the *Annals* without being cluttered up with lost plays, Latin academic plays, and other material irrelevant to the analysis. There is close correspondence between the *Cambridge Companion* and the contents of 'Literature Online'.

[15] The anonymous *Thomas Lord Cromwell* (1600), attributed on the 1602 title page to the Chamberlain's Servants and 'W. S.', and the Admiral's Men's *Sir John Oldcastle* (1599, published 1600), by Drayton, Hathway, Munday, and Wilson, are among the fifteen non-Shakespeare plays with three or more links to Hand D. Both, like *More*, dramatize episodes from the lives of prominent citizens and both have long been recognized as having significant points of contact with it. See, for example, Levin L. Schücking, 'Shakespeare and *Sir Thomas More*', *Review of English Studies*, 1 (1925), 50–9, especially at pp. 49–53. *Oldcastle*'s opening closely parallels Hand D's scene: a street fight has broken out with the Sheriff and the Mayor trying to restore peace.

FERDINAND'S WIFE AND PROSPERO'S WISE

RONALD A. TUMELSON II

In the last quarter of a century, no textual variant in the works of Shakespeare has captured the attention of his serious readers quite like *The Tempest*'s wise / wife crux. During the wedding masque presented by Juno, Ceres, and Isis in Act 4, Ferdinand either praises both Miranda and Prospero's powerful magic –

> Let me live here euer,
> So rare a wondred Father, and a wife
> Makes this place Paradiſe.

–or he praises exclusively his father-in-law's magic and ignores altogether his newly betrothed:

> Let me live here euer,
> So rare a wondred Father, and a wiſe
> Makes this place Paradiſe.

Both textual scholars (bibliographers and textual critics) and literary critics have invested considerable time and energy to debating the issues concerning the variant. In preparation for the Shakespeare Electronic Archive, Peter S. Donaldson gave it a remarkably high profile: 'In the early stages of planning the digital Folio collection', he recounts, 'I used this variant in our first prototype, creating digital images of the line from several of the Folger copies'.[1] Similar status is accorded to the crux by the Arden3 editors, who find in it a fitting conclusion to their introductory discussion of *The Tempest*. For them, the crux 'encapsulates several of the play's major issues: the role of a chaste female (daughter/wife) in Prospero's generative project; the magician's wisdom and control of events (or lack thereof); and, most centrally, the question of

what it takes to turn a paradise into a "brave new world" in a universe corrupted by greed and egoism'.[2] As the editors suggest, the crux cuts across the lines of inquiry initiated by both textual scholars and literary critics; the Vaughans are, after all, both editing *The Tempest* and commenting on the implications the crux has for interpretations of the play as a whole.

Despite this critical interest, however, most discussions of the variant have less to do with readings of the play and more to do with the ideological control of Shakespeare's text(s). Like these critics, I do not offer a reading of the crux or of its implications for interpretations of the play as a whole; rather, I offer a meta-critique of recent arguments concerning its treatment. Foremost in these discussions are the implications for feminist struggle in relation to textual scholarship and literary criticism. Using the crux to subtend this ideological agenda, several critics have debated at length the research of bibliographers and the choices of editors. I will attend to recent arguments that prefer the reading *wife* in order to demonstrate how the rhetoric in these arguments replicates conventional, 'masculinist' rhetorical strategies when attempting to justify that choice. And I will attend to recent, bibliographically grounded counterarguments that

---

[1] Peter S. Donaldson, 'Digital Archive as Expanded Text: Shakespeare and Electronic Textuality', in *Electronic Text: Investigations in Method and Theory*, ed. Kathryn Sutherland (Oxford, 1997), p. 194.

[2] *The Tempest*, ed. Virginia Mason Vaughan and Alden T. Vaughan (Walton-on-Thames, 1999), p. 138.

favour the reading *wise* in order to demonstrate how the rhetoric in these arguments attempts to forestall debate. Examining the rhetoric on both sides of the issue will, I hope, enable the play's future editors and commentators to weigh more carefully their rationalizations of the choice between variants.

Attention to the Folio *Tempest*'s multi-lexical texture was brought prominently to the fore by Jeanne Addison Roberts in 1978. Unlike those feminist critics of Shakespeare in the late 1970s who were 'like the great astronomers of the Renaissance . . . see[ing] new worlds by looking through new lenses',[3] Roberts turned her back to the heavens' luminaries and directed her attention to more mundane objects: the numerous folios in the Folger Shakespeare Library. For Roberts, at issue in Ferdinand's encomium is whether the reading *wife* is sanctioned by bibliographical evidence. Relying on standard accounts of the crux, Roberts noted that the reading *wife* began with Nicholas Rowe's emendation in 1709, and it remained the reading in editions of the play throughout the eighteenth and well into the nineteenth century. However, because copies of the First Folio – the earliest and therefore the most authoritative text of the play – read 'wiſe', not 'wife', editors since the mid nineteenth century have been hesitant to privilege this reading. Yet, as Roberts set out to demonstrate in her essay, not all copies of the first Folio are in agreement regarding the crux. After increasing the candle-watt power in a room at the Folger Shakespeare Library, she scrutinized the documents 'under high-intensity light', and discovered traces of damage to the *f*'s left crossbar (right in inked impressions). Roberts surmises that the letter fractured early in the press run and the crossbar eventually separated from the letter's stem. Consequently, according to Roberts, what began as an *f* became a long *s* (ſ), 'thus transforming "wife" to "wiſe"'.[4] The empirical data set forth in her essay sought to demonstrate once and for all that 'wife' was the original setting, and that 'wiſe' was the result of typographical damage. Hence, subsequent seventeenth-century folios of Shakespeare perpet-

uated the latter, incorrect reading until Rowe emended the passage.

Roberts's (re)discovery of this brave new word was celebrated as an index of feminist progress not only on the text of Shakespeare but also within the male-dominated field of bibliography. In the manuscript of her published essay, Valerie Wayne had written: 'The confirmed sighting of this "wife" took a woman and 355 years.'[5] In a similar vein, Jonathan Goldberg approvingly notes that Roberts's investigation was 'bibliographic work done with a feminist agenda', an implicit challenge to the old regime. Goldberg goes on to add, parenthetically, 'it hardly needs to be pointed out that the field of bibliography has been and remains still heavily male dominated'.[6] It is certainly hard to deny that textual studies have been dominated by a male/masculinist community of scholars: in his 1985 presidential address to the Society for Textual Scholarship, the late Fredson Bowers summed up centuries of masculinist control over this field of study when he quipped, 'textual criticism . . . is not for sissies'.[7] Still, however much we may wish to praise the progress of feminism or to celebrate its triumphs, such simplistic, formulaic explanations for the variant's loss, recovery, loss, and recovery are inadequate. Such arguments merely betray their own ideological bias.

---

3 Carolyn G. Heilbrun, book review, *Signs*, 8 (1982), p. 185.

4 Jeanne Addison Roberts, '"Wife" or "Wise" – *The Tempest* l. 1786', *Studies in Bibliography*, 31 (1978), 206, 207.

5 Wayne's essay was printed as 'The Sexual Politics of Textual Transmission', in *Textual Formations and Reformations*, ed. Laurie E. Maguire and Thomas L. Berger (Newark, 1998), pp. 179–210. The typescript's title continues, 'Wherein are described certain villainous practices of faithless compositors and foul editors who have debased, defamed, and decomposed women in Renaissance texts'. Here I cite the typescript, p. 15. Unless specified, further citations are from the essay as published.

6 Jonathan Goldberg, 'Under the Covers with Caliban', in *The Margins of the Text*, ed. D. C. Greetham (Ann Arbor, 1997), p. 123. This essay is reprinted, with revisions, in Goldberg's *Tempest in the Caribbean* (Minneapolis, 2004); for his discussion of the crux, see pp. 55–62. I cite the earlier publication throughout.

7 Fredson Bowers, 'Unfinished Business', *Text*, 4 (1988), p. 3.

In his frequently reprinted essay 'Prospero's Wife', Stephen Orgel concluded with a coda in which he summarized the salient aspects of Roberts's bibliographic investigation.

[A]fter 1895 the wife became invisible: bibliographers lost the variant, and the textual critics consistently denied its existence . . . Even Charlton Hinman with his collating machines claimed there were no variants whatever in this entire forme of the Folio. And yet when Jeanne Roberts examined the Folger Library's copies of the book, including those that Hinman had collated, she found that two of them have the reading 'wife', and two others clearly show the crossbar of the *f* in the process of breaking. We find only what we are looking for or are willing to see. Obviously it is a reading whose time has come.[8]

This passage has a rhetorical strategy whereby the triumphs of feminism can be all the more extolled. But the only unobjectionable claim I find here is Orgel's penultimate observation: 'We find only what we are looking for or are willing to see.' I want to turn this phrase back on Orgel's own rhetoric in order to examine the ideological agenda his rhetoric espouses. The rhetoric succeeds (if it succeeds at all) by inventing and exaggerating details, as well as by misrepresenting and suppressing evidence. As Goldberg points out, it 'is not, in fact, quite true' that textual critics denied the variant's existence: Orgel fails to mention that Morton Luce, Northrop Frye, and Frank Kermode recorded the variant in their respective editions of the play (p. 119). There are more troubling ways in which Orgel misrepresents the facts, however. Both his suggestion that there was a conspiracy to cover up the variant's existence and his claim that *wife* 'is a reading whose time has come', are belied by the fact that there were editions between 1895 and 1984 that read *wife*. Apart from the various reprints of nineteenth-century editions of both Shakespeare's works and the play, several twentieth-century editions of the play have the reading as well: The Windsor Shakespeare, The New Readers' Shakespeare, The Laurel Shakespeare, and the New Swan Shakespeare Advanced Series are just a few. The reading *wife* also appears in several anthologies that include *The Tempest*: *The Living Shakespeare*, *Five Plays of Shakespeare*, and *An Essential Shakespeare*.[9] Truly, we find only what we are looking for or are willing to see.

Suppressing *wife*'s twentieth-century textual history is only one way in which Orgel misrepresents the historical record. This tactic relates to a larger rhetorical strategy to criticize the male-dominated new bibliography, whose primary scapegoat in Orgel's coda is Charlton Hinman. Hinman, who played a profound role in the new bibliography's examination of the first Folio, became a symbol for bibliography's old, phallocratic order. He was thus an obvious target, and Orgel is not alone in scoping him out. Wayne opines: 'Although Jeanne Roberts makes no association between her discovery and her gender, she was probably more moved to recover this variant than Charlton Hinman.'[10] Blaming Hinman on account of his gender is hitting below the belt; his so-called failure to detect the reading *wife*, I submit, lies not in his sexual but in his mechanical equipment. Hinman's optical collating machine was designed to detect vertical and lateral typographical displacement. When images of both states of the page in the first Folio *Tempest* are superimposed, we cannot detect any displacement whatsoever. As Roberts herself had remarked, 'enlarged and

---

8 Stephen Orgel, 'Prospero's Wife', in *Representing the English Renaissance*, ed. Stephen Greenblatt (Berkeley, 1988), p. 229. Orgel's essay originally appeared in *Representations*, 8 (1984), pp. 1–13.

9 The Windsor Shakespeare, ed. Henry N. Hudson (London, c. 1905), p. 70; The New Readers' Shakespeare, ed. G. B. Harrison and F. H. Pritchard (New York, c. 1927), p. 81; The Laurel Shakespeare, ed. Charles Jasper Sisson (New York, 1961), p. 127; New Swan Shakespeare Advanced, ed. Michael J. C. Echeruo (London, 1980), p. 97; see also *The Tempest*, ed. Ian Stuart (London, 1933), p. 119. Collections include *The Living Shakespeare: Twenty-two Plays and the Sonnets*, ed. Oscar James Campbell (New York, 1949), p. 1189; *Five Plays of Shakespeare*, ed. Hardin Craig and Waldo F. McNeir (Chicago, 1965), p. 453; and *An Essential Shakespeare: Nine Plays and the Sonnets*, ed. Russell Fraser (New York, 1972), p. 467.

10 Wayne, 'Sexual Politics', typescript p. 15. Roberts may not have referred to her gender/sex because she was participating in an empirical discourse that was ostensibly genderless.

superimposed photographs of various copies reveal general co-incidence of the outlines of the letter, except for the crossbar, and *absolutely no disturbance in the setting of the line*' (p. 207; emphasis added). Hinman's collating machine would not have detected any displacement either: due to the similarity between the shapes of ſ and f the former could be masked by the latter. What we can or do see often relies on the capacities and limitations of the apparatuses we devise to aid us in our scholarly research.

What we can or do see also depends on how we use those prosthetic devices. Another reason 'Hinman with his collating machines' may have failed to discover the reading *wife* is related to the method of his investigation into the printing and proof-reading of the first Folio. His primary objective in collating the Folger copies was to locate specifically press-variants that were due to proof-correction, variants that would have resulted in typographic disturbance in a line's type-setting; Hinman was not interested (initially) in variants that were caused by typographical damage. For this reason alone it would be irresponsible to fault him for failing to notice the type damage discussed by Roberts. We can go further, I think, in defending Hinman from ideologically motivated attacks. Roberts remarks in her essay that he had collated only one – Folger Folio no. 6 – of the two copies she examined in which there are 'clear examples of "wife"' (p. 206). She claims to find further, albeit less conclusive, evidence of crossbar fragments in Folger folios '2, 12, 18, 54, and 62' (pp. 206–7), the last of which Hinman had also not collated. All told, he collated five copies of the Folio in which the reading *wife* is more or less clear; that is, he collated one clear copy (no. 6) and four not-so-clear copies (nos. 2, 12, 18 and 54). I submit that Hinman never saw the reading *wife* because he never looked systematically for type-damage in the entire Folger collection. In the same note to which Roberts refers while directing her readers' attention to the folios he had not collated, Hinman offers a compelling, personal view of the labour he devoted to analysing the Folger copies of the first Folio.

Having spent more than two full years collating Folger Folios, I speak feelingly on this subject. The great bulk of the variants I ever found I had of course found by the time I had gone through some 20 or 25 copies. Thereafter the going was very tedious, and almost no new variants were turned up during the last six months I devoted to full-time collation. And morale suffers as returns diminish – especially when such further returns as there may be cannot reasonably be expected to add much to our understanding of the problem in hand. Long before I had collated fifty copies, moreover, it had become apparent that a great deal was to be learned about the printing of the Folio by a study of its types. After searching for evidence of proof-correction throughout only two-thirds of the Folger Folios, therefore, I turned my attention to types – and not, I trust, too soon.[11]

Hinman's own account runs counter to the claims (and usually accompanying critiques) that bibliography is an objective, un-emotive, mechanical application of scientific methods. The image presented here is not of some phallocratic automaton, but of a disheartened human being engaged in unrewarding labour. When he turned at last to an examination of type – having nearly exhausted his search for evidence of proof-correction, the 'problem in hand' – Hinman had already collated two-thirds of the Folger folios. Given the labour involved in collating them, I suspect his subsequent work on type and type-damage – which he mentions elsewhere was 'noticed by chance' (vol. I, p. 56)[12] – did not entail re-collating the entire collection. Thus, I surmise Hinman's preliminary work on type-damage was done on the last third of the Folger's folios; the odds are very high that the sole copy he collated containing the 'clear' reading *wife* was in the earlier two-thirds of the collection. Clearly, there are alternative – i.e., not ideologically motivated – explanations as to why Hinman 'failed' to detect typographical variation in Ferdinand's lines.

---

[11] Hinman, *The Printing and Proof-reading of First Folio of Shakespeare* (Oxford, 1963), vol. I, pp. 245–6. Roberts calls attention to this passage on p. 206, n. 4.

[12] Hinman's method for locating type-damage is discussed in vol. I, pp. 67f.

A defence of Hinman seems necessary at this time given similar ideological criticisms that have been directed at Peter W. M. Blayney's subsequent work on the first Folio's typography. Examining the same copies Roberts had scrutinized twenty years earlier, Blayney magnified the type impressions 'to the 200th power', according to the Arden editors (p. 137). 'As a typographer', he concluded, 'I cannot agree that what resembles a crossbar in Folger copies 6 and 73 [the two clear examples identified in Roberts's essay] is in fact part of the type at all, or that the marks in the supposedly intermediate copies were impressed by the remnants of a crossbar'.[13] The so-called crossbar Roberts had ostensibly discovered is, according to the Arden editors' summary of Blayney's investigation, little more than 'blotted ink' (p. 137). Shoring up the Arden3 editors' preference for the reading *wise*, Richard Proudfoot 'celebrate[s] the [variant's] solution, by material bibliography', adding that Blayney's 'solution' was 'perhaps the last such triumph of the twentieth century'.[14] Despite this hyperbolic praise, Blayney has been taken to task by Wayne, who complains that he 'employed an electron microscope to view the Folger copies, so what Roberts saw with the naked human eye is called into question through the use of advanced scientific equipment and the specialized knowledge of typography' (p. 187). While the critique itself may be just, the irony here is rich: whereas Hinman and his 'machine' were blamed for not discovering the reading *wife*, Blayney and his electron microscope are blamed for discovering the reading *wife*. It is difficult to understand why Wayne considers Blayney's findings so objectionable. I suspect that objection has more to do with the binary, essentialist discourse underlying her rhetoric: men have a penchant for the world of science and its gizmos, whereas women are intuitively closer to nature. Yet, like Orgel, Wayne also suppresses information. She neglects to mention that Roberts's 'naked human eye' was aided by 'high intensity light'. Moreover, Wayne neglects to account for the 'enlarged' images of the Folger copies Roberts superimposed and examined, and that accompanied the essay when it was published in *Studies in*

Bibliography. These omissions serve the ideological project of Wayne's feminism, in which 'sexual politics' determine the outcome of bibliographical research. She opens the essay by calling attention to the 'objective, empirically based' assumptions of textual scholarship, and proposes to question further its seemingly 'impartial nature' by attending to 'the gendered process of textual transmission' (p. 179). Like Wayne, I am convinced that gender plays an important role in textual scholarship. However, because I am not convinced of its role in determining finally whether an edition of *The Tempest* should read 'wife' or 'wise', I want to propose that the issue of gender is as problematic in Wayne's discussion of the crux as it is in the decisions of the male editors and bibliographers she criticizes.

As with Orgel's coda, Wayne's rhetoric in this politically charged preference for the reading *wife* is especially prone to logical inconsistency. She begins her discussion of *The Tempest*'s variant by chastising twentieth-century editors who prefer *wise* for the reason that 'none of those editorial decisions was made on bibliographical grounds' (p. 184). Editorial choices without bibliography cannot be good, she appears to argue. But Rowe's decision to emend to *wife* was not made on bibliographical grounds, either; and the decisions of editors who adopted Rowe's emendation were also not similarly grounded.[15] If we hold to the premise that textual criticism must rely on bibliography, then the reading *wife* in these earlier editions – or in any edition not reliant on bibliographical analysis – ought to be rejected. However, Wayne does not pursue that argument; rather, she expresses the desire for our modern editions to reflect 'diversity' insofar as the wife/wise crux is concerned (p. 187). This desire is voiced, however, as a rejection of Blayney's

---

[13] Peter W. M. Blayney, introduction, *The Norton Facsimile: The First Folio of Shakespeare*, 2nd edn (New York, 1996), p. xxxi.

[14] Richard Proudfoot, *Shakespeare: Text, Stage and Canon* (London, 2001), p. 30.

[15] In his reading of the crux, Goldberg argues that Rowe and his followers emended to 'wife', not to restore Miranda to the play but as part of a project 'to police the male–male relations between Ferdinand and Prospero', p. 120.

examination of the bibliographic 'evidence'. Her dissatisfaction with Blayney's interpretation of that evidence creates a conundrum around which her rhetoric wavers. In sum, Wayne appears to argue, modern editors are damned if they do not rely on the bibliographical work of Roberts, and damned if they rely on the bibliographical work and typographical expertise of Blayney. In other words, she appears to argue, modern editors are damned if they choose *wise* over *wife*, however they make that choice.

Logical inconsistency in Wayne's thinking is compounded by her subsequent rhetorical move, a move that flatly contradicts the argument set forth in Roberts's essay, whose premise explicitly challenges the primacy of editorial judgment. Referencing at the beginning of her essay the tension between 'literary judgments and bibliographical study' (p. 203), Roberts returns to this discourse near the end where, having argued the bibliographical foundation for the reading *wife*, she concludes (apparently triumphant): 'the literary judgments of critics and editors [who emended to "wife"] are revealed as ingenious but useless flounderings' (p. 208). It was, in other words, on the incontrovertible evidence of bibliography that Roberts founded her argument for the reading *wife*. Roberts argued that bibliography would have the final say insofar as the crux is concerned; Wayne eventually comes around to arguing precisely the opposite of this position. Continuing her criticism of Blayney's use of a microscope and his typographic expertise, Wayne writes (apparently conceding),

technology in this instance can only offer information about what was printed in the First Folio; it cannot achieve certainty about which word was used in the earliest performances or manuscript versions of the play. Since the manuscript for the Folio printing was a transcript, the possibilities for error in copying or typesetting this word remain extraordinarily high: long *s* and *f* could be confused in handwriting, and those letters lay side by side in the typecase. So the larger issue about whether 'wise' or 'wife' was used in the first productions or in playscripts or should appear in our own texts remains open to question and is not a material 'fact' fully available to the assessments of science. (p. 187)[16]

There is an element of truth expressed here: we cannot 'achieve certainty' with respect to the readings in non-extant material. Yet, an appeal to a string of intermediaries – the variables of which are unknown – cannot resolve the issue, either. For, allowing Roberts's discovery to stand for the moment, the reverse claim is equally plausible: the setting *wife* could have been due to misreading by either the transcriber or the compositor.[17] We simply cannot know what Shakespeare's intentions were. Nor can we know whether or not some intermediary thwarted or reproduced those intentions. We have only the texts which have come down to us. In the final analysis, then, 'bibliographical grounds' seem very far from Wayne's concerns, for she endorses the results of Roberts's work while eschewing its means. If we were to establish our editorial choices on a bibliographical foundation, then Blayney's discovery would enjoin editors to choose the reading *wise*.

With this rhetorical sleight of hand, Wayne returns us to the kind of suspicions with which bibliography had long been regarded by textual critics – even when those textual critics happened to be grouped beneath the rubric New Bibliography. Fredson Bowers, the belated godfather of new bibliography, put little faith in the proposition that bibliographical evidence would be the final arbiter in issues of textual criticism. On the contrary, he argued consistently in his Sandars Lectures at Cambridge (1957–8) for the primacy of an editor's individual judgment: 'When we inquire what agent decides to which range we may assign the individual words of Shakespeare's text, just about

---

16 Even as she criticizes it, Wayne appears here to accept tacitly the New Bibliography's work in such areas as scribal transcript, copy-text, and printing-house practices. For a critique of the unquestioned acceptance of New Bibliography's findings, see Paul Werstine, 'McKerrow's "Suggestion" and Twentieth-Century Shakespeare Textual Criticism', *Renaissance Drama*, 19 (1988), pp. 149–73.

17 The potential for 'error' returns us, in fact, to one of the points John Jowett had raised in the Oxford edition's *Textual Companion* (Oxford, 1987), p. 616. Wayne discusses Jowett's note on pp. 185–6. For a similar discussion, see Goldberg's 'Under the Covers', pp. 123–5.

the only answer is *critical judgement* or *common sense*. No linguistic or bibliographical argument has any operative validity until the results of its application are accepted by the critical judgement.'[18] Similarly for Wayne, literary judgment will win out over bibliographical analysis of phenomena.

If new bibliographers like Bowers desire the non-extant manuscripts underlying the printed text, Wayne expresses a similar desire for 'the earliest performances or manuscript versions of the play' in order to legitimate her concomitant desire for the reading *wife*. This appeal to non-extant material introduces into Wayne's reasoning other masculinist discourses. In particular there is a striking correspondence between that appeal and Platonism's epistemological romance. In this kind of circular reasoning, the material texts that survive (copies of the First Folio) are posited as the copy not the f/actual source of an ideal, non-extant 'text' (e.g. Shakespeare's manuscript, performance, Crane's transcript). The extant, material texts are deemed debased, fallen representations of those non-extant, idealized manuscripts or performances.[19] As Julia Flanders notes, in a related context: 'anyone familiar with neoclassical aesthetics will have already predicted that in the body-spirit dynamic we are confronting, the body will be gendered female and the spirit male'.[20] In seeking non-extant, pre-publication, masculine essences (spirit), Wayne denies the extant, material, feminized body. In doing so, she may be linked again with Orgel who acknowledges Platonist discourse operating on another level within textual criticism. Orgel argues, 'all our attempts to produce an authentic, correct, that is, stable text have resulted only in an extraordinary variety of versions. Their differences can be described as minor only if one believes that the real play is a Platonic idea, never realized but only approached and approximately represented by its text' (p. 220). This is sound reasoning, but its rhetorical force weakens when Orgel suggests in the essay's coda that we attempt to fix the reading *wife*. Choosing *wife* clearly delimits the potential for 'an extraordinary variety of versions' offered by the other variant competing for this lexical space. Choosing this variant attempts to produce

'an authentic, correct, that is, stable text'. Choosing *wife*, despite Blayney's bibliographical evidence to the contrary, entails committing oneself to the notion that 'the play is a Platonic idea', a masculine essence never realized in the feminine, material bodies of the surviving material witnesses.

Masculinist discourse emerges elsewhere in Wayne's discussion of the crux. In her critique of *The Tempest*'s editors who prefer the reading *wise*, Wayne remarks: 'behind the burden of editorial evidence they bring to bear on their arguments lies a notion of paradise as more felicitously equipped with a wise father, alone, than one accompanied by the diviner's wife. Many utopias in our culture are created specifically without women, and most of our master narratives grant women at best a very tenuous status' (p. 186). However insightful her remark may be, I would argue that many nineteenth-century editors could rationalize the reading *wife* by appealing to a similar Edenistic ideology. In its nineteenth-century form this reconceptualization of 'Eden without Eve', Susan Morgan suggests, meant 'returning to paradise . . . without her, replacing Eve with a less adventurous, less dangerous, partner, in order to reach a higher level of innocence which protects that achieved Eden from becoming the beginning of a new fall in a ceaseless cycle'.[21] In choosing the reading *wife*, earlier editors may have implicitly aligned themselves with this Edenistic ideology. It

---

[18] Bowers, *Textual and Literary Criticism* (Cambridge, 1959; rpt. 1966), p. 68. Bowers is more explicit in *Bibliography and Textual Criticism* (Oxford, 1964), where he argues that 'To disbar critical judgment from the editorial process would be an act of madness, for there will come a time when literary criticism is necessary to assist in the interpretation of bibliographical evidence' (p. 19).

[19] For the Platonic assumptions behind textual criticism, see for instance Margreta de Grazia's 'The Essential Shakespeare and the Material Book', *Textual Practice*, 2 (1988), 69–86.

[20] Julia Flanders, 'The Body Encoded: Questions of Gender and the Electronic Text', in *Electronic Text: Investigations in Method and Theory*, ed. Kathryn Sutherland (Oxford, 1997), p. 129.

[21] Susan Morgan, 'Paradise Reconsidered: Edens without Eve', in *Historical Studies and Literary Criticism*, ed. Jerome J. McGann (Madison, 1985), p. 266.

certainly informs Anna Jameson's rapturous portrait of Miranda in the remarkably influential *Characteristics of Women*. Crowning the classification of what she calls 'characters of passion and imagination', Jameson turns to *The Tempest*'s 'Eve of an enchanted Paradise':

The character of Miranda resolves itself into the very elements of womanhood. She is beautiful, modest, tender, and she is these only; they comprise her whole being, external and internal. She is so perfectly unsophisticated, so delicately refined, that she is all but ethereal. Let us imagine any other woman placed beside Miranda . . . there is not one of them that could sustain the comparison for a moment; not one that would not appear somewhat coarse or artificial when brought into immediate contact with this pure child of nature, this "Eve of an enchanted Paradise."[22]

It is perhaps tempting to dismiss entirely Jameson's hyperbolic sketch of Miranda. But doing so runs the risk of ignoring the striking comparison she draws between Miranda and Eve, a comparison that is striking for its sheer incongruity. Conventional representations of Eve rarely consider her in such glowing terms. In her character sketch, however, Jameson celebrates a different kind of Eve in order to effect the replacement Morgan discusses. Jameson does this by substituting Miranda, the 'beautiful, modest, tender' exemplar of impeccable womanhood, for the recalcitrant Eve. The influence of Jameson's description is indicated by several nineteenth-century editors who cited it in their introductions or notes to the play. Her image of not-Eve Miranda arguably influenced the perspective of editors like Richard L. Ashhurst, who opined, 'Miranda must be the chief cause of Ferdinand's finding the Island a Paradise'; or like Henry N. Hudson who commented: 'The old reading [i.e., *wise*] has been stoutly maintained; but I can hardly think that Ferdinand would leave the wife out of such a reckoning, especially the wife being Miranda, or the Wonderful.'[23] Indeed, as late as the mid 1920s, F. H. Pritchard asks in the exercises to The New Readers' Shakespeare (an edition that reads 'wife'), to which of the play's characters does the phrase 'The Eve of an enchanted Paradise'

apply; then, he encourages readers to 'comment on the justness' of the remark (p. 116). Editors often preferred the reading *wife* while frankly acknowledging that 'Paradise', as Shakespeare conceived it, is better served by having the meek, demur Miranda replace Eve.

The desire for an Eden without Eve, or for a return to a prelapsarian world, is not exclusive to nineteenth-century discourses. Indeed, this trope was quite familiar to bibliographers and textual critics of Shakespeare in the twentieth century. As Bowers put it nearly half a century ago, a textual critic 'can no more permit "just a little corruption" [in the works of Shakespeare] than "just a little sin" was possible in Eden'.[24] For Bowers and others who follow the editorial principles mapped out by W. W. Greg, the object of editorial desire is the always already lost paradise of authorial intent deemed to exist in a holograph manuscript. Thus, just as for Jameson the 'all but ethereal' Miranda is more desirable than the material Eve, the holograph manuscript is the textual critic's desired object, a lost object posited as hovering above the printed editions deemed by their very nature to be 'fallen' representations of the idealized work. Insofar as issues of textual criticism are concerned, Wayne appears problematically aligned with the new bibliography's re-conceptualization of Eden without Eve.

Although Jameson might have considered replacing Eve with a more fitting partner, she could not exclude Miranda from Ferdinand's vision of Paradise: when she wrote *Characteristics* in the early 1830s, available editions of *The Tempest* read 'wife'. Jameson, who designed the images published in the book's earliest editions, clearly had the play in mind while designing the frontispiece for the second edition of 1833, in which she celebrated the placidity of a distant Paradise, 'felicitously equipped

---

[22] Anna Jameson, *Shakespeare's Heroines: The Characteristics of Women* (London, 1889), pp. 170–1.
[23] Ashhurst is cited both in Rolfe's edition (p. 151) and by Roberts (p. 204); see Hudson's Windsor Shakespeare, p. 103.
[24] Bowers, *Literary Criticism*, p. 8.

with a [woman], alone'. In Miranda-like fashion, the etching depicts a forlorn female figure (seated on an exotic shore, beneath a prominent palm tree), who watches a ship sailing away over calm waters.[25] Like Jameson's character sketch of Miranda, this was not an unmotivated portrait. The dedication itself indicates that Jameson created this image for Fanny Kemble, the esteemed nineteenth-century Shakespearian actress. A few months before the second edition was published, Kemble had embarked with her father, Charles, on a theatrical tour of America. Kemble's life, the etching suggests, was becoming more and more like Miranda's. Indeed, knowing that *The Tempest*'s narrative was at the centre of one of Kemble's earliest and most vivid of childhood memories, or that the play was her 'favourite of Shakespeare's Dramas', it is surprising to learn that she considered the tour with her father equivalent to 'unhappy exile'.[26] Moreover, for someone who regarded this play as her 'first possession in the kingdom of unbounded delight' (p. 128), and who was perhaps the first woman to write about the wife/wise crux, it is also surprising to learn that no one has paid any attention to Kemble's remarks in *Notes*. Her discussion of the variants is analogous to our present situation.[27]

The wife/wise crux became an issue for Shakespearians in the years between the publication of Jameson's and Kemble's books. When Jameson etched her vision of a placid paradise in 1833 she could not have anticipated the crux-storm brewing on the horizon; by the early 1880s, however, Kemble could read 'wise' or 'wife' in a variety of editions of the play. Signs of trouble began in 1842 when John Payne Collier announced, '[*wise*] is the reading of every old copy, from which modern editors have varied'.[28] Serious reconsideration of the seventeenth-century Folios' reading was thus instigated. From that time forward the wise/wife crux became tempest-tossed as editors wavered in their preference for one or the other variant. William J. Rolfe surveyed the crux's erratic, nineteenth-century textual history: 'D[yce] gave "wise" in his 1st ed., but he changes it to "wife" in the 2d; and so does H[udson; ("Harvard" edition)]. K[night], on the other hand, has "wife" in the 1st ed. and "wise"

in the 2d.'[29] Even Collier later retracted the reading *wise*, after claiming to have discovered a copy of the second Folio (1632) that contained notes and corrections written in a seventeenth-century hand; Collier ascribed authority for the reading *wife* in that Folio's anonymous 'corrector'.[30]

Forty years after the first signs of textual instability, Kemble began her discussion of the play by summarizing for readers of *Notes* both the initial reception of Collier's discovery and the current state of affairs concerning his Folio 'corrector'. Reporting on the analyses of the British Museum's experts in bibliography and paleography (Hinman and Blayney are in the not-too-distant future), Kemble writes: 'The ink in which the annotations are made has been subjected to chemical analysis, and betrays, under the characters traced in it, others made in pencil, which are pronounced by some persons of a more modern date than the letters which have been traced over them' (p. 108). Kemble did not accept wholly the bibliographic expertise of 'some persons', as her subsequent remarks suggest. 'While the question of the antiquity and authority of these marginal notes remains thus undecided', she continues, 'it may not be amiss to apply to them the mere test

---

[25] The image is reproduced in Ann Thompson and Sasha Roberts, eds., *Women Reading Shakespeare 1660–1900: An Anthology of Criticism* (Manchester, 1997), p. 68.

[26] For the significance of the story, see Kemble, *Notes upon Some of Shakespeare's Plays* (London, 1882), pp. 123–8, 132. Thompson and Roberts, who include excerpts from Kemble's account (pp. 121–2), remark that Kemble regarded the trip as exile (p. 68). My references to Kemble's *Notes* are to the 1882 edition.

[27] Thompson and Roberts do not include Kemble's discussion of the crux in their selections; they mention only that she discussed several variants in the context of John Payne Collier's infamous 1632 Folio (p. 116).

[28] Cited in Roberts, '"Wife" or "Wise"', p. 203.

[29] See William J. Rolfe, ed., *Shakespeare's Comedy of The Tempest* (New York, 1899), p. 137. At least one modern production was equally equivocal: in true Shakespearian fashion, Nicholas Hytner's 1988–9 RSC production departed for London and left the 'wife' in Stratford. See Christine Dymkowski, ed., *The Tempest* (Cambridge, 2000), p. 282

[30] See John Payne Collier, *Notes and Emendations to the Text of Shakespeare's Plays* (1853; rpt. New York, 1970), p. 34.

of common sense in order to determine upon their intrinsic value' (p. 109). After expressing her dissatisfaction with the expert claims of bibliographers and paleographers, Kemble appeals to 'common sense' or judgment (Bowers and Wayne are in the not-too-distant future, too). Via Collier's commentary on the second Folio's alleged corrector, Kemble turns to the wife/wise crux in her third and final chapter on *The Tempest*. The reading *wife* was accepted by Kemble thus: 'The change of the word "wise" for "wife" . . . receives the sanction of Mr Collier's Folio. The passage is so printed by Hanmer, Malone and the later editors all concur in the change, so that the authority of the Folio corrector seems hardly needed to recommend it' (pp. 153–4). 'Common sense', insofar as it was already reflected in standard editions of the play, had, for Kemble, decided the issue beforehand.

Kemble's rationale for accepting the reading *wife* concerns me little here; after all, even if a serious consideration of Collier's so-called corrector were not fraught with difficulty,[31] her appeal to an editorial tradition that had already preferred the reading *wife* but had not done so on 'bibliographical grounds' might give us pause. Nevertheless, I am intrigued by the context in which Kemble discusses the variant. In the pages immediately preceding her remarks she has taken pains to demonstrate Shakespeare's knowledge and use of the English Bible. In the paragraph concluding this discussion and immediately preceding her comment on the crux, Kemble writes: 'The copious inspiration Shakespeare drew from this source [i.e., the English Bible] has made his plays the lay Bible of Englishmen; and it is curious enough that the ignorant among them misquote him for Holy Writ sometimes . . . seduced . . . by the similitude of speech and spirit, into substituting the words of poetical for those of sacred inspiration' (p. 153). Implicitly, Kemble suggests we stop (mis)taking Shakespeare for Holy Writ. Then, without any kind of transition she launches into her discussion of the variant. Her suggestion can be linked to late twentieth-century critiques of the Greg-Bowers line of textual criticism, critiques that propose we discontinue treating extant Shakespearian texts as

fallen objects requiring the divination of authorial intent.[32]

Unlike Kemble, however, I want to resist the temptation to appeal to 'common sense'. Investing in such appeals in the pursuit of consensus can be problematic, politically charged rhetorical ploys. For Bowers, judgment and common sense were explicitly tied to issues of masculine power:

critical judgement means the judgement of more than one man – ultimately what we can only say is common consent. Of course, we must not require common consent to include every ultimate consumer of a text: we need not secure the assent of every teacher in every school before agreeing that a reading is acceptable. We may take it that common consent embraces chiefly those critics and editors whose opinion is powerful enough eventually to shape the form of the edited texts that penetrate the schools. These might be as many as fifty scholars. They might well be fewer, perhaps considerably fewer.[33]

Although I have argued above the similarity of Wayne's and Bowers's positions on bibliographical evidence and its relation to textual criticism, I suspect she would find his rhetoric here as masculinist as I do. Desiring to counter it with equally politically charged rhetoric would be a mistake, however. Doing so would serve only to replace an old, phallocratic order with a new gynocratic system that insists on its own ideological control over and dissemination of Shakespeare's texts. In this respect, Wayne's desire for 'diversity' is dubiously argued when she also complains, 'perhaps the time has not yet arrived for this reading of "wife" in some quarters' (p. 186). For many textual scholars, stability is no longer a widely shared goal; we have come to celebrate multiple versions of Shakespeare's works.

---

[31] The story of the Collier forgeries is well known. For a full account and plausible defense, however, see Dewey Ganzel's *Fortune and Men's Eyes: The Career of John Payne Collier* (Oxford, 1982).

[32] The seminal text that galvanized the debate over Greg's author-based approach to copy-text and the social reception of literary works is Jerome J. McGann's *A Critique of Modern Textual Criticism* (Chicago, 1983).

[33] *Literary Criticism*, p. 68.

Solving this textual crux in *The Tempest* by using evidence of type deterioration (or the apparent lack thereof) to shore up one's choice between the readings may no longer be a widely shared goal either.

As suggested above, 'the textual condition' in which Kemble wrote *Notes* indicates critical judgement had not achieved total, absolute consensus. Indeed, Kemble does not appear to have achieved consensus within her own discussion of the play. Despite her preference for the reading *wife*, she refers repeatedly to Prospero via the reading *wise*. The variant appears to haunt her interpretation of the play, an interpretation whose centre is God-like father, Prospero. He is 'the representative of wise and virtuous manhood', 'the wise and good man' (p. 132), and 'the wise Magician' (p. 133). She notes further the effects of his 'wise discipline' (p. 133), his 'wise will that teaches forbearance and self-control' (p. 134), and his 'wise severity' (p. 136). Because the crux is the only instance in the play in which the word *wise* is used to describe Prospero, Kemble appears to want both readings. If her remarks will serve as a model for current discussion of the crux, then I propose we allow the presence of both readings not only to tempt us from the Eden desired by textual critics but also to haunt our editions and interpretations of the play. Like Kemble's, our present textual condition resembles nothing like consensus. Orgel's edition of the play for Oxford differs from the same press', *Complete Works*: the former reads 'wife', the latter 'wise'; and even more recent editions perpetuate the passage's multi-lexicality.[34]

Unilexical consensus might be a consequence of Blayney's more recent reexamination of the bibliographical evidence adduced in favouring the reading *wife*, and his subsequent pronouncement on the dubious status of this 'reading'. This seems to me Wayne's greatest concern: although 'the time has not yet arrived for this reading of "wife" in some quarters', it may be more disconcerting to learn that the time for the reading *wife*, to return to the language of Orgel's coda, may have come and gone. Indeed, persuaded by Blayney's expertise, the Arden3 editors privilege the reading *wise* in their text. In concluding their introduction, the editors write 'However much one would like to read the word as "wife" in some copies of the Folio, we have been persuaded by Peter W. M. Blayney's exegesis of early seventeenth-century casting and printing techniques' (p. 137). Like the Arden editors, I too am prepared to accept Blayney's typographical evidence for the setting *wise*. Nevertheless, there are two problems with their rationale for accepting his argument. My first objection is terminological: by calling Blayney's pronouncement 'exegesis', the Arden editors introduce the discourse of Holy Writ; considered thus, Blayney's remarks are tantamount to biblical commentary. But in what exactly does that commentary consist? Presumably the editors refer here to the discussion of the crux in his introduction to the reissue of Hinman's Norton Facsimile of the first Folio. After rejecting the possibility that any of the Folger folios read 'wife', Blayney adds: 'the way in which ink is deposited by metal type on damp paper is too specialized a subject to examine in detail here, and proper resolution of the matter must await a much more thorough discussion'.[35] To my knowledge, that discussion has not been forthcoming. Thus, his so-called exegesis amounts to little more than a deferral of discussion and an assertion about typecasting and 'the way in which ink is deposited by metal type on damp paper'. It is perhaps a consequence of the absence of this discussion that David Lindley, the New Cambridge editor of *The Tempest*,

---

34 For select series of the play that read 'wife', see The New Folger, ed. Barbara A. Mowat and Paul Werstine (New York, 1994), p. 129; The Applause First Folio Editions, ed. Neil Freeman (New York, 1998); Case Studies in Critical Controversy, ed. Gerald Graff and James Phelan (Boston, 2000), p. 69; Shakespeare in Production, ed. Christine Dymkowski (Cambridge, 2000), p. 282; The New Cambridge, ed. David Lindley (Cambridge, 2002), p. 188. See also *The Necessary Shakespeare*, ed. David Bevington, 2nd edn (New York, 2005), p. 871. Series whose edition reads 'wise' include, in addition to the Arden3 (p. 251), The Pelican Shakespeare, ed. Peter Holland (New York, 1999), p. 65; The Cliffs Complete, ed. Sidney Lamb (Foster City, 2000), p. 115; Barron's Simply Shakespeare (Hauppauge, 2002), p. 164. See also *The Norton Shakespeare*, ed. Stephen Greenblatt, et al. (New York, 1997), p. 3094.

35 Blayney, Introduction, p. xxxi.

misjudges the nature of the debate: he attributes the reading *wife* to 'an ink blot' (p. 229).[36] Lindley's misjudgement is instructive, for we are not dealing with a singular blot of ink but with at least two clear, and four not-so-clear *blots*.

The presence of these inkblots in some copies of the first Folio leads me to my second objection to the Arden editors' rationale. This objection concerns their prefatory clause in the sentence cited above: 'However much one would like to read the word as "wife" in some copies of the Folio'. Put simply, their rhetoric confuses the scientific application of bibliographical analysis with normal *reading* practices: There is a difference between (a) reading words on a page and (b) examining under high-intensity light or with an electron microscope the serifs, ascenders, descenders, stems and cross-bars that make up the letters that make up the words on a page. Blayney does not offer a 'reading' of the passage in any conventional sense of the word; rather, he attempts to discover by means of micro-scopic examination an impression left by an inked piece of metal type on wet, absorbent paper. In the final analysis, letters on a page are little more than blotted patterns of ink. Whether that paper absorbs the patterns of inked type-impressions or stray inkblots, readers can only respond to the ink on the page in front of them regardless of how the ink got there (or, conversely, how it failed to get there). On the face of it, this is not so 'specialized a subject' that it requires an academic scholar with typographical expertise. Whether we like it or not, readers discover in the inking of a page static and meaning-bearing signals quite apart from the inten-tions of authors, scribes, typesetters, proofreaders or editors.[37]

The lexical space in various copies in the Fol-ger can be read at least two ways. In addition to the predominant reading *wife*, it is possible to read *wife* in some copies of the first Folio. This remains the value of Roberts's study: discovery of at least two clear copies of the first Folio that do *read* 'wife', and four others that have been and may still be read so. If we resist the temptation to examine minu-tia microscopically and if we resist the temptation to read such passages 'under high-intensity light' – particularly since the overwhelming majority of readers engages in neither of these so-called read-ing practices – we can better celebrate the lexi-cally rich environment of Shakespeare's unstable text, and the textual variety the singularly con-ceived construct 'The First Folio' provides us. The time for appeals to a singular First Folio *Tempest*, or for claims that it *reads* a certain way, has come and gone. Our editions of Shakespeare continue to choose multi-lexicality over univocality. If it is true that 'we find only what we are looking for or are willing to see', then perhaps we should re-examine our delimited field of vision, and attend more carefully to the rhetorical strategies that serve to patch over the blind-spots in our perceptions of Shakespearian text.

---

[36] Lindley unnecessarily distorts the material record further when he writes, 'F unambiguously reads " . . . wise". F2, however, printed "wife", a reading followed by Rowe, and adopted in most eighteenth-century editions' (p. 229).

[37] For the Korean Panmun Shakespeare, Suk-koo Koh seems to have annotated an edition different from that secured by the publishers at Panmun; whereas the text reads 'wife', Koh's notes read, 'So . . . wife = a father so wise and rarely won-derful' (Seoul, 1969), pp. 71, 130.

EDITING STEFANO'S BOOK

ANDREW GURR

As Walter Ong said in his study of the interface between oral and literate cultures, 'Print encourages a sense of closure.'[1] Editors are bound to aim at identifying and fixing a single version of their play, chiefly for reasons that acknowledge the current dominance of the reader over the listener. They elevate the literate culture over the oral that still was just about dominant when Shakespeare composed his plays. We live now in the literate culture's hope of attaining so-called 'definitive' editions, in the process closing, as Ong suggests, the range of possibilities that are inherent in any text designed for speaking rather than reading. The real problem is not so much a simple consequence of the literate culture's prioritization of writing over speaking as the effect of long reliance on the written word for its superior precision. Writing allows precise memorization to become the top priority. The original Shakespeare company lacked such a priority and such precision. Perhaps we really are enriched by the concern our editors share, that they must fix the precise wordings of Shakespeare's plays. But we should recognize at the same time that a lot can be lost by such a priority.

Editors need not only closure but consistency, and it can be dangerous. All modern editors assume, for instance, that Caliban must always speak in verse, despite the case that can be made against it. This assumption requires us to ignore completely the alternative that Stefano, whom he takes as his new master in 2.2, offers him instead. Much has been made in recent years of the curse that Caliban says Prospero laid on him, his language. Much less has been made, though, of the language

Stefano offers him in its place. At their first meeting, at 2.2.79 (TLN 1125),[2] after wondering how such a beast came to 'learn our language', Stefano gives Caliban his bottle, and says 'Here is that which will give language to you, cat.' His cure for Trinculo's and Caliban's fear is his invitation to drink, that is, as he says (blasphemously), to 'kisse the Booke' (TLN 1174). Stefano's book has obviously different attractions to Caliban from Prospero's. His subsequent over-use of the new book makes him drunk. Should that not mean that he gradually adopts a new language, drunken prose, in place of Prospero's elevated verse? Such a change seems to be written as a design into Stefano's euphemisms about a new language for Caliban through his use of Stefano's 'Booke'.

As befits their class status, Stefano and Trinculo consistently speak their lines in prose, and an increasingly drunken prose as the language of the bottle prevails on them. So it would be understandable if Caliban's language changed too, as he gradually loses the influence of Prospero's book by dropping into the alternative fed by Stefano's liquid book. But does he? According to most editors

---

[1] Walter J. Ong, *Orality and Literacy. The Technologizing of the Word* (London, 1982), p. 129. He goes on to define closure as 'a sense that what is found in a text has been finalized, has reached a state of completion.' That is clearly the ideal of Shakespeare editors.

[2] Act and scene divisions are registered here from the Oxford and Norton Shakespeare editions, the through-line numbers (TLN) from the second edition of the Norton Folio text (New York, 1997), which is also used here for the reproduction of significant lines.

he largely continues to speak the verse of his first master. That may reflect some failure of editorial attention to the possibly intended effects of Stefano's alternative book, and to its implications for Caliban's speech. Any study of *The Tempest*'s verse ought to inspect the rhythms of Caliban's speeches, not just as Prospero's verse but to see what effect the language of the bottle has on his lines. Such a study might call into question the rightness of the adjustments editors routinely make from the Folio text, and their representation of Caliban's speeches at different points in the story as verse or as prose. Stefano's alternative book can test both the possible application of a critical theory identified in the play to make the text consistent with the theory, and of the dangers of the ruling preconceptions that dominate editorial practices.

All editors make consistency their primary aim because readers need to know where they are and why. Shakespeare had no such need, which in any case must have fluctuated over his twenty and more years of acting and production. His inconsistency thus creates a problem for every editor, first of choosing what to be consistent about, and secondly what to do when the author is evidently not always following the same priority. Even such attractive concepts as the effect of Caliban's alternative book on the speaking of his verse, when Prospero's dignified rhythms are befuddled by the effects of his new master's bottle, raise the question whether an editor should seek seriously to emend the text in order to make it more consistent. He or she might well choose to reline the Folio text of *The Tempest*, which itself shows fluctuations in the identification of which lines are verse, in order to be consistent with the idea that Caliban should drop from Prospero's verse into Stefano's prose when he is drunk. Almost all editors have commonly made all of Caliban's speeches into verse on the assumption that he keeps to the language he learned from Prospero, while Stefano and Trinculo stick to the less dignified prose that editors assume befits their lower class status. Perhaps future editors will seek to make Caliban's drunken lines prose in order to suit his drunken condition. Whatever that might say about the credibility of the idea of two books and

two languages taught by Caliban's different masters, it raises large questions about the rules that editors set for themselves, and how consistently they should observe them.

Technically, the question of Caliban's drunken language raises a long sequence of hurdles for editors. To start their race they have to ask just what the company scribe, Ralph Crane, did with his authorial manuscript's division of verse and prose.[3] Like most scribes of the time, he was not in the habit of automatically capitalizing the initial letter of the first words of verse lines. After that generation of doubt, the next hurdle is what the compositors might have made of their scribal copy. Beyond such technical hurdles is a much broader and deeper question: what were the standards of versification that, in turn, Shakespeare, Crane, the Folio compositors, and more than three centuries of subsequent editors might have had in mind when they created their texts? Finally in this long steeplechase we ought to ask what a modern edition should end up with if it is to present a properly judicious version of the text to its readers, one that is regulated by consistency. How should editors allow for authorial inconsistency?

Such a sequence of questions raises the whole issue of Shakespeare's verse in his last plays, and editorial policy when translating it into modern editions. We are confident that *The Tempest*'s verse is the most mature and sophisticated in all Shakespeare. It is therefore the least responsive of any to the identification of a standardized verse-line and absolutely regular metre. Responsive in the main, as it must be, to the laws governing both dramatic and non-dramatic verse in the early seventeenth century, it nonetheless displays great rhythmic and even structural variety, and the relationship between its verse and prose is complex and fascinating. Inevitably the variety of its form caused problems for its first editors, who relied on

---

3 T. H. Howard-Hill, *Ralph Crane and Some Shakespeare First Folio Comedies* (Charlottesville, 1972), p. 109, notes that 'Crane's habitual use of minuscules at the beginning of lines, mingled with emphasis capitals, might well have obscured the distinction of prose and verse at some points.'

standardizing rules developed long after the play was written. Modern editors, looking for slips in the transmission of the original that need correction and hounded by doubts over compositors' errors and alterations, need an extrinsic law that can test the accuracy of the verse as it ends up on the printed page. Sadly, they can find little that helps them when they apply the 'rules' of regular versification to this play. Powerfully rhythmical, with potent help from line-breaks, it is still almost impossible to tell whether any of the variations in *The Tempest* from the rhythmical norm of the decasyllabic line is a deliberate shift or the result of an accident in the transmission process.

Alexander Pope, the most consistent and insistent of all editors in preferring to govern his text by the rules of rhythmical regularity rather than what he thought were the aberrant practices of seventeenth-century compositors, altered an average of one line in twenty from his main source, the Second Folio text. He did his Procrustean work of stretching or shrinking lines into iambic pentameters out of his respect for regularity in metre and his assumption that Shakespeare was poorly served by his original printers. The thoroughness of his alterations prompted objections even in his own time, rooted though his practices were in the neoclassicist concept of the 'correct' rules for making verse that Edward Bysshe set out in 1709.[4] Other editors of Shakespeare, most notably Lewis Theobald, found such re-inscriptions of the holy text offensive. But Pope's principle had a greater force than Theobald could admit even in his own more cautious approach to the anomalies in *The Tempest*'s verse. Subsequent editors such as Johnson and George Steevens applied those metrical norms even more rigorously and tunelessly than had Pope. No editor can be happy with the need to make a choice of priorities between the metrical rules and likely authorial variation from those rules. The Popish rules do have the easy virtue of consistency.

The eighteenth-century expectations of poetic 'correctness' that Pope upheld are easy to dismiss today. We accept that perfect regularity, either of metre or style, is inherently unlikely in any dramatic text by Shakespeare. The variety of speakers, the range of situations in which the verse is spoken by different characters and in different dramatic settings, even the modulation from verse into prose, all impose variations from consistently 'correct' versification. That is an easy assertion to make today. The difficulty that modern editors find, however, is that without some version of the eighteenth-century expectation of 'correctness' that defines a standard pattern for the metre, nobody working on a text such as *The Tempest* can have much confidence in identifying slips of transmission of the verse made in the error-prone process of transcribing the author's original text. The copy was what we ought to call 'translated', rather like Bottom, first from the authorial draft into a manuscript at one or more removes from it, and thence into the only surviving printed version with any authority, the First Folio (FI).

The FI version of *The Tempest* is dominated by its first transcriber. It shows far more signs of Crane's modifications of his source manuscript for the reader than, for instance, any evidence of stage practices, not least in Crane's insertion of the explanatory stage directions that R. C. Bald and John Jowett identified as typical of his alterations to his original text.[5] Crane's consistent scribal practices put an overlay onto Shakespeare's apparent habit of ranging through different ruling ideas. The FI compositors had their own pattern of consistency, which they can be seen using through

---

4 It is easy to make fun of Bysshe's hugely popular and durable *Art of English Poetry* (1702, revised with examples from Pope in 1709). Copies remained in unquestioning use at least until Shelley, who owned one. Essentially a do-it-yourself handbook on how to write rhyming verse, it comprised a set of rules for making verse, a rhyming dictionary, and an anthology of the best thoughts drawn from poets and philosophers of the past: a book of instructions, the chief tool, and some raw material to work on. Bysshe's 'rules' for verse are fairly close to what is here identified as Pope's concept of versification.

5 John Jowett, 'New Created Creatures: Ralph Crane and the Stage Directions in *The Tempest*', *Shakespeare Survey 36* (Cambridge, 1983), pp. 107–20. R. C. Bald had previously suggested in his edition of *A Game at Chess*, 1929, p. 42, that the descriptive character of the stage directions in Crane's transcripts meant that they could not be theatrical.

Compositor B's attempts at setting the text, the first play in the book. But even the idea of the text as a translation squeezed out through such layers of different minds is something that editors inevitably force into a regular pattern, in order to suit their own concepts of what the author originally conceived. Above all, Pope's Procrustean principle with versification lives on, effecting predictable and sometimes regrettable changes to the original body of the text we have from F1.

The spirit of eighteenth-century neo-classical poetic theory was very different from the Jacobean spirit, but the non-dramatic verse of Spenser, Sidney and even of Shakespeare himself was every bit as regular as Pope could have desired. Even dramatic blank verse was fairly regular in its earlier versions. Certainly the might of Marlowe's mighty line derived in part from an obsessive uniformity of verse rhythm. Our reading of *The Tempest*'s verse still depends heavily on the Popish assumption and hope that apparent metrical irregularities in the verse came not from authorial inventiveness but from scribal or compositorial misrepresentations. Before we can affirm any such assumption or hope, though, we must identify the broad terms within which these complex dramatic lines lived, the familiar and particular patterning of the speeches that were designed to be heard in 1610. We need to begin with a (necessarily concise) attempt to set down the basic parameters of verse speech within which Shakespeare appears to have been operating by the time he wrote the verse of *The Tempest*. This account is, of course, intended to be descriptive rather than prescriptive.[6]

The dramatic line used by Shakespeare and other playwrights contemporary with him was a pentameter in generally rising duple rhythm, maintained, where necessary, by speech contractions familiar at the time and by other metrical compressions. In *Henry VIII* it is possible to find a few undoubted trisyllabic feet mixed in with the disyllabic, and it is not impossible that one or two might occur in *The Tempest*, though the general style of this play, however flexible it is in so many ways, does not encourage the supposition. Most of the

verse is demonstrably tightly controlled. After the chaos of the opening storm scene's gabbled prose, for instance, we hear its designed contrast in the orderly verse of Prospero and Miranda. Here are eight precisely controlled lines (TLN 100–7):

I haue done nothing,but in care of thee
(Of thee my deere one; thee my daughter) who
Art ignorant of what thou are, naught knowing
Of whence I am : nor that I am more better
Then *Prospero*,Master of a full poore cell,
And thy no greater Father.
    Mira. More to know
Did neuer medle with my thoughts.

The 'feet' generally used in these lines are the disyllabic combinations the language gives us: the iamb (x/), the pyrrhic (xx), the spondee (//), and the trochee (/x). The first three may appear in any place in the line, preceded by any of the others and as freely followed except (without intervening pause) by the trochee. That foot, since it reverses rising rhythm, is and must be the most carefully controlled in the line.

It seems that, conventionally, the trochee does not appear in the last place in lines of whatever length in any of the syllabo-tonic metres. In the pentameter it appears most commonly, and least dangerously, at the line-beginning, or after a midline pause in the third or fourth position. The most daring poets (Donne, Milton, some others) used the iamb-trochee and spondee-trochee sequences without a dividing pause, but in these instances the trochee is not ordinarily a trochaic word. Double trochees are possible but rare, triple trochees non-existent, though a line may in one form

---

[6] The best of the current books on Shakespearian metrics is George T. Wright, *Shakespeare's Metrical Art* (Berkeley, 1988). Russ McDonald, *Shakespeare and the Arts of Language* (Oxford, 2001) supplies a sensitive overview, especially for the purposes of this article in the chapter, 'Here Follows Prose'. The account of Shakespearian prosody that follows here, however, is largely, indeed hugely indebted to Edward R. Weismiller, the doyen of prosodists and Miltonists in the USA, with whom I have enjoyed wonderfully extensive discussions about the verse in this play. Much of its wording is taken directly from his comments and observations, though sadly without any of his immaculately precise ability to sound out the nuances of the stress in particular lines.

consist entirely of iambs, or in another largely of spondees.

Many critics now feel that the analysis of rhythm in the English line requires the recognition of four degrees of stress, not two. If we use the traditional two in the analysis of metre, we must postulate the existence of a stress threshold, above which syllables are heard as stressed, though not necessarily equally stressed, and below which they are heard as relatively unstressed, though here too there may be differences in prominence. Stress is not, it should be said, the only component of prominence. Probably it is relative prominence in the even-numbered syllables of the line, rather than stress alone, that assures our sense of the generally rising rhythm.

The sequence | xx | /x | x/ | without a pause between the first two feet is the only possible one in English that actually breaks the metre, for to the reader or listener it divides | xx/ | xx/ |. A striking example is the last four words of

| x   x   / | x   x   / | |
Blasted | with sighs, | and surround | ed with teares |
(Donne, 'Twicknam Garden', line 1)

Donne was a mischievous poet. The first lines of all the succeeding stanzas are unquestionably ten-syllable pentameters. But this line seems to be a tetrameter ending with two trisyllabic feet, a line, that is, in a different metre from later lines presumably identical with it in metre, for a tetrameter cannot seem identical metrically to a pentameter. It was easy for the Italian *endecasillabo* from which the English iambic pentameter descended to accommodate the x x / x x / sequence. That the English line cannot is the clearest proof that it is heard as composed of disyllabic 'feet', though these are not, of course, classical quantitative feet, as Elizabethan critics and their successors well into the nineteenth century thought they were, since they could not distinguish the iambic line from the concept of Latin quantity they had learned about in school.

Technically pause plays no metrical, as distinct from rhythmic, part in the English line except as it is required to keep the pyrrhic-trochee sequence from breaking the metre. But there are a few suites

of ten syllables in English that are not broken by a pause, sometimes more than once. The early custom among English poets of having grammatical pauses in the line after the fourth or sixth syllable, in effect a caesura, plus perhaps the familiarity of shorter lines in stanzaic verse, seems to have suggested to Shakespeare, by the time he wrote *The Tempest*, that he could use the grammatical sub-division of lines in a number of ways to make his versification more flexible, and its results therefore more akin to speech. First, an unusually large number of speeches in this play end with a part-line. If a part-line is picked up and completed by another character, the completion emphasizes some kind of harmony, or complicity, between them, or the dependence of the second on the first. Other dramatists have characters share lines, but surprisingly (to devotees of consistency) in *The Tempest* Shakespeare will sometimes end a speech with a part-line that no one completes. This effect – of formal uncertainty, or of brevity and assurance, or of something unfinished, something yet to come – shows us one of the ways in which simple form and its breaking can qualify or enrich articulated meaning.

If we have a sense of the line as often being constructed of part-lines, roughly or even usually half-lines, new possibilities open. The full line may end with an extrametrical unstressed syllable (a 'feminine ending'), which does not disturb the audience's sense of the metre. If the first half-line seems to have a strong grammatical form and formal identity of its own, why not allow it a 'feminine ending'? This could be recognized for what it is, an extrametrical syllable at the caesura, in verse which does not admit trisyllabic feet; otherwise the extrametrical syllable, though followed by a strong pause, would attach itself to the following disyllabic foot in rising rhythm. The caesura is unlikely to be followed by a trochee, since that would compound, confusingly perhaps, the sense that the line movement is being interrupted or negated by a switch to falling rhythm. The reader or hearer must always have an exact sense, conscious or unconscious, of where he or she is in the line, or the metre is at least temporarily lost.

Additionally, the full line may occasionally be headless:

> Twelue | yere since, | (*Miran* | *da*) twelue | yere since,
> (TLN 144)

After a strong and clear midline break, might not the second half of a line be headless too? In fact Shakespeare does not take this liberty in the pentameter verse of *The Tempest*. He uses it twice, however, in the tetrameter verse of the Epilogue (TLN 2324 and 2334). That verse, like the verse of the songs in the play, is not really dramatic verse, though its forms must be accounted for.

The tetrameter, unlike the pentameter, does divide easily into precise halves, and one might think that there need be no ambiguity about the structure of FI lines 2324 and 2334. Unfortunately, that is not quite true. Tetrameters in English are often headless, or a mixture of full lines and headless lines; and indeed the Epilogue to *The Tempest* begins with two headless lines. One may well assume, then, that the following line, 2324, is to read

> *Which* | *is most* | *faint: now* | *'tis true*

But the next line is a full tetrameter, reading

> *I must* | *be heere* | *confinde* | *by you,*

Where the omission of '*heere*' would make the line headless. If a full line in mixed 8s and 7s begins with a trochee, we cannot understand at once whether we are reading / x | or (x) / | x. The fact that 2325 is of eight syllables may make us reconsider 2324. A reading

> *Which is* | *most faint*: | (*now*) | *'tis true*

does seem a better arrangement of emphases. Line 2334 confirms this preference, almost, it would seem from its phrasing, intentionally:

> *Which was* | *to please*: | (x) *Now* | *I want* . . .

It is certain, however, that the omission of syllables from a line may sometimes leave the structure ambiguous.

The metre of the songs, fortunately, is made clear by the music that accompanies them. But what if one does not hear the music?

> *Full fad* | *om fiue* | *thy Fa* | *ther lies,*
> *Of his bones* | *are Cor* | *rall made*: . . .

That will not work because of what follows.

> *Of* | *his bones* | *are Cor* | *rall made*:
> *Those* | *are pearles* | *that were* | *his eies* . . .

In short, if a headless tetrameter begins with an unstressed syllable followed by an iamb, there may be some difficulty in keeping the two from combining into an anapaest. Mixed 8s and 7s may produce other problems; but sufficient unto the play.

And so to what we have, the printed FI text of *The Tempest*, the first and one of the shortest plays set in that long sequence of brilliant verse and prose. Presenting verse on a page has always been a complex process, subject to standard rules that vary between one house-style and another. Styles of formatting and of page design can vary quite radically, even when printers are familiar, as were the Folio compositors in 1622, with the customary ways of setting dramatic verse. The use of different configurations for speech-headings, either centred or at the left margin, the various ways of indenting speeches, the spacing of lines, the depth of margins, the use of italics and roman type and in the early texts blackletter, differing founts or italics for quotations, letters and stage directions, capitalization, a justified right margin for prose as against an unjustified margin for verse, all these variables give ample scope for different layout and design. Not until the first rush of play-texts into print in 1594 began to initiate a standard format for dramatic dialogue did the look of playscripts begin to develop much uniformity on the page.

In Shakespeare's texts both the early Quarto page layout and the two-column Folio layout set down a line-length short enough to demand occasional run-overs or run-unders. Limitations of line length forced compositors to use a variety of abbreviations, ampersands and ligatures to signify letters meant to be doubled, and some compressed spellings, such as 'ye' (with a superscript 'e') in place of 'the'. Before spelling became standardized, orthography could be varied to help justify a line, especially when setting prose. To help fit the text into the composing stick a word might be expanded with extra letters such as a terminal 'e'. That saved on the leads used for spacing between words. On the larger scale, the use of cast-off copy meant that the compositor might come to the end of a page and find he had too much or too little space left for the quantity of copy he still had to set on his page. So he compressed or expanded it to make it fit, varying the standard format and perhaps altering his copy, or at least its lineation. *The Tempest* shows compression of that kind on Compositor C's page A2v, where in the first column at TLN 376 Ariel's monosyllabic reply is set on the same line as the end of Prospero's question, and in the second column three stage directions are squeezed into the ends of lines at TLN 453, 456 and 458. It has also been noted that quite frequently manuscript copies given to typesetters failed to make a clear distinction between verse and prose, either by failing to use a capital letter to start a line, or by ending the lines at the right-hand margin, with the result that a confused compositor might easily set verse as prose and vice versa.[7] Setting verse from any manuscript whose scribe economized on the amount of paper used by marking the line-breaks instead of physically separating them into the verse lineation that the poet intended also meant at the least a frequent risk of mislineation.

In this context it is also worth developing Lukas Erne's point about distinguishing between texts prepared for use in staging and those meant for reading.[8] Most dramatic verse, and certainly all of Shakespeare's, was composed in the original manuscripts not to be read but to be spoken, and never to be read on the page except by the player learning his part, the second of the two points in the process where the literate culture came to rule the oral. Blank verse can afford to be less insistent than rhyming verse in its lineation, since it lacks the rhyme-words that mark each transition from one line to the next. The introduction of blank verse in

plays set a new challenge for the layout of pages in verse. Play quartos have a notably different appearance on the page from poems, especially rhyming poems, written for print. Blank verse does not need the formality of division into stanzas or couplets, and the manuscripts the printers were given were not composed with any concern for the look of the verse on the page and the other aids for the reader that poets like Spenser, Sidney and Daniel expected. Even in the cheapest and most popular forms of verse, the broadside ballads, their stanzaic forms made them look more like formal verse on the page than did the verse of any play manuscript, and in consequence of any printed playtext. Moreover a page from a play using speech prefixes to denote the speakers gave priority to its text as dialogue rather than as verse. Dramatic verse was continuous, occupying less space on paper than a formal poem with its stanzaic divisions.

Not many listeners can distinguish the line-breaks in blank verse simply by listening to them. In the earlier plays, when Marlowe's mighty line was the model and verse rhythms were more emphatic, it was usually possible because the lines were mostly end-stopped. Speakers used the line-ends to take breath, which encouraged them to keep the metre regular and so recognizable. Thus the mnemonic and hypnotic function of emphatic rhythm in the earlier plays helped the listener to identify where the line-breaks came. Later, though, when more frequent elision and enjambement softened those

---

[7] The 1600 Quarto of *Henry V* was set entirely as verse, a result, I believe, of one player dictating the script to a copyist one line at a time, without telling him which passages were verse and which were prose. Hence the uniform transcription of the comic prose as verse in Pistol's metrical prose as well as Mistress Quickly's flowing malapropisms, and even Henry's long dispute with his soldiers, a characteristic that has devalued thinking about the quarto text. How many other early printed texts might have suffered from this kind of mistranscription we can only guess.

[8] See Lukas Erne, *Shakespeare as a Literary Dramatist* (Cambridge, 2003), pp. 20–5. I think that Erne overstates the case for Shakespeare's personal concern to see his plays into print, since their owner was the company, not the author, but he is surely right so far as Ralph Crane's transcripts are concerned, as can be seen from Crane's treatment of some stage directions.

hard edges, and Marlowe's 'mighty line' became archaic enough to be parodied by characters like Ancient Pistol, that function was much reduced. The verse in Fletcher's plays has its own powerful rhythmic sway, but all too often his editors find it impossible to differentiate between an eloquent speech by a commoner in prose and the normative verse spoken by the noble characters.[9] The burlesques of Marlovian speech by Ancient Pistol, and the consequent question whether his lines should be set as verse or prose, are a rock on which editors of Shakespeare still founder.

An additional curious and potentially awkward fact about *The Tempest* is that much of its prose, whether spoken by noble characters or by the lowest of the stage low, is almost scannable as verse. An occasional misplaced syllable, or the compositor's omission of an initial capital for the first word in the line, is all that distinguishes the two. In hectic and gabbling scenes like the opening storm, attempts to identify lines as verse can easily get lost in the marshes of iambic prose. We have no explanation for prose sounding like verse, except that rising rhythms are pervasive in English, and while English prose is in general made up of non-repeating sequences, an unstructured flow of disyllabic and trisyllabic groups in rising rhythm, the habits of a writer accustomed to expressing himself in iambic pentameter might well dispose the flow of prose towards the iambic.

The editorial steeplechase in the transition from Shakespeare as a spoken text to FI's page poses quite a few further problems with versification. Ever since Pope imposed his standardization of the verse-line, editors have had trouble when speeches end in a part-line. The early printed texts always started the verse of a new speaker immediately after the speech-prefix, creating a problem visually when the new speaker keeps the decasyllabic rhythm by completing the part-line of his interlocutor. Not until Capell in 1768 developed Pope's logic and began to indent the second half of a verse line when it was delivered by another speaker, so that it stood below and just after the end of the previous half-line, was the so-called 'white space' layout invented. Steevens made it into a standard

feature of his variorum edition in 1793, a practice upheld by Fredson Bowers, and still followed in all modern editions.[10] A Procrustean insistence on rhythmic continuity authorizes the apparent symmetry of such a layout. It emphasizes the regular flow of the verse, and by giving both half-lines the same line-number editors allow the line-count to reinforce the flow. The fact that this system breaks down when a part-line at the end of a speech is followed by a full line, or by prose, and that completing half-lines was a practice of the earlier years of blank verse that gradually vanished as verse came closer to prose in the Jacobean years, identifies it as one of the standardizations that editorial practice finds so necessary but which obscures the original design of the verse. Three centuries of this formulaic setting-out of dramatic verse have made it into a convention that we now question at our peril. Quite a few versions of Pope's Procrustean bed are still with us, some better disguised than others.

The versification of *The Tempest* in the one text we have is complicated by the two overlays that distort the authorial design: transmission into the FI copy first through a transcript containing the well-known habits of Crane the copyist, and secondly through the equally well-studied practices of the Folio compositors. These two layers of change complicate in their distinctive ways the process of identifying the author's original intentions when writing his copy for the King's Men, which we assume is the principal objective of most editions.

---

9 In quite a few of Fletcher's plays editors have difficulty distinguishing verse from prose, especially when the speaker is a proletarian. See for instance the differing editorial presentations of the old Captain's speeches to the crowd of citizens throughout 5.4 of *Philaster*.

10 Paul Bertram, *White Spaces in Shakespeare: The Development of the Modern Text* (Cleveland, 1981), gives a careful analysis of the changes that he sees Steevens rather than Capell introducing to line formatting in the Variorum edition of 1793. He shows how it was influenced by eighteenth-century ideas of scansion and affected all subsequent editorial line formats, especially the still-influential nineteenth-century Cambridge and Globe editions.

While Crane's and the compositors' general practices are identifiable, their specific practices with this text are still not easy to identify. Crane seems to have had no consistent rule about how to begin a line of verse.[11] His failure to use capitals to mark the start of a verse line left the compositor having to judge whether it was verse or not chiefly by the line-end's proximity to the right margin, not an easy basis for choice. This would seem to make the decision to set any passage as verse or prose, and particularly the shorter speeches, hopelessly subjective. Whether that should be seen as freeing modern editors to versify or de-versify some sections of the Folio text on the grounds that two sets of interpretations have already confused the issue is the question here. A general rule of thumb might seem a useful guideline, but thumbs vary too much in width and length to justify confident choices.

Two examples of the apparent merging of verse into prose, and vice versa, will illustrate the nature of the main challenge of *The Tempest*'s versification to readers and editors. The first is the shift from verse into prose and back by Gonzalo in the conspiracy scene, 2.1, where a deliberate pattern does seem to have been imposed. Lines addressed to the king appear to be in verse, and he himself always uses verse, whereas the mockers Sebastian and Antonio inject their asides in prose, as does Gonzalo when he is provoked into speaking to them reprovingly. Setting the lines in this pattern, of course, is an editorial imposition based on the traditional rules for Shakespearean speech. Responsible addresses to one's ruler belong in verse while asides and interjections, and replies to the interjectors, can stand as prose. Such an assumption raises the question of how clearly the compositor might have recognized such a patterning and followed it in setting the Folio text. The alternative likelihoods, either that such patterning is a modern misinterpretation, or that it arises from confusion following scribal or compositorial interference, are both present equally in my second example, which returns us to our initial question, Caliban's conceivably drunken speech after he has imbibed his new 'book'. When Caliban's verse is mingled with the prose of Stefano and Trinculo in the clown scenes, we might expect the drunken prose of Stefano's book to replace the verse of stately Prospero in Caliban as well as in the clowns. But does it? How far might the compositors' assumptions in setting F1 have influenced the setting of those pages? And how far might editorial rules of thumb have dictated the lineation in current editions? How deeply, in other words, might our editors' need to create consistency in the identified patterns have taken us into an excess of textual emendation?

Act 2 Scene 1, the conspiracy scene, my first example, raises the question how confidently we can identify the apparent pattern of Antonio and Sebastian interjecting their comments in prose against the verse the other courtiers are using. The rhythms as well as the F1 lineation do suggest that their initial mockery of Gonzalo and Adrian is in derisive prose, in clear contrast to Gonzalo's ponderous attempts at addressing his king in verse. Finally Gonzalo seems to be provoked into replying to their mocks with his more dignified version of their own derisive prose. Only later, when Antonio so delicately broaches to Sebastian the idea of killing Alonso and Gonzalo, do the two mockers return to verse. As a scene manned entirely by the nobles of the Neapolitan court, in the king's presence, where formal verse would be the norm, the speeches appear to have been modulated very deliberately between verse and prose. Such an apparently clear patterning is a good basis for testing whether the compositor recognized it when he set the printed text.

The scene starts with eight and a half lines of verse, as Gonzalo tries to comfort the king (TLN 675–83). At the start, Sebastian and Antonio clearly speak their prose as asides (referring to Alonso as 'he' and 'him'), deriding the attempts to cheer Alonso up, and increasingly letting Gonzalo overhear their mockery. Like Gonzalo, the courtier Adrian addresses Alonso in a sort of verse,

---

11 T. H. Howard-Hill, *Ralph Crane*, p. 36, notes that if a line of verse starts with a capital 'it is generally because the first word was a noun or adjective which he would ordinarily have capitalized'.

at TLN 710 and 713, and Alonso replies in good verse.[12] But Adrian's third speech, TLN 717–18, is, however rhythmic, certainly prose ('It must needs be of subtle, tender, and delicate temperance').[13] The compositor chose to set this as prose. His setting of the run of speeches in prose or short verse lines may have influenced him to go on and set Gonzalo's next speeches as prose too. Subsequently, once Sebastian and Antonio join in the speeches addressed to the king, they speak to him in verse, only reverting to prose once Gonzalo starts up again. What starts as verse in the second column of page A4 (TLN 811–42) in the Folio apparently becomes consistent prose when Sebastian and Antonio resume their mockery.

The setting of all this section was by the leading compositor, B. Without taking too much note of his lineation as verse or prose, we might conclude that from the moment Gonzalo is provoked into responding to his mockers in prose, at TLN 694–5, their interruptions allow him only to address Alonso in short verse lines, his speeches declining more and more into prose as the asides grow louder. At TLN 727–8 he speaks an apparent line of verse, mis-set because of its over-run as two verse lines in F:

> *Gon.* How lush and lusty the grasse lookes? How greene?

But his next speech, at 733–34, reads as unmistakable prose, and is set as such by Compositor B:

> *Gon.* But the rariety of it is, which is indeed almost beyond credit.

So is his continuation at 736–39, after Sebastian interjects:

> *Gon.* That our Garments being (as they were) drencht in the Sea, hold notwithstanding their freshnesse and glosses, being rather new dy'de then stain'd with salte water.

The speeches to Alonso that follow by both Gonzalo and Adrian are also clearly prose. Gonzalo's 'widdow *Dido*' reference draws both of them away from Alonso into a prose argument with Sebastian

and Antonio, until Gonzalo turns back to Alonso at TLN 767–9 and 773–4. He then speaks prose, losing the formality of his earlier lines up to 743–5 as if Antonio has made him lose control. It is King Alonso who returns the language to verse at 777–84. Francisco, speaking for the first time, answers him in verse, and Sebastian, at last addressing his brother directly, also now appears to change into verse.

The same pattern of Gonzalo's verse degenerating under Sebastian and Antonio's influence into prose seems to recur in the sequence that follows his 'Commonwealth' speech, TLN 819–42. When their jeers force him to turn from addressing Alonso to acknowledging them again he drops into prose. Alonso says 'Pre-thee no more: thou dost talke nothing to me' (set as prose in F, although Capell made it verse), and Gonzalo's response at 850–3 is strong prose:

> *Gon.* I do vvell beleeue your Highnesse, and did it to minister occasion to these Gentlemen, who are of such sensible and nimble Lungs, that they alwayes vse to laugh at nothing.

The king again lapses into silence, and Gonzalo continues his quarrel with Sebastian and Antonio in prose until after Ariel's entry they feel the need to sleep. Alonso then speaks in verse, and the others, including Sebastian, reply to him in obvious verse, set as such by the F1 compositor.

From then on Sebastian and Antonio undoubtedly address each other in verse. Full though it is of short speeches and linked half-lines, the versification makes it superbly expressive of Sebastian's lax indolence (notably the slow voicing of 'Hereditary Sloth'), resonating against Antonio's quiet

---

[12] Theobald and Capell struggled with Gonzalo's second two-line speech (TLN 691–2), spoken in the middle of Sebastian and Antonio's prose exchanges, making it one and a half decasyllabic lines instead of one shortish line followed by a full one. Both were clearly ruled here by the prescript that formal speeches must be verse.

[13] The addition of 'a' before 'subtle' might turn it into a verse line and a half, but that is the kind of conjectural emendation justifiable only by a circular argument. It should surely remain what it sounds like, prose.

insinuations and innuendos. Possibly the clearest expression of the manipulation of verse rhythm is TLN 932. Set in F1 as 'What great hope haue you? No hope that way, Is', it has ten monosyllables all stressed in varying degrees to establish Antonio's subtle meaning. This is a supreme example of a line where all four of the identifiable levels of stress in English verse have to be invoked. The comma preceding the capitalised 'Is', which is a characteristic Crane form of transcription, marks the break of the emphatic verb at the line-end from the phrase before it, initiating the new thought.[14] Picking up Sebastian's short statement that he has no hope that his nephew Ferdinand is alive, Antonio echoes his phrase 'no hope' in completing Sebastian's half-line, and develops it in the next. The line reverses Sebastian's conventional thought with a radically opposite idea. Inverting Sebastian's phrase, it starts with a rising spondee followed by a series of spondees and trochees in a line of monosyllabic and almost uniformly emphatic words, in which the quoted words recur once in each opposed meaning.

Perhaps the tidiest way to identify these stresses is by using the markers for the four degrees of stress now conventionally acceded to English verse, in their sequence of increasingly heavy emphasis: x \ ^ /. The line could thus be made to sound, spaced out in its five extraordinary feet:

\ / | \ ^ | / / | / / | \ \
What great | hope haue | you? No | hope that | way, Is

The caesura breaks the third foot into two, though not with any great length of pause. A rather different reading of Antonio's meaning might conceivably mark the second foot the other way, as a trochee, and the third as an iamb, reducing the stress on 'you' and thus minimizing the caesura. 'No hope' is then highlighted as a quotation. That would shift the meaning a little, moving the priority from Sebastian himself ('you') to his future ('haue'). Either way, the line is scored for Antonio to now bring his plan into the open. Sebastian is slow to comprehend, slower by dozens of lines than the audience. 'I remember / You did supplant your Brother Prospero', he eventually registers, at

TLN 968–9. Antonio is very cautious in broaching his scheme. The line is rigid with his intensity and excitement under the carefully emphatic and clearly enunciated language. Such precisely controlled speech has to be in verse.

The multitude of adjustments that editors have made in this scene from the F text's setting in verse or prose call the principles used in making any such emendation into question. The second of my examples, the prose of the second scene when Stefano's 'book' is dictating the speech, puts the choice of verse or prose at an extreme. Judging by the evidence just considered in 2.1.'s conspiracy scene, the rhythmical patterns that become apparent in Caliban's longer speeches of the parodic and drunken 3.2 do appear to make him speak, like Gonzalo, in a consistently different mode from the two clowns. The others start in ponderously drunken prose – 'debosh'd Fish' cannot but sound drunkenly ponderous and slurred – but Caliban, for all Stefano's claim that 'thy eies are almost set in thy head', seems to improve his language enough in the course of the scene first to use the accents that we find in the prose of the conspirators in 2.1, and then, when he offers his new master the plan to kill Prospero, to adopt the verse of Antonio plotting with Sebastian. At the end of the scene he rises to Prosperian eloquence when he describes the island's music, setting his language firmly off from the colourfully idiomatic prose of Stefano and Trinculo. It is tempting to think that this three-step transition in Caliban's language is evidence of the author's deliberate adjustments to his accents, calculated to make them match the shift in his role from Stefano's servant to conspirator, and to match the transitions of the scene it parodies, 2.1.

This brings us back to the question whether editors ought to assume that Caliban always speaks in verse. In his first scenes, Caliban certainly uses the same flowing verse rhythms as Prospero and

---

[14] F's capitalization of the initial letter of the last word may be a compositor error, but is more likely to be Crane's standard practice of isolating the noun phrase before it.

Miranda. His verbal downfall, and his first descent into prose, we might argue, is the result of Stefano's bottle-book, studied between 2.2 and 3.2. The F1 text, however, is not entirely helpful with this theory. In 2.2 (A5v) after his sober first seventeen-line speech Compositor D or F began to print his verse as prose. Some of it clearly does seem to have been composed as prose, especially after Stefano first gives him wine at 1138. The compositor, however, set TLN 1113–14 and 1121–3 as prose, which may do no more than suggest his uncertainty about his text, later affirmed when he made Trinculo's prose at 1203–04 into verse. After imbibing, Caliban at 1159–61 has two pentameters followed by a line in which the last five syllables collapse into prose. Lines 1169–70 are evident prose, as are 1184–5, and 1193–4. TLN 1205–9 are a mix of verse and prose, and 1212–17 is verse. These speeches need careful and sceptical scrutiny.

Caliban certainly appears to be intended to show the effect of the drink in his speeches, since Trinculo says 'the poore monster's in drinke' at TLN 1203. The change is marked most clearly in the three lines 1159–61. This speech, however, while set in the Folio as prose, does sound like verse:

> _Cal._ Thefe be fine things, and if they be not fprights:
> that's a braue God, and beares Celeftiall liquor : I will
> kneele to him.

On the other hand, lines 1169–70 are certainly prose:

> _Cal._ I'le fweare vpon that Bottle, to be thy true fub-
> ieƈt, for the liquor is not earthly.

Its slurred consonants and the slow delivery it demands certainly make it sound like drunken speech. Later the compositor turns Trinculo's prose into a verse couplet (TLN 1203–4), followed (1205–9) by five lines of Caliban set confusedly in prose and verse. Most editors make these five lines into verse, usually on no stronger grounds than that Caliban's speech is always distinguishable from

that of the others.[15] It is certainly rhythmic, and it no longer has the drunken slurring of his former speeches such as 1169–70.

> _Tri._ But that the poore Monfter's in drinke :
> An abhominable Monfter.
> _Cal._ I'le fhew thee the beft Springs : I'le plucke thee
> Berries : I'le fifh for thee ; and get thee wood enough
> A plague vpon the Tyrant that I ferue ;
> I'le beare him no more Stickes, but follow thee, thou
> wondrous man.

But Caliban's next speech, TLN 1212–17, set by almost all editors as verse, was set by the compositor unambiguously as prose:

> _Cal._ I'prethee let me bring thee where Crabs grow;
> and I with my long nayles will digge thee pig-nuts;
> fhow thee a Iayes neft, and inftruƈt thee how to fnare
> the nimble Marmazet : I'le bring thee to cluftring
> Philbirts, and fometimes I'le get thee young Scamels
> from the Rocke : Wilt thou goe with me ?

It is impossible to determine here whether the compositor's manuscript copy from Ralph Crane was unclear at this point about verse lineation, or whether he worked under the assumption that Caliban should now be sharing his new master's prose.

The two main influences on the patterning of verse against prose, the practices of the compositors and editors, are both most clearly evident in Act 4 Scene 1, when Caliban, Stefano and Trinculo enter 'all wet' and cursing. The first part of the scene occupies the second half of the second column on Folio page B2 (TLN 1870–1901), set by Compositor C. Caliban speaks first, and the compositor set his two lines as prose. Yet all the subsequent speeches, those by Stefano and Trinculo as well as Caliban's, he set as verse. On the next

---

[15] Pope was the first editor to versify these lines. Of his followers, the Arden3 editors justify their conversion of F1's prose into iambic pentameters by arging that 'Because Miranda and Prospero were members of the nobility and taught him their language, Caliban's poetic idiom reflects their characteristic speech rather than the lower-class prose of Trinculo and Stephano' (note to 2.1.157–61). This of course ignores any effect of Stefano's book on Caliban's speech.

1 An assembly from Caliban's list of fruits and nuts, drawn by Adèle Rossetti Morosini of the Schools of Art and Design of the Liberal Arts of the Pratt Institute, NIC.

page (B2v), the same compositor reverted to prose in setting Stefano and Trinculo but gave verse to Caliban, the differentiation that every editor since Pope has subsequently applied to the whole of the scene.

Crane's inadequate differentiation of verse from prose cannot have been any help to Compositor C. Much of our problem here is the inconsistent setting of the lines in F with or without initial capitals, as verse or as prose, as in Crane's surviving manuscripts. How consistently the compositors were following their standard practices in these scenes is open to considerable doubt. So far as the main Caliban scenes are concerned, the compositorial sequence entailed 3.2 being set first, followed by 2.2, and then 4.1, with other material intervening. We know that at least three compositors were employed on these pages.[16] The leading compositor, B, set the first page, while two lesser compositors, C and F, set the others. Compositor B's A6v (TLN 1382–1512), the bulk of Scene 3.2, was the first page of the play to be set. A subsequent stint also included the first part of 3.2, from TLN 1352 to 1381. It is worth looking more closely into this scene, because Compositor B showed a lot of uncertainty over setting the lines as verse. After beginning with Caliban's drunken one-liners,

none of which shows much sign of a verse rhythm, Caliban speaks some prose that is printed as prose. Another speech appears to be prose set as verse. In the remainder of 3.2 and through the rest of the play most of Caliban's speeches return to verse set in the same handsome form as Prospero and Caliban's first scenes. From then on, despite several stumbles, the compositors appear generally to have accepted his speeches as verse while Stefano and Trinculo speak prose.

Compositor B's setting of 3.2 starts with Stefano and Trinculo in prose, with Caliban speaking only when addressed by his new master Stefano. His first reply is two lines of perfectly regular if ponderous decasyllabics:

> *Cal.* How does thy honour? Let me licke thy fhooe :
> Ile not ferue him, he is not valiant,

(TLN 1373–4)

His previous silence and the heaviness of these two lines with the over-enunciation of the three

---

16 According to the Oxford edition's *William Shakespeare. A Textual Companion* (Oxford, 1997), p. 149, F1's Compositor C probably set B2–B2v, while A5–A5v may have been set by D rather than C.

syllables of the last word, 'valiant', are auditory marks of his drunken condition. They may have been set as verse, although the fact that the first word of the second line would have been capitalized whether it was meant to be verse or prose leaves it indeterminate. Caliban's second speech is more distinctly prose:

> *Cal.* Loe, how he mockes me, wilt thou let him my
> Lord?

(TLN 1380–1)

Here again the capitalized 'Lord' at the beginning of the second line could be taken as a marker for the line being thought of as verse, though not by any poet. Caliban's next lines, on Compositor B's page 12 (A6b), the first one he set, were certainly seen as prose:

> *Cal.* I thanke my noble Lord. Wilt thou be pleas'd
> to hearken once againe to the suite I made to thee?

(TLN 1388–9)

Here the absence of a capital at the beginning of the second line seems to contradict the compositor's evidence of the apostrophe in the last word of the previous line, normally used in verse to indicate an elision. The first line is perfectly good verse and would have been heard as such before the speech collapses into prose. It is of course possible to embed a pentameter in prose; we sometimes briefly use verse rhythms when speaking what is overall prose. And the first of these lines is without question a pentameter. The second line, on the other hand, has no sign of verse rhythm, unless it is a gabbled hexameter. It is quite conceivable that as elsewhere the two lines were originally meant to begin as verse and descend into stumbling prose.

The setting of the speeches that follow is confused and confusing. In the dramatic situation, with Caliban trying to broach his plan to kill Prospero while Ariel uses Trinculo's voice to interrupt and upset all three speakers, we might expect some confusion between the voices. But Compositor B was confused too, since he set at least nine of Stefano's longer speeches as verse, and only four as prose.

Even Trinculo has one speech set with capitals at the beginning of each of his lines.[17]

None of the speeches in the first thirty-five lines of the scene, on F's A6 (TLN 1352–81), composed later than TLN 1382 onwards, is set as verse. Crane's transcript evidently left Compositor B unsure, having initiated his setting of the play with A6v's muddles of prose and verse before he did the opening section of the scene, just about what was expected. On the new page, from 1382 onwards, it seems that Caliban begins with prose, but moves on (or back) to verse. He begins his narrative prosaically, yet several lines, including Stefano's 1390–1, were set as verse. Caliban's response is also set as verse:

> *Cal.* As I told thee before, I am subiect to a Tirant,
> A Sorcerer, that by his cunning hath cheated me
> Of the Island.

(TLN 1393–5)

The rest of his response after Ariel's interjection 'Thou lyest' at TLN 1396 is conceivably the compositor's prose, although it is not justified to the right margin:

> *Cal.* Thou lyest, thou iesting Monkey thou:
> I would my valiant Master would destroy thee.
> I do not lye.

(TLN 1397–9)

Of these, the first is a foot short of becoming a verse line, but 1398 is a pentameter with a feminine ending. It would even be possible to hear the first exclamation in TLN 1397 as Caliban's completion of Ariel's dissyllabic half-line, if 'liest' could be contracted into a monosyllable.

Caliban's next speeches are good verse, and none are justified to the right margin:[18]

---

[17] Trinculo's name has recently been given to a satellite of Uranus, a fact that has absolutely nothing to do with the subject of this article.

[18] Pope made them verse. Stephen Orgel in his New Oxford edition set them as prose.

> *Cal.* I say by Sorcery he got this Isle
> From me, he got it. If thy Greatnesse will
> Reuenge it on him, (for I know thou dar'st)
> But this Thing dare not.

(TLN 1404–7)

The first of these lines is a pentameter, although the rhythm stumbles slightly in what follows. After this, Caliban's subsequent speeches become more and more distinct from the prose of Stefano and Trinculo, rising to his seventeen-line speech about how to kill Prospero and take his daughter. Then after the drunken song, its correct tune supplied by Ariel, Caliban delivers his wonderful speech of nine rhythmical lines, 'the Isle is full of noises', which FI does set as verse.

The other scenes involving Caliban, Trinculo and Stefano are on Folio pages A5 and A5v (2.2), B2 and B2v (4.1), and B3v (5.1, where Caliban and the others are brought to book, and where Stefano's lines are all set as verse). If we compare A5, A5v and B3v, set by Compositor F, and B2 and B2v set by Compositor C, with Compositor B's initial setting of FI's A6v, it seems that F and C made similar mistranscriptions of verse as prose or vice versa to those of Compositor B on his first page. This seems to confirm that the verse/prose confusion started with Crane's lost transcript. Identifying the apparent mislineations of verse and prose in these scenes becomes much more difficult for editors if it was not the compositors who were responsible.

A little light can be made to glimmer in this apparent confusion between verse and prose introduced by Crane's lost transcript. Two matters in particular might suggest that FI as printed does stand up against every subsequent editorial attempt to adjust it. One is at TLN 1780–91, when Ferdinand interrupts the rhymes and songs by the masquers to speak to Prospero. Here half-lines are used to impressive effect, although a textual crux has caused major editorial modifications. This is an example that puts to the test any reading of the assumptions we make about the principles of dramatic versification that Shakespeare was using in 1610.

The first gleam of light is at TLN 1779 when Ferdinand comments on Ceres singing the masque's tetrameter song of blessing. He speaks two and a half lines:

> FER   This is a most majesticke vision, and
> Harmonious charmingly: may I be bold
> To thinke these spirits?

Prospero assents, completing Ferdinand's half-line, and leaving him another:

> PRO   Spirits, which by mine Art
> I haue from their confines call'd to enact
> My present fancies.

Ferdinand responds with a half-line that matches Prospero's perfectly:

> FER   Let me liue here euer,

and adds another one and a half lines, the half-line inviting further harmonious concurrence:

> So rare a wondred Father, and a wise
> Makes this place Paradise.

The full line here has exercised editors since Rowe, who followed the F2 reading and installed the alternative 'wife' for 'wise' in his 1709 edition. Editors since then have wavered between the two. The problem starts with a few copies of FI which may have altered the text with a broken long 's' in 'wife', since most copies of FI make it 'wise', with a half-stroke across the long s, whereas two copies seem to have the full stroke which makes it 'wife'.[19] If this apparent variant was in the original copy, subsequent editors are right to follow this change and thus add an Eve to the Eden Ferdinand finds on the island. If so, Rowe and his successors must be correct when they accept the variant reading and

---

[19] The case for 'wife' was first analysed by Jeanne Addison Roberts, '"Wife" or "Wise" – *The Tempest* l.1786', *Studies in Bibliography* 31 (1978), 203–8. She identified two Folger copies of FI, Nos. 6 and 73, as having the 'f'. Peter Blayney, however, in the new Norton Facsimile (*The First Folio of Shakespeare: The Norton Facsimile*, Second Edition [New York, 1996]), dismissed the view that the 'long s' is a broken 'f' (p. xxxi). The history of the long debate over these alternatives is nicely assessed by Ronald Tumelson in this volume.

augment it by emending the singular 'Makes' of FI to the plural 'Make', on the grounds that Ferdinand is citing not the singular rare and wise Prospero but the plural rare father and his daughter. These editors read the praise that Ferdinand gives to Prospero about living forever in this paradise with his wise and wondered-at father-in-law as praise of his daughter too, who in Ferdinand's vision of the blissful future is his wife. The single piece of broken or misread type thus calls for an editorial emendation of the verb. Such an emendation has large implications for interpretation of the text. By this reading FI's comma after 'Father' seems to separate him (Him?) off from the signified 'wise' / 'wife'. Prospero becomes God the Father, and Eve will join Adam in Eden.

In the case for the substantive FI reading, 'wise', allowing for uncertainty or at least variance in usage over voiced and unvoiced consonants, we have to ask whether a rhyme was intended, and whether a half-line ending can be heard to rhyme with a full line-end: wise / Paradise. It is true that Shakespeare sometimes used heavily-emphasised rhyming couplets to close off a scene or an unanswerable speech; verse half-lines usually make less formal and alternative types of closure. There are almost no instances in Shakespeare where half-lines are made to rhyme with the preceding full line. But *The Tempest* is distinctive in its use of half-lines, and innovation, especially in such possible uses of half-lines as this, is a feature of its verse. The reading 'wife' has the attraction of not rhyming, and so frees the text from this charge of eccentricity. But it needs stronger support as a reading than the eighteenth-century editors were prepared to allow it, and the need consequentially to emend the verb in order to make a necessary grammatical adjustment is a strong counter-argument. Given the intricate control shown in Prospero's next lines, the balance of evidence here seems to support FI's 'wise' over FI/F2/F3's 'wife'.

Prospero answers Ferdinand's half-line with a check, 'Sweet now, silence:' (TLN 1788). Two inverted feet, trochees with an apparently falling rhythm, bring the dialogue to a careful halt. Pros-

pero's next line has a pun in it: '*Iuno* and *Ceres* whisper seriously' making Ceres serious in this solemn visual fantasy. The real seriousness is of course yet to come, with Prospero's interruption of the masque. His two falling trochees at TLN 1788 halt Ferdinand's excited yet elegant compliments, and turn attention to the reapers' dance, hardly, as a version of the courtly anti-masque, a truly serious vision. Prospero's two lines, preceded and followed by half-lines, are immaculately metrical. The last half-line is an emphatic closure: 'Or else our spell is mar'd.' The control over the speaking voice that is evidenced in these lines should justify a preference for the Folio text over the various adjustments that editors have made. In this instance the principal Folio version can be upheld, not because it fits the editors' Procrustean metrical norm but because the sound and meaning of the text they seek to modify is fully justifiable as it stands.

Given such evidence for the master's control of metre, used with impeccable correctness and yet with such exceptional originality, it is evident that the editorial urge towards 'correct' scansion by 'rules' of metre in *The Tempest* will never be applied satisfactorily enough to explain the infinite variety of modulation and emphasis that the different dialogue situations demand. That is the case whether we look at the transitions between verse and prose shown here, or revise the verse rhythms that appear in sections set in FI as prose but sound like verse, such as Gonzalo's final four lines in the opening scene. To use the familiar metrical norms and the ostensible rules of thumb they provide as a means to identify copyist errors in transmission of the text is likely only to obscure qualities of the 'heard' text for which the original manuscript was composed. The basic trouble is that, as our study of Caliban's apparent fluctuations between Prospero's and Stefano's books suggest, perfect consistency was an achievement that seems to have eluded even the author. Behind the impositions of their own patterns by editors, compositors and scribe, stands the author's own patterning. But even the prose/verse pattern developed between Gonzalo and his mockers in 2.1. seems not to have been followed with perfect regularity in the drunken clown scenes. Perhaps Shakespeare abandoned it because he did not want complete consistency. Perhaps his own patterning was more subtle than anything we have identified here. If so, for all the value that we think we can gain from identifying what underlies Ralph Crane's or Compositor B's practices, the F1 text as it stands remains the only reliable source we have for Shakespeare's original soundscript. Editors should listen carefully to his verse rhythms, never forgetting that Procrustes enjoyed the tortures he imposed on his victims.

MANUSCRIPT, PRINT AND THE AUTHENTIC SHAKESPEARE: THE IRELAND FORGERIES AGAIN

TOM LOCKWOOD

Where do we locate the authentic Shakespeare? This was the question asked, rather less bluntly, by Stephen Orgel in his influential *Representations* essay of 1988. Taking and testing Shakespearian examples in manuscript, in print, in the theatre and in portraiture, Orgel asked how the category of the authentic varied historically in, and was varied historically by, these different but clearly related contexts. Orgel argued that although these locations can perform authenticity they cannot themselves be authentic; despite their variety, Shakespearian authenticity oddly still exists elsewhere:

What is authentic here is something that is not in the text; it is something behind it and beyond it that the text is presumed to represent: the real life of the characters, the actual history of which the action is a part, the playwright's imagination, or the hand of the master, the authentic witness of Shakespeare's own history. The assumption is that texts are representations or embodiments of something else, and that it is that something else which the performer or editor undertakes to reveal. What we want is not the authentic play, with its unstable, infinitely revisable script, but an authentic Shakespeare, to whom every generation's version of a classic drama may be ascribed.[1]

What we want, as Orgel put it, others have wanted also; and this article explores an earlier version of those desires for Shakespearian authenticity: the Shakespeare forgeries of William-Henry Ireland. The story of those forgeries has been often told, and the narrative of the young William-Henry Ireland's 'discovery' of a trunk of papers containing not only Shakespeare's long-lost correspondence with Queen Elizabeth, Lord Southampton,

Richard Burbage and others, but also manuscripts of *King Lear* and *Hamlet*, with, to top it all, two 'lost' plays, *Vortigern* and *Henry II*, does not need retelling here.[2] Rather my argument focuses on the relation between the forgeries and their most devastating exposure, Edmond Malone's *An Inquiry into the Authenticity of Certain Miscellaneous Papers and Legal Instruments* (1796). My argument will be that this episode is less about Shakespeare than it is about how we understand his place within a wider account of the materiality of early modern textual culture; in making that argument, I want to suggest that the history of the authentic Shakespeare need not be only (here in Orgel's phrase) 'something that is not in the text', but rather that it might need precisely to account for the text and its materiality.[3]

I am grateful to audiences at the Universities of Sheffield and Birmingham for their comments on earlier versions of this paper; Robert Jones, Marcus Nevitt, and *Shakespeare Survey*'s anonymous readers all helped to improve it.

[1] Stephen Orgel, 'The Authentic Shakespeare', *Representations*, 21 (1988), 1–25, collected in his *The Authentic Shakespeare and Other Problems on the Early Modern Stage* (London, 2002), pp. 231–56 (at p. 256).

[2] The two standard accounts, now both dated, are John Dunbar Mair, *The Fourth Forger: William Ireland and the Shakespeare Papers* (London, 1938) and Bernard Grebanier, *The Great Shakespeare Forgery: A New Look at the Career of William Henry Ireland* (London, 1966), superseded by Samuel Schoenbaum, *Shakespeare's Lives*, 2nd edn (Oxford, 1991), pp. 130–68; Peter Ackroyd's novel, *The Lambs of London* (London, 2004), testifies to the continuing appeal of the affair.

[3] Orgel, of course, has in other essays paid precisely this attention to what Margreta de Grazia and Peter Stallybrass have elsewhere called 'The Materiality of the Shakespearean

In the Preface to the first print publication of the 'discovered' Shakespearian documents, *Miscellaneous Papers and Legal Instruments under the Hand and Seal of William Shakspeare* (1796), their editor, Samuel Ireland, father of William-Henry, discounted all claims about their inauthenticity, taking to italics to assert that '*these Papers can be no other than the production of Shakspeare himself*'.[4] 'The production of Shakspeare', of course, cuts two ways: these papers are not only produced by Shakespeare but, at the same time, are involved in the business of producing Shakespeare. Allowing that double claim on the Shakespeare papers, and allowing them a double claim on the late sixteenth and late eighteenth centuries, opens out a way of reading their materiality more closely akin (I will argue) to the ways in which they were read by their contemporaries. This way of reading the Shakespeare papers removes them from the (sometimes constraining) sphere of individual agency – who did and knew what, when – and places them instead within the more diverse, more collaborative agencies of a dispersed textual culture. Rather than the Ireland affair being one to be explained, and in which we ought to adjudicate, at the level of individual blame, this way of reading derives from the papers an account which recognizes that their materiality matters: rather than locating the individual at their centre, be that individual Ireland or Shakespeare, we can, by locating the document at the centre of this affair, take it seriously as an account of Shakespeare and textual culture.

Ireland's forgeries occupy spaces in their contemporary culture that hold increasing interest for scholars today and serve, too, to locate Shakespeare in those same, earlier spaces. They occupy not only the world of manuscript, print and the theatre, as discussed by Orgel, but those previously marginalized spaces that record the history of reading.[5] The closing paragraph of the preface to the *Miscellaneous Papers* nicely captures the variety of textual and cultural locations in which Shakespeare moved across this dual chronology:

The Editor further informs the Public, that (besides the Play of Vortigern now preparing for representation at Drury-Lane Theatre) another, and more interesting, historical Play has been discovered among the other papers, in the hand writing of Shakspeare: this will in due time be laid before the Public. He likewise acquaints them, that he is in possession of a great part of Shakspeare's Library, in which are many books with Notes in his own hand, and those of a very curious nature. Some of these he, most probably, will reprint: they exhibit him in a new character, – unite with the Bard, the Critic and the Moralist, and display an acute and penetrating judgment, with a disposition amiable and gentle as his Genius was transcendant. Such a view of our immortal Poet must prove highly acceptable to every sincere admirer, who will doubtless concur with the Editor, that nothing should be lost, scarce even "One drop which fell from Shakspeare's pen."[6]

Different kinds of textual and cultural authority are engaged here by the Irelands, as are different kinds of display: the stage and institution of the Theatre-Royal at Drury Lane; the page with the 'hand writing of Shakspeare'; and the manuscript annotations keyed to the printed texts of his library, comprised of 'many books with Notes in his own hand'. Curiously it is not in *Vortigern* or the unnamed *Henry II* that Shakespearian Genius is laid before the public, but here the annotations: the messy material record (apparently) of Shakespeare's engagement with the material production of the contemporary book trades. Like the Shakespearian annotations in the printed books, or like the manuscripts of *King Lear* and *Hamlet*, these papers move intriguingly between the worlds of manuscript and print, terms whose interrelation they question and entangle. They suggest that, as well as a discursive understanding of the forgeries which would link them to the Ossian and Chatterton affairs of the mid- to

---

Text', *Shakespeare Quarterly*, 44 (1993), 255–82 (see particularly p. 256 n.3).

[4] Samuel Ireland, ed., *Miscellaneous Papers and Legal Instruments under the Hand and Seal of William Shakspeare* (London, 1796), p. vi; quotations, unless otherwise indicated, follow the octavo rather than the folio edition of the *Miscellaneous Papers*, a distinction discussed below.

[5] Explored provocatively by William H. Sherman, '"Rather Soiled By Use": Attitudes Towards Readers' Marks', *The Book Collector*, 52 (2003), 471–90.

[6] Ireland, ed., *Miscellaneous Papers*, p. xix.

late-eighteenth century, or to developing contemporary formations of Shakespeare, we need also to locate them in relation to their materiality.[7] Produced by and at the same time producing Shakespeare, Ireland's forgeries complicate not only our understanding of the authentic Shakespeare, but also of manuscript and print.

The Ireland forgeries were the subject of much discussion in their time; neither have they wanted for later commentators. In fact, repetition has curiously become the condition of these supposedly once-only, unique discoveries. William-Henry Ireland himself is as guilty in this as any subsequent commentator: as well as the account of the papers and their discovery he and his father mounted alongside their first printing in the *Miscellaneous Papers*, he later offered variant accounts of the episode in his *An Authentic Account of the Shaksperian Manuscripts, &c.* (1796),[8] in his *Confessions of William-Henry Ireland* (1805),[9] and in the reprinted *Vortigern* (1832).[10] Behind these stands a host of other modes in which the matter of the forgeries was repeated and circulated, among those modes a conversational habit that Ireland recalled in the 1805 *Confessions*. As justification for their publication, Ireland wrote that he was merely putting into print an account of his actions that earlier audiences had enjoyed: the making and success of the forgeries had been 'frequently detailed in the circle of my friends, who have invariably stated the entertainment they have received, and the full conviction that the public would experience an equal portion of amusement were the whole to be collected and placed before them'.[11] Full conviction, there, carries its own, wide-eyed scrupulousness in this *confession*, with its title-page motto, 'THE WHOLE TRUTH, AND NOTHING BUT THE TRUTH.'; but Ireland is equally aware of the various different modes of publication with which his writing engages: the coterie of 'the circle of my friends', set within, and partly against, 'the public'. The tale repeated in one medium has its meaning in relation to other earlier and later tellings of the same tale, in this and other media; as it is reproduced, so it is also altered by its contexts and mode. Audience and reproduction are terms here conditioned

precisely by context and mode: as conversation and print publication are linked here by Ireland, so will different kinds of manuscript and print publication be seen to bear on the meaning and making of the forgeries, and the meaning and making of their exposures. But, at the same time, I want to insist – as do the forgeries themselves – that the different kinds of reproduction create different kinds of meaning for different kinds of audience. Reproduction becomes a part of the forgeries' meaning; the telling of their stories over again becomes part of the story they were originally supposed to tell. The 'new' account of Shakespeare and his texts that they offered becomes, in turn, new accounts of where the impulse to make those texts and meanings came from.

Recent writers on the Ireland affair have struggled either to break the forgeries free from reproduction or to contain them within it. Margreta de Grazia argued that Ireland's activities and texts participate in a Foucauldian rupture with early traditionary understandings of Shakespeare that also marks, as it is in part produced by, the editorial work of Ireland's antagonist, Edmond Malone; more recent accounts, chief among them that by Paul Baines, have sought to reintegrate the Ireland forgeries into a less violent, 'gradualist' development of forgery that, in contrast to the Foucauldian model, invests 'no single revolutionary moment' with explanatory force.[12] As well as these

---

7 See, for instance, Paul Baines, *The House of Forgery in Eighteenth-Century Britain* (Aldershot, 1998) and Margreta de Grazia, *Shakespeare Verbatim: The Reproduction of Authenticity and the 1790 Apparatus* (Oxford, 1991); David Fairer, *English Poetry of the Eighteenth Century, 1700–1789* (Harlow, 2003), pp. 167–91, usefully locates contemporary versions of the 'authentic' and the 'genuine'.

8 W. H. Ireland, *An Authentic Account of the Shaksperian Manuscripts, &c.* ([London], 1796).

9 W. H. Ireland, *The Confessions of William-Henry Ireland* (London, 1805).

10 W. H. Ireland, *Vortigern* (London, 1832).

11 Ireland, *Confessions*, sig.A3r.

12 Paul Baines, *The House of Forgery*, pp. 183, 4; compare also David Scott Kastan, *Shakespeare and the Book* (Cambridge, 2001), p. 103.

historiographical concerns attendant on reproduction, as de Grazia in particular has argued, there are particular contemporary technological concerns: the development of the facsimile in the last quarter of the eighteenth century gave particular focus to the forgeries and their mechanical reproduction.[13] Facsimile, as it moves between manuscript and print, between the authentic and the inauthentic, is vital to an understanding of the authentic reproduction of the forgeries, as I will argue; it is just one of the material recoveries necessary for our full understanding of the forgeries.

I

How, then, might we arrive at such a material account of the Ireland forgeries? Even to ask the question in those terms is to recapitulate an earlier mode of response. Take, for instance, the response of Thomas Caldecott. In a letter to John Mander of 30 November 1797, Caldecott passed grumpy judgement on Ireland's forged Shakespearian documents (he may have been especially grumpy having subscribed four guineas towards their publication in the belief that they were genuine). As commentators at the time and since have noticed, the excitable orthogaphy of Ireland's multiply consonanted texts represents a severe challenge to their genuineness: it quickly became their parodic, identifiable feature, the columns of the daily newspapers and quarterly periodicals abounding in elaborately double and triple-lettered correspondence, as well as running reports on the controversy and from its participants.[14] For Caldecott at least, however, the texts's orthography was contingent upon more basic features of their materiality. Caldecott discussed Samuel Ireland's decision to make the Shakespeare papers public in his *Miscellaneous Papers and Legal Instruments Under the Hand and Seal of William Shakspeare*, a decision taken in the face of Caldecott's earlier advice as to 'the impolity of printing or any longer producing' the texts in public:

From an idea that it was improper to suppress any thing that had been extensively circulated & known, &, I verily believe, an honest conviction that they were genuine (for

he thought it was very fine, & there were some foolish people who told him so, & he was not capable of judging upon the subject himself) this advice was rejected; & the opinion, which coincided with his own persuasion & his sense of duty, prevailed. But the Publication of the papers at once decided the question of their Authenticity: Till then, in the illegible state of MSS. (for such it was to almost every one, & in consequence a translation or deciphering of the crabbed text was always placed beside it) a comparison of the mode of spelling of the several supposed writers was impracticable: but upon Publication it was seen, that not only Shakespeare, but *others*, whose writing were exhibited as Originals & not Transcripts, were made to spell in the same way, & that a way not only unknown to any particular period, but unknown to all times; & in which no one ever was ever known to have printed any more than to have written[.][15]

The relationship of manuscript and print, and their relation to 'the authentic', are at the very centre of Caldecott's objections. The authenticity of the 'illegible' documents themselves, Caldecott insists, is problematic; they require 'translation or deciphering', in effect different kinds of 'Publication', for that question to be decided. As the texts move between manuscript and print, so are those two worlds those by which they are finally judged: they exist in a state in which 'no one ever was ever known to have printed any more than to have written'.

There is what amounts to a studied archness in Caldecott's letter; his unblinkingly neutral reference to Samuel Ireland's 'honest Conviction' should alert us to some words having more than one meaning in this text. 'Publication', though less pointed, is no less key: it spans in Caldecott's usage a whole range of modes and locations, in manuscript and print, in which a text is made

---

[13] De Grazia, *Shakespeare Verbatim*, p. 87.

[14] Edmond Malone bound together his 'press cuttings' of the affair; they are now Bodleian Library, Oxford, Malone F III.44 (bound as 'Extracts From Newspapers Relative to the Ireland Forgeries of Shakespeare.').

[15] I quote from my own transcription of Folger Shakespeare Library, PR 2950 B5 Cage Copy 2; the letter was first printed by Samuel Schoenbaum, 'The Ireland Forgeries: An Unpublished Contemporary Account', in his *Shakespeare and Others* (London, 1985), pp. 144–53.

public, and in which it encounters an audience. Think, for instance, of the process of public inspection during which the forgeries were 'extensively circulated & known'; think, too, of the exercise in 'translation or deciphering' by which the forged original manuscripts were faced with modern representations or reproductions of their text, again in manuscript; and finally think of print publication, which must be the local meaning of Caldecott's term. The single term does many services, as the letter discloses the extent to which those three categories are themselves variable: publication, as well as indicating the difference between modes, indicates also the differences within them. Though it is deployed rather than described, Caldecott's is a way of reading that anticipates D. F. McKenzie's insistence that we describe not only 'the technical but the social processes' by which texts are transmitted, recognizing that the processes by which texts are transmitted are necessarily part of their ongoing meaning.[16] The modes in which the Shakespeare papers were made public drive home this point.

James Boswell, when he first saw the Shakespeare papers at the Irelands' house on Norfolk Street, knelt to kiss them. By William-Henry Ireland's account, Boswell announced: 'I now kiss the invaluable relics of our bard: and thanks to God that I have lived to see them.'[17] This kind of '*ocular demonstration*' (the phrase Boswell used of Samuel Johnson's inspection of the chest from which Chatterton's Rowleian forgeries were said to have appeared) makes one context for the authenticity of the papers their social display.[18] James Macpherson's Ossian forgeries had similarly been displayed at the shop of his publisher, Thomas Becket, in 1762; the Irelands' exhibition of their Shakespeareana at Norfolk Street have as well a contemporary parallel in the Shakespeare Gallery of John Boydell in Pall Mall, which opened in 1789.[19] As well as display, the Shakespeare papers also gave rise to debate; one held at the Westminster Forum on 9 January 1797 asked pertinently: 'Do the Shakespearean Manuscripts, the Play of Vortigern and Rowena, and the Apology of Mr. Ireland Jun. exhibit stronger Proofs of Authenticity, flagrant Imposition, or the Credulity of Persons of Genius?'[20] This social context for authenticity – a context that both locates and produces the authentic – is vital to an understanding of the Shakespeare papers; it need not be to situate the papers in 'the public sphere' (or to argue over how such a sphere might be constituted or contextualized); but it is to insist that one of their earliest contexts is sociable, their publication at least as much a matter of display and debate as of reproduction.

As manuscript is another of the fields within which the forgeries move so is it, too, a field complicated by their presence. Caldecott's letter reminds us that the forged documents were not displayed without context; because of 'the illegible state of MSS', he wrote, 'a translation or deciphering of the crabbed text was always placed beside it [*sic*]'.[21] These alternatives, themselves in apposition to the original forged documents, allow for historical variation within the world of manuscript: the imprecision about terms – 'a translation or deciphering' – recognizes that a shift has taken place in English script between the 'sixteenth' and eighteenth centuries, a shift so radical as almost to be a difference in kind. Are these supposedly sixteenth and seventeenth-century texts in a foreign language to be translated? Are they in a code to be deciphered? The antiquary Francis Douce, the later owner of one such forgery and its transcription, wrote on the transcription: 'As it was impossible

---

[16] D. F. McKenzie, *Bibliography and the Sociology of Texts* (Cambridge, 1999), p. 13.

[17] W. H. Ireland, *Confessions*, p. 96.

[18] James Boswell, *Life of Johnson*, ed. R. W. Chapman (Oxford, 1991), p. 752.

[19] Howard Gaskill, 'What Did James Macpherson Really Leave On Display at his Publisher's Shop in 1762?', *Scottish Gaelic Studies*, 16 (1990), 67–89; Jonathan Bate, *Shakespearean Constitutions: Politics, Theatre, Criticism 1730–1830* (Oxford, 1989), pp. 45–60.

[20] John Philip Kemble's copy of the bill advertising the debate is now bound in Folger Shakespeare Library, PR 2950 M32 Cage Copy 5, following sig.3I2; Edmond Malone's copy of the bill is now bound in Bodleian Library MS Malone 41, fol.20.

[21] S. Schoenbaum, *William Shakespeare: Records and Images* (London, 1981), reproduces one paired forgery and transcription as facsimile 62; I discuss another example below.

that any one except the impudent fabricator of the Shakespeare papers could read the hand writing of them, to save the trouble of those who exhibited them, as well as that of the numerous inspectors, he had made transcripts of them himself, and these were usually read to the spectators.'[22] The mode of their display makes the forgeries' illegibility a condition of their authenticity: these documents must be genuine because they look so unlike contemporary documents, to be deciphered only by an expert. A visitor to Norfolk Street would have been faced with, on the one hand, the preserved records of a manuscript culture that had apparently perished into illegibility; on the other, the manuscript records of a contemporary textual culture, the transcriptions in a modern hand, that insists on the vitality and continuity of that very manuscript culture with its earlier stages.

Print publication, as might now be expected, is also more variable than Caldecott's letter concedes, but it is a mode of publication that relies on forging links between its own status and that of the 'recovered' culture it proposes to make available. The categories through which the *Miscellaneous Papers* produce their own authenticity in print are vitally linked to the categories through which William-Henry Ireland's forgeries produce their authenticity in manuscript. The *Miscellaneous Papers* were first printed in a subscription folio volume, to which 122 credulous (or simply keen) names were affixed; later the papers were printed in a 'commercial' octavo, without subscribers. The imprints to both editions list the same pair of printers, 'COOPER and GRAHAM, Bow Street, Covent Garden', and the same syndicate of five London publishing firms, but the books themselves address very different audiences. The folio edition of the *Miscellaneous Papers* makes a claim to authenticity in two ways: socially, by name, and bibliographically, by format. This is a large book: printed throughout on a single stock of paper, the pages of the folio measure upwards of 420 × 320 mm in uncut copies. And it makes correspondingly large claims: its dedication, signed by '*SAMUEL IRELAND*. | Norfolk Street, | *Dec.* 1795.' offers itself 'TO THE | INGENU-OUS, INTELLIGENT, AND DISINTERESTED, |

WHOSE CANDOUR, CONVICTION, AND SUP-PORT | HAVE GIVEN A SANCTION | TO THE PUBLICATION OF | THESE PAPERS'. Those supporters are then listed in two full columns per page over the recto and verso of the following leaf, from 'Angerstein, J. J. Esq.' to 'Yarborough, Lord': the individual and institutional subscribers invest the project not only with their four guineas payment but the prestige of their name and participation. The octavo edition, by contrast, is altogether a smaller thing: it lacks both the dedication and the list of subscribers, as typical a piece of late eighteenth-century printing as the folio spectacularly is not. It is the collocation of bibliographical and social claims to authenticity, as we will see, that most clearly marks the folio *Miscellaneous Papers*: the dedication and subscription list situates the book within a plausible social network that can be read off against, and confirmed by, a plausible textual network.[23] In this, the published *Papers* make, through the medium of the print, a claim to authenticity that parallels the claim made, through the medium of manuscript, by the papers themselves.

The materiality of these texts is again at the centre of their meanings; in support of such a claim as they make, even watermarks matter. The single stock of super royal paper, watermarked 'JWHATMAN | 1794', on which the folio *Papers* were printed gives evidence of forethought and expense in their production: paper, as it had been since the advent of printing, continued to be the major publication cost in any

---

[22] Bodleian Library, MS Douce e.8, fol.2v; the forgery and transcription were extracted from a genuine sixteenth-century annotated book, *The Newe Testament of Our Lord Iesus Christ, Translated Out of Greeke* by Theo. Beza, *and Englished by* L.T. (London, 1581), now Bodleian Library, Douce N.T. Eng. g. 1581, whose provenance Douce wryly records as 'From the supposed library of Masterre Wyllyamme Shakespeare.'

[23] The notion of such networks is discussed by Jason Scott-Warren, 'Reconstructing Manuscript Networks: the Textual Transactions of Sir Stephen Powle' in Alexandra Shepard and Phil Withington, eds, *Communities in Early Modern England: Networks, Place, Rhetoric* (Manchester, 2000), pp. 18–37; and Harold Love, *Attributing Authorship: An Introduction* (Cambridge, 2002), p. 71.

venture.[24] The machine-made, woven Whatman paper was more common in the mid 1790s than it had been earlier in the century when used by the Shakespearian editor Edward Capell, but here no less than there, it ought to be understood (in Marcus Walsh's terms) as 'a condition of the typography' of the volume.[25] The Irelands, as this example demonstrates, were acutely aware of paper and its material relationship to authenticity. In his *Confessions*, William Henry Ireland explored paper as a condition of authenticity:

As I was fully aware, from the variety of water-marks which are in existence at the present day, that they must have constantly been altered since the period of Elizabeth, and being for some time wholly unacquainted with the water-marks of that age, I very carefully produced my first specimens of the writing on such sheets of old paper as had no mark whatsoever. – Having heard it frequently stated that the appearance of such marks on the papers would have greatly tended to establish their validity, I listened attentively to every remark which was made upon the subject, and from thence I at length gleaned the intelligence that a *jug* was the prevalent water-mark of the reign of Elizabeth: in consequence of which I inspected all the sheets of old paper then in my possession; and having selected such as had the jug upon them, I produced the succeeding manuscripts upon these; being careful, however, to mingle with them a certain number of blank leaves, that the production on a sudden of so many water-marks might not excite suspicion in the breasts of those persons who were most conversant with the manuscripts.[26]

In the Preface to the *Miscellaneous Papers* Samuel Ireland made a similar although inflationary point in defence of the recovered manuscript of *King Lear*: 'It may not be improper to add, that in the paper, on which this Play is written, more than twenty different water marks appear.' Are few watermarks more authentic than many? If the questions of scale have not been fully resolved, this attention to paper is not simply a matter of history in the Irelands's hands; rather they are pressing against a conception of paper as a documentary proof of authenticity that has many modern relations.[27] Many watermarks are not more authentic than a single watermark, we might argue today,

unless they can be read in conjunction with the known habits of the paper archive and its producers: as the single stock of paper bearing the folio *Miscellaneous Papers* serves to authenticate the book, so the 'more than twenty' watermarks bearing the *Lear*, in fact, serve rather to question it.

But it is the conjunction of paper and a second term, facsimile, that is particularly strained by the folio *Miscellaneous Papers*. Thirty pages earlier in his *Confessions*, under the heading 'A SHEET OF OLD PAPER', William Henry Ireland described the circumstances under which he sat down to produce Shakespeare's 'profession of faith':

The sheet of paper on which the profession of faith was written was the outside of several others, on some of which accounts had been kept in the reign of Charles the First; and being at that time wholly unacquainted with the water-marks used in the reign of queen Elizabeth, I carefully selected two half sheets not having any mark whatsoever, on which I penned my first effusion; keeping the *facsimiles* of Shakspeare's original autographs before me.[28]

Ireland confessed here to a charge levelled against him by Edmond Malone in his *Inquiry*: that the model for his forged documents had been,

[24] See Peter Blayney, 'The Publication of Playbooks' in John D. Cox and David Scott Kastan, eds, *A New History of Early English Drama* (New York, 1997), pp. 383–422.

[25] Marcus Walsh, 'Form and Function in the English Eighteenth-Century Literary Edition: The Case of Edward Capell', *Studies in Bibliography*, 54 (2001), 225–42 (at p. 232).

[26] W. H. Ireland, *Confessions*, pp. 71–2.

[27] See De Grazia and Stallybrass, 'Materiality', pp. 280–2; Paul Needham, 'Concepts of Paper Study', in Daniel W. Mosser, Michael Saffle and Ernest W. Sullivan II, eds., *Puzzles in Paper: Concepts in Historical Watermarks* (New Castle, Delaware, 2000), pp. 1–36; and B. C. Barker-Benfield, comp., *Shelleyan Writing-Materials in the Bodleian Library: A Catalogue of Formats, Papers and Watermarks*, Bodleian Shelley Manuscripts, 23 (New York, 2002), pp. 7–23.

[28] W. H. Ireland, *Confessions*, p. 56. Malone's copy of the *Confessions* is now British Library C.182.aa.7; an initialled note in his hand on the front free endpaper announces that 'There is as much *falsehood* in this Rogue's *Account* of his impudent forgery, as there was in the forgery itself; for scarcely a single circumstance is represented truly in all its points. E. M.' (title-page –2r).

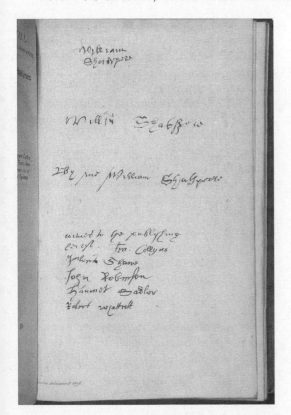

2 Facsimiles of Shakespeare's signature traced by George Steevens for *The Plays of William Shakespeare*, ed. Samuel Johnson and George Steevens, 10 vols. (London, 1778), plate facing vol. 1, p. 200.

paradoxically, the authenticating facsimile reproductions of Shakespeare's genuine signatures in the 1778 Johnson-Steevens edition. 'In the year 1776', Malone recalled, 'Mr. Steevens, in my presence, traced with the utmost accuracy the three signatures affixed by the poet to his Will.'[29] These tracings became the basis for an engraved plate first published in 1778 (see illustration 2). But a later dispute about whether the signatures spelled *Shakspeare* or *Shakspere* caused Malone to reassess and consult again the original documents; by 1796 he was convinced that Shakespeare wrote his name 'SHAKSPERE'. From this followed, he argued, a fact devastating to Ireland's claims to authenticity:

it is manifest that he wrote it himself SHAKSPERE; and therefore if any original Letter or other MS. of his

shall ever be discovered, his name will appear in that form. The necessary consequence is, that these papers, in which a different orthography is almost uniformly found, cannot but be a forgery.[30]

It is one of Malone's happiest moments in the *Inquiry*: 'if Mr. Steevens and I had maliciously intended to lay a trap for this fabricator to fall into, we could not have done the business more adroitly', he chuckled without humour. Yet the means of that trap, the facsimile on which Ireland relied, remains undiscussed here.

At one level there is an unremarked circularity to these textual transactions: the Shakespeare papers created with a facsimile as their model came themselves to be facsimiles, expensively reproduced in the *Miscellaneous Papers*. But that relation of manuscript and print here placed under tension only activates a longer-running tension in the genealogy of the word, which moves between manuscript and print across its history of use. Thomas Fuller, in his *Worthies*, remarked of one who, 'though a quick Scribe, is but a dull one, who is good only at *fac simile*, to transcribe out of an original' (1667; *OED*). Fuller's terms resonate with those that the Ireland forgeries put in play at the close of the eighteenth century: scribal culture and print culture are entangled as texts move between modes. Ireland, as he 'penned his effusion', participates in a continuity of scribal practice – transcription from an original – that he, at the same time, subverts. Ireland's 'making like', though it is still a matter of transcription, is also a matter of invention.

[29] Edmond Malone, *An Inquiry into the Authenticity of Certain Miscellaneous Papers and Legal Instruments* (London, 1796), p. 117; William Carstairs, *Lectures on the Art of Writing* (London, 1816), p. 106, provided advice on '*Directions for preparing Paper to trace on*. Take a sheet of bank [sic] post paper, and rub it well all over on both sides with a feather dipt in sweet oil; take a small linen cloth, and rub the sheet perfectly dry, and then hold it before the fire a few minutes, when it will be ready for use. Then lay the prepared sheet upon the copy you intend to trace, and the writing will appear clear and perfect through it. In this manner, any form of writing whatever may be copied or imitated.'

[30] Malone, *Inquiry*, p. 121.

The twenty-two plates of Shakespeare's authentic hand were engraved for the folio *Miscellaneous Papers* by John Girtin, brother of the watercolourist Thomas Girtin.[31] Girtin was perhaps an odd choice to engrave the plates, or perhaps merely unusual: certainly he does not figure among the engravers most associated with the trade and publications of writing-masters and their copy books surveyed by Ambrose Heal in 1931.[32] Heal reveals the extent of the trade, which had its origins back in the late sixteenth-century, contemporary with the presumed date of the Ireland forgeries.[33] Facsimiles of engraved hands were not at all uncommon in the years around the Ireland forgeries: in the previous year, 1795, for instance, William Milns's *The Penman's Repository*, 'CONTAINING | Seventy Correct Alphabets, | a Valuable SELECTION of flourishes | *and a* | Variety of new Designs', was produced entirely without letterpress, each of its plates engraved with model alphabets and exercises.[34] These engraved hands and alphabets were designed to facilitate precisely that imitative transcriptional practice adopted and subverted by Ireland in his forgeries: keeping the engraved hand in front of him, the new scribe was to copy and make his own the hand in front of him.[35] But Ireland's forgeries work in the opposite direction: the engraved hand in front of him is reproduced in the forgeries, and with it a claim to status. To recognize as much is to be reminded again of the persistent way in which his forgeries work to unsettle relationships between manuscript and print, both historically and practically. As facsimiles of handwriting were a recognized, if now little discussed, part of the book trade, Ireland, the trainee attorney's clerk, disturbs even as he reinscribes those relationships.[36]

This can be seen clearly in the *Miscellaneous Papers*, where the relation of its letter press to its engraved facsimiles is another of the areas in which the folio differs from the derivative octavo edition. Where the octavo edition presents its transcriptions of the letters in standard left-to-right, descending type lines, the folio edition offers its readers what presents itself as a fully diplomatic transcription of the texts. The opening which faces the facsimile of 'Queen Elizabeth's Letter' with its letter press transcription is a case in point. The book keeps the italic heading, '*Queen Elizabeth's Letter*', on the recto as expected in the headline of the page; but it uses different sized fonts, set vertically from the foot to the head of the page to transcribe the text of Elizabeth's letter and Shakespeare's endorsement; this aligns it with the facing facsimile of the 'original' letter. A third font is set, inverted, at the foot of the recto to transcribe the Queen's direction 'For Master William | Shakspeare | atte the Globe bye | Thames'. A similar principle is evident in the facing facsimile and typographic transcription of Shakespeare's '*Verses to Anna Hatherrewaye*': the five stanzas, set one below another in the octavo edition, are here set in the folio as they appear on the facsimile, at ninety degrees to the regular portrait orientation of the page in an x-shape, stanza 3 at the centre, with stanzas 1 and 4 at the head, and 2 and 5 at the feet, of the cross lines. This is not the same conception of 'significant space' in manuscript as Jonathan Gibson has recently outlined; but it is nonetheless a conception of the ways in which space

---

[31] Biographies of John Girtin are provided alongside his brother's life in Thomas Girtin and David Loshak, *The Art of Thomas Girtin* (London, 1954); *Oxford Dictionary of National Biography*, gen. eds H. C. G. Matthew and Brian Harrison, 60 vols (Oxford: Oxford University Press, 2004), vol. 22, pp. 351–54.

[32] Ambrose Heal, *The English Writing-Masters and Their Copy-Books, 1570–1800: A Biographical Dictionary & A Bibliography* (London, 1931).

[33] See H. R. Woudhuysen, *Sir Philip Sidney and the Circulation of Manuscripts, 1558–1640* (Oxford, 1996), pp. 29–45; as Woudhuysen notes, 'the links between writing-masters, engravers, heralds, painters, and silversmiths deserve further investigation' (at pp. 35–6).

[34] William Milns, *The Penman's Repository* (London, 1795), first published in 1787; on Milns, see Heal, *English Writing-Masters*, p. 76, and on Ashby, Heal, *English Writing-Masters*, p. 6.

[35] Tamara Plakins Thornton has some provocative thoughts on this relationship in *Handwriting in America: A Cultural History* (New Haven, 1996), pp. 3–41.

[36] Also involved is the relationship between letterpress and copperplate printing, on which see Roger Gaskell, 'Printing House and Engraving Shop: A Mysterious Collaboration', *The Book Collector*, 53 (2004), 213–51.

(*mise-en-page*) creates meaning in texts.[37] Typography and page make-up are here used to create an authentic typographical representation of an engraved facsimile that is itself claiming and creating a version of manuscript authenticity. What is more, the situation recreates in print that described at Norfolk Street in Caldecott's letter, with the 'original' forgeries being accompanied by documents that move between being translations, decipherings or transcriptions.

The legal documents printed in the *Miscellaneous Papers* use their materiality to similar effect. The '*Agreement with John Lowine*' and the '*Agreement with Henry Condelle*', both letter press transcriptions, have at their foot engraved plates of the signatures and wax seals of the parties making them. In these pages, the distinction that had been maintained between the separate printing of the engravings and the letterpress – one on a rolling press, the other on a screw press – has been broken. These two 'agreements', though they contain letterpress, are included under the 'DIRECTIONS TO THE BINDER', suggesting that they were machined twice, separately from those sheets containing only letterpress. Here we see the *Miscellaneous Papers* reminding us of the many book trades, plural: the sheets run off on the rolling press rely upon the sense of the book's binder – not its author, its printer, or its publisher – to link them up with the body of the text. The allied book trades here place and contain the energies of the forgeries which are at work to disturb those locations and containments: the whole of Ireland's textual culture – by which I mean manuscript, print, and all the institutions, discursive and material, that produce texts and readers – are engaged by the forgeries.[38] Even the ink in which they were written had a provenance in the trades. The ink was obtained, Ireland wrote, from 'a bookbinder of the name of Laurie, who had bound many books for me, and resided in New Inn Passage, within two minutes' walk of the gentleman's chambers under whom I was articled to study the law as a chancery conveyancer'; it was made up for him from 'three different liquids used by bookbinders in marbling the covers of their calf bindings'.[39]

From these examples it is clear that the relation of the forgeries to their own textual culture – the contemporary ways in which texts are produced by, and circulate in, a culture – is complicated and dynamic; they work not only to unsettle the distinction between authentic and *in*authentic, but to uneasy effect between manuscript and print. The forgeries serve, too, to unsettle the relationships between the various allied book trades. We are all growing tired even of the *ambiguous* triumph of print; but here is a moment, precisely when by recent accounts, that triumph takes ambiguous effect, that we might again question it, precisely because of the apparent persistence of early modern manuscript and print culture into these later events and institutions.

For these reasons Caldecott's letter, too, has its own unexamined textuality, a textuality that takes us a good way back into the matter of the forgeries themselves: Ireland's forgeries, like Caldecott's letter, depart from, and find their way back into, books. Ireland, stirred by the success of his first forgeries, needed more blank paper on which to produce others: 'I applied', he confessed, 'to a bookseller named Verey, in Great May's Buildings, St Martin's Lane, who, for the sum of five shillings, suffered me to take from all the folio and quarto volumes in his shop the fly-leaves which they contained.'[40] Later participants in the affair often chose to interleave their copies of the

---

[37] Jonathan Gibson, 'Significant Space in Manuscript Letters', *The Seventeenth Century*, 12 (1997), 1–9, and his 'Letters' in Michael Hattaway, ed., *A Companion to English Renaissance Literature and Culture* (Oxford, 2000), pp. 615–9; Maureen Bell, '*Mise-en-page*, illustration, expressive form', in John Barnard and D. F. McKenzie, with the assistance of Maureen Bell, eds., *The Cambridge History of the Book in Britain, Volume 4, 1557–1695* (Cambridge, 2002), pp. 632–5; Sue Walker, 'The Manners of the Page: Prescription and Practice in the Visual Organization of Correspondence', *Huntington Library Quarterly*, 66 (2003), 307–29.

[38] William St. Clair, *The Reading Nation in the Romantic Period* (Cambridge, 2004) explores the full range of these institutions and their relationships.

[39] W. H. Ireland, *Confessions*, pp. 39–40; I intend to write elsewhere on the textual culture of the law in this period.

[40] W. H. Ireland, *Confessions*, pp. 70–1.

publications with original forgeries, or, on occasion, later forgeries deliberately produced by Ireland for the purpose.[41] This interleaving of manuscript and print binds in Caldecott's letter, too: it is now bound as a two-leaf flyleaf in a composite collection of octavo tracts relating to the Shakespeare papers owned by the Folger Shakespeare Library. The volume, still in its eighteenth-century calf binding, contains in fact two manuscript letters, one at either end as front and endpapers; they hold between them ten printed interventions in the controversy, among them William-Henry Ireland's *An Authentic Account of the Shaksperian Manuscripts, &c* and his father, Samuel Ireland's *Mr. Ireland's Vindication of his Conduct* (both 1796) and *An Investigation of Mr. Malone's Claim to the Character of Scholar, or Critic* (1797).[42] Caldecott's letter, as front endpaper, offers a summative response to the printed debate that it precedes; the second letter, apparently unpublished, was addressed to Caldecott by an unidentified correspondent, and describes the first and only performance of Vortigern at Kemble's Drury Lane (this letter is dated 4 April 1796). Holding between them the printed record of the controversy, the two letters remind us that yet another institution besides the cultures of print and manuscript was involved in the Ireland affair: the theatre, its audience yet another witness to the matter of Shakespearean authenticity.

Moreover, like Caldecott's letter, Ireland's forgeries are social texts: they create and record social as well as textual relationships. That it should be two letters that enclose and moderate the printed pamphlets serves to bind them securely in the world of manuscript, and particularly the manuscript letter. For the letter is characteristically the genre which Ireland's forgeries inhabit, the *letter* being a form that requires us axiomatically to understand it socially as well as bibliographically. This was an understanding, however unexamined, clearly available to Ireland: his forged Shakespearean correspondence is from the very outset social. 'Queen Elizabeth's Letter', the first of the miscellaneous papers printed, immediately locates itself within a manuscript economy of textual exchange: 'WEE didde receive youre prettye Verses goode Masterre William through the hands off oure Lorde Chamberlayne', the queen writes, 'ande wee doe Complemente thee onne theyre great excellence' (see illustration 3, where this portion of the letter is illustrated from the facsimile in *An Inquiry*, set against Malone's authentic examples of Elizabeth's hand).[43] This letter, addressed 'For Master William | Shakspeare | atte the Globe bye | Thames', moves back to Shakespeare from the queen just as his verses made their way to her through the Lord Chamberlain; texts are transmitted through offices and to locations by named and nameless intermediaries in this fictive manuscript economy. Shakespeare's endorsement to the letter – 'Thys Letterre I dydde receyve fromme mye most gracyouse Ladye Elyzabethe and I doe requeste itte maye bee kepte with alle care possyble' – casts that manuscript economy forwards into the future of its discovery by Ireland: once transmitted by, it now serves as a material record of, a network of manuscript and social exchange between the poet and the theatre, the queen and her court, and the courtiers whose offices bridge those two locations. This economy is imagined as it is forged by Ireland, but it looks very like those exchanges that form the basis of the work by Harold Love, Arthur Marotti, Henry Woudhuysen, and Peter Beal that has recovered such real historical exchanges in vibrant detail.[44]

Shakespeare's correspondence with the Earl of Southampton again links the court with the

---

41 British Library Add. MSS 12501–2 contain 'original' forgeries bound alongside printed sheets from their publication; Folger Shakespeare Library MSS w.b.496 and w.a.209–10 are interleaved and extra-illustrated exempla of Ireland's *Confessions* (1805), the last his own copy.

42 PR 2950 B5 Cage Copy 2; the second letter is not mentioned by Schoenbaum, 'The Ireland Forgeries'.

43 Samuel Ireland *Miscellaneous Papers*, sig. A1r; further references follow in text.

44 See Harold Love, *Scribal Publication in Seventeenth-Century England* (Oxford, 1993); Arthur Marotti, *Manuscript, Print, and the English Renaissance Lyric* (Ithaca, 1995); Woudhuysen, *Sidney and the Circulation of Manuscripts, 1558–1640*; and Peter Beal, *In Praise of Scribes: Manuscripts and their Makers in Seventeenth-Century England* (Oxford, 1998).

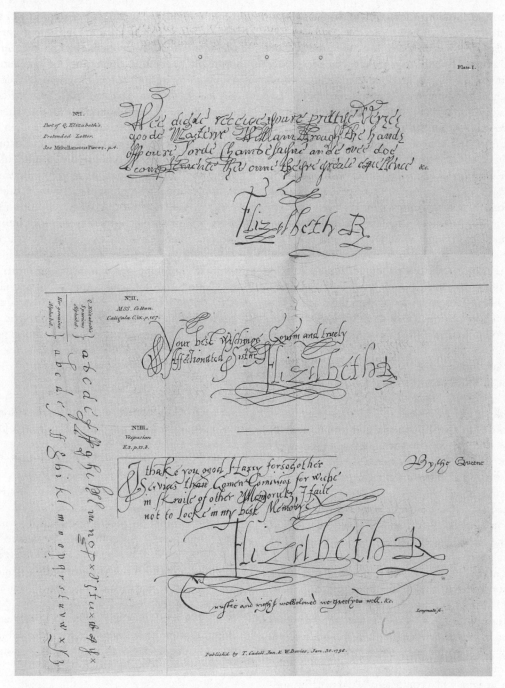

3 Facsimiles of William-Henry Ireland's forged 'Elizabethan' hand set against authentic facsimiles of her hand engraved by Barak Longmate for Edmond Malone, *An Inquiry into the Authenticity of Certain Miscellaneous Papers and Legal Instruments* (London, 1796), plate facing p. 111.

theatre as locations of textual exchange. Shakespeare's '*Copye of mye Letter toe hys grace offe Southampton*' is at one level (as Schoenbaum points out) a ruse of Ireland's to account for the presence of a letter in the supposedly discovered archive whose original could not have been retained by Shakespeare (sig. A3v); but, ruse or not, copied letters were common in the early modern period, part not only of a secretary's role but of many other authors' and collectors' too.[45] There is an irony, moreover, in this document's itself being notionally a *Shakespearian* copy of a Shakespearian original: even in their initial contexts, the discovered Shakespeare papers were caught up in reproduction. Southampton's reply, addressed 'To the Globe Theatre | Forre Mast' Willam | Shakspeare', creates the theatre again as a site of ongoing manuscript activity (sig. A4r); Shakespeare's letter to his '*Worthye Freynde*', Richard Cowley, widens the reach of this manuscript culture to include Cowley's 'dwellynge atte oune Masterre | Holliss a draperre inne | the Wattlynge Streete | Londonne', this letter enclosing another text with it, 'a whymsycalle conceyte whiche I doe suppose thou wilt easylye discoverre' (sig. B1v). Ireland's conceit in all of this is anything but whymsical: these letters remain as a record of the paralleled social and manuscript networks within which they and other texts might have moved. Letters delivered to the court, the theatre, or a draper's shop for their addressees to collect; retained copies of letters; manuscript ephemera enclosed with other texts: all point towards the socialised textual practice reflected and at the same time created by the letters and their circulation.

These are forgeries not so much of text, then, as of context: they are forgeries of a textual culture that is set within, and serves as an earnest of, a wider culture. As such they represent an attempt to understand, at the same time as to produce, an account of how texts function within a much wider economy of exchange. Ireland's forgeries, at the same time as they imagine and reconstruct a world of early modern textuality, point up for us today the continuities between that imagined early modern culture of circulating texts and their own late eighteenth-century textuality, itself not less a product of textual exchange and circulation. One support for this argument is, oddly enough, the text that served primarily to destroy the claims for authenticity mounted by Ireland's forgeries: Edmond Malone's *An Inquiry into the Authenticity of Certain Miscellaneous Papers and Legal Instruments* (1796). There is at one level, here, a familiar enough paradox: that forgery, the category of the *in*authentic, actually serves to produce and establish the category of the authentic; the production of forgery produces at the same time the means of its detection.[46] But this paradox does not quite account for the insistent ways in which the determining factors of Ireland's forgeries then reach out to include the text that apparently refutes them, Malone's *Inquiry*. This, as we shall see, is no less a text whose authenticity is produced not only textually but socially – it is couched as a letter to Malone's Irish patron, James Caulfield, first earl of Charlemont – and one whose own textual practices bring together print and manuscript to unsettling effect.

II

The Earl of Charlemont was an awkward addressee for Malone's *Inquiry*, not least because, as a footnote on its first page acknowledged, the name of Malone's 'noble friend' had 'appeared in the List of Subscribers prefixed to the MISCELLANEOUS PAPERS'. (Malone himself, he makes clear elsewhere, had 'been forced to buy it (though no subscriber) in order to confute it'.) Malone's footnote continues: 'I am authorized by him to say, that he subscribed to that work at the request of a gentleman who furnished him with a splendid PROSPECTUS of it, which he carried hence to Ireland; and that if Lord C. had known as much of it as he now does, he would not have given either his name or his money to the publication.'[47] Malone's 'authorized' here pits one version of

---

[45] Gibson, 'Letters', p. 617.

[46] The paradox is well-described by De Grazia, *Shakespeare Verbatim*, pp. 86–7, 111.

[47] Malone, *Inquiry*, p. 1n.

authority, Charlemont's personal communication, against other earlier ones: the splendid prospectus, with its bibliographical claims for its subject, and more particularly the collocation of 'name' and 'money' that subscription publication brings together. Behind the fiction of the *Inquiry*'s generic status as 'A | LETTER | TO THE | EARL OF CHARLEMONT', a fiction only incidentally presented in a thick octavo volume of over 400 pages, are a series of manuscript letters from Malone to Charlemont, that give us another perspective on the textuality of this *Inquiry* and the forgeries it exposes.[48]

Writing from London on 29 December 1795, Malone told Charlemont of his progress in the composition of the *Inquiry*. The folio edition of the Shakespeare papers, he noted, 'were published last Thursday': 'the perusal of them has fully confirmed', he added, 'what I always thought, that they are direct and palpable forgeries.' The intention he announced to Charlemont was 'to draw up all my objections in form, and to address them to you in the way of a letter'; this, 'surrounded with dictionaries, etc.', he was in the process of doing, having 'advertised yesterday' the publication of a text that was not yet written. But that process of composition and publication is worth more attention, as Malone's account makes clear:

I hope to have finished the manuscript by Thursday night (I am now writing on Tuesday), to get to press on Friday, and to publish my letter on the 8th of January. I did intend to have sent you a written copy as soon as it is finished, but as that will create some delay I am sure you will excuse it, and instead of that, as soon as all the sheets are worked off at the press, I will transmit a copy to you (before publication) through Mr. Lees of the post office. I mean to have a fac-simile of lord Southampton's handwriting engraved, which I think may be done within the time. They have had the impudence to print a letter as his without a single trace of resemblance. The fact is, they had no archetype, and did not know there was any existing. The editor, a Mr Ireland, a broken Spitalfields weaver, aided by his son, an attorney's clerk, are without doubt the inventors, though to avoid being pelted in the newspapers by such men, I shall leave that matter in uncertainty, and merely confine myself to prove the forgery, let it come from where it may.[49]

Malone's account of the genesis of his *Inquiry* stands provocatively in relation to the textuality of the forgeries that it identifies. The text, as it is imagined moving from compositional manuscript to presentation transcript, momentarily occupies precisely that space of privileged, patronised textuality marked out by Shakespeare's forged correspondence with Southampton, the writer addressing his patron directly and particularly. Malone held back from creating such a presentation manuscript only for reasons of speed: it was the 'delay' of creating such a manuscript copy, rather than the inconvenience of producing one, that halted him. That such long transcripts could (apparently) easily be produced at this date makes me think that the persistence of manuscript and its functionaries still might not have been solidly enough stated: Malone's letters are full of such casually noticed gestures at a scribal culture within easy and unspectacular reach.[50]

As easily reached was Malone's engraver, Barak Longmate, who produced for the *Inquiry* the three plates that serve as Malone's primary tools in his demolition of the forgeries.[51] With Longmate's engraved plates, Malone demonstrated (as we have seen) Ireland's reliance on earlier facsimiles of Shakespeare's signature as the model for his own imitation hand. 'In copying his *name*', Malone wrote, 'the fabricator had for his direction the autographs with which we have furnished him, and therefore it is not at all surprising that here there should be some little resemblance to the archetypes before him; though even there the imitation, partly from inability and partly from caprice, is bungling and incorrect enough.'[52] The authentic is under

---

[48] In his working copy of *An Inquiry* (now British Library c.45.e.23), Malone struck through this generic fiction in his revisions towards a never-realised second edition.

[49] Edmond Malone to James Caulfield, 29 December 1795: *Charlemont Papers*, *HMC*, pp. 267–8.

[50] Other examples are discussed in my 'Edmond Malone and Early Modern Textual Culture', *The Yale University Library Gazette*, 79 (2004), 53–69.

[51] *Oxford Dictionary of National Biography*, vol. 34, pp. 408–9, under Barak Longmate (1737/8–93), his father.

[52] Malone, *Inquiry*, pp. 124–5.

pressure here from inability, but more pressingly from itself: Ireland's forgeries, prompted by and therefore identifiable by their reliance upon earlier facsimiles of Shakespeare's hand, are both produced by and work to complicate authenticity's later reproductions. For it is facsimile that complicates the opposition or interrelation I have been maintaining between manuscript and print, terms our understanding of which – just as much as 'Shakespeare' or 'the authentic' – are at the centre of the Ireland affair. Scholarly attention has recently returned to the status of the facsimile.[53] Here we see that the engraved hands of the eighteenth century copy book, or the facsimiles of Shakespearian signatures in eighteenth century editions of Shakespeare, are neither simply print *or* manuscript: they unsettle any neat opposition that might obtain between the two terms. Manuscripts and their culture persisted alongside print, as we are increasingly recognizing; but here we can see manuscripts and their culture not only persisting alongside but actually permeating print, copper engraved plates of hands making 'manuscript' something that can be produced on the press.

Yet it was not manuscript that Malone took, in the end, to authenticate the exemplum of the *Inquiry* that he sent to Charlemont, but the press and the postal service: 'as soon as all the sheets are worked off at the press', he told his patron, 'I will transmit a copy to you (before publication) through Mr. Lees of the post office.' In the way that 'publication' slipped referents in Caldecott's letter, so too does 'publication' waver in Malone's usage here. The generic pose of the *Inquiry*, a letter to the Earl of Charlemont, here becomes literalised: the *Inquiry* is confirmed again as a text whose meanings and whose authority are created socially as they are created bibliographically. This urge on Malone's part towards the personal and so therefore authenticated copy of the *Inquiry* is seen again in the exempla of the book that he presented to his friends and associates: books marked out not only by their manuscript inscriptions, but by their paper stock and their binding.[54] It is seen again, too, in the copy of the *Inquiry* that Malone kept for himself and massively annotated towards a never-realized second

edition: this copy, later owned by John Payne Collier – whose reasons for ownership must have been complex – is now in the British Library, interlined, enriched with marginalia, and often both interand extra-leaved.[55] This annotated copy refuses to let print remain stable: it pulls print's apparent fixity back into the fluidity of manuscript.[56] And even this copy, too, has its own reproductions: a text of the *Inquiry* now in the Beinecke Library at Yale is what we might call a twentieth century 'manuscript facsimile' of this annotated copy, with Malone's annotations transcribed word-for-word into it.[57]

The categories of manuscript and print, and the drives behind them, are those of the forgeries themselves. As should now be evident, the forgeries and their responses are recognisably the product of a late eighteenth-century textual culture even as they emphasize the connections between that culture and its Shakespearian precedents; as they imagine and reconstruct a Shakespearian textual culture, so do they create links between the textuality of their

---

[53] Joseph A. Danes, '"Ideal Copy" versus "Ideal Texts": The Application of Bibliographical Description to Facsimiles', *Papers of the Bibliographical Society of Canada*, 33 (1995), 31–50; H. R. Woudhuysen, '"Works of permanent utility": Editors and Texts, Authorities and Originals' in Lukas Erne and Margaret Jane Kidnie, eds, *Textual Performances: The Modern Reproduction of Shakespeare's Drama* (Cambridge, 2004), pp. 37–48.

[54] Presentation copies include those at the Beinecke Library, Yale, to Edmund Burke (Ig 6z y796mb), Albany Wallis (Osborn pc 46), Thomas Astle (Osborn pc 67), and James Boswell, junior (Tinker 1520); at the British Library, to the Rev. Clayton Cracherode (682.d.27); at Delaware University Library, to Francis Dudley Fitzmaurice (SC PR2950.M3 Copy 2); at the Folger Shakespeare Library, Washington DC, to Mrs Crewe (PR 2950 M32 Cage Copy 1), the Rev. Mr Mason (PR 2950 M32 Cage Copy 3), Miss Emily Jephson (PR 2950 M32 Cage Copy 4), and John Philip Kemble (PR 2950 M32 Cage Copy 5); and at the Lewis Walpole Library, Farmington, CT, to Isaac Reed (77 6z y796M).

[55] British Library c.45.e.23; Collier's later forged manuscript addition to this copy is discussed by Arthur Freeman and Janet Ing Freeman, *John Payne Collier: Scholarship & Forgery in the Nineteenth Century*, 2 vols (New Haven, 2004), p. 1139

[56] As David McKitterick has argued, the supposed fixity of print is itself increasingly recognised to be fluid: *Print, Manuscript, and the Search for Order* (Cambridge, 2003).

[57] It is now Beinecke Library, Yale University, Osborn pc 147.

present and the textuality of the past they fabri-
cate. Authenticity is in part, at least, a function of
technology in the Ireland forgeries: technologies of
manuscript, print, and facsimile both underwrite
and later expose the claims towards the authentic
that the documents caught up in the controversy
embody. But as authenticity is located precisely in
the documents at the centre of the Ireland affair,
so do they suggest that, if we are to locate the
authentic Shakespeare beyond or behind the documents that transmit him to us, it ought only to
be when we have a clearer sense of the materiality
of those documents themselves and of the spaces,
locations, and institutions in which they moved.
The Shakespeare who emerges from Ireland's *Miscellaneous Papers*, and Malone's *Inquiry*, might be a
poet and dramatist who spelled in a manner 'in
which no one ever was ever known to have printed
any more than to have written', but he is unavoidably a poet and dramatist who must be approached
directly through the evidence of manuscript and
print.

THE AUTHOR, THE EDITOR AND THE TRANSLATOR: WILLIAM SHAKESPEARE, ALEXANDER CHALMERS AND SÁNDOR PETŐFI OR THE NATURE OF A ROMANTIC EDITION

JÚLIA PARAIZS

Sándor Petőfi (1823–49), a major Romantic poet writing in Hungarian, translated William Shakespeare's *Coriolanus* in 1848. Whose *Coriolanus?*, we should pause and ask, bearing in mind the long and distinguished tradition of editing Shakespeare. Is it the *Coriolanus* of John Heminges and Henry Condell, Nicholas Rowe, Alexander Pope, Lewis Theobald, William Warburton, Thomas Hanmer, Samuel Johnson, Edward Capell, George Steevens and Isaac Reed, Edmond Malone and James Boswell, Samuel W. Singer, Charles Knight or John Payne Collier? Any historical survey on editing Shakespeare will reveal the differences between these editors, and monographs on the individual achievements often present the edition in question as a paradigm shift.[1] The corpus we know as 'Shakespeare' is redefined by each editor and in each edition.

However, some editions receive more and some less attention in this process of redefinition. The historiography of editing Shakespeare has its privileged areas of research. The textual schools of the twentieth century, New Bibliography and the post-structuralist schools triggered a new theoretical interest in both the seventeenth-century early printings and in the 'long eighteenth-century' of Shakespeare-editing (1709–1821).[2] On the contrary, the history of nineteenth-century editions is an under-researched field. Although Andrew

I would like to thank Dr John Jowett, the Library of the Shakespeare Birthplace Trust and the European Society for the Study of English for their help.

[1] See, for example, Barbara Mowat, 'The Reproduction of Shakespeare's Texts' in *Cambridge Companion to Shakespeare*, eds. Margreta de Grazia and Stanley Wells (Cambridge, 2001); Andrew Murphy, *Shakespeare in Print: A History and Chronology of Shakespeare Publishing* (Cambridge, 2003); Gary Taylor, *Reinventing Shakespeare: A Cultural History, from the Restoration to the Present* (New York, 1989); Paul Werstine, 'Shakespeare' in *Scholarly Editing: A Guide to Research*, ed. D. C. Greetham, (New York, 1995); Margreta de Grazia *Shakespeare Verbatim: The Reproduction of Authenticity and the 1790 Apparatus* (Oxford, 1991); Peter Martin, *Edmond Malone, Shakespeare Scholar: A Literary Biography* (Cambridge, 1995); G. F. Parker, *Johnson's Shakespeare* (Oxford, 1989); Peter Seary, *Lewis Theobald and the Editing of Shakespeare* (Oxford, 1990); Arthur Sherbo, *The Achievement of George Steevens* (New York, 1990).

[2] See for example: Matthew W. Black and Matthias A. Shaaber, *Shakespeare's Seventeenth-Century Editors 1632–1685*, (New York, 1937); Lukas Erne and Margaret Jane Kidnie, eds., *Textual Performances: The Modern Reproduction of Shakespeare's Drama* (Cambridge, 2004); Joanna Gondris, ed., *Reading Readings: Essays on Shakespeare Editing in the Eighteenth-century* (Madison, NJ, 1997); Simon Jarvis, *Scholars and Gentlemen: Shakespearean Textual Criticism and Representation of Scholarly Labour, 1725–1765* (Oxford, 1995); David Kastan, *Shakespeare and the Book* (Cambridge, 2001); John Jowett and Gary Taylor, *Shakespeare Reshaped, 1606–1623* (Oxford, 1993); Marcus Walsh, *Shakespeare, Milton and Eighteenth-Century Literary Editing: The Beginnings of Interpretative Scholarship* (Cambridge, 1997).

Murphy in his indispensable *Shakespeare in Print* devotes two chapters to the popular and scholarly editions in the nineteenth-century from the perspectives of editing and publishing, by the nature of such a comprehensive historical account it cannot extend to case studies.

In the literature, nineteenth-century editors are either perceived as derivative of the grand eighteenth-century traditions or as representatives of an interim period (in want of theory) falling in between two great centuries of Shakespearean editorial theory. For the first attitude I quote Andrew Murphy who writes that 'the eighteenth-century editorial tradition cast something of a long shadow beyond its own immediate period' and '[m]ost of the editions produced for the popular market over the course of the 1800s were highly derivative'.[3] To illustrate the second claim, Paul Werstine notes when comparing the editions of Charles Knight (idealizing the Folio) and John Payne Collier (championing the Quartos) that '[t]he wide differences between the editions of Knight and Collier testify to the lack of consensus on the relations among the early printed texts. No theory was available in the absence of documents that could be construed as the ground of such a theory.'[4]

Alexander Chalmers (1759–1834), the editor whose 'Shakespeare' Sándor Petőfi used in translating *Coriolanus*, does not appear in the historical surveys. In this article I set out with the objective of establishing him as a major Romantic editor of Shakespeare. His absence from these histories may be attributed to the same reason why editions in the nineteenth-century (especially the first three decades) have received less scholarly attention. Since most histories on editing Shakespeare are written with an interest in editorial and textual theories the nineteenth century features as a shadowy period. Seen from a cultural and reception history point of view, however, an early nineteenth-century edition like Chalmers's opens up new insights into the premises of editing yet another 'Shakespeare', a new editorial response to the previous tradition, and into the way Shakespeare was read and produced in Romanticism.

To start with: how do we ascertain which edition Petőfi used when translating *Coriolanus*? There are a number of pieces of external evidence. There is an English language Shakespeare edition which in 1848 was in Petőfi's library of several hundred books.[5] As the title page announced it was printed from the 'Correct and Esteemed Edition of Alexander Chalmers' and published by Baudry's European Library in Paris in 1838.[6] Chalmers based his edition on the Johnson–Steevens–Reed variorum edition of 1803. When in 1850 Austrian authorities confiscated Petőfi's property the Shakespeare edition of 1838 appeared on the list of his confiscated books carefully recording all the bibliographical details.[7] Only twenty-eight books of his collection survived the turns of Hungarian history, and fortunately the edition is available in the Literature Museum's Library, Budapest. The edition contains Petőfi's holograph signature saying 'Petőfi Sándor's' on the beginning waste page of the edition. There is also a preliminary plan drafted by Petőfi on the division of labour between himself and fellow poet, Mihály Vőrősmarty, the translator of the first classical Shakespeare translation in Hungarian, *Julius Caesar*. Petőfi lists the plays, attaching the name of the translator and the number of pages. The page numbers coincide with the page numbering of the Chalmers edition.

Textual evidence also proves that Petőfi used this particular edition. Zoltán Ferenczi, the first textual critic to have the Chalmers edition in hand, compared a few textual cruces and emendations in *Coriolanus* and the way Petőfi translated them in the notes of his 1916 edition such as 'heart' vs 'herd', 'hope' vs 'holpe', 'waves' vs 'weeds', 'scale' vs 'stale', 'contending' vs

---

[3] Murphy, *Shakespeare in Print*, p. 188.

[4] Werstine, 'Shakespeare', p. 263.

[5] *Petőfi Sándor Összes Művei* (PSÖM), (Collected Works of Petőfi), ed. Béla Varjas, Vilma B. Nyilassy, József Kiss (Budapest, 1956), vol.5, p. 250.

[6] *The Complete Works of William Shakespeare with Explanatory Notes by the Most Eminent Commentators. Accurately Printed from the Correct and Esteemed Edition of Alexander Chalmers, F.S.A.* 2 vols. (Paris, 1838).

[7] PSÖM, vol. 5, p. 251.

'contenning' with the Chalmers edition opting for the former (always following the textual choices of the Johnson-Steevens–Reed edition). The importance of establishing the source edition of the translation is evident from the critical reception of Petőfi's translation. The first two critics who carried out the philological work to compare the translation with the original, Gyula Haraszti in 1889 and Adolf Havas in 1895, admittedly did not have the Chalmers edition in hand (as it was in the private ownership of the Szigligeti family at that time), and made several charges against Petőfi mistranslating the play on the grounds of different editions, and different textual choices.[8]

There is no indication how much Petőfi knew about the textual history of Shakespeare's plays or the number of editions available in English. The only remark concerning his Shakespeare translation is found in his correspondence with János Arany, poet and translator of Shakespeare plays:

I am sending on the following page excerpts from *Coriolanus*. From these you will be able to determine what liberties I had taken with its form and content; I do not think one could ask any more from the Hungarian language than what I have given here . . . Here and there I end up with a line that is longer than the original, but even the famous Schlegel, who is a German, does this, and to translate English into German is a veritable child's play in comparison to translating it into Hungarian.[9]

Yet Petőfi would have been aware of some of the problems of the Shakespearean text, had he read through Chalmers's 'Life of Shakespeare' in the 1838 edition. It includes a passage about textual problems:

It is unfortunate, however, for all wishes and all conjectures, that not a line of Shakespeare's manuscript is known to exist, and his prose writings are no where hinted at. We are in possession of printed copies only of his plays and poems, and those so depraved by carelessness and ignorance, that all the labour of all his commentators has not yet been able to restore them to more than a probable purity. Many of the difficulties which originally attended the perusal of them yet remain, and will require, what it is now scarcely possible to expect, greater sagacity and more happy conjecture than have hitherto been employed.

No matter how well-informed or uninformed a Hungarian poet was about Shakespearian textual studies he had an edition on his desk in its materiality. We have no information on how Petőfi acquired the edition in question, whether it was a conscious choice or he got hold of it accidentally, and whether he knew anything about the quality of the edition he was working from. Yet, do we know more? What do we know about Alexander Chalmers as a Shakespeare editor? What was the scholarly value of Chalmers's edition and where does it fit in the editorial tradition of English language 'Shakespeares'?

There is hardly any literature on Alexander Chalmers and on his activities as a Shakespeare editor. As Edward P. Willey notes, even though Chalmers was a man of reputation among his contemporaries as a result of his writings for periodicals and his wide range of work for the London booksellers, he is usually 'associated with the shadowy laborers of the age of early literary scholarship.'[10] Willey adds that there is no satisfying primary bibliography on Chalmers as the two existing sources are an obituary notice in the *Gentleman's Magazine* (*GM*) by John Bowyer Nichols, and the second a *Dictionary of National Biography* (*DNB*) entry on Chalmers, which is a selective reprinting of *GM* information with no revision of scholarship.[11] In his article Willey attempts to provide a sketch of his journalistic work, and a chronological bibliographical listing of his editorial work for the booksellers with annotations.

---

8 Gyula Haraszti, 'Petőfi Coriolánja' in *Egyetemes Philologiai Közlöny* 1889; Adolf Havas, ed., *Petőfi Sándor Vegyes Művei*, (I.) (Athenaeum, 1895). On the history of the ownership of the Shakespeare edition see *Beszéli tárgyak: a Petőfi család relikviá* (Budapest, 1997).

9 Thomas Raymond Mark, *Shakespeare in Hungary. A History of Translation, Presentation, and Reception of Shakespeare's Dramas in Hungary, 1785–1878.* (Doctoral Dissertation: Columbia University, 1955), p. 231.

10 Edward P. Willey, 'The Works of Alexander Chalmers, Journalist, Editor, Biographer', *Bulletin of Research in the Humanities* 86 (1983), p. 94.

11 Willey, p. 94.

The sources above reveal that Chalmers had written extensively for the periodical press (*St James Chronicle, Morning Chronicle, Gentleman's Magazine*), edited three London newspapers (*London Packet, Public Ledger, Morning Herald*), and superintended approximately thirty editions for the London booksellers. As John Bowyer Nichols noted, 'no men ever edited so many works as Chalmers for the booksellers of London'.[12] His first work as editor appeared in 1793 and the last dated edition in 1826. Chalmers edited (among others) the works of Robert Burns (1804), William Shakespeare (1805, 1823), Samuel Johnson (1806, 1823), and Henry Fielding (1806). In his edition *The British Essayists: With Prefaces Historical and Biographical* in 45 volumes he reprints the entire runs of the *Tatler, Spectator, Guardian, Rambler, Adventurer, World, Connoisseur, Idler, Mirror, Lounger*, and *Observer*. As Willey remarks, the collection 'even today is the means by which many libraries maintain on their shelves these early journals'.[13] As Bonnie Ferrero notes, Chalmers was an active participant in determining the authorship of Johnsonian works in the periodical press, most of which Johnson published anonymously.[14] Chalmers's own essays were printed monthly in the *Gentleman's Magazine* for eight years under the title 'Projector' and are, according to Willey, in direct line of descent from the *Tatler* and *Spectator*.[15]

Bonnie Ferrero in her article shows the impact of Chalmers on the formation of the Johnson canon as we know it today, and it also sheds light on the quality of Chalmers's literary scholarship. As Ferrero writes, 'Alexander Chalmers's 1823 edition of Johnson's Works contributed in many ways to advance what we know of Johnson the writer' by discovering new pieces and excising incorrectly attributed ones. Ferrero adds that Chalmers 'by 1823, produced a collection that had stood the test of time'[16] since '[m]ost of the pieces attributed to Johnson by Chalmers have met with acceptance by Johnsonian scholars'.[17]

Ferrero and Willey both point out a recurring motif in Chalmers's afterlife. While his notes are often incorporated in subsequent editions, often without crediting him, 'many of Chalmers' contributions to Johnsonian studies are anonymous'.[18] Willey notes in regard to Chalmers's edition of *The Works of the English Poets, from Chaucer to Cowper* (1810) that while 'many of the works by minor writers are available in no other edition' full or selective reprints give either no or very brief mention of Chalmers.[19] One notable exception, pointed out by Ferrero, is a credit to Chalmers's scholarly work by Edmond Malone. Malone in a note to his own edition of James Boswell's *Life of Johnson* (1807) states that certain pieces in the chronology of the works had been suggested to him by Chalmers (who later published his own edition of Boswell's *Life* in 1822).[20]

Ferrero claims that 'one continuous thread throughout this career is his engagement with works by, and about Samuel Johnson'.[21] We may also consider Chalmers's work on Shakespeare as a further advance on his contributions to the Johnson canon since he based his first Shakespeare edition on the Johnson–Steevens–Reed variorum of 1803, an edition tracing back its origins to Johnson's landmark edition of 1765. Steevens was collaborating with Johnson already in the 1765 edition as he added a list of the extant Shakespeare quartos to the end of volume 8 and forty-nine notes to the appendix.[22] Steevens's own editions were revisions of Johnson's 1765 edition.

The next link in the chain of the editorial tradition was Isaac Reed. As Arthur Sherbo points out, the literary executor of the Steevens tradition was Isaac Reed since Steevens left his notes

---

[12] *The Dictionary of National Biography*, p. 1353.

[13] Willey, p. 99.

[14] Bonnie Ferrero, 'Alexander Chalmers and the Canon of Samuel Johnson', *British Journal for Eighteenth-century Studies* 22 (1999), p. 173.

[15] Willey, p. 98.

[16] Ferrero, pp. 183–84.

[17] Ferrero, p. 186.

[18] Ferrero, p. 178.

[19] Willey, pp 101–2

[20] Ferrero, p. 184.

[21] Ferrero, p. 186.

[22] Arthur Sherbo, Arthur, *The Achievement of George Steevens* (New York, 1990), p xi.

and the completion of his last edition to Reed. Reed wrote that the 1803 edition contained 'the last improvements and corrections by Mr Steevens, by whom it was prepared for the press'.[23] This edition was published three years after Steevens's death in 1800, and it is the so-called fifth variorum following the 1773, 1778, 1785 and 1793 Steevens editions. George Steevens was involved in the editions of 1765, 1773, 1778, 1785, 1793 and Isaac Reed in the 1785, 1793 and 1803 editions.

The established tradition had become mainstream. Jaggard's *Shakespeare Bibliography* lists 352 complete works of Shakespeare (including all English language editions published in the United States, Leipzig and Paris etc.) between the year 1803 (when the last edition of George Steevens appeared) and 1847 (when Petőfi started the translation).[24] The two editors dominating Shakespeare editing from the last third of the eighteenth century to the second half of the nineteenth are George Steevens and Edmond Malone. While today Malone is perceived as the first modern editor, especially since the publication of Margreta de Grazia's *Shakespeare Verbatim* (Oxford, 1991), in the period Steevens seems to have been more popular, at least when it comes to the quantity of Shakespeare editions. Between 1773 (the publication year of the first Johnson–Steevens variorum) and 1847 Steevens's editions were published fifty-six times, whereas between 1780 (Malone's publication of his *Supplement* to the 1778 Johnson–Steevens variorum) and 1847 the Malone editions were published twenty-five times.[25]

As Andrew Murphy shows in *Shakespeare in Print* the rate of publication of Shakespeare editions accelerated dramatically during the nineteenth century.[26] He adds that '[m]ost of the editions produced for the popular market over the course of the 1800s were highly derivative, with a great number of them – at least in the first half of the century – being based on the later Johnson-Steevens-Reed and Malone texts'.[27] Following Murphy's categorization, the Chalmers edition would be one of these derivative texts, based on the scholarly edition of the Johnson–Steevens–Reed variorum published in 1803. Murphy mentions

Chalmers only in the appendix in his listing of complete editions up to 1821.[28]

Chalmers himself recognizes his indebtedness to Steevens, yet we should be careful to understand derivative as a derogatory term. Even the editions of Steevens and Malone have a clear line of succession to the Fourth (and not the First) Folio. As Paul Werstine reminds us, the first major eighteenth-century-editor, Nicholas Rowe marked up a copy of the Fourth Folio in 1709; Alexander Pope based his edition on Rowe, Theobald used Pope's edition. Johnson turned to Theobald's fourth edition of 1757.[29] Steevens used Johnson's, and Simon Jarvis draws our attention to the fact that Malone's 1790 edition relied on the Steevens–Reed edition of 1785. Malone collated this Steevens edition line by line with the First Folio and those quartos he considered authoritative.[30] The variorum tradition itself comprises, in the words of Joanna Gondris, the 'interpretative comprehensiveness' of eighteenth-century editing, which is the peak of the received text tradition and is emblematic of the continuity of the work of various editors.[31]

As Chalmers admits in the Preface to his first Shakespeare edition published in 1805, his work is largely indebted to George Steevens in at least two major ways. First, the work, as Chalmers recalled, 'was suggested by the Proprietors of Mr Steevens's elaborate edition' (in 1802 as we learn from his revised Preface of 1823), a claim investing some legitimacy in Chalmers as editor originating from Steevens through the edition's proprietors. Second, Chalmers added that he derived some of his editorial principles directly from Steevens's remark in

---

23 Sherbo, p. 199.
24 William Jaggard, *Shakespeare Bibliography* (Stratford-on Avon, 1911), pp. 509–26.
25 Jaggard, pp. 644–5 (Steevens), p. 206 (Malone).
26 Murphy, p. 167.
27 Murphy, p. 188.
28 Murphy, p. 342.
29 Werstine, p. 256.
30 Jarvis, p. 185.
31 On the variorum tradition see Joanna Gondris, '"All This Farrago": The Eighteenth-Century Shakespeare Variorum Page as a Critical Structure', in *Reading Readings*.

his own preface; as Chalmers writes, 'Mr Steevens in his Advertisement to the edition of 1793, after apologizing for the prolixity and number of his notes, seems to anticipate the time when "a judicious and frugal selection may be made from the labours of all".'

In his preface Chalmers explicitly confessed a continuity with the Johnson-Steevens tradition yet at the same time he introduced significant changes to the variorum style of editing. Colin Franklin points out Chalmers's contribution to the history of Shakespeare editing by starting his entry on the 1805 edition as follows:

[t]his admirable edition in nine volumes had a finer pedigree and more interesting place in the canon than has usually been acknowledged . . . his Shakespeare is remarkable in many ways. The 'Series of Engravings, from the original design of Henry Fuseli, Esq. R. A., Professor of Painting' has not passed unnoticed, but Chalmers was responsible for what he called 'the first attempt that has been made to concentrate the information given in the copious notes of the various commentators within a moderate space, and with an attention rather to their conclusions than to their premises'.

At the end of his evaluation of the 1805 edition Franklin judges that '[i]t was the first modern edition, departing from the habit of variorum commentary'.[32]

In the history of editing Shakespeare I propose to see Chalmers as a Romantic editor. On the one hand Chalmers relied on the grand tradition of neo-classical editing in the eighteenth century and on the other hand broke with that tradition in various ways. Chalmers reduced the sizeable variorum apparatus to reflect only its conclusions, to emphasize the poetry rather than commentary, both suiting the needs of a general readership. He reduced the introductory materials, wrote a glossary and a new Shakespeare biography, both having a successful afterlife as reprints in future editions. Chalmers as a scholarly editor made the decision to synthesize some of the Steevens and Malone textual variants in the notes in his 1823 edition. In his editorial practice Chalmers treated the received 'Shakespeare'

apparatus in a selective way and emphasized the individuality of his choices in his prefaces.

Willey records the bibliographical data of Chalmers's first Shakespeare edition published in 1805 as follows: '[t]his is the first of the Shakespeare editions to employ any of the Chalmers apparatus. Chalmers put the Steevens material through press and wrote the accompanying brief life. The 1811 edition prepared for J. Nichols includes glossarial notes by Chalmers. In 1823 Chalmers again saw Shakespeare's works through the press, revising his earlier notes. Many editions of the day utilized the various Chalmers apparatus – prefaces, glosses, life.'[33] It is evident from Jaggard's *Shakespeare Bibliography* that the Chalmers editions were very popular in the nineteenth-century, and were published long after his death in 1834 up to the 1860s.

Chalmers's first Shakespeare edition in 1805 came out as a large-paper copy of ten volumes as well as an issue on small paper in nine volumes, both by the London publisher, Rivington.[34] As David Alexander notes about the edition 'this was a major undertaking: 3250 sets were issued in no less than 46,000 numbers, while further copies were sold in other formats.'[35] The title was *Plays of William Shakspeare accurately printed from the Text of the corrected Copy of the late George Steevens, Esq. with a series of engravings, from original designs of Henry Fuseli, Esq. R. A. Professor of Painting: and a selection of explanatory and historical notes, from the most eminent commentators; A History of the Stage, A Life of Shakspeare etc. by Alexander Chalmers, A.M.* London: Rivington, 1805, 10 vols.

The ordering of material and the way the illustrations are placed are different in the ten- and nine-volume editions. The large-paper octavo

---

[32] Colin Franklin, *Shakespeare Domesticated: The Eighteenth-Century Editions* (Menston, 1991), p. 52.

[33] Willey, 'Chalmers', p. 99.

[34] Throughout the article references to the 1805 edition refer to both the 10 and the 9 volume issues, unless they are specified.

[35] David Alexander, 'Shakespeare and the British Print Market 1700–1860' in *Shakespeare in Art*, ed. Jane Martineau and Desmond Shawe-Taylor (London, 2003), p. 25.

copy of ten volumes starts with Chalmers's Preface and continues with his 'Sketch of the Life of Shakespeare', 'Shakespeare's Will', 'Chronology of Shakespeare's Plays' by Edmond Malone and a different version by George Chalmers, Samuel Johnson's 'Preface', 'An Historical Account of the English Stage' by Malone and closes with Alexander Pope's 'Preface'. *Coriolanus* is in Volume VIII with *Timon of Athens* and *Antony and Cleopatra*. There are thirty-seven illustrations by Henry Fuseli, one for each play. In the ten-volume edition each illustration is placed by the scene it illustrates.

The nine-volume, smaller paper edition exhibits a slightly different arrangement of the same introductory materials. Johnson's 'Preface' is the first text, followed by 'An Historical Account of the English Stage' by Malone, Pope's 'Preface', Chalmers's 'Preface', his 'Life of Shakespeare', 'Shakespeare's Will' and finally Malone's 'Chronology'. *Coriolanus* is in volume VII with *Timon of Athens, Julius Caesar* and *Antony and Cleopatra*. The rearrangement of the order of the introductory texts may reflect a more hierarchical ordering as it starts with Johnson's Preface pointing to the *origo* of the tradition. Johnson was the unquestionable authority for the age, and certainly for an editor working in the frame of the Johnson–Steevens–Reed tradition; therefore 'his celebrated preface seems indispensable to every edition of Shakspeare in which illustration is at all admitted. It is at his recommendation, likewise, that the Editor has prefixed Mr Pope's Preface.' Chalmers also made the decision to reduce the quantity of introductory materials. While the Prolegomena of the Steevens edition of 1803 in three volumes contains twenty-five texts (prefaces, early modern documents, etc.) in volume 1 alone, fourteen in volume 2, and five in volume 3 (volumes 4–21 containing the plays), Chalmers selected the seven texts listed above. The nine-volume edition moves the illustration to the beginning of each play as a frontispiece.

The 1805 edition was an illustrated edition, and was illustrated by Henry Fuseli (1741–1825). Both make the edition unique, especially in supporting the claim to see Chalmers as a Romantic editor. Fuseli was an illustrator who was a member of the proto-Romantic *Sturm und Drang* movement of nationalist writers and intellectuals.[36] To Moelwyn Merchant Fuseli already belonged to the Romantic generation together with Blake.[37] Also, in the eighteenth-century illustrated Shakespeare editions were rare, while they thrived in the nineteenth-century. As Lucy Oakley notes '[i]llustrated editions of Shakespeare's plays first produced during the eighteenth-century reached the peak of their popularity during the mid-Victorian period.'[38]

The choice of Fuseli as the illustrator of the edition may be indicative of the novelty of the inventions introduced by Chalmers in his apparatus. As Merchant writes, 'every painting or engraving based on a poem or a play is a critical gesture towards its source, a critical gesture the more potent in that it does not cease to be an original creative act.'[39] Rivington's combination of Fuseli as the illustrator and Chalmers as the editor may be interpreted as a critical gesture pointing to an innovative style of editing.

Fuseli (Johann Heinrich Füssli) was also a man of literature. He had translated *Macbeth* into German before going to England.[40] When he arrived in London from Switzerland in 1764, he was already known to the reading public as the author of the essay *Remarks on Rousseau* (1767), which used the example of Shakespeare as a counterbalance to the rationalism of Hume and Locke.[41] Fuseli's theories expanded upon earlier eighteenth-century philosophers' (mostly Burke's) 'devaluation of the

[36] Edward Hodnett, 'Images of Shakespeare' in *Image and Text. Studies in the Illustrations of English Literature* (Menston, 1982), p. 70, and Lucy Oakley, 'Words into Pictures: Shakespeare in British Art, 1760–1900' in *A Brush with Shakespeare. The Bard in Painting 1780–1910* (Montgomery, Alabama, 1985), p. 5.

[37] W. Moelwyn Merchant, *Shakespeare and the Artist* (London, 1959), p. 77.

[38] Oakley, 'Words into Pictures', p. 12.

[39] Quoted in Oakley, p. 3.

[40] Oakley, p. 5.

[41] Maria Grazia Messina, 'Shakespeare and the Sublime' in Martineau, *Shakespeare in Art*, p. 61.

beautiful in favour of the "sublime", evoked by the threatening aspects of nature, the terror of the immeasurable, the supernatural, the fear of injury or death.'[42] As Maria Grazia Messina notes, Fuseli 'stood out from his fellow artists in London precisely because of his rich literary apprenticeship. In his native Zürich, Fuseli studied with two writers, Johann Jakob Bodmer and Johann Breitinger, both of whom anticipated the culture of Sturm und Drang, which taught that poetry was born out of the invention of the imagination and the power of sympathetic feeling, justifying on this basis the genius of Shakespeare.'[43]

The 1805 edition received more praise and attention due to the illustrator than to the editor. Edward Hodnett in his chapter on 'Images of Shakespeare' entitles the third section of the chapter 'The Fuseli Shakespeare (1805)', omitting the editor's name from the subtitle. This omission is given some rationale when Hodnett writes, '[o]n the title-page of the ten-volume *Plays of Shakespeare* (1805) published by a consortium of forty-one booksellers, Fuseli takes precedence over Alexander Chalmers, the editor. The thirty-seven designs (c. 165 × 90 mm) were admirably engraved by fourteen engravers, including William Blake.'[44]

Today some critics perceive Fuseli as 'England's most prolific and influential eighteenth-century artist-interpreter of Shakespeare.'[45] In Hodnett's evaluation '[t]he enormous vitality of Fuseli's drawings makes his Shakespeare series exhilarating even today. He brought Elizabethan passion into book illustration (as he had already into painting), the violence, sexuality, and the darker sides of the human spirit as well as its nobler.'[46] Moelwyn Merchant commented on Fuseli's work that, while his seven drawings for the Boydell Shakespeare Gallery[47] are the best in the collection, 'there is more power, movement, and original interpretation in the drawings that he made for the Rivington edition of Shakespeare in 1805.'[48] According to Messina, 'Fuseli approached Shakespeare not just as source material to be translated into painting, but as a kind of sparring partner with whom to compete

in psychological penetration and dramatic intensity.'[49]

The novelty may be found not only in the illustrations but also in the independence of Fuseli as illustrator compared to previous artists, yet another Romantic trait. Edward Hodnett notes that, in illustrating *Coriolanus*, Thomas Hanmer in his Shakespeare edition of 1744 elected to follow the two earlier illustrated Shakespeares published in 1709 (editor: Nicholas Rowe, designer: Francois Boitard, engraver: Edward Kirkall) and in 1740 (editor: Lewis Theobald, designer: Gravelot [Hubert Francois Bourguignon], engravers: Gravelot and Gerard Vander Gucht).[50] The scene in all three cases depicts Volumnia successfully imploring her son to spare Rome and make peace.[51] Marcia Allentuck's discovery of Hanmer's instructions to Francis Hayman, the illustrator for twenty-seven of the designs and his criticism of the first versions of three of them[52] showed that Hayman did not have a free hand in the illustrations and that it was Hanmer as the editor who determined which scene (one for each play) should serve as an illustration. The case is interestingly different from the Chalmers edition. As Hodnett notes, Fuseli did not get instructions from Chalmers as to which scenes to illustrate: '[u]nlike Boitard and Hayman, he made his own decisions

---

[42] Oakley, p. 6.

[43] Messina, p. 61.

[44] Hodnett, p. 70.

[45] Oakley, p. 5.

[46] Hodnett, p. 70.

[47] The Boydell Shakespeare Gallery was the most ambitious undertaking of the print publisher John Boydell. It first opened to the public in 1789 with 34 pictures; by 1802 there were 167 paintings by 33 different artists, among them the major artists of the time: West, Fuseli, Romney, James Barry, John Hoppner, Angelica Kauffmann, James Northcote and John Opie.

[48] Merchant, *Shakespeare and the Artist*, p. 77.

[49] Messina, 'Shakespeare and the Sublime', p. 62.

[50] Hodnett, 'Images of Shakespeare', pp. 62, 46, 54.

[51] Hodnett, p. 62.

[52] Hodnett, p. 52.

about which passages in Shakespeare's plays to illustrate'.[53]

In Chalmers's edition of 1805 the Fuseli illustration to *Coriolanus* diverts from the previous tradition of depicting Act 5, Scene 3. We find Aufidius seated on a throne and Coriolanus standing to his left illustrating Aufidius's lines in 4.5 'Say, What's thy Name? / Thou hast a grim appearance.' In *Pericles*, *Coriolanus*, *Julius Caesar*, and *Timon of Athens*, writes Hodnett, 'Fuseli indulges a whim for drawing seated figures in the style of Michelangelo.'[54] Fuseli usually filled his space with one central character and one or two supporting figures, with little detail about settings. In spite of his interest in theatre, Fuseli also broke with the tradition of depicting figures like actors on stage in costume.[55]

Jaggard praised the 1838 Paris edition for the nearly two hundred wood and steel engravings of fellow actors and commentators.[56] The 1838 edition has two illustrations for *Coriolanus*. The first serves as a frontispiece to the play depicting the most popular scene, Volumnia pleading to Coriolanus in the company of Virgilia, Valeria and young Martius. Under the picture the inscription says 'Act V.-Scene 3', and we find Volumnia's speech below: 'O, stand up bless'd! Whilst, with no softer cushion than the flint, I kneel before thee.' The second illustration depicts 4.5, with the inscription 'Coriolanus and Aufidius' and it is the same illustration by R. K. Porter, which had appeared in Boydell's 1802 Shakespeare Gallery. Jaggard describes it as follows: 'this set contains Boydell's series of one hundred large copperplates from paintings by leading British artists like Reynolds, Smirke, Northcote, Porter, Stothard, Hamilton, Bunbury, Opie, and Westall'.[57] Jaggard notes that the edition matches the grandiosity of the Boydell Shakespeare Gallery as it was published as an extra-large folio, and according to the prospectus to the edition a type foundry, an ink factory and a printing house were all specially erected for the production of this edition.[58]

After 1805 the next Chalmers edition was brought out in 1811 (in nine volumes). Although the title-page claims it was a 'new edition' it is a reprint of 1805. The order of prefaces, notes, etc. follows the ten-volume edition of 1805. The main difference is that it is not an illustrated edition, at least not the copy in the library of the Shakespeare Birthplace Trust, although Jaggard claims it is 'with engravings after Fuseli.'[59] The title-page of 1811, however, does not any longer advertise the engravings by Fuseli. The explanation for this difference lies in David Alexander's information on contemporary book-binding '[t]hose with the means would have had the sheets bound to their own specifications, giving them the opportunity to have additional illustrations bound in at the same time.'[60]

The 1823 edition marks important changes in the editorial practices of Chalmers, which also influence the 1838 Paris edition in question. Chalmers in his new preface introduces a few novelties to the Chalmers apparatus:

[t]he text of the edition of this selection, printed in 1803 [*sic*] and 1811, was that of the corrected copy left by Mr. Steevens, and edited by Mr. Isaac Reed, 21 vols. 1803. In the present republication, we have availed ourselves of the various readings pointed out by Mr. Malone in his last edition (1821): and thus, by repeated collations, and every mode of critical investigation, the text may now be thought to be fixed beyond the hope, or at least the probability, that any future discoveries will be able to add much to its purity.

Chalmers seems to be the first editor to combine the Steevens variorum of 1803 and the Malone variorum published in 1821 (by James Boswell Jr. after Malone' death in 1812) to a certain degree. Chalmers, although having already radically reduced the number of notes and textual commentary in 1805, made the decision to recreate some of the dialogical nature of the variorum

---

[53] Hodnett, p. 70.
[54] Hodnett, p. 73.
[55] Hodnett, p. 70.
[56] Jaggard, p. 522.
[57] Jaggard, p. 508.
[58] Jaggard, p. 508.
[59] Jaggard, p. 512.
[60] Alexander, 'Shakespeare and the British Print Market', p. 22.

tradition in 1823. While the textual base for his edition remains Steevens 1803, Chalmers introduces some 'various readings' suggested by Malone. These textual notes are always credited to Malone (as opposed to commentary, which is usually not credited, except Johnson's). The change from 1805 to 1823 may be attributed to the publication of the 21-volume Malone variorum after the death of the editor. Chalmers envisaged his text as final after the publication of the two grand variora of 1803 and 1821, reflecting his hope ('or at least the probability') that 'the text may now be thought to be fixed'.

One example, using Malone's notes as a test case, will serve to illustrate that the 1838 Paris edition was printed after Chalmers's 1823 edition. In 1.2 in the note to the lines 'Auf: Is it not yours? / What ever hath* been thought . . .', in the 1823 and 1838 editions we find a textual footnote by Malone, 'whatever have been', while there is no note yet in 1805 (nor in the 1811 reprint). The only difference (other than that Chalmers 1823 is not an illustrated edition and the 1838 Paris edition is) between the 1823 and 1838 editions is that while the 1823 edition works with footnotes the Paris edition operates with endnotes.

Chalmers in his editorial practice separated the received critical apparatus and the received text of Shakespeare. He kept the evolved text but broke with the apparatus of the variorum tradition, which accumulated materials in their historic and narrative succession. Chalmers made his selection about the introductory materials on the basis of what he deemed to be either canonical (prefaces by Pope and Johnson) or recent and essential scholarship (Malone's writings and his own biography). Even though by including some of Malone's textual notes Chalmers reestablished the dialogical aspect of the variorum tradition, he did that to keep only the Steevens 1803 and the Malone 1821 variora in conversation. He reintroduced the dialogical aspect of the variorum edition in a selective way (as he dealt with the reduction of the prolegomena material and the notes of Steevens 1803), including only credited textual notes by Malone which differ from the Steevens' edition. Chalmers, of course, had

commentary from Malone in his edition but as in the case of other commentators it many times went without credit. As Chalmers explains this in the preface, '[i]n selecting the notes, the names of the authors have seldom been retained, unless where they relate to contested points. Notes of criticism, however, have generally their authors' names, and it is hoped that the preservation of all Dr Johnson's remarks of this kind will not be thought superfluous, since they are almost universally quoted as authorities.'

Other than uniting two textual traditions and the work of two competing colleagues (who had actually been contributing to each others' editions) Chalmers also published a glossary to the 1823 edition, which had a lasting impact on subsequent Shakespeare editions. As he remarks, '[i]nstead of verbal index, a complete glossary of Shakespearian language has been compiled, at no small labour, for the present edition'. It gives the definition of the word and the place of reference in his volumes. For example, we find that *abate* means to 'depress, sink, subdue' and may be found at volume 3, p. 219.

A Shakespeare edition from 1838, edited by Thomas Campbell and published in London, contains a glossary like Chalmers's. Ernst Fleischer's English-language Shakespeare edition published in Leipzig (1840) announces on the title-page that it contains Chalmers's Shakespeare biography: *Plays and Poems of William Shakspeare with notes critical, historical and explanatory selected from the most eminent commentators by the Edmond Malone with Dr Johnson's Preface, A Life of the Poet by A. Chalmers and a copious glossary*. Jaggard adds that the glossary is also by Chalmers, and the 1823 Chalmers glossary and the one in the Leipzig edition look identical (except for the referencing given to Chalmers's volumes). Even though Chalmers's own claim in his preface was that he compiled the glossary only for the 1823 edition, the DNB article on Chalmers mentions a *Glossary of Shakspeare* dating from 1797, which may have been the basis for Chalmers's own glossary in the 1823 edition. It could have also served as a source for its earlier publications in other editions before 1823, which appear in Jaggard's Shakespeare bibliography.

Chalmers made another important and lasting contribution (in his 1805 edition) in printing his *Sketch of the Life of Shakespeare*, an attempt, and the first of the kind, to collect the *disjecta membra* of his biography scattered over the volumes of Johnson and Steevens. It may be useful as shewing the reader at one view all that is known of the personal history of our great bard, and it can pretend to no other merit.' Here Chalmers did not assume the role of the first biographer, as it was the *Life* of Nicholas Rowe (1709) which remained the standard biography throughout the eighteenth-century. Chalmers merely filled the gap for the need of an up-to-date biography. He was an acclaimed biographer of his time, the editor of the 32-volume *The General Biographical Dictionary* (1812), a work that 'remained standard for years and was Chalmers' principal claim to fame during his lifetime'.[61] Judging by the bibliographical data in Jaggard's *Shakespeare Bibliography* the 'Sketch of the Life of Shakespeare' by Chalmers became the standard biography in the first half of the nineteenth century and there are several editions even in the 1850s and 1860s, which print Chalmers's Sketch (e.g. an 1856 Longman edition, and an 1864 New York edition), and we still find two Chalmers editions published in 1864 in London (Bell and Daldy) and in Cincinnati.[62] A book printed in German combines Chalmers's biography with William Hazlitt's *Characters*.[63] Chalmers yet again appears in a Romantic context.

Chalmers as a Romantic editor responds to a long-standing need to reform the apparatus. Andrew Murphy notes that '[w]hile the text established by these editors [i.e. Johnson-Steevens-Reed and Malone] was accepted as standard, a backlash set in against their sprawling apparatus.'[64] Although Murphy mentions Chalmers only in the appendix Chalmers could be the earliest example to illustrate his claim that

[b]y the early decades of the nineteenth-century . . . editors themselves were beginning to feel that the limits of commentary had been reached and that a rationalization of the editorial apparatus was now necessary. Thus

Manley Wood, in his edition of 1806, observed that 'The present Editor did not set out with the design of making notes, though in a few places he could not avoid it. His purpose was to retrench: and to attach to his author such remarks only, from the various annotators, as are really illustrative of his dark passages.'[65]

Chalmers relied on the variorum tradition of scholarly editing in the latter third of the eighteenth century; yet he questioned the rationale for variorum editing with a view to a widening readership and the need for a more poetic and less scholarly Shakespeare. Editing a Romantic Shakespeare is editing Shakespeare in an individually selective way as opposed to the 'interpretative comprehensiveness' or universality of the eighteenth-century neoclassicist variorum editing. As Chalmers writes in the 1805 Preface, he as an editor 'can only say that in the whole progress of his labours, he endeavoured to place himself in the situation of one who desires to understand his author at the smallest expense of time and thought, and who does not wish to have his attention diverted from a beauty, to be distracted by a contest. In thus assuming the character of a general reader, who is neither a scholar nor a critick, he found no difficulty; but it would have been arrogant, had it been possible, to measure the understanding of others by his own, and therefore from the opinions that he is given too much, or too little, he can have no appeal.'

Editing Shakespeare is more than a poetic or a scholarly exercise; the editions are documents of literary history, cultural history and book history. An edition always reflects some implicit or explicit theories about the text, the editor's relationship to the tradition, perceptions about the author and the potential readership. Theories and practices of a particular edition packed into the

---

[61] Willey, 'Chalmers', p. 103.

[62] Jaggard, pp. 532, 537.

[63] *Supplement zu Shakespeare, enthaltend: Shakspeare's Leben von A. Chalmers. Charakteristik der Shakspeare'schen Dramen von William Hazlitt* [Translated by A. Jäger] (1838).

[64] Murphy, p. 188.

[65] Murphy, p. 189.

materiality of the book travel through time (as reprints) and in geographical space. The edition a Hungarian Romantic poet used for his translation in the middle of the nineteenth century, at the height of Hungarian Romanticism, was the product of late eighteenth-century English textual scholarship relying on the tradition of the received text. At the same time it was an edition which redefined the received 'Shakespeare' by suiting it to the taste of an emerging general readership, breaking with the variorum tradition and revealing more poetry. Travelling across time and space the edition furnished Sándor Petőfi working on the translation of *Coriolanus* a reliable Romantic edition in creating his own Romantic Shakespearian poetry.

WOMEN EDIT SHAKESPEARE

JEANNE ADDISON ROBERTS

Between the years of 1903 and 1913 two remarkable women, Charlotte Endymion Porter and Helen Armstrong Clarke, published three editions of the complete works of William Shakespeare.[1] Before that they had already edited the complete works of both Robert and Elizabeth Barrett Browning and founded a literary journal still in existence called *Poet-Lore*.[2] Throughout their careers they were extraordinarily productive. The Library of Congress catalogue lists sixty-nine titles for Porter and sixty-seven for Clarke.

The publishing careers of these two amazing women began in Philadelphia. In 1875 Charlotte Porter had been one of the graduates of Wells College in Aurora, New York (illustration 4) where she had created scale models of Shakespeare's stage (illustration 5) and planned to write a series of essays on 'Staging Shakespeare's Wit'.[3] She had studied briefly at the Sorbonne and then settled in Philadelphia. There, in 1883, with the encouragement of Horace Howard Furness, she became editor of a new periodical called *Shakespeariana* (begun by the Shakespeare Society of New York). Among the articles she published in the journal was one on Shakespeare's music by Helen A. Clarke, a young scholar with a certificate in music from the still all-male University of Pennsylvania.[4] Porter and Clarke formed a life-long friendship.

The two women lived unconventional lives. The best source of information about them is a long account of their friendship written by Porter and published in their journal *Poet-Lore* after Clarke's death.[5] The Wells College archive contains not only the early photographs, but also some letters and poems; and the Folger copy of the women's First Folio Shakespeare has, pasted into

I am extremely grateful for the help of the Folger Shakespeare Library staff: Dr Georgianna Ziegler, the Reference Librarian, has been constantly helpful in locating materials both from the Folger and from Wells College and the University of Pennsylvania; Betsy Walsh and the circulation staff have been wonderfully helpful and unfailingly patient in dealing with the forty volumes in the Shakespeare Collection. The staff of the American University Media Center performed miracles of reproduction. I am also indebted to Professor Edward Kessler who has located information about Porter and Clarke in Boston. I especially want to thank Professor Patricia Parker for her persistent nagging and Professor Valerie Wayne for her useful suggestion about the history of criticism.

[1] (1) Charlotte Porter and Helen A. Clarke, eds., *The Pembroke Edition* (New York, 1903), 12 vols. (2) *The First Folio Edition of the Works of William Shakespeare* (New York, 1903–1913), 40 vols. (3) *The Complete Works of William Shakespeare Reprinted from the First Folio*, Introduction by Churton Collins (London, 1906), 12 vols. These volumes were greeted with praise by many critics. H. H. Furness included the editors in the notes of his last Variorum, *Cymbeline*, in 1913, and his son lists them in his Works Collated in the editions which he edited. Two recent critics, both writing in the series *Shakespeare: The Critical Tradition*, have notably discussed the introductions of these editions: Joseph Candido in his 1996 volume on *King John* and Charles Forker in his 1998 study of *Richard II*. Both found them important contributions. Indeed Candido considers Charlotte Porter's 'neglected essay one of the most important in the interpretative history of *King John*' (p. 16).

[2] The journal is currently published by the Writing Center in Bethesda, Maryland.

[3] I am grateful to Helen T. Bergamo of the library at Wells College, who sent me pictures of Porter and her design for a model of the Globe stage.

[4] Clarke's article, 'A List of Shakespeare Operas, Operatized Dramas and Overtures', *Shakespeariana*, 5 (1888), 457–62,

4 Charlotte Porter as an undergraduate

A Midsummer Night's Dream (vol. 8), three fascinating photographs of the two women (illustration 6). One shows them in a study with a reproduction of Shakespeare's epitaph among the pictures on the wall. A second one shows the two
women standing with a First Folio and one of the
volumes of their own First Folio edition in their
hands. The third shows the two women standing behind an iron rail fence with hands extended
through the fence holding the two volumes,
now open, on the other side. No explanation is
provided.

Both women had early developed an interest in
Shakespeare but, by 1888, Porter had begun to find
the limits of *Shakespeariana* confining, and she proposed broadening its focus to include other writers.
When the proposal was rejected, she resigned as
editor, and in 1889 she and Clarke announced the
formation of the new monthly journal called *Poet-
Lore*. They moved with the magazine to Boston
in 1891. They had not lost their interest in Shakespeare, but they had broadened it to include the
Brownings and the comparative study of literature.
Porter's account reflects vividly their excitement in
starting this new adventure:

Did ever two women before dare embark so independently on publication of a periodical so unprecedented?
When so young in experience, moreover so recently
through some special courses, Miss Clarke at the University of Pennsylvania and I after graduation at Wells
College, briefly in Paris at the Sorbonne, before we met
in Philadelphia . . . To venture upon an unoccupied
field requiring arduous ploughing up, we liked . . . We
were singular in our belief in Genius and the excelling in
the Arts, as the true breadth and incentive of the larger
progress in life.[6]

Their belief in the importance and evolutionary
nature of art and criticism is evident in all their
work. Porter says,

Our standards were evolutionary and relative in principle in a day when the static and the has-been rather than

---

540–5, is cited by Richard Knowles twelve times in his New
Variorum edition of *As You Like It* (New York, 1977).

[5] 'A Story of *Poet-Lore*', a first-hand account by Charlotte Porter
of her long friendship with Helen Clarke, was published in
Poet-Lore, 37 (1926), 432–53, after Clarke's death.

[6] 'A Story of *Poet-Lore*', 438. Perhaps because of her relative
freedom from academic influences, Porter writes in a distinctive and original style.

5 Porter's design of an Elizabethan Theatre.

the dynamic and coming-into birth constituted the measure in criticism. As it looks to me it is better now, and worse. It is possible now to be as intolerant to excellence through much adherence to 'up-to-dateness' as a fixed measure as then it was to fail to discern fresh merit or even aliveness in a new direction. We were champions then for what is still needed, it may be – the standards that relate all aesthetic expression to evolving life. This we were convinced is the only criterion capable of looking before and after. Because it is aware of flux it alone can be trusted to anticipate and also encompass the genuinely progressive.[7]

Porter and Clarke's interest in how individuals and societies change and how art may influence those changes is pervasive throughout their work. It was perhaps their belief in genius that led them to focus

again on Shakespeare and, in 1903, to begin their publications of his works. They see his genius as raising him above time-bound contemporaries and critics and producing works which literally evolve like pictures seen under changing lights as individuals and societies change. It is not certain when their Shakespeare editing projects were started, but in 1901 they reproduced from *Poet-Lore* a whole volume of Study Programmes devoted to *Macbeth*.[8]

---

[7] 'A Story of *Poet-Lore*', 439.
[8] Charlotte Porter and Helen A. Clarke, *Shakespeare Study Programs: The Tragedies* (Boston, 1914), p. 101. A second volume, *The Comedies*, appeared in the same year. Charlotte Porter and Helen A. Clarke, *Shakespeare Study Program:*

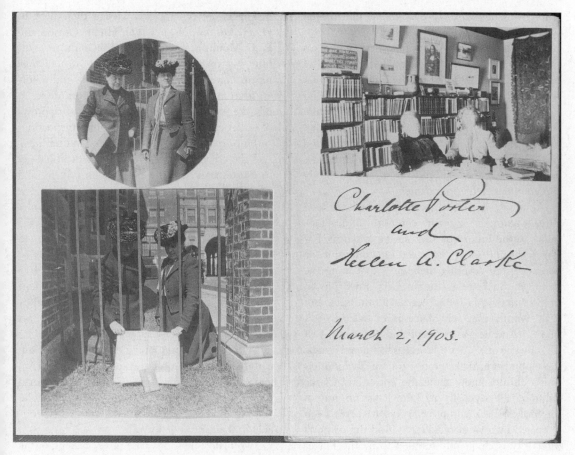

6 Photographs pasted into the front of *A Midsummer Night's Dream* in Porter and Clarke's First Folio edition.

They later collected two more volumes devoted respectively to comedies and tragedies. The most striking feature of these programmes is their use of questions rather than answers, a policy consistent with the authors' conviction that critical principles should not be engraved in stone. However, the questions often imply only one answer. For example they ask about Shakespeare whether it is true that his 'mind was not confined to the level of most of his contemporaries' or audiences then or now. And they conclude with a query about the possibility that critics who object to Shakespeare's extravagances in diction or design may simply 'make it clear to the modern eye that their critical powers were for a day, the subject of them

for all time.'[9] The expected answer is hardly in doubt.

The editions of Shakespeare's complete works began to follow soon after the first Study Programmes. In 1903 in New York and in 1906 in London the two women published the

---

Macbeth (New York, 1901) is the only single play programme. The Preface records their debt to their male mentors and an advertisement enclosed in the Folger copy includes enthusiastic blurbs from some of them. Rolfe says the programmes are the best he has ever seen.

[9] *Programs: Tragedies*, p. 131. Porter and Clarke see Shakespeare, Shelley in 'The Revolt of Islam' and Browning as precursors of Darwin and his evolutionary theory. See also *First Folio* edition, *The Tempest*, vol. 1, pp. viii–ix.

twelve-volume *Pembroke Shakespeare* with several plays to a volume. The first volume of the forty-volume *First Folio* edition of single plays and poems was also published in 1903 and the last in 1913. The volumes did not come out in the order of the First Folio, but the volume numbers follow the Folio order. Porter writes that the first four volumes were jointly edited by both women, but that after that Clarke developed other interests and Porter edited the rest alone.[10] However, many of the later plays still bear the names of both women, and the Study Programmes credit both names.

Although their Shakespeare editions have been largely ignored, they represent a crucial development in the history of Shakespeare criticism. For the first time smart, educated, and free-spirited women were devoting themselves to editing the complete Shakespeare canon. Gary Taylor, in an important essay in 1988, begins with the statement that 'Women may read Shakespeare, but men edit him.'[11] And he points out, I think correctly, that the absence of women editors has hampered critical development in Shakespeare criticism. Taylor obviously did not know about the Porter and Clarke editions. He says, 'To my knowledge no edition of Shakespeare's complete works has ever been prepared by a woman'(p. 196). (And the edition's obscurity is eloquently testified to by the Folger Library edition, which still includes a large proportion of uncut pages.) But Taylor's conclusions seem to me accurate. Within the value system which rates textual scholarship as the most important activity of academic humanism, he finds that 'editing is work, criticism is play; editing is primary, criticism is parasitic.' The paucity of women 'in the Shakespearean editorial club tends to perpetuate various myths about editing and about gender' (p. 197). Thus, he contends that the whole history of Shakespeare scholarship has been warped by the relative absence of female views.

The presence of female views is abundantly evident in the women's *First Folio* Shakespeare edition. It is intriguing to try to discover what these views are. I should like to begin an exploration of how such views are expressed by two enlightened women at the start of the twentieth century.

The two women acknowledge their debt to H. H. Furness, W. J. Rolfe, Hiram Corson and R. G. Moulton, and the publication of the first volume was well received. *A Midsummer Night's Dream* reprints twelve rave reviews by critics and scholars from major publications. The editors' desire to edit the works was sharpened by their disapproval of earlier editions with their multiple emendations and modernizations. They expressed in their prefaces the conviction that the closest one could get to Shakespeare was the original First Folio, and argued that 'there is practically nothing in the First Folio . . . which should cause the present-day reader to stumble'. Chaucer and Spenser are not modernized, they say, and Shakespeare should not be. To add to the problem of later editions they report that all modernized editions trace their ancestry back to the worst of the Folios, the fourth.[12] A few modern scholars have dismissed their texts because 'They reprint the First Folio, so what's to edit?' In fact the editors do edit and supply many textual notes as well as sections on sources, date of composition, early editions and examples of selected criticism and variorum readings. The whole texts are worth study, and some of their defences of restored Folio readings are notable; but the chief interest is probably in their introductions.[13]

Two major questions arise in my reading of the Porter and Clarke editions: (1) what is the evidence of their application of their evolutionary theory?, and (2) to what extent can the criticism can be considered 'feminist'? Obviously in this limited space my discussion of these two issues will be severely selective, and the two issues inevitably overlap. Both invite further study.

---

10 'A Story of *Poet-Lore*', 451.

11 Gary Taylor, 'Textual and Sexual Criticism: A Crux in *The Comedy of Errors*', *Renaissance Drama* n.s., 19 (1988), 195–225 (p. 195).

12 The Editors' Prefaces at the beginning of many of the volumes spell out their reasons for a new edition.

13 The volumes of the *First Folio* edition are numbered in the order of the original First Folio and not in the order of publication. Hereafter all notes citing short forms of titles of plays with volume numbers refer to the women's *First Folio* edition.

Perhaps the more difficult of the two questions is the effort to analyze the nature of the editors' 'feminism'. They are certainly interested in female characters and often see them in different light from male critics, but I find no evidence of complaint against Shakespeare as sexist for his portrayal of women as victims or inferiors because of their gender. The editors do declare an interest in freeing themselves from academic 'old fogeyism' and 'the learned idiots who inveigh upon fixed standards, "central figures", etc'.[14] and, in fact, their most striking conclusions are refreshing because of their freedom from inherited wisdom.

Although they do hope to interrogate patriarchal values, in my view they treat all characters of the plays, male and female, primarily as people, and in general dwell on women only when they see them differently from earlier critics. For example, they spend more time than one might expect on Adriana and Luciana in *The Comedy of Errors*, portraying them as two important types of woman, 'the new woman', and 'the man's woman'. Adriana, the wife, is described as 'a thoroughly human type, who expects completely to possess her husband, and whose jealous affection for him conjures up the vision of a rival when he does not happen to come home on the moment'. And when the Abbess suggests that her jealous behaviour may not be the best way to improve a man, reminding her that a man is master of his liberty, she makes a retort worthy of a new woman, 'Why should their liberty be more than ours?' On the other hand the editors praise Luciana as 'the type called "the man's woman", who longs to be a sweet and passive recipient of some man's love, willing to obey him and let him have all the liberty he wants'. The editors conclude, 'That Shakespeare in this early stage of his work should have sketched so truly two opposite types of womanhood, making them at once human and loveable is one of the most powerful indications that a great genius had arisen – one who . . . would surely in the end portray, more fully, greater women.'[15]

But other women pass more quickly. Helena and Hermia in *A Midsummer Nights Dream* are declared 'hardly worth considering'.[16] The editors say almost nothing about the wives in *The Merry Wives of Windsor*. Although they admire the play, they say very little about Beatrice in *Much Ado About Nothing*, and there is little analysis of women in *Measure for Measure*, *King Lear* or *Hamlet*. Katherine in *The Taming of the Shrew* is singled out briefly but curiously because 'her proud and sensitive shrewishness arouse interest'. When tamed she develops 'wariness and judgment, self-control and poise, and finally, finesse and stratagem . . . in order to gain by policy . . . a surreptitious purpose'. 'The tamer and the tamed . . . exhibit a congenial interplay . . . while they win . . . over all the competitors in the final scene'.[17] This is not so much 'feminism' in the modem sense as an analysis of how a smart woman may succeed in a patriarchal society.

A few women are blamed for their destructive behavior. Ophelia represents an 'undertow dragging fatally at [Hamlet's] heart and vital force'.[18] Other women are overlooked or accepted with their limitations. Volumnia does not even get mentioned by name in the discussion of *Coriolanus*. Cressida in *Troilus and Cressida* is 'too passive, too weak and wavering' but is nonetheless praised for her 'charming ingenuousness', her 'exquisite naivete' and the 'beautiful timidity and innocent artifice which grace and consummate the feminine character'.[19]

A few strong women are praised specifically for traditional 'feminine' qualities. Portia in *The Merchant of Venice* receives high praise as an 'exemplar of all that is beautiful in womanhood'. 'She is exalted and alluring and equipped to lead the best specimens of present day womanhood'. Jessica is beautiful and fascinating with an 'intuitional perception of higher laws of justice'.[20] Helena in *All's*

---

[14] *King John*, vol. 15, p. viii. See also the *Comprehensive Index of Poet-Lore, 1–58*, compiled by Alice Very with an introduction by Melvin H. Bernstein, which records that the goal of the founders was to 'undercut academic "Old Fogeyism"' (p. 16).

[15] *Err*, vol. 5, pp. xxxii–xxxiii.

[16] *Programs: Comedies*, p. 74.

[17] *Shr*, vol. 11, pp. xii. 18.

[18] *Ham*, vol. 31, p. xxvii.

[19] *Tro*, vol. 24, pp. xv, 20.

[20] *MV*, vol. 9.

Well That Ends Well is an especially interesting case. The editors see her as a young woman who knows what she wants and is true to herself, but as such she excites the 'repulsion felt for such a nature'. Bertram, the crude young male, sees her as the average man sees men of genius or culture in a realm beyond his range. To such a rough youth the powerful is 'manly' and the weak is 'girlish'. 'Masculine sex pride . . . contemns the feminine to exalt the soldierly', but the talented Helena finally becomes 'our surety for the latent capacity of Bertram'.[21]

In general Porter and Clarke see the men of the plays in more need of evolution than the women. The editors show an unusual sympathy for the widely neglected Posthumus of *Cymbeline*, seeing him as mistaken but not evil, and in the end susceptible to change. They ask 'Is only the brain of genius acquainted with error and equal to the task of the offending it?'[22] Falstaff in *1 Henry IV* and Parolles in *All's Well* are classed together as exponents of 'male' principles which need to be superseded,[23] and Ford of *The Merry Wives*, Othello, and Leontes of *The Winter's Tale* represent progressive stages of the 'male' problem of jealousy.[24] In the comedies such as *Love's Labour's Lost* and *Much Ado About Nothing*, probably the editors' favourites and, they suggest, the favourites of their author, Berowne and Benedick, the scholar and the soldier, are brothers under the skin. In the 'twin plays' they credit the poet with the sceptical point of view of the artist toward 'certain intellectual assumptions', a view which facilitates change – in this case it modifies the 'exclusiveness of the ultra masculine view of life and love' by the introduction of feminine opposition to masculine ideas. In these two plays, they suggest, the poet reveals 'more relish of his work than is necessary to achieve the plot's predestined end – in order to reveal the supremacy of love as an emotional motive power in life to those who have decried, depreciated, and opposed it'. The plays celebrate the powers, not necessarily rational, which lie behind evolutionary change.[25]

The focus on the need to change men does perhaps constitute a form of feminism, but it is interestingly joined with the insistence that the interpretation of art is not bound by rules or reason and that

it is shaped by evolutionary forces both personal and social. Feminism and evolutionary theory are merged. I will return to the two most interesting and extensive analyses of women in the introductions to *Antony and Cleopatra* and *Macbeth* but, since these involve both critical subjects, I will first say a bit more about the editors' critical principles.

Perhaps the only constant theme in Porter and Clarke's criticism is that every work of art should be interpreted by its own standards. They insist that

in fixed methods in art no virtue exists but in the harmonious correlation of changing material, organic design, under the molten handling of genius, all virtue.

Criticism, they insist, has no independent grounds of exercise. It is therefore 'still suggestive of new patterns to the present age'. They consistently oppose didacticism in art, seeing Shakespeare as superior, for example, to Ben Jonson's evident desire to teach. Shakespeare's strength, they say, is that 'he contented himself without condemning or taking sides with any one way of art' and 'thus is able to humanize, refine, and idealize history, comedy, and tragedy'. And his work did not suffer in its moral significance from his refusal to adopt Jonson's conscious aim at teaching. Shakespeare wrote, they say,

Not limiting his mimic world to the objectively known side of life commending itself to the rational mind, always transcending realistic action by making it suggestive, the inner light of idealism graced it with gifts bearing better fruit in men than a conscious didacticism could urge or conceive.[26]

Porter and Clark's rejection of the idea of Shakespeare as moralist, and their conception of his freedom from rigid adherence to the restrictions of the prevailing social, political, intellectual, and literary

---

21 *AWW*, vol. 12, p. xv.
22 *Cym*, vol. 35, pp. xiv, vii.
23 *AWW*, vol. 12, p. xv.
24 *Wiv*, vol. 3, p. vii.
25 *Ado*, vol. 6, pp. x–xx.
26 *WT*, vol. 14, xvii–xxvi. This introduction contains one of the editors' most sustained discussions of their theories.

conventions helps them to see in his works evolutionary insights in individual plays but also broader trends throughout the works. They ask, for example, whether the sequence of events in *The Winter's Tale* may indicate a passing from aristocratic to democratic ideals and whether the play may even show signs of the changing status of women by its movement away from self-sacrifice toward self-development.[27] In *Coriolanus* they query whether this play also may be ahead of its times in depicting the serious foes that block 'moral growth to genuine democracy.'[28] They compare Shakespeare to Ibsen in being the defender of the enemies of the 'compact majority'. In *1 Henry IV* they find a partisanship for the outlaw in the representation of Falstaff, which may reflect memory of the Saxon defeat by the Normans, but still hampers progress.[29] They see signs of changing culture in the rise of covert puritanism in *Twelfth Night* and *Measure for Measure*.[30] *The Tempest* shows Shakespeare's consciousness of 'a new breath blowing over the sea', and Caliban reveals signs of ability to 'pass through stages of evolution'.[31]

Romantic love does seem to be an ultimate good for Porter and Clarke – either in itself as a human achievement or as guide to fuller humanity. *Troilus and Cressida* and *Love's Labour's Lost* show both its successes and its limitations. *Love's Labour's Lost* shows the victory of natural emotion over the artificial elements of educational schemes. Porter and Clarke ask in their study programme whether love should be seen not as the only thing in life but as the 'typical experience of life that should open up the depths of knowledge not of love alone but of death and suffering in relation to it?' Women in general seem better at love than men, and they are left in charge in *Love's Labour's Lost*.[32] However, Porter and Clarke do suggest that the sonnets are Shakespeare's 'most absolute expression of self' and that they 'permit the inference that Shakespeare or else an imagined self loved a fair and gifted youth.'[33] And in *Troilus and Cressida* the editors see Shakespeare's adaptation of the inherited story as revealing 'a tragic effect peculiar to himself'. They argue that the gentler, kindlier, artless Troilus, although defeated in war by the hard,

keen, dominating and cunning Greeks, and in love by the passive weak Cressida's vulnerability to 'the crude masculine ways' of young Diomed, nevertheless represents 'the slow human up-struggling of romantic love'.[34]

Porter and Clarke's studies of Cleopatra and Lady Macbeth are both feminist in their detailed examination of two leading women and evolutionary in their interpretation of the plays. Both are specifically related to their historical moments and credited with foreshadowing the future. The editors see them as not just strong and distinctive portraits of women but also as focuses of their conviction that drama operates as an evolutionary force. For Cleopatra the force is primarily personal but also points to changing human values which transform Antony, while Lady Macbeth fails to change her society but foreshadows the retreat from superstition in later culture.

Porter's analysis of *Antony and Cleopatra* begins with an evocation of the Queen based on the picture of her face on an ancient coin: a face with a 'thick, strong, aquiline nose, a presence of imperial vigour, rather than feminine softness', the face of a self-assertive woman, a face which does not seem consistent with views of her as 'the sensuously alluring and suavely fascinating woman' usually imagined in the play. Porter argues that the view of critics that Cleopatra is 'the betrayer of Antony's higher self through his corporeal weakness' cannot be reconciled with the 'indubitable Cleopatra of the historic coin'. Although the face on the coin does not quarrel with the idea of culture, cleverness, or 'the artistic quality of her luxuriousness', it does not allow for 'mere feminine seductiveness'.[35] On the contrary, she argues, it is Cleopatra who

---

[27] *Programs: Comedies*, pp. 138, 132.
[28] *Programs: Tragedies*, p. 29; *Cor*, vol. 25, p. vii.
[29] *1H4*, vol. 17, p. viii.
[30] *TN*, vol. 13, pp. xvii–xviii.
[31] *Tmp*, vol. 1, pp. xxvii, xiv.
[32] *Programs: Comedies*, p. 53.
[33] *Son*, vol. 39, pp. viii–xiii.
[34] *Tro*, vol. 24, pp. viii–xv.
[35] *Ant*, vol. 34, p. vii.

inspires Antony and helps him to realize his higher self.

Porter's view of Antony in the beginning is that he is quintessentially a Roman male. Although aware of Cleopatra's charms, he is in no sense enmeshed in them:

Queen as this rare woman is, he regards her as an alien as men have long been able to regard women outside the protection of their own class or outside the pale of laws and customs accepted merely because they were born into them.

Porter goes on to elaborate the gradual development of Antony's change:

Shakespeare's Antony was crude when he first met Cleopatra. He regards her as a Roman would; leaves her without dreaming that he has yielded her any encumbering allegiance; meets the test proposed for him by Caesar and Agrippa in the way a Roman would applaud; and only develops a nobility of soul passing the the limitations of temporal situation, race, or fortune because of the subtler power latent within his relation to Cleopatra. This transforms his disposition into that of a lovership so devoted that no Roman could approve it and but few Englishmen besides Shakespeare appreciate it without reservations.

In the beginning the Roman Antony is obsessed with ambitions of domination and conquest of the east, but this ambition gradually yields to the influence of Cleopatra. His transformation takes place gradually. As he leaves Cleopatra in Act I, after the start of their love, Porter believes that she means to tell him she is pregnant, but breaks off because she sees he is not ready for such news. 'That she would have told him that she was with child comes out clearly . . . to the audience, but not to Antony when she says it is "sweating Labour to beare such Idlenesse so neere the heart."' But she realizes that he is deaf to such a message and she 'is too mature a woman not to accept the fact'.

It is evident then that Shakespeare's Cleopatra 'did not purse up Antony's heart when first they met'. Modern critics' belief that she has done this is 'due to the modern borrowing of the Roman standpoint'. Antony's turning point comes when he follows Cleopatra away from the sea battle, a moment which signals not defeat, but victory. He chooses love over war, and Porter sees that

In the end, it appears that Anthony is spiritually indebted to Cleopatra and she to him. Their loss was merely a material mess of pottage . . . In the deepest sense of values to the individuality he is saved and not ruined by the development through her of those higher heroic capacities of the soul that render it superior to loss.

Finally in her conclusion Porter returns to the image on the coin:

The quality in Shakespeare's Cleopatra that despite a tragic clash with the Roman majority educes such nobility of soul, and that meets it with the like heroism, successfully challenges life-likeness with the ripe imperious woman whose effigy on her ancient coins demands a deeper conception of her power?[36]

Porter does not argue for Shakespeare's intention but rather that his texts present visions large enough to evoke an ambiguous world which persistently invites new ideas and promotes evolutionary thinking.[37]

Porter and Clarke's introduction to *Macbeth* is feminist in the sense that again it devotes special attention to a female character, Lady Macbeth. It is evolutionary in that it sees her as a voice of the future, countering the superstition and credulity of her age. As others have done, they interpret the whole play as a negotiation between King James's belief in witchcraft as set forth in his 1599 *Demonologie* and the sceptical views of Reginald Scot as adumbrated in his 1594 *Discoverie of Witchcraft*. They conclude that Banquo is as piously credulous as James. Macbeth is as wickedly credulous as any doomed soul addicted to black magic. And Lady Macbeth, 'no such baby prey to credulity', is 'as cool-headed as Scot, without a trace of his piety'. Lady Macbeth 'does not bother with the supernatural'. She moves efficiently to effect her husband's vague and feeble desires. The only fear she shows is not of prophecy or murder, 'but the very rational fear, as events prove,

---

[36] *Ant*, pp. xxi–xxiv.
[37] See especially *WT*, pp. x–xxii.

of the "compunctious visitings of Nature" within herself'. They conclude that

Such natural visitings do indeed make up the permanent conscience of the most liberated and enlightened intelligence; and it is one of Shakespeare's profoundest revelations that the boldest mind in his play and the freest from superstition suffers the quickest and most inwardly by outraging its own finer quality and descending from its right level of spiritual leadership to put itself at the service of violence.[38]

The editors argue that Shakespeare had a vision broader and more imaginative than most of his contemporaries and that *Macbeth* has been misread because '[i]t naturally takes a long time for the generations to grow up to a sympathetic level with a poet "for all time" on a subject involving a profound conception of human life'.[39] Shakespeare uses the views of both Scot and James without prejudice as matters of psychological human fact of the profoundest human interest. Unlike the others in the play, however, Lady Macbeth 'does not bother with the supernatural'. She focuses instead on 'reckoning up the difficulties' of effecting her husband's desires and marshalling her forces to supplement his often vague and feeble ones. Porter and Clarke find that Lady Macbeth is 'more entirely Shakespeare's creation than either Macbeth or Banquo'. The author enhances the value of her executive ability and credits her with a 'magnetic wifely allegiance' to her husband's powerful ambition, 'an allegiance the more captivating in that it appears not in a weak but a strong feminine nature, rich in resources and resolution'. Finally they ally Lady Macbeth with Shakespeare himself: 'Shakespeare's own creative touch upon her is the natural temper of her mind toward supernaturalism. It suggests the breadth of his own attitude as necessary to animate hers.'[40]

The editors recognize that many later critics have seen the play differently. In their study guide they quote Dr. Johnson's view that 'Lady Macbeth is merely detested . . . while the courage of Macbeth preserves some esteem.'[41] But it is a view they challenge. They sympathize with her suffering, noting: 'Her unrecriminating silence through all she took

no part in . . . and her shielding of Macbeth as long as she could.' And they quote her last words of sanity as showing her 'agonized conviction of the stupidity of her husband's stubborn quest to secure peace of mind by violence':

> 'Tis safer, to be that which we destroy
> Then by destruction dwell in doubtfull joy.
>
> (3.2.6–7)

Their conclusion is:

This psychical quality of Lady Macbeth's hell, together with the unusual rationalism of her mind make her antichristian almost, as judged by the Elizabethan standards Scot and James furnish of the witch-superstition. And the pagan mode of her death, 'by selfe and violent hands', as reported by Malcolm, is the accordant final trait in the awful majesty of Shakespeare's picture of her.

She is clearly seen as the aspect of the play which points to the future. By contrast they characterize her husband as 'the slave of fortune . . . the abject creature of bewitchment [and] . . . the laughing stock of witches'. They judge that his bloody head in Macduff's hands is 'the just and necessary sentence upon so unconscionable a beast of prey'. But they also concede that the 'self-innocence of the man at the start' and the power of his language 'always sets him in intimate favor with the common understanding'.[42] Porter and Clarke's singling out both Cleopatra and Lady Macbeth as the voices of the future seems both feminist and evolutionary.

I have focused especially in this preliminary study of the First Folio Shakespeare on only a selection of commentaries which seemed to me of special interest because of their examples of early feminist criticism, their insistence on the uselessness of

---

[38] *Mac*, vol. 30, pp. xxxii–xxxiv. The whole introduction returns frequently to the relation of James and Scot.

[39] *Mac*, p. xxv.

[40] *Mac*, pp. xxxiii.–xxxv.

[41] *Programs: Tragedies*, p. 129.

[42] *Mac*, xxxv–xxxvii. Dr Johnson's view is still pervasive. My students regularly blame Lady Macbeth for Macbeth's tragedy, and a recent newspaper critic refers to Lady Macbeth as 'a total monster'.

fixed standards of criticism, their rejection of didactic intention in Shakespeare's work, and their application of principles of revolutionary change in the perception of literary productions. Their discussions of all the plays provide new and provocative interpretations of Shakespeare's works, and challenging insights into the functions of drama in general. Finally, they offer intriguing views of the remarkable minds and careers of two remarkable women. Their work should be belatedly recognized as a landmark in the history of editing, and the women should be recognized as a welcome addition to the long-standing brotherhood of 'the Shakespearian editorial club'.

THE SHAKESPEARE EDITION IN INDUSTRIAL CAPITALISM

CARY DiPIETRO

In 1924, E. K. Chambers delivered his British Academy Lecture, 'The Disintegration of Shakespeare', whose title neatly categorized a range of textual activities associated with the reattribution of Shakespeare's plays to non-Shakespearian sources.[1] Among these were the attribution studies of F. G. Fleay and J. M. Robertson, both of whom receive significant critical attention in the lecture. Robertson had been famously praised by T. S. Eliot in his earlier 1919 essay on *Hamlet* for 'moving in the other direction' of romantic idealization in favour of historical and intellectually rigorous scholarship.[2] In what would become a remarkably sustained attempt to decode the authorship of Shakespeare's lesser plays and passages through metrical and stylistic analysis, Robertson completed his five-volume analysis of the Shakespeare canon in 1930.[3] Despite their claim to objective methodical analysis, Robertson and his contemporaries such as E. E. Stoll relied on preconceived ideals of Shakespeare's literary quality and were, Chambers noted, as equally idealistic as the defenders of the canon. After 1924, despite Eliot's praise, Robertson and his contemporaries would be better remembered as 'disintegrating' critics. This label is really rather remarkable, if only insofar as the idea of canonical disintegration entirely misrepresents such studies of attribution in a language antithetical to their (however misguided) pursuit, that is, identifying and characterizing the authentic Shakespeare text. More significant, though, is the rather morbid metaphoric dimension of Shakespeare's disintegration. 'Shakespeare' appears in the title synonymous with the extant printed texts attributed to his name – a common enough trope in literary criticism, but conspicuous in a discussion of textual attribution – as a unitary author whose 'disintegration' suggests an assisted decomposition or decaying of his corporeal body, a deliberate and irreverent disturbing of the grave which, as any early twentieth-century Shakespeare enthusiast would have known, the inscription on Shakespeare's gravestone explicitly cautions against.

The metaphoric dimension of Shakespeare's authorship in the title of Chambers's lecture discreetly reaffirms the romanticist belief in Shakespeare as the unitary imaginative and intellectual centre of the canon, and allegorizes textual activities which question that unity as 'disintegrating' the assumed whole. Interestingly, the lecture goes on to discuss what Chambers termed the doctrine of 'continuous copy' as developed in a series of books and articles by Alfred W. Pollard and John Dover Wilson, as well as the New Shakespeare edition series, begun by Cambridge University Press in 1921 under the editorship of Dover Wilson and Arthur Quiller-Couch. Quiller-Couch bowed out of the series in 1925, giving Dover Wilson more

---

[1] E. K. Chambers, 'The Disintegration of Shakespeare', in *Aspects of Shakespeare: Being British Academy Lectures (1923–1931)*, ed. J. W. Mackail (Oxford, 1933), pp. 23–48.

[2] See T. S. Eliot's summary of Robertson's *The Problem of 'Hamlet'* (London, 1919) and E. E. Stoll's *Hamlet: An Historical and Comparative Study* (Minneapolis, 1919) in *The Sacred Wood: Essays on Poetry and Criticism* (1920; repr. London, 1934), pp. 95–103.

[3] J. M. Robertson, *The Shakespeare Canon*, 5 vols. (London, 1922–32).

or less free rein to implement his highly unorthodox editorial principles and to produce one of the more unusual and extraordinary scholarly edition series in the twentieth century. Indeed, given the relative eccentricity of the New Shakespeare, it is unsurprising that Chambers would categorize Dover Wilson's efforts alongside the impressionistic judgements of enthusiasts such as Robertson. But beyond impressionistic misrepresentation of the canon, 'disintegration' clearly refers to a much broader process of canon reconfiguration, potentially including a new bibliographic approach to the texts, as exemplified in a new Shakespeare edition series, which is articulated in the conflict between the 'disintegrating' impulses of contemporary scholarship and a pre-existing idealized author/canon.

Numerous contemporary critics have demonstrated how the tension between the material practices of textual production and the romanticist ideologies of authorship characterized early bibliographic studies. Laurie E. Maguire, for example, has noted that while the New Bibliography introduced a twentieth-century scientific approach to textual analysis, their methodologies were mixed with nineteenth-century presuppositions about authors and texts, the result of which was a combination of material analysis and textual interpretation, the certainty of attitude appropriate to the former being transferred to the latter.[4] Hugh Grady has also suggested how scientific bibliography concealed a humanism – reasserting the traditional authenticity and unity of the canon in the face of textual disintegration – in a language and methodology which resonated with the scientism inherent in late-Victorian literary culture. The ready and near universal acceptance of bibliography, he argues, 'in the light of the far from certain and stable nature of its proofs argues strongly that it fulfilled ideological functions and was welcomed as a legitimator of a desired authoritative Shakespeare'.[5] Grady places scientific bibliography in the context of early twentieth-century modernism, a modernism advertising its newness by appealing to the modern technologies and scientistic methodologies which were otherwise disintegrat-

ing the traditional, romantic culture which modernism sought to reinscribe: in the case of bibliography, the organic unity of the canon and the singular authorship of Shakespeare as a marker of high culture. While we tend to think of the early twentieth century as a period given to the rise of the New Bibliography and its determining effects upon the practices of textual production, what I would like to do here is, first, recast the edition in this period in the context of a dialectical tension between modernization and the ideologies of literary culture, and then explore the issues surrounding the reception of Dover Wilson's New Shakespeare series, the title of which arguably demonstrates that tension between a modernizing impulse to 'make new' and a romanticist dedication to preserving Shakespeare's authorship.

The 'disintegrating' tendencies of Dover Wilson's editorial practices were, I would argue, demonstrative of a broader 'disintegration' which saw Shakespeare's texts reproduced, disseminated and diversified through unprecedented modernized and massified media. With improvements made in printing and book production technology, Shakespeare editions proliferated through the late eighteenth and nineteenth centuries. These editions were mostly inexpensive pocket and abridged or expurgated family editions, but also included elaborately illustrated decorative and performance editions. The growth of a mass market for editions of Shakespeare reflected not only the introduction of Shakespeare into the national school curriculum in the nineteenth century, but more broadly, and especially by the early twentieth century, the assimilation of working class and

---

[4] Laurie E. Maguire, *Shakespearean Suspect Texts: The 'Bad' Quartos and their Contexts* (Cambridge, 1996). See also Margreta de Grazia, 'The Essential Shakespeare and the Material Book', *Textual Practice*, 2 (1988), 69–86, who employs Michel Foucault's concept of the 'author function' to expose the ironies of bibliography's materialism; and Andrew Murphy, 'Texts and Textualities: A Shakespearean History', in *The Renaissance Text: Theory, Editing, Textuality*, ed. Andrew Murphy (Manchester, 2000), pp. 191–210 (especially p. 205).

[5] Hugh Grady, *The Modernist Shakespeare: Critical Texts in a Material World* (Oxford, 1991), p. 61.

bourgeois culture in a growing urban middle-class culture in which Shakespeare proved a respectable and entertaining past-time.[6] Improvements in photographic technology in the latter half of the nineteenth century had also allowed for the first photographically reproduced original texts, from the very limited and expensive lithographic Quarto reproductions of J. O. Halliwell and William Ashbee, produced between 1861 and 1871, to the first full and widely available photolithographic reproduction of the First Folio, produced by Howard Staunton in 1866.[7] While the increasing dissemination of photographically reproduced original printed texts exposed contemporary stylistic superfluities such as bowdlerization, extra-textual illustration and editorial emendation as inauthentic, the unmediated photographic reproduction of what were still largely regarded with an eighteenth-century pessimism to be corrupted texts, magnified the necessity to establish criteria for modern editing and textual production.[8] In working to establish those criteria, the emerging scientific bibliography, even while it espoused scientific progress (and the teleology of the modern in its self-proclaimed newness), would seek to contain the ever-expanding diversity and heterogeneity of the Shakespeare edition.

As the growth of a domestic reading market coupled with technological developments in book production facilitated the expansion of the Shakespeare publishing industry, the diversification of the Shakespeare text in an emerging mass market economy was not confined to the edition. Shakespeare's popularity was also in evidence both in the late-Victorian music-hall, and later, in the feature cinema, where Shakespeare proved consistently popular fare for working-class and, with the growth in number and size of cinemas, increasingly middle-class audiences.[9] As non-theatrical venues for Shakespeare continued to grow in popularity through the early twentieth century, theatrical production was increasingly seen to be in a state of crisis. During this time, a broad range of discourse about theatrical reform, beginning in the 1880s with the social reforms proposed by Matthew Arnold and continuing through to the

legislation of the National Theatre Act in 1948, commonly articulated an anti-capitalist socialism characteristic of the Fabian society, whose members in the period included two of the most vocal campaigners for theatre reform, George Bernard Shaw and Harley Granville-Barker.[10] Between 1904 and 1907 at the Court Theatre, under the joint management of Granville-Barker and John Vedrenne, Shaw would produce some of his most successful and influential naturalist drama, including *Candida*, *Man and Superman* and *Captain Brassbound's Conversion*.[11] Prompted by the success of this

---

[6] Andrew Murphy, in his recent *Shakespeare in Print: A History and Chronology of Shakespeare Publishing* (Cambridge, 2003), notes that this growth of a mass market for editions of Shakespeare, in addition to nineteenth-century educational reforms, was partly due to the growth of a domestic reading culture in Victorian England (p. 179). Murphy also notes the simultaneous growth of an edition market in America, resulting in a significant cross-Atlantic trade.

[7] Murphy, *Shakespeare in Print*, p. 194. The photographic editions are also listed in the comprehensive chronological index provided at the end of the book.

[8] Randall McLeod, 'UN *editing* Shak-speare', in *Shakespeare and the Editorial Tradition*, ed. Stephen Orgel and Sean Keilen (London, 1999), pp. 60–90, calls this a process of 'unediting': 'For us to witness the vast difference between the evidence of text conveyed by photofacsimiles and what stands revealed as editorial rumours and irrelevant improvements of it, is immediately to unedit Shakespeare' (p. 71).

[9] A distinction should be made here between middle-class culture and mass culture which, rather than suggest a specific class association, refers to a process of class reorganization and cultural massification precipitated by the industrialization, urbanization and democratization of English society. Richard Halpern, in *Shakespeare Among the Moderns* (Ithaca, 1997), defines mass culture more explicitly (esp. p. 54), drawing further reference to Jürgen Habermas.

[10] On the Fabian critique of culture, see Ian Britain, *Fabianism and Culture: A Study in British Socialism of the Arts c. 1884–1918* (Cambridge, 1982).

[11] *Candida* was first performed in 1897 and revived under the Barker-Vedrenne management at the Court Theatre with Granville-Barker in the cast of 1904; *Man and Superman* was first performed, again with Granville-Barker, in 1905; *Captain Brassbound's Conversion*, for which Shaw finally persuaded Ellen Terry to take the role of Lady Cicely, was revived in 1906. The playbills are included in Desmond McCarthy, *The Court Theatre 1904–1907: A Commentary and Criticism* (London, 1907).

experiment, Granville-Barker and William Archer published their scheme for a national repertory theatre system in 1907.[12] Their envisioned goal of establishing a national English repertory theatre was conceived as a countermeasure to a theatrical crisis precipitated by the growing commercialism of the West End. Similar theatrical discourse throughout the period commonly articulated a hostility towards actor-managers such as Henry Irving and Herbert Beerbohm Tree, whose ever more lavish scales of production were seen to necessitate an appeal to the broader and less-critical tastes of a growing urban middle-class audience. The introduction of film technology and its ready acceptance by mainstream actor-managers, from Tree to Frank Benson and Johnston Forbes-Robertson, further heightened an anxiety about the multiplication of bourgeois tastes and values through such mass media to a new mass audience. At the centre of this debate was Shakespeare: for actor-managers like Tree, an agent in the cultural enfranchisement of the lower classes; for theatre reformers, in contrast, a national dramatist whose cultural and racial superiority would legitimate state-sponsored institutions such as the proposed national theatre, institutions which would extend the tastes and values of an elite cultural minority to the larger public.[13]

Similarly, the improvement of photographic and print technology coupled with the increasing mechanization of book production, the growth of a mass market for relatively cheap editions of Shakespeare, and the subsequent rise of a modern publishing industry to meet that market, would all give rise to specialized scholarly editions which, as authorized by the authenticating practices which they would eventually necessitate (such as scientific bibliography), would similarly secure the tastes and values of a traditional high culture against a threatening mass culture. This idea of encounter between a romantic aesthetic idealism and the degrading mechanization and massification inherent in the corporate stage of capitalism draws directly from the aesthetic theories of Walter Benjamin, who first expressed his concern for 'The Work of Art in the Age of Mechanical Reproduction' in 1936.[14] We

can see how Benjamin's notion of the artwork's 'aura', a singularity and originary aesthetic function located in the edition in that elusive essence of the author, the 'what-Shakespeare-wrote', would be potentially degraded by the endless capacity of the text for reproduction, derivation and dissemination in modern industrialized society. In his critique of capitalist society, Benjamin was applying a central tenet of Marxist theory to the aesthetic; in particular, the constant revolutionizing of the means of production inherent in bourgeois society, the relentless modernization affecting all instruments and relations of production, and all the relations of society.[15] Of the resulting effects – urbanization, massification, expansionism – the idea of industrial mechanization in the mass market posed, for Benjamin, one of the greatest threats to the aura of the artwork. Benjamin was not strictly critical of mechanization or mass culture, but more so of the 'bourgeoisification' of the artwork: under capitalist conditions of production, he argued, the work of art became a work designed for reproducibility, and was therefore preconditioned by the mass-audience market for which it would be intended. Later Marxists have further refined concepts of cultural production in industrial capitalism, but we can see how Benjamin's earlier theory might characterize the Shakespeare edition in the context of print mechanization and the growth of the edition market through the nineteenth and twentieth centuries: in the face of the unregulated proliferation of Shakespeare editions, the equally

---

12 William Archer and Harley Granville-Barker, *A National Theatre: Scheme and Estimates* (London, 1907); it would be revised by Granville-Barker in 1938 under the shorter title *A National Theatre* (London, 1938).

13 See my own article, 'Shakespeare in the Age of Mechanical Reproduction: Cultural Discourse and the Film of Tree's *Henry VIII*', *New Theatre Quarterly*, 76 (November 2003), 366–80.

14 Walter Benjamin, 'The Work of Art in the Age of Mechanical Reproduction', in *Illuminations*, trans. by Harry Zohn (London, 1973), pp. 211–44.

15 This understanding of Karl Marx in *The Communist Manifesto* is developed by Marshall Berman in *All That Is Solid Melts Into Air: The Experience of Modernity* (London, 1983).

affordable scholarly edition offered to secure the aura of a genuine Shakespeare text, and the elite cultural values associated with his authorship, against the threat of canonical 'disintegration' posed by the mass market edition.[16] If scientific bibliography espoused a problematic materialism which concealed the tensions between a modernizing scientism and a romanticist dedication to Shakespeare's authorship, the resulting scholarly edition would come to efface its own commodity status in the capitalist market – ever-new, ever-improved – by bracketing itself off as an academically authorized text.[17]

In 1924, however, the year in which Chambers derided the New Shakespeare series, scientific bibliography had yet to secure its claim to academic authority vis-à-vis the Shakespeare edition. Certainly by this time, the textual optimism of the New Bibliography had taken hold. One year earlier in 1923, Pollard had delivered his British Academy Lecture on *The Foundations of Shakespeare's Text*, a revision of his earlier full-length study in 1909, *Shakespeare's Folios and Quartos*, which made the ill-fated distinction between 'good' and 'bad' quartos.[18] 1923 was also the year in which he published a volume of collected essays on *Shakespeare's Hand in the Play of Sir Thomas More*.[19] Pollard, whose interest in Shakespeare bibliography began when a librarian at the British Museum, was a leading member of the Bibliographic Society, and editor of its journal *The Library* from 1904. Like similar scholarly societies of the nineteenth century, the Bibliographical Society encouraged the methodical and scientific study of literary texts as a social occupation for its largely non-academic members.[20] Following the further establishment of the Malone Society in 1906, which had grown to a membership of nearly 250, Pollard and his contemporaries, including Chambers, had produced nearly fifty single-play editions of non-Shakespearian Renaissance drama by 1924.[21] Despite their involvement in such formally ordered societies, however, bibliographic scholarship was still largely regarded by academic contemporaries to be the least conservative of textual practices and, though references were often made to the New Bibliography's com-

paratively unconventional conclusions in textual notes, it was not directly associated with the established editions of Shakespeare. The two major edition series of the period, the Arden Shakespeare begun in 1899 (under the general editorship of W. J. Craig in 1923), and the American Yale Shakespeare begun in 1917, remained cautious in their application of bibliographic speculations. Both nearing completion in 1924, these two series represented the second generation of scholarly editions after the landmark nineteenth-century Cambridge, which was issued again as the Globe Shakespeare in 1864,

---

[16] Early Marxist texts share both an ideological and chronological framework with the narratives of late modernity, and therefore Benjamin's analogous writing (often labelled modernist) usefully highlights the anxieties generated by the appearance of new technologies and modes of production in traditional spheres of culture. I would be reluctant, however, to endorse fully the negative characterization of modernization and mass culture as developed by some later Marxists, especially including, among others, Jürgen Habermas in *The Structural Transformation of the Public Sphere: An Inquiry into a Category of Bourgeois Society* (1962), trans. by Thomas Burger (London, 1989); and later, Perry Anderson in *A Zone of Engagement* (London, 1992).

[17] Terry Eagleton, in 'Capitalism and Post-Modernism', *New Left Review*, 152 (July/August, 1985), 60–73, characterizes modernist artworks as in conflict with their own material status, denying their own economic reality: 'Modernism is among other things a strategy whereby the work of art resists commodification, holds out by the skin of its teeth against those social forces which would degrade it to an exchangeable object' (p. 67). See also Fredric Jameson, 'Reification and Utopia in Mass Culture', *Social Text*, 1 (Winter 1979), 130–48.

[18] Alfred W. Pollard, *The Foundations of Shakespeare's Text*, The Annual Shakespeare Lecture, 1923 (London, 1923); *Shakespeare's Folios and Quartos: A Study in the Bibliography of Shakespeare* (London, 1909).

[19] Alfred W. Pollard, ed., *Shakespeare's Hand in the Play of Sir Thomas More* (Cambridge, 1923).

[20] The history of scientific bibliography in relation to nineteenth-century scholarly societies has been noted repeatedly. See especially Gary Taylor, *Reinventing Shakespeare: A Cultural History from the Restoration to the Present* (London, 1989), pp. 162–230; Grady, *The Modernist Shakespeare*, pp. 28–73; and, most recently, Murphy, *Shakespeare in Print*, pp. 208–36.

[21] See 'List of Publications: 1907–1956', in The Malone Society's *Collections, Volume IV* (Oxford, 1956), pp. 17–26.

the first inexpensive and widely available scholarly edition.

A third on-going major series in 1924 was the New Shakespeare, also published by Cambridge University Press, and like both the Arden and Yale, serialized in single-play volumes. Initially under the editorship of Quiller-Couch and Dover Wilson, this was the only edition series to acknowledge an intellectual debt to the New Bibliography: 'No moment', Quiller-Couch wrote in his General Introduction, 'has been more favourable for auspicating a text of the plays and poems than that which begets the occasion of this new one'.[22] Clearly, the editors conceived of their series as an answer to the contemporary popular editions, the next generation of *new* Shakespeare texts informed by the twentieth-century scientific approach of the New Bibliography. In his review of the first edition for the series, *The Tempest* (1921), Sidney Lee praised the scientific principles which the editors endeavoured to employ, but Lee remained far more cautious about Dover Wilson's controversial textual theories.[23] Dover Wilson held, for example, that the punctuation of the extant Folio texts for the most part reproduced the punctuation of the prompt copy and, furthermore, reflected the dramatic quality of that copy. The punctuation, he argued, represented Shakespeare's instructions to the actors: 'The stops, brackets, capital letters in the Folio are in fact stage-directions in shorthand. They tell the actor when to pause and for how long, they guide his intonation, they indicate the emphatic word, often enough they denote "stage-business".'[24] For Lee, Dover Wilson's conclusions about the dramatic quality of the text rested not on empirical deduction, but on 'unstable foundations of conjecture and hypothesis'.[25]

Moreover, far from being a performance-oriented text, reviewers also noted the editors' proclivity for narrative elaboration, demonstrated especially by the frequent 'supererogatory' stage directions inserted into the text for the benefit of the modern reader.[26] Dover Wilson's extra-textual narrative *mise-en-scène* directions were not to be confused with the stage directions of the extant texts, nor the authorial dramatic punctuation, both of which allowed a guess as to the stage business required at any given moment. Instead, the *mise-en-scène* directions were necessary for the understanding of the modern reader: 'Editorial stage-directions will always evoke the laughter of the actor and will never completely satisfy the judgement of the scholar', he wrote in 1929, 'Yet no editor can avoid the responsibility; he must either compose them himself or endorse those of his predecessors by reproducing them.'[27] Characteristically, Dover Wilson chose the former route, introducing his own elaborate narrative directions to aid the imagination of the reader. This was not to suggest, however, that the *mise-en-scène* directions had no basis in the authorial text: Shakespeare, he argued, 'almost always formed a clear-cut and definite picture of the surroundings amid which his characters moved, and it is generally possible to reconstruct this scenery from incidental references in the play'.[28] The eccentricity of Dover Wilson's editorial policies magnified for critics such as Chambers the sense in which textual theorization, such as also typified by scientific bibliography, could be seen to disintegrate the traditional canon. For most critics and reviewers, the Arden remained the more conservative and reliable series of Shakespeare editions.

By the 1923 New Shakespeare editions of *Much Ado About Nothing* and *Love's Labour's Lost*, Arthur Reed was noting that critical appreciation of the

---

[22] In the General Introduction to William Shakespeare, *The Tempest*, ed. by Arthur Quiller-Couch and J. Dover Wilson (Cambridge, 1921), p. ix.

[23] Sir Sidney Lee, 'Shakespeare', in *This Year's Work in English Studies, Volume II 1920–1*, ed. for the English Association by Sir Sidney Lee and F. S. Boas (London, 1922), pp. 66–80 (pp. 68–71).

[24] In the Textual Introduction to *The Tempest*, pp. xxxvii–xxxviii.

[25] Lee, p. 70.

[26] Lee, p. 68.

[27] J. Dover Wilson, 'The Elizabethan Shakespeare', in *Aspects of Shakespeare*, pp. 202–26 (p. 217).

[28] In the Textual Introduction to *The Tempest*, p. xxxix.

series was 'hardening to an issue between conservative scholarship and the new bibliography'.[29] The departure of the series from previous editions demonstrated what he perceived to be a growing schism between two modes of textual methodology. For Lee, the series was itself indicative of that schism between a modernizing scientism and a more conservative nineteenth-century approach, particularly in the pairing of Dover Wilson with Quiller-Couch. The presence of Quiller-Couch arguably demonstrated the kind of edition the Shakespeare-reading public was willing to buy. In addition to the character studies of A. C. Bradley and the criticism of Algernon Swinburne and Edward Dowden, the Shakespeare book market still witnessed frequent reprints of essays by William Hazlitt, Samuel Taylor Coleridge and Samuel Johnson.[30] At the turn of the twentieth century, the new chairs being established in English literature at major universities were dominated by Victorian scholarly essayists such as Bradley and Walter Raleigh, whose styles descended directly from English and German romantic essayists such as Coleridge.[31] If mainstream Shakespeare criticism was still predominantly demonstrative of the literary tastes and textual concerns of eighteenth- and nineteenth-century romanticism, scholarly editions of Shakespeare also required validation by the presence of a conservative scholarship which placed primary emphasis on the cultural, intellectual and literary superiority of Shakespeare, rather than the kind of scholarship typical of the scientific literary societies. Thus, Quiller-Couch, the King Edward VII Professor of English Literature at Cambridge, wrote in his General Introduction to the series: 'It were merely feeble compliment today to call him our "great National Playwright." He is that: but he is much more – he is very much more – he is more by difference of quality. He is our great national Poet.'[32] This association between nineteenth-century literary high culture and the twentieth-century edition was further evidenced by both Dowden, who initially fronted the Arden and who produced an edition of *Hamlet* as the first in that immensely successful series, and by Raleigh,

who sought to produce a series of Folio-based editions through Oxford University Press, an initiative which would culminate finally in the 1986 Oxford Shakespeare.

While the concept for the New Shakespeare, whose series title once again advertised a newness predicated upon a modernizing principle, demonstrated the ideological friction between traditional humanist scholarship and modernization, the series also demonstrated the degree to which the practices of textual 'authorizing' were seen more generally to be indicative of modernization. This was not merely symptomatic of bibliographic scholarship. Editing itself, particularly when it was as heavy-handed as in the New Shakespeare series, retained the stigma associated with the adaptation and revision characteristic of the numerous derivative editions, a perception of tampering with the text. In contrast to the New Shakespeare series,

[29] Arthur W. Reed, 'Shakespeare', in *This Year's Work in English Studies, Volume IV 1923*, ed. for the English Association by Sir Sidney Lee and F. S. Boas (London, 1924), pp. 74–92 (pp. 82).

[30] Of the many editions of Hazlitt, particularly relevant to this discussion is a 1916 edition of *Characters of Shakespeare's Plays*, introduced by Arthur Quiller-Couch (London); see also *The Best of Hazlitt*, compiled by P. P. Howe (London, 1923); and in twelve volumes, *The Collected Works of William Hazlitt*, edited by A. R. Waller and Arnold Glover and introduced by W. E. Henley (London, 1902–4). Several editions of Coleridge on Shakespeare appeared in home library edition series, most notably *Lectures and Notes on Shakespeare and Other English Poets*, compiled by T. Ashe (London, 1890), reprinted at least five times up to 1914. In addition to a thirteen-volume series by the American publisher Pafraets of *The Works of Samuel Johnson* (1903), see also Walter Raleigh's 1908 edition of *Johnson on Shakespeare: Essays and Notes* (London). These represent a mere sampling of the numerous volumes and collected editions by these three writers in print in the early twentieth century.

[31] Johnson, Coleridge, Hazlitt, Swinburne and Dowden all receive significant critical attention in A. C. Bradley's *Shakespearean Tragedy: Lectures on Hamlet, Othello, King Lear, Macbeth* (New York, 1904). The significance of both Bradley and Walter Raleigh's *Shakespeare* (London, 1907) are discussed by Terence Hawkes in *That Shakespeherian Rag: Essays on a Critical Process* (London, 1986).

[32] Arthur Quiller-Couch in the General Introduction to *The Tempest*, p. xxv.

the Yale Shakespeare, which made few notes to the text and presented the text first, leaving textual notes to the appendices (thus following the example of the un-annotated text in the Globe series) was praised for its prudence. Reviewing the Yale series, Arthur Reed noted: 'It is pleasant to handle a Shakespeare . . . in which the reader has a full page of text, bating only a modest array of glosses at the foot, and in which the editor retires to the relative obscurity of the appendices.'[33] The effect produced in most major scholarly editions was an appearance of the text as having been unmediated.[34] The self-effacement of textual editing was perhaps indicative of the pessimism inherited from the eighteenth and nineteenth centuries regarding the authority of Shakespeare's extant printed texts, a pessimism amplified by the contemporary theories of disintegration. Editorial glosses were simply efforts to tidy up very untidy texts with a series of best guesses founded upon conjecture and literary taste. Not unlike the 'disintegrating' critics, the earliest scholarly editors sought to rescue Shakespeare from the vagaries of print and performance based on a largely impressionistic belief in Shakespeare's literary quality. If bibliography was reinvigorating Shakespeare scholarship with a renewed faith in the extant texts and a non-impressionistic methodology in 1924, that optimism had not yet translated into a protocol for textual editing. Published in 1935, McKerrow's *Prolegomena for the Oxford Shakespeare* was the first systematic consideration of editing practice to define explicitly an editing procedure against a bibliographic criterion of authenticity.[35] The ideal text, McKerrow argued, 'should approach as closely as the extant material allows to a fair copy, made by the author himself, of his plays in the form which he intended finally to give them, and . . . should not in any way be coloured by the preconceived ideas or interpretations of later times'.[36]

Although McKerrow's Oxford edition never materialized, his prolegomena finally defined bibliographic scholarship within a traditional humanist program, instituting a set of criteria for editing according to the non-disintegrating conception of a wholly authorial copy-text. The New Shakespeare series, by comparison, was predicated upon a far more fluid sense of copy-text, demonstrated by Dover Wilson's theories about the stylistic tendencies of Shakespeare's hand and his theory of dramatic punctuation. Taken together, his conclusions about the transmission of individual plays would come to be known as 'continuous copy'. Much of his thinking prior to the New Shakespeare series had been tested in a series of articles jointly written with Pollard and printed in the *Times Literary Supplement* in 1919, although the three plays discussed therein were not published in the New Shakespeare series for several years.[37] This series of five articles was concerned primarily with the transmission of the 'bad' or surreptitious Quartos, as categorized by Pollard in 1909; though, significantly, insofar as the three quarto texts discussed were derived from 'shortened versions of the plays used by Shakespeare's company on tour' (*TLS*, 19 January 1919), they therefore also reflected performance versions of the plays. Moreover, argued Pollard and Dover Wilson in the following week, the bibliographical links between the bad and the good Shakespearian texts proved 'not only that the former were to some extent derived from playhouse manuscript, but that these manuscripts possessed some kind of organic connexion with those

---

33 Arthur W. Reed, 'Shakespeare', in *This Year's Work in English Studies, Volume V 1924*, ed. for the English Association by F. S. Boas and C. H. Herford (London, 1926), pp. 108–27 (pp. 115).

34 This point is made of the Globe Shakespeare by Murphy, *Shakespeare in Print*, p. 191, who cites Margreta de Grazia, 'The Question of the One and the Many: *The Globe Shakespeare*, the *Complete "King Lear"*, and the *New Folger Library Shakespeare*', *Shakespeare Quarterly*, 46:2 (1995), 245–51 (p. 247).

35 Mention might be made here of W. W. Greg's earlier *Principles of Emendation in Shakespeare* (London, 1928).

36 Ronald B. McKerrow, *Prolegomena to the Oxford Shakespeare: A Study in Editorial Method* (Oxford, 1939), p. 6.

37 A. W. Pollard and J. Dover Wilson, 'The "Stolne and Surreptitious" Shakespearian Texts' for *The Times Literary Supplement* in 1919 (9, 16 January, 13 March, 7, 14 August). The Quartos discussed include, in order, *Henry V* Q1 (1600), *The Merry Wives of Windsor* Q1 (1602), and *Romeo and Juliet* Q1 (1597).

which formed the copy for the latter' (16 January 1919). The articles generated a significant interest insofar as they explained the 'corruption' of the surreptitious texts in the context of piracy, which Pollard had initially proposed in his 1917 *Shakespeare's Fight with the Pirates*, but also in the possibility of theatrical revision.[38] In further suggesting that the bad texts possessed an organic connection with the good, these initial articles established a strong correlation in all the extant texts between textual mutability and performance.

As Chambers noted in 1924, the doctrine of 'continuous copy' was based primarily on the principle of theatrical precaution and economy: the copy-text used by the printers for the 'good' Quartos reflected the fewest possible number of expensive transcriptions, and were, therefore, primarily authorial fair copies. Given the fear of printing piracy, these manuscripts were closely guarded by the theatrical companies over long periods of time, and subsequently reflected the numerous, possibly non-authorial, revisions occasioned by revivals and provincial tours. Returning in 1923 to the question of the Folio's authority, Pollard thus surmised that, when the copy-texts used by the printers were not the revised authorial fair copies themselves, then the earlier 'good' Quartos used as copy-text may have either served as playhouse prompt-books, which would then bear the marks of dramatic revision, or may have been checked against authorial or revised manuscript or play-house prompt-books. In any case, the Folio text might reveal important information about the way the plays were performed, recording alterations which had been made in performance. Thus, the 'foundations of Shakespeare's texts' demonstrated a continuity between authorial and performative versions. In 1923, Pollard's *Shakespeare's Hand in the Play of Sir Thomas More* offered the extant manuscript of *Sir Thomas More* as the most concrete evidence of such theatrical revision. Insofar as the claim of Shakespeare's hand was true, then it represented the possibility that the copy-texts used by the printers for Shakespeare's First Folio were, like the manuscript of *Sir Thomas More*, socially conditioned, possibly multi-authored, and dramatic in nature.

Dover Wilson's theories on dramatic punctuation comprise a significant chapter in the volume on *Sir Thomas More*, theories which also served as the basis for his highly unorthodox editing of punctuation in the New Shakespeare series. In 1929, he would also summarize the notion of continuity in copy; the Shakespearian playbooks as 'in a constant state of flux' only achieving their final state in print without 'any considered preparation by the author', a final printed state which merely recorded 'the conditions of the last performance before the printing was taken in hand'.[39] The term 'continuous copy', however, was coined by Chambers in 1924, when he denounced these theories as another form of textual disintegration: 'and so we arrive at the notion of the long-lived manuscript in the tiring-house wardrobe', Chambers derided, 'periodically taken out for a revival and as often worked upon by fresh hands, abridged and expanded, recast to fit the capabilities of new performers, brightened with current topical allusions, written up to date to suit new tastes in poetic diction'.[40] According to Chambers, bibliographical scholarship was a useful addition to the equipment of scholarship, but he was highly sceptical of the 'superstructure of theory', the supposition and conjecture, piled on the plays in the New Shakespeare series. Indeed, Chambers was among the first to note the absence of material evidence supplied by bibliographic scholarship, as he was equally unsure of the burden of proof borne by the manuscript for *Sir Thomas More* which, he argued, was an exceptional and unusual rather than exemplary text. The main difficulty of Dover Wilson's theories regarding the transmission of the seven plays taken on in the New Shakespeare series up to 1924, however, was that not one was 'allowed to be an integral and untouched product of Shakespeare's creative energy, in the form in which he first conceived and wrought it'.[41] In contrast to such

---

[38] Alfred W. Pollard, *Shakespeare's Fight with the Pirates and the Problems of the Transmission of his Text* (London, 1917).
[39] Dover Wilson, 'The Elizabethan Shakespeare', p. 204.
[40] Chambers, 'The Disintegration of Shakespeare', p. 42.
[41] Chambers, p. 40.

disintegrating scholarship, hardly less perturbing than the Baconians, 'the rock of Shakespeare's reputation', he argued, reaffirming a belief in the organic and inviolable unity of Shakespeare, 'stands four-square to the winds of Time'.[42]

Dover Wilson was given his turn to respond to Chambers in his 1929 British Academy Lecture, which, like the New Shakespeare series itself, represented both a culmination of the theories which he espoused with Pollard, as well as, given the highly speculative nature of their theories, a significant schism in the ranks of the New Bibliography over the question of 'continuous copy'. Following the Oxford *Prolegomena*, the notion of 'continuous copy' would be firmly denounced by more conservative bibliographers such as McKerrow and Greg as 'a figment of the editorial brain'.[43] In contrast, their principles for editing would come to mean seeking to reconstruct the final authorial fair copy, significantly, before it entered the playhouse for performance. As Greg noted in 1955, both Pollard and Dover Wilson also seem to have withdrawn from the idea after 1924, the latter writing in his introduction to the New Shakespeare *3 Henry VI* that 'continuous copy' was 'a doctrine which the said Wilson long since abandoned, without, to the best of his recollection, ever consciously holding it'.[44] If Chambers unfairly polarized the New Bibliography by coining the term 'continuous copy', nevertheless Dover Wilson's efforts in the New Shakespeare series seem to have reflected a time when the bibliographic conception of text was negotiating a precarious balance between what were understood to be the material realities of Elizabethan theatrical production and the reaffirmation of a nineteenth-century humanist belief in singular authorship implicit in the scholarly edition. The series itself might therefore be said to contain the ideological frictions produced by the conflicting appeals made to newness, scientific progress, textual authority, and the genuine Shakespeare text.

The New Shakespeare series – initially fronted by the odd combination of Quiller-Couch and Dover Wilson, both equally eccentric in their editorial visions, traversed by a series of different motivations, and characterized throughout by Dover Wilson's imaginative speculations – was far from representative of contemporary scholarly editions, and has long since fallen out of print and further out of fashion. The issues surrounding its reception, however, would seem to have anticipated many of the textual concerns and controversies which characterize contemporary editing and textual production. Theories of multiple authorship and revision, the practice of publishing parallel-text editions, the endless possibilities for hyper-text annotation in the internet edition, and concepts of performance in textual editing and book production, all threaten to compromise or expose a persistent romantic ideal, the authorial 'aura' which otherwise serves to construct the Shakespeare text as the genuine work of its author rather than a mechanically reproduced (and endlessly reproducible in any conceivable version) commercial product in the capitalist market economy. Even while contemporary editors remain far more cautious in their mediation and dissemination of an indeterminate textual ideal, the scholarly publishing industry will continue to generate a series of ironies and ideological tensions as it endeavours to produce ever-new, ever-improved editions of Shakespeare.

---

[42] Chambers, p. 23. A similar point is made by Michael Taylor, *Shakespeare Criticism in the Twentieth Century* (Oxford, 2001), p. 7.

[43] See, for example, W. W. Greg's *The Editorial Problem in Shakespeare: A Survey of the Foundations of the Text* (Oxford, 1942), p. 42.

[44] As cited in W. W. Greg, *The Shakespeare First Folio: Its Bibliographical and Textual History* (Oxford, 1955), p. 102.

PRINT AND ELECTRONIC EDITIONS INSPIRED BY THE NEW VARIORUM *HAMLET* PROJECT

BERNICE W. KLIMAN

THE THREE-TEXT HAMLET: PARALLEL TEXTS OF THE FIRST AND SECOND QUARTOS AND FIRST FOLIO

At the beginning, there was the Modern Language Association's New Variorum *Hamlet* project. The original team, which began working before 1990, included Paul Bertram as text editor.[1] Almost immediately, he and I realized that having the three early texts of *Hamlet* in front of us in a compact and legible form would be useful for textual collations as well as commentary notes based on textual variants – the material we were collecting for the variorum edition. Encouraged by the many vital works that AMS Press had made available through its reprints, we approached Gabriel Hornstein, President of AMS, with a plan for publishing a *Three-Text* Hamlet, which he readily accepted. Though the idea of electronic versions of our new variorum work was very much a part of my original planning, Paul Bertram and I also felt that we needed a book to place by our computers for easy consulting. The flow between paper and electrons is a hallmark of our efforts in all our texts.

The first edition of The *Three-Text* Hamlet appeared in 1991 and was useful beyond our expectations not only to us but to the many scholars, students, and theatre practitioners who wrote to tell us how much they valued it.[2] Though many of the users had facsimiles of the First Quarto (Q1), the Second Quarto (Q2) and the First Folio (F1), our book simplified comparing the three texts through the parallel columns in which we arranged them.[3] If we had chosen to model our work on the exam-

ple of Michael Warren's excellent *Lear* books,[4] we might have xeroxed the facsimiles and cut them up to produce the parallel texts, but given the

---

[1] For the Modern Language Association's New Variorum Editions, I proposed the *Hamlet* project and with the permission of the Variorum Committee enlisted the team, which included William Hutchings, Harry Keyishian and Marion Perret. For life and career reasons, this entire first new variorum *Hamlet* cohort, including Paul Bertram, had dropped out of the project by 1993. Luckily, I persuaded F. Nicholas Clary of St Michael's College to join me, and he recruited Hardin Aasand of Dickinson State University; Eric Rasmussen (University of Nevada Reno) joined us in 1994. Our collaboration is unusual in that each of us takes responsibility for about one-fourth of the play – text, textual notes, commentary notes. We each also take a share of appendix essays. Our unique approach has garnered us several important grants, including three from the National Endowment for the Humanities, which we thank for its confidence in all of us, and we thank the Nassau Community College Foundation for administering the grants. All our institutions have been more than helpful. We also have been lucky since 1993 to have on the team Dr Jeffery Triggs (Rutgers University), our gifted web master. I thank all four colleagues for their consultations and support in the writing of this paper.

[2] Paul Bertram and Bernice W. Kliman, eds., *The Three-Text Hamlet: Parallel Texts of the First and Second Quartos and First Folio* (New York, 1991).

[3] Wilhelm Vietor's three-text version: Hamlet: *Parallel Texts of the First and Second Quartos and the First Folio* (Marburg, 1891) has, in the top two-thirds of facing pages, Q1 on the verso and Q2 on the recto, effectively making it easy to compare only these two. Below them F1 appears, spread in the last $\frac{1}{3}$ of facing pages. Vietor thus varies the arrangement made by the Bankside *Hamlet*, ed. Appleton Morgan (New York, 1890), which placed in parallel Q1 and F1, eliminating Q2 altogether.

[4] Especially his *The Parallel King Lear, 1608–1623* (Berkeley, 1989).

technology available at that time we would not have been able to generate electronic texts from facsimiles. Like many editions, ours served more than one purpose: the benefit to our project of having electronic texts for all three versions has proved itself over and over since then. Besides, word-processed texts can be relatively inexpensively reproduced in book form, and, eventually, as low-cost paperback books (AMS released a paperback of *Three-Text* in 2003 as part of the second, revised edition). Now, with the emergence of PDF files and inexpensive optical character reading (OCR) software, web sites and CDs can display facsimiles with electronic texts behind them.[5] But even if the technology had been up to it, printed facsimiles would have given us a text difficult, at times, to read.

To produce the electronic texts, we had two proficient typists each prepare word-processed copies of the three facsimiles. We explained to them that they should substitute a short s for each long ∫ from the originals; though the ∫ is easily confused with lower-case f, it remained in use until John Bell, the eighteenth-century publisher, abandoned it. We would have liked to retain the long ∫ for our seventeenth-century editions, but our computers had no character able to represent it well. It is not a character that translates from computer to computer. We retained u for v and v for u and as many other letters as possible as they were in the originals (double capital vvs for capital w, for example). Clearly, however, the modern font we used, Times, does not look like the original; we had a diplomatic text rather than a facsimile. As such, our text is cleaner and clearer, all the better for a reading text; the fact that it does not obscure its *edited* nature was, to our way of thinking, a good thing.

Once the texts were copied onto floppy disks and loaded into our computers, we used comparison software to pick out differences between each set of two versions and to flag the variants, which we could then check against the facsimiles. If any doubt remained, we compared the corrected word-processed copies to originals. I recall a pre-dawn visit to the British Museum, where by appointment a librarian led me to a display case that held their

copy of Q1 (one of the two so far discovered; the other is at the Huntington Library in California) to allow me to see if a mark on my facsimile was a bleed through or a punctuation mark.[6] After all our checking, I produced the *Three-Text* volume with Quark XPress software. To simplify the publishing process, we prepared camera-ready copy. Once we had determined each letter and punctuation mark, we had no wish to entrust the work to a typesetter.

We decided that the order in which the three *Hamlet* editions had been published would work for the order across the page spread: On the verso pages, Q1 (1603) and Q2 (1605) in left and right columns, respectively, and on the recto pages, F1 (1623) in the first column. Quite possibly the manuscript upon which Q1 is based is a version of the manuscript behind either the Q2 or the F1 or a combination of the two. Or, less likely, it is an earlier draft by Shakespeare or someone else with some Shakespeare intermixed. We might have suggested one idea of 'true chronology' rather than 'print chronology' by placing Q1 to the far right; but the certainty of the publication dates as opposed to the speculativeness of the dates of composition made print chronology more attractive.

Though the work is not formally 'edited' as many understand the term (text modernization, introduction, notes), we made many choices. We attempted to indicate the spacing, the line length and the justified right edge of the prose sections, at least suggesting the original look though we could

---

[5] 'Invented by Adobe [see adobe.com], Portable Document Format (PDF) is the published specification used by standards bodies around the world for more secure, reliable electronic document'. OCR software can produce a searchable electronic text but PDF files are best searched when clean electronic files underlie them – not OCR files. See the CD version of *The Winter's Tale*, the 2005 Variorum Edition, ed. Robert Kean Turner and Virginia Westling Haas (New York, 2005), and the web version of *The Century Dictionary* in http://www.hamletworks.org.

[6] The team owes a debt of gratitude to many libraries, especially the Folger Shakespeare Library, the Huntington Library and the British Library; as well as the libraries at the University of Pennsylvania; the Nassau Community College Library, Interlibrary Loan Department; and The Rutgers University Library.

not, of course, duplicate it with available fonts. Quartos have about thirty-five lines per page in a single column while folios have over 100 lines of text on each page in double columns. We had no staggered lines, the device that editors have used since George Steevens began the trend in his 1793 edition to put together complete verse lines where he perceived them. One of our main innovations beyond using a modern font and modern spacing between letters (disconnecting ligatures) was to provide Through Line Numbers (TLN) for all three texts as well as Continuous-Through-Line-Numbering for Q1 (Q1CLN). TLN appear to the left on every line (rather than every five or ten lines). We kept in mind two facts: one is that it is easier for readers to find a specific line when a number appears on every one, and easier for readers to compare texts when we had already done part of the task by placing the Through Line Number next to all three texts. Another is that we knew that our electronic version of the three texts would require a number with every line for tagging purposes. The number would be the chief means to call up specific lines from a CD or web site.

Though our using F1's Through Line Numbers (as in Hinman)[7] for all three texts seems to reify its position as our primary text (as does its position on the recto page), we did so because they were going to be our new variorum *Hamlet*'s numbering system. Paul Bertram preferred Q2 as our copy-text, but the *Shakespeare Variorum Handbook* specifies the use of Hinman's Through Line Numbers for the print edition regardless of copytext.[8] Like any edition in a series, then, ours had to adhere to rules made for all the plays in the new variorum project, half of which of course have no Quarto version.

In *The Three-Text* book we might have, perhaps, provided a double set of numbers for Q2 (TLN and CLN) as we had for Q1. But Q2 lines are long compared to those for Q1 (which are all verse) and F1 (which are double columned), and numbering to the right as well as the left of Q2 would have required us to compress the font size. Since our variorum project does not require separate numbering for Q2, we opted for maintaining full font size. F1 with its shorter lines allowed

us to place at its right a complete set of *Riverside* line numbers, with the act and scene opposite the first folio line on each page and at the beginning of scenes.[9] Our choice of *Riverside* line numbering was, again, dictated by the *Shakespeare Variorum Handbook*.

Line numbers are useful once scholarly manipulation of texts come into play. When Nicholas Rowe, the first Shakespeare editor credited by name for an edition, produced his edition in 1709, he envisioned a reader who would pick up one of the handy octavo volumes and read a play from beginning to end or dip into it as one might dip into the Bible. Rowe's ideal readers needed no line numbers because they had no reason to refer to specific speeches by anything more than page number; like the folios, the Rowe was meant to be *the* standard edition. The readers Rowe (and his publisher Tonson &c.) envisioned needed no notes; variant and explanatory notes are the chief force impelling the numbering of lines. From the publisher's perspective, the main thing Rowe did was lend his famous name as a dramatist to a reprinting project that was evidently needed, since the last complete plays had been published as the Fourth Folio in 1685, twenty-four years before, but he also made choices among the fourth folio and those that had come before it, and, for *Hamlet*, from the Quarto tradition. The first to number lines was Samuel Ayscough, Assistant Librarian, British Museum,[10] perhaps inspired by Edward Capell's separately published notes for his 1768 multi-volume edition of

---

7 Charlton Hinman, ed., The Norton Facsimile, *The First Folio of Shakespeare*, Prepared by Charlton Hinman (New York, 1968). Through-Line-Numbers are used in *Three-Text* with permission from the W. W. Norton Co. I believe this is the first instance of a numbering system held in copyright.

8 *Shakespeare Variorum Handbook. A Manual of Editorial Practice*, ed. Richard Hosley, Richard Knowles and Ruth McGugan (New York, 1971); 2nd edn. revd. and enlarged by Richard Knowles (New York, 2003). The second edition is available on the mla.org website; search "Riverside".

9 G. Blakemore Evans *et al.*, eds. *The Riverside Shakespeare* (Boston, 1974). The 1997 2nd edn supplies TLN in brackets at the tops of pages.

10 Ayscough's first one-volume Shakespeare, published by Stockdale, appeared anonymously in 1784.

the plays.[11] In his notes published years later in large quarto format, Capell referred to the edition's page and line numbers (which readers had to count for themselves). In Ayscough's 1790 and 1807 one-volume editions of the complete plays (sometimes published in two volumes), the numbering linked the plays to a separate index volume. Moreover, each page heading for the first time indicated act and scene, a scheme followed by, among others, the 1819 Thomas Caldecott edition of *Hamlet* and *As You Like It*, without emulating the line numbering. Not until the 1864 Globe edition did the idea take hold of numbering the lines (every five lines) consecutively (omitting stage directions), and beginning anew in each scene rather than at the top of each page.[12] Here, too, act and scene appear on page headings. This is the most emulated numbering system now in spite of some disagreement among editors about what constitutes a Shakespearean line. The line numbering facilitated access to the notes featured in these editions. This numbering practice depended on the stable scene divisions promulgated by Capell in his 1768 edition and taken up by almost every editor. Numbering by scenes instead of pages responded to the huge expansion in the number of editions. No longer did any one edition rule the market; it was no longer possible to mention to a wide audience a specific line of a play by page numbers. Much later the idea of Through Line Numbers began to appear in new variorum editions, inspired by Charlton Hinman's Norton Facsimile of the First Folio (1968). TLN include stage directions, and since a line is defined by FI's lineation, the numbers are the same in all editions. *The Three-Text* Hamlet numbering system builds on these previous editorial practices.

The necessity for comparing three texts in parallel mandated a landscape $11'' \times 8\frac{1}{2}''$ format rather than the smaller portrait format of most books. Since our three texts filled only three of four columns, Paul Bertram had the brilliant idea of repeating in the fourth column any QI lines that corresponded to the Q2 or FI lines on that spread but did not appear in the first column. As is well known, the order of the lines in QI does not correspond at every point with those in the other texts.

Moreover, some of its lines contain mere hints of the other texts.[13] We agreed that each text would be printed from beginning to end, with spaces left blank if necessary. But we eased the comparison between QI and the other texts through the fourth column.

Of course, no choice is purely innocent or immaterial. Each conveys something to the user. On our cover, the three identical portraits of Shakespeare derived from the First Folio's frontispiece, for example, suggest that all three texts are by Shakespeare and that all three texts are somehow equal in value. One reviewer criticized the subliminal effect of the cover, but we agree with the publisher that it includes both a recognizable image and a teasing suggestion about worth: all three texts merit our study if not our allegiance.

The placement of texts, the cover picture, the spacing and the numbering – all our choices were just so much more conspicuous in that we offered no notes, emended nothing, not even obvious mistakes. Our thinking was that if mistakes are obvious, anyone can see them as mistakes. We were determined to allow the texts to display at least some of their strangeness. Nor did we want to pre-empt our textual history that was to be the fruit of our variorum work. We settled for a short preface.

Careful as we were in reproducing the texts, we inevitably discovered some misreadings, places where the two typists and both of us had misread the facsimiles we had used (demonstrating if nothing else how difficult it can be to read grey-on-grey facsimiles). When a second edition of the *Three-Text* Hamlet was called for, we corrected the

---

[11] Capell's *Notes and Various Readings to Shakespeare*, vol. 1, part 1 (1774); a three-volume edition of the notes, including the 1774 publication, appeared from 1779 to 1784.

[12] The Globe Edition. *The Works of William Shakespeare*, ed. William George Clark and William Aldis Wright (Cambridge, 1864).

[13] One of the differences between the 2nd edn (2003) and the first is that we recognize more QI lines as being reminiscent of Q2 and/or FI lines than we had, conservatively, allowed in 1991.

errors we and helpful readers had found,[14] supplied a more complete list of the Q1, Q2 and F1 print variants (having since discovered some previously unknown), and Eric Rasmussen, who had supervised Dee Ann Phares-Matthew's work on textual variants, provided a succinct history of the editions in his introduction. Peter Donaldson of the Massachusetts Institute of Technology gave us access to beautiful electronic facsimiles of all seven extant Q2 texts. Four illustrations from the Folger Shakespeare Library and one from the Huntington Library enhance this second edition.

THE ENFOLDED HAMLET

In the meantime, however, before the first edition of the *Three-Text* appeared in print, I had discovered another, even more compact way to present the two main texts, one that has become a steady companion in word-processed, print and web versions. This is *The Enfolded* Hamlet, a text that has served the project well. With the Q2 text as the base (chosen because that was the text we had decided to use as our new variorum copytext), and with material variations[15] between it and F1 enclosed in brackets (curly for Q2, pointed for F1), it was possible to see the most important variations immediately. Putting aside immaterial variants, such as capital letters in F1, misspellings in Q2, and the differences in line length, the two texts are more alike than different. That is what makes enfolding possible. The enfolded edition presents variants of single words and whole passages with equal ease. In *The Enfolded* Hamlet, to read the Q2 text one reads all the words that are unbracketed with the ones in curly brackets. To read something approximating the F1 text, one reads all the unbracketed words plus the words in pointed brackets.

At first the brackets for Q2-only variants were square; in this version I gave copies to several scholars, one of whom was Jesús Tronch-Pérez, who drew inspiration from it for his important *Synoptic* Hamlet edition (2002), a fully edited, modernized text, and even before that for his doctoral dissertation (1996).[16] Realizing that the team would be using square brackets for any editorial additions in

our notes, I shifted to curly brackets for Q2. At first I called the text 'The Conflated *Hamlet*' because the folio variants were added to the quarto text. But an ordinary conflated text, like most twentieth-century editions, makes choices between Q2 and F1, using now one and now another. Even John Dover Wilson, who argued strenuously for the superior provenance of Q2, admitted that the press in 1604/5 had produced one of the most error-ridden of Shakespeare's plays, and for his emendations his Cambridge edition of 1934 drew both upon F1 and his own suppositions. My new edition was not conflated in the same way because it did not choose sometimes one, sometimes another edition, with or without notice; it was Q2 with Q2 and F1 variations integrated and highlighted. Thus, I named it 'The Enfolded *Hamlet*'. At one point, Randall McCleod, who has a passion for unmediated texts, called it 'The Encrusted *Hamlet*', but 'Enfolded' suggests the method I used.

In 1994, I asked the editors of *The Shakespeare Newsletter* if they would be interested in publishing *The Enfolded* Hamlet. They were, and with the help of generous donors, they produced in 1996 an extra issue of the journal containing the entire text in two-column format.[17] The easily portable

---

[14] Among the many who offered suggestions were Mike Jensen, Barry Kraft and Ron Rosenbaum.

[15] See Bernice W. Kliman, 'Considering the Terminology of the New Bibliography and After', *Analytical and Enumerative Bibliography* n.s. 10 (1999), 148–65, on using the terms 'material' and 'immaterial' variants rather than 'substantives', 'semi-substantives', and 'accidentals'.

[16] Jesús Tronch-Pérez, *A Synoptic* Hamlet: *A Critical–Synoptic Edition of the Second Quarto and First Folio Texts of* Hamlet (Valencia, 2003), and 'El Editor Ante El Enigma Textual de "Hamlet" . . . ', Tesis Doctoral, Julio, 1996.

[17] 'The Enfolded *Hamlet*', *Shakespeare Newsletter* Extra Issue, 1996, with Introduction, pp. 2, 44. Again, I prepared print-ready copy. I thank the editors Thomas Pendleton and John Mahon and donors Robert Macdonald and Troland Link, who made the publication possible. Thanks to a grant from the Gladys Krieble Delmas Foundation, Jeffery Triggs, our web master, was able to put it on our private web site, established so that the new variorum *Hamlet* editors and contributors could have access to our database. There Jeffery Triggs used color-coding, green for Q2, purple for F1, but he retained

print edition became available immediately to *Shakespeare Newsletter* subscribers. The team could refer to either the word-processed or the print version as we proceeded in our work of collating. Though created to ease our own work, *The Enfolded* Hamlet has turned out to be helpful to others as well.

Modern marketers try to suggest that every edition has to suit all purposes: general reading, study, scholarship and performance. Our *Enfolded* edition is in this respect distinctly retrograde: a text for a specific audience – which as it turns out is not as narrow as one would think: relatively little of the text's peculiarity, compared to modern editions, is unfathomable. Readers who require notes can easily look elsewhere, as can those who require modernized spelling. The best example they can find if they also want to preserve the play's multiplicity is Tronch-Pérez's *Synoptic* Hamlet, mentioned above.

Long lines in Q2 coupled with enfolded variants led to some strange looking passages. Polonius loses the thread of his thought as he speaks to Reynaldo in 2.1. The first line below is a single line in Q2 and two lines in F1 (the vertical line '|' indicates the line break in F1). Then the next two lines appear as one line in F1 (thus both have the same Through Line Number). F1 may have omitted *By the masse* because of regulations about profanity on stage, but if so the text is remarkably uneven, admitting many an oath.

942–3	*Pol.* And then sir doos {a this, a} <he this? | He> doos, what was I about to say?
944	{By the masse} I was about to say something,
944	Where did I leaue?

Polonius in Q2 falls into prose while in F1 he maintains a semblance of the verse line. Of course (as Graham Bradshaw has pointed out),[18] characters do not know that they are speaking either prose or verse; the difference is a clue to a reader or performer: the verse stumbles as Polonius's mind stumbles. The Q2 text is sometimes described as the more literary one, F1 the more stage-oriented, but for these lines their position is reversed: Q2, perhaps inadvertently, suggests how the lines might be played.

THE ENFOLDED HAMLETS: PARALLEL TEXTS OF <F1> AND {Q2}, EACH WITH UNIQUE ELEMENTS BRACKETED

While there is no doubting the usefulness of *The Enfolded* Hamlet, I regretted the text's inability to show the folio's immaterial elements. In the introduction, I expressed this caveat about enfolding only material variants:

In a larger sense, there are no immaterial variants: every spelling, turned letter, space, and punctuation mark is a material code for some purpose – providing, as Peter Blayney, Randall McLeod, and others have demonstrated, information about booksellers, print shops, intonation, and much more. Thus, by 'immaterial', I mean those variants the new variorum project as a whole considers immaterial to the purpose of the edition.

(p. 2)

By creating a double enfolded edition, a combination of parallel texts and enfolded texts, I could show both material and immaterial elements of both Q2 and F1, thus providing diplomatic versions of both originary texts and also highlighting their variations from each other. On the verso side of a page the F1 text enfolds material F1-only variants (still in pointed brackets) followed by material Q2-only variants (still with curly brackets). On the recto side of the page, the text appears pretty much as it had in *The Enfolded* Hamlet, with Q2-only variants preceding F1 variants. Again, AMS Press was interested and in 2004 published the texts in hardcover as *The Enfolded* Hamlets: *Parallel Texts of* <F1> *and* {Q2}, *Each with Unique Elements Bracketed*. Here all of the material and most of the immaterial variants are on display; yet a modern font

---

the brackets both to reinforce the display and to allow for printing in black and white without losing the variant signals. We have continued that practice for the open web site hamletworks.org: see below.

18 Graham Bradshaw, 'Metaferocities: Representation in *Othello* and *Otello*', *The Shakespearean International Yearbook 3: Where are we now in Shakespearean Studies?*, 3 (2003), 336–56.

and clear spacing facilitate reading. Either text may be read alone or with reference to the other. The shorter FI line dictated that it go on the verso page where the *Riverside* line numbers could appear near the alley between the two pages, thus providing two kinds of numbering for every line, TLN and act.scene.line numbers. In *The Shakespeare Newsletter*, *Riverside* numbers had been limited to the tops of pages and beginnings of scenes.

While preparing the text, again using Quark XPress, I discovered that, with the texts in parallel, I did not require as many brackets. There was no need to indicate FI's line breaks (as I had, above for line 942 in *The Enfolded* Hamlet). Of course, in another sense there had been no need to indicate line breaks at all, since they are so often dictated by printing necessity and probably are not significant to many readers – though at times they seem noteworthy.[19] Other differences that *The Enfolded* Hamlet had ignored show up in *The Enfolded* Hamlet*s* for anyone who wishes to note them. The differences, for example, in speech prefixes, such as *Pol.* in Q2 and *Polon.* in FI are on display. Again there are no notes, only a generous 'Preface' by Jesús Tronch-Pérez, and a short introduction.[20]

http://www.hamletworks.org

The website, an offshoot of the new variorum *Hamlet* project, is itself an edition of the play, an encyclopedic gathering of opinion and speculation about individual words, phrases, lines and passages, expressed in Commentary Notes (CN), Material Textual Notes (TNM) and Immaterial Textual Notes (TNI). For the Modern Language Association's print edition, the four editors are distilling the essence of the CN and TNM and omitting TNI altogether. Obviously, having a summary of opinion, crafted by the editors, can be more valuable for many readers than surveying a long collection of commentary notes on each line. But seeing the whole story of the development of Shakespearian literary criticism in the writers' own words can illuminate how interests change. Early editors were concerned with 'correct' metre, with what could and what

could not be Shakespearian language, and with ways to emend. These interests have become newly fascinating to editors who want to return to the openness of the originary texts rather than follow editorial custom and accept eighteenth-century emendations.

We envision readers using both the website and the printed copy of the forthcoming 'New Variorum *Hamlet*'. The print edition will feature as its *Hamlet* text a diplomatic version of Q2 adorned only with FI additions (not variants), marked with asterisks as mandated by *The Shakespeare Variorum Handbook*. On our open web site, *search HW* on the homepage allows users to look up words or sets of words from the play as well as names of commentators; *browse HW* on the homepage enables users to access CN, TNM and TNI arranged by Through Line Numbers. The number of bytes tells readers how much data to expect in each document. With *The Enfolded* Hamlet at the top of each note-document, users can see the Q2/FI variants from which significant editions have selected.

The website also has facsimiles of several editions (and in one instance a diplomatic transcript), and there will be more as we have the opportunity to have them scanned and mounted. Some of the editions are fairly rare, such as Jennens's *Hamlet* (1773), an important, though underrated, edition.[21] For a description of the site,

---

[19] See Paul Bertram, *White Spaces in Shakespeare: The Development of the Modern Text* (Cleveland, 1981).

[20] In preparing the edition, I did not notice what I call my Elmer Fudd error at the top of the recto page, where I typed 'Second Quarto *Hamlet* with {Q2}<FI> wariants enfolded' as the running head. (Elmer Fudd is a cartoon character who pronounces *v*'s as *w*'s.) My obedient program repeated this heading for every recto page. Eric Rasmussen, whose eagle eye is famous, was the first to notice the error in the published book. Gabriel Hornstein insisted on reprinting the lot, but no doubt there are some defective copies floating around.

[21] We scan works other than *Hamlet* when they come to hand: e.g. since Charles Jennens's 1773 *Hamlet* and 1770 *Lear* are bound in one volume, we scanned both. We own copies of most of the scanned-in texts. We thank Saint Michael's College's Jeremiah Durick Library for its loan of its complete run (twenty-five years) of *Hamlet Studies* for scanning.

see http://www.hamletworks.org, especially the introduction.[22] We also have several essays written especially for the web edition, including 'Global *Hamlet*' essays; unlike essays that appear in print collections, these essays are on the top layer, existing in present tense (rather than receding into back issues), and they are updatable. Thanks to Jeffery Triggs, we also have a facsimile of the excellent, nineteenth-century *Century Dictionary*, which he recently described as rivalling 'the *OED* in size and scope and surpass[ing] it in certain respects'; many scholars, he affirms, consider it 'to be the greatest American dictionary ever produced'.[23]

In early days, when we knew there would be an electronic version of our work but did not know how it would come together, we agreed that we would prepare our documents in a disciplined way. This is not as easy as it sounds, but we made the effort to build one document per one or two Through Line Numbers, using specific Microsoft Word styles that we designed and named for each area of the document. Like the print edition, the web edition uses *sigla* for editions, standard abbreviations in small caps as defined by the *Shakespeare Variorum Handbook*.

In our documents, the string of editions that are materially like Q2 are in *hanging* style, and the textual collations are in an *indented paragraph* style. In our working documents, we separated material variants (TNM) from immaterial variants (TNI) by *striking-through* the latter. Strike-throughs are useful because a later commentary could change our minds about materiality (as we defined it), and a string of editions could be unstruck easily. On the site they are in separate TNI files where they are not struck through. Here is a material textual note (TNM), beginning with the *Enfolded* Hamlet:

3001-2   {So} <He> that thou knowest thine | Hamlet.

Next, a string tells the reader how many texts followed Q2:

3001-2   Q3, Q4, Q5 = Q2 (*subst.*)

Finally, there are lists of variants compared to the Q2 choice:

3001 *So . . . thine]* Om. Q6, Q7, Q8, Q9, Q10, WILK1, WILK2, GENT

So] *He* F1, F2, F3, F4, ROWE1, ROWE2, TJOH1, ROWE3, TJOH2, POPE1, POPE2, THEO1, THEO2, HAN1, HAN2, WARB, THEO4, JOHN1, CAP, HAN3, V1773, JEN, V1778, V1785, MAL, RANN, V1793, V1803, V1813, CALD1, V1821, SING1, CALD2, VALPY, KNT1, COL1, VERP, COL2, DEL2, HUD1, SING2, DYCE1, ELZE1, COL3, STAU, WHI, GLO, KTLY, C&MC, HAL, DYCE2, CAM1, TSCH, RUG1, DEL4, HUD2, CLN1, DYCE3, V1877, COL4, HUD3, ELZE2, WH2, MULL, IRV2, OXF1, ARD1, RLTR, NLSN, VAND, CRG1, CAM3, RID1, KIT1, PARC, N&H, CLN2, ALEX, CRG2, SIS, PEL1, PEL2, EVNS1, PEN2, ARD2, CHAL, CAM4, OXF3, OXF4, BEV2, FOL2[24]

In the print edition, the TNM sigla will be compressed; F1, F2, F3, F4 will compress to Ff.

Because every TNM file has a record of the fully-collated editions that are materially the same as Q2 (including 0 = Q2), there is a TNM record for every line. Textual notes for immaterial variations (TNI) do not appear for every line, and there is none for 3001–2. Here are TNI for 3003, starting with the line from *The Enfolded* Hamlet:

3003   {*Hor.*}Come I will <giue> you way for these your letters,

3003 *Hor.*] *Hora.* Q3, Q4, Q5, Q6, Q8, Q9; *Horat.* Q7
Come∧] ~, F1, F2, Q5, F3, Q6, Q7, Q8, F4, Q9, Q10, ROWE1, ROWE2, TJOH1, ROWE3, TJOH2, WILK1, POPE1, WILK2, POPE2
letters] Letters F1, F2, Q5, F3, Q6, Q7, F4
letters,] ~; WILK1, WILK2

---

[22] Though the site has not been launched officially, we have had some publicity, including an article in the online *Chronicle of Higher Education* 27 May 2005; also it was selected as 'Site of the Week for Wednesday, September 14, 2005' by eSchool News Online.

[23] 'Exploring the Edward J. Bloustein Dictionary Collection', *The Journal of the Rutgers University Libraries*, 61 (2005), http://jrul.libraries.rutgers.edu/viewissue.php?id=3. Connect to *The Century Dictionary* from the hamletwork.org homepage.

[24] As I write this, the bibliography on the site contains only the fully-collated editions, listed by sigla.

TNI such as these serve to remind readers of historical and personal variations in optional graphics.

Each commentary note (CN) has three parts. The first part indicates year and siglum of edition or other source (in what we call *sigla style*), with sigla of editions in small caps, authors of other works in plain font. The second part (in *hanging* style) indicates which if any edition or other work has similar notes; it starts with the siglum or author's name again and then lists prior works that he or she refers to in the CN, with attribution or not; we call this the *genealogy*. The third part, in *indented paragraph* style, starts with TLN, lemma in bold, with a bracket if that lemma comes from Q2, and then the commentary note, starting with the author of the note and the year of edition or the year and page number of a source other than an edition or dictionary.

I mention these protocols at length because they attest to our leap of faith. We knew that we were going to gather a large amount of information that would not enter the print edition. We wanted to record as much as we could because we knew that the project would continue for years and that we might find too late that we needed more quoted material than we had gathered from a book or article or manuscript annotation at some distant library. Early on, when there was hardly a Web, scarcely an Internet, people told us we would have to provide tags to indicate every kind of typography: tabs, italics, small caps, large caps, and so on. Tags are codes that allow any computer to translate into the appropriate format. Without tags, they said, our data would not be universally readable by all computers. But we believed that by the time our job was finished there would be an easier way, and indeed Jeffery Triggs has developed a program that automatically changes the invisible Microsoft Word tags to XML, which provides flexibility for display and allows us to do reliable field searches of the texts: the XML tags are dynamically converted to HTML for display in a Web browser.

Our file for TLN 313 commentary notes begins again with *The Enfolded* Hamlet:

313*Ham*. O that this too too {sallied} \<solid\> flesh would melt, {*but Hamlet*}

1578   Cooper[25]
313 **sallied**] *solidus* in COOPER (1578): Ovid and others used the word in various senses, meaning *whole* (a solid year), *hard*, *perfect*, *sound* (not hollow), *full*, etc.

1613   Cawdry
313–43 **soliloquy** CAWDRY (2nd 1613 ed.) was the first, according to *OED*, to use the word in English, meaning to speak to oneself. With respect to non-dramatic utterance, the word or cognates had long been in use.[26]

1723– MTBY2
313 **sallied**] THIRLBY (1723-) provides a quarto variant note: 'Q sallied It is in many places very faulty as well as here'.[27]

1730   Bailey
313 **sallied**] BAILEY (1730): no suitable definition for *sally*; for *sully*: 'to defile, to dirty, to dawb, to foul'.[28]

1739   Smith
313–43 SMITH (1739, pp. 157–8), \<p. 157\> referring to Longinus's definition of *hyperbaton*, comments: Longinus's 'fine remark may be illustrated by a celebrated Passage in *Shakespeare's Hamlet*, where the Poet's Art has hit off the strongest and most exact Resemblance of nature. The Behaviour of his Mother, makes such Impression on the young Prince, that his Mind is big with Ab-\</p. 157\> \<p. 158\> horrence of it, but Expressions fail him. He begins abruptly, but as Reflexions croud thick upon his Mind he runs off into Commendations of his Father. Some time after his Thoughts turn again on the Action of his Mother which had raised his Resentments, but he only touches it, and flies off again. In short he takes

---

[25] Thomas Cooper, *Thesavrvs Lingvæ Romanæ et Britannicæ . . .* STC 5688. 1578. Huntington Library 601433. Unless otherwise noted, London is the place of publication for all books. In the interest of saving space, in these CN the 2nd part of the record (the genealogy) is omitted or added to the first part.

[26] Robert Cawdry [or Cawdrey], *A Table Alphabeticall, containing and teaching the true vvriting, and vnderstanding of hard vsuall English words*. The lemma has no right bracket because it does not come from Q2.

[27] Styan Thirlby (Jesus College, Cambridge, 1692–1753), who was apparently planning an edition of Shakespeare in the early to mid-eighteenth century, wrote notes in editions by Rowe (lost), Alexander Pope (1723–5); Lewis Theobald (1733); William Warburton (1747).

[28] N[athan] Bailey, *Dictionarium Britannicum*, 1730.

up eighteen Lines in telling us that his Mother married again, in less than two Months after her Husband's Death. [quotes 322–40, ending with 'Oh most wicked speed!]'. </p. 158>[29]

1752 Dodd refers to Smith indirectly
313–43 DODD (1752, 1: 217): 'The late translator of *Longinus* observes, upon that *section* (the 22d) where his excellent author is speaking of the *Hyperbaton*, . . . '.[30]

1770 Gentleman
313–43 Gentleman (1770, 1: 16): 'The first soliloquy of Hamlet is particularly striking and essential, as it is lays open in a pathetic, beautiful manner, the cause of his melancholy, and paints his mother's frailty with strong feeling, yet preserves a delicate respect'.[31]

313–43 Gentleman (1770, 2: 483) says of Garrick, 'in his soliloquies he happily avoids that absurd method of speaking solitary meditation to the audience; he really appears alone'.

1773 GENT
313–43 GENTLEMAN (ed. 1773): 'This soliloquy is admirably adapted to the situation of *Hamlet*'s mind; which is oppressed with grief, not only for the loss of a father, but by the sudden and strange second mariage of his mother'.[32]

and so on, eventually through 2001, our closing date for the print edition, and beyond for the web site. One can see immediately why the print edition will rely on compressions of commentary: the notes for 313 already stretch to some thirty single-spaced pages. The website can afford to be expansive so as to provide users with the raw data. By comparing the full commentary to the printed narrative summary of the commentary, readers can judge for themselves what they need to know.

The entries above begin before the date *c.* 1600 of *Hamlet*'s composition with Cooper's 1578 dictionary, which suggests that F1's *solid* might mean 'sound' rather than 'fat' as Dover Wilson famously explained in his argument for *sullied*[33]; Cooper's definition, however, works well: Hamlet laments his all-too healthy body. TLN 313 begins what has been called Hamlet's first soliloquy; Shakespeare's texts, however, never use the term *soliloquy* in any stage direction. The first to use *soliloquy* as an English word is Cawdry in 1613, and a glance at

Francis Gentleman (1770) shows that actors before Garrick did not speak the lines as if they were alone. As a theatre critic, Gentleman naturally keeps the stage in mind as he writes his commentary notes. Pope's 1723 edition of the play in which Thirlby wrote his notes uses the F1 variant; Thirlby provides the Q2 variant and judges it. Bailey, who does not refer to Shakespeare specifically, defines *sully*, a possible spelling of *sally*. William Dodd quotes 'The late translator of *Longinus*' without naming him; part of our mission is to uncover references like this one. Thus, we also record Smith, above Dodd.

Beyond commentary and textual notes, users can also read whole books and essays on the web site. There are various ways to approach the electronic texts. One way is to 'turn the pages' of a book more or less as one would a printed book. Few of my generation expect to read very long from a computer screen, but younger people seem to be comfortable reading websites. Our dynamic web interface

---

[29] William Smith, trans. and ed. *Dionysius Longinus On the Sublime . . .*, 1739. Rpt. New York, 1975. The note's pointed brackets for page numbers are not true SGML tags but are meant to show readers where pages begin and end for their ease in referring to the sources from the web site.

[30] William Dodd, *The Beauties of Shakespear Regularly Selected from Each Play with a General Index Digesting them under Proper Heads, illustrated with explanatory Notes, and Similar Passages from Ancient and Modern Authors*. 2 vols. (1752). Dodd's *Beauties* was frequently republished, but with 'beauties' alone, without his commentary. He ended badly, publicly hanged in spite of pleas for clemency by Samuel Johnson and others. Our web site will eventually include short biographies of the commentators. Another of the great pleasures of variorum work is encountering a splendid array of characters, good and bad.

[31] Francis Gentleman, *The Dramatic Censor; or, Critical Companion*, 2 vol. (1770). Notice that there are two notes from the same work and therefore no sigla line for the second one.

[32] Francis Gentleman, ed., Hamlet, Prince of Denmark: *A Tragedy, by Shakespeare. As Performed at the Theatre-Royal, Covent–Garden. Regulated from the Prompt-Book . . .*, Bell's Shakespeare. An Introduction, and Notes Critical and Illustrative, are added by the *Authors* of the *Dramatic Censor* [i.e., Francis Gentleman] (1773; 2nd edn revd, 1774).

[33] J. Dover Wilson, *The Manuscripts of Shakespeare's* Hamlet *and the Problems of Its Transmission: An Essay in Critical Bibliography*, 2 vols., (Cambridge, 1934), especially vol. 2, 307–15.

will provide links from the entries to the many facsimiles we intend to include. Furthermore, Jeffery Triggs has arranged the site in a way that both encourages users to find exactly what they need as well as to discover information they did not know they would want. Using the *search HW* function, to the left on the home page, a reader can locate instances, for example, of *Lr.* (*Lear*) or *Johnson* in CNS. In a way, this easy means of approaching the site is less daunting than a 1000-page book – though there too a reader can and probably will look up one aspect at a time. For the next few years, while we are completing the work for the print edition, we will also be refining the website, correcting and adding – as ever depending on readers for corrections and suggestions.

Altogether it seems our dream has come true – the project has already generated books and, free to all, an abundance of electronic data, not only the raw material for the print edition but much more as well. My present concern is for the website's future. We are certain that print editions of *Hamlet* will serve readers for many years. To quote myself,[34] the print edition of the variorum *Hamlet* 'should be as indestructible as the Folio itself, now almost four hundred years old. A New Variorum book will take up its five inches of space on a library shelf, and barring theft, flood or fire it can remain ready for use without expert supervision. It will exist in hundreds of inviolable copies. Can we say the same for our cyberspace book? The site needs a stable server, and the software that supports it may need upgrading. Someone has to be on watch. We gather our data thinking of the long term, but we do not know what the future of our project will be beyond our own lifetimes'.

I would like to foster in myself and the team the same sanguine faith about the web site's robust future as I had that technology would catch up with us if we prepared our data consistently. In the meantime, we hope to make DVDs of the data and trust that they continue to be readable or updatable. If a donor materializes, perhaps he or she will endow a chair at a favourite university that will give a stream of scholars release-time to guide graduate students who can add to the data as new editions and literary studies appear and to direct the technicians who can tend the servers. I compare the website not to a book but to a journal, like *Shakespeare Survey*, that has behind it the strength of a lasting institution, that hands over the task of overseeing it to new scholars as time goes on.

---

34 See Bernice W. Kliman, 'A Plan for www.hamletworks.org: An Offshoot of the New Variorum *Hamlet* Project', *The Shakespearean International Yearbook 4: Shakespeare Studies Today*, 4 (2004), 135–67. Though the website stems from the preparatory work for the New Variorum Project, the Modern Language Association is not responsible for it and the other independent editions described in this essay.

THE EVOLUTION OF ONLINE EDITING: WHERE WILL IT END?

CHRISTIE CARSON

In his keynote address on the Future of Shakespeare at the inaugural British Shakespeare Association conference in Leicester in September 2003, Jonathan Bate argued that future scholarly editions of Shakespeare would be online, because only the digital environment can show the depth and complexity of the scholarly project. This acknowledgement of the influence of the online environment follows a period of resistance to and upheaval in the development of the digital dissemination of Shakespeare's work. What this statement acknowledges is the emergence of a series of what have been termed second-generation projects in digital editing, projects that have learned from the mistakes of the past. The question remains, however, of what form the online edition in this new stage of development will take. This essay attempts to bring that question, which has been debated for too long among only a small group of specialists, to a wider audience.

The history of digital editing is relatively short but filled with activity and drama. Given that many of the early digital projects were created on CD and are only available in the collections of those who purchased them at the time, it is important, at this crucial juncture, to document work that might otherwise disappear without a trace. The development of the online edition owes a great deal to these early experiments in that they mapped out the difficult and complex terrain of the digital world. The contested questions of copyright, intellectual property and ownership of the final edited texts has meant that even in the open environment of the Internet there remain only a handful of serious attempts to

address the issue of what a scholarly online edition of the plays should look like and how it should function. In this essay, I will outline the nature of the crossroads we currently face by placing it into its historical context. I will present my own developing approach to the issues involved in online editing alongside other serious attempts to make materials available digitally for the study of Shakespeare as a means of illustrating several different approaches to the questions faced. I suggest that the issues of copyright and intellectual property, in particular, in this area should be discussed widely and vigorously since the outcome of these questions will have a significant impact on the future of Shakespeare studies. The model most widely adopted for the digital edition will determine the form and availability of Shakespeare's texts, inevitably privileging specific contexts. We ignore such developments at our peril.

Some of the early projects I will examine expose assumptions that are naïve and idealistic. However, they also raise fundamental questions, such as which texts are being made available, by whom, and for what purposes? What online publishing has had to face squarely is the question of what a general, as well as a scholarly, user of a Shakespeare text might want if freed from the conventions and restrictions of publishing within the established print models and given the opportunity of free distribution. When technically freed of constraints can we – should we – be intellectually freed of the established ways of working?

The projects that were developed in the first stage of this debate broke essentially into two camps. The first were based on the model of the digital library and concentrated on making as many primary texts available as possible. The second emulated the print-based edition and so were more concerned with making connections between carefully selected primary and secondary materials. The first type of project focused on the ability to search freely large corpora of texts. The second kind of project focused on the possibility of making a wide variety of links between related materials. This essay will focus on the second kind of project but will acknowledge the fact that these efforts were developed in an environment in which an increasing breadth of primary material was being made available. Another difference that must be acknowledged in the projects described is the motivation and funding of the producers. At the beginning of this adventure publishers imagined that the digital dissemination channel would be their own and that traditional relationships with academics would remain unchanged. Many scholars, and increasingly libraries and universities, are recognising the advantages of translating Shakespeare from the page to the computer screen for their own ends, and so new and complex relationships are developing with publishers.

What the digital environment offers is a way of looking towards the future that encompasses the past. The complexity of creating a model that incorporates past, present and future methodological approaches perhaps explains why a clear way forward for digital editing has been hard to find. There has been a good deal of ground to prepare. There has also been a debate about who should be responsible for developing standards in this new environment. The traditional relationships between not only academics and publishers, but also between theatrical producers of Shakespeare, teachers of Shakespeare and the archivists of Shakespearian history, are rapidly breaking down in the digital world. Theatre companies are becoming archivists, libraries are developing teaching materials and literary scholars are working with software developers to publish their work directly on the web. Now that structures and strategies have started to emerge, I suggest that the development of

new standards will happen quite quickly. Increasingly, scholars will need to be aware of, even if not involved in, the debate about the intellectual property both of the work we want to use in our teaching and research and of the work we ourselves create. The debate surrounding the digital edition presents a practical illustration of the way these issues are being negotiated between publishers, libraries, theatre companies and individual academics.

THE DEVELOPMENT OF THE DIGITAL EDITION: THREE EARLY EXAMPLES

Looking at three early projects produced on CD will provide an example of the kind of approaches that have been taken and the problems that inevitably arise in terms of structure and the control of distribution. Each of these projects tackled the question of the purpose and form of a digital edition. The first of these projects, Voyager's *Macbeth*, was produced by a commercial company in 1994. The second and third projects, *The Arden Shakespeare CD-ROM: Texts and Sources for Shakespeare Studies*, published in 1997, and *The Cambridge King Lear CD-ROM: Text and Performance Archive*, published in 2000, are two of only a handful of digital projects created as an extension of existing academic editions in CD format. All three of these projects, while the result of a great deal of work and thought, did not anticipate the fact that the technology and audience expectations were evolving so quickly during this period that it was impossible to devise a template that would endure. However, the lessons that can be learned from these earlier projects should not be discarded.

Voyager's *Macbeth* combined an academic text edited by A. R. Braunmuller with a full audio recording of the play by the Royal Shakespeare Company, starring Sir Ian McKellen and Dame Judi Dench. The CD also included extracts from film adaptations of the play that highlight different interpretations of individual scenes. The CD included an introduction and commentary by David S. Rodes as well as a concordance and additional essays on the play. Somewhat more fancifully, the CD also included a karaoke *Macbeth* which allowed the user to speak the lines of Macbeth or Lady Macbeth while Sir Ian McKellen or Dame Judi Dench responded. The design of the CD was elegant in pale grey. It was attractive and functional. And yet it was not a success. Aimed at the general public, it anticipated needs that had not yet been felt. It involved academic texts but the design was created using computer conventions that were not yet established in the academic world. The film clips that were reproduced were at a very low resolution and in a postage stamp size. While the imagination behind the project is obvious, neither the technology nor the audience were prepared for the materials in this form.

The Arden Shakespeare CD-ROM: Text and Sources for Shakespeare Studies included not only all of the texts of the plays and poems included in the Arden second series but also facsimile reproductions of Folio and Quarto editions of most of the plays to provide comparisons for close readings of individual lines or speeches. This was accomplished with a clever interface that introduced the user to the possibilities of the split screen. This project's inclusion of a range of other useful source texts and reference material such as David Bevington's *Shakespeare's Bibliography* and Geoffrey Bullough's *Narrative and Dramatic Sources of Shakespeare*, to name just two, provided the user with the opportunity to draw together collections of material around particular aspects of the plays. As Jean Chothia writes in a review of this CD:

Chief among the various potential delights offered is the capacity to read one or more of these on-screen [reference texts], adjacent to the modern spelling Arden text and to make direct comparison between Folio and Quarto versions of a speech or scene.[1]

Ray Siemens in his review states that 'the CD is in many ways a pioneering effort'[2] acknowledging the technical capabilities of this work. However, both Siemens and Chothia lament the decision to include only the Arden second edition texts, many of which were considered out of date even at the time of publication. Chothia states: 'here, then, we

have the latest technology and some pleasing features offered to us with an outdated core'.[3]

The Cambridge King Lear CD-ROM: Text and Performance Archive can be seen to be comparable to *The Arden Shakespeare CD-ROM* in a number of ways. This project, which I co-edited with Professor Jacky Bratton, and the Arden CD-ROM had a much clearer audience in mind than the Voyager *Macbeth* but both of these scholarly projects faced a number of difficult questions in terms of the content chosen and the publishing software available (Dynatext was used in both cases). While both of these projects offered materials that were aimed at scholars and university level students, the *Arden CD* tried to replicate existing scholarly practices. The *Cambridge CD*, by contrast, tried to do something quite new by drawing together the interests and concerns of textual scholars working in English Departments with performance history scholars working in Drama and Theatre Departments. Like the Arden project the textual material included was largely taken from already existing editions of the play. The *New Cambridge Shakespeare* Quarto (1994) and Folio (1992) editions edited by Jay Halio and the *Plays in Performance* edition edited by Jacky Bratton in 1987 (but updated for this project) formed the basis of this project.

The *Cambridge Lear CD* took a detailed look at the textual and performance history of just one play and was therefore able to concentrate on the creation of a new approach that was made possible through this new technology. One considerable innovation developed at the heart of this project was the newly conflated 'Finder' text, which used colour coding to differentiate the Quarto- and Folio-only lines, providing a quick visual key to the major textual variations. The lineation in the

---

[1] Jean Chothia, 'Review: *The Arden Shakespeare*', *Computers and Texts*, 15 (August 1997) (http://users.ox.ac.uk/~ctitext2/publish/comtxt/ct15/chothia.html).

[2] Siemens, R. G., 'Review of *The Arden Shakespeare CD-ROM: Texts and Sources for Shakespeare Study*', *Early Modern Literary Studies*, 4.2 (September, 1998), 28.1–10 <http://purl.oclc.org/emls/04-2/rev_siem.html>.

[3] Chothia, 'Review'.

Quarto, Folio and Finder texts were regularised to facilitate cross-referencing between the texts and to indicate the relationship between them. The notes from the three original print editions were also added to the Finder text so that clicking on an individual line brought up three types of notes to describe it, commentary, apparatus and staging notes. Cross-references within the texts and between them were also made possible through an extensive network of hypertext links. To this central text five full acting and edited versions of the play were added, including the complete text of Nahum Tate's happy-ending adaptation, which held the stage for nearly 150 years. The Quarto and Folio texts were also reproduced in facsimile in full. Reference material from the *Cambridge Guide to Theatre* and production reviews from *Shakespeare Survey* added a further level of complexity and support.

While significantly enhanced, most of the material on the CD was available in print. There was just one section of the project which was the product of entirely new research, the Shakespeare in performance area of the CD. This section included 500 images of the play in performance, arranged chronologically and by act and scene, and a selected list of performances from 1605–1998, which included production details from performances in Australia, North America and the United Kingdom. All of the images illustrating a particular scene were linked to the beginning of that scene in the Finder text, and individual images were also used to illustrate the staging notes throughout the text illuminating particular moments in the play. The three critical essays included on the CD, which discussed performance history, also included links to illustrate particular productions. Together all the information on the disk was designed to allow for a study of the play which emphasized textual and performance history, helping to map out the overlap between these two approaches. Unfortunately, this resource, like the others described above, did not receive very wide distribution. The CD format was seen by some as prohibitive and the cost of these early experiments also exceeded expectations. As a result, the

influence of these initial projects is often overlooked.

What all of these projects did, through offering specific manifestations of the idea of the digital edition, was raise questions about the purpose and function of this new form. The scholarly study of Shakespeare and the casual or commercial approach to Shakespeare have always met through the edition. The conventions used and approaches taken by Arden, Oxford, Cambridge and others all have their champions and their detractors, but their form and function are well established. These early attempts to digitise Shakespeare raised the fundamental question: if a new form of online edition is to be created, which, if any, of the already established conventions should be translated into the new medium? Each one of these projects involved innovative new work in terms of the design and function of the digital display. The *Macbeth CD* introduced a clever speaking text, *The Arden CD* pointed out the usefulness of the split screen comparison and the *Lear CD* created the first colour-coded conflated text. Yet much of the content was recycled textual material that was adapted to this new form of delivery. The only materials that were not also available in print were those which addressed performance history. With the *Macbeth CD* this included the full RSC audio recording of the play and with the *Lear CD* this included the images of performance and the performance database.

These early CD projects were an attempt by publishers to find a distinctive role in the digital world and therefore the advantages of these projects, both in terms of form and content, were unfortunately buried in the difficulties of distribution that were presented by working in an unstable technology. During the 1990s, the Internet was not seen as a viable option for most publishers. The slow realisation of the fact that the Internet bypasses established publishers as the only route to an audience caused an enormous crisis in the publishing industry. CDs were embraced initially by publishers because they seemed to present a way forward which did not involve losing control. The public, however, were quick to spot the limitations of this distribution system and opted instead to support the developing online culture.

SHAKESPEARE RESOURCES ON THE INTERNET FOR TEXTUAL STUDIES: AN OVERVIEW

The advent of the Internet as the dominant medium of distribution and communication in the years that followed the first phase I have described has changed, in radical ways, the nature of the materials that are now available for the study of Shakespeare. The principle of public access has pushed publishers to develop new ways of working and pressure has been placed on libraries and archives to make the materials they hold more widely available. The result of this shift has been that the number of resources available online has greatly increased: there are now hundreds of sites from a range of sources making materials available online. In response to the new resources, scholars and students are beginning to change the way they work. Looking briefly at the resources currently available will help to illuminate some of the choices involved and issues at stake for the creators of online editions. What the Internet has, in fact, made available is an unprecedented opportunity for a range of producers to present very particular approaches to the work of the Bard in a very public way. A general audience has never been more approachable; there has never been more scope for diversity in the ways in which Shakespeare is presented to this audience.

Providing an overview of the wealth of resources available is the aim of a number of reliable gateways. Each gateway tries to bring the array of resources into coherence. In doing this, however, they inevitably redefine the boundaries of the subject for their particular audiences. The UK based Touchstone site run by the Shakespeare Institute Library (http://www.touchstone.bham.ac.uk/) focuses on resources of use to a British academic audience while Mr William Shakespeare and the Internet (http://shakespeare.palomar.edu/) is aimed at a more general North American audience. Only Sh:in:E (Shakespeare in Europe,

http://www.unibas.ch/shine/), run by the University of Basel, has a European focus. The title of these gateways illustrates their differing tone and emphasis. These first resources begin to highlight an important problem when creating online Shakespeare resources. While the resources on the Internet are international most scholars continue to be very specifically culturally located. Belying somewhat the ideal of universal access, these gateways must define their audiences and their disciplinary approaches very clearly.

In the Internet environment, of course, there are still resident authorities. The established Shakespeare Libraries, the Folger Shakespeare Library in Washington (http://www.folger.edu/Home_02B.html), the Shakespeare Centre Library (http://www.shakespeare.org.uk/main/3) and the Shakespeare Institute (http://www.is.bham.ac.uk/shakespeare/) in Stratford all have websites which consolidate their international reputations for Shakespeare scholarship. These sites make a wider public audience more aware of their home institutions. However, creating an interesting public presence is not quite the same as presenting the online audience with a valuable service. In terms of making resources usefully available online for the study of Shakespeare these institutions have been surpassed in a number of ways.

From the very earliest days of the Internet there have been a plethora of Shakespeare texts (as distinct from editions) available online, though they vary considerably in terms of their sources and objectives. Some of these texts are commercially produced as part of large digital services such as Literature Online (http://lion.chadwyck.com/), some are made freely available as a scholarly service such as the *Complete Works* produced by the Massachusetts Institute of Technology (http://www-tech.mit.edu/Shakespeare/) [4] or the Electronic Text Center at the University of Virginia (http://etext.virginia.edu/shakespeare/works/),

---

[4] Developed by MIT, this modern spelling complete works of Shakespeare is freely available on the web, based on a generic text released to the public domain in the early 1990s called the 'Complete Moby Shakespeare'.

and some are made available by ama-teur enthusiasts such as Project Gutenberg (http://www.promo.net/pg/). In each case, the source of the text and the information that accompanies it varies to suit the intentions of the producers and illustrates the nature of the intended audience.

A relatively new and very welcome resource that has been made freely available to scholars is facsimile reproductions of the Quarto and the Folio editions. A number of individual libraries have given access to their holdings in this area. First to do so was the University of Pennsylvania Library. The full 1623 Folio edition plus limited Quarto editions are freely available and presented in a way that makes them both attractive and easy to use (http://dewey.library.upenn.edu/SCETI/PrintedBooksNew/index.cfm?TextID=firstfolio&PagePosition=3).[5] More recently the British Library's *Treasures in Full: Shakespeare in Quarto* site has provided scholars with an extremely valuable online resource (http://www.bl.uk/treasures/shakespeare/homepage.html). This resource makes available the Library's entire collection of Quartos before 1642. Again, the materials are displayed in a way that is both useful and intuitive. As a public library the British Library has developed a wide range of accompanying information about Shakespeare's life, the printing and theatrical practices of the time and the social context for the plays. In addition short essays by academics have been commissioned that highlight specific variants in three plays that might be of interest to a general audience. My own short essay on *King Lear* points users who are unfamiliar with the play to the changes made to the last scene from the Quarto to the Folio, changes that I argue may well have been made to accommodate early audience responses to the play.

Writing this short essay clearly revealed to me that producing material for the Internet is a very different exercise from writing exclusively for an academic audience. The style, content and approach of the work all have to accommodate an international non-specialist audience. That is not to say that resources on the Internet have to be sim-ple or simplistic. Rather I suggest that they need to acknowledge their public position. Looking at a range of the examples above will illustrate that often several levels of complexity are offered by scholarly resources online. What differentiates a digital schol-arly resource from a scholarly monograph is the fact that it might be discovered by a variety of different levels of students and scholars and used in a number of different ways. Allowing for that kind of flexi-bility, while maintaining rigorous academic stan-dards of practice, presents a challenge. There are, of course, a great many resources that do not aim for an academic audience and do not try to claim academic depth or rigour. There are, however, an increasing number of very detailed and expansive projects that are likely to have a large impact on the future of scholarly research. In fact the digital environment allows for an unprecedented level of detail and encourages the sharing of both the mate-rials and the outcomes of large research projects.

There are three examples of existing digital edi-tion projects that I would like to highlight which illustrate this principle. The first is the *Internet Shakespeare Editions* (http://ise.uvic.ca/index.html) produced at the University of Victoria, which include texts of all of the plays both in Quarto and Folio editions. This project does not simply reproduce out-of-copyright texts but rather pro-vides a genuine attempt to edit these texts for the digital environment. In addition to conventional annotations these texts are placed in the context of other resources made available to discuss the work of Shakespeare in an international context, housed both on the site and elsewhere. Here, then, is an example of an attempt to create new research prac-tices through online editions of the plays rather than simply making available digital texts.

A second example of a currently avail-able online edition is *The Enfolded Hamlet*

---

5 Produced by the University of Pennsylvania Library this site provides free access to a high quality facsimile reproduction of the Furness Shakespeare Library copy of the First Folio. The Furness Shakespeare web page also contains facsimile repro-ductions of other important texts from the period including Quarto texts of *King Lear* and *Othello*.

(http://www.global-language.com/enfolded.
html)[6]. This edition, which is edited by Bernice
W. Kliman, offers the user a choice of five *Hamlet*
texts, FI, FI Only (the variants without the full
text), Q2, Q2 Only (again including only the
variants) and the Enfolded text. Much like the
colour-coded Finder text, which I developed for
the *Lear CD*, the Enfolded text includes variants
from FI and Q2, which are displayed in pink and
green respectively. As a result, all of the variants
in the play can be noted in a single viewing of
the central text but complete alternative texts also
exist, as do complete lists of variants. For plays with
substantial variations this system of layering texts
provides a new kind of approach to editing and
points out one of the key advantages of working
online. Digital technology allows an editor to
maintain the integrity of the original texts while
at the same time showing their relationship to one
another. The Enfolded text, like the Finder text
on the *Lear CD*, is not a primary authoritative text
but rather a navigational device and an illustrative
model that points out the relationships between
the other texts made available. This approach
makes clear the editorial process and gives users
the freedom to make their own editorial choices.

Finally, the third project area I would like to
highlight is, in fact, two separate attempts to create
a digital Variorum edition. The first is an extension of *The Enfolded Hamlet* project already mentioned which was recently described at the 2005
Shakespeare Association of America conference by
Eric Rasmussen:

The four editors at work on the New Variorum edition
of *Hamlet* – Bernice W. Kliman, Hardin Aasand, F. Nick
Clary, and myself – have spent the last decade assembling
a database of interpretative commentary from over one
hundred editions of the play, along with all known commentary on *Hamlet* from the 18th century, most of the
commentary from the 19th century, and much of that
from the 20th – all linked to the through-line-number of
the play that the comment addresses.[7]

This project is still a work in progress but the current prototype shows the great potential of such a
detailed approach to one play. The second project

in this area that was described at the same seminar is a Variorum edition of *The Winter's Tale*.
Working under the guidance of NVS Co-General
Editor Paul Werstine, Alan Galey has developed
a complex structure of tables to hold and display
the wealth of information that a Variorum edition
entails.[8] Paul Werstine, who chaired this SAA seminar, made clear his view that the fundamental purpose of these editions can be greatly enhanced by
digital technology:

the essential purpose of the New Variorum Shakespeare
has always been to provide a detailed history of critical
commentary together with an exhaustive study of the
text. . . . In its inclusiveness and its historical orientation
the NVS differs from regular scholarly editions.[9]

What these two projects amply illustrate, although
both are still in development, is the fact that the
digital environment can facilitate access to an enormous amount of detailed information about the
plays that can then be variously displayed for a wide
range of users.

Through these new online editions, therefore,
the tremendous advantages of this new delivery
mechanism are becoming apparent. Each provides
additional information by publishing more content
than a traditional edition would allow. But more
fundamentally they test the underlying assumptions of current print publishing conventions. *The
Enfolded Hamlet* project illustrates the possibility of
presenting parallel texts in a non-hierarchical way
and the Variorum projects show the capacity of

---

[6] These texts are made available online by a company entitled
Global Language Resources, who have also made available
The Illustrated Shakespeare, edited by G. C. Verplanck (1847),
a collaborative project involving the New Variorum Hamlet
Project and Princeton Imaging.

[7] Eric Rasmussen, 'Hamletworks.org' conference paper
Shakespeare Association of America, Bermuda, 17 March
2005. A trial version of the website is available at
http://www.leoyan.com/global-language.com/ENFOLDED/

[8] Alan Galey '"Alms for Oblivion": Bringing an Electronic
New Variorum Shakespeare to the Screen' conference paper
Shakespeare Association of America, Bermuda, 17 March
2005.

[9] Paul Werstine, quoted in Patrick O'Kelley, 'To Tag or Not to
Tag' http://www.xml.com/lpt/a/2004/05/26/totag.html

digital technology to hold and variously display vast sums of information. Yet still, I would argue that each one of these projects aims to extend access to existing materials and research practices rather than radically altering the idea of what an edition can do. What these examples illustrate is how current print conventions and research practices can be enhanced in the online environment. The functionality these projects offer, as well as their free distribution, begins to suggest that the online edition could potentially present a very new kind of venture indeed. In fact, all of the above resources indicate that the collaborative and public nature of the Internet provides a forum for a very different kind of scholarly debate. It is a debate that is open to public as well as scholarly scrutiny. It is a debate that is funded and distributed usually by academic institutions or public funding bodies rather than by publishers. It is a debate that presents openly both the materials and the methodologies of research in this area. All of the online edition projects I have described work in this open and collaborative way, a way that contrasts starkly with the motivation behind the original publishing ventures on CD.

COPYRIGHT: A SERIOUS CHALLENGE TO INNOVATION?

Despite the many opportunities offered by digital technology there remain a number of hurdles that have limited the creation of a truly innovative online edition. The key hurdle is copyright. Publishers' initial drive to work on CD was fuelled by a desire to restrict access to their copyright-protected editions. Scholars, who until recently have readily handed over their work to publishers are becoming more aware of the value of their own intellectual property, but so too are their employing institutions. The key challenge for the scholar of performance has always been that the subject of our research is a saleable product. Images of performance are regularly sold on postcards, T-shirts, coffee mugs and programmes. Vested in these images are several levels of copyright. There are the rights of the actors, the director, the designer and the theatre company involved in the production. There are

also the rights of the photographer of the image. Obtaining permission to use these materials is often a complex and costly business. But increasingly, libraries and archives, which used to encourage free access to their collections, are finding a useful source of funding through licensing access to their holdings online. Thus the use of all of the materials involved in the creation of an edition raises a number of important questions; if a profit is to be made from these materials who should make it? Perhaps more importantly, if a profit is not to be made who should bear the cost of producing and distributing these materials? Who should bear the responsibility of collecting, selecting and making available digital Shakespearean textual and performance history?

Increasingly the issues of copyright and of intellectual property must be of interest and of concern for the individual scholar. When working on these projects it is always essential to determine where the copyright in the final edited-mediated text will lie. While public research councils or charitable foundations often fund large research projects, they are usually housed and distributed through the universities that hire the academics working on them. The fact that these projects are collaborative creates a problem for the individuals involved when it comes to crediting the work. Unlike a scholarly monograph, the work of an individual who contributes to a large research project is often difficult to quantify. Given that the university, in essence, becomes the publisher of the work, the individual academic is also in danger of losing access to, or involvement in, the work if he or she moves institutions. While many universities have been eager to publish this work, few have committed themselves, in the long term, to solving the intellectual property issues at stake or to putting in place the infrastructural support necessary to maintain large projects that may endure over decades. All of these factors make working in this area a precarious business. It is perhaps little wonder then that so few working models have evolved. However, given that what is at stake is an opportunity to wrestle back from commercial forces the responsibility, as well as the credit, for our own work this seems a battle that is eminently worth fighting.

THE DEVELOPMENT OF PERFORMANCE MATERIALS ONLINE: THREE CURRENT EXAMPLES

The issue of copyright is not one that will go away. Rather than throwing up our hands in despair, I suggest this issue needs to be addressed head-on. Looking at three examples of performance-oriented projects it is possible to see how working collaboratively with copyright holders can create productive new working relationships as well as new kinds of resources. Working in the digital environment one quickly discovers that the Internet is as much a communications medium as a distribution channel. As a performance-history scholar I saw, from the outset, that digital technology would provide an opportunity to access the experience of live theatre both past and present. This technology allows theatre practitioners to become actively involved in the critical debate about the interpretation of Shakespeare plays. By looking at three examples of work that involves creative practitioners it is possible to envision an edition that would develop an entirely new collaborative relationship between the academy and the professional theatre.

The first example, then, of a performance-oriented resource is my second large digital project, a project which I feel represents a development in my understanding of the medium in which I am working as well as the institutional structures that support this work. Following on from the research involved in the *King Lear* CD-ROM, but also as a result of the contacts beyond the academy which I made in the process, I went on to develop a new collaborative digital research project which received funding from the Arts and Humanities Research Council in the United Kingdom. The aim of this new project, the official title of which is *Designing Shakespeare: An Audio-visual Archive 1960–2000*, (http://ahds.ac.uk/performingarts/designing-shakespeare), was to collect performance-based material that focused attention on the temporal and spatial aspects of production. There are no texts of the plays in this case but rather four databases which include: production credits and reviews for all professional productions of Shakespeare in London and Stratford from 1960–2000, 3500 pictures of these productions in performance, interviews with designers, and virtual models of the theatres most often used for Shakespearean performance. The database is freely available through the Arts and Humanities Data Service of Performing Arts at the University of Glasgow, which as part of the national AHDS is dedicated to preserving these materials for public access in the long term.

In this project I chose to move away from the specificity of the *Lear* CD to address the entire canon. In fact, what the *Lear* CD does in terms of covering one play in depth is contrasted in this case with a project that aims for breadth on a narrower subject. The key aim of the project was again to give students and scholars access to performance-related information but the material was much more focused both historically and geographically and the information was made freely available online. The material is accessible through a play-based hierarchy or can be more specifically mined through a search facility. Each image, video clip and 3D model has a unique url so users can embed links to it in their own work. Alternatively, the material can be saved locally. In order to address the challenge of copyright this project set up a collection that is copyright-cleared for educational purposes. The majority of the photographs come from three central archives: the personal archive of the theatre photographer Donald Cooper, the archive of the RSC held at the Shakespeare Centre Library and the private archive of Janet Arnold, former lecturer in Drama at Royal Holloway. This project also uses oral accounts of the creative process. Interviews were specially commissioned with designers who signed the rights to their memories over to the project. Similarly, the theatre designer who created the VRML models, Chris Dyer, who was also a co-investigator on the project and a colleague at Royal Holloway, granted the right to the free use of the models online.

Thus, all of the material in the Archive was designed with reuse in mind, acknowledging the collaborative nature of the web in its structure. The project addressed the issue of intellectual property directly by working with copyright holders in a collaborative way. As a result *Designing Shakespeare*, when it was launched in February 2003, was one of the first sites to offer free access to information about British Shakespearian performance that had been copyright cleared for educational use. The addition to this archive of sound, video and 3D models changed the nature of the research materials available to scholars and teachers and therefore this archive opened up the potential to change the way the plays are studied. This Archive is publicly available but it is also a resource that acknowledges the public position and the multiple uses that public access entails. The *Designing Shakespeare Archive* is dedicated to the idea of creating a creative dialogue, a debate rather than a single persuasive argument.

The second example of a project that helped to shift the digital landscape for Shakespeare studies is the 'Picture and Exhibitions' site launched by the Royal Shakespeare Company as an offshoot of its main site. Through this new venture the RSC has made available online 3500 images from its archive and from the collection of the Shakespeare Centre Library, funded by the New Opportunities Fund of the National Lottery (http://www.rsc.org.uk/picturesandexhibitions/jsp/index.jsp). The front page of this project states: 'This archive is for anyone interested in Shakespeare performance, including exhibitions and a searchable collection of paintings, photographs, costumes, and prompt books from RSC productions.' The material is available as a searchable database or through a series of twelve exhibitions. The material includes nineteenth-century playbills and illustrations from a range of theatre companies, as well as more recent materials relating to the RSC's own productions. The appearance of such materials online represents a wonderful new resource for students and scholars of performance history. However, the breadth of the audience addressed and the lack of a published selection criteria results in a project that is somewhat eclectic in its approach. Nevertheless, as a development in the online debate, the appearance on the scene

of a theatre company as a new source of archival information is intriguing. It helps to open up the dialogue about archival responsibility while at the same time making available new resources for teaching and research.

The third example I would like to highlight again is not aimed specifically at a scholarly audience but, I would argue, has important consequences for that audience. It is a government-sponsored initiative to develop broadband materials for schools entitled *Stagework* (http://www.stagework.org.uk/). This project offers students, scholars and the general public access to interviews with actors and directors and provides unprecedented insight into the creative process of theatre making. The work of three theatre companies, the National Theatre, The Bristol Old Vic Theatre and the Birmingham Repertory Theatre, on four productions is documented in detail. Nicholas Hytner's acclaimed production of *Henry V* at the National Theatre starring Adrian Lester is the focus of one quarter of this project. The user has the opportunity to access extensive interviews with the actors and director. Video clips of rehearsal and performance document the creative process. The resource also includes an extensive rehearsal diary and a series of thematic approaches to the play that are illustrated through this production. These thematic areas include sections on 'Nationality and Race' and 'Images of War'. As an example of an in depth archive of audio-visual material related to a particular production this project is unprecedented in its thoroughness and availability. With this project the full capabilities of the technology begin to be realised.

Like the RSC project, the *Stagework* project indicates that copyright holders are increasingly keen to experiment with the possibilities the technology offers, largely, I suggest, because they are increasingly keen to maintain control of the ways in which their copyright materials are distributed. As with the resources available for the study of texts on the Internet, performance-history materials have, over the past five years, become much more widely available. The variety of resources now accessible online, such as those described above, raise interesting questions about the position and influence of copyright holders in this debate. These examples also, I believe, open up the possibility of thinking in radical new ways about what an online edition could look like and how it could function.

THE DEVELOPMENT OF A NEW MODEL FOR THE DIGITAL EDITION

If digital resources are to be created which are both rigorous in their standards but also inclusive in their approach, then new ideas about what is desirable in a scholarly edition must be debated. I suggest digital resources could be seen as a means of engaging a new generation of scholars and students in the history of representation of the plays both in textual form and in performance. The challenge for the individual scholar in this complex environment is finding a way of working that moves current thinking and practice forward. One possible approach for the creator of an online edition lies in finding a way of drawing together the existing and developing resources in a coherent way. A second opportunity lies in working in partnership with copyright holders to develop entirely new kinds of projects. Working with commercial publishers is one possibility, but I suggest that commercial practices are inherently conservative. Therefore I insist that it must be the role of the academy to push the boundaries of what is possible in this new area.

Two recent developments have helped to form my thinking about the possibilities of a very new kind of digital edition. The first was the live broadcast by BBC 4 of *Measure for Measure* at the Globe Theatre (2004) for which Kiernan Ryan provided interactive commentary. The second is a new broadband project launched by the Royal Shakespeare Company in June 2005 that uses the performance text as a navigational device to direct users to a wide range of materials that helps the user understand the interpretative choices and the theatrical process involved in the productions of *Hamlet* and *Macbeth* performed in Stratford and London in 2004 (*Exploring Shakespeare: Hamlet and Macbeth* http://www.rsc.

org.uk/learning/hamletandmacbeth/). Harkening back to the original speaking text of the Voyager *Macbeth* CD and the *Lear* CD's Finder text, these two examples illustrate that increasingly it is possible to think of a performance text as the anchor for a complex multilayered presentation of information about the plays. I suggest that the integration of performance-related materials with an authoritative annotated text of the play, which includes editions, sources and adaptations, all linked through a current theatrical production would create an unparalleled resource which could provide a model for the future, not just for Shakespeare texts but for other performance texts online. The new kind of edition I propose, in fact, in many ways combines the full realisation of the embryonic approaches of the early experiments.

This new kind of edition, if it could be realized, would bring together the interests and the expertise of textual scholars, performance-history scholars and creative practitioners to create a productive dialogue. The aim of such a project would be not only to create a useful resource but also to engage in a discussion about the nature of interpretation and creativity. The work of theatre practitioners could, in this environment, be highlighted as interpretive and the creativity of scholars could also be made clear. This model would provide a productive collaboration between the individuals and institutions involved in the creation and dissemination of Shakespeare resources through the development of an integrated online resource.

CONCLUSIONS: THE FUTURE

Clearly there are many parties involved in the development of online resources for the study of Shakespeare each with their own agendas and priorities. There continues to be a debate about who is responsible for the presentation of Shakespeare's work and the textual and performance history this work has inspired. Where publishers fit into the new environment is still undetermined. The role of libraries and the individual as well as the institutional role of scholars and universities remains unclear. From my own research work in this field I have drawn two fundamental lessons. First, that the lessons of the past cannot be overlooked in this new environment and second, that a movement into a new medium must work with both the advantages and the restrictions of that medium. In the future there will certainly emerge a series of new examples of online editions of Shakespeare developed by individual or groups of academics. The work of the *Internet Shakespeare Editions*, the Variorum projects and my own work on performance history offer three possible existing models. But I suggest that there are also more radical possibilities available through the bringing together of these and other working methods through the collaboration of academics and creative practitioners.

If innovation is to be encouraged there must be an open debate about the form these resources should take which crosses over traditional institutional barriers. Until now this debate has taken place amongst a small group of specialists who have been absorbed by the immediate pressures of the projects they are working on. I count myself among this group but I have increasingly come to see that what is needed instead is a more inclusive, more dispassionate critical debate about the nature of these resources and their influence in the long term. This debate must include archivists, librarians and theatre companies if it is to truly address the potential that is offered by the digital revolution. The central question of the public nature of the debate that faces Shakespeare studies, and the cultural impact and investment in the study and production of Shakespeare, mean that any critical debate must discuss engagement with both a public and a commercial audience. The issues of copyright and intellectual property must therefore be at the centre of this debate.

We are at a crossroads. I suggest that the most successful models for the future will be those that find the best combination of old and new ways of working and bring together the greatest number of potential audiences. An adaptation of the edition form that moves forward and makes use of the tremendous advantages of distribution and communication that digital technology allows will prove a benefit to both the scholarly community and the general public. Scholars have never before been given the opportunity to wrest control of the subject, and of their own work, away from the jaws of commercialisation. I suggest that this is now possible through the opportunity provided by digital technology and the free distribution channel of the Internet. The online edition could also provide an opportunity to break down the barriers that have traditionally existed between scholars and theatre practitioners. As a result I suggest that the online edition could be seen to have the potential to be one of the greatest collaborative scholarly projects of this century. Is it not, then, worthy of some serious consideration and debate?

WEBSITES CITED

Gateways
 Touchstone Links List http://www.touchstone. bham.ac.uk/links.html
 Mr. William Shakespeare and the Internet http://shakespeare.palomar.edu/
 Sh:in:E http://www.unibas.ch/shine/

Specialist Shakespeare Libraries
 Touchstone http://www.touchstone.bham. ac.uk/
 Shakespeare Institute Library, University of Birmingham http://www.is.bham.ac.uk/ shakespeare/
 Shakespeare Centre Library, Stratford-upon-Avon http://www.shakespeare.org.uk/main/3
 Folger Shakespeare Library, Washington http:// www.folger.edu/

Literature repositories
 Literature Online http://lion.chadwyck.com/
 Oxford Text Archive http://ota.ahds.ac.uk/
 Project Gutenberg http://www.promo.net/pg/

Electronic Texts produced by Scholars and University Libraries
 The Complete Works of William Shakespeare, MIT http://www-tech.mit.edu/ Shakespeare/

Electronic Text Center, University of Virginia http://etext.virginia.edu/shakespeare/works/

Renaissance Electronic Texts http://www.library.utoronto.ca/utel/ret/ret.html

Facsimile Reproductions produced by Libraries

British Library *Treasures in Full: Shakespeare in Quarto* http://www.bl.uk/treasures/shakespeare/homepage.html

University of Pennsylvania Library facsimile reproduction of the Furness Shakespeare Library copy of the First Folio http://dewey.library.upenn.edu/SCETI/PrintedBooksNew/index.cfm?TextID=firstfolio&PagePosition=3

Online Editions

University of Victoria *Internet Shakespeare Editions* http://ise.uvic.ca/index.html

The Enfolded Hamlet http://www.global-language.com/enfolded.html

Concordances

Shakespeare Concordance http://www.languid.org/cgi-bin/shakespeare

The Works of the Bard http://www.it.usyd.edu.au/~matty/Shakespeare/test.html

Open Source Shakespeare's Concordance http://www.opensourceshakespeare.com/concordance/

The Oxford Shakespeare on the Bartleby.com site http://www.bartleby.com/70/

Shakespeare in Performance

Scholarly Research Projects

Designing Shakespeare (http://ahds.ac.uk/performingarts/designing-shakespeare)

Biographical Index to the Elizabethan Theater http://shakespeareauthorship.com/bd/

Canadian Adaptations of Shakespeare www.canadianshakespeares.ca

FESTE Database the Shakespeare Birthplace Trust www.shakespeare.org.uk/main/3

Library Projects

RSC Archive – Pictures and Exhibitions http://www.rsc.org.uk/picturesandexhibitions/jsp/index.jsp

Cleveland Press Shakespeare Photos, 1870–1982 from the Cleveland State University Library http://www.ulib.csuohio.edu/shakespeare/

Collaborative Research Services

Touchstone's Traffic of the Stage and Database http://www.touchstone.bham.ac.uk/performance.html http://www.touchstone.bham.ac.uk/database.html

Backstage http://www.backstage.ac.uk/

Compiled Lists of Theatre Company websites

Theatre companies worldwide on the Virtual Library site: http://vl-theatre.com/

Theatre Companies performing Shakespeare worldwide http://dmoz.org/Arts/Performing_Arts/Theatre/Shakespeare/Theatre_Companies/

Touchstone list of Theatre Companies performing Shakespeare in the UK http://www.touchstone.bham.ac.uk/links/theatre.html

Shakespeare Festivals List from the Mr William Shakespeare and the Internet site http://shakespeare.palomar.edu/festivals.htm

Individual Theatre Company websites

Royal Shakespeare Company http://www.rsc.org.uk/home/index.asp

Globe Theatre http://www.shakespeares-globe.org/

National Theatre http://www.nt-online.org/home.html

Stratford Festival, Ontario Canada http://www.stratford-festival.on.ca/

Bremer Shakespeare Company, Germany http://www.shakespeare-company.com/

Higher Education Teaching Resources

Hamlet on the Ramparts, MIT Shakespeare Project in collaboration with the Folger

Shakespeare Library http://shea.mit.edu/ramparts

The Higher Education Academy English Subject Centre Shakespeare resources:
http://www.english.ltsn.ac.uk/designshake/completed/index.htm

Media Education Resources
BBC Resources: *King Lear* site
http://www.bbc.co.uk/education/bookcase/lear/

Channel 4 Learning Resources: *Twelfth Night* site
http://www.channel4.com/culture/microsites/T/twelfth_night/index.html

Broadband projects
Stagework
http://www.stagework.org.uk/

Exploring Shakespeare: Hamlet and Macbeth
http://www.rsc.org.uk/learning/hamletandmacbeth/

THE DIRECTOR AS SHAKESPEARE EDITOR

ALAN C. DESSEN

To discuss directors and their productions in relation to editors and their editions is at first glance to mix (or conflate) apples and oranges, cuts and emendations. To the scholar, the differences may far outweigh any similarities, but the essential problem facing both groups remains the same: when putting quill to paper, Shakespeare was fashioning his plays for players, playgoers, playhouses, and (perhaps) play readers that no longer exist. How does or should an editor or theatrical professional factor in the gap between the 1590s–early 1600s and the 1990s–early 2000s? To focus on the preparation of early modern English plays for presentation in today's theatre is to bring into focus the problems and choices involved in a species of 'editing' geared to a larger arena and a less predictable audience.[1]

When mounting a production of a Shakespeare play, today's theatrical professionals take a wide range of approaches in choosing which words, speeches, and scenes to perform. Occasionally a textual adviser or dramaturg will be on hand to sort through the various options; some actors and directors deal directly with the Quarto or First Folio texts; others rely on a particular series as their chosen authority (e.g., the Arden, Oxford or Cambridge editions). One director told me that, after various paperbacks fell apart during the rigours of the rehearsal process, he chose a particular edition for its durable binding. During the rehearsal process some directors encourage their actors to use as many different editions as possible so as to highlight choices and anomalies, whereas others hand their personnel a playscript that contains pre-established cuts

and transpositions, so that some cast members may never consult a full text of the play in question.

The problems in for-the-stage text work are comparable to yet different from those facing the on-the-page editor. One major difference is the question of length, for editors dealing with *Hamlet* or *Richard III* are not under pressure to reduce the number of lines in their texts, whereas directors must worry about running time and playgoers' staying power. Issues central to scholarly introductions (textual history, sources, style, performance history) are not irrelevant to the thinking that lies behind a good production (and such material regularly turns up in programme notes), but, unless a theatrical company is prepared to resort to opera supertitles, no onstage equivalent is available for textual glosses on hard words, mythological or historical allusions, and difficult syntax. To

---

[1] I do not claim any special credentials for writing this chapter, for in both arenas my role has been that of consumer rather than practitioner. I have never edited a play, but as teacher and scholar I have made extensive use of editions of English Renaissance drama for over four decades. Similarly, I have no rehearsal room experience, but over that same period I have sat through more productions of the plays of Shakespeare than is healthy or fruitful. In the comments that follow I draw upon that playgoing experience, the many conversations I have had with theatrical professionals in the United Kingdom and North America, and terms and distinctions found in my *Rescripting Shakespeare: The Text, the Director, and Modern Productions* (Cambridge, 2002). To avoid merely recycling material, I have concentrated largely upon post-2000 productions not covered in that book. With one exception (see note 4) I have limited myself to productions I have seen.

hold the attention of playgoers (and, in commercial theatre, to keep bums in seats) a director must find an onstage vocabulary that is shared by actors and audience.

And thereby hangs my tale. The spectrum of choices I have witnessed in my playgoing does not lend itself to easy summary (and much of this play-going took place before the recent scholarly arguments that postulate 'maximal' Shakespeare scripts that do not correspond to what would actually have been played at the Globe or Blackfriars).[2] At one extreme is a director such as Deborah Warner who has provided strong productions with few if any cuts from the received text. At the other extreme are those productions that for a variety of reasons (e.g., theatrical exigency, a directorial 'concept') exhibit substantive, even radical changes (what I term *rewrighting*). In between these two poles lie most current productions.

The most common form of directorial editing is the omission of lines, speeches and even entire scenes in order to reduce the running time of long scripts. Examples are plentiful and will be evident in the accounts that follow. Next in line are the many adjustments generated by a director's fear that auditors will be mystified by the words spoken by the actors. Will a significant number of playgoers unaccustomed to blank verse, early modern English and difficult syntax and accustomed to processing information through the eye rather than through the ear give up when confronted with a daunting line or passage and assume that they cannot follow what is happening onstage? This assessment is reinforced by the familiar sight during a performance of audience members turning to their programmes or a copy of the play in the hope of relocating themselves in the plot.

Easiest to categorize are changes to individual words and phrases that are deemed opaque, politically incorrect, or otherwise troublesome (as when they conflict with a play's casting or design). Exactly what is deemed daunting or unpalatable to the consumer can vary widely. Typical is Leon Rubin's *Measure for Measure* (Stratford Festival Canada 2005) where *stock-fishes* became *codfish* (3.2.109) and *gyves* became *chains* (4.2.11).[3] To heighten the comedy

generated by the mechanics in his *A Midsummer Night's Dream* (Globe 2002) Mike Alfreds had his actors say *turtle pigeon*, not *sucking dove* (1.2.82–3); *prolapse*, not *prologue* (3.1.17); *transcommunicated*, not *translated* (3.1.119); and *parasite*, not *paramour* (4.2.12). In his *Antony and Cleopatra* (RSC 2002) Michael Attenborough had Enobarbus say 'And for his *nourishment* pays his heart', not *ordinary*, and 'Mine honesty and I begin to *cross*', not *square* (2.2.225, 3.13.41); had Antony say 'Like boys unto a *game*', not *muss* (3.13.91); and, most strikingly, had Cleopatra say 'Then put my *robes and sandals* on him', not *tires and mantles* (2.5.22).

As to political correctness, the best known passage deemed potentially offensive is Portia's comment on the departing Morocco 'Let all of his complexion choose me so' (*The Merchant of Venice*, 2.7.79) which is regularly omitted, as is the third witch's 'Liver of blaspheming Jew' (*Macbeth*, 4.1.26). Harder to cut, because it is the climax to a comic sequence, is Benedick's 'if I do not love her, I am a Jew' (*Much Ado About Nothing*, 2.3.263), so that Gregory Doran (RSC 2002) changed *Jew* to *jack* (other alternatives have been *knave*, *fool* and even *jerk*). To avoid any semblance of a racial slur, the director of a 1995 *Macbeth* (Shakespeare Theatre, Washington, DC) changed Macduff's 'Be not a *niggard* of your speech' (4.3.180) to *miser*; and the director of a 1989 *A Midsummer Night's Dream* (San Francisco Shakespeare Festival), which featured an Asian-American actor as Snout–Wall, changed references to the *chink* in the wall (e.g., 'Show me thy chink', 5.1.177) to *hole*.[4]

Other comparable editing of words, phrases, and stage directions can best be classified as pragmatic. If *Henry V* is to be presented in modern dress with modern weaponry, the apology for 'four or five

2 See Andrew Gurr, 'Maximal and Minimal Texts: Shakespeare v. The Globe', *Shakespeare Survey 52* (Cambridge, 1999), pp. 68–87; and Lukas Erne, *Shakespeare as Literary Dramatist* (Cambridge, 2003).

3 Citations from Shakespeare are from the revised Riverside edition, ed. G. Blakemore Evans (Boston and New York, 1997).

4 For this example I am indebted to Michael P. Jensen.

most vile and ragged foils / (Right ill dispos'd, in brawl ridiculous)' (Chorus to Act 4, 50–1) is a likely casualty, as in Nicholas Hytner's 2003 National Theatre production. To avoid an unwanted laugh at what may seem initially an incongruous image, the same director had Paulina in *The Winter's Tale* (National Theatre 2001) say not 'I, an old *turtle*, / Will wing me to some wither'd bough' (5.3.132–3) but *turtledove*. In Steven Pimlott's *Hamlet* (RSC 2001) references to 'young Osric' (5.2.196, 259) were omitted because the same older actor who had played the Ghost doubled as Osric (who therefore was definitely not a junior Polonius in the making). Jupiter's descent '*sitting upon an eagle*' (*Cymbeline*, 5.4.92.s.d) is a perennial problem when staging this script, but that problem was compounded for Rachel Kavanaugh outdoors in Regent's Park in 2005 with no acting area above. Her solution: she eliminated Jupiter completely so that one of the ghosts produced and then delivered the tablet with the prophecy. In Rubin's Stratford Festival Canada modern dress *Measure for Measure* the clerical figures wore dark suits with no hoods, so that all references to *friar* were changed to *father*. In an action-related adjustment, Mariana, pleading with Isabella to speak in behalf of Angelo, may say 'O Isabel! will you not lend a knee?' (5.1.442), but in this show the *knee* reference was gone so that this Isabella did not have to kneel.

Along with running time, obscurity, and pragmatism, another factor in preparing a script for the stage as opposed to an edition for a reader is theatrical exigency, most commonly a shortage of personnel. A director in 2005 presenting *As You Like It* or *The Tempest* at the Festival Theatre in Stratford, Ontario need not economize on actors (especially given the availability in the same theatre of singers and dancers from *Hello Dolly*), so that the Act 4 masque in *The Tempest* could have ten nymphs and reapers – as opposed to other productions I have seen where Ferdinand and Miranda had to be enlisted in the dance. Smaller companies, however, must confront significant logistical problems that in turn lead to editing of the script. Changes linked to exigency are most common in productions of non-Shakespeare items,

as seen regularly in London Fringe shows. The 2002 Southwark Playhouse production of *The Changeling* with a cast of nine had some actors play a single role (Beatrice, Alsemero, De Flores, Lollio) but doubled Diaphanta–Isabella, Antonio–Tomazo, Vermandero–Alibius, and Jasperino–Franciscus. Given such recycling of figures in the two plots, various adjustments followed: the first two madhouse scenes (1.2, 3.3) were combined; Vermandero and Tomazo spoke with Isabella, not Alibius in 5.2 (so that Vermandero–Alibius need not talk to himself); and to avoid the coming together of figures from the two plots in the same scene the final forty lines were cut, so that this show ended with Beatrice's dying words. At the same venue the 2005 production of *'Tis Pity She's a Whore*, also with a cast of nine, omitted Bergetto, Philotis, Richardetto and Grimaldi (in 1.2 Vasques fought with Donado, not Grimaldi) with the same actor playing Donado and the Cardinal. The result was a gain in intensity and pace (the show including interval lasted less than two-and-a-half hours), but at a price (gone were the unintended death of Bergetto and the Cardinal's shielding of Grimaldi), and in the final moments the Cardinal was literally the only figure left standing. The Landor Theatre production of *Women Beware Women* (2002) with a cast of ten cut Sordido (so that the Ward's role was much diminished), had the same actor play Fabritio and the Cardinal (so that the former disappeared from the final third of the script), and made a series of adjustments to the climactic masque-within-the-play (in addition to the limited cast, this pub theatre had no above for Livia–Juno and no trap door for the caltrop).

Comparable adjustments were provided by David Lan in his *Doctor Faustus* (Young Vic 2002) presented with seven actors (six men, including Jude Law, and one woman) and incorporating elements from both the A and B texts along with many omissions. The two major casualties were Helen of Troy and the Old Man. The display of Helen to the scholars was offstage, a lighting effect rather than an actress, so that she was not seen by the playgoer. Her subsequent appearance to Faustus was represented by a mirror on a chair; Faustus therefore could not exit with her, and the full resonance of his big speech (e.g., 'Her lips suck forth my soul, see where it flies', A-1360, B-1877)[5] was diminished. To omit the Old Man is to eliminate the trigger for Mephistophiles offering the dagger to Faustus (a moment that therefore seemed abrupt) and to lose the speech describing an angel with 'a vial full of precious grace' hovering over Faustus (A-1320–3, B-1835–8), a major statement in this final sequence of the alternative.

Such severe compression owing to a shortage of actors is not as common with Shakespeare's scripts; nonetheless, the merging of less than central figures is standard practice, particularly in the history plays. Tim Carroll made a variety of such adjustments in his *Richard II* (Globe 2003) where several smaller roles were curtailed or telescoped together. For example, Berkeley in 2.3 became Salisbury, so that the same figure interacted with Bolingbroke in 2.3, the Welsh Captain in 2.4, and Richard in 3.2; the Willoughby and Ross lines were gone from 2.3; the Abbot was gone from 4.1 along with the three-figure coda to that scene involving the Abbot, Carlisle, and Aumerle that echoes the end of 2.1 with Northumberland, Willoughby, and Ross. Far more extreme (and hence atypical) was the Riverside Studio's *Measure for Measure Malaya* (2002) adapted for seven actors. Gone were such figures as Escalus, the Provost, Elbow, Froth, and Friar Peter-Thomas; Barnadine was renamed Pompey and absorbed some of the latter's lines about other inmates (4.3.1–19). Key speeches from Escalus and the Provost were given to Lucio so that this composite figure spoke both Escalus's praise of the Duke (3.2.232–7) and Lucio's own denigrations (3.2.116–40, 4.3.156–66).

To economize on the number of actors can generate new problems. In his 2005 *Measure for Measure* Leon Rubin chose in 2.1 (the comic display of 'justice' at work that involves Escalus, Pompey, Froth, and Elbow) to eliminate an anonymous justice in the script with whom Escalus converses about Claudio's fate after Elbow's departure. These closing lines, in which Escalus invites the justice to dinner and the latter says 'Lord Angelo is severe' (2.1.276–86), were still included, but Escalus's lines

were addressed not to a fellow justice but to Elbow (the bumbling constable addicted to malapropisms). Since both the situation (why would Escalus confide in Elbow?) and the language were totally inappropriate, I found this choice jarring.

Several recent productions can demonstrate the range of adjustments linked to running time and exigency. Consider first the 2003 RSC and Globe productions of *Richard III*, a long script that places heavy demands on a theatrical company and its audience. For the RSC, Sean Holmes did much eliding but cut no scenes, so that included were 2.2 (even some of the children's lines that are almost always omitted), 2.3 (for two rather than three citizens), and the Stanley-Urswick 4.5 (with the latter part pared back), while atypically Richmond kept many of his lines in Act 5. At the Globe, where there was a collision between a lengthy script and the presence of many standees in the yard, Barry Kyle cut the citizens (2.3) and the children in 2.2 and moved some key 4.5 lines to 5.3. Both directors factored lines from Richard's soliloquies in *3 Henry VI* into the opening of 1.1; both (to save on personnel and costumes) created a composite clergyman who combined the Cardinal of 3.1 and Bishop Ely of 3.4 (at the Globe this same figure figured in 2.4 as well). In Stratford, Ratcliff rather than Brackenbury refused the women entry to the Tower in 4.1 (the goal was to create more of a through-line and set up a greater threat to the two boys).

Not all directors follow the same paths. In his *Coriolanus* (RSC 2002) David Farr did not make various adjustments I have come to expect (e.g., having the boy play silently during the women's dialogue in 1.3; cutting the servants at the end of 4.5; rescripting the elements of the final scene) though he did cut 4.3, the Roman traitor scene. Rather, he made his own distinctive moves – for example, cutting most of 4.1 and 4.2 and moving the women's attack on the tribunes in 4.2 to 4.6. Most unusual was his omitting Valeria from 5.3 so as to change the classic story that attributes the saving

---

5 Citations from *Doctor Faustus* are from *Marlowe's Doctor Faustus 1604–1616*, ed. W. W. Greg (Oxford, 1950). I have modernized the spelling.

of Rome to three women and a child, not solely to the mother figure. Also atypical were the choices in the 2005 West End *As You Like It* where David Lan cut 5.1 (the only scripted appearance of William) and also Touchstone's discourse on the degrees of the lie (often a show-stopping tour de force, as with Stephen Ouimette's rendition in Stratford Festival Canada 2005) and, in a highly unusual choice, repositioned Jaques' famous speech on the seven ages of man *after* the arrival of Orlando and Adam. In this production, Jaques' final disparaging lines on old age ('second childishness, and mere oblivion, / Sans teeth, sans eyes, sans taste, sans every thing' – 2.7.165–6) were not juxtaposed with Adam being borne in by a caring Orlando.

A director's editing linked to obscurity, exigency, or running time calls attention to the gap between the 'real world' of commercial theatre (where saving one actor's salary, I was told by a US artistic director, can pay for a set) and the more rarefied world of editing on-the-page. Of even greater interest are directorial changes to solve or resolve perceived problems. Editors may deal with apparent anomalies in terms of the faulty transmission of a text or unrevised first thoughts in an authorial manuscript (and may suggest alternatives), whereas a director can actually rescript the scene or omit it entirely. For example, readers who puzzle over the presence of Christopher Sly in the first two scenes of the First Folio's *The Taming of the Shrew* would have found no 'solutions' at the Globe or in Stratford-upon-Avon in 2003, for those scenes were gone from both productions. Similarly, I have seen several productions of *The Merry Wives of Windsor* where directors have sought to 'improve' the underwritten sub-plot in Act 4 that involves horses, Germans, and revenge on the Host by Doctor Caius and Parson Hugh, but in her rendition (RSC 2002) Rachel Kavanaugh took the Gordian knot approach and omitted this material entirely. She also cut the 4.1 language lesson, thereby sidestepping the need to recruit a child actor to play William Page.

Some of these adjustments or 'improvements' have become commonplace, even standard practice. In Sam Mendes's *Twelfth Night* (Donmar 2002)

Malvolio, when reacting to the letter supposedly from Olivia, did not say 'She did commend my yellow stockings of late, she did praise my leg being cross-garter'd' (2.5.166–7). Yes, these lines are contradicted by Maria's subsequent comment ('He will come to her in yellow stockings, and 'tis a color she abhors, and cross-garter'd, a fashion she detests' – 198–200) so that actors and directors often eliminate the apparent anomaly. However, I am not the only reader of the scene who believes that, as with the crushing of M.O.A.I., this contradiction is at the heart of the sequence (here, to reassure myself, I sounded out a series of actors including several who had played Malvolio). How far will Malvolio go to hold onto his dream, his 'what you will' approach to reality? Is an invented memory so alien to early twenty-first-century playgoers?

To present the two parts of *Henry IV* as back-to-back productions with the same personnel can lead to some exciting theatre, as with the English Shakespeare Company (1988), the RSC (2000), and the National Theatre (2005), but to offer the two items as a unit generates problems that can lead to editing of Part One. At the National Theatre in 2005, Nicholas Hytner's acting script for *1 Henry IV* contained various elisions I have come to expect; for example, gone were Prince Hal's list of the words learned from the drawers (2.4.15–20), Falstaff's invocation of the camomile (2.4.400–2), and much of Worcester's politic speech to Hotspur (3.1.175–87). The only surprise was the omission of Hotspur's pre-battle speech (5.2.81–8) which can be a stirring, charismatic moment that also reinforces the issue of 'time'. Often cut elsewhere but included here were the carriers discussing fleas in 2.1, the practical joke involving Francis in 2.4, and the Archbishop-Michael scene (4.4) which looks forward to Part Two and is therefore often a casualty when Part One is presented alone.

To present the two parts in sequence, however, is to confront a problem: how do you move from Prince Hal's triumph in various senses at Shrewsbury at the end of Part One to his backsliding in his next appearance, what I think of as the 'small beer' scene with Poins (*2 Henry IV*, 2.2)? In the final moments of Michael Bogdanov's *1 Henry IV*

(English Shakespeare Company 1988) Falstaff, after wounding Hotspur in the thigh, exited with the body (5.4.129), at which point the action shifted to the fate of Worcester and the ransom of Douglas in 5.5. With Henry IV still onstage, Falstaff re-entered with his claim that he, not Hal, had killed Hotspur, so that the king, overhearing most of this exchange (5.4.138–53), could depart no longer believing in his son. A stunned Hal, again estranged from his father, threw down his sword, and Falstaff had the final lines in the production (5.4.162–5), so that the playgoer was prepared for a diminished view of Hal when next seen in Part Two.

Hytner's choices were comparable albeit less extensive. The actions involving Hal, Falstaff and Hotspur's body in 5.4 were not changed, but 5.5 (not a memorable scene for most readers) was rescripted. First, the King's opening speech (5.5.1–10) was directed not at two figures, Worcester and Vernon, but at three, for Douglas was included here among those sentenced to death. Prince Hal's subsequent two speeches and Prince John's response (17–33) were gone, so that not only the account of Douglas' flight and capture was eliminated but, more significant, so was the example (in John's words) of Hal's 'high courtesy' (32) in awarding the ransom of Douglas and the honours of the day to Prince John in keeping with his earlier praise (5.4.17–20). Rather than publicly giving credit to both his brother and Douglas, Prince Hal had no role in the closure of this production – and the final image was of the Falstaff Hal had promised to help 'if a lie may do thee grace' (5.4.157) rifling the onstage corpses. Any sense of a 'new' Hal in the final moments was thereby repressed.

Some problems can be resolved by inserting stage business. Readers of *Henry V* have wondered about the absence in the received text of the Dauphin from the negotiations in the final scene (one director told me that he and his cast had puzzled at length over this absence). In his 1988 English Shakespeare Company production Michael Bogdanov did include the Dauphin here and had him nonplus both the English and French figures by storming off the stage just as the treaty was being announced and celebrated. In contrast, Nicholas Hytner (National Theatre 2003) 'solved' the problem by having a fleeing Dauphin shot after the killing of the boys in Act 4.

Sometimes stage business can complete actions left unresolved in the script. In *Romeo and Juliet* a belligerent Tybalt, after overhearing Romeo, calls for his rapier before his confrontation with father Capulet (1.5.55) – a request left unfulfilled in the script. But in a 2002 production (Mercury Theatre, Colchester) a Peter relishing the prospect of violence hurried back with the weapons just as Capulet finished his demolition of a chastened Tybalt. Similarly, at the outset of 2.3 in *Much Ado About Nothing* Benedick sends off his boy to fetch a book from his study, but the Quarto provides no completion to this action. In both the Actors from the London Stage Fall 2002 five-actor production and Gregory Doran's RSC 2002 rendition the boy returned with the book while Benedick was trying to remain invisible to Don Pedro, Claudio and Leonato – and in the latter this returnee created an even greater degree of comic awkwardness by refusing to leave until given a tip.

In his *Much Ado* Doran made another distinctive move linked to stage business. Scholars have speculated about a supposed missing scene midway in this play which in turn directors have supplied, so playgoers should not be surprised to see a dumb show wherein Claudio and Don Pedro are seen observing Margaret in the guise of Hero being wooed by a man. Doran, however, went a step further by placing that man not below but above embracing a female figure. This interpretation was presumably linked to Don John's claim: 'Go but with me to-night, you shall see her chamber-window ent'red' (3.2.112–13) rather than Claudio's query: 'What man was he talk'd with you yesternight / Out at your window betwixt twelve and one?' or Don Pedro's subsequent 'Talk with a ruffian at her chamber-window' (4.1.83–4, 91).

Two related passages in *Measure for Measure* pose a problem that has led to adjustments in the theatre: the Duke's soliloquy in tetrameter couplets (3.2.261–82) and his subsequent soliloquy during the brief conference between Mariana and Isabella (4.1.59–64). A long note in the New Variorum edition[6] records dissatisfaction going back to the eighteenth century with the latter passage, a meditation on how 'place and greatness' are vulnerable to 'millions of false eyes' (4.1.59). Why does the Duke express these sentiments at this point? Moreover, in practical terms is this speech long enough to allow for the Isabella–Mariana conference that takes place offstage? Similarly, does the tetrameter couplet speech, which starts 'He who the sword of heaven will bear / Should be as holy as severe' and moves to a plan of action in 'Craft against vice I must apply' (3.2.261–2, 277), make sense in its Folio position? In defence of the 4.1 speech Katherine Lever notes: 'The time has obviously been foreshortened, but this was permitted by the theatrical convention that time could be presumed to elapse during a soliloquy', but many directors agree with A. P. Rossiter that the earlier speech in couplets 'could equally well go in here – providing a necessary explanation and at a point where the Duke must be alone'.

To deal with this perceived problem directors have resorted to a variety of solutions. Steven Pimlott (RSC 1994) chose to omit the Duke's 4.1 Folio soliloquy but not to replace it with a section of the 3.2 speech; rather, his choice was elegant in its simplicity – the Duke stood silent onstage and looked impatiently at his watch. Jim Edmondson's solution (Oregon Shakespeare Festival 1986) was more elaborate than most: he repositioned the 4.1 speech as the Prologue and broke up the 3.2 speech so that one part was placed at the end of 3.1 just before his interval and the remainder replaced the original soliloquy in 4.1 – and no lines were left at the speech's original placement at the end of 3.2. Simon McBurney (National Theatre 2004) went a step further by switching from the mid scene *exeunt* of the two women to the beginning of 4.2 (the segment involving the Provost, Pompey, and Abhorson), then returning to the remainder of 4.1, then back to 4.2. Leon Rubin (Stratford Festival Canada 2005) omitted almost all of the 3.2 speech (because, I was told, of the odd rhythm generated by the metre and couplets) and also cut the final section of 4.1, so that an *exeunt* of the Duke, Mariana and Isabella before the Duke's soliloquy concluded the

scene. As a result, two speeches that help to define the Duke were missing from this show as well as the closing segment of 4.1 that helps to set up the Isabella–Mariana 'sisterhood'.

Such resolution of perceived problems or anomalies falls under the larger category of 'improvements' that theatrical professionals deem necessary or advisable. Here, moreover, is where directors can achieve what scholars can only dream of: correct apparent errors; supply what is seen as missing; and enhance a particular effect. Such adjustments or improvements take many forms. For example, in the received text of *Measure for Measure* Mistress Overdone reveals that Lucio's bastard child by Kate Keepdown 'is a year and a quarter old come Philip and Jacob' (3.2.201–2) but in Rubin's Stratford Festival Canada production that age was changed to thirteen so that in the final moments not only Kate Keepdown but also an actress playing a teenaged girl emerged to corral Lucio.

The most extensive editing or rescripting is generated not by obscurity, exigency, or perceived problems but by a director's overriding thesis or 'concept'. An extreme example is Phil Willmott's *Measure for Measure Malaya* (Riverside Studios 2002) where (as noted in the programme) the action took place 'In and around the prison headquarters of the newly appointed District Officer for an isolated British Colony in 1930s Malaya', with the Duke 'the Malayan High Commissioner', Angelo 'recently instated as the first District Officer of an isolated Malayan province', Lucio 'A British soldier assigned to the prison', Juliet 'A disgraced young English woman', Claudio 'A Eurasian civil servant working for the British', Overdone a Eurasian prostitute, and Isabella and Mariana also Eurasian. To summarize briefly the wholesale rewrighting, the show opened not with 1.1 but with material from the Duke's speeches in 1.3 reshaped into an expository soliloquy (but gone was a key

[6] See *Measure for Measure*, ed. Mark Eccles, New Variorum (New York, 1980), p. 190 from which I have taken the Lever and Rossiter quotes. Similar questions have been raised about the 3.1 positioning of the 'to be, or not to be' soliloquy in the Second Quarto and the Folio.

couplet: 'hence shall we see / If power change purpose: what our seemers be', 1.3.53–4). In the action that followed, 2.2, 2.3 and 2.4 remained intact, but speeches elsewhere were cut, transposed, or reassigned. Race was a constant unspoken issue, given the three British men (the Duke, Angelo and Lucio) and three Eurasian women (Isabella, Mariana and Overdone). Most transformed was Act 5, for in this version Lucio, Mariana and Isabella were aware of the Duke being Friar Lodowick from the outset (many of the revelations therefore were repositioned earlier before Angelo was involved); with no Escalus and no Friar Peter, the Duke never left the stage, Angelo did not exit with Mariana to be married and then return, and the testing of various figures was much diminished.

Few productions in major venues take the editing or rescripting process this far. Nonetheless, significant cuts and changes are to be found in such productions, so that an account of several recent examples can serve as the final section of this essay. Extensive changes were evident in Edward Hall's *Julius Caesar* (RSC 2001). The Folio's first scene involving Flavius, Marullus and the cobbler (a scene not prized by many theatrical professionals with whom I have talked) was gone completely to be replaced by the singing of a Fascist hymn ('We bring forth the new world from the ashes of the old . . . The republic makes us strong') by an ensemble that included a host of black-shirted figures. A strong Forum scene (3.2) started with those same black-shirted figures scattered throughout the theatre; during Antony's oration they made their way onto the stage so as to be unleashed on Rome (and maul Cinna the poet). I missed the display of the power of oratory by Flavius and Marullus to sway a crowd (an early demonstration of real 'Romans' in action), but Hall's opening was theatrically exciting, and the mob in 3.2 was as strong an onstage presence for this moment as I have seen.

Hall's severe streamlining of Acts 4 and 5 was less successful. Other directors have omitted the second account of Portia's death by Messala, an omission supported by a scholarly argument[7] (albeit one with which I disagree), but Hall also eliminated other features of this scene (gone completely were Mes-

sala, Titinius, Varrus, and Claudio). Brutus directed at Cassius a few lines about Cicero and other dead senators, but the playgoer did not hear Messala's assessment of Brutus' reaction to Portia's death ('Even so great men great losses should endure') or Cassius's comment: 'I have as much of this in art as you, / But yet my nature could not bear it so' (4.3.193–5). In addition, in the Folio Brutus accuses Cassius of having 'an itching palm' (10) and later notes that 'I did send to you / For certain sums of gold, which you denied me' (69–70), but most of this latter speech (69–82) was cut, including 'For I can raise no money by vile means. / By heaven, I had rather coin my heart / And drop my blood for drachmaes than to wring / From the hard hands of peasants their vile trash / By any indirection' (71–5). At several points in this scene the script choices therefore increased the pace and economized on personnel at the expense of a more nuanced portrait of Brutus. How is Cassius (or a playgoer) to react to a Brutus who is apparently playing the part of the great (Stoic) man or who criticizes the fundraising methods used by Cassius but still demands money from his ally?

To pare back Act 5, particularly the 5.4 action with Cato and Lucilius, may be standard practice, but Hall took out far more. Not only was the brief 5.2 gone, but also 5.3.9–35 where Cassius announces 'my sight was ever thick' (21), sends Pindarus above, and gets a false report of the capture of Titinius. Hall's dialogue started up again with the Cassius speech to Pindarus and Cassius's death (36–50), but the remainder of the scene was gone (the Titinius–Messala reaction, Titinius's suicide, Brutus's finding of the two bodies). A key death was therefore included, but much of the logic behind

---

[7] In a long note in his Arden2 edition (London, 1955) T. S. Dorsch accepts the traditional view 'that the copy from which the Folio was printed contained two versions of the account of Portia's death, of which one was a revision, and that both were printed by mistake', so that the second account provided by Messala is the original and the first provided by Brutus himself is the revision (pp. 106–7). In recent years directors, who no longer hold an idealized vision of Brutus, usually keep both accounts of Portia's death, so that Hall's adjustment is the exception, not the norm.

that death was eliminated. Similarly, Clitus, Dardanius, Volumnius and Strato were gone from 5.5, so that Brutus's suicide was set up as a series of appeals to the same figure, Lucilius, a change that yielded a sequence with a very different theatrical rhythm. Antony then spoke his epitaph for Brutus, but Messala did not question Lucilius-Strato about the manner of Brutus's death nor did Octavius offer to 'entertain' those that had served Brutus (5.5.60) – and during this abbreviated final sequence Caesar appeared upstage with his wounds visible. The story-telling here was very effective, but the story told in the last two acts was a diminished version of the full narrative found in the Folio.

Less extensive but also of interest are the changes, omissions and transpositions in Michael Attenborough's *Antony and Cleopatra* (RSC 2002). To streamline this long script the director eliminated some scenes (2.1, 2.4, 3.1, 3.5) and pared back others. The show started not with Philo's speech (as in the Folio) but with an exchange between the two title figures (1.1.14–17); gone from the final scene were Seleucus and the Romans' piecing out how Cleopatra died. Gone too were Pompey and Menas, so, in addition to 2.1, large chunks of 2.6 and 2.7 disappeared (some of Menas's lines were given to other figures), and Enobarbus's famous speech on Cleopatra (2.2.191–239) was moved to 2.6 which was combined with 2.7. The raucous and entertaining galley or party scene (2.7) featured in lieu of the scripted song an all-male African dance led by Eros and some drunken sword fights wherein a macho Antony embarrassed a standoffish Caesar, but, without Pompey's refusal of Menas's proposition ('Wilt thou be lord of all the world?' – 2.7.61), the meat of the scene disappeared.

Three small adjustments to the dialogue are worth noting. First, omitted from 1.2 was Enobarbus's 'Hush, here comes Antony' (79) spoken at Cleopatra's entrance, a line apparently deemed confusing or anomalous rather than suggestive or metaphoric. In Antony's death scene Cleopatra's 'we must draw thee *up*' (4.15.30) became *down*, for the director solved a notoriously difficult staging problem by having Antony lowered to Cleopatra below rather than raised to her above. Also of

interest was the omission of the final line of 4.9, 'Come on then, he may recover yet' (33), spoken by one of Caesar's watch over the body of Enobarbus. The Folio provides no specific signal for how this remorseful figure is to die (other than perhaps a suggestion of a broken heart), but this Enobarbus stripped off his shirt to reveal many self-inflicted wounds. In the final sequence Iras did die with no such specified cause (in the past I have seen Iras sneak an asp in advance of Cleopatra) but, in this production, with the genesis of Enobarbus's death made clear, no connection existed between the two events – a potential link that I, for one, find meaningful as a window into the distinctive appeal or stature of the two title figures.

The two 2004 productions of *Hamlet*, directed by Trevor Nunn (Old Vic) and Michael Boyd (RSC) also provided many items of interest. Both shows included Barnardo not solely as scripted in 1.1 and the end of 1.2 (the report to Hamlet of the ghost's appearance) but also along with Horatio and Marcellus in 1.4 and 1.5, again to fashion a larger through-line for the actor. Both directors moved 'to be, or not to be' earlier, although not to the same position. Boyd spliced both the soliloquy and the subsequent nunnery scene into 2.2 after Polonius's report to the king and queen, then reverted to the fishmonger exchange and the remainder of 2.2, then the beginning of 3.1. Nunn chose an even earlier placement. After Hamlet's 'The time is out of joint' lines that end Act 1 (1.5.188–90), the playgoers saw Ophelia regarding herself in an imaginary mirror and dancing to music only she could hear, at which point Hamlet entered as later described by her in 2.1; this dumb show was followed by 'to be, or not to be' delivered by Hamlet seated on a bench with a dagger on one side and pills and water on the other.

Overall, both directors did much cutting and reshuffling. Nunn moved Ophelia's 'O, what a noble mind is here o'erthrown!' speech (3.1.150–61) from the end of the nunnery exchange to the end of the next scene after Hamlet's 'Now could I drink hot blood' soliloquy (3.2.388–99) where he ignored her entrance, so that her lament became a response to the Hamlet of the play-within. In 5.2

Nunn included Claudius's aside ('It is the pois'ned cup, it is too late' – 292) but omitted Laertes's 'And yet it is almost against my conscience' (296), whereas Boyd cut the former and kept the latter. Boyd used a full text in his first half (the interval was taken after 3.2), but did considerable streamlining thereafter so that 3.3 through to the end took only one hour and a quarter. The Second Quarto–Folio's 4.6 (Horatio and the sailors) was replaced by the First Quarto's Horatio–Gertrude scene, so that Q1's compressed exposition of events replaced much of the material at the beginning of 5.2; also heavily pared back was the beginning of 4.7 (Claudius–Laertes). Nunn also did much streamlining, though this show including the interval still ran around three hours and forty-five minutes compared to the RSC's three and a half hours. Horatio lost many lines starting in 1.1 where Marcellus was often the beneficiary (so the latter spoke 'So have I heard, and do in part believe it', 165). Much of the Hamlet–Horatio dialogue in 5.2 was gone, so that this Horatio was not a key building block (e.g., the playgoer did not witness his reaction to the deaths of Rosencrantz and Guildenstern), in decided contrast to a militant and active Horatio in Stratford who was quick to draw his sword in 1.1 and 5.2 and was a forceful presence throughout.

For my final example I turn to what I found to be a highly successful piece of directorial editing, Gregory Doran's RSC 2005 rendition of Ben Jonson's *Sejanus His Fall*. I had never expected to see this script staged, for I am surely not the only reader to have concluded that what has survived in the 1605 Quarto and the 1616 Folio is not a play but rather a poem in dramatic form. That Doran and his cast at the Swan found a stageable play in this script with strong in-the-theatre moments (including some racy and very funny bits) represents for me a remarkable achievement. Over 800 lines from the received text were streamlined from the acting script, but the scene structure remained intact (much of the omitted material came from long speeches) and the personae and issues came across forcefully. As expected, less than central figures were telescoped together (e.g., Gallus was folded into Sabinus, Pomponius into Afer). A series

of onstage adjustments added significantly to the impact of the narrative. Providing a dumb show of Drusus's death was a gift to the playgoer; having a visible Tiberius read his Act 5 letter (the turning point in the downfall of Sejanus) turned a good on-the-page moment into an even stronger theatrical one, especially with Caligula standing behind him.

Of particular interest are the adjustments made to a key Tiberius–Sejanus encounter in Act 2. The usual interpretation of this sequence is that Tiberius, who throughout the play appears to be consistently a step ahead of Sejanus, is here testing his protégé, but that was not the approach here. The alternative presented forcefully at the Swan is therefore worth exploring.

To establish the Tiberius to be displayed to the playgoers, Doran made two related choices (I am ignoring the eliding of several long speeches). First, to start the scene Doran inserted a nightmare vision so as to set up a shaken Tiberius who could then be instructed by Sejanus on how to proceed against Agrippina and other potential threats. The second key choice was to cut two lines from the passage cited below, a speech that conditions our view of the Tiberius–Sejanus relationship. The words in bold type were omitted from the production, whereas *We are* was added for continuity:

> We can no longer
> Keep on our mask to thee, our dear Sejanus.
> **[Thy thoughts are ours in all, and we but proved**
> **Their voice, in our designs, which by assenting]**
> {We are} [**Hath**] more confirmed [**us**] than if heart'ning Jove
> Had, from his hundred statues, bid us strike . . .
> 2.278–83[8]

My understanding of 'we but proved [i.e., *tested*] / Their voice' is that the scene up to this point had been a testing of Sejanus, to see if he would come up with the strategy at which Tiberius (the grand master always several moves ahead) had already

---

[8] Citations from *Sejanus* are from the Yale edition, ed. Jonas A. Barish (New Haven and London, 1965).

arrived. Doran's shaken, troubled Tiberius, how-ever, is more theatrical (and perhaps more faithful to the historical records), albeit not as sly and there-fore less insidious. For the two actors and many auditors the rescripted speech made excellent sense in terms of psychological realism (a basic part of the vocabulary shared by players and playgoers in 2005) – and I suspect only the occasional old school Jonsonian noticed any difference. I found the scene as staged telling, so I leave the verdict about possible pluses and minuses to other readers.

This last example brings into focus several key issues linked to editing for the theatre. Unlike the on-the-page editor, whose goal is to offer readers a text that preserves and clarifies the original, the director's goal is to make that text comprehensible so that it can come alive for playgoers who are both viewers of onstage activity and auditors of verse in early modern English. Moreover, the director must achieve this goal without exceeding the lim-its imposed by the available resources, an imper-ative not faced by the editor. A director will not stay a director for very long if he or she misjudges the capacity and tastes of that targeted audience or the practicalities of the situation. The various in-the-theatre changes I have noted, even the most extreme ones, would not have been made had those mounting the production not perceived gains to be achieved, whether practical (to reduce obscurity, to conserve time and personnel, to solve apparent problems) or conceptual (to enhance a particular interpretation). To edit for the theatre is often to cut the Gordian knot so as to save on running time,

economize on personnel, and make Elizabethan–Jacobean language, culture, and onstage conven-tions more accessible to today's playgoers. The pro-cess can also involve translation into our idiom, as witnessed by Doran's adjustment to the Tiberius–Sejanus scene so as to establish clearly a psycholog-ical progression in a pivotal moment.

Some years ago an RSC director, reacting to what he interpreted as implied criticism in one of my questions, stated with some force: 'We are not vandals!' I confess that as a theatre historian my purist gene is never recessive, but I retain a healthy respect for the challenges facing theatrical profes-sionals staging Shakespeare today. Choices must be made, choices that inevitably carry with them a price tag, for to gain X one may end up sacrificing Y. I therefore keep returning to the same questions. Wherein lie the trade-offs? What, if anything, is lost or blurred in this process? Given a gap of four hun-dred years, is directorial editing inevitable? When is the price tag too high? Since the director has far more latitude than the editor, the most chal-lenging questions are generated by real or supposed improvements, for here is where the theatrical pro-fessional can move beyond the role of interpreter and closer to the role of translator or playwright. To streamline, massage or reconceive the editor's text is to chart a smoother journey for today's play-goer at the risk of eliminating something integral to the play. Such editing or rescripting may be inevitable in the 'real world' of commercial theatre, but are there lines to be drawn? Whose play is it, anyhow?

THE EDITOR AS TRANSLATOR

BALZ ENGLER

In a world in which scholarly communication is increasingly monolingual and where scholars no longer need feel embarrassed if they only consult studies in one language, it may be strange to raise the issue of translation in editing Shakespeare. But there are at least two reasons to do so: it is much more common than one may think, and it offers opportunities that may lead to useful contributions to Shakespeare studies. Provocatively, an edition might be called a translation *manqué*.

Even editors of 'monolingual' editions, of course, keep translating, from early modern English into the language of their twenty-first-century audience. They may not see their work as such, because of their sense that Shakespeare and their audience are part of the same culture; indeed, one of the motives for editing and re-editing his works is certainly to keep this sense alive. But just because editors are aware that this commonality of culture has its limits they will add glosses, where necessary; in N. F. Blake's words, 'the impression is given that provided the odd difficult word is translated, there should be no difficulty in understanding what Shakespeare wrote'.[1]

Translation also plays a subtle, but consequential role in the modernization of spelling. The issues involved are particularly difficult where modern spelling forces the editor to narrow down early modern meanings, e.g. when having to choose between the modern spellings *travel* and *travail*, or *metal* and *mettle*. According to Stanley Wells a modernizing editor should select what he regards as the primary meaning, irrespective of the original spelling, print this, and annotate the secondary meaning.[2]

This makes good sense, but there are two problems: editions do not usually have enough space to annotate all the instances;[3] and, more importantly, making the very distinction between a primary and a secondary meaning is a modern one; in Shakespeare there may be a single meaning that includes everything modern English forces us to keep apart. The decision whether a note is necessary, and, if so, which of the meanings distinguished should be the primary one, will be based on the editors' interpretation of the context in which the word occurs, which in turn, reflects their search for coherence.[4] The losses incurred in the process are the same as in translation.

The search for coherence will also guide the writing of glosses and explanatory notes. When Ernst Leisi, the Swiss scholar in semantics, published his pioneering *Measure for Measure: An Old-Spelling and Old-Meaning Edition*,[5] he listed several criticisms of existing editions in his introduction, some of which continue to be pertinent.

---

[1] N. F. Blake, *The Language of Shakespeare* (Basingstoke, 1989), p. 2.

[2] Stanley Wells, *Re-Editing Shakespeare for the Modern Reader* (Oxford, 1984), p 10.

[3] The one-volume *Oxford Shakespeare* Stanley Wells was preparing when he formulated the rule has no notes at all.

[4] Shoshana Blum-Kulka, 'Shifts of Cohesion and Coherence in Translation', in Lawrence Venuti, ed., *The Translation Studies Reader* (London, 2000), pp. 298–313, p. 298.

[5] William Shakespeare, *Measure for Measure: An Old-Spelling and Old-Meaning Edition*, ed. Ernst Leisi (Heidelberg, 1964).

(1) *Gaps*: existing editions leave unexplained a good many words that have changed their meanings and consequently need an explanation.

(2) *'Lump translations'*: it often occurs that an editor translates an entire passage into a phrase of his own without discussing the individual words of which it is made up.

(3) *Lack of evidence*: as a rule, editions . . . present no evidence in support of their definitions; they simply state that the meaning of the word is such and such . . .

(4) *Evidence from dictionaries*: some editors . . . gather their evidence mainly from dictionaries, especially from the Oxford Dictionary. Dictionaries . . . have a tendency to split up words into a number of (seemingly unrelated) 'meanings', thus missing their individual and unique essence. They usually tell us nothing about the frequency or importance of one meaning as against another, nor, in the case of general dictionaries, about the specifically Shakespearean use of words . . .

(5) *No full meanings*: very often, the editor's explanation is merely a 'situational equivalent', i.e. a definition which fits the particular passage but does not catch the full meaning, or essence, of the word.[6]

The last point, of course, takes up the issue of coherence mentioned earlier. But the most serious criticism is probably the first, concerning gaps. It is also the one most difficult to deal with in an edition. In many passages, every single word would need an explanatory note, every sentence one for the syntax and the cultural context. We would actually need a *translation* of the whole text in all its details. Then again, a translation into modern English would often be difficult because the often subtle shifts in meaning may not be reflected by adequate changes of the vocabulary.

This is where the translation between languages becomes an opportunity: the vocabulary and the structure of the target-language may make it easier to catch the early modern meanings. Such a translation, which of course may need its own explanatory notes, can then serve as a commentary on Shakespeare's text.

Bilingual editions of Shakespeare's works, like those of other classics, have been quite popular; in many European languages readers may even choose between several.[7] They are familiar to an English-speaking audience from the *Loeb Classical Library*, which began to appear in 1912, and they usually follow the programme formulated by James Loeb:

To make the beauty and learning, the philosophy and wit of the great writers of ancient Greece and Rome once more accessible by means of translations that are in themselves real pieces of literature, a thing to be read for the pure joy of it, and not dull transcripts of ideas that suggest in every line the existence of a finer original from which the average reader is shut out.[8]

Two contradictory aims are pursued: the translated text is supposed both to stand on its own (offering 'pure joy') and to serve as a commentary on the source-language text (making it 'once more accessible').[9] The programme does not say anything about the complex issues created by the fact that the texts appear on facing pages, usually with the source-text on the left, the translation on the right.

Discussion of these issues is surprisingly rare, and we have to go to an Italian translator of Hölderlin for some insights; Luigi Reitani observes:

When the translated text and translation are printed together [. . .] the reader can easily move from one language to the other, opening up the possibility of

---

[6] Leisi, *Measure for Measure*, p. 15.

[7] Editions that come to mind are those by Agostino Lombardo and by Giorgio Melchiori in Italian, the series edited by Michel Grivelet and the translations by Jean-Michel Déprats in French, by Ángel-Luis Pujante in Spanish – the list is by no means complete. The first bilingual English–German edition of Shakespeare appeared in 1912, edited by L. L. Schücking, and has remained in print ever since. Interestingly, it has continued to use the Schlegel/Tieck translation (with some corrections). A list of Shakespeare translations into European languages can be found on the Shakespeare in Europe website http://pages.unibas.ch/shine/.

[8] Quoted by John St. John, *William Heinemann, A Century of Publishing, 1890–1990* (London, 1990), p. 152.

[9] One exception to this is Sinclair's edition of Dante's *Divine Comedy*. He states in his preface: "I have tried to serve readers who have little or no knowledge of Italian and who wish to know the matter of Dante's poem." Dante, *The Divine Comedy*, trans. by John D. Sinclair (New York, 1939), p. 9.

reverberative effects. Not only does the translation become functional to the reading of the 'original', but the 'original' may help give a better understanding of the choices made in the translation. The starting text therefore also loses its autonomy: in bilingual editions it 'lives' by the translation.[10]

This means that in a bilingual edition of the type described the juxtaposition of texts, by inviting comparison, affects both; in some cases, the function of the juxtaposition may even be to bring out the art of the translator. As such it is something quite different from a translation that is meant to stand on its own – the kind of translation that a gloss should offer.

The relatively high status of the translation is supported by its position on the right hand side of the book, where important information is traditionally placed, like the title or the beginning of a chapter. This may be due to the mechanics of reading: as we read from left to right and economize on our eye movements, we tend to get caught on the right-hand page.

Bilingual editions of the type described then cannot really offer the kind of complete commentary that an edition might offer. There is a bilingual edition, however, that tries to solve the problems mentioned, the series *Englisch-Deutsche Studienausgabe der Dramen Shakespeares*, an edition that has been progressing slowly but steadily since the 1970s, and in which twenty-five volumes have been published so far.

In the late 1960s the founders of the series, Werner Habicht, Ernst Leisi and Rudolf Stamm, all board members of the Deutsche Shakespeare-Gesellschaft West, saw themselves confronted with a specific situation in the West German theatre: after a period of celebrating the classics as a mainstay of humanist culture, directors, whose influence was growing, began to rebel against the limitations this imposed on them and increasingly insisted on their own freedom in shaping productions. In the eyes of the bard's devotees, as they would meet in the Gesellschaft, these were only nominally Shakespearian. Directors freely adapted the

classical Schlegel/Tieck translation or used versions like those by Hans Rothe, which claimed to bring across Shakespeare's spirit rather than the meaning of his supposedly disfigured texts. One of the lazy arguments used by directors was that one did not really know anyway what Shakespeare had written, in the absence of manuscripts and single authorized editions. At the meetings of the Gesellschaft there were heated debates on the issues, in typical German fashion pitching scholars, who dominated the Gesellschaft, and 'practitioners' against each other. But what was the proper scholarly response to be? It was felt to be an edition, which made available the considerable amount of sound knowledge we have about Shakespeare and his plays to an audience with some command of English, as it had become common in Germany after the Second World War. This led to the project of an edition of a special kind. It was to offer a critical introduction, a scene-by-scene commentary modelled on Wolfgang Clemen's *Commentary on Shakespeare's 'Richard III'*, a good English text with variants, a prose translation and explanatory notes. Not surprisingly, the specific scholarly interests of the founders became part of the edition's programme: Ernst Leisi's interest in historical semantics, and Rudolf Stamm's interest in the way performance is inscribed in the text, what he called their *theatrical physiognomy*.[11]

A key feature of the edition is the translation, which aspires neither to stand on its own, nor to be performed, nor to invite comparison with the source text as in other bilingual editions. It solely serves, together with the explanatory footnotes, as a guide to understanding Shakespeare's English

---

[10] Luigi Reitani, 'Face to Face. Hölderlin in a New Italian Bilingual Edition', *Modern Language Notes* 117 (2002), 590–8, p. 591. On the manner in which readers may move between the texts see Lance Hewson, 'The Bilingual Edition in Translation Studies', *Visible Language*, 27, no. 1–2 (1993), 139–60.

[11] Cf., e.g., Rudolf Stamm, 'The Alphabet of Speechless Complaint', in Joseph G. Price, ed., *The Triple Bond: Plays, Mainly Shakespearean, in Performance* (University Park, 1975), pp. 255–73.

text. To mark the contrast to common bilingual editions the English text is printed on the right, the German translation on the left; and the footnotes, which claim the same status as the translation, are only referenced in the German text. Readers are expected to use their knowledge of English to read off common stylistic features, like verse, alliteration and rhyme, from the English text; less familiar ones are explained.

The translation thus helps to offer readers an unrivalled amount of information about Shakespeare's text. But, as we have seen, translation, by forcing editors to choose, also makes them give serious thought to the use and meaning of each word. What Stanley Wells observes *apropos* modernizing texts is even more pertinent for the interlingual type of translation: it may be seen 'as a means of exploring Shakespeare's text that can make a real contribution to scholarship'.[12]

Reitani even claims that

only the translation brings to light problems that on first glance are hidden. In order to write a genuine commentary, it would perhaps always be necessary to translate a text into another language and then ask what it means.[13]

As every word has to be understood to be translated, the *Studienausgabe* has stimulated a great deal of research; some might say, perhaps less charitably, that it has proved to be a philologists' playground. Many of the editions provide explanations for passages passed over in silence in English language editions, or new explanations where these have relied on the work of earlier editors.

Inconspicuous problems that do not perturb the annotators often catch the eye of the editor-translator and may have far-reaching consequences. To give just one example: the patient student of Shakespearian usage will discover that *ha* at the end of a sentence may be a question rather than an excited exclamation. This clearly affects, for example, the way in which the development of Othello's reactions to Iago's insinuations is presented:

OTHELLO By heaven, I'll know thy thoughts.
IAGO You cannot, if my heart were in your hand;
  Nor shall not whilst 'tis in my custody.

OTHELLO Ha![14]
IAGO O, beware, my lord, of jealousy.

(3.3.167–9)

Unfortunately such findings may be difficult to access for many scholars for linguistic reasons, and because librarians in the English-speaking world would classify the edition as a translation and fail to acquire it. Some of them have also been published in English, in articles and notes, and catalogued in *English and American Studies in German*;[15] and Werner Brönnimann has offered a selection of examples in an article on the edition.[16]

The translation as a part of the edition thus achieves two goals: it contributes to a better understanding of the source text, and it leads to a reconsideration of many passages. But even though it aims at being strictly scholarly, it cannot avoid problems that, at first sight, have little to do with its aims. As Michel Grivelet, the editor of one of the French bilingual editions puts it:

D'une bonne traduction on attend qu'elle soit fidèle, fidèle à la pensée du texte. [. . .] Mais la pensée dans

---

[12] Wells, *Editing*, p. 34.
[13] Reitani, 'Face to Face', p. 591.
[14] This is the punctuation of the Oxford edition. F has a '?' (which in early modern English may stand both for a question and an exclamation mark). Q1 does not have the word. *Othello* in the *Englisch-deutsche Studienausgabe* has a note on *ha* at 3.3.35. Ernst Leisi, *Problemwörter und Problemstellen in Shakespeares Dramen* (Tübingen, 1997), pp. 85–6, discusses *ha* and *ha, ha* in more detail.
[15] *English and American Studies in German: Summaries of Theses and Monographs. A Supplement to Anglia, 1968–* (Tübingen: Max Niemeyer, 1969–). The entries may be found as follows: *The Comedy of Errors* 1982, no. 30; *Julius Caesar* 1988, no. 30; *King John* 2003, no. 31; *King Richard II* 1980, no. 31; *Love's Labour's Lost* 1998, no. 36; *Measure for Measure* 1977, no. 41; *Much Ado About Nothing* 1989, no. 32; *The Merchant of Venice* 1982, no. 31; *Othello* 1976, no. 31; *Romeo and Juliet* 1996, no. 37; *Timon of Athens* 1996, no. 38; *Troilus and Cressida* 1986, no. 42; *Twelfth Night* 1992, no. 29. Many of these findings are also dealt with in Leisi, *Problemwörter*, which discusses 972 words and phrases in all.
[16] Werner Brönnimann, 'Think-Along Edition: The Bilingual Studienausgabe of Shakespeare', in A. J. Hoenselaars, ed., *Shakespeare and the Language of Translation* (London, 2004), pp. 184–98.

Shakespeare n'est pas désincarnée, loin de là. Elle a un corps, un corps sonore si l'on veut, qui réclame lui aussi fidélité.[17]

There is no meaning without body, and no text without style. Even though translation as commentary does not emulate the style of the source text, it must have one of its own: a word-for-word, 'literal' translation without a consistent style would suggest incompetence, even helplessness, and therefore lose the reader's trust in its accuracy. Because of this, and because of the reverberative effects mentioned by Reitani, which not even book design can avoid, the style will be deliberately different from that of the source text: avoiding archaisms and sound effects, as factual and brisk as possible. This reminds us that even translating as comment is a creative task, one that a scholar can cope with. But then, so is all editing.

---

[17] William Shakespeare, *Oeuvres Complètes: Tragédies I*, ed. Michel Grivelet and Gilles Monsarrat (Paris, 1995), p. 13.

PERFORMANCE EDITIONS, EDITING AND EDITORS

ELIZABETH SCHAFER

The most interventionist, inventive, outrageous, radical and immediately accountable editors of early modern texts are those preparing a play text for a specific performance event, usually directors and dramaturgs. Away from the constraints of a publishing series house style, although often limited by the requirements of a theatre house style, directors can treat early modern texts with a daring that can sometimes seem by traditional scholarly editing standards to border on the reckless: what modern editor would actually dare leave out the first two scenes of *The Taming of the Shrew* (although continuing to label what the Folio text calls 'Actus Primus. Scaena Prima' an 'Induction' does invite the reader to discount these scenes)?[1] But how many theatre directors, including Jonathan Miller in the so-called complete works broadcast by the BBC, have discarded *The Taming of the Shrew*'s first two scenes? How many of those editors who are convinced of the significance of the full Sly framework have actually had the nerve to plough straight on from 5.2 into Sly's final scenes from the Quarto *Taming of A Shrew*? Robert Atkins does, in his 1925 edition for Samuel French, but this is a specialist edition aimed at performers, and Atkins was only guesting as an editor: most of his working life was spent as a theatre director.[2] Atkins was also the first director bold enough to bring the full *Shrew* epilogue back on to the stage, in 1922 at the Old Vic, but while in relation to the theatrical restoration of Sly, Atkins the director has many followers, Atkins the editor has few disciples.[3]

Nevertheless editors and theatre directors are often performing closely related cultural work:

they are both subjecting a dramatic text to intense scrutiny, possessing it, testing it, repoliticizing it, representing it and preparing it for a readership or audience that will, mostly, need some help or persuasion to engage with that text. They are agonizing over very similar issues, some absolutely fundamental, such as who says what line. For example, in *Twelfth Night* 2.5, while the Folio has Fabian, on his first official entrance into the play, and Toby both admonishing each other to keep the 'peace', and so not risk disrupting the plot against Malvolio, the 1930 Cambridge edition of the play gives every single 'peace' to Fabian.[4] But in 1947

Thanks to Richard Proudfoot, Jacky Bratton, Richard Cave, Chris Dymkowski and Christie Carson for discussing ideas and earlier versions of this chapter with me. Jo Robinson's paper 'Theatre History and the Elusiveness of Performance', presented at the inaugural Theatre and Performance Research Association conference, Manchester 2005, was also a stimulus.

[1] Alexander Pope first proposed the 'Induction' label; it is astonishing that this heavily value laden term persists in modern editions. The Quarto does not have scene divisions or headings.

[2] Robert Atkins, ed., *The Taming of the Shrew* (London, 1925).

[3] For Atkins's restoration of the Sly 'Epilogue' see Elizabeth Schafer, ed., *Shakespeare in Production: The Taming of the Shrew* (Cambridge, 2002), pp. 26, 54.

[4] All references to *Twelfth Night* here are to the text edited by Elizabeth Story Donno (Cambridge, 1985, reprinted (with revisions) 2001). It is John Dover Wilson's text (introduced by Arthur Quiller-Couch) of *Twelfth Night*, (Cambridge, 1930) which gives Toby's 'peace's to Fabian. Although this is Fabian's first marked entrance, some productions (see, for example, the prompt copy of the Benson company's production, Shakespeare Centre library) do allow him to enter earlier as an attendant on Olivia in 1.5, and some (for example, the film

Walter Hudd's production of *Twelfth Night* at Stratford went in the opposite direction: Hudd cut 'peace' in lines 26, 29, 33, 37, 43, 48, making Fabian's repetitiveness less manic, and thereby suggesting just how difficult it might be for an actor of Fabian, uttering his very first speeches of the performance, to repeat the same word over and over again.[5] After scrutinizing the same section of the play, and asking who ought to be saying what, both the scholarly editor and the director here responded with active intervention, but in very different ways.

Given the close relationship between the job of editing a play for book publication and editing it for the public event that is theatrical performance, it would seem logical to connect these two activities in performance editions, which for the purposes of this discussion I am defining as editions of the play that are grounded in what the plays have been made to do in performance. Such a connection, however, has been comparatively rare. Some scholarly editors do try to keep in touch with performance – Horace Howard Furness, for example, in the Variorum *Twelfth Night*, is attentive to what can be learnt from stage practice – and some series, such as the most recent New Cambridge Shakespeares, allow their editors room to discuss performance in their introductions.[6] More usually, however, scholarly editors do not respect theatrical responses to the texts they are working with, ignore or marginalize these responses and, in effect, reconstruct the texts as literary, rather than dramatic, works.

This has important implications, as Laurie Osborne demonstrates in her incisive analysis of how *Twelfth Night* was reshaped in eighteenth and nineteenth-century performance editions, a term which, in her discussion, refers to published editions closely based on eighteenth- and nineteenth-century productions and prompt copies.[7] Osborne contests the routine neglect of these performance editions by scholarly editors and critics, arguing that these texts attest to important aspects of *Twelfth Night* in action. Certainly these editions, simply by providing evidence as to what is acceptable and unacceptable at a given cultural moment, seriously explore the play's potential – to offend, to amuse, to confuse – and some of their editorial decisions

still find adherents today: for example, John Philip Kemble's decision to open *Twelfth Night* with 1.2 clearly still resonates, as so many directors continue to follow his lead.[8] And while, personally, I prefer *Twelfth Night*s to open with 1.1, it is important to acknowledge that the frequency with which *Twelfth Night* has opened with 1.2 does raise important issues about the play: even on the potentially fast-moving unlocalized stage of the Elizabethan playhouse *Twelfth Night* opens with a challengingly quick succession of different locations and quite short scenes that give the audience a lot of information very quickly, while withholding some important information, such as the name of Viola (the audience do not learn Viola's name until 5.1.237). These first scenes *are* difficult to process for a first-time audience, and opening with 1.2 offers an understandable response to this problem, simply because of the reassuringly (although rather deceptively) clear declaration of the second line (1.2.2): 'This is Illyria, lady'. While Osborne points out some of the ramifications of opening with 1.2, which can have a serious impact on how the central characters and their narrative lines will be seen, she also argues cogently that the 1623 Folio is itself a performance edition, because it includes so many features that are responses to very specific performance conditions, and, in this, the Folio 'initiates an editorial tradition which the nineteenth-century performance editions develop'.[9] So the complete and absolute privileging of the editorial work of scholars such as Edmond Malone over and

---

of Kenneth Branagh's production) allow him to join in the revels of 2.3.

[5] Prompt copy for Hudd's production held at the Shakespeare Centre library.

[6] Horace Howard Furness, *Twelfth Night*, A New Variorum Edition of Shakespeare (London, 1901). Furness attends to theatrical interpretations intermittently pp. 392–412 and in footnotes.

[7] Laurie Osborne, *The Trick of Singularity: 'Twelfth Night' and the Performance Editions* (Iowa City, 1996).

[8] For example, Alec Guinness (Old Vic 1948), Kenneth Branagh (redirected for television by Paul Kafno, Thames Television 1988).

[9] Osborne, *The Trick of Singularity*, pp. 47–8, 16.

above the editorial work of theatre practitioners such as John Philip Kemble imposes a hierarchy on these two men's work in relation to the texts they generated which is not always appropriate. Their work should not be seen in terms of better or worse but in terms of different targets; they are selling the text of *Twelfth Night* to different constituencies: Malone to readers who can see from the speech prefixes that they are dealing with a character called Viola, and Kemble to audiences who may have to wait until the end of the play to find out the heroine's name.

Apart from the publication of texts closely based on eighteenth- and nineteenth-century prompt copies, such as those Osborne examines, there have been a range of different approaches to the challenge of editing Shakespeare's plays with a performance-centred approach. Although not conventionally 'editions' of the plays, the four volumes produced by Marvin Rosenberg – on *Othello* (1961), *King Lear* (1972), *Macbeth* (1975) and *Hamlet* (1992) – reveal Rosenberg's thinking, as it evolved over three decades, on how best to incorporate theatre history into detailed, often line-by-line analysis of the play, an analysis which approaches editing even though the play text is not represented as such.[10] Rosenberg's earliest volume, on *Othello*, works chronologically, surveying production work in sections, century by century. Eleven years later, in the volume on *King Lear*, Rosenberg had found the basic format he was to retain for *Macbeth* and *Hamlet*: scene-by-scene, often line-by-line commentary on the theatrical potential and the history of what has been done to these lines, with excursions for essays on the major characters. Rosenberg is often beguilingly enthusiastic about productions he has seen or observed in rehearsal and declares his interest in plurality: he aims for 'polyphony', or 'the sense of the many notes in the character designs, and their dynamic, changing patterns';[11] he hopes to include responses by 'naive spectators', by which he means those who do not know the play before they see it.[12] However, there is often an intrusive sense that Rosenberg has his own, personal ideal production of the plays in mind, and that his theatre history is shaped by all other pro-

ductions' relationship to this ideal production. He writes specifically for what he declares to be an 'actor-reader', but, for example, he is completely clear that *Hamlet* opens thus:[13]

Midnight, on a high platform, a castle battlement. A deep bell tolling out the uneasy hour. A lonely sentinel, distraught. Something is wrong with this night.[14]

Of course 'distraught' is not the only possible mood for the performer playing that (possibly not 'lonely') sentinel to enact.

Prescriptiveness is particularly difficult to avoid in editions which offer staging commentary in terms of potential performance readings.[15] The Applause Shakespeare Library claims to avoid this problem by offering:

a continuous commentary on the text by a professional director or leading actor that considers the stage life of the play as its action unfolds . . . A reader can 'feel' what the play would be like in action . . . It does not try to provide a single theatrical reading of the text. Rather it offers a range of possibilities, a number of suggestions as to what an actor might do.[16]

---

10 *The Masks of 'Othello'* (Berkeley, 1961); *The Masks of 'King Lear'* (Berkeley, 1972); *The Masks of 'Macbeth'* (London, 1975); *The Masks of 'Hamlet'* (London, 1992).

11 Rosenberg, *'Macbeth'*, p. x.

12 Rosenberg, p. xii.

13 For 'Actor–reader' see, e.g. Rosenberg, *Hamlet*, p. xi.

14 Rosenberg, *'Hamlet'*, p. 1.

15 For example, even in a staging commentary that is, in general, admirably permissive, Paul Edmondson moves from proposing in relation to *Twelfth Night* 3.4.154 ff. 'Perhaps we see [Sir Toby] tear up the letter', to prescribing at l.310 that 'Antonio humbly requests "to speak a little"', when it is in the actor's and director's gift as to whether or not this speech is spoken humbly, angrily, desperately, heart-brokenly, frantically etc. etc. etc. (Paul Edmondson, *The Shakespeare Handbooks: 'Twelfth Night'* (Houndmills, 2005), p. 142, 146). The forthcoming online edition of the plays of Richard Brome (2005–8, general editor Richard Cave), by promising to publish excerpts of action performed in a variety of different ways by a group of professional actors, suggests one possible way of discussing potential staging without risking prescriptiveness.

16 'General Preface to the Applause Shakespeare Library' by John Russell Brown in John Russell Brown, ed., *Twelfth Night* (New York, 2001), p. vi. Brown's edition mostly offers commentary on staging potential with occasional forays into

This series seeks to invoke that old friend 'the theatre of the mind' but downplays the usefulness of performance editing grounded in theatre history, claiming that historical knowledge 'unavailable' to the general reader 'is required to interpret records of earlier performances'.[17] However, the diversity that theatre history inevitably documents is also very liberating, and it certainly makes nonsense of prescriptiveness, even though extremely detailed and specific records of theatrical practice can produce information overload; this is certainly my experience of working with William P. Halstead's monumental performance editions, which chart the cutting of 5,000 acting editions.[18]

The most extensive and sustained attempt to produce theatre history-centred editions of Shakespeare's plays is to be found in the Shakespeare in Production series published by Cambridge University Press under the general editorship of Jacky Bratton and Julie Hankey. The series, despite its publisher, has an element of being alternative to the Shakespeare establishment: Bratton is best known for her seminal New Readings in Theatre History, and for her work on cultural history and nineteenth-century popular culture – music hall, melodrama, clowns and female contortionists – as well as her work on the stage history of King Lear;[19] Hankey, who has edited two volumes for the project, Richard III and Othello, is a freelance writer and researcher. The series originated with Jeremy Treglown, the then editor of the Times Literary Supplement, who set up the series to be published by Junction Books and commissioned the Richard III and King Lear volumes. The series then relocated to Bristol Classical Press, as 'Plays in Performance', and also published The Duchess of Malfi and Othello.[20]

The fact that Cambridge University Press took this series on says a lot for increasing scholarly interest in theatre history, and publishers' willingness, during the mid 1990s, to believe there might be a market for theatre history books. Interestingly, however, Cambridge University Press quailed at the idea of performance editions of all of Shakespeare's plays and commissioned only a third of the canon: A Midsummer Night's Dream, Much Ado About Nothing, Antony and Cleopatra, Hamlet, The Tempest, Macbeth, King Henry V, The Taming of the Shrew, The Merchant of Venice, As You Like It, Othello, Troilus and Cressida, Romeo and Juliet, Twelfth Night. King Lear is now only available in CD-ROM format. It seems extraordinary that plays such as Measure for Measure, Henry IV 1 and 2, The Winter's Tale, Coriolanus and Richard II, all of which have compelling theatre histories and which are also much studied, have been omitted from the series.

The great advantage of the Shakespeare in Production series is that it allows for extremely detailed commentary on stage business running alongside the Shakespeare text.[21] The series bravely abandons all helpful notes on the meanings of words and replaces glosses with discussions of who did what when.[22] The Bristol Classical Press editions

---

production history and he keeps the commentary predominantly in the conditional tense; however, when he notes (p. 71) at 2.5.76–8 'Malvolio does not hesitate to open the letter' he ignores the fact that, for example, Donald Sinden built up comic business around precisely such hesitation (Donald Sinden, 'Malvolio in Twelfth Night', in Players of Shakespeare [1], ed. Philip Brockbank (Cambridge, 1989), pp. 55–6).

[17] Brown, pp. vi, v.

[18] William P. Halstead, Shakespeare as Spoken: A Collation of 5000 Acting Editions and Promptbooks of Shakespeare (Ann Arbor, 1977–83).

[19] Jacky Bratton, New Readings in Theatre History (Cambridge, 2003).

[20] Information taken from Shakespeare in Production, 'Series Editors' Preface' by J. S. Bratton and Julie Hankey, and private communication with Jacky Bratton. This series was intended to include The Alchemist, The Country Wife, Cymbeline, Measure for Measure, The School for Scandal. The volume on The Duchess of Malfi was edited by Kathleen McLuskie and Jennifer Uglow (Bristol, 1989). The Richard III volume, edited by Hankey, first appeared with Junction Books in 1981, was revised for Bristol Classical Press in 1988, but Cambridge have not taken this volume on.

[21] In all cases except for the Lear CD-ROM the Shakespeare text was actually edited in the sense of establishing copy-text, spelling, punctuation, lineation, etc., by the editor for the Cambridge University Press Shakespeare editions. The New Cambridge Lear text was edited by Christie Carson, something which highlights the inadequacy of traditional scholarly texts for performance-history editing, as productions of Lear almost all abandon the scholarly text they are based on and use a conflation or adaptation.

[22] The Bristol Classical Press editions did publish brief glossaries at the back of the book.

had play-text on the left-hand page and staging commentary on the right-hand, which resulted in a lot of white space on the right-hand side, and while this allowed for photographs to appear alongside appropriate moments in the text, it was clearly uneconomic. By contrast Cambridge place all commentary at the foot of the page. While the Cambridge commentaries are often packed with information, they can be daunting to read and, as Jonathan Statham argues, the 'price' for interweaving text and performance in this format is 'a textualized concept of performance'.[23] The texts are also quite difficult to use in workshop/rehearsal reading conditions – as a hefty staging footnote may result in a few lines being spread across several pages, which would then need to be turned very fast for a fluent reading.

The Shakespeare in Production series claims to offer

the reader, the student and the scholar a comprehensive dossier of materials – eye-witness accounts, contemporary criticism, promptbook marginalia, stage business, cuts, additions and rewritings – from which to construct an understanding of the many meanings that the plays have carried down the ages and across the world.[24]

While the claim to be 'comprehensive' flies in the face of the strict word-length limitations imposed on the editors, the documentation of staging commentary sources does pave the way for future scholars to investigate the productions cited in greater detail.[25] There is, however, a tension, between Bratton's stance as general editor of Shakespeare in Production, insisting on precision in source documentation, and her less conventional, more ambitious approaches in *New Readings in Theatre History*. Some of Bratton's most exciting work here – her historicization of the historians that so many of the Shakespeare in Production editors rely on for their work on the seventeenth and eighteenth centuries; her exploration of the idea of intertheatricality and the contextualization of theatrical events in terms of the entire theatrical and cultural milieu in which they originated;[26] her expansion of the notion of the anecdote and the job of work it might be able to perform – such approaches have

to be excluded from the Shakespeare in Production volumes because of the pressures of space and the text-bound requirements of the series. While Bratton's work on the CD-ROM of *King Lear* indicates her growing interest in moving beyond the limits of book-bound theatre history, the Shakespeare in Production series under the imprint of Cambridge is still more troubled by the limitations of commercially aware book publication than it was while published by Bristol Classical Press. The series is also constrained by the limitations of the archive and of conventional source materials, areas I would like now to look at in turn.

Archives, of course, are not value free. When Derrida offers a Freudian reading of 'Archive Fever', he alerts us again to the fact archives are so deliberately constructed, funded, legitimated and maintained.[27] Theatre archives are particularly subject to space constraints and, put crudely, sets and costumes are less likely to be well archived because they are difficult to preserve, bulky, costly and eminently recyclable. In addition, large and comparatively wealthy institutions, such as the RSC, or star actors, such as Henry Irving, are always likely to be among the better archived. Consequently, aberrant productions at Stratford, Warwickshire will be well archived, while ground-breaking, seminal,

---

[23] Jonathan Statham 'After Ariadne: From Stage History to Cultural Immaterialism' (unpublished MA dissertation, Royal Holloway, University of London, 2004), p .12

[24] J. S. Bratton and Julie Hankey, Cambridge Series Editors' Preface.

[25] This is made explicit in Christine Dymkowski's introduction to *The Tempest* (Cambridge, 2000), pp. 1–2, where she states her work is 'intended to serve as a primary resource for further research'.

[26] For intertheatricality see especially Bratton 37–8.

[27] Jacques Derrida, *Archive Fever: A Freudian Impression*, trans. by Eric Prenowitz (Chicago, 1996). Derrida (p. 1) points to the 'Arkhē' as naming 'at once the *commencement* and the *commandment*'. He also suggests (p. 17) 'The archivization produces as much as it records the event' and links 'archive fever' with the threat of the 'death drive' (p. 9f), while positing that 'the question of the archive is not . . . a question of the past . . . It is a question of the future, the question of the future itself, the question of a response, of a promise and of a responsibility for tomorrow' (p. 36).

poverty-stricken fringe productions at, for example, Stratford East, will not. Thus, Milton Rosmer's use of dancing-girls during Orsino's opening speech in *Twelfth Night* at Stratford in 1943 strikes me as aberrant, but it is carefully documented in promptbook, reviews, cast lists etc. This well-archived reading survives, whereas Joan Littlewood's 1953 *Twelfth Night*, which actually inaugurated Theatre Workshop's residency at Stratford East, can hardly be accessed, simply because maintaining an archive was never a priority at Theatre Workshop: they needed to spend their money on other things.

Within the various archives, the material remains available, for consultation and analysis also pose a variety of challenges. Prompt copies are particularly extraordinary artefacts, written by stage managers for a very specific and pragmatic purpose, stage managers who might well be disconcerted to find academics now peering over their shoulders pondering their doodles, or the clinical severity of 'LX15'.[28] It is also important to note that for some theatre practitioners, the thought of academics plodding through long-abandoned prompt copies attempting to revisit a long-dead moment of theatre is risible. When Peter Brook maintained 'theatre is always a self-destructive art, and it is always written on the wind', he was pointing to the importance of the live event, and it is crucial for Brook that this live event is something which can never be resurrected from the bones of the prompt copy.[29] It is pragmatic for theatre practitioners to adopt this romantic posture because they have to sell the live event: theatre as the unique, extraordinary moment. That is their job – and then they sell the next unique, extraordinary theatrical moment, and then the one after that. By contrast, theatre archaeology suggests that activities such as the reading of material remains like prompt copies, and interpreting them, have the potential to give the past a kind of presence which can then be usefully and critically considered.[30]

It is also worthwhile remembering that one reason prompt copies survive is because in the past theatre practitioners have found them so useful: for example, pioneering director Margaret Webster, the first woman to direct at the New York Metropolitan Opera House, was disappointed, when making the crossover from Shakespeare to opera, to find there were no old prompt copies of *Don Carlo* for her to consult.[31] At the two Stratfords, because it is often possible to trace lines of cutting and related matters, such as emendations and substitutions of modern words for early modern vocabulary, through successive productions, it is clear that some directors, or their dramaturgs, look through old prompt copies.[32] Establishing, or even documenting, such traditions may contribute significantly to the process by which some lines are very rarely performed: if everyone in the last twenty years has cut a certain line (e.g. *Twelfth Night*, 2.5.104–5, 'Sowter will cry upon't for all this, though it be as rank as a fox'; *Taming of the Shrew*, 1.2.251, 'And let it be more than Alcides' twelve'),[33] then directors may be less inclined to work at keeping those lines in their productions.

---

[28] See also Russell Jackson's discussion of promptbooks, souvenir books, note books, preparation books etc. in his introduction to *Shakespeare and the Stage, Series One: Prompt Books from the Folger Shakespeare Library* (Brighton, 1985). Maria Delgado (private communication) also points out to me the particular challenges posed by prompt copies which had to be submitted under Spanish censorship laws during the Franco period, prompt copies which were often quite deliberately inaccurate.

[29] Peter Brook, *The Empty Space* (Harmondsworth, 1972), p. 18.

[30] Although Michael Shanks is discussing devised theatre, his arguments, as an archaeologist viewing theatre are suggestive for Shakespeare theatre history as well. See Shanks's contributions to *Theatre/Archaeology* by Mike Pearson and Michael Shanks (London, 2001). Shanks (11) argues for an archaeology that is not 'a reconstruction of the past from its surviving remains' but 'a work of mediation with the past', a crafting of the past and the creation of 'something – a meaning, a narrative, an image – which stands for the past in the present', linear but 'turbulent, past and present percolating'. See also his *Experiencing the Past: On the Character of Archaeology* (London, 1992).

[31] Margaret Webster, *Don't Put your Daughter on the Stage* (New York, 1972), p. 205.

[32] Russell Jackson uses the term 'Family likenesses' to describe such genealogies ('Introduction', p. 12).

[33] References to *The Taming of the Shrew* are to the text edited by Ann Thompson (Cambridge, 1984).

And yet when faced with genuine staging puzzles, old prompt copies can provide help. They can illuminate vital questions such as who, in *Twelfth Night* 5.1, is to go after Malvolio? Orsino's instruction 'Pursue him, and entreat him to a peace' (5.1.357) has been addressed to Fabian; sometimes Orsino's officers are expected to act; as in Harley Granville Barker's 1912 production. But then the 'Duke hands sword to Antonio who receives it kneeling'.[34] This last reading opens up the even larger question of what happens to Antonio at the end of the play, which, theatre history demonstrates, runs the gamut from being led off to execution (as in Denise Coffey's 1983 Young Vic production) to an apparently comfortable integration into a final tableau of happy families (as in John Philip Kemble's production where Orsino even explicitly thanked Antonio for protecting Cesario in the duel scene).

Prompt copies are perhaps most useful in the evidence they can provide on a production's cutting, but the risk here is logocentrism, and a literary focus on the words, rather than the three-dimensional, moving, sounding, smelling action of theatre. Laurie Osborne's work on patterns of cutting in performance editions offers a partial corrective here, using cutting as a basis for cultural analysis of the possible meanings of *Twelfth Night*. So, for example, Osborne argues that cutting around the character of Antonio reflects nineteenth-century homophobia.[35] This is undoubtedly true, although I would add that it is also the case that it is far easier in *Twelfth Night* to cut anything to do with Sebastian and Antonio simply because they are set apart from the main action and they are not plot drivers. Again, Osborne argues that the cuts to the recognition sequence between Viola and Sebastian in 5.2 aim at getting Cesario back to being Viola as quickly as possible, and she suggests that this is why so many nineteenth-century Violas did not stop to discuss the fact that her father had a mole upon his brow.[36] Osborne makes an important point here, but I would add that after the success of *Box and Cox*, which makes fun of precisely this kind of recognition scene, this sequence was far more likely

to generate unwanted laughter and may also have been cut to prevent this.

In order to consider something of the real potential value of prompt copies, however, I want to consider a non-Shakespearian example, Jules Wright's prompt copy for her 1991 *The Revenger's Tragedy*, for the Sydney Theatre Company at the Sydney Opera House. Wright is a feminist, and this was evident in every aspect of her production and her engagement with a play remarkable, even by early modern standards, for its misogyny. Scholarly editions, and indeed literary analyses of the play, have rarely taken up the challenge of interrogating the play's misogyny vigorously, but Jules Wright's prompt copy subjects the play to an excoriating feminist critique.

Wright's prompt copy is remarkable partly because it is extremely detailed in its marking up of motivations for each scene.[37] For example, in 2.1, when Vindice, as the pimp Piato, attempts to prostitute his sister, his mother Gratiana is identified as seeking 'to resist the one option open to her for her family's survival', that is, the only avenue open to Gratiana if she does not want her family to starve. Such a sympathetic approach to Gratiana is rare in criticism of the play, as is in-depth analysis of the oppressive patriarchal world in which Gratiana attempts to stay alive. Castiza's motivation in 2.1 is identified in the prompt copy as 'to resist taking the . . . option' that Gratiana eventually reluctantly accepts. Vindice's motive is noted as 'to corrupt Castiza and Gratiana', something which flatly rejects Vindice's own stated explanation that it is for 'policy' that he tries 'the faith' of both women close to him (1.3.177–8).[38]

---

[34] The prompt copy of the 1912 Harley Granville Barker production of *Twelfth Night* is held at the University of Michigan.

[35] Osborne, *The Trick of Singularity*, pp. 80–9, 'Displacing Antonio'.

[36] Osborne, p. 73.

[37] The production prompt copy is in the Sydney Theatre Company archive. All scene references are to *The Revenger's Tragedy* edited by Brian Gibbons, New Mermaids, 2nd edn (London, 1991).

[38] This belief in Vindice as both agent and victim of corruption is also signalled in Wright's programme comments: 'Vindice's

7 Gillian Jones as the Duchess, Lech Mackiewicz as Spurio, Max Cullen as the Duke, Geoff Morrell as Vindice and Stuart Robinson as Hippolito in Jules Wright's production of *The Revenger's Tragedy*, Sydney Theatre Company, 1991.

The motivations marked in the prompt copy for 4.4, where Vindice and Hippolito confront and assault their mother, are also unequivocal: Gratiana's motivation is defined as 'to survive/ to find a way of re-meeting Castiza', which places heavy emphasis on the need for reconciliation between the women. Castiza's motivation, which is usually seen to be problematic here (has she really succumbed to the lure of gold, or is she testing her mother?) is stated to be entirely woman-centred; it is simply 'to please Gratiana'. As Wright claims in the production programme,

the play happens because a woman has been murdered because she refused to sleep with the Duke; another woman has been raped and committed suicide as a result, because the man who raped her has gone unpunished.

Gratiana's and Castiza's motivations consequently include not only fear of abject poverty, but also the basic hope of staying alive and the hope of staying together.

At the end of the production Castiza, Gratiana and the Duchess slowly walked across the stage, drawing after them a veil-like half curtain, which covered up the ungainly pile of dead male bodies. This provided a fitting epilogue to and implicit final comment on Wright's feminist editing of the play, which was not interested, as so much editing is, in privileging supposed authorial intent. What Wright was interested in was understanding and re-presenting the misogyny of

revenge is not a crime of passion, it's nine years since his fiancée was murdered'.

the world in which Gratiana is trying to survive, and in stressing the cost, to both women and men, of living in a macho culture dedicated to violence. Of course her approach sees characters in terms of 'real' people, with coherent psychologies, but this post-Stanislavskian approach, although much critiqued by theorists, is still, understandably, not uncommon in mainstream theatre production.

If Wright's prompt copy, her, as it were, performance edition of *The Revenger's Tragedy*, is compared with the work of most scholarly editors of the play, the results are startling. Wright's prompt copy offers an exemplum of editing and interrogating the text, by an intelligent, politically committed woman asking extremely searching questions of the play. Given that *The Revenger's Tragedy* is studied by large numbers of women students in English literature and drama programmes, such a robustly women-centred response to the text would seem to warrant a wider readership. But, unlike eighteenth and nineteenth-century publishers, publishers today generally see little market for prompt copy texts.[39]

An individual and fascinating prompt copy such as Wright's *Revenger's Tragedy* might offer a significant interpretative and critical response to a canonical tragedy, but prompt copies in general also offer great potential for analysis of the way that comedy, especially physical comedy, can work. In general, Shakespeare's (usually male-centred) tragedies and histories are routinely privileged over (often woman-centred) comedies.[40] This extremely persistent hierarchy of genre is connected to the fact that it is actually quite hard to read and understand physical comedy on the page. Most readers of Shakespeare, through education and/or training, are highly literate, and so they are good at reading the words, the poetry and the famous speeches. But to imagine just how silly a chase could look, how visually ludicrous a pair of cross-gartered yellow stockings might appear, or how very funny stuffing a fat old man into a washing basket full of dirty linen could be for an audience to witness, takes a special kind of reading skill. Consequently, the funniness of Shakespeare's broad comedy (with the proviso that what is funny and what is not changes

over the years and is culturally specific) tends to suffer when it is being discussed by a highly literate editor who would rather be dealing with verbal pyrotechnics than pratfalls. Editions which privilege performance can elucidate for those of a cerebral disposition how jokes have worked in the past and can do something to combat the prejudice against broad comedy that still pertains in Shakespeare studies. Thus *The Merry Wives of Windsor*, which I would actually argue is Shakespeare's best play, in the sense of its consummate mastery of 'play-full-ness', would benefit enormously from a production-history-driven edition. The problem is that this is not likely to happen, because the play is not studied and so not purchased in large quantities and so will not be attractive to publishers. But one reason *Merry Wives* is not studied is because its appeal is not to literary values but to theatrical ones, so the play's very theatricality and physicality create a vicious circle ensuring its neglect in studies even of Shakespeare's comedies.[41]

Broad comedy, however, just like choreography and physical theatre, is hard to document, to analyse or to appreciate fully, away from the moment of performance, and in the attempt to elucidate it there is the risk that the play will disappear in a welter of 'biz'. For example, Bridges-Adams's production of *Twelfth Night*, which ran from 1920 to 1934 at Stratford-Upon-Avon, interpolated comic business in 2.5 whereby, when Malvolio first enters the scene, the eavesdroppers

drop a berry of the box hedge on his hat. He takes his hat off looks at it suspiciously waves his fingers at a possible bird and speaks.[42]

---

[39] There are exceptions: the English Touring Theatre have published the adapted texts they have used for their productions of *King Lear* (2002), *Romeo and Juliet* (2003), and *Twelfth Night* (2004) with Oberon Books.

[40] See Penny Gay's prefatory remarks (p. x) to *As She Likes It: Shakespeare's Unruly Women* (London, 1994).

[41] Similar arguments might be applied to the plays of robustly, physically and visually comic writers such as Ben Jonson and his disciple Richard Brome whose virtuoso theatricality is often undervalued in literary studies.

[42] Prompt copy held at the Shakespeare Centre, Stratford-Upon-Avon.

8 Richard O'Callaghan as Sir Toby Belch, John Ramm as Malvolio and Jonathan Bond as Sir Andrew Aguecheek in Lucy Bailey's production of *Twelfth Night*, Royal Exchange Theatre, Manchester, 2003.

The *Stratford-Upon-Avon-Herald* very much enjoyed this business but, reading about it now, it seems desperately unnecessary, a completely extraneous gag, introduced into what is already an extremely funny scene.[43] While such business can provide evidence about what previous generations found funny, it is also important that such 'biz' also blatantly chips away at the notion of the inviolability of the text. Indeed the meaning of the text could even become completely changed: for example, for decades reviewers complained that the joke about the meat at Petruchio's house in 4.1 of *Taming of the Shrew*, where Petruchio rails about its burnt state, only works if the meat is *not*, in fact, burnt. But theatrical practice proved the opposite. The 'trad. biz' of using incinerated meat and having Petruchio blacken the cook's face with it would have been dropped a long time before it was – it persisted at least from 1844 to 1931 – if audiences had stopped

laughing at the joke; so the gag did, in despite of the words on the page, work theatrically.[44]

While prompt copies offer an often completely unpredictable and unexpected range of resources and challenges, another standard resource for performance editions, the reviews, is more convention-driven: reviews can provide snapshot, eye-witness accounts, usually of the peculiarly pressured first night, but they will also target the readership of the publication in which they appear. Ideally, reviews can themselves be re-viewed in the light of as much other evidence as possible: material traces of Lucy Bailey's 2003 *Twelfth Night* for the Manchester Royal Exchange, for example, can be accessed by means of its reviews but also

---

[43] *Stratford-Upon-Avon-Herald*, 22 July 1927.
[44] For details see Schafer, ed., *Shakespeare in Production: Taming of the Shrew*, p. 178.

its prompt copy, production photos, programme, lighting and sound plots, nightly reports, etc. However, the reviews on their own do create a vivid impression of certain aspects of Bailey's production, despite occasional self-evidently Tynanesque moments, where rhetoric, wit and the desire to entertain readers begin to dominate. Certainly a glimpse of John Ramm's Malvolio manages to emerge from the reviews: he was 'ranting and spluttering like a demented schoolmaster'; 'Malvolio masquerading as Basil Fawlty'; a 'John Cleese-like Malvolio'; a 'Basil Fawlty-like Malvolio'; 'a straight take on Basil Fawlty, and all the poorer for it'.[45] Director Bailey herself is quoted as saying 'I see him as a nasty school prefect. If you had the chance to humiliate him you'd jump at the chance.'[46]

Whether or not it is appropriate to read Malvolio as an ancestor of Basil Fawlty, there was clearly a useful consensus here that the manic presumption and desperately comic but perpetually doomed overreaching of Basil Fawlty helped make the character of Malvolio readable to Bailey's reviewers and probably to many of her audience. Memories of the excruciatingly embarrassing antics of Fawlty certainly helped Ramm deliver a Malvolio that was not steeped in sentimentality and that was teetering on the edge of the tragic, without actually beginning the journey towards tragic hero that some Malvolios post-Irving have taken.[47] However, it remains an open question as to whether the reviewers' comments on Ramm's Malvolio and their unanimity concerning his Fawlty-like antecedents actually prejudged the character for many audience members, predisposing them to see Basil Fawlty in Ramm's Malvolio.

While the range of resources for performance editions is excitingly unpredictable – biographies and autobiographies, scholarly theatre history, theatre ephemera, choreographic notation, fanzines, personal memories, oral histories, scandal – these multi-faceted resources inevitably suffer when being processed down into the service of staging commentary grounded in a text. Film productions, which tend to cut very deeply, or radically reworked theatre productions are also ill suited to line-by-line commentary: when the text is so fla-

grantly rearranged there seems little point in detailing all the rearrangements.[48] The theatrical dimension that I would argue suffers the most in the Shakespeare in Production approach, however, is design, and the series has often been quite tentative in its attempts to deal with the spatial: theatre space, set, costume and blocking. While Helen Kelly's extremely detailed work on the Shakespeare productions of Harley Granville-Barker indicates how reconstructions of stage blocking can risk sinking under the weight of detail, it is still a limitation that in the Shakespeare in Production series blocking, scenography and design are represented only by a few two-dimensional photographs of a very few productions, something which can give only a very limited sense of the setting, periodization, costuming and theatre space, which are so crucial to a production's impact.[49]

An example of design work by Pamela Howard – who defines herself as a scenographer rather than a designer[50] – provides a particularly vivid example of how marginalizing design can limit interpretation of a production's cultural work. Howard designed the set and costumes for Jude Kelly's 1992 production of *The Revenger's Tragedy*, and several visual aspects of this production stand out as absolutely critical in the interpretative challenges the production posed. Firstly, there was the insertion

---

[45] Quotations taken from: *Sunday Times*, 28 September 2003; *Stage* 2 October 2003; *Oldham Evening Chronicle*, 16 September 2003; *Morning Star*, 25 September 2003; *Chorley Guardian*, 17 September 2003. *Fawlty Towers* was also involved in *Stage*, 2 October 2003; *Guardian*, 19 September 2003; *Morning Star*, 25 September 2003.

[46] *City Life*, 17 September 2003.

[47] For example, Donald Sinden in John Barton's 1969 RSC production; Antony Sher in Bill Alexander's 1987 RSC production.

[48] See Dymkowski's (*The Tempest*, p. 1) decision to omit films such as *Prospero's Books* from her edition. Productions such as those examined by Andy Lavender in *Hamlet in Pieces* (London, 2001) are also fairly intractable in terms of line-by-line commentary, as are ballets, musicals and operas etc.

[49] Helen M. Kelly, 'The Granville–Barker Productions. A Study Based on the Promptbooks' (unpublished PhD thesis, University of Michigan, 1965).

[50] Pamela Howard, *What is Scenography?* (London, 2002).

9 Reece Dindsdale as Vindice (foreground), David Crellin as a Noble in Jude Kelly's production
of *The Revenger's Tragedy*, West Yorkshire Playhouse, 1992.

into the play of a large, silent chorus of thirty-five women, dressed in headscarves and smocks, who were frequently to be seen clearing, servicing and maintaining the ducal palace. Unable to speak, uncomplainingly doing the real dirty work of cleaning up the mess the men created, these women were always on the fringes of the action. Howard explained the chorus as 'illustrating the

unspoken presence of females quietly expected to accomplish menial tasks, while the men at the forefront of the stage get on with murdering, betraying and avenging one another'.[51] Howard also cited Brecht's poem 'A Worker Reads, and Asks These

---

[51] *Yorkshire Post* 19 February 1992. There was also a smaller chorus made up of whores who were associated with Vindice.

Questions' as an inspiration for the chorus, and she argued that this production posed an extension of Brecht's question 'Who built Thebes with its seven gates?': Howard and her director Kelly were asking 'Who made the beds, who did the washing up, who services the men in the play?'[52]

The second crucial aspect of the design was the set, which basically consisted of several huge yellow walls, end-on to the audience, walls which dominated the theatre space and which were spotted with masks 'of women's faces . . . It's as if once they've been used and discarded they disappear to become part of the furniture.'[53] For the *Guardian* reviewer these walls were evocative of the killing fields of Cambodia or of victims buried by their murderers in concrete, and they sustained an ongoing atmosphere of horror.[54] When the walls were side-lit, the face masks bubbling and erupting through the smooth surface were very pronounced and, in front of this wall of death, Gloriana's remains suggested a fate that was commonplace in a world of casual violence.

Howard's costume designs also had a significant interpretative impact. She dressed the production's black actors, playing the Duchess and her sons, as high-class, elegant fashion icons, complicating responses to these beautiful, deadly and markedly 'othered' characters. She also costumed the final deadly masque as high camp, ironizing and commenting on the proceedings. The designer's input in this production was crucial in terms of the meanings that *The Revenger's Tragedy* generated but, while a single photograph or illustration can ground the discussion of the 'high camp' masque, without such an illustration, the discussion is liable to drift. 'High camp' will conjure up very different images in different readers' minds. However, the question then remains whether it is appropriate for three-dimensional art work to be routinely represented in stage histories solely by means of two-dimensional design sketches or photographs? and sometimes discussed by literary critics who have more of a flair for the verbal than for the visual?

Barbara Hodgdon has meditated recently on the uses of photography in theatre history, teasing out implicit and covert meanings that can be found in powerful and memorable theatrical images.[55] One pragmatic reality that Hodgdon does not confront completely is full cost. Photographs are getting more expensive to use not just in terms of cash but also in terms of time: when faced with chasing through complicated permissions procedures, or even just tracking down a busy photographer and extracting copy, it is tempting just to settle for an image that is easy to obtain, rather than one which more fully evokes a production's ethos. My ideal would be to reproduce a production's (often hectic) contact prints, which will impart far more useful information than the single image that usually has to be selected for book publication. Although the technology used is no longer fashionable, the Theatre in Focus series came closest to this approach by extensive publishing via slides and microfiches of images that provide the maximum information about a production rather than, more conventionally, display a photogenic star in a flattering pose.[56] A precursor to this series' approach might be found in W. R. Fuerst and S. J. Hume's *XXth Century Stage Decoration*, which, in 1928, was very deliberately published in two volumes:[57] one volume houses their written text and the other the lavish illustrations. The written text can thus always be read with the appropriate illustrations open at

---

52 Pamela Howard, private communication.

53 Howard, *Yorkshire Post*, 19 February 1992.

54 *Guardian*, 22 February 1992.

55 Barbara Hodgdon, 'Photography, Theater, Mnemonics; or, Thirteen Ways of Looking at a Still', in W. B. Worthen with Peter Holland, eds., *Theorizing Practice: Redefining Theatre History* (Houndmills, 2003), pp. 88–119. The irony is that throughout this thoughtful and provocative essay the written text lags behind the photographs being discussed and the reader is constantly flicking backwards and forwards to set image alongside analysis.

56 Theatre in Focus was published by Chadwyck-Healey (Cambridge, 1974–94) in association with The Consortium for Drama and Media in Higher Education (UK). Richard Allen Cave was the General Editor. The resources offered by this series are quite astonishing but are less likely to appeal to researchers more comfortable with computer-centric approaches.

57 W. R. Fuerst and S. J. Hume, *XXth Century Stage Decoration* (New York, 1928). I would like to thank Richard Cave for drawing this publication to my attention.

the reader's side. The application of this approach to performance editions of Shakespeare could be revolutionary: play text and commentary could be read comfortably alongside a separate volume of photographs, designs, and ground plans. However, the fact that Fuerst and Hume's volumes are now collectors' items says a great deal about the high cost, as well as the value, of good reproductions of visual materials.

In 1952, Herbert Marshall published a *cri de coeur* demanding that all theatre productions:

publish a complete Production Record using the existing prompt copies; the notes of the producer; sketches and final drawings of the designer; material from the actors and participants; selected reproductions of every scene design; action photographs of the high spots of every scene, together with every critical review worthy of the name and special articles from the leading protagonists.[58]

The abundance of Marshall's profusely illustrated photographic record of *Hamlet* through the ages could never be emulated in the Shakespeare in Production series in the current format, but the seductive possibilities of online archiving may suggest ways forward: perhaps a kind of online Über-Variorum really could provide access to designs, photographs, 3-D images of model boxes, etc. In hyperreality, a performance edition might offer a passage from a play and everything that was ever done to it/with it; it might play all recorded versions of that moment; it might access all plays produced around the same time in the theatrical environment where the production appeared; it could offer general cultural histories of the time and access to main news events of the moment (so, for example, the torture of John Ramm's Malvolio in 4.2 of Lucy Bailey's 2003 *Twelfth Night* involved suspending him from the ceiling of the Royal Exchange Theatre, a staging decision contextualised by the production's proximity to magician David Blaine's recent performance of suspension over the Thames). But in such an Über-Variorum professional film productions would inevitably gain a disproportionate dominance and then pity the fate of *The Merry Wives of Windsor*, represented by

a BBC production that leeched comicality and theatricality from the play.

I would argue, however, that performance editions also, despite their limitations, have, potentially, a great deal to contribute to editing and reading of Shakespeare in general. Because *different* readings/renditions/versions are being documented, performance editions immediately and inevitably destabilize the text and question the possibility and, indeed, desirability of a stable text. Authorial intention *cannot* be an unproblematic goal when the proverbial blue pencil is seen so clearly in action, countermanding what it is thought the author may have written. In addition, however, performance editions also help render more explicit the often unscrutinized power of the scholarly editor in compiling commentary and footnotes.

Performance editions by choosing to comment, for example, on one bit of business by one particular actor, in the context of a work engaging with the entire production history of a play, and the performance choices of hundreds of actors across hundreds of years, are always, and self-evidently, *extremely* selective. If we hear about Helena Faucit's Miranda in Christine Dymkowski's commentary on 3.1.54 of *The Tempest* but not elsewhere in the scene then, self-evidently, the reader is missing out on the sum total of the extant information on Faucit's performance, and Dymkowski has, of course, selected only a tiny proportion from her production research for publication.[59] What is more, performance editions may select and document readings that look between, behind and under the words, at subtext and back stories, which can provide a license to fantasize and disrupt, but which are importantly, and self-evidently, not authorial. Yet the very overtness of the theatrical practitioner's input, and the overtness of the performance editor's selection of that input, makes the processes of

---

[58] Herbert Marshall, 'Introduction' to *'Hamlet' Through the Ages: A Pictorial Record from 1709*, compiled by Raymond Mander and Joe Mitchenson (London, 1952), pp. xi–xii, xiv.

[59] Dymkowski, *The Tempest*, p. 238.

editing easier to acknowledge than the covert input of scholarly editors. When Laurie Maguire brilliantly historicized New Bibliography, she 'outed' the editors who set the pattern for much modern scholarly editing, making explicit what can be known about their background, education, biases and prejudices.[60] However, even during the height of the theory wars when it became *de rigueur* for commentators to parade their political and critical affiliations, editors were *not* expected to come out about their prejudices, which, of course, impact not only on the introduction but, even more tellingly, on the glossary and footnotes.[61] While everyone knows that the glossary and footnotes are politicized and potentially extremely powerful in swaying a reader's, director's or actor's response to the play, it is still very hard to remain vigilantly alert to this when struggling through an unfamiliar text, grateful for any helping hand.[62] The risk then is that, for example, editors who choose not to challenge the anti-feminism (and racism, and homophobia, and classism, etc.) of the play texts themselves may radically influence the reader's or actor's interpretation, without the politics in play being fully acknowledged.

Overall the Shakespeare in Production series offers a quite diverse set of responses to the challenge of discussing the stage histories of a group of Shakespeare's plays – the individual editors even provide extremely different kinds of information in their opening 'List of Productions' – but, as a whole, the series raises important issues about theatre history in general, and about who exactly reads theatre history.[63] At their best, the volumes document how the plays have been reworked to speak to particular cultural moments, and offer bridges between the theorisation and the materiality of theatre practice, presenting opportunities to analyse, revive, revisit, recontextualize, reconstruct and renovate plays at work and at play in the theatre.

[60] Laurie E. Maguire, *Shakespearean Suspect Texts: The 'Bad' Quartos and their Contexts* (Cambridge, 1996), especially Section 2 'The rise of the New Bibliography'.

[61] See, for example, Ann Thompson's comments in 'Does it Matter which Edition you Use?' in *Shakespeare in the Changing Curriculum*, ed. by Lesley Aers and Nigel Wheale (London, 1991) on editors' '[b]ias in the notes' masquerading 'as neutral glossary' (p. 84).

[62] This reservation also, of course, applies to the ultimate powers, and politics, of the general editor. It also seems likely that the comparative paucity of women editors of early modern drama (*pace* the prolific Alice Walker and Evelyn Simpson) until the last twenty years of the twentieth century may have had an impact of the evolution of editorial practice.

[63] For recent interventions in debates over theatre history see, for example, Bratton *New Readings in Theatre History*; W. B. Worthen with Peter Holland, eds., *Theorising Practice*; Peter Holland and Stephen Orgel, eds., *From Script to Stage in Early Modern England* (Houndmills, 2004). A crucial earlier text is Thomas Postlewait and Bruce McConachie, eds., *Interpreting the Theatrical Past: Essays in the Historiography of Performance* (Iowa City, 1989).

EDITING COLLABORATIVE DRAMA

SUZANNE GOSSETT

He was delated by Sr James Murray to the King for writting something against the Scots jn a play Eastward hoe & voluntarly Imprissonned himself w^t Chapman and Marston, who had written it amongst y^m.

Jonson, *Conversations with Drummond*[1]

No reading of the play can be satisfactory that does not also take account of its remarkable imaginative unity.

Lois Potter, Introduction to *The Two Noble Kinsmen*[2]

I have become, apparently, a specialist, if not an expert, on editing collaboratively written drama. Although I profess surprise, the path is not really difficult to trace. I began my professional life writing on Beaumont and Fletcher for G. E. Bentley; I was soon editing; and, as many scholars, usually citing Bentley, have reiterated, the majority of early modern plays were collaboratively written.[3] Ergo, to edit, logically enough, is to edit collaboration.

But no, not for most people, or at least not willingly. Most scholars want to edit Jonson, not *Eastward Ho!*, Middleton, not *A Fair Quarrel*, Shakespeare, not *Pericles*.[4] Although I was flattered when Gary Taylor asked me to write the Introduction to *The Spanish Gypsy* for the Oxford *Collected Middleton*, perhaps no one else was foolish enough to undertake 5,000 words on a play whose 1653 title-page names Middleton and Rowley as the authors but which has been convincingly attributed primarily to Ford and Dekker. And now I find myself, in a satisfying return to origins, editing *Philaster*. Partly on the basis of my own editing experience, but also because as a General Editor of Arden Early Modern Drama, I, and my co-General Editors John Jowett and Gordon McMullan, have been faced

with the complications that arise in the collaborative editing of collaborations, I will here offer a meditation on the practical consequences, for the real and lonely editor, of the mantra we all now repeat. The English early modern theatre was a site of collaboration, from the composition of the drama through the unpredictable transmission, by a multitude of agents, of at least some of its plays through the printing process. But what do we *do* with that recognition?[5]

FRAMEWORKS

Today, and in fact since the Jonson Folio of 1616, the editing of most individual plays, especially plays from earlier periods, occurs as part of a 'collected works'. Jonson, Webster, Marston, Middleton and of course paradigmatically Shakespeare are edited, or re-edited, for the constantly receding 'modern

---

[1] *Ben Jonson*, ed. C. H. Herford and Percy and Evelyn Simpson, 11 vols. (Oxford, 1925–52), 1: 140.

[2] Lois Potter , ed., *The Two Noble Kinsmen* (Walton-on-Thames, 1997), p. 101.

[3] Gerald Eades Bentley, *The Profession of Dramatist in Shakespeare's Time 1590–1642* (Princeton, 1971), p. 199.

[4] Douglas A. Brooks generalizes: 'for editors and scholars of Renaissance drama the desire is to reduce the multiple and dispersed intentions that shaped play-texts in the playhouse and the printing house into idealized, single-author works' (*From Playhouse to Printing House: Drama and Authorship in Early Modern England* (Cambridge, 2000), p. 153).

[5] In addition to the specific citations that follow, I wish to acknowledge gratefully the influence on my thinking of conversations over many years with Jeffrey Masten, Gordon McMullan, Gary Taylor and Paul Werstine.

reader'. But what that reader is assumed to want varies. In Shakespeare editions the tendency has been to move back and forth between purity and inclusiveness: *Pericles* was one of the seven plays added to the second issue of the Third Folio (1664) but, because it had been excluded from the First Folio, it did not appear in the successive Tonson collections and was only restored or admitted by Malone. Readers, of course, have no 'collected Wilkins' to make up the omission. But *Eastward Ho!*, published in 1605 with three authors on the title-page, appears, sometimes but not always, in collected works of Jonson, of Marston and of Chapman. And where will we look for *The Spanish Gypsy*? It appeared in A. H. Bullen's 1885 *Works of Thomas Middleton*, but was almost omitted from the forthcoming *Collected Middleton*, until Gary Taylor and MacDonald P. Jackson determined that Middleton was responsible for at least some lines and in all likelihood the plotting. However, you will not find the play in the last collected works of its primary authors: it does not appear in Alexander Dyce's 1869 *The Works of John Ford* or in Fredson Bowers's 1958–64 *The Dramatic Works of Thomas Dekker*, although Dekker's less extensive contribution to *Sir Thomas More* is included there.

An editor commissioned to prepare a collaborated, or allegedly collaborated, play, is likely to find that someone else, the general editor or an attribution scholar persuasive to that general editor, has previously determined on the inclusion. As the recent collected Shakespeares (e.g. second Riverside with *Edward III*, second Oxford with *Edward III* and *Sir Thomas More*) and the *Collected Middleton* with *Revenger's Tragedy* and *Spanish Gypsy* demonstrate, inclusion, sometimes to excess, is our current position: if a persuasive case can be made, even for a play where external evidence points to a different author or does not name the author in question, in it goes.[6] This contrasts with the usual nineteenth-century procedure. Dyce, for example, included *The Two Noble Kinsmen* in 1846 in his edition of *The Works of Beaumont and Fletcher*, but then, despite the 1634 title-page attribution to Fletcher and Shakespeare, waited twenty years to take the radical step of editing it for the first

time for a collected Shakespeare, and only then in deference to 'the opinion of more than one literary friend, who think that the works of the great dramatist can hardly be considered as complete without it'.[7] And which collected edition the editor participates in will inevitably affect how he or she approaches the play and the task at hand. David Kay and I were not asked to edit *Eastward Ho!* because of our previous work on Chapman and Marston, even though Percy Simpson himself suggested that the play was initiated by Marston.[8] A Jonson scholar and a previous Jonson editor sitting down to write about *Eastward Ho!* for the *Cambridge Works of Ben Jonson* implicitly assume that at least one part of the task is to fit the play into Jonson's *oeuvre*.

Thus it is not uncommon for plays of dubious provenance, sometimes another name for collaborative authorship, to be relegated to a final volume or the back of the book. Inclusion of a collaborated play in the collected works of a named author tends to create a hierarchy: Middleton *assisted by* Rowley; Jonson *bringing in* Chapman and Marston, Shakespeare and *the hack* Wilkins. Beaumont and Fletcher only appear to complicate this paradigm. No other collected edition that I am aware of has gone as far as the Bowers *Beaumont and Fletcher*, which arranges the canon according to Cyrus Hoy's division of the plays by authorship, but in fact the much-attested presence of unannounced authors from Jonson to Shirley in that canon again demonstrates hierarchy and singular dominance, in this case really Fletcher's.

Having agreed to the commission, editors are expected to fit their play into the general format of the edition or series, and here we reach the first paradox facing editors of collaborated plays. Most new editions of early modern dramatists, for example the *Collected Middleton*, the *Cambridge Works of Ben Jonson*, and the volumes commissioned for

---

[6] See Jeffrey Masten, '*More* or Less: Editing the Collaborative', *Shakespeare Studies*, 29 (2001), pp. 109–31.

[7] Alexander Dyce, ed., *The Works of William Shakespeare*, vol. 8 (London, 1876), p. 117.

[8] *Ben Jonson*, vol. 9, p. 637.

Arden Early Modern Drama, are being published in modernized texts. The goal of this format is to clear away the screen of old spellings and unfamiliar punctuation that obscures the material for potential readers and actors, and, in the case of the other dramatists, to level the playing field with Shakespeare, now always published, even by the Oxford *Shakespeare*, in this way. Yet modernizing tends to mask or remove precisely the evidence employed to determine authorship and/or collaboration. Some of the information pertinent to the methods of attribution scholars – the proportions of function words or a preference for certain interjections, for instance – survives the modernization process, but much, like spellings or variant elisions (*'um/'em*), is likely to be erased. When, as in the case of *The Spanish Gypsy*, an editor believes that the play has also been expurgated, the resulting edition can end up arguing for unannounced collaboration demonstrated by internal evidence even while erasing some of the fragile evidence that has survived various interventions.

The second paradox for the editor of a collaborated play is that she is charged with being an advocate for her play (a goal sometimes overtly encouraged in editorial guidelines) while simultaneously expected to describe the effects of, or present the evidence for, collaboration, depending upon whether the collaboration is accepted or still contested. The keywords that emerge from her first charge are coherence and unity. From M. C. Bradbrook demonstrating that the connection between the plots of *The Changeling* is 'very carefully worked out', to Lois Potter arguing that in *The Two Noble Kinsmen*, 'complex as the collaboration process was, the end product can be discussed as a coherent work', to David Gunby finding that in *A Cure for a Cuckold* 'The story of Compass . . . is related significantly, both in theme and language, to the main action', to my own description of *Pericles* as 'complete in outline and carefully structured by repetition, parallel and contrast of characters and events', editors have not abandoned the traditional view that a successful work of art, no matter how many persons participated in its creation, is ultimately singular.[9] In other words, a collaborated

play, to be worthy of our attention, must conceal or override its own multiplicity. Deconstruction, for most editors of collaboration, refers to 'disintegrating' authorship, not to finding '*aporia* or impasses of meaning, where texts get into trouble, come unstuck'.[10]

This leaves an editor needing to correlate two kinds of evidence and two views of authorship. The first looks for stylistic and linguistic markers and assumes that dramatic documents were composed by individuals with discoverable histories, habits and canons. The second stresses that collaboration was a different kind of composition, blurring distinctions and constricting the agency of the individual subject. In this view collaboration led to something more like a chemical melding than a simple accumulation of parts, undermining analysis that begins from the presumption of identifiable personal work. An editor's attitude towards these issues will affect every part of her edition: the introduction, both in its account of the play's composition and in the 'reading' offered; the text, in such matters as lineation and punctuation; and the commentary, where the case for collaboration can be subtly supported or weakened.

COLLABORATION AND THE TEXT

Although the ordinary reader hardly notices the text or understands the decisions that go into making it, editors know that this is the heart of their work. And the extent to which the text itself is

---

9 M. C. Bradbrook, *Themes and Conventions of Elizabethan Tragedy* (Cambridge, 1935), p. 213; Potter, p. 1; *The Works of John Webster*, ed. David Gunby, David Carnegie, MacDonald P. Jackson, vol. 2 (Cambridge, 2003), p. 277; Suzanne Gossett, ed., *Pericles* (London, 2004), p. 9. All references to *Pericles* are from this edition.

10 Terry Eagleton, *Literary Theory* (Minneapolis, 1984), pp. 133–4. Even in '*The Witch of Edmonton*: A Model for Teaching Collaboration in the Renaissance', in *Approaches to Teaching English Renaissance Drama*, ed. Karen Bamford and Alexander Leggatt (New York, 2002), pp. 59–64, the aim of the authors, Jayson B. Brown, William W. E. Slights and Reta Terry, is to show students how 'theatrical cooperation and integration, not authorial individuality and competition', drive a collaborated play.

altered by the presence of collaboration varies considerably. The underlying issue, only sometimes addressed directly, is one of circularity: once we decide that *Pericles* is by Shakespeare and Wilkins, how much do we alter, or not alter, the text because a peculiarity, an incoherence, even an 'error', is a stylistic tic of Wilkins? If we make our determination on that basis and adjust the text accordingly, we strengthen the Wilkins 'case'; if we return to a more 'Shakespearian' formulation, we weaken it. The editor, even when she claims not to participate in attribution scholarship, is inevitably drawn into the argument

The extent, of course, varies. Dyce, editing *The Two Noble Kinsmen* for his *Shakespeare*, makes only a few alterations in the text that had appeared in his *Beaumont and Fletcher*. These changes fall into two major categories. First, over two decades he simply changes his mind, sometimes in places where he had earlier played with a second possibility (e.g., in 1.4. the Herald's 'Wi' leave' becomes 'We learn' in the transition between editions, but in the notes to the *Beaumont and Fletcher* Dyce writes, 'Heath would read "We learn", and rightly perhaps.')[11] But other changes seem to be based on Dyce's reading of William Sidney Walker's *Critical Examination of the Works of Shakespeare*. (This was apparently not published until 1860, although Walker died in 1846.) Thinking of *The Two Noble Kinsmen* as Shakespeare's evidently encouraged Dyce to accept new suggestions based on that author's works. In any case, even when the words and their arrangement are little changed, the text looks different in its new environment. It brings up the rear in the final volume, after, of course, *Pericles*.

Modern editions of collaborated plays do tend to alter words and their arrangement based on beliefs about the authorship. For example, Lois Potter, after careful consideration of the lineation problem in *The Two Noble Kinsmen*, decides to 'retain a basic blank-verse shape' where other editors have printed certain scenes as prose, because 'Both Shakespeare and Fletcher . . . were blank-verse virtuosos who seem to have enjoyed creating smooth lines out of apparently disparate elements'.[12] Her text, therefore, implicitly strength-

ens the case for their virtuosity, although it does not distinguish between them on these grounds. In our forthcoming edition of *Eastward Ho!* David Kay and I change the placement of a number of the 1605 Quarto's entries. We are the first to do so at the beginning of the second act. The Quarto opens the scene with '*Touchstone, Quickesiluer, Goulding and Mildred, sitting on eyther side of the stall*'; it gives a second entrance direction for Quicksilver at line 2. We believe that Touchstone enters alone, Quicksilver thereafter, and Golding and Mildred forty lines later. We support our change partly by looking at the play's other massed entries, noted by previous editors (at 4.2.88, '*Touchstone, Mistresse Touchstone, Gyrtrude, Golding, Mildred, Syndefie*', where Golding and Touchstone are already on the stage; 5.3.1, '*Holdfast. Bramble. Security*', where Security is called out from his prison cell at line 4; and 5.3.54, '*Enter Petronel, Bramble, Quickesiluer, Woolfe*', where Wolf has another, correct entrance at 67), and our argument is sustained by our understanding of how the collaboration proceeded. Similar massed entrances are common in the plays of Jonson, and although *Eastward Ho!* scenes with massed entries probably vary in their authorship – 2.1 being primarily by Marston – Jonson, we believe, as shown also by the distribution of certain elisions, was in control of the copy for the play and inclined to write mass entries even when these occlude the actual order of the action.

More typical, and more extensive, consequences of believing a text is collaborated and adjusting to what is known or believed about the collaborators' styles are found throughout my Arden3 *Pericles*. Sometimes my attitude towards the authorship leads me *not* to emend. For example, where editors from Steevens to Taylor and Jackson have rearranged several of Antiochus's speeches to make them rhyme – changing 1.1.11–12 to conclude *sit/ knit* instead of *sit/perfections*, and 1.1.120–1 to conclude *be/degree* instead of *be/worth* – I follow the Quarto, noting that Wilkins's 'erratic use of rhyme

---

[11] Alexander Dyce, ed., *The Works of Beaumont and Fletcher* (London, 1846), vol. 11, p. 350, note d.
[12] Potter, 122.

is visible throughout the scene'. I also do not emend the often changed 3.0.7–8, 'And crickets sing at the oven's mouth / Are the blither for their drouth' because the source of the trouble 'is a zero relative typical of Wilkins, *sing* = which sing. Thus *Are*, not *sing*, is the main verb'. At 1.2.119, a line that is a syllable short, I adopt F3's emendation, 'will sure crack', over other suggestions because, 'as Taylor and Jackson say, the alliteration of shuns and sure seems characteristic of Wilkins'. And I could certainly be accused of inconsistency by someone who rejected collaborative authorship for this play. My emendations to 2.1.161 and 2.4.29–32 are justified on the grounds that Wilkins tends to repeat himself. Yet, in emending Gower's *Where* to *Whence* at 5.0.14, I cite Taylor and Jackson on the 'clutter of repetition' in the surrounding lines and conclude 'Undoubtedly some comes from the reporter'. Wilkins, who I do not believe participated in this chorus, for once is not scapegoated.

The circularity of my methodology is not unusual: modern editors who believe that they have identified the author of passages needing adjustment will naturally proceed in this way. For example, in the 'General Textual Preface' to the second volume of *The Works of John Webster*, MacDonald P. Jackson writes, 'Some of our decisions on how to arrange the verse have been affected by our attributions of authorship in collaborative plays. *A Cure for a Cuckold* was published as by John Webster and William Rowley, but our own investigations have confirmed . . . that Thomas Heywood contributed . . . Heywood's blank verse is more regular than Webster's, and Rowley's habit of at times dealing out ten-syllable lines with scant regard for patterns of stress has influenced our lineation in *A Cure for a Cuckold*'.[13]

A more radical example of textual intervention comes from Gary Taylor's editing of *The Spanish Gypsy*.[14] Taylor argues that Q, 1653, represents a censored text, as shown, for example, by the absence of the oaths *faith* and *marry*. The absence of *faith* is 'unparalleled in the Dekker or Rowley canon, found in Middleton only in the censored texts of *Game at Chess*, and in only three plays of Ford'. *Marry* is found in 'every other tabulated play

of the four canons except Middleton's very short *Yorkshire Tragedy* and Ford's *Perkin Warbeck*'. Taylor acknowledges that some editors would accept the statistical evidence that the text 'has been censored, without wishing to restore the expurgated oaths conjecturally' but objects that such apparently cautious editing will be 'globally injudicious, in offering readers a text which certainly contains too little profanity'. Consequently, decisions on whether and how to emend must be based on 'analysis of authorial practice elsewhere'.[15]

Accepting Taylor's emendations requires previous acceptance of the arguments for multiple authorship and of the attributions proposed. For example, the note to 4.3.52 explains the insertion of '*Swounds* thus: 'A "rake-hell" should employ lots of offensive oaths; the extant text gives [Roderigo] none. This is a particularly strong oath, which immediately establishes his character, and is relevant to the rest of the sentence; it is used elsewhere by Rowley (who probably wrote this scene)'. This procedure is even more striking in the case of the authors whose names do not appear on the title-page: to justify the insertion of *faith* at 5.1.68, Taylor writes, 'Metrically the line is awkward, as editors have recognized . . . such irregularity is particularly suspicious in a passage apparently written by Ford. A word like "here" might have been omitted by simple eyeskip, but given other evidence that the text has been expurgated the problem may be censorship. . . Ford uses *faith* as an expletive at least fifteen times elsewhere'. Even a reader who accepts Taylor's argument for Ford's presence, his analysis of Ford's metrics and the statistics suggesting expurgation – as I do – may wonder whether any other one syllable oath could have been omitted here. Taylor's response is that, 'An editor is better placed to point

---

[13] Gunby, Carnegie and Jackson, vol. 2, p. xiv.

[14] I am grateful to Gary Taylor for permitting me to use quotations from the latest version of the proofs of this edition, which is not yet published.

[15] Taylor has a fuller discussion of his method in ''Swounds Revisited: Theatrical, Editorial, and Literary Expurgation', in Gary Taylor and John Jowett, *Shakespeare Reshaped 1606–1623* (Oxford, 1993), pp. 51–106.

to probable expurgation, and probable solutions, than any unassisted reader.' He thus reveals a general challenge to the editor of any collaborated play. To ignore the consequences of collaboration in the text may not elicit objection, but it can be a failure of courage. If editors do not follow through on what they believe about the collaboration, no one else can be expected to do so. Nevertheless, as the differences between my *Pericles* edition and the Taylor and Jackson 'reconstruction' of that play reveal, there will always be differences regarding how and how much editors embody their knowledge in their texts.

The modernized text, as already mentioned, is likely to eliminate some or all of the traces of collaboration that the editor believes she recognizes. Good examples come from *The Two Noble Kinsmen* and *Sir Thomas More*. In the former case Potter convincingly identifies the role of one of Paul Werstine's 'close contrivers' or 'playhouse functionaries' in the creation of a text.[16] She suggests that the colons separating the characters in the first stage direction in the 1634 Quarto, '*Enter* Hymen: *a Boy, in a white Robe before singing, and strewing Flowres:*' indicate an insertion, and that their form specifically 'corresponds to the manner of Edward Knight, the book-keeper for the King's Men from 1625 to 1633'.[17] These colons, of course, disappear in modernized punctuation, concealing traces of this diachronic collaboration. A more complex example concerns the *Jailor* of Q's 2.1, who becomes Q's *Keeper* in 2.2. Arguing that it is in the discrepancies between these two scenes 'that the change from one writer to the other shows most clearly', Potter suggests that Fletcher refers to the *Keeper* of the prison in 2.2. but 'in the rest of the play he calls him "Jailor" – presumably because he discovered that this was what Shakespeare had already called him in 2.1'.[18] This sequence is an important piece of the evidence for Potter's theory that the two collaborators worked separately and 'did not expect to have much opportunity to talk about the work in progress'.[19] Yet the reader of her edition who does not study the introduction and textual notes finds only a consistent *Jailor* in the stage directions

and speech prefixes of 2.2: such a reader is unlikely to consider Palamon and Arcite's use of the term *keeper* at 2.2.221, 223, and 225 significant. Perhaps it merely marks them as Thebans in Athens.

For Potter, variant spellings of Pirithous's name 'are one of the clearest indicators of dual authorship';[20] such spelling distinctions also vanish in modernized texts. To some theorists this doesn't matter. Jeffrey Masten, objecting to the fundamental attributional procedure of taking 'textual habits' as conveying 'individual identities', asserts that 'the difficulty of linking spelling and "identity" is suggested by the fact that nearly a fifth of the words Hand D [in the *Sir Thomas More* manuscript] writes more than once are spelled in more than one way'.[21] His stunning example, 'Shreiue moor moor more Shreue moore', is meant to undermine 'old historicist' methods of editing. Masten proposes replacing these with newly historicized 'models of "agency", "individuality", "style", corporate effort, contention, influence and so forth'. He does mention that such new models will require 'the invention of new kinds of editorial apparatuses, criteria for and modes of emendation, etc.', but unfortunately he tosses this acknowledgement into a parenthesis, offering no methodological specifics.[22] Thus the editor is left to her own devices, usually determined by the series, which no doubt requires characters to have one designation, consistently spelled. It will be interesting to see in what ways the texts of *Sir Thomas More* in the Oxford Shakespeare second edition and that in the Arden3 series vary. They are both entrusted to John Jowett.

[16] See Paul Werstine, 'Close Contrivers: Nameless Collaborators in Early Modern London Plays', in *The Elizabethan Theatre XV*, ed. C. E. McGee and A. L. Magnusson (Toronto, 2002), pp. 3–20.

[17] Potter, p. 26.

[18] Potter, p. 26–7.

[19] Potter, p. 25.

[20] Potter, p. 133.

[21] Masten, '*More* or Less', p. 115–16; pp. 130–1, note 74.

[22] Masten, p. 116.

COLLABORATION AND THE INTRODUCTION

It is in the introduction that the editor will directly confront the question of authorship and collaboration. For editors it is normally impractical to operate as if there were no author, especially if that author has given his name to the commissioning series. Yet discomfort with, and the elimination of, collaboration is not an invention of modern editorial practice. Notoriously, Jonson eliminated the second hand in *Sejanus*; Marlowe's printer may have done something similar with *Tamburlaine*.[23] In deciding how to present *The Spanish Tragedy* as a volume in Arden Early Modern Drama, the General Editors found themselves facing the question of diachronic collaboration. Should we publish an historical artefact of the Elizabethan drama – whereby the additions belong in an appendix – or the play in its more interesting later adaptation – whereby the additions can be treated as part of the text? Is this play by Kyd, or by Kyd and Jonson, or by Kyd and Anon? Should it appear in the *Cambridge Works of Ben Jonson*? But whether the authorship question is put first, as in R. A. Foakes's 1957 Arden2 *King Henry VIII*, or last, as in Gordon McMullan's 2000 Arden3 edition of the same play, the topic is inescapable. The reader, rightly or wrongly, wants an explanation of why, for example, the jacket blurb for Foakes's *King Henry VIII* promises 'new arguments . . . to support the attribution to Shakespeare' and the only title-page identification offered is 'The Arden Edition of the Works of William Shakespeare. *King Henry VIII*', while McMullan's title-page lists the authors as William Shakespeare and John Fletcher. No matter what the final decision is about *The Spanish Tragedy*, our readers will expect the Introduction to discuss how the play came to be.

The editor of a collaborated play who maintains a traditional attitude towards authorship is nevertheless likely to realize the inappropriateness or, at least, the uncertain applicability of biographical and psychological paradigms to her material.[24] Even if all critics agree on the distribution of attributions, the presence of a second writer in any section complicates a one-to-one connection between 'life' and 'text', between individual intention and dramatic result, throughout. It seems that everyone is willing to give the splendid recognition scene of *Pericles* (5.1) to Shakespeare, but no matter how pertinent the lost child motif was to the older author, could he, or the scene, have been entirely unaffected by the presence of Wilkins, who had recently become a father himself? Political and religiously inflected readings can be as problematic in this context as psychoanalytic ones: if Fletcher, as McMullan and Finkelpearl agree, is 'country', but Shakespeare is by some readings the 'King's playwright', or Fletcher is the Anglican bishop's son and Shakespeare perhaps secretly longs for the old religion, should these distinctions be invoked in a discussion of, for example, the three long prayer scenes towards the end of *The Two Noble Kinsmen*?[25] Or when two men who disagree about such matters write a play set in ancient Athens, do they put their differences aside and, by Venus, Mars and Diana, mean merely Venus, Mars and Diana?

In writing about collaborated drama, studies of individual psychology can be usefully replaced with accounts of interpersonal relations and theatrical developments. *Eastward Ho!* seems to be the product of a brief interval of peace in the ongoing hostilities between Jonson and Marston, and Marston's flight from London while Chapman

---

[23] See 'To the Gentlemen Readers', where R[ichard] I[ones] Printer explains that he has 'omitted and left out some fond and friuolous Iestures, digressing (and in my poore opinion) far vnmeet for the matter' although they have been 'greatly gaped at, what times they were shewed vpon the stage in their graced deformities' (1590, A2).

[24] These difficulties also affect feminist and 'queer' approaches. See Jeffrey Masten, *Textual Intercourse: Collaboration, Authorship, and Sexualities in Renaissance Drama* (Cambridge, 1997), for fuller discussion.

[25] See Gordon McMullan, *The Politics of Unease in the Plays of John Fletcher* (Amherst, MA, 1994); Philip Finkelpearl, *Court and Country Politics in the Plays of Beaumont and Fletcher* (Princeton, 1990); Alvin Kernan, *Shakespeare, The King's Playwright: Theater in the Stuart Court, 1603–1613* (New Haven, 1995).

and Jonson were imprisoned – a flight that Jonson occludes in his recollections to Drummond – may well have something to do with the later failure of the relationship. Similarly, Leeds Barroll argues that Shakespeare was unwilling to start new projects when the theatres were closed by plague, but could the eagerness of Wilkins, frustrated because he had finally had his own play produced by the King's Men only to see the theatres shut down, explain how the *Pericles* project began?[26] Especially if, as Katherine Duncan-Jones suggests, Shakespeare ate regularly with Wilkins?[27] Proposing that we must see dramatic collaboration as 'historically embedded but personally inflected', Heather Hirschfeld cogently examines the institutional frameworks, including competition between the public and private theatres, in which these plays developed.[28]

Even traditional sections of an introduction, such as analysis of a play's use of its sources, may in the case of collaborated drama be affected by possible circularity in the use of evidence. McMullan points out that in *Henry VIII*, where the 'Shakespeare' scenes depend on Holinshed but the 'Fletcher' scenes also use Speed, 'a convincing narrative can be created in which the younger man uses the fashionable new history book where his older colleague carries on using the tried-and-trusted chronicle'. But, McMullan objects, since analysts disagree about whether collaboration was done by entire scenes or collaborators revised each other's works, and since statistical methods can't be trusted on scenes of fewer than about a hundred lines, we risk using this observation about the distribution of source material to confirm a predetermined division, rather than creating new evidence.[29]

Finally, it is in the introduction that an editor's conflicting charges are most likely to reveal themselves. Even such brief pages as Richard Dutton's introduction to *The Changeling* in the Oxford World's Classics try to emphasize both the significant presence of separate authors and the coherence of the resulting text: 'Rowley deserves at least an equal billing with Middleton . . . the castle plot and the madhouse plot [are] closely integrated.'[30] To an editor less comfortable with the concept of

collaboration, or one wedded to a vision of hermetically sealed separations between scenes, the result is more likely to be a variation on, 'despite collaboration, play xxx is aesthetically satisfying'. Of course, if the editor believes, as I do, that collaboration of various kinds, and thus an inevitable complexity in the trajectory between inspiration, creation and production was the norm, the caveat is unnecessary.

COLLABORATION AND THE COMMENTARY

There are numerous ways in which the commentary notes to any edition can support a view of the play in question. The first question for the editor of a collaborated, or allegedly collaborated, text, is whether to include a running annotation on the authorship. Such 'information' as there is has presumably already found a place in the introduction, but one never knows whether the reader will have consulted the introduction or plunged in at Act I, Scene I. A typical note is found at the beginning of 3.1 in my edition of *Pericles*: 'The opening speech of this scene is generally taken to be the moment when Shakespeare's poetic force and form becomes apparent.' When authorship alternates, one finds, for example, McMullan's first note to *Henry VIII* 2.2, 'generally considered a Fletcher scene, though Hoy thought it Shakespeare's writing reworked by Fletcher' and his opening note to 2.3, 'Generally considered a Shakespeare scene'.[31] Our variants on 'generally taken to be', 'generally considered', acknowledge the possibility of

---

[26] Leeds Barroll, *Politics, Plague, and Shakespeare's Theater* (Ithaca, NY, 1991), pp. 17–19.

[27] Katherine Duncan-Jones, *Ungentle Shakespeare: Scenes from his Life* (London, 2001), p. 208.

[28] Heather Anne Hirschfeld, *Joint Enterprises: Collaborative Drama and the Institutionalization of the English Renaissance Theater* (Amherst, MA, 2004), p. 1.

[29] McMullan, private communication.

[30] Richard Dutton, ed., *Thomas Middleton, Women Beware Women and Other Plays* (Oxford, 1999), pp. xxvii–xxviii.

[31] Gordon McMullan, ed., William Shakespeare and John Fletcher, *King Henry VIII* (London, 2000), pp. 279, 289.

disagreement, but the very presence of these attributions in the commentary indicates the editor's endorsement of the authorship suggested, as well as a belief that the reader may wish to track changes in authorship while reading the play.

Potter apparently believes that such notes are detrimental to the editor's charge to demonstrate coherence. Concluding that *The Two Noble Kinsmen* is neither confused nor contradictory, she explains that her edition will reflect the consequences of this evaluation in its format: 'that is why, having "deconstructed" the play in this section [of the introduction], I have chosen not to do so in the text or the notes, which, as far as possible, will refrain from identifying the assumed author of each scene'.[32] Although no similar justification is offered, in Dutton's edition of *The Changeling* the reader who actively wants to follow the alleged authorship changes must keep turning back to the introduction.

Even without repeated attributions, the notes may consciously or unconsciously reflect the editor's views on the nature of the collaboration or of the collaborators. An amusing example of the latter emerges from Dyce's notes in his two editions of *The Two Noble Kinsmen*. One striking difference is the omission, in the Shakespeare edition, of quite a few notes that explicate the more sexual material. Although he continued to assign the scenes of the country dance to Fletcher, Dyce omitted from the Shakespeare volume explications of *bavian*, *long tool* and *dowcets*. Similarly, in the first scene, usually conceded to be by Shakespeare, when the First Queen asks Theseus how he will think of 'rotten kings and blubber'd queens' while making love to Hippolyta, in the Beaumont and Fletcher volume a note on *blubber'd* admonishes, 'The reader ought to recollect that formerly this word did not convey the somewhat ludicrous idea which it does at present.'[33] When the play appears among the works of Shakespeare, the note disappears, one suspects because merely to suggest the 'ludicrous' in the presence of 'the great dramatist' was unacceptable.

Parallel passages, even if ostensibly selected only to demonstrate similar usage or attitude, will inevitably influence the reader's view of the likelihood of composition by one author or another. The availability of the Shakespeare concordance, first in print and now online, as well as the disproportionate citation of Shakespeare in the *OED*, creates an easy trap for editors, who can most conveniently identify parallels in those reference works. But if one really believes that collaboration could override hierarchy, the temptation must be resisted. In my note to *Pericles* 2.1.1–4, I attempt to complicate the tendency to refer only to the 'major' collaborator. 'These lines are frequently compared to *King Lear* 3.2.14–19 . . . The lines also anticipate the "Shakespearean" opening of 3.1. However, Wilkins too paralleled danger at sea to the vicissitudes of life. Compare Katherine's lines in *Miseries*.' The advent of new electronic sources, particularly *LION*, makes it more possible to search easily for parallels in Beaumont and Fletcher for *Philaster* or in Chapman, Marston and Jonson for *Eastward Ho!*, which may in future mean that parallels do not unintentionally give unbalanced attention to one author.

Often, however, parallel passages are invoked explicitly to support the editor's theory of authorship. In the case of *Eastward Ho!* David Kay and I are persuaded that many scenes of the play, at least by the time they reached their final form, had been worked on by more than one author. Some, like 3.2, appear to combine sections composed separately. These hypotheses are not irreconcilable: assuming that the men planned the play together (or perhaps agreed to work from one of 'Benjamin's' plots) and each then made a preliminary draft of his assigned sections, they might nevertheless have had meetings at which they improved each others' drafts. Consequently, as much as possible we disturb the tendency to cite only parallels to the 'primary' author of each scene. For example, we point out that Marstonian elements and echoes in the acts usually claimed for Chapman and Jonson run the gamut from a

---

[32] Potter, p. 34.

[33] Dyce, *Beaumont and Fletcher*, vol. 11, p. 338.

paradoxical praise of usury, to favourite words, proverbs and Shakespearian echoes, to a cluster of his preferred form, 'them', in 'Chapman's' 3.3.[34] Again, the staging of the 'Jonson' prison scenes (5.3 and 5.5), in which Security, heard but not seen, tells Bramble that his case 'is stone walls, and iron grates', seems to be based on Marston's *Antonio's Revenge*, where Mellida, imprisoned, 'goes from the grate', and it is Chapman who had previously used the proverbial 'cut your thongs unto your leather', found at 5.5.110. On the other hand, in 'Marston's' Act 1 there are conspicuous echoes of Chapman and Jonson, including Golding calling Quicksilver a 'common shot-clog', a Jonsonian coinage (see *OED*), first found in *Every Man Out Of His Humour* (1599) and again in *Poetaster* (1601). A vivid manifestation of the collaborative theatrical and authorial milieu occurs when the drunken Quicksilver, in this 'Marston' act, quotes a line from Chapman's *Blind Beggar of Alexandria* (1596); the line had already been quoted by Jonson in *Poetaster*.

One can, of course, use parallels selectively to spin any kind of interpretation, not just one about authorship. For example, one could imagine editions of *The Maid's Tragedy* with different notes to the scenes between Melantius and Amintor depending upon whether the editor believed Beaumont and Fletcher slept with each other or took turns with the wench. Indeed it is difficult to write notes longer than mere glosses that do not in some way reflect the editor's intellectual positions about authorship, as well as his or her view of the play's cultural and theatrical environment. Potter, who rejects listing authors scene by scene, includes parallels to the plays of Shakespeare in notes to the 'Fletcher' scenes of *The Two Noble Kinsmen*. And how could she not? The Jailor's Daughter's madness is clearly descended from Ophelia's, no surprise as Fletcher, like Wilkins, was deeply indebted to works of Shakespeare written well before the collaboration took place. But Potter also points out resemblances 'between the Daughter and Viola in Beaumont and Fletcher's *The Coxcomb*', allowing another glimpse of the complexities of theatrical influence by noting that 'this part of the

plot is thought to be the work of Beaumont'.[35] The roaring boy school of *A Fair Quarrel* (1615–16) is indebted to Jonson's *Bartholomew Fair* (1614), but the scenes of both authors reflect real rowdies causing trouble on the London streets. A careful note reader will form a different picture of Middleton and Rowley's 'originality' depending upon which piece of the play's background is cited or emphasized.

CONCLUSION

In the end, there is one way in which editing collaborated plays is the same as editing plays unquestionably originated, if never completed by, a single author. Every play is different.[36] The editorial problems of *Pericles* and the problems of *Eastward Ho!* represent, in useful ways, the extremes. In one case we have a play that appears with only one name on the title-page, yet where much of the play or the writing does not seem 'like Shakespeare', whether that means the text has been distorted during the production process or that another author is responsible for some of the writing. Consequently, much scholarly energy has been expended trying to determine whether transmission or collaboration is the cause of the play's peculiarities, and, if the latter, the identity of the other author. In the case of *Eastward Ho!*, the play has three names on the title-page, and at least some of the history of the writing, theatrical production and publication is known. We have letters from Chapman and Jonson, Jonson's somewhat obfuscatory acknowledgement of his participation in his conversations with Drummond, and even the fortuitous survival of two exemplars of the cancel page. The rest of the text is very 'clean', so clean in fact that

---

[34] We thus contest some of the conclusions of D. J. Lake, '*Eastward Ho!*: Linguistic Evidence for Authorship', *Notes and Queries*, 28 (1981), 158–166.

[35] Potter, p. 49.

[36] 'All playwriting is collaborative in nature: all collaborative playwriting is like any playwriting', Charles Cathcart, 'Plural Authorship, Attribution, and the Children of the King's Revels', *Renaissance Forum* 4 (2000), p. 5.

there are large white spaces on some of the pages. According to Herford and Simpson, these blanks were caused by a first round of censorship, probably by the printer.[37] A fuller list of the possible agents responsible can be deduced and, David Kay and I believe, may include Jonson and Chapman themselves, trying rather desperately to censor what they realized had been left in the text, once they were released from prison and saw the printer's working manuscript. Even the role of the company is clearer than in *Pericles*. That play was inaugurated at the Globe but shortly afterwards was being taken around the provinces by the recusant Cholmley players, in a text that may or may not have been altered and for reasons that either do or do not have to do with the company's religious orientation. *Eastward Ho!*, on the other hand, was produced by the Children of the Queen's Revels, not surprising for players who seem regularly to have been so willing to risk offence that three years after *Eastward Ho!* they put on another Marston play and succeeded in having their company suppressed.

The real question for the editor, then, is what to do with all this information. For example, in the case of *Eastward Ho!*, should a modern edition print the original material, on the grounds that it was heard on the stage sometime between 16 July and 30 August 1605, or the revision, on the grounds that it represents the socialized, that is, censored, text? One cannot lean on the authors' intentions: aside from the more general objection that such intentions are unknowable, an editor is faced with the contingency of the collaboration and 'its' intentions. Marston, fled westward, may have had different intentions for the play than his associates, just as we do not know if the second author of *Sejanus*, often assumed to be Chapman, intended that his contribution to the play disappear in the printing. In the case of *Eastward Ho!* intentions may well have been fluid: having at first 'intended' the scurrilous attack on James, the letters that Jonson and Chapman sent to various powerful courtiers reveal that soon their overriding intention was to get out of jail and save their ears and noses. Furthermore, we do not know who wrote the sub-

stitute passages in *Eastward Ho!* – he might have been anyone in the printing shop, but he might just have been one of the authors. The additions in question are only, respectively, two words and thirty-one words long, not meeting a minimum requirement for statistically meaningful analysis of language. Meanwhile, the example of *Pericles* shows how widely editors may vary in their reactions to collaboration, from the Cambridge edition, which does what it can to ignore what the editors would clearly prefer to deny, to the Oxford reconstruction, whose editors practically become collaborators themselves.[38] About all one can ask is for an editor to take a coherent position and share it clearly with the readers.

Perhaps the last word should go to another Bentley, one Thomas, a little noted collaborator in the editing of *Pericles*. A notorious crux in 2.2, a 'Wilkins scene', is Simonides's sententious comment on the Knights' objections to the unknown Pericles' dusty appearance as he presents his device to Thaisa. Q 1609 prints, 'Opinion's but a foole, that makes vs scan / The outward habit, by the inward man'. In the diachronic collaboration of successive editors, my emendation comes from Ernst Schanzer, who changes only 'by' to 'for'.[39] Such a reading seems confirmed by Wilkins's *The Painful Adventures of Pericles Prince of Tyre*, another possible participant as we try to develop a text of *Pericles*, claiming as it does to be the 'true History of the Play of *Pericles*, as it was lately presented'. If this is true, and many have doubted it, *Painful Adventures* is an account of King's Men's production, although it also includes a good deal of material plagiarized from Lawrence Twine's *The Pattern of Painful Adventures*, which thus must also be considered as a predecessor/collaborator. Wilkins has the King

---

[37] *Ben Jonson*, vol. 4, pp. 495–7.

[38] 'We as editors don't really care who wrote *Pericles* (though we do believe it to be the product of a single creative imagination)', Doreen DelVecchio and Antony Hammond, eds., *Pericles* (Cambridge, 1998), p. 15; compare *A Reconstructed Text of Pericles, Prince of Tyre*, in Gary Taylor and Stanley Wells, *William Shakespeare* (Oxford, 1986).

[39] Ernst Schanzer, ed., *Pericles* (New York, 1965), p. 76.

report that 'the outward habite was the least table of the inward minde'.[40] But Bentley, our annotator, writes at the end of his copy of Chapman's 1599 *A Humorous Day's Mirth*, now owned by the Folger Shakespeare Library, 'Thomas Bentley owes this booke / he is a foole that scann / The Inward habitts by the outward man / Shackesphere'.[41] In Bentley's mind and Shackesphere's text, Wilkins has vanished, the final line is reversed, and *habit* changes from a mode of apparel (*OED* I) to a mental construction (*OED* III). Yet the change creates the same emendation. Duncan-Jones proposes that 'Bentley's garbled version suggests recollection of a performance'.[42] If so, we end where we started, with the collaboration of theatrical agents and readers, and an author whose name, while delightfully reminiscent of the Globe in which he acted, will have to be regularized in a modern edition.

---

[40] Geoffrey Bullough, *Narrative and Dramatic Sources of Shakespeare*, vol. 6 (London, 1966), p. 509.
[41] Duncan-Jones, 205.
[42] Duncan-Jones, p. 303, n. 28.

WILL IN THE UNIVERSE: SHAKESPEARE'S SONNETS, PLATO'S *SYMPOSIUM*, ALCHEMY AND RENAISSANCE NEOPLATONISM

RONALD GRAY

Shakespeare's debt to Plato is often seen as not much more than an acquaintance with the meaning of 'substance' and 'shadow', relating to 'ideal' and 'real'. A few wider explorations have been made,[1] and more importantly W. H. Auden took the view that 'the *primary* experience – complicated as it became later – out of which the sonnets to the friend spring was a mystical one', of which 'the classic descriptions . . . are to be found in Plato's *Symposium*, Dante's *La Vita Nuova* and some of these sonnets'.[2] G. Wilson Knight also referred to the *Symposium* in *The Mutual Flame*. I return to Auden's view later.

Platonic allusions are not prominent in the whole of the Sonnets, which are often the thoughts and feelings of a lover like other lovers, who protests his love, doubts his worthiness, denounces infidelity, is reconciled. There are, however, occasionally surprising phrases: the friend is 'the grave where buried love doth live' (31.9), he will 'pace forth' against death (55.10), he is 'a God in Love' (110.12), the poet 'hallows' his name, as though in the Lord's Prayer (108.8). And there are close resemblances to a passage in the *Symposium* which speaks of a vision of universal love.

Shakespeare could have read the *Symposium* in Ficino's Latin translation, and have discussed it with Ben Jonson, who owned a copy. It takes the form of a banquet, in which each of the speakers hold forth on the nature of Love,[3] the most important being the wise woman Diotima, as reported by Socrates. Diotima denies that Love is merely love between human beings: it 'includes every kind of longing for happiness and for the good'. It is found not only in poetry, but in business, athletics, philosophy.

But then comes a passage in which Diotima asks why men are so deeply interested in prolonging their own selves through intercourse, why 'the mortal does all it can to put on immortality'. It can only do so, she says, by breeding 'and thus ensuring that there will always be a younger generation to take the place of the old' (para. 207). Here we come close to the concerns of the opening sequence of Sonnets, in which begetting a child is of such importance that the poet spends nearly three hundred lines on it. As Diotima goes on, she draws closer still to the profound meaning Shakespeare is moving towards. Everyone, she says, 'no matter what he does, is longing for the endless fame, the incomparable glory that is theirs, and the nobler he is, the greater his ambition, because he is in love with the eternal' (207). Some will go on to raise a family, but 'those whose procreancy is of the spirit, rather than of the flesh – and they are not

---

I cite the following editions of the *Sonnets* in the article: J. Kerrigan, ed., *The Sonnets and A Lover's Complaint* (Harmondsworth, 1986); G. Blakemore Evans, ed., *The Sonnets* (Cambridge, 1996); K. Duncan-Jones, ed., *Shakespeare's Sonnets* (London, 1997); C. Burrow, ed., *The Poems* (Oxford, 2003).

[1] E.g. C. and M. Martindale, *Shakespeare and the Uses of Antiquity* (London and New York, 1990), p. 11, and Anne Baldwin and Sarah Hatton, eds., *Platonism and the English Imagination* (Cambridge, 1994).

[2] W. H. Auden, 'The Sonnets' in *The Complete Signet Classic Shakespeare* (New York, 1963), p. 1726.

[3] I quote from the translation by Michael Joyce in *Five Dialogues of Plato* (London, 1938).

unknown, Socrates – conceive and bear the things of the spirit. And what are they? You ask. Wisdom and all her sister virtues: it is the office of every poet to beget them, and of every artist whom we may call creative' (209). She adds: 'to love is to bring forth upon the beautiful, both in body and soul' (206), insisting on the sexual metaphor.

Every man who comes to manhood and whose first ambition is to be begetting will go in search of the loveliness on which he may beget, and having found it in another man – for this homosexual (not homoerotic) love is greater in their eyes than heterosexual love – a friendship will follow, and a communion more complete than that which comes of bringing up children, 'because they have created something, lovelier and less mortal than human seed' (209). Who, she asks, would not prefer such fatherhood to merely human propagation, if he stopped to think of Homer and Hesiod, and all the greatest of our poets? Who would not envy them their immortal progeny, their claim upon the admiration of posterity? (209). Diotima goes on, however, to say that falling in love with one individual body must lead to the lover setting himself 'to be the lover of every lovely body', and from thence to the beauty of every kind of knowledge, in laws, institutions and sciences, and so be saved from slavish and illiberal devotion to the individual loveliness of a single boy, a single man, or a single institution, coming at length to a final revelation:

And now, Socrates, there bursts upon him that wondrous vision which is the very soul of the beauty he has toiled so long for. It is an everlasting loveliness which neither comes nor goes, which neither flowers nor fades; for such beauty is the same on every hand, the same then as now, here as there, this way as that way, the same to every worshipper as it is to every other.

Nor will his vision of the beautiful take the form of a face, or of hands, or of anything that is of the flesh; it will be neither words, nor knowledge, nor a something that exists in something else such as a living creature, or the earth, or the heavens, or anything that is, but subsisting of itself and by itself in an eternal oneness; while every lovely thing partakes of it in such sort that, however much

the parts may wax and wane, it will be neither more nor less, but still the same inviolable whole.

(para.211)

This is close to the love spoken of in 116, as unalterable and unchanging, 'an ever fixed marke, That lookes on tempests and is never shaken', that is 'not Time's foole', even though lovers die, but 'beares it out even to the edge of doome'.

In Sonnet 124 the poet defines his love in just such terms as Diotima uses. It comes after a Sonnet in which he speaks of a love that is unchanging, and will survive even the death of his lover (123.14). It is a love not 'subiect to times hate, but was 'buylded far from accident' (124.5), that is far from the accidentals of the real as opposed to the ideal in Plato's sense. ('Built far from the chance of any accident happening' is also a possible reading, on an unphilosophical interpretation, and is invited by the solidity implied in 'building'). This Sonnet is the most telling evidence I can find that Shakespeare is speaking not only of ordinary human love, but also of a love that is not restricted to bodily manifestations and is part of the higher world of 'Ideas', supra-sensual, perfect, eternal, and therefore not subject to the 'smiling pomp' (124.6) of ordinary achievements, or liable to be overthrown by some civil uprising of 'thralled discontent' (124.7). It does not fear Policy, that '*Hereticke*' so-called because it is not, in some canny, calculating adaptiveness, working for brief temporal aims ('leases of short numbred howers') but a true representative of that Policy that governs by supreme adaptiveness, so greatly adaptive, one might say, as to be imperceptible – 'all alone stands hugely pollitick'. Diotima's words just quoted (it 'neither comes nor goes nor fades', 'however much the parts may wax and wane, it will be neither more nor less; subsisting of itself and in itself and by itself in an eternal oneness') evidently inspired the lines:

all alone . . .
it nor growes with heat, nor drownes with
    showres

(124.11–12)

In the first nineteen Sonnets the poet is concerned at the eventual and inevitable loss of the young man's beauty, and in the first seventeen he urges him to beget a child who will preserve it. There are verbal resemblances to Erasmus's *De Conscribendis Epistolis* here, in which a young nobleman is urged to marry, and this group may conceivably have begun with such a purpose. But in Sonnet 15 the poet is already hinting at a new development, when he writes

> And all in war with Time for love of you,
> As he takes from you I engraft you new.

In the sequence it is not yet clear what 'I engraft you' means: the horticultural verb relates to the Rose of Sonnet 1, but the significance of this does not appear till 17, where the poet reflects that in time to come nobody would believe that the youth had such beauty, and the poet's verse would be scorned.

> But were some childe of yours alive that time,
> You should live twise, in it and in my rime.

With this, the beauty of the young man, still present in his child, is seen to be equal with the beauty of the poet's verse and both are the Rose (although, in a typical contradiction, found all the way through the Sonnets, he has just spoken of his verse as 'my barren rime', 16.4). More boldly then, in 18, one of the most beautiful of the Sonnets, the poet declares that Death will never brag of conquering the youth,

> When in eternall lines to time thou grow'st.

Now for the first time, by means of a pun, the poet not only equates the beauty of his poem with that of the child yet to be born, but establishes his claim, so far as the poetry is concerned, by the incontrovertible beauty before our eyes, the Sonnet itself, which still lives today. Just as the genealogical links of descent will preserve that beauty in the child, so also will the lines of verse. The two kinds of beauty, human and poetic, are one, and as 19 continues, concluding the sequence of nineteen Sonnets:

> My love shall in my verse ever live young

where 'my love', as always in the Sonnets, means both the love the poet has for the youth, but also the youth himself.

This goes beyond anything said by Erasmus or by any supposed request to Shakespeare from a mother to encourage a son of hers to foster the dynasty of some noble family. There is as yet nothing of the experience of which Auden speaks as the origin of the Sonnets. But a first step – if we regard the Sonnets as in any degree sequential – has been made on the way to greater fulfilment. In the *Symposium* the love of two men is better than the love of a man and woman, for 'it will produce something lovelier and less mortal than human seed' (see p. 226 above). Similarly here the need for the young man to have a child by a woman is superseded, in Plato's terms, by the poet producing beauty in his homosexual love.

Immediately after 1–19, Sonnet 20 strikes a new note. The man is praised here for his feminine looks and woman's gentle heart, and yet is 'the Master Mistris of my passion'. If there is a man whom Shakespeare had in mind here it could well be the Earl of Southampton. But his appearance is difficult to imagine: he has a 'woman's face', and yet is 'a man in hew [hue]', and after being praised for his superiority to women, who are fickle and whose eyes are not so bright as his, he emerges in complete ambiguity in line 9: 'and for a woman wert thou first created'. As Burrow argues, this means '(a) you were originally intended to be a woman, and (b) you were made to belong to a woman', and, I would add, not merely to belong to but to please or satisfy a woman. This is one of many significant word-plays to which I will return. In the ensuing quotation, however, the man is said to have had a woman's body, so beautiful that Nature fell in love with it, and so seductive, that Nature added to that body 'one thing to my purpose nothing', a penis that can only serve to give pleasure to women. He has been 'prickt out', chosen, and provided with a prick, and is to be enjoyed only by women, not by the poet.

Lines 9–12 speak of a feminine body, but this is as ambiguous as the woman's face that is also male in hue. It appears to be that of a hermaphrodite in the symbolical sense of alchemical and other writings, the poem gliding from the description of a real man with feminine features to a female body with female breasts and hips, but with male genitals. To say this is not altogether to dismiss speculation about the identity of the young man. It does, however, introduce in its ambiguity the wide range of images of a similar kind found world-wide, in a profusion of sculptures, paintings and poems, and in alchemy.[4]

The most likely source of this symbol is alchemy, which produced visible equivalents for many of the concepts of neoplatonism. We are so influenced by Ben Jonson's portrayal of gullible fools that the religious or philosophical meaning goes unnoticed. Jonson was aware that there was more to alchemy than Sir Epicure Mammon supposed. To gain the Philosophers' Stone, says Surly, requires

> A pious, holy and religious man,
> One free from mortal sin, a very virgin.
>
> (*The Alchemist*, 2.2.97–8)

Jakob Boehme, almost a contemporary of Shakespeare's, wrote his mystic works entirely in alchemical terms, becoming the originator of the Pietist sect in Germany that strongly influenced Goethe. Isaac Newton studied alchemy with no intention of making money by it, expecting to be vouchsafed the key to the Philosophers' Stone, just as he had been granted the discovery of the laws of gravity and the infinitesimal calculus. At its simplest the theory was that each metal except gold, a perfect, unchangeable metal, contained a 'kernel' of gold, which could be released from its outward 'dross', and allowed to permeate the whole, in other words, for Christian alchemists, to transform the sinful mortal into Christ.[5] The Stone was also called Sol, the sun, an image often used by Shakespeare in the Sonnets, and Gold, as the one unchanging metal that could only remain itself however much it was drawn upon, and yet was a necessary ingredient in the chemical process. But the Christian allusion was only one aspect of a many-faceted tradition,

which did not attempt to show any way of reconciling one belief with another. Alchemists saw no difficulty in linking Christ with images of men and women in sexual intercourse: the Stone was often illustrated as a copulation. (Sir Epicure Mammon was ambitious to have it for just that reason.) A combination of so-called Mercury and Sulphur, it was a complete unity-in-duality, a synthesis.

A more respectable source of such ideas was the neoplatonist tradition, beginning with Plotinus in the third century CE and passing with continual modifications through Proclus, Iamblichus, Petrarchan poetry, the supposedly Egyptian Hermes Trismegistus, the Kabbala, Castiglione's *The Courtier* and many others. The principal features are the need to embrace the death of self, leading by stages to union with the One or Good, the former represented in alchemy by the 'nigredo', or blackening of metals, and the latter, the Stone itself, or Elixir of Life. The hermaphrodite resembles, for instance, the 'coincidence of opposites' in the teaching of Nicholas of Cusa, which was also symbolical. All these philosophers and Hermetic adepts saw their quest in terms of paradoxes and contradictions. Thus Nicholas, a contemporary of the fifteenth-century Florentine Platonic Academy, rejected the philosophy of Aristotle, according to which if two statements contradict each other, one at least must be false. His central insight was that 'all oppositions are united in their infinite measure, so that which would be logical contradictions for finite things, can exist without contradiction in God, who is the measure of (i.e. is the form or essence of) all things, and identical to them inasmuch as he is identical with their reality, quiddity, or essence'.[6]

It is not arguable that Shakespeare knew anything directly of Nicholas's thought. He may well,

---

[4] See Marie Delcourt, *Hermaphrodite, Myths and Rites of the Bisexual Figure in Classical Antiquity* (London, 1956) and Elémire Zolla, *The Androgyne* (London, 1981).

[5] See chapters 1–3 in my *Goethe the Alchemist* (Cambridge, 1952); also C. G. Jung, *Psychologie und Alchemie* (Zurich, 1944).

[6] Robert Audi, ed., *The Cambridge Dictionary of Philosophy*, 2nd edn (Cambridge, 2005), p. 612.

however, have at least heard some details of the visit to Oxford of Giordano Bruno, in 1583 and 1584, when the Italian became associated with Sir Philip Sidney, Fulke Greville and Robert Dudley, Earl of Leicester. It was because of his defence of the Copernican theory that Bruno aroused incredulity in Oxford, but his teaching in *De gli eroici furori*, 1585, used neoplatonist imagery, and treated the attainment of union with the infinite One by the human soul. Like Nicholas of Cusa, Bruno rejected the dualism of Aristotle, preferring a monistic conception of the world. For him too all substances were in a basic unity, and opposites coincided in the infinite unity of Being.[7] Shakespeare was twenty-one at the time this book appeared, and although he is unlikely to have read it, the stir it caused may very well have come to his attention. The frequency of coinciding opposites – a useful term – in his work certainly suggests that he had some knowledge of the neoplatonist tradition as represented in Bruno, although it may have come from several sources, including alchemy.

In 53 the fulfilment spoken of by Diotima is treated, not as an achievement of the poet, but rather of the poet's ability to see the universal figure of love in the friend. It begins, using Plato's two concepts of real and ideal, shadow and substance, as in the myth of the cave, where mortals in the cave see only shadows of the real world beyond, with the awe-struck question:

> What is your substance, whereof are you made,
> That millions of strange shaddowes on you tend?
> Since every one, hath every one, one shade,
> And you but one, can every shaddow lend?

The answer might well be the sun, with whom the young man is sometimes identified, as in 33 and 34 (to be treated later), and which casts shadows all about itself. Is there a suggestion too that the poet, who, as we have shown, is also the man he loves, his Will, is also intended? Is Shakespeare the dramatist musing on his own amazing ability to create not millions, but perhaps thousands of characters, born and unborn? In the next quatrain the male and female characteristics again point to the hermaphrodite of Sonnet 20, although once

again a man of feminine beauty may be seen. It is in the third quatrain that the more than human friend emerges more clearly. Like the sun, he is the provider of 'spring, and foyzon [harvest] of the yeare'. Taken literally, this is beyond the power of any human being. And more, he is 'in every blessed shape we know', and is part of 'all externall grace'. Here is the vision of Diotima again: in the friend the lover perceives the ideal that is present in all beauty, and insofar as he is identified with the friend, the poet may be claiming as much for himself.

The last line: 'But you like none, none you, for constancy', then brings us back to mundane reality. For although the friend is praised for his constancy, the words of praise are once again a significant pun. We know from Sonnets earlier than this that the man is not constant in his love, and it is after all otiose to say 'you like none, none [like] you' if 'like' is an adjective, for the one implies the other. There is some point, however, in understanding not only 'you are incomparable for constancy', but also 'you like nobody, and nobody likes you for being constant' (Duncan-Jones and Burrow make a similar point.) In the tradition of Bruno and Nicholas of Cusa, such a coincidence of opposites ought not to seem impossible. The ambiguity of gender in Adonis–Helen is reflected in the duality-in-unity in the language of the same Sonnet. This accords with the way the poet always praises his lover as perfect while showing up his defects.

Shakespeare does not follow Plato in every respect. Though the poet's love is symbolically so illimitable, the man he loves is not only blemished, to say the least, but has stolen the poet's mistress. It is as though Shakespeare intended to put to the test Diotima's vaunted love, to confront it in human terms, in a common enough human situation. The theme of betrayal of love begins in a short sequence starting with 33, where Shakespeare writes of the obscuring of the sun's glory by a passing cloud. The sun here is like a monarch presiding over his

---

[7] Frances A. Yates, *The Occult Philosophy in the Elizabethan Age* (London, 1979), ch. 1 and 2, and *Giordano Bruno and the Hermetic Tradition* (Chicago, 1964).

court, flattering them with his 'sovereigne eie', though dis-graced by the cloud which hides him, but also like 'my Sunne', the lover, who was hidden in a comparable way from the poet. For this the poet forgives him in what seems an arbitrary way: 'Suns [sons] of the world may staine [grow dim, but with an implication of disgracing oneself, if not sinning] when heaven's sun staineth', as though the inattention (not the infidelity) of the lover could be excused on meteorological grounds. In the next Sonnet, however, there is a surprise, when the poet turns angrily on the lover for having promised such a beauteous day, making him travel forth without his cloak only to let him get drenched. It is not a man that he is blaming, but rather the sun – 'thy brau'ry' (34.4) is the sun's – although this is said in such a matter-of-fact way as almost to escape attention. For the poet his love *is* the sun, not merely metaphorically, and the sun can be upbraided as though it were a human being. In a casual way, this reflects the theme of the cosmic lover.

In the next Sonnet the poet finds truly metaphorical excuses: the lover should not be grieved at what he has done (still not defined), since roses have thorns and silver fountains create mud, and clouds will 'stain' (make dim) both sun and moon, though the connection of this with whatever it is that the lover must not grieve over remains obscure, as the poet admits himself, when he confesses to making faults by 'Authorizing thy trespas with compare' (35.6). The comparisons with roses, fountains and clouds are really inadequate to any 'trespass' the lover may be guilty of, and seem to be made only so that the poet may take blame on himself also, for so much as making the comparisons – 'My selfe corrupting, salving thy amisse' (35.7). He is corrupt, making these lame excuses.

It is not until 40 that it becomes clear how the lover has betrayed the poet: he has taken his mistress, as becomes even clearer in 42 – 'That thou hast her it is not all my griefe.' It now also becomes clear why he has blamed himself for exonerating the young man. He is taking perfectly seriously the idea that he and his lover are one, that he speaks from the awareness of a fusion joining them both, and can thus launch into a cascade of double-meanings:

Then if for my love, thou my love receivest,
I cannot blame thee, for my love thou usest

(40.5–6)

– where 'my love' means not only 'the love I bear you', but also 'the woman I love', and the first line means not only 'if, out of love for me, you receive the gift of my love', but also 'if you accept my mistress as a sign of my love for you', while the second line means 'I cannot blame you for making love ['usest' has this sense often in the Sonnets] with my mistress' as well as 'I cannot blame you, since it is my own love for you that you are making use of.' Towards the end of the Sonnet the poet does confess to the pain this causes him. But the assumption of two-in-one-ness continues in the couplet:

Lascivious grace, in whom all il wel showes,
Kill me with spights yet we must not be foes

(40.13–14)

'In whom all il wel showes' encapsulates the unity of a meaning that embraces opposites: the lascivious grace – itself an oxymoron – shows (all too) well what ill it shows, and yet that ill 'shows well', is apparently good.

These double-meanings are not all playful, nor are they self-indulgent lapses. They may appear to us today as of no great consequence, but as Mahood observes, 'To Elizabethan ways of thinking, there was plenty of authority for these eloquent devices. It was to be found in Scripture (*Tu es Petrus* . . .) and in the whole line of rhetoricians, from Aristotle and Quintilian, through the neo-classical texts that Shakespeare read perforce at school, to the English writers such as Puttenham.'[8] In the Sonnets they carry a serious point if we regard them as not simply about a lover in real life, but a superhuman or even a divine being, with whom the poet feels himself at one. A lover who consents to being deceived in such easy terms, using the stock phrase of lovers, that both are one, sounds hypocritical. If he is speaking in a religious or mystical sense, he sounds less so, or not

---

[8] M. M. Mahood, *Shakespeare's Wordplay* (London, 1957). Mahood cites none of the examples I give.

at all. Seeing the good even in what appears evil is often said about a god rather than about a human being.

Yet more ambiguities follow, as in 42, when the poet acknowledges that his exoneration of his friend's disloyalty can be reinforced by the fact that they are both one and the same and thus the friend's mistress can only love the poet himself:

> But here's the joy, my friend and I are one,
> Sweete flattery, then she loves but me alone.

Coming out of the clouds, the poet sees what flattery is involved in claiming to be identical with his lover, and the naivety of 'she loves but me alone' is obvious, unless we interpret that the lover is (sometimes) imagined, not real, and in this sense identical with the poet, a projected self. But this is yet another example of the ambitious combination of opposites that runs all through the Sonnets. Admittedly, that ambition can at times sound unconvincing. Yet the puns state in so many incontrovertible meanings what ambition is claiming. The poet may be open at other times to Johnson's charge, that punning was Shakespeare's will o' the wisp that led him into marshes of unnaturalness, but in these instances he uses them in full awareness for a serious purpose.

He can be faulted (even in an Elizabethan context, one would think) for 'as you were when first your eye I eyde' (104.2), which puns on 'eye' as 'I' and makes their identities. The intention is bold. The line can mean 'when first I looked at your eye', but also 'when first I made your "I" ', that is, as a poet, if not as a god, as he appears to be later. The spelling 'Eyde' rather than 'Eyed', if not a misprint, invites a daring reading here, since the 'I' is also, thanks to the duality-in-unity, the poet's own 'I', which he has 'I'd' in the other. I confess, this interpretation may out-William William.

Even more awkward are the lines:

> What wretched errors hath my heart committed
> Whilst it hath thought it selfe so blessed never?
> How have mine eies out of their spheares bene fitted
> In the distraction of this madding fever?
>
> (119.9–12)

'Fitted' is known to the *OED* nowhere but in this instance, where it means perhaps that his eyes have been wrenched or taken out of their sockets. But the separation into two words 'bene fitted' suggests, although only visually, 'benefitted'. ('Benefit' appears two lines later.) This produces the desired paradoxical combination, but at some cost.

Another word-play relying on the look of the written or printed word is in a line criticising the lover even as it adores him. The poet has just said he corrupts himself by 'salving' the lover's wrongdoing:

> For to thy sensual fault I bring in sence.
> Thy adverse party is thy Advocate.
>
> (35.9–10)

That is, he brings his rational faculty to bear on the 'sensual fault', and excuses it thereby. Almost all editors produce the first of these lines as here. But Burrow, who also prints 'in sense', notes without comment that in 1714 Gildon interpreted 'in sence', the curious Quarto spelling, as 'Incense'. The poet does not merely use reason here, he worships the fault. (The stress falls on the wrong syllable, as it does in 'bene fitted', if 'benefitted' is meant, but the 'c' for an 's' is surely deliberate, and the ambiguity is typical.) Even in saying that he and the lover are separate, the poet says they are one, as in

> Let me confesse that we two must be twaine,
> Although our undevided loves are one
>
> (36.1–2)

which says both that they are separate, in the sense of 'twain' meaning 'two', 'asunder', 'separate', but also 'a group of two', a pair, a couple' (*OED* II.2). Thus even as the poet confesses separation he denies it, since, although '*a* twain' would strictly be called for to make the second sense – 'we two must be a twain' – there is an intimation of the pun.

A similar pun is in the couplet of 39, where the poet, who has just lamented his absence from the lover, comforts himself with the thought that

> . . . thou teachest how to make one twaine
> By praising him here who doth hence remaine.

The lover thus shows how to make 'one', a single individual, be 'twain', both a pair and a divided pair, and does so by praising the poet as though 'here', even though he remains 'hence', somewhere else. But 'hence' in the sense of 'therefore' provides the meaning 'who, being praised here, therefore remains here'. As the poet has just said, 'And what is't but mine own when I praise thee?' (39.4): the self that addresses itself is divided yet still the same self, and in one sense the lover is that imagined *alter ego*.

This 'alter ego' has striking reverberance when the poet writes:

> So true a foole is love, that in your Will
> (Though you doe anything) he thinkes no ill.
>
> (55.13–14)

'In your Will' means not only 'whatever is in your will to do', but also 'whatever your will does in Will Shakespeare': the lover's will activates the poet, is part of him. A religious or metaphysical significance, expanded later, begins to emerge here.

In 113 and 114 he questions whether he is not being led astray by his love, since it allows him to disregard the faults in the lover. Nothing that he sees now appears ugly or savage to his mind or eye:

> For if it see the rud'st or gentlest sight,
> The most sweet-favor or deformedst creature,
> The mountaine, or the sea, the day, or night:
> The Croe, or Dove, it shapes them to your feature.
>
> (113, 9–12)

Thus his 'true' mind, true because loyal in love, makes his mind 'untrue', and this he ascribes to a kind of alchemical transformation:

> Or whether shall I say mine eie saith true,
> And that your love taught it this *Alcumie*?
> To make of monsters and things indigest,
> Such cherubines as your sweet selfe resemble,
> Creating every bad a perfect best.
>
> (114. 2–7)

In alchemical terms, as I have said, base metals could be transformed into gold (and, in the higher sense, human error or sin transformed into loving perfection). But just as alchemy was suspect in its secular guise as a means of deceiving the gullible, so too was the capacity to transform in a godly way. It is just such a transformation, such a coincidence of opposites, that the poet has been guilty of in speaking of the man as 'lascivious grace, in whom all il wel showes' (40.13) and of the mistress too, when he asks whence she has 'this becomming of things il . . . that in my mind thy worst all best exceeds' (150.5 and 9). In effect, Shakespeare is questioning here the whole Platonist vision of love, the illimitable loveliness of which Diotima speaks, since it apparently disregards, in overcoming, the ugliness present in the world. Does it appeal, he asks, because it flatters him to think he is 'crowned' like a monarch with his love, or should he renounce the 'poison' it truly is? His answer, ironically aware of his continued self-interest, is that 'my great minde most kingly drinkes it up' (114.10), and he tries to escape the full meaning of this in the couplet:

> If it be poison'd, tis the lesser sinne,
> That mine eye loves it and doth first beginne.
>
> (114.13–14)

The reasoning here is specious – what is the sin compared with which his own sin is lesser, and how does his eye, beginning first, make the deceptive vision any the less sinful? But the theme of poisoning is not exhausted in 114; it recurs in 118, where the poet admits he is simply poisoned (118.14), only to be dismissed in 119 – 'now I find true/That better is, by evil still made better' (119.9–10). The opposites coalesce and divide continually, just as Mercury did in alchemical laboratories. Not content with the Platonic vision, Shakespeare rejects and accepts duality-in-unity, passing on from the 'ever-fixed mark' of Love to explore the tempest with which Love has to contend, and never remaining absolutely with either of the opposites.

It may seem that the Dark Lady or, as she should rather be called, the black mistress, black not only in her hair and eyes, but sometimes black morally, can have no connection with any kind of Platonic love, which in the *Symposium* is entirely homosexual between men. But Platonism had undergone some transformation since the publication in 1527 of Baldassare Castiglione's *Il Cortegiano*. Shakespeare can scarcely not have known it, and the witty dialogue between Beatrice and Benedick in *Much Ado* may well have been inspired, as Peter Burke suggests, by the exchanges between Castiglione's lords and ladies.[9] (The Balthasar who attends Don Pedro in the same play, the one in *The Comedy of Errors*, Romeo's servant, Portia's servant and Portia's adopted name, again Balthasar, reflect Shakespeare's awareness of Castiglione's first name.) Unlike Plato, who speaks only of the love between men leading by degrees to the universal vision of love, the *alter ego* of *The Courtier*, quoting the same words of Diotima's that Shakespeare echoes in Sonnet 124, inspires the question 'Whether women be not as meete for heavenlie love as men'. Since he also argues that kissing may be a bond between souls, which 'poure them selves by turne the one into the other bodie, and bee so mingled together, that each of them hath two soules',[10] he comes close to suggesting a spiritual union of man and woman (each sharing in both sexes) with strong similarities to sensual love. This may help to explain how Shakespeare came to present the Dark Lady as in many ways, despite her sexual allure, akin to the male lover.

All the Sonnets addressed to or about a woman are numbered after 126. Those numbered early in the sequence say merely that she is black in mourning, or that her beauty is not the conventional one, or play with fanciful ideas, although 129 is a savage denunciation of lust (contradicted in later Sonnets). In 141 he denies contradicting 128, that he has any sensual desire for her. In 132, however, he announces a theme that has a large part to play in the Sonnets later in the sequence, the paradox that 'beauty her selfe is blacke' (132.13), and again 'Thy blacke is fairest in my judgments place', where the last four words can mean 'in the place where my judgment stands', as well as 'in place of', 'instead of' my judgment. The poet is both committed and not committed to his paradox.

The mistress also resembles in this paradoxical way the young man, whose infidelity is lamented and yet justified, with incense, in the same breath. (Some interpretations ignore this, presenting the love for the man as pure and for the woman as corrupt.) The theme becomes more important as it involves moral blackness as well as lack of beauty.

In 133 and 134 the woman is drawn into the 'plot': it is to her that the young man turned in 40–2, and the poet confesses now that he has lost her (134.1). Yet in later Sonnets in the sequence he still woos her.

135 and 136 bring in, startlingly, a new development of the paradox. We have seen how Shakespeare puns on his own name, Will, confessing that Will in a broad sense of potency is at work in his own self. Will now becomes the Will of the woman (identical with that of the man, in a hermaphrodite sense?), and leads to a fantastic variety of meanings.

Commentators have regarded both 135 and 136 deprecatingly – 'Shakespeare quibbles compulsively' and 'two frankly bawdy and frenetically witty exercises'– and it is true that by the time the several meanings of 'will' have been explained the reader needs little to discourage himself from working out every possible combination of interpretations. Kerrigan, Evans agreeing, lists six meanings of 'Will' and 'will': what is wanted (thou hast thy *Will*); penis; vagina; carnal desire (hide my will in thine); shall (Will, will fulfil) and William, i.e. Shakespeare (but some say another man of the same first name). The ribaldry, once the multiple meanings are appreciated, may take over and produce astonished laughter.

There is no 'very woe' here (129.11), no despising (129.5) of sexual love, and in the light of so many other combinations of opposites we do best to allow each, 135 and 136, with 141, to stand in its own right, neither in this context invalidating the other, and this is easier to do if the often accepted view that the mistress is a prostitute is looked at closely. To her 'will in others seeme[s] right gracious', which suggests a lover rather than a prostitute. There is no mention of payment; and the

---

[9] Peter Burke in his *The Fortunes of the 'Courtier': The European Reception of Castiglione's Cortegiano* (Cambridge, 1995).

[10] Baldassare Castiglione, *The Book of the Courtier*, trans. by Sir Thomas Hoby, intro. by J. H. Whitfield (London, 1928), end of Book 4.

poet cares for *her* enjoyment – 'so it please thee hold . . .'; he looks for 'faire acceptance', and wants her to love him 'still' (i.e. always), implying a personal rather than a commercial relationship. It is a 'loue-sute' (136.12) that he presents. The tone is one of a beseeching lover, not of a customer.

The couplet of 135

> Let no unkinde, no faire beseechers kill,
> Thinke all but one, and me in that one *Will*.

is usually emended by editors (as in 'Let "No", unkind, no fair beseechers kill' or 'let no unkind [person] kill any fair beseechers') so as to mean in the first instance 'do not unkindly put off fair beseechers with a denial'. This is an understandable emendation, reducing the line to a more usual and easily acceptable sense. But if 'kill' means 'destroy your desire' the unemended sense reads 'Do not let either unfeeling or fair wooers keep you from accepting them.' The poet is asking her to accept them all, in a spirit of love like that in which he himself transforms the 'rud'st or gentlest sight' (113.9) so as to make both beautiful. Both unkind and fair wooers are to be thought of as one, and he himself, whether as male organ or as his name suggests, is one also with them.

A serious part of this extravaganza arises from the similarity of the mistress to the male lover of the earlier Sonnets. Just as he has a more than human presence and has all the poet's lovers in himself, so she has her Will in super-abundance, suggesting a kind of goddess that is the epitome of loving unions. Vendler indeed asks 'Is she an idealized Petrarchan goddess, above good and evil? Is she a natural essence, like the ocean? Or is she a calculating accumulator of goods?'[11] In another poem than this, she observes, lines 5–10 (in 135) 'could be addressed to God', while the whole Sonnet has 'echoes of liturgical prayer'.[12]

That the mistress's will is 'large and spacious' (135.5) is meant both physically and mentally, yet no woman's will is capable of accepting more than one will at a time. The impossibility of 'I fill it full with wils and my will one' (136.6) is no impossibility if it means that the mistress accepts

lovers metaphorically in thousands or millions. She resembles the male lover in this, when he is urged by the poet to 'take all my loues' (40.1) and is asked what he would have thereby more than he already has; she resembles him again in that he contains in himself all the 'parts' of the poet's former lovers (31.11). 'And thou (all they) hast all the all of me' (31.14) is a tribute to an all-enveloping love that the mistress also enfolds in herself in her own way.

The mistress is asked to be like the sea, all accepting:

> The sea all water, yet receives raine still,
> And in aboundance addeth to his store,
> So thou being rich in *Will* adde to thy *Will*,
> One will of mine to make thy large *Will* more.
>
> (135.9–12)

The parallel with Orsino's speech suggests itself:

> O spirit of Love, how quicke and fresh art thou,
> That notwithstanding thy capacitie
> Receiveth as the Sea . . .
>
> (*Twelfth Night* 1.1.9–11)

And similarly Romeo says

> My bounty [capacity for giving] is as boundless as
>   the sea,
> My love as deep; the more I give to thee,
> The more I have, for both are infinite.
>
> (*Romeo and Juliet* 2.2.133–5)

– again expressing the idea that both love and the sea do not grow greater or less by being added to or subtracted from. The mistress is being asked by the poet to accept his love, which will not increase her own.

The poet takes her part against himself ('I against my self with thee pertake' (149.2)), just as he does with the male lover ('Thy adverse party is thy Advocate, And against my selfe a lawfull plea commence' (35.10–11)). What this means is not spelled out,

---

[11] Helen Vendler, *The Art of Shakespeare's Sonnets* (Cambridge, Mass., 1997), p. 574.
[12] Vendler, *The Art*, p. 574.

although the male lover is, of course, not only celebrated by the poet as the true Rose (67.8) but is also guilty of gross betrayal of his friendship. But the way to understand is to remember the poet's insistence that he is blinded by love, at the same time insisting that love teaches him to see truly. It is this paradox that underlies the relation with both mistress and male lover. 136 differs, however, from 135, introducing more clearly something other than sexual love in the ordinary sense. We have seen that the male lover is spoken of in 53 as 'in every blessed shape we know', while the harvest is spoken of as his bounty, as though he were like Ceres. Since the poet thinks of himself as identical with his love, the same godlike attributes must be his also, and he is in the same way identical with the mistress, whose Will he is. Duncan-Jones interprets 135.6: 'fill [your sexual organ] full to the brim with male sexual organs', Burrow adds: 'the poet becomes one universal appetitive will'. The opening lines of 136 are easier to follow if this is borne in mind:

> If thy soule check thee that I come so neere,
> Swear to thy blind soule that I was thy *Will*,
> And will thy soule knows is admitted there,
> Thus farre for love, my love-sute sweet fulfill.

But the poet is speaking here of the soul, not the body: he is courting not merely for sexual pleasure, but for something spiritual. Saying 'I was thy *Will*' can mean 'I, Will Shakespeare, was yours.' Yet when he argues that Will is admitted 'there', he seems to mean in her soul. The soul knows that such a Will is certainly accepted, and a seventh, religious sense, in addition to the six already listed, becomes more apparent still. The Bible has many references to God's will directing the believer, who is encouraged always to act in accordance with it, and the relationship, as in *Ezekiel* 16, can be sexual. The verses thus say 'you know that this kind of will is proper for the soul to receive'. From the views just quoted this is a small step, and yet a hugely different one.

Shakespeare goes on to say

> Will, will fulfil the treasure of thy love,

where the meaning is sexual (compare 20.13, 'women's *treasure*') but adds

> I fill it full with wills, and my will one.

That is: 'I, Will, will fulfil'. One may prefer to emend, as editors naturally do, 'Aye, fill it'. But Shakespeare likes to play with this meaning too. We have seen how he plays on 'eye' and 'I' in 104.2, 'when first your eye I eyde' (p. 231 above), and he makes similar use of 'Aye' and 'eye' elsewhere. So, 'I, Will will fulfil' is acceptable as it stands, even though he adds 'and my will one'. He is both microcosmically and macrocosmically present in the same line, both one of many wooers and the power that informs all their wooing. Shakespeare seems to go beyond both Plato and Neoplatonism here. For Plato, or rather for Diotima, the supreme vision is attained by renunciation of the love of women. In Castiglione both men and women may realise together, though chastely, in a version of Diotima's own words, 'the originall of all other beautie which never encreaseth nor diminisheth, alwaiess beautifill, and of it selfe.'[13] Diotima also, however, to Socrates's bewilderment, adds:

> to love is to bring forth [also translated 'begetting in'] upon the beautiful, both in body and soul
>
> (para.206)

which brings in a sexual meaning she earlier denied or avoided. This may help to account for the implied wish of the poet to join 'Will' in all three senses, including the divine or superhuman, in a single act. Such a combination is well known in accounts of mysticism and in alchemy.[14] As Zaehner says, 'There is no point at all in blinking the fact that the raptures of the theistic

---

[13] Castiglione, p. 320.

[14] C. G. Jung reproduces one of many alchemical illustrations showing coition as the conjunction of 'male' and 'females' in the Philosophers' Stone. One in particular shows a naked, crowned king and queen, in sexual intercourse, both winged like angels. C. G. Jung, *Psychologie und Alchemie* (Zurich, 1944), p. 638.

mystic are closely akin to the transports of the sexual union.'[15] Many instances of such a union, as described by St Teresa,[16] however, show only one pair, of male and female. Shakespeare differs in imagining a large number sharing with his own Will. This is not Plotinus's 'flight of the Alone to the Alone', although the 'all alone' of 124.11 suggested something like that.[17] It sounds rather egalitarian, and lusty, as though Rabelais had written Plato. It is a counterpart, if not a contradiction of Plato's vision, which appears, but for the strange intrusion in Plato, of 'begetting upon', to be without sexual participation, and yet has the same universal scope.

Two of the plays have scenes reminiscent of 136, but in a contradictory sense. Othello says he could be happy 'if the generall Campe, Pyoners and all' could have 'tasted' Desdemona's body, so long as he knew nothing of it, but is of course tormenting himself with the thought. When Cressida arrives in the Greek camp, the Greek captains, so many wills, one after another enact a similar tasting, so far as the public stage will allow. Troilus is not present at this communal wooing, but soon afterwards sees Cressida flirting with Diomed and loathes her (5.2.154–8). The Sonnet and the plays are poles apart on this theme. Is it a question of the Sonnet being macrocosmic while the plays are microcosmic, human rather than metaphysical?

Auden speaks of the origin of the Sonnets in a mystical experience. In the light of much that has gone before, 33 may be seen in that way. Here the sun appears like a sovereign flattering his subjects by the glory he lends them, 'guilding pale streams with heavenly alcumy' (33.4), but then disappearing behind clouds. The poet sees in this his own relationship with the young man:

Even so my Sunne one early morn did shine
With all triumphant splendor on my brow

(33.9–10)

This sun, as we have seen in 34, is one and the same as the young man: he sends heat to dry the poet's tears and rain to express his remorse. But 'all triumphant splendor on my brow', some might say, could (just?) be meant as gross flattery for someone like the Earl of Southampton, or any other lover, although the magnitude of the splendour suggests more. Was the sun shining *on* or even from a brow that itself shone, sending its ray back? The 'celestiall face' is the face of the Sun, but the friend is also 'my Sunne': the confusion between the two in 34 continues, for the poet is now also 'turned into gold', like the streams, by heavenly alchemy. The Stone, or Elixir of Life, is his.

And 'but one hour mine'? Is that all? It is a brief meeting for ordinary lovers, but just the sort of momentary glimpse that mystics speak of. The vision is often connected with the sun. Boehme famously '"gazed fixedly upon a burnished pewter dish which reflected the sunshine with great brilliance" and fell into an inward ecstasy'.[18] Underhill cites numerous examples, when 'a new sun rises above the horizon and transfigures their twilit world'.[19] The preparation for such a moment comes later in the printed sequence of Sonnets. All mystics speak of the necessity for complete loss of selfhood, and so does 146, with its message to the poet's soul, that it is spending too much on making itself beautiful outwardly. 'Buy tearmes divine in selling houres of drosse' leads to an unusually powerful couplet:

So shalt thou feed on death, that feeds on men,
And death once dead, ther's no more dying then.

(146.13–14)

It does not follow that Shakespeare himself made such a self-denial. He counsels his soul in this way. But whether or not the vision in 33, one of the most telling and beautiful poems in the whole collection, is play-acting, or poetry, which, as Touchstone says, is 'feigning', it appears that he knew

---

[15] R. C. Zaehner, *Mysticism Sacred and Profane* (Oxford, 1957), p. 151.
[16] Evelyn Underhill, *Mysticism*, 12th edn revised (London, 1930), p. 356: 'It is impossible for her [the soul] to doubt that she has been in God and God in her.'
[17] *Enneads*, v.vi in G. R. S., Mead, ed., *Select Works of Plotinus: Thomas Taylor's Translation* (London, 1914), p. 171.
[18] Underhill, *Mysticism*, p. 58.
[19] Underhill, p. 249.

what self-abnegation was needed for the vision to be engendered.

Parallel with 33, reflecting it as the scene of the Greek captains' greeting Cressida reflects the many Wills of 136, is the scene in which Bottom reflects on his own 'most rare vision', as he calls it. He relates his climactic erotic encounter with a queen named after a great god in terms of the 'hidden wisdom', which, St Paul wrote, 'God ordained before the world unto our glory' (1 *Cor.* 2: 7): 'as it is written, Eye hath not seen, nor ear heard, neither have entered into the heart of man, the things which God hath prepared for them that love him'. Bottom garbles it, transposing the verbs to the wrong senses. But why does he speak not only of his 'dream' but of a 'vision', and why does he think of it in terms of a so well-known and surpassingly sublime biblical passage?

As in 136 there is here almost a goddess, and in her embrace there is a revelation comparable to the one in 33. This all looks very much like another parallel between the plays and the Sonnets, as though Shakespeare, being conscious of the conceivably overweening claim he made in the Sonnet, balanced it in another place with bathos. Alternatively, he may have seen the two visions as, once again, coinciding opposites.

If Shakespeare ever did feel himself capable like Hamlet of being king of infinite space, he no doubt was frustrated, as Hamlet was. He offers no clue about the way in which one Sonnet can be reconciled with another. Rather, he seems to have used his imagination to range over many aspects of love. He never confronts the troubling question of the ease with which contraries are declared identical, whether in the identity of two lovers, or of a human being and a deity, or, perhaps most troubling of all, of good and evil. It is easily said that the mistress's foulness is in the poet's judgement fair, or that love keeps him blind so that he cannot see her foul faults (148.14), that in his mind 'thy worst all best exceeds' (150.8). This is uncomfortably close to the Witches' chorus, 'Fair is foul, and foul is fair', which no one ever takes to be anything but a downright expression of evil. Without some substantiation such as, I shall argue, some of the plays

provide, the coincidence of opposites may be seen as mere philosophizing.

One other role of the lover remains. It is Christian rather than Platonic, and yet not irrelevant to the Platonic themes. This is natural enough, given Shakespeare's interest in duality-in-unity, bearing in mind this passage in the Gospel of St John:

> Believe me that I am in the Father, and the Father in me . . . At that day [of Judgment] ye shall know that I am in the Father, and ye in me, and I in you.
>
> (John 14:11 and 20)

The origin of this idea in Greek philosophy, found earlier in Plato and the pre-Socratics, is not disputed. In the Gospel, however, the words 'I am' have an unusual implication. They are the subject of Sonnet 121.

121 includes the self-defence by the poet ('Noe, I am that I am'), rejecting all criticism of himself and recalling Parolles 'simply the thing I am shall make me live' (*All's Well That Ends Well*, 4.3.369), but expressed in such terms as again give rise to debate on whether they have any biblical connection. 'I am that I am' are the words used by God in speaking to Moses (*Exodus* 3: 14) and alluded to by Christ, asserting his divinity, in 'Before Abraham was, I am' (*John* 8: 58).[20] They can of course be used simply to affirm one's own identity, but it is remarkable that Shakespeare should have used them in this cluster of Sonnets with their similarly freighted senses. Burrow observes that 'This is not to claim divinity'. Duncan-Jones refers to the use of the same words by 'the demi-devil Richard III' (although this would make yet another coinciding opposite) and quotes Booth: 'the biblical echo makes "the speaker sound smug, pretentious and stupid"'. But the poet has, after all, in several Sonnets identified himself with the lover, who is sometimes the sun, sometimes 'a God in love'; he is 'Will', perhaps the substance of a million shadows, and although he at other times is

---

[20] Iago's 'I am not that I am' may be taken as reflecting on the biblical 'I am', confessing his alienation.

conscious of his weakness as an individual, and of his separate identity, he is not thereby disqualified, given the paradoxical nature of his meditations, from asserting in his poetry even a sameness with God the Father such as Christ himself is represented as making. Mystics have always been accused of heresy in claiming to have God in them. But in the neoplatonist tradition the transcendent is also the immanent, and both coincide, like all opposites. It is still possible to read the Sonnet as an assertion of divinity, though contradicted by a self-criticism of huge proportions, for throughout the Sonnets there is, alongside the great pretensions to universality, the theme of being called to judgment. The beloved man is not only a dear friend, he is a fearsome critic, required by his love to condemn the poet, who even accepts the justice of this:

> When as thy love hath cast his utmost summe,
> Cauld to that audite by advis'd respects . . .
> Against that time I do insconce me here
> Within the knowledge of mine own desart,
> And this my hand, against my selfe unpreare . . .
>
> (49.2–3, 9–11)

The ferocity imagined in the lover is astonishing. If a normal human relationship were involved, it would hardly survive such a plea as this:

> Accuse me thus, that I have scanted all,
> Wherein I should your great deserts repay,
> Forgot upon your dearest love to call . . .
>
> (117.1–3)

Thus all the praises of the lover, which in part are praises of the poet himself, sharing in the universality, are at the same time a means of affirming the poet's subjection and unlawfulness, the opposite of the assertion in 'I am'. And in 90, with such fearful pleading as 'Then hate me when thou wilt, if ever, now', 'make me bow', 'Ah doe not come in the rereward of a conquerd woe', 'in the onset come', although they are suited to a real man, we seem to hear Job suffering the blows of the Almighty.

How far do the combinations of contraries reach? How often are they to be found in the plays, in individual lines and scenes? Should we include the two long poems, one about a goddess trying to seduce a man, the other about a man trying to seduce, and raping, a woman? How about the hilarious tragedy of Pyramus and Thisbe, so similar in outline to the real tragedy of Romeo and Juliet? And Hamlet's ability to speak of the world as 'this majestical roof fretted with golden fire', and at the same time as 'a foul and pestilential congregation of vapours'?

Do we not feel at certain points the need for some curb to be put on the contraries and their fusions found in the Sonnets? The witches' chorus, 'Fair is foul and foul is fair' – does that reflect on the poet's ability to see the mistress as 'black as hell' (147.14) and yet excuse himself as blinded by love (148.13)? Is it a requirement that he should take sides here against the witches? Is there any possibility of reconciling this with 'Love is not love that alters' (116.2–3)? We should rather, I submit, see that any alteration in love indicates the absence of love.

GIANTS AND ENEMIES OF GOD: THE RELATIONSHIP BETWEEN CALIBAN AND PROSPERO FROM THE PERSPECTIVE OF INSULAR LITERARY TRADITION

LYNN FOREST-HILL

This chapter engages with a growing body of criticism that analyses early modern drama from the perspective of insular literary tradition. Its eventual focus is on Shakespeare's *Tempest* but it begins in Anglo-Saxon literature, before moving on to the foundation myth that appears in the medieval *Brut*, or *Chronicles of England*. These sources illuminate the play's engagement with political and religious controversies that were current in England when the play was first performed in November 1611. This approach adds another dimension to the established post-colonial critique of the play and adds depth and complexity to the relationship between Prospero and Caliban as it exposes additional cultural significance in the manipulation of images deployed in the play. Although these images reflect traditional eschatological and mythical sources, those sources have hitherto been obscured by the overwhelming preoccupation of earlier critics with classical influences.[1]

The best-known form of the mythical founding of Britain recounts the coming of Brutus, grandson of Aeneas of Troy, from Armorica, with a band of Trojans. They kill the giants they find when they land at Totnes in Devon and settle down to create a city-based society. European foundation myths citing Greek or Roman ancestors first appear in the work of the seventh-century Frankish chronicler, Fredegar.[2] These myths offer explanations of how a society, civilization or realm came into being and include etiological material and eponymous characters. Many British myths, legends and stories include giants. From the work of Anglo-Saxon poets to that of sixteenth-century antiquarians, giants appear as the original inhabitants of the island of Britain. They are, of course, part of many foundation myths. The Titans of Greek legend are the classical version, and Genesis 6: 4 tells us that before the Flood 'there were giants in the earth in those days'.[3] Giants are the quintessential primary inhabitants in the myths of many realms and regions. They are Other by virtue of their size, monstrosity,

I should like to thank Professor Greg Walker and Dr Jane Cowling for reading and commenting on an earlier version of this chapter as well as thanking other colleagues at the Centre for Antiquity and the Middle Ages (CAMA) at the University of Southampton for their support and encouragement during the development of this research.

[1] The significance of eschatological and apocalyptic tradition has, however, been noted in *King Lear* although the contexts for interpretation naturally differ. See Joseph Wittreich, '"Image of the horror": the Apocalypse in *King Lear*', in *The Apocalypse in English Renaissance Thought and Literature*, ed. C. A. Patrides and Joseph Wittreich (Manchester, 1984), pp. 175–206.

[2] Susan Reynolds, 'Medieval *Origines Gentium* and the Community of the Realm', *History*, 68 (1983), 375–90. Reynolds observes that 'origin stories . . . were unlikely to have had a single common descent' (378).

[3] *Gigantes autem erant super terram in diebus illis*. Gen. 6: 4. Other biblical references to giants: Sap. 14: 6; Ecclus. 16: 8; Bar. 3: 26. *Biblia sacra iuxta vulgatam versionem*, rev. Robertus Weber, (Stuttgart, 1969).

and animosity towards the humans who displace them and become the founders of the society to which each myth refers. The fact that they are savages vanquished and destroyed is always important as a sign of the beneficial process of establishing the society that succeeds them.[4] The political potential of such a mythology was constantly exploited, and indeed appears as the motivating factor in the development of the British founding myth after the Norman Conquest.

The history of one particular giant introduces the potential for an analysis of *The Tempest* in terms of early modern eschatological anxieties, but in insular literature there are two views of giants, both of which offer insights into the relationship between Caliban and Prospero. The first conforms to the pattern of the hostile Other. In *Beowulf*, the hero's first opponent is Grendel who is a troll, from Northern European tradition, and the enemy of God because he is one of Cain's kin from the Christian tradition.[5] From him, we are told, arose all those monsters 'who joined in long wars with God'.[6] Grendel is a giant in size and animosity, while his role as Other in the manuscript includes his opposition to Christianity. As the resentful outcast, he poses a threat to the ideal human community of Heorot, which he also envies.[7]

However, this poem, like others in the Old English corpus, also gives a less threatening view of giants, *enta* or *eotenas*. Their ancient works are the objects of wonder. Grendel's vengeful mother is killed with the sword whose hilt is described as being *entisc* or the ancient work of giants.[8] Another ancient *entisc* sword splits Ongentheow's helmet, which is also described as the work of giants. In all these references to giant artefacts, including the masonry of the dragon's lair, age, strength and wonderful skill are indicated, and the craft of giants elicits comment in other Old English poems. In *The Ruin*, the *Gnomic Verses*, and *The Wanderer*, ruined Roman architecture is described imaginatively as *orþanc enta geweorc*, the wonderful, or cunning, work of giants, and the Old English translation of Orosius's fifth-century story of Cyrus of Persia, declares that 'Membrath the giant first began to build Babylon.'[9] This skill in building remains a feature of

giants in post-Conquest versions of the founding of Britain and throughout implies their original tenure and settlement of the land.

The Germanic tribes may have known the real source of Roman ruins but in England these are depicted as a sign of mutability in the work of the Anglo-Saxon poets who create an absent giant race characterized by its skill rather than its overt aggression. The sense of wonder associated with an imagined race of giants suggests a mythologizing impulse consistent with the trend observed by Susan Reynolds among people who participated in the great migrations of the first millennium.[10] The Anglo-Saxon view does not, however, constitute a coherent founding myth, perhaps because having established their own control over the land they faced successive waves of northern raiders who provided a more immediate Other against which to define Anglo-Saxon society and tenure, but this view interrogates later myths of savage giants.

The Norman invasion modified the perception of giants in accordance with the political interests of the conquerors. In his *Historia regum Britanniae*

---

4 Walter Stephen, *Giants in Those Days* (Lincoln and London, 1989), pp. 31–2.

5 Fr Klaeber, ed., *Beowulf and The Fight at Finnsburg*, 3rd edn. (Lexington, 1922), line 107.

6 *þanon untydras ealle onwocon, /eotenas ond ylfe ond orcneas, /swylce gigantas, þa wið Gode wunnon / lange þrage* [from him an evil brood all arose, ogres and elves and monsters, as well as giants who joined in long wars with God]. The poem uses both OE *eotenas* and *gigantas* from Latin although both may be translated as 'giants'. All translations are mine. Klaeber, ed., *Beowulf*, lines 111–14.

7 Andy Orchard suggests that 'given Grendel's central role as a man-eating monster, it seems extraordinary that the *Beowulf*-poet should choose to depict him as a character with a point of view, one that is capable of evoking sympathy, at precisely [the] key moment in the battle, when the predator becomes prey.' Orchard, *A Critical Companion to Beowulf* (Cambridge, 2003), p. 192. I would like to thank Professor David Hinton for this reference.

8 *enta ærgeweorc.* Klaeber, ed., *Beowulf*, line 1679.

9 *Membrað se ent angan ærest timbran Babylonia.* Henry Sweet, ed., *King Alfred's Orosius*, part 1 EETS OS 79 (1883), 74. In this parallel edition Sweet also gives the Latin original: *Namque Babyloniam a Nemrod gigante fundatam.*

10 Reynolds, '*Origines Gentium*', 375.

of *c.* 1136, Geoffrey of Monmouth not only asserts that the name of Britain was once Albion, but that Brutus found giants inhabiting the island when he and his expedition arrived. He found the germ of Brutus's story in Nennius's ninth-century *Historia Brittonum*,[11] but a claim of descent from the Trojans was already an established continental *topos*. As the pre-existence of giants has biblical authority from the Genesis passage, Geoffrey offers no further explanation.

In Geoffrey's *Historia*, the only giant to survive the invasion is named Gogmagog and he is described very briefly as 'particularly repulsive' and strong enough to uproot an oak tree.[12] He is kept alive to wrestle with the Trojan champion, Corineus, who eventually throws him over a cliff. The unusual name Gogmagog is a contraction of the names of two biblical opponents of God – Gog and Magog. Confusion arises over these names, because their first mention, in the Book of Ezekiel, is of a person and a place: Gog is a defiant prince from a land called Magog.[13] However, in The Book of Revelation, Gog and Magog are the names of the peoples of the earth who will be deceived by Satan into fighting for him in the last days. Their eschatological significance is developed in medieval texts and becomes part of the legend of the coming of the Antichrist. It is found in the influential sixth-century text known as the *Revelationes* of Pseudo-Methodius,[14] and in one early redaction of Adso of Montier-en-Der's even more influential early eleventh-century *Libellus de Antichristo*. From the twelfth century onwards, English manuscripts gathered together versions of Adso's treatise and copies of the Pseudo-Methodius *Revelationes*.[15]

The story of Gog and Magog as servants of the Antichrist and heralds of the end of days was widely disseminated to a non-clerical audience in the medieval story of Alexander the Great.[16] In all these texts, however, Gog and Magog remain separate entities. The authority for the conflation of the names into Gogmagog is Bede's eighth-century *Expositio Apocalypsis* in which he says that Gog and Magog in the Book of Revelation are to be understood as 'parts of the whole', and not differenti-

ated, because they are alike enemies of God.[17] They will not, however, suffer the same fate as Satan and the Antichrist.[18] The contraction of their names encapsulates the undifferentiated negative significance attributed to them in their eschatological context, and when applied as a name to the last giant in Albion, creates a creature that is not only Other, but whose destruction could be regarded as righteous because he is an enemy of God, not simply an opponent of those who invade his land and usurp his autonomy.

The definition of Gogmagog as an enemy of God is stated plainly in Laȝamon's early thirteenth-century vernacular *Brut*. This verse chronicle of the British kings in alliterative form retains elements of Old English vocabulary.[19] Laȝamon's Gogmagog is huge, strong enough to use trees as weapons,

---

[11] Geoffrey of Monmouth, *History of the Kings of Britain*, ed. Lewis Thorpe (London, 1966), p. 71.

[12] Geoffrey of Monmouth, 72.

[13] Magog on its own is the name of a son of Japheth in Gen. 10: 2. All biblical references are to the Authorized Version unless otherwise noted.

[14] George Cary, *The Medieval Alexander* (Cambridge, 1956), p. 130. Adso Dervensis, *De Ortu et Tempore Antichristi*, ed. D. Verhelst, Corpus Christianorum, XLV (Turnhout, 1976), p. 139.

[15] Adso Dervensis, *De Ortu et Tempore Antichrist*, ed. Verhelst, 11.

[16] For the history and development of this myth see George Cary, *The Medieval Alexander*. Also D. J. A. Ross, *Alexander Historiatus: A Guide to Medieval Illustrated Alexander Literature* (London, 1963).

[17] *Porro Gog et Magog uel a parte totum significant, uel iuxta interpretationem, quae <tectum> et <de tecto> dicuntur, occultos et apertos indicant hostes.* Bede, *Expositio Apocalypsis*, Corpus Christianorum, CXXIA (Turnhout, 2001), 20: 8–9.

[18] 'Satan shall be loosed out of his prison. And shall go out to deceive the nations which are in the four quarters of the earth, Gog and Magog, to gather them together to battle: the number of whom is as the sand of the sea. And they went up on the breadth of the earth, and compassed the camp of the saints about, and the beloved city: and fire came down out of heaven, and devoured them. And the devil, that deceived them, was cast into the lake of fire and brimstone, where the beast and the false prophet are' Rev. 20: 7–10. For an exposition see for example, St Augustine, *The City of God*, trans. Henry Bettenson (London, 1972), pp. 919–21.

[19] Laȝamon, *Brut*, ed. G. L. Brook and R. F. Leslie, EETS OS 250 (London, 1963). Kenneth J. Tiller suggests that Laȝamon

---

and he is defined as *wiðersaca*, arch-enemy of God. Laȝamon writes that Brutus and his Trojans

> funden I þon londe'/ twenti eotandes stronge.
> Heora nomen ne herdi neuer tellen a leoda ne a
>   spella.
> Boten þes anes name'/ þa heore alre lauerd wes.
> Geomagog ihaten'/ þat was þe heiste.
> Godes wiðersaka'/ þe Wrse hine luuede.[20]

The translation of 'wiðersaca' in Old and Middle English is 'arch-enemy, especially the devil or Antichrist'.[21] This recalls the biblical depiction of the separate beings Gog and Magog. The plural noun appears in three manuscripts of Archbishop Wulfstan's eleventh-century *Sermo Lupi ad Anglos*,[22] which warns that: '*her syn on earde a Godes wiðersacan apostatan abroþene*' [there are always in this land God's arch enemies, degenerate apostates].[23] Laȝamon's explicit depiction of Gogmagog retains the connection with the Antichrist, as the giant takes on the mantle of God's adversary.[24] Later versions of the founding myth construct Gogmagog's oppositional condition from a less explicit direction.

The particular version of the foundation myth that surfaces in *The Tempest* derives from a fourteenth-century development of these earlier versions. In about 1333, the Brutus myth was reworked in Anglo-Norman, in the form of a *lai* rather than a Chronicle. It is known as *Des Grantz Geanz*,[25] and it explains, *without* reference to biblical sources, how giants came to be on the island of Albion before Brutus arrived, and how it got the name Albion. It tells the story of a king and queen of Greece who had thirty daughters, the eldest of whom was called Albina. When the girls came of age they were married to noble kings. However, the young wives, because of their proud and noble upbringing, objected to being subservient to their husbands, and plotted to kill them while in intimate embrace. The youngest sister, however, told the plot to her husband, and then to her father, who had all the other sisters arrested for treason. In his rage, he condemned them to death, but the other judges, considering the honour of the parents and husbands, commuted this to exile for life.

So the sisters were set adrift in a rudderless ship without food.[26] For three days and nights the ship was battered by a storm. When this abated the ship fetched up on an island and Albina stepped ashore. Later, she declared that as the eldest sister she was taking possession of the land, using the legal term '*seisin*' at this point, and that it was to be called Albion after her own name.

The sisters found wild herbs, fruit, game and fish in the rivers, and fresh water to drink, but found no other inhabitants. They made fire with flints to cook the game they caught and ate so well that they

---

uses the mythical history of Britain to encourage resistance against post-Conquest suppression of Anglo-Saxon culture. Tiller, *Translating Conquest* (Cardiff, forthcoming 2006).

20 '[They] found in that land twenty great giants. I never heard their names told or spoken by people, except for the name of the one who was their lord. He was called Geomagog who was the greatest adversary of God, the worst creature alive', Laȝamon, *Brut*, lines 902–6. My translation. OE 'ent', 'eoten', and 'gigant' from Latin, occur in *Beowulf*. See Klaeber, ed. *Beowulf*, Glossary. 'Wiðersaca' is not found there. In OE eoten = giants; but 'eotan' = Jute; in ME eotandes = giants. This may be influenced by dialect or uncertain othographic transmission, like the variant spelling 'Geomagog' for Gogmagog.

21 J. R. Clark Hall, *A Concise Anglo Saxon Dictionary*, 4th edn (Toronto, 1894). Hans Kurath, and Sherman M. Kuhn, *Middle English Dictionary* (Ann Arbor, 1956–).

22 Bede's *Expositio Apocalypsis* influenced Adso's treatise, which was itself a source for Wulfstan's eschatological homilies. Adso Dervensis, *De Ortu et Tempore Antichristi*, ed. Verhelst, 156.

23 Dorothy Bethurum notes 'apostatan' is only recorded in Wulfstan's works: Mss. Corpus Christi Cambs 419 (eleventh century) and Bodleian 343 (later twelfth century) read 'Godes wiðersacan' only. Ms. Corpus Christi Cambs 201 (late eleventh century) combines both. See *The Homilies of Wulfstan*, ed. Dorothy Bethurum, (Oxford, 1957), 363n.

24 Bernard McGinn notes: 'The conception of Antichrist as a giant was common in the early Middle Ages, as Bede and other commentators demonstrate.' 'Portraying Antichrist in the Middle Ages', in W. Verbeke, et al. *The Use and Abuse of Eschatology in the Middle Ages*, Medievalia Lovaniensia Series 1; *Studia*, 15 (Leuven, 1988), 1–48, 7.

25 Georgine Brereton notes that the vocabulary of the poem and errors in versification are 'an unmistakable indication of insular origin'. *Des Grantz Geanz*, ed. Georgine Brereton, Medium Aevum Monographs II (Oxford, 1937), xxxi–ii. More than 20 manuscripts are extant. Cotton Cleopatra D IX is the longer redaction.

26 *Des Grantz Geanz*, ed. Brereton, 12.

became grossly fat. This provoked the women's lust and they desired male company. The Devil saw this and, taking human form, satisfied their lust. Giants were born from these unions with the Incubus. More giants were born from subsequent incestuous relationships. They were excessively large and massively strong. They were also hideous to look at, because they were fathered by the Devil and their mothers were already gross. This huge supernatural race lived in caves and on mountains. Like the giants in earlier versions of the myth, they built great walls and deep ditches around their dwelling places, but, the story tells us, the defences these giants built have fallen through tempest and storm.

This was the race that held the land when Brutus and his men arrived, but because there was strife between the giants, when the Trojans landed there were only twenty-four of them to oppose the invaders. Brutus destroyed all but Gogmagog who was allowed to live because the Trojan not only marvelled at his size and wanted him to wrestle the Trojan champion, as in Geoffrey's and Laȝamon's versions, but wanted to know how giants came to inhabit the land. When Gogmagog had told his story and been killed, Brutus obliterated the name Albion, called the island Britain after himself, and established cities.[27]

This story became hugely popular. An abridged version became the basis for two prose translations *into* Latin,[28] and for the prologue to a Latin prose translation of the *Brute Chronicle*.[29] A metrical version in English forms the prologue to Castleford's *Chronicle of England*.[30] A version of the story in which Albina and her sisters are the offspring of the King of Syria accompanies ten of the fourteen extant texts of the Anglo-Norman prose *Brut*; and this Syrian version became the most widely known form because it was used, in translation, as the preface to the Middle English *Brut*.[31] This form of the story was printed in *Caxton's Chronicle*. The popularity and dissemination of *The Chronicles of England* is testified by the 167 manuscripts still extant in English, French and Latin, as well as the thirteen editions printed between 1400 and 1528.[32] Wynkyn de Worde included the Syrian version in his 1528 *Chronicles of England* as did John Rastell.

The many versions of the Albina revision to the Brutus myth demonstrate continuous interest in this story of the foundation of Britain. Its Anglo-Norman *lai* form suggests an intention to entertain, but the translation into Latin suggests a more serious purpose. As Geoffrey of Monmouth's *Historia* sought to legitimate the Norman Conquest,[33] so the anonymous *Des Grantz Geanz* addresses a later topical political problem. Commentators suggest that the Albina revision was a response to Scottish assertions of independence in the 1320 *Declaration of Arbroath*.[34] This claimed, in the face of English incursions, Scotland's ancient independence by reason of its foundation by Scota, daughter of a king of Egypt. By claiming a separate founding myth, Scotland portrayed an ancient authority for its independence from England. In response, the Albina myth challenged Scottish separatism through what James Carley and Julia Crick describe as an 'expression of the natural state of the island polity'.[35] The Latin form gave the myth the aura of authority.

[27] My paraphrase throughout.

[28] *Des Grantz Geanz*, ed. Brereton, xxxvi.

[29] The versions of the *Brute Chronicle* dating after 1333. *Des Grantz Geanz*, ed., Brereton, xxxiii.

[30] Caroline D. Eckhardt argues that Castleford's *Chronicle* was composed shortly after 1327. If so, this challenges the date of *Des Grantz Geanz*. See *Castleford's Chronicle or The Boke of Brut*, ed. Caroline D. Eckhardt, EETS os 305 (Oxford, 1996).

[31] James P. Carley and Julia Crick, 'Constructing Albion's Past: An Annotated edition of *De Origine Gigantum*', in *Arthurian Literature* 13, ed. James P. Carley and Felicity Riddy (Cambridge, 1995), pp. 41–114, 47

[32] I am most grateful to Richard Barber for additional information about sources. He includes the story of Albina in his book *Myths and Legends of the British Isles* (Woodbridge, 1999).

[33] Geoffrey wanted 'to give "a precedent for the dominions and ambitions of the Norman kings".' *The History of the Kings of Britain*, ed. Thorpe, 10, citing J. S. P. Tatlock, *The Legendary History of Britain: Geoffrey of Monmouth's Historia Regum Britanniae and its early vernacular versions* (California, 1950), p. 426.

[34] See for example, Lesley Johnson, 'Return to Albion', *Arthurian Literature*, 13, ed. James P. Carley and Felicity Riddy (Cambridge, 1995), 19–40, 25. Also Carley and Crick, 'Constructing Albion's Past', pp. 55–9.

[35] Carley and Crick, 'Constructing Albion's Past', p. 42.

In all cases, the Brutus myth appears to legitimate conquest and usurpation by depicting the original inhabitants of the island as violent cave-dwelling monsters, while the classical authority implied by the mythical Greek origins of Brutus and his men suggest that they represent the coming of civilization, order and patriarchal law to an otherwise barbaric land. Most versions of the Albina revision preserve this idea. However, *De origine gigantum*, a reworking in Latin prose of the abridged version of *Des Grantz Geanz*, renders the giants differently, depicting them as living a peaceful life until Brutus invades.[36] This version alters the perception of the actions of Gogmagog and his comrades as these hitherto peaceful first inhabitants of the island unsuccessfully confront an invading Trojan fighting force. From this perspective, Brutus is the violent colonizer usurping the giants' inheritance.[37] This is the perspective found in later versions of the myth where Gogmagog and his kin are said to have 'dwellyd in caues and in hylles atte ther wylle And hadde the londe of Albyon as them lykyd/unto ye tyme that Brute arryued.'[38]

The freedom of the giants within their own land is important as a context for reviewing *The Tempest*, but it is only one aspect of the political potential of the Albina myth. That potential is significant for understanding the extraordinary popularity of the story. It influences Chaucer's late fourteenth-century *Man of Law's Tale*. The story of the Roman maiden Constance, taken from Nicholas Trevet's chronicle of world history written *c.* 1334,[39] has heavy overtones of hagiography, but in Chaucer's version Constance is set adrift from Syria rather than from Trevet's Saracen land,[40] and she speaks a form of Latin,[41] rather than Saxon as she does in Trevet's story.[42] In both versions, however, she travels in a ship that cannot be steered and eventually arrives on the coast of Northumberland, bringing Christianity specifically to the region that had frequently been contested between the English and the Scots.

Chaucer, following Trevet, apparently contributes to an ongoing political debate about unified control of the island of Britain. He may also have perceived the problem with the Albina story,

which had then been part of insular literary tradition for some sixty years. In the process of claiming insular unity, the myth depicted the first inhabitants as monstrous adversaries of God akin to the Antichrist, who would be born, according to one version of his genealogy, from the union of a human mother and the Devil. Chaucer, however, appears to conflate the Albina myth with the story of Constance to rewrite it in terms of the re-establishment of Christianity. Like Trevet, he depicts the prior existence of British Christianity declaring that

> In al that lond no Cristen dorste route;
> Alle Cristen folk been fled fro that contree
> Thurgh payens, that conquereden al aboute
> The plages of the north, by land and see.
> To Walys fledde the cristyanytee
> Of olde Britons dwellynge in this ile.[43]

---

[36] *Et perdurarunt gigantes pacifice in hac terra usque as aduentum britonum. De origine gigantum*, ed. Carley and Crick, 'Constructing Albion's Past', 113. Ruth Evans notes the specific and continual 'toning down' of the giants' violence in line with more political purposes. Ruth Evans, 'Gigantic Origins: An Annotated Translation of *De Origine Gigantum*', *Arthurian Literature* 16, ed. James P. Carley and Felicity Riddy (Cambridge, 1998) pp. 197–211, p. 211.

[37] Anke Bernau, 'Problematic Origins: The Struggle over Nation and Historiography in Medieval and Early Modern England', in Gordon McMullan and David Matthews, eds., *Reading the Medieval in Early Modern England*, forthcoming.

[38] *The Chronicles of England and St Alban's Chronicle* (1485), printed by Julian Notary (1515) STC 9995; and by Wynkyn de Worde (1528) STC 9986.

[39] *The Riverside Chaucer*, ed. Larry D. Benson, 3rd edn. (Oxford, 1987), p. 857. Trevet was writing for Marie, daughter of Edward I.

[40] *The Life of Constance from the Anglo-Norman Chronicle of Nicholas Trevet, Originals and Analogues of some of Chaucer's Canterbury Tales*, ed. and trans. Edmund Brock, part 1, The Chaucer Society (London, 1872), line 136.

[41] 'A maner Latyn corrupt was hir speche', *The Man of Law's Tale*, in *The Riverside Chaucer*, ed. Benson, line 519. Constance's use of a form of Latin reflects her origins in Rome and suggests her function as a symbol of the Roman Church.

[42] 'And she answered him in Saxon . . . as one who was learned in divers languages'. *The Life of Constance*, ed. Brock, 12. A translation into Middle English from Trevet's French original dates *c.* 1430–40, too late to be Chaucer's source, but still preserves the Saracen-land location, 221.

[43] *The Riverside Chaucer*, ed. Benson, *MLT*, lines 540–45.

Chaucer's version of Constance's arrival taints Scottish incursions with the stigma of paganism as well as challenging Scottish separatism by alluding to the Albina myth. It justifies English control by asserting a Christian agenda against the gross sin implied by the myth, depicting the Roman Church in the image of the Latin-speaking daughter of Rome *restoring* the faith of the unified island. At the same time it challenges the implicit Anglo-Norman suggestion that Britain needed the civilizing process of the Conquest.

The significance and dissemination of the Albina myth in late medieval and early modern England is not yet widely recognized. Gogmagog's name, on the other hand, occurs not just in literature,[44] but also in topographical legends.[45] He is one of the giants adopted from legend and romance to serve as mascots. The claim to have a protecting giant, or to have overthrown one during the founding process, may be a playful sign of civic status but Gog and Magog are London's giants and were historically associated with the city's claim to great antiquity. In 1859 in his discussion of the significance of the London Guildhall figures of the giants, Frederick Fairholt noted that:

Tales of Albion and Brutus were so much valued by our forefathers that they were transcribed as well-authenticated and sober early history in their *Liber Albus*, as well as in the *Recordatorium Civitatis Speculum*; and advanced in a memorial presented to Henry VI, and now preserved in the Tower of London, as an evidence of the Great Antiquity, precedency and dignity of the City of London, even before Rome.[46]

There is no mention of Albina in the *Liber Albus*, only Brutus, but the preservation, transmission and explicit purpose attached to these legends increased in political significance during the fluctuations of the Reformation. The *Liber Albus* asserts the preeminence of London over Rome through its prior foundation by Brutus and derives all the liberties, laws and customs of London from the Trojan, ignoring his pagan condition.[47] Similarly, the depiction of the prior inhabitants as offspring of murderous women who in their lust were impregnated by the devil, did not prevent transmission

in official and popular texts, and Victor I. Scherb has argued that whether as Gogmagog or Gog and Magog, this biblical phenomenon came to define English consciousness.[48] The pride or pleasure late medieval English people evidently took in their foundation myth, including the story of Albina, clearly continued because it became the subject of controversy. John Rastell in his early sixteenth-century *Chronicles of England* rejects it; Holinshed remarks upon it in the late sixteenth century, as does the antiquarian John Trussell in the seventeenth.[49]

The Albina story appears in the second edition of Holinshed's *Chronicles*, which Shakespeare used as a source for *Henry IV Part II*, *Cymbeline* and other plays. Holinshed condemns with some force writers who used inappropriate myths of the founding of Britain, declaring irritably,

most of all they erre in that endevour to fetch it from Albine the imagined daughter of a forged Dioclesian, wherein our ignorant writers have of late not a little stained our historie.[50]

---

[44] The story of Brutus and Gogmagog also surfaces in the Anglo-Norman prose romance *Fouke Fitz Waryn*. Gogmagog is slain in the Payn Peverel episode and a devil enters his body. Thomas E. Kelly, 'Fouke Fitz Waryn', in *Medieval Outlaws*, ed. Thomas H. Ohlgren (Stroud, 1998), pp. 106–67, pp. 113–15.

[45] 'Gogmagog's Hill (Cambridgeshire) was called Windlebury beforetime'. William Harrison, *A Description of England* (1576), ed. Georges Edelen (Ithaca, New York, 1968), p. 224. No explanation is suggested for the change of name.

[46] Frederick W. Fairholt, *Gog and Magog: The Giants in Guildhall* (London, 1859). The *Recordatorium* is lost.

[47] *Haec prius a Bruto in similitudinem magnae Trojae condita est quam illa a Remo et Romulo; unde adhuc ejusdem antiquae civitatis Trojae libertibus, juribus, et consuetudinibus utitur.* Munimenta Gildhallae Londoniensis: *Liber Albus, Liber Customarum, Liber Horn*, ed. Henry Thomas Riley, 2 vols. (London, 1860), vol. 1, *Liber Albus*, p. 61.

[48] Victor I. Scherb, 'Assimilating Giants: The Appropriation of Gog and Magog in Medieval and Early Modern England', *Journal of Medieval and Early Modern Studies*, vol. 32, no.1 (Winter 2002), 59–84.

[49] John Trussell, *Touchstone of Tradition* (1617), condemned those who 'haue endeavoured to question the truth' of the Brutus myth. Hampshire Records Office, W/KI/12, f.19ʳ.

[50] Raphael Holinshed, *The First Volume of the Chronicles of England, Scotlande, and Ireland*, 2nd edn (1587), p. 3.

The objections perhaps explain why the Albina myth disappeared. Nevertheless, Shakespeare would have known it and the controversy surrounding it. Indeed, much of the imagery he uses in *The Tempest* seems chosen to prompt a Jacobean audience to recall Albina, Gogmagog and Brutus, the controversy over the myth, and its significance in the context of Jacobean religious and political sensitivity.

It is not hard to read *The Tempest* in terms of the Albina story. Sycorax, for 'mischiefs manifold and sorceries terrible',[51] was exiled and shipped off to the unnamed island. Her monstrous son Caliban was fathered by a devil, and she was 'grown into a hoop'. Although Prospero claims it is through age and envy, the image is still of a grossly fat female,[52] like Albina and her overfed sisters. However, Prospero implies that Sycorax's lust was directed towards the reluctant Ariel when he reminds the airy spirit 'thou wast a spirit too delicate / To act her earthy and abhorred commands' (1.2.284). The Jacobean audience would have known Satan's title: 'prince of the power of the air',[53] so despite Ariel's comic reluctance,[54] this airy spirit is still an echo of the demonic Incubus that the *Chronicles* assert took a body of air and the nature of men in order to impregnate Albina and her sisters.[55] After Sycorax's death, Caliban inherits the island, which is then wrested from him by an invader who makes him live in a cave.[56] Although there is no evidence that Caliban lived in one previously, nor that he built, as the originary giants built walls and ditches, nevertheless, the relationships and intertextual echoes imply his equivalence to the giant Gogmagog,[57] and, by reference to the printed *Chronicles* at least, confirm his peaceful prior tenure of the island.[58]

There are admittedly problems with using the Albina myth as an interpretive tool for *The Tempest*. Sycorax originates from Algiers, but although the Syrian version of the myth would have been known from the English *Chronicles* and from Caxton's edition of *The Canterbury Tales*, Algiers would have been just as exotic and would have had more entertaining political significance for the Jacobean audience than Syria. Algiers, like Tunis, had been under

Catholic (Spanish) control in the mid-sixteenth century and was linked to Milan and Naples. Philip II of Spain, who was also King of Naples and Duke of Milan, had lost the North African territories in the second half of the sixteenth century and had been unable to regain control of them, much to the displeasure of Pope Pius IV.[59] Sycorax, moreover, is not the only character in the play to reach the island by boat. The resonance between Prospero's tale and *The Man of Law's Tale* signals a Christian aspect to his biography, casting him, briefly, as evangelical victim. Prospero and Miranda were set adrift in an uncontrollable ship,[60] and their circumstances resemble those of Constance and her

[51] William Shakespeare, *The Tempest*, ed. Virginia Mason Vaughan and Alden T. Vaughan (London, The Arden Shakespeare 3rd series, 1999), 1.2.264. All quotations are from this edition.

[52] Shakespeare, *The Tempest*, 1.2.258–9. There is no evidence in the *OED* nor in other plays by Shakespeare that anything other than horizontal rotundity is implied by 'hoop' at this time.

[53] 'Ye walked according to the . . . prince of the power of the air, the spirit that now worketh in the children of disobedience', Eph. 2:2

[54] Comic because it suggests that Sycorax is so fat this minor incubus is deterred.

[55] 'þe Deuyll . . . nome bodyes of þᵉ eyre & likyng natures shad of men, & come into þᵉ land of Albyon and lay by þe wymmen.' *The Brut, or The Chronicles of England*, ed. Friedrich W. D. Brie, part 1, EETS os131 (London, 1906), p. 4.

[56] Caliban complains to Prospero: 'you sty me / In this hard rock' (1.2.343–4).

[57] His knowledge of the island's resources: the plants, berries, and springs also echo the resources Albina and her sisters initially lived on.

[58] *The Chronicles of England* and the *St. Alban's Chronicles* (1485), STC 9995, printed by Julian Notary (1515), STC 9986, and Wynkyn de Worde (1528), STC 10002, all assert the peaceful prior tenure of the giants.

[59] Peter Pierson, *Philip of Spain* (London, 1975), pp. 66 and 152. By 1591, originating from Milan, Pope Clement XIV known in England as Philip's 'milanoise vassal'. See *A Declaration of Great Troubles Pretended Against the Realme*, Bodleian Library, Arch Bodl. G.C.6, 18 October 1591. STC 565.

[60] Prospero declares he is set adrift, not assassinated, because 'So dear the love my people bore me' (1.2.141). The mitigation of the punishment of Albina and her sisters is cast as a similar rejection of excessive violence in *The Brut*, where the king their father 'wolde hem all haue brent; but alle þe

child. Their ship is provisioned and Prospero claims to be innocent of any sin, except the desire for occult knowledge.

Equally problematic is Prospero's assertion that Sycorax is a witch. This could be merely spiteful slander in support of his claim to the island. In *The Man of Law's Tale*, Constance is defamed as an evil spirit, and her infant son is called a monster, but this is a malicious lie.[61] However, Ariel and Caliban support Prospero's assertion. The airy spirit acknowledges that he had been imprisoned in a tree. Caliban's ineffectual curse is less convincing evidence but certainly suggests Sycorax's occult activity when he says:

> As wicked dew as e'er my mother brushed
> With raven's feather from unwholesome fen
> Drop on you both.
>
> (1.2.322–34)

Furthermore, in early modern terms mating with a devil was characteristic of a witch.[62] Caliban is born of this union and is thus the dramatic descendant of the giant Gogmagog, the adversary of God. However, in spite of his parentage, he has no magic or occult powers; his curse, unlike Prospero's, has no effect, a detail worthy of note in the light of Keith Thomas's observation that

In Shakespeare's plays, the curses pronounced by the characters invariably work. This is not just for dramatic effect; it was a moral necessity that the poor and injured should be believed to have this power of retaliation when all else failed.[63]

Caliban's impotent expressions of violence bring him closer to the earlier tradition of peaceful giants who had prior possession of their island, inherited from monstrous mothers, and could not drive out the invaders. In addition, although demonic paternity and adversarial condition were well known attributes of the Antichrist, despite these characteristics, Caliban does not show any of the Antichrist's other defining features. He does not perform any of the tricks or false miracles for which the Antichrist was famed. He does not create storms, upturn trees, or raise the dead, all of which are actions associated with the Antichrist in all the versions of

his biography from Adso's eleventh-century treatise to the late fifteenth-century Chester *Play of Antichrist*. Caliban may be viewed, therefore, from a mythical perspective, as a descendant of the usurped and hitherto peaceful giant, but he may also be seen from an eschatological perspective in terms of the deceived undifferentiated figure of the apocalypse.

A number of medieval and early modern plays of the Antichrist have been identified.[64] The earliest is the massive twelfth-century Tegernsee Play.[65] The medieval English representative is the Chester play, in which Antichrist boasts of his ability to invert trees, open graves and resurrect the dead. This play is included in the five manuscripts of the complete Chester cycle dating from 1591 to 1607.[66] By reference to this earlier tradition *The Tempest* may be considered as a more subtle version of Antichrist drama in which the eschatological pre-occupations of early modern Protestant England are conflated with the Albina myth in a series of semiotically complex and unstable but familiar images.

All the actions that traditionally characterized the Antichrist are those which Prospero in his renunciation speech declares he has previously performed. He boasts,

---

barouns & lordes of Sirrye conseilyd hym not so for-to don suche sternys to his owne doughtres.' *The Brut* ed. Brie, 4.

61 *The Riverside Chaucer*, ed. Benson, *MLT*, lines 743–79.

62 Keith Thomas, *Religion and the Decline of Magic* (London, 1971), p. 521.

63 Thomas, *Religion and the Decline of Magic*, p. 605.

64 Klaus Aichele finds twenty-five Antichrist plays across Europe during the Reformation and Counter-reformation, but does not identify *The Tempest* as one. See Klaus Aichele, *Der Antichristdrama des Mittlealters, Reformation, und Gegenreformation* (Den Haag, 1974). See also, Richard Emmerson, *Antichrist in the Middle Ages* (Seattle, 1981).

65 Alboin who revised Adso's *Libellus c.* 1026 was abbot of Tegernsee. It is hardly surprising then that the earliest play emerged from this location.

66 David Mills, 'Chester', in *The Cambridge Companion to Medieval English Theatre*, ed. Richard Beadle (Cambridge, 1994), p. 110. The play alone is in the late fifteenth-century Peniarth ms.

I have bedimmed
The noontide sun, called forth the mutinous winds,
And 'twixt the green sea and the azured vault
Set roaring war; to the dread-rattling thunder
Have I given fire and rifted Jove's stout oak
With his own bolt: the strong-based promontory
Have I made shake, and by the spurs plucked up
The pine and cedar; graves at my command
Have waked their sleepers, ope'd and let 'em forth
By my so potent art.

(5.1.41–50)

His subsequent promise to Alonso to 'bring forth a wonder' takes the form of Ferdinand's apparent 'resurrection' (5.1.70), a stage trick like the 'resurrections' in the Chester play. In addition, the torments the Antichrist is prophesied to inflict on the faithful in all versions of his biography are, in part, those of which Caliban complains in homely terms. Ancient tradition asserts that during Antichrist's reign, 'every Christian who is discovered will either deny God or perish in the fire of the furnace, or by the sword, or by snakes or wild animals, or by some other kind of torment'.[67] Caliban does not suffer the capital punishments associated with apostasy and religious dissent which are suggested by references to the fiery furnace and the sword, but complains of Prospero's spirits,

For every trifle they are set upon me:
Sometime like apes that mow and chatter at me
And after bite me, then like hedgehogs which
Lie tumbling in my barefoot way and mount
Their pricks at my footfall. Sometime am I
All wound with adders, who with cloven tongues
Do hiss me into madness.

(2.2.8–14)

I have argued elsewhere that Caliban's torments may be read in terms of contemporary deprivation,[68] but an eschatological interpretation relates closely to the wider politico-religious situation of England in the early seventeenth century. Caliban's torment may be read through apocalyptic imagery to shed new light on the extent to which his characterization reflects the giant adversary of God. He is troubled by visions of apes, a colloquial reminder of apocalyptic deception: the Devil, because of his perverted nature, was called God's ape.[69] An even more familiar image of the Devil as a serpent takes the homely form of the adders with cloven tongues, and demonic deceit is again implicit in this nightmarish vision.

Insofar as his characterization echoes the legends of Gogmagog, Caliban may suggest the barbaric giant usurped by a violent invader. He may also be considered in terms of the *wiðersaca*, the enemy of God, as he was seduced into being Prospero's willing servant. As Gog and Magog are deceived by Satan and serve his purpose Caliban is deceived into servitude by Prospero who then usurps his autonomy; his enslavement is the extreme form of this servitude. In his folly, or innocence, Caliban recalls male characters in earlier drama who were allegorical representations of the English nation. Commynnalte, son of the widow Englande in John Bale's *King Johan* (1538, revised 1560),[70] and People, in *Respublica* (1553),[71] are also intimidated by illegitimate authority. However, if Caliban is considered in terms of Gog and Magog, the undifferentiated servants of Antichrist, his relationship with Prospero suggests the conflict of the end of days, but while his negative signification is enhanced through this relationship with Prospero, the Antichristian aspect of the magus's characterization is confirmed. Although together they imply eschatological

---

[67] See for example *Liber Anselmi de Antichristo*: *Tunc omnis christianus, qui unuentus fuerit, aut Deum negabit, aut siue per ignem fornacis, siue per ferrum, siue per serpentes, siue per bestias, siue per aliud quodlibet genus tormentorum, iteribit*. Adso Dervensis, *Ortu et Tempore Antichristi*, ed. Verhelst, 163. My translation. The insular writer known as Pseudo Anselm took the version of Adso's work written by Alboin and altered the mode to address a public audience. The text was frequently copied. A version from Worcester Cathedral library was lost in 1624 en route to London. Adso Dervensis, *Ortu et Tempore Antichristi*, ed. Verhelst, 156.

[68] Lynn Forest-Hill, 'Prospero's Art: Magic or Mycotoxicology', *Times Literary Supplement*, 23 April 2004, pp. 12–13.

[69] Stuart Clark, *Thinking with Demons* (Oxford, 1997), Chapter 6, 'The Devil, God's Ape'.

[70] John Bale, *King Johan*, ed. Peter Happé, *The Complete Plays of John Bale 1* (Cambridge, 1985), lines 1548–1600.

[71] *Respublica*, ed. W. W. Greg, *EETS* os 226 (London, 1952), 5.7.1580–1605.

conflict, a comment perhaps on the turmoil of the Reformation, when Prospero torments Caliban the slave's negative characterization is redefined by eschatological legend and insular mythology. Caliban, the earlier inhabitant, in the tradition of the peaceful giant freely inhabiting his own land, who then willingly serves an invader, evokes an image of the Christian English nation as first misguided, and then persecuted, by a demonic tormentor.

Beginning with Adso's treatise on the Antichrist, the coming of this enemy of God was a recurring image deployed to address politically contentious situations.[72] In England in 1014 Archbishop Wulfstan's *Sermo Lupi ad Anglos* warned the English that the Danish raids were a sign of the Antichrist's coming because of the disobedience and sins of the people.[73] Wulfstan cites Gildas's earlier warning to the British that God would give victory to the Angles because of the laziness of priests and bishops.[74] This sense of a Christian nation wilfully bringing about its own suffering echoes in *The Tempest*, where the division of the Albina and Antichrist myths between Prospero and Caliban delineates their shared but unequal culpability. As the learned magus and male conqueror, Prospero may have offered Jacobean audiences a comforting image of the imposition of patriarchal order on an island formerly in the chaotic state of being ruled by successive Others – an Albina figure and her monstrous offspring.[75] But this magisterial image of Prospero is challenged by his characterization as the violent colonizer, expressed in his threat to Ariel, which reiterates Sycorax's cruel spell, and the violent exchanges he initiates with Caliban, even before it is disrupted by the eschatological revelations of his renunciation speech. In Caliban's case, his enslavement seems justified by his assault on Miranda. Like Grendel, he is depicted as a resentful outcast, but unlike Gogmagog or Grendel, he once participated as a willing servant in a loving relationship with the object of his hatred.

In addition to the standard view that Prospero's renunciation speech derives from Ovid's *Metamorphoses*, well-known Christian traditions reveal the presence of Antichristian attributes in this speech. A Protestant Jacobean audience would not only

have perceived the fashionable humanist Ovidian source but would also have been able to identify the more familiar and traditional references in it to the Antichrist's 'false miracles' for which Prospero's magic may be regarded as a euphemism.[76] That audience would also have been familiar with the religious and political conflict attributed to the Antichrist in sixteenth and seventeenth-century England when this character was constantly used as a metaphor for the abuse of power by the papacy.[77]

In *The Obedience of a Christian Man*, in 1528, William Tyndale remarked that 'we borrow likenesses or allegories of the Scriptures . . . to express our miserable captivity and persecution under antichrist the pope'.[78] The conflation of the Antichrist with the Pope in Protestant polemic also served as a metaphor for usurped power. As the Antichrist usurped the role of Christ, so, Protestants alleged, the Pope usurped the power of temporal monarchs. Indeed, Cranmer said at his trial that 'he had devoted . . . many years to proving

---

[72] Bernard McGinn, *Apocalyptic Spirituality* (London, 1979), 87.

[73] *Ne dohte hit nu lange inne ne ute, ac wæs here and hete on gewelhwilcan ende oft and gelome, and Engle nu lange eal sigelease and to swyþe geyrigde þurh Goddes yrre, and flotmen swa strange þurh Godes þafunge þæt oft on gefeohte an feseð tyne and . . . eal for urum synnum.* Wulfstan, *De Antichristo*, ed. Bethurum, *Homilies*, 106. Quoted by permission of the Oxford University Press.

[74] *An þeodwita wæs on Brytta tidum, Gildas hatte, se awrat be heora misdædum, hu hy mid heorasynnum swa oferlice swyþe God gegræmedan þæt he let æt nyhstan Engla here heora eard gewinnan and Brytta dygeþe fordon mid ealle . . . þurh biscopa asolcnesse and þurh lyðre yrðhe Godes bydela þe soþes geswugedan ealle to gelome and clumedan mid ceaflum þær hy scoldan clypian.* Wulfstan, *De Antichristo*, ed. Bethurum, 92. Quoted by permission of the Oxford University Press.

[75] Bernau, 'Problematic Origins'.

[76] William Tyndale had commented on the Church's use of Latin 'as a form of magic'. David Daniell, *William Tyndale: A Biography* (New Haven, 1994), p. 44.

[77] For the Elizabethan interest in the Antichrist, see Peter Lake, 'The Significance of the Elizabethan Identification of the Pope as Antichrist', *Journal of English History*, 31 (1980), 161–78.

[78] William Tyndale, *The Obedience of a Christian Man*, Christian Classics Series V (London, n.d.), p. 271.

that the Pope was Antichrist (the particular mark of whom was usurped power over princes)'.[79] By 1609 King James was using the same identification in his own anti-papal treatise *An Apologie for the Oath of Allegiance* and with some justification.[80] In opposition to James's assertion of divine right, the political theories of leading continental Jesuits such as Juan de Mariana and Cardinal Robert Bellarmine proposed the legitimacy of regicide.[81] In 1610 James engaged in public controversy with the Cardinal over his treatise *De potestate summi pontificis in rebus temporalibus*, in which he asserted the pope's right to depose monarchs.[82]

Although Prospero presents himself as rightful ruler of the Island, Caliban's complaints of usurpation can be upheld by reference to the well-known myths and chronicle traditions. In the context of Bellarmine's assertions a threat to the body politic may then be perceived as the Antichristian aspect of Prospero's persona, alluding to a view of the papacy as a threat to the authority of the rightful monarch, which simultaneously inflicts oppression upon the native Christian population. Prospero's occult practices and oppression hint at the abuses of power of which the Roman Catholic Church stood accused by Protestants, while Caliban may be read as the abused population awed but resentful of its authority.[83] From within these politicized contexts, their relationship then redefines the relationship between the Catholic Church and the faithful as that between a tyrannical master and his rebellious slave and in turn contextualizes Prospero's comment concerning Caliban: 'this thing of darkness I / Acknowledge mine' (5.1.275–6). The proprietorial confession offers a view of the Catholic Church as unwilling to relinquish its grasp on the English people, and defines its responsibility for those it has oppressed, and who rebel against it.

Caliban is not a comfortable metaphor for the English nation's devotion to the Catholic Church, but this characterization is significant in the context of sixteenth and early seventeenth-century attempts to strengthen the legitimacy of the Protestant Church. John Bale commented on the 'purity of the ancient British Church', in his *Vocation* of 1553,[84] contrasting it with later Roman Catholicism, and in the same cause, William Camden in his *Britannia*,[85] drew attention to the continuation of the first English Church.[86] Although he deplores the Albina myth, Camden's historical work nevertheless echoes Chaucer's and Trevet's revision of the story. Both medieval writers note the existence of British Christianity before the arrival of the Roman Church symbolized by Constance the daughter of Rome, and Camden reports that Halyston in Northumberland was regarded as the place where 'Paulinus in the primitive Church of the English nation baptized many thousands.'[87] From this perspective, Caliban's resentful recollection of Prospero's former affection offers a brief lyrical metaphor for the relationship between that

---

[79] Diarmaid MacCulloch, *Thomas Cranmer* (New Haven, 1996), p. 576.

[80] Bernard Capp remarks 'It was a major step for a reigning monarch to give public endorsement to Protestant apocalyptic teaching'. Capp, 'The political dimension of apocalyptic thought', in *The Apocalypse in English Renaissance Thought and Literature*, ed. C. A. Patrides and Joseph Wittreich (Manchester, 1984), pp. 93–124, 102.

[81] Juan de Mariana's *De rege et regis institutione* (1599) put forward the thesis of the 'permissability of regicide'. John W. O'Malley, *The First Jesuits* (Cambridge, Mass., 1993), pp. 233–4. W. B. Patterson, *King James VI and I and the Reunion of Christendom*, Cambridge Studies in Early British History (Cambridge, 1997), p. 93. Robert Miola mentions very briefly Mariana and Suarez, but does not note their significance with respect to *The Tempest*, nor does he mention Bellarmine. See Miola, *Shakespeare's Reading* (Oxford, 2000), p. 45.

[82] David Wootton, ed., *Divine Right and Democracy* (London, 1986), p. 92.

[83] Caliban's complaint that he is tormented by adders recalls earlier Protestant polemic in which 'adder' was used as a term of abuse for the Catholic clergy. See for example, John Bale, *King Johan*, ed. Happé, lines 2428–30.

[84] Peter Happé, *John Bale* (New York, 1996), p. 38.

[85] First published in 1586. Last edited by Camden himself in 1607. Hugh Trevor-Roper, *Elizabeth's First Historian* (London, 1971), p. 8.

[86] Trevor-Roper, *Elizabeth's First Historian*, p. 6.

[87] William Camden, *Britain, or a Chorographicall Description of England, Scotland, and Ireland*, trans P. Holland, 2 parts (London, 1610), p. 813. Paulinus was consecrated bishop in A.D. 625. Bede, *A History of the English Church and People*, trans. Leo Sherley-Price, rev. R. E. Latham (London, 1955), p. 115.

early Church and the people. Caliban reminds Prospero

> When thou cam'st first,
> Thou strok'st me and made much of me; wouldst give me
> Water with berries in't . . .
> And then I loved thee.

(1.2.333–7)

This image of reciprocal affection challenges both the interpretation of Caliban as the violent originary giant and that of Prospero as the brutal colonizer. Nevertheless, this invader, later configured in Antichristian terms, usurps Caliban's inheritance, and it is against this that Caliban rebels, his violence, like that of the giants in *De origine gigantum* and the later *Chronicles*, being directed against the usurping oppressor.

So we return to Caliban's assault on Miranda. Although the play does not encourage allegorical readings, this attack may be read allegorically as both an attempt to gain control of the island, and an attack on the Roman Catholic Church. The image of the nubile daughter may be approached from two ancient and allegorical traditions. The mythical and secular tradition perceives the land allegorically as female and as the bride of the ruler. The biblical and allegorical tradition uses the image of the daughter as the Church, which is the bride of Christ.[88] Both perspectives suggest potentially political interpretations of Miranda's relationships with Caliban and Prospero. As an allegorical representation of the island, she is desired by Caliban but controlled and denied to him by her father, the usurper; this depiction of patriarchal control then problematizes the interpretation of Miranda's relationships from within the Christian allegorical tradition.

As Constance symbolizes the church in *The Man of Law's Tale*, Miranda too may be read as symbolizing the Church, but her role in the play suggests the problematic view of the Roman Catholic Church as the dependent of the papacy that controls it. Reformers such as Tyndale and Bale distinguished the 'papal church' from the church of Protestantism,[89] and this distinction is significant for its implication of papal control. Insofar as Miranda may be taken to reflect the familiar image of the Church, she is not defined by her relationship to Christ but by the control of her earthly father, with all his echoes of pagan magic and eschatological arrogance. Nevertheless, in his assault on Miranda, Caliban evokes an image of culpable English violence against that Church. His culpability, punishment and rebellion then offer a comment on the condition of the nation that fell temporarily into the role of Gog and Magog – God's lesser adversaries and servants of the Antichrist, who engage in a conflict that is typical of the end of days.

However, by the end of the play, Caliban is no longer rebellious. His willingness to serve Prospero again not only takes place in the context of Prospero withdrawing from the island, but signifies Caliban's acceptance of his place in what is now a temporary insular hierarchy. His reaffirmation of obedience to an oppressive master should be seen in terms of the traditional theory that tyrants were God's punishment on a sinful people.[90] After his humiliating devotion to the clowns, and still awed by Prospero, he declares 'I'll be wise hereafter / And seek for grace' (5.1.295–6). This brief reference not only acknowledges Caliban's acceptance

---

[88] In biblical allegory, 'daughter' signifies the Church of God, Ps. 45: 9, 10; Cant. 5: 8. Alexander Cruden, *A Complete Concordance to the Holy Scriptures of the Old and New Testament* (London, 1831). St Augustine commented on the Song of Songs and described 'the marriage of the king and queen . . . namely Christ and his Church.' St Augustine, *City of God*, trans. Henry Bettenson (London, 1984), p. 757. In spite of Protestant complaints regarding Catholic glossing and exegesis, the King James or Authorized Version of the Bible retains in its chapter heading the interpretation of the Song of Solomon as the mutual love between the Church and Christ.

[89] David Daniell, *William Tyndale: A Biography*, p. 207. Bale called it the 'churche of the pope'. Happé, *Bale*, p. 50.

[90] King James reiterated the view when he wrote 'I grant in deede that a wicked king is sent by GOD for a cursse to his people, and a plague for their sinnes. But that it is lawfull to them to shake off that cursse at their owne hande, which God has lain on them, that I denie.' James VI and I, *The Trve Lawe of Free Monarchies* (1598), in James Craigie, ed., *Minor Prose Works of King James VI and I* (Edinburgh, 1982), p. 77.

of the will of God, but simultaneously introduces the difference between Catholic and Protestant doctrine concerning the need for God's grace in order to be saved,[91] and signals religious differentiation between the usurper and the usurped native.[92] Prospero has already renounced his most superstitious practices that connote the Antichristian aspect of his characterization and concomitantly the usurping power of the papacy: the storms, inversion of trees and resurrections, and he is leaving the island.[93] He nevertheless appears obstinately Catholic in his need for the prayers of others when he begs the audience in his Epilogue, 'release me from my bands / With the help of your good hands.' He then tells them, 'my ending is despair / Unless I be relieved by prayer' (Epilogue 9–10, 15–16). These comments suggest continuing adherence to the old religion with its belief in the power of other people's prayers to aid the soul of the deceased through the pains of Purgatory. They therefore engage with the 1606 Oath of Allegiance that was 'intended to separate Roman Catholics who adhered to the doctrine that a pope could depose a temporal ruler from Roman Catholics who did not hold this view and could be therefore considered loyal subjects'.[94] This implication of unreformed Roman Catholicism sets Prospero apart from Caliban, who, like a good Protestant, will seek for grace personally.[95]

The train of revelation that emerges in *The Tempest* may be seen as mimetic of the process by which the nation moved from the earliest form of 'primitive' Christianity, to willing servitude under Roman Catholic hegemony, through awakening resentment, to a more rational selfhood grounded in the Protestant doctrine of grace. By looking back to literary traditions, Caliban's prior claim to the Island is established in mythical terms and Prospero takes on the characteristics of an Antichrist figure as well as a usurper: a perversion of the evangelical Constance. The magic he uses has long polarized critical opinion. It has been read as benign white magic used to bring about reconciliation,[96] but it has also been seen as black magic used to torment and terrify,[97] in the tradition of the *maleficium*

that defined witchcraft throughout its history.[98] This darker interpretation of Prospero's magic is consistent with, and enhanced by, the eschatological references even more than by the Medea connection that taints him with pagan witchcraft. His Antichristian aspect is thus an extension of his equivocal role as magus that also comments on papal intervention in British politics. Caliban, however, insofar as he may be considered a dramatic descendant of Gogmagog, is not without blame. Like Gildas's Britons and Wulfstan's English, he is punished for his sins: his violence, rebellion, and disobedience. The same sense of the nation being punished occurs in a pamphlet of 1607 describing the inundation of large parts of southwest England and Wales. The anonymous author exhorts 'England, be not ouercome with thine owne folly . . . neyther sinke thou thy selfe in thine owne sinne; For since . . . the time of Noy, neuer the like Inundation or watery punishment then hapned . . . as by this sequell it shall heare appear.'[99] However, although Caliban is

---

91 *The Book of Common Prayer*, The Articles of Religion, articles XI and XII, cited the Protestant view of grace.

92 In 1586 and 1593 Bellarmine had published a statement of Catholic doctrine including grace. See Philip Caraman, *Henry Garnet 1555–1606 and the Gunpowder Plot* (London, 1964), p. 17

93 Prospero also destroys his book of 'magic' in the same year that the new Authorized Version of the Bible displaced the older Bishop's Bible and Geneva Bible.

94 W. B. Patterson, *King James VI and I and the Reunion of Christendom*, Cambridge Studies in Early Modern British History (Cambridge, 1997), p. 124.

95 The opposing doctrines had long been controversial. In 1534 Cranmer stipulated that no one should preach for a year either for or against the view that 'faith only justifieth', since these 'things have caused dissension amongst the subjects of the realm already.' Nicholas Tyacke, ed., *England's Long Reformation 1500–1800* (London, 1998), p. 6.

96 See for example, John Mebane who refers to Prospero as 'Benevolent Artist'. Mebane, *Renaissance Magic and the Return of the Golden Age* (Lincoln, Nebraska, 1989), p. 180.

97 See for example, Stephen Greenblatt, *Shakespearean Negotiations* (Oxford, 1988), p. 143.

98 Thomas, *Religion and the Decline of Magic*, p. 519.

99 *God's Warning to His People of England* (London, 1607), STC 10011.

sinful and tainted by association with the Antichrist myth this association also defines him as victim of both apocalyptic deception and of political usurpation.

The traditions of insular literature, and particularly the Albina myth, open up suggestive new perspectives on *The Tempest* and the relationship between its ambiguous main characters. These perspectives have hitherto been obscured by theories derived from twentieth-century politics, and by a persistent critical emphasis on interpretations from classical tradition. They would nevertheless have been familiar to the early modern audience. Shakespeare's division of the myth between Sycorax and Prospero is not exact, because that would engage too closely with early-modern controversy surrounding the origins of Britain, but it provides insights into other areas of controversy,[100] as well as illuminating the characterizations of Caliban, Sycorax, and Prospero. The dramatic recapitulation of the ancient foundation myth may also have been taken as an allusion to the unifying presence of James VI and I on the throne of England. While Jacobean audiences would have recognized the echoes of the secular myth, the familiarity of Shakespeare and his audience with eschatological myth is not an issue in this reading. In addition to the eschatological pre-occupations of the prevailing official Protestantism, Shakespeare and his audience, 'lived in a world still permeated with a Catholic vision of life expressed through traditions developed over centuries'.[101] The conflation of the Antichrist with the pope, and their association with usurped power had long been a Protestant motif and had grown in political popularity in the early Jacobean era; but Shakespeare does not create overt anti-papal propaganda in *The Tempest*. Nor does he satirize a contemporary pre-occupation with anti-Catholicism, as Ben Jonson did in 1610 when the Puritan Ananias, in *The Alchemist*, tells Surly the gambler 'Thou look'st like Antichrist in that lewd hat.'[102] The eschatological myth provides a trenchant means of apportioning blame from within the contexts that governed early modern religious controversy. Although time and changing culture may have obscured them from us, Shakespeare's allusions and their political potential would have been accessible to a Jacobean audience familiar with both the Albina and the Antichrist traditions and this approach via insular literary tradition illuminates further the complex hermeneutics of *The Tempest*, enabling a view of the play's reflection of the politically sensitive issues of the day, just as the Albina and Antichrist myths had traditionally been used.

---

[100] Virginia and Alden Vaughan have observed 'Controversy has marked the play almost from the outset.' Vaughan and Vaughan, eds, *The Tempest*, p. 1.

[101] Velma Bourgeois Richmond, *Shakespeare, Catholicism, and Romance* (New York, 2000), p. 16.

[102] *Ben Jonson: Four Comedies*, ed., Helen Ostovich (Harlow, 1997), *The Alchemist*, 4.7.55.

SHAKESPEARE'S AGES

RUTH MORSE

Most of this article teases out Shakespeare's ideas about pasts, and sets those ideas in verbal and intellectual context. The latter part is therefore directly concerned with the implications of periodization, and the long history of recruiting period appellations to suit the present. I am particularly concerned with the consequential estrangement of a 'Middle Ages', because I believe we are moving to an intellectual position where ignorance encourages sweeping generalization. Our over-arching tri-partite model (Antique, Medieval, Modern) threatens to turn convenient strategies into unexamined certainties and anachronisms. To begin with a polemical contradiction: there were no Middle Ages but we cannot do without them. In the sense we think we know, 'Middle Ages' is, like Shakespeare's birthday, a modern invention; the 'middles' of our inherited period label were shifting signifiers whose denotations and connotations changed with passing time. Shakespeare wrote about *what we call* a middle ages, but which he did not, because he could not. When we discuss history, or Shakespeare's history, or 'history plays', we are constantly caught in the problem of using the word-to-be-defined as part of the definition, and Shakespeare is part of what created that definition. Thus, if we go looking for 'a middle ages', in the *OED*, for example, we will certainly find one, but we may then fail to see what we think we recognize. Shakespeare may have written about events which we think happened in the middle ages, but *he* cannot so have conceptualized them. Our middle ages were still in the future. Shakespeare refers to a ground bass of pastness which is not our sense

of historical periodization – but it is not a continental European sense either.

If we are to believe the *OED*, and what scholar does not?, the first appearance in English of 'the middle age' in the sense relevant to this discussion comes in a sermon on 1 Timothy 15: 'It is a perplex'd question in The School (and truly the Balance in those of the middle age, very even) whether if Adam had not sinned, the son of God had come into the world, and taken our nature and our flesh upon him.' The citation is from Donne, and when he preached that sermon, Shakespeare had been dead for five years.[1] The middle age, *le moyen âge*, comes into English as both singular and plural, and by the early eighteenth century English has settled, happily, although inconsistently, for the plural.[2] We are all well aware of the dangers of anachronism in thinking about Shakespeare's inheritance from and attitude to 'the' Middle Ages, but

---

I am particularly grateful to Professors Sukanta and Supriya Chaudhuri for their invitation to give an early version of this chapter at a seminar at Jadhavpur University in Calcutta. As always, I thank Professor Stefan Collini for careful reading of the text.

[1] An earlier citation from Thomas James, Bodley's first librarian, was said to appear in *A Treatise on the Corruption of Scripture, Councels, and Fathers*, Advt. to the Christian Reader, *3: 'The open or secret wrongs done unto Fathers, auncient, *middle-aged*, or moderne writers by the Papists' (1611, not used by *OED*).

[2] See G. S. Gordon, '*Medium Aevum* and The Middle Age', *Society for Pure English Tract*, 19 (Oxford, 1925), pp. 1–25. Fragmentation can be an advantage, of course, and suggests a category a little more tentative than the singular.

if we start with a phrase or its non-existence, we confront difficulties greater than tracing it might seem to imply. The non-existence of a word does not, of course, disprove the existence of a concept for an early period, but nor does the existence of the word attest the concept, or concepts, or not what we might think. In fact, as it happens, *OED* is wrong, and I shall offer a modest corrective, but I want to begin by explaining why Shakespeare was most unlikely to have had the word or words designating the concept or concepts that most of us probably use. In order to do that, it makes sense to begin with a historical sketch before turning to Shakespeare.

A MONTH OLD AT CAIN'S BIRTH BUT NOT FIVE WEEKS YET

Dull's riddle (*Love's Labour's Lost* 4.2.35) about the moon is a timely reminder, a reminder that time, in agricultural former ages, was largely a matter of days and months, annual seasons as registered in the almanac. In riddle-time, Cain is a story which comprehends permanence, the *constant* moon. Time meant different things to persons of different status, in different places, and the interpretabilities of reference texts could have serious consequences, such as the invasion of France in *Henry V*, 1.2. The comedy of Henry's deference must not distract us from legal and religious searches through unclear chronicles of conflicting pasts; the Archbishop's scholarship is parodic, but it is also not clear what it is a parody *of*: unscrupulous scholarship, perhaps, rather than what we name the instruments or documents of scholarship. In Shakespeare's usage a little learning may be dangerous, but much learning is never safe; like courage in a bad cause, or even meaning itself, learning is only as good – or as bad – as the way it is used, as *Henry VIII*'s multiply-conflicting pasts also make clear. Henry Plantagenet fears that his Archbishop might

> fashion, wrest, or bow your reading,
> Or nicely charge your understanding soul
> With opening titles miscreate, whose right
> Suits not in native colours with the truth.[3]

> (1.2.14–17)

The arguments are geographical, legal and genealogical: the place called Salic is not France; even if the inheritance bar was a precedent there are important precedent exceptions; therefore Henry's genealogical claim is good, even clothed in native colours. The law, elsewhere often appealed to as permanent and unchanging, here appears in its full contradictory glory, consistent with J. G. A. Pocock's descriptions of varying attitudes to the law in the sixteenth century.[4] We might prefer to call the Archbishop's retrospect and examples historical; but no one in the play does so. Shakespeare had been reading Holinshed, but he says nothing of Canterbury's sources (in performance he often has a scroll or a dusty tome to hand); in arguing from legal evidence as contained in charters, Canterbury demonstrates – creates in interpretation – continuity with the past in the sense in which legal precedent represents it. But in the theatre he is equally demonstrating the difficulty of hearing one system of measurement. Canterbury's obfuscation includes mixing types of time reference: arithmetic ('land/Until four hundred one-and-twenty years', 1.2.56–7), incarnational ('year of our redemption/ Four hundred twenty-six' 1.2.60–61, 'river Scale in the year/Eight hundred five' 1.2.64, and 1.2.57), and regnal ('eleventh year of the last king' 1.1.2).[5] British 'chroniclers' tend to speak of reigns since the Conquest. Unusually in Shakespeare, England's Archbishop supports his authority with dates. Canterbury urges the Black Prince's

---

[3] *King Henry VIII (All is True)*, ed. Gordon McMullan (London, 2000).

[4] 'The essence of custom was that it was immemorial, and the argument could with equal facility be used that, since the people retained a given custom through many centuries, it had proved itself apt to meet all the emergencies which had arisen during that period. Custom was *tam antiqua et tam nova*, always immemorial and always perfectly up-to-date', writes J. G. A. Pocock, *The Ancient Constitution* (Cambridge, 1957), p. 15. 'Antiqua' and 'nova' need no further comment.

[5] Understandably enough, starting from modern assumptions about reckoning time, annotators of this scene continue the tradition of correcting the dates, or at least making them coherent. See *Henry V*, ed. Andrew Gurr (Cambridge, 1992); ed. Gary Taylor (Oxford, 1994).

'playing' of 'tragedy' in France against the future writing of 'chronicle' (in a slippery progression of pronouns which function to evade explicit argument). The play, of course, is full of theatrical reference, but so, too, were books about the past: it was a learned question if each age were not implicated in cycles of ambition and fall. The tacit appeal is to the continuities in the law and in the line.

If, then, law, religion and genealogy all militate against rupture, how does Shakespeare divide times and ages, how does he periodize? Are his characters consistent, or have they options? Is the speaker of the Sonnets special? What senses has he of placement in time or contrasts with 'now'? Unsurprisingly, 'Shakespeare' is tacit about periodizing time, even if we equate the man with the voice of the sonnets. Shakespeare's characters characterize time depending on who they are, when and where. Time, like love or the sea, is an abstract force capable of concrete devouring. It might be thought that stage practice would help; although there may be evidence of togas among costumes, there is no clear 'ancient' English dress (what *is* Posthumus's disguise?), and characters refer enough to the varieties of contemporary vestimentary differences, by individual taste, rank or local custom, to reduce time passing to a kind of sumptuary spectrum. In this sense, clocks and togas are conventions more like asides than anachronisms, because they are conventional indications of time, as costumes are of age, status and country of origin. References to architecture are no more precise, including the apparently troublesome monastic ruins around Aaron. The same continuities which preserved Caesar's Tower reached back to Antique orders of priests, translated into the familiar linguistic archaism which conveyed pastness. Ruins were also tourist attractions, including for the Second Goth who caught Aaron because he 'strayed / To gaze upon a ruinous monastery . . . wasted building' (5.1.20–4). Rome is the place where those ruins were thickest. Posthumus is there, too, as well as not there, for his Rome is also confounded with a more contemporary Italy, which located both the enviably continuous Remains which were also the

ruinous waste. When Shakespeare regularly displaces his Italy into Rome he conjures up that combination. If this seems to indicate a very past Antiquity and a continuity to now, that must imply something in between, but not yet a 'Middle' in the period sense.

Ruins matter in this story; they were all around, evidence of time's rage, the disintegration of monuments in stone or brass. Roman roads linked English cities and Saxon and Norman fortifications defined English towns; abandoned villages witnessed to the ravages of natural pestilence, famine and plague; the literal dilapidation of selected monuments of the Old (meaning 'former') Religion marked the countryside while they enriched some of its denizens. This layering of change encourages ideas of cycles, rather than ideas of 'a' middle. Bacon's *Novum Organum* pursues this idea of recurrences, times of the advancement of learning with great troughs of darkness in between. Cycles, almost by definition, are not linear development, and that double-referential descriptive possibility survived and throve. Visual evidence is particularly intriguing where architectural continuity is concerned, since there was clearly an expressive stylistic convention which we call Tudor Gothic. Non-visualized buildings can be important, too. The precocious York Prince of Wales wonders if Julius Caesar built the Tower and asks

> Is it upon record, or else reported
> Successively from age to age he built it? . . .
> But say, my lord, it were not registered,
> Methinks the truth should live from age to age,
> As 'twere retailed to all posterity[6]
>
> (3.1.72–3, 75–8)

Buckingham's polite rewording that Caesar began what 'since succeeding ages have re-edified' (71) is, in context, a dark reference to the Tower's history of executions which both boys instinctively feel. Whether the truth is registered, recorded or retold from age to age, the question is indeed whether the shadow of death contains a promise that what

---

[6] *Richard III*, ed. John Jowett (Oxford, 2000).

is done shall be revealed. But there is no sense of a middle here. Architecture leaps a millennium. If the only artist Shakespeare mentions by name is Giulio Romano, he mentions him in the surprising context of the freshly painted statue of Hermione in *The Winter's Tale*. Yet any backward glance could perceive a sequence of disruptions: colonizing conquest by Romans and Saxons, Danes and Normans; aristocratic civil war; theological controversy once contained but now triumphing over another foreign oppressor. Like Bolingbroke in the secular world, successful rebellion in religion becomes a new legitimacy. Religion, like law, must be *tam antiqua et tam nova*.

Henry worried about misinterpretation, and even a woman, even a young one, could share Henry's – or the Prince of Wales' – doubts about reliability. *As You Like It*'s ages belong to a discourse of analogy and relationship, not to a discourse of history. Rosalind knows the world's age and speaks of 'the foolish chroniclers of that age' with cavalier lack of exactness (4.1.85–98), as Jacques knows the cycles of men's ages, but there is no appeal to specificity or exactitude. Transforming their commonplaces into learned disquisitions is rather the work of editors and scholars, and uncomfortably close to Holofernes.

From *OED* to Concordances, then, the search continues, but each occurrence is in a character's mouth, and is therefore to be discriminated accordingly. What follows can easily be checked in Marvin Spevack's indispensable volume, though one must remember here, too, that one searches in an absence of semantic field.[7] Is there a consistent, non-festive, vocabulary of time passing? A metaphor or a metonym appeals to the imagination and offers a way around particularity. Nothing is less identical than 'likeness'. François Laroque's paradoxical references to festival as an alternative to linear time are themselves situated in pasts which are not exact, but which do allow for ranges of reference.[8] Shakespeare's usual meaning for 'past' is 'previous', and he speaks only rarely of 'the past' (as in Sonnet 123), which is of indefinite distance and duration. 'History' is close to French 'histoire', and often means story, although story which may

be true – like Cesario's sister's. The 'former golden days' which are invoked in *3 Henry VI* (3.3.7) utilise a set expression for subsequent decline, but given that the speaker is Margaret of Anjou there is likely to be a certain irony. Whatever Rosalind or Jacques think, there is no sign that the three or four or seven Ages of the World were useful to Shakespeare (but I shall return to them below in 'The Former Age'). In the Vale of Evesham Falstaff finds nostalgia, but decline is entirely personal. In Shakespeare's characters' perspectives there is often no middle distance – in the Sonnets time is now, recent or eternity. This, too, is personal rather than historical time. Cleopatra likewise juxtaposes now, then, eternity. There is a comfortable vagueness about time, as there is about space, and linguistically the markers belong with 'this, that, t'other' or 'hither, thither, yon' – location by reference to the speaking body. Overall, one can say that in small units Shakespeare has hours (undivided into clock minutes) and days, months and years, but that his precisions are usually imprecise, functioning only to give a sense of specificity without tying him to one, as in the double time-scheme of *Othello* or the felt haste in *The Tempest*. Similarly, although there is the occasional ninth of next month or eleventh of this, Shakespeare's 'date', like 'period' is a fixed point rather than a numbered or labelled day, further modified by the necessities of the equally elastic two hours' traffic. The body's beating pulse offers a polar opposite to a 'scientific' world of chronomensuration.

Like Montaigne, Shakespeare uses 'age' to mean 'a long period of time'. As Margreta de Grazia has stressed, he never uses century to mean one hundred years, and 'thousand' almost always indicates

---

[7] *The Harvard Concordance to Shakespeare* (Cambridge, 1973). I cite book rather than website, because there is a methodological point here about being able to see whole columns of quotation, which must then be recontextualized.

[8] *Shakespeare's Festive World: Elizabethan Seasonal Entertainment and the Professional Stage*, trans. Janet Lloyd (Cambridge, 1991 [orig. *Shakespeare et la fête* (Paris, 1981)]), esp. ch. 7.

a very big number.[9] If he makes few comments on regnal or ecclesiastical dating, or the calendar (which is a synomyn for the almanac), his characters indifferently invoke the commonest festivals: Hollowmas and Holyrood Day (*Richard II* 5.1.80 and 1.1.52 and *Measure for Measure* 2.1.120); Michaelmas, which might have arisen for renting, moving or hiring, appears only twice (*Merry Wives* 1.1.188 and *1 Henry IV* 2.4.54 where it is part of a calculation of age). Church festivals are less apparent than tenacious custom would have led one to expect, though I shall have something to say about [John] Gower's view of them below. We find St David's Day (but not St Andrew's) and St George's; Ophelia sings of St Valentine; there are about four references to Lent/lenten; and only one to Easter (in *Romeo and Juliet*'s Italy – but clearly recognizable in Shakespeare's England); two of the three references to Christmas have to do with the games or shows associated with that holiday; and, of course, King Harry's nostalgic future veterans acquire their speaking wounds on St Crispin's Day.

His father's desire to take the cross recalls that it is fourteen hundred years since Christ lived, which is remarkably exact given Shakespeare's usual practice (1.1.26, quoted above). It is also unusual. In passing it should be remarked that if Shakespeare was a Catholic he was remarkably discreet about his characters' attitudes to the cycles of the year. Reformed 'feast days' are not quite the old Holy Days renamed, but whatever the arguments about observance, they held the calendar in place.[10] Shakespeare is even-handed about the pre-reformed clergy, or clergy elsewhere: Canterbury and Wolsey may be movers, but Friars Lawrence and Francis are good men.

Like everyone around him, Shakespeare knew that what we call Classical Antiquity was different from us, but that is not an awareness different in kind from twelfth or even ninth-century educated men, who also translated vestals into nuns. In historical time, in which medieval men argued the parallels between pagan and Old Testament chronologies, there was a fluidity which was not resolved – because, of course, it was not resolvable. One could sense that Rome declined into Italy,

despite the advantages of Christianity, but Shakespeare is neither a philosopher nor a historian, and he might be said to use what is available rather than to reflect much upon it, as indeed *Cymbeline* suggests. 'Antique' means 'extremely old' for Shakespeare, as 'antiquity' means very long ago, including 'antique Rome' (*Henry V*, Chorus, prologue to Act 5, 26), where the distinction is between the pagan and the Christian cities, as indeed it is when Horatio uses it. The 'Two Cities' have always coincided.

Of the possible practices which might be thought to offer 'measure', it would be very difficult to show that Shakespeare had affiliations with the new learning (as it called itself), despite the inkhornery in *Love's Labour's Lost*. He is not concerned with changes in handwriting, or spelling, and if he himself plays with some of the innovations of early modern English, such as auxiliary 'do' ('They that have pow'r to hurt, and will do none,/Who do not do the thing they most do show', Sonnet 94), or retains conservative features such as the genitive without 's' (as in 'some lady trifles' in *Antony and Cleopatra*), even if he mixes third person singulars in -eth and in -es, there is nothing special in that. The place where we might expect to find a middle ages in Shakespeare is in the legendary Britain of Kings Cymbeline and Lear. But we do not.

THE KING'S ENGLISH

Ancient English authors offer the most promising avenue of enquiry into Shakespeare's possible concepts of the past. English changed. Its

---

[9] 'Fin-de-Siècle Renaissance England', in *Fin de Siècle: English Poetry in 1590, 1690, 1790, 1890, 1990*, ed. Elaine Scarry (Baltimore and London, 1995), pp. 37–63.

[10] As Judith Maltby, among other historians, has recently stressed in work on the slow modification of 'Old Church' practices. See her *Prayer Book and People in Elizabethan and Early Stuart England*, Cambridge Studies in Early Modern British History (Cambridge, 1998) and 'Prayer Book Protestantism in the 1640s-50s', *Studies in Church History*, ed. R. N. Swanson (Woodbridge, Suffolk, 2004). Here, too, gradualism, rather than strong periodization, supports a triumphal Protestant interpretation.

instabilities were a matter of continuous comment from Chaucer's admonition to his scribe. It would appear that Shakespeare (or Shakespeare and Fletcher) knew something about older forms of English, but here, too, there are problems, since it may be Shakespeare's older contemporary, Spenser, whose linguistic re-formations they imitate.[11] Spenser was one among many to insist on the threefold-founder origin-story through which the modern vernaculars claimed cycles of establishment. He had already created a precedent, as well as a method, for inventing, or perhaps reviving, an archaizing style, in *The Shepheardes Calender* and, to a less extent, his *Faerie Queene*, and Shakespeare learned from him. Shakespeare knew two at least of those founding fathers, Chaucer and Gower. In *The Two Noble Kinsmen* the speaker of the Prologue says,

We pray our play may be so [modest], for I am sure
It has a nobler breeder and a pure,
A learned, and a poet never went
More famous yet 'twixt Po and silver Trent.
Chaucer, of all admired, the story gives;
There, constant to eternity, it lives.
If we let fall the nobleness of this
And the first sound this child hear be a hiss,
How will it shake the bones of that good man
And make him cry from under ground, 'Oh, fan
From me the witless chaff of such a writer
That blasts my bays and my famed works makes lighter
Than Robin Hood!'

(Prologue 9–21)[12]

The evidence of *Pericles* is rather more interesting.[13] Shakespeare brings Gower back from dust: 'From ashes auncient Gower is come' announces the poet-chorus. From ancient days, the distant past, ancient Gower, the old story-teller, appears. Vocabulary, syntax and morphology contribute to a cod English which is certainly intended to make style give an impression of pastness. 'Ember eves' and 'holy days', verbs of motion with 'to be', a slightly higher incidence of subject–object–verb order, phrases such as 'I tell you what mine authors say', obsolete vocabulary or vocabulary used in old-fashioned senses (I wis, certainly, peer, wife, benison, derne, attent); careful absence of the

innovative auxiliary 'do'; plurals, infinitives and pasts expressed by the suffix -en (including incorrectly, 'he spoken can' for 'he knows how to speak'); prefix y- to indicate the preterite (y-slacked, y-ravished). These marked words tend to come grouped, further to call attention to themselves, and sometimes the thickness of these evocations becomes quite startling, as 'All perishen of men, of pelf/ Ne aught escapend but himself' (Act 2 Prologue) – and it is quite clear, looking at a sequence of editions, that not all editors have seen what Shakespeare would be at and have corrected or 'clarified' Gower's speech.[14] While Gower's English demonstrates that Shakespeare (or Shakespeare + Wilkins), had some awareness of language change through time, that is not, however, awareness that the past to which Chaucer or Gower belonged might be labelled a Middle Ages. Just as Shakespeare writes country-convention speech without calling it stage yokel, so his archaizing English is never explicitly Old or Middle.

---

[11] The story of Spenser's – and Shakespeare's – Chaucer is told by Alice Miskimin, *The Renaissance Chaucer* (New Haven, 1975) and Ann Thompson, *Shakespeare's Chaucer: a study in literary origins* (Liverpool, 1978).

[12] I quote from the Arden 3rd series edition of Lois Potter (London, 1997); she thinks the prologue is Shakespeare's. Eugene M. Waith's Oxford edition (1987) concurs. Dr Gordon McMullan considers that the section which follows this quotation 'may be a form of *occupatio*, but it seems to me to exhibit a degree of anxiety which is due to a particular conjunction of historicity and Englishness, i.e. an anxiety which would not be produced in the same way by a more recent foreign writer' (p.c.). I am grateful to Dr McMullan not only for a careful reading of this paper, but also for allowing me to read the introduction to his *Henry VIII* before publication.

[13] Ideas of collaboration vary, and I do not think we will ever know who, precisely, is responsible for what. Although a few scholars name Fletcher as Shakespeare's collaborator, Jonathan Hope believes the prologue to be George Wilkins's, in *The Authorship of Shakespeare's Plays: A Socio-Linguistic Study* (Cambridge, 1994), but the prologue contains a shortage of telltale markers such as auxiliary "do", and there are stylistic reasons (archaizing) to make it unlike Shakespeare, Wilkins or Fletcher. See now Dr Hope's *Shakespeare's Grammar* (London, 2003).

[14] As does the Arden series edition of F. D. Hoeniger (London, 1963).

Henry VIII is nicely mixed in its references to men of religion, and to religion, and its characters refer to 'the law' as if there were one thing, and it immemorial; as so often in Shakespeare there is something for everyone, no sharp definitions, and no moment of revolution. Rather, like other plays, *Henry VIII* succeeds in its balance and ambiguities by structural repetitions which elevate ambition and envy over the dangers of discussing doctrine. The question of Reform is necessarily of moment, but it is absorbed in Wolsey's and Gardiner's human and personal machinations, and is made to seem contingent to the play's human dramas. Yet this in turn leads us to consider that the desire to push back the origins of British church reform, erasing any sudden divide which might be deemed innovation rather than restoration, also suggested the potential contradiction of a need for continuity, issues important in *King John* as well as *Henry VIII*. This is also not the place to trace the valorization of the word 'Protestant', or even its history, but quick recourse to *OED* will reveal now-familiar problems. 'Puritan' offers similar vicissitudes, as, for that matter, does 'catholic'. One could write a new history in which England kept the faith throughout benighted times, in the face of foreign opposition.

Relations between King Henry, Cardinal Wolsey and Cranmer capitalize on a series of stresses, not all of which are religious and none of which describe a rupture. What we see is Shakespeare exploiting up-to-date arguments without explicitly naming them. Henry dismisses Wolsey's exaction of a tax because there is no legal precedent, that is, no evidence of custom successive from age to age (1.2.88–94), and Buckingham appeals similarly to the law and then accepts its judgement, if not its justice; when he compares his fate to his father's he makes no distinction of time. Since the action of the play is resolutely present for its participants, the immemorial question is that of betraying one's master, as Wolsey himself eloquently recognizes. So the multiple accusations against Cardinal Wolsey are that he is a 'new' man, and has no guide through descent or upbringing; that, at the same time, he is not only an

upstart, but backed by a foreign power (*Henry VIII*, 2.2.54–6); and that he plays both ends against the middle (the Dukes' accusations in 3.2). He is finally ruined when Henry sees his ambition. Our hindsight emphasizes Rome or Latin as 'Catholicism' at 2.4.233–5 or 3.1.40–50, when it is 'Lutheranism' which is the marked position, e.g. 3.2.99, as is Wolsey's accusation, repeated later by Gardiner, that Cranmer is a heretic. Yet the king swears 'By my Holydame' and by 'God's blest mother' (5.1.116, 153 and 5.2.32). The most important ambiguity is Katherine's vision of the heavenly banquet, which is not even necessarily Christian, let alone sectarian. If anything the play merely refers to the arguments about continuity and discontinuity in the scene of Cranmer's trial (5.2), where he gets the better of Gardiner's accusations of novelty (114), sectarianism (104,114), disloyalty (114,116). There is a reference to *Limbo Patrum*, which may be a confusion with 'Lime House', 'limbs', and the license which attends the rejoicing over Elizabeth's christening (5.3.59–65), and Cranmer the visionary sees the newly christened baby achieving company with the saints. If the play ends on the word Holy-day, that is an old-fashioned, not a 'medieval' touch. There is, however, one crucial caveat in the preceding analysis: if Cyrus Hoy and Jonathan Hope are right, the legal examples I have quoted are probably Shakespeare's, while the religious ones are Fletcher's.[15]

'THE FORMER AGE'

Thus far I have often referred to the law, to religion and reform, to dynastic change and to the roots of semantic and morphological language-change without formally addressing the historiographical problem. For Shakespeareans the stakes are high, because in dealing with texts which are apparently, deceptively, accessible, widely circulated in school, stage, and screen, and replacing other senses of national and linguistic pasts, the risks

---

[15] Hope, *Authorship*, pp. 67–83.

associated with anachronism are so acute. Shakespeare is accused of inventing the human, shoring up imperialism, stimulating capital-formation. Surely more scepticism is required, and the good service of history is a vaccine against bad masters. Shakespeare does not contrast himself, his characters, his times with a historical past of darkness, and this matters for us. In this last large section I shall try to answer Roberto Calasso's question in *The Marriage of Cadmus and Harmony* about another kind of story, How did it all begin?

A much-quoted epigram makes a good introduction: 'The Renaissance invented the Middle Ages in order to define itself; the Enlightenment perpetuated them in order to admire itself; and the Romantics revived them in order to escape from themselves.' This is witty and appealing, but it threatens to cloud the very problem it identifies by its own assumptions not only of periodization but of agency.[16] If one translates into something less elegant, the claim appears to be that there was a Renaissance, that 'it' self-consciously invented a period (or rather, two periods), and that that act became preservation and revival, in implied chronological (and discrete) sequence. There are cycles here, too, especially if one reaches beyond the borders of the English language and the British Isles.

In Ireland, but thinking of London, Spenser's celebration of 'Dan Chaucer, well of English undefyled / On Fames eternall beadroll worthie to be fyled' (*The Faerie Queene* (1595), 4.2.32) echoes earlier returns to the purity of Cicero, and Cicero's own Republican values. What is less obvious in the parallel is that Chaucer is, for Spenser, an origin, not a middle. It is also an essential observation that whatever it is that is legitimated, the appeal, via rebirth or resuscitation, is to the preeminence of origin, to 'pure' aristocratic descent. This argument is a genealogy, but it is a genealogy with a difference. Between us and the good old days there is always darkness and decline. The measure of that distance may, or may not, be counted arithmetically, as Margreta de Grazia has recently pointed out, reminding us of the 'bundling' connotation of

such familiar concepts as 'decade' or 'century'. And as she, from one point of view, or as James Simpson, from another, has also reminded us, the periodizations which we utilize function to legitimate our own approaches to history.[17]

The divisions of time and history are already focused for students of Shakespeare by varieties of 'lates', 'posts' and, above all, 'earlies'. Among the intriguing consequences of 'the millennium', one has been an accelerating attention to periodization, beginning with the calendar and radiating outwards. Was the man of the millennium also a renaissance man? It depends, of course, on what you mean by 'renaissance'. This is far from trivial, given how much, how far and how often 'renaissance' has prompted its apparent opposites for denigration and denial. Books of date-equivalences and the habit of scholarly corrections mean that although we know we *might* name Shakespeare's birth date as in the first month of a calendar which still began in March, or as part of an 'old style' calendar, or in a regnal year counting from Elizabeth's accession, we almost always avoid such labels as antiquarian: we still consider that he was born (or not) on 23 April 1564. In the larger perspective the shift in nomenclature from 'renaissance' to 'early modern' has brought with it its own seismic resettlements, not least of which is the canal which separates the fast-receding dark medieval continent from the bright birth of what eventually becomes recognizable as now. It is worth remembering that 'early modern', itself, has a previous identity

---

[16] Brian Stock, 'The Middle Ages as Subject and Object', *New Literary History*, 5 (1974), 527–47; reprinted in his *Listening for the Text: on the uses of the past* (Baltimore, 1990), p. 69, and now regularly quoted by medievalists trying to fight the *cordon sanitaire* of exclusion.

[17] In 'Ageism: Leland, Bale, and the Laborious Start of English Literary History, 1350–1550', *New Medieval Literatures*, 1 (1997), 213–35 and expanded in his volume for the New Oxford History, *Reform and Cultural Revolution: 1350–1547* (Oxford, 2002). His detailed, and valuable, assessment of the antiquarians Leland and Bale well illustrates many of the historical problems raised by any description or analysis of what we unavoidably term Humanist scholarship.

denoting language change, and that our map of 'medium aevum' is barely a century – for we are bound to such periods – old.[18]

Rediscovery of the growth of ideas of middle ages requires a double perspective: a binocular sympathy with what authors thought they were doing at the time, and a retrospect which attends to those once-taken-for-granted metaphors which reveal so much. *OED* cites Donne and Sir Henry Spelman as first users of a 'middle age(s)'; both invoke the learning of the schools *with approval*, emphasizing the continuities we have already seen in Shakespeare.[19] The problem about dictionary definitions is always that the dictionary cannot discriminate the complex and different usages and associations it cites, or plot the dynamics of historical semantics where 'the middle ages' changes, slightly but significantly, its connotations. When Petrarch spoke of a long dark loss of learning he thought it *coincided* with the Christian dispensation, from which he himself, within that darkness, could hope to see a new dawn.[20]

The idea of restoration avoids the accusation of innovation by appealing to arguments of prior superiority, and implies a curious false humility which replaces something lost while re-placing the less-gifted losers of it. Revivals of poetry, language (that is, philology), art, architecture, of learning more generally, of ideas of history, of political structures or legal systems, above all, theology, the return to the pure source of the Gospels, – these many headings identify areas where claims to renovation, renewal, re-formation were focussed by different men at different times in different countries. Their strengths as description, which imply strengths as demonstration, as argumentative force, grow at different rates, depending upon subject, time and place. They do have things in common, but by and large they have different meanings depending upon when, where, and by whom they were used. One cannot simply trace a phrase back in time and write that history, as historians have begun to insist.[21] All of these 're-'s' turn on that unspecified area of darkness I have already invoked, but that is only to observe that now is a contrast to some time ago. Both 'medium aevum' and 'le moyen âge' antedate usage in English, but there, too, problems arise which have not always been fully appreciated in surveys of the question. Like that other 'unit idea', 'courtly love', which also came into prominence at the end of the nineteenth century, 'middle ages' is problematic at the very least because if we pose it as a question we impose it as a thing.[22]

---

[18] 'Middle age(s)', comes into English as both singular and plural, and does not settle for the plural until the earlier twentieth century, and the 'received' history of the designation stems, unquestioned, from G. S. Gordon's article cited in n. 1 above, a mere eighty years old, but subsequently accepted as authoritative, as in Nathan Edelman, 'The Early Uses of *Medium Aevum, Moyen Age, Middle Ages*', *Romantic Review*, 19 (1938), 3–25; and Fred C. Robinson's 'Medieval, the Middle Ages', his Presidential Address to the Medieval Academy of America, *Speculum* 59 (1984), 745–56. Gordon himself quotes from Paul Lehmann, *Vom Mittelalter und von der lateinischen Philologie des Mittelalters: Quellen und Untersuchen zum lateinischen Philologie des Mittelalters*, vol. 1 (Munich,1914), pp. 9–10. It is time to dismantle such apparent authority.

[19] 'But thus the eldest and newest expositors are wholly for me, many also (and of the best of them) of the middle ages', *De non temerandis ecclesiis, a tract of the rights and respect due to churches* (London,? second edition, expanded, 1646 [not in edition of 1613]) (ULC Bb*.9.40), Appendix, p. 40, rather differently quoted by Edelman, p. 6. The *OED* citation from 1 Timothy 15 (see p. 254) is from 'A Second Sermon Preached at White-Hall', April 19. 1618, *The Sermons of John Donne*, ed. George R. Potter and Evelyn M. Simpson (Berkeley and Los Angeles, 1953–), vol. 1, p. 303.

[20] See the well-known, even authoritative, article by Theodor Mommsen, 'Petrarch's Conception of the Dark Ages', *Speculum*, 17 (1942), 226–42.

[21] See Jürgen Voss, 'Le Problème du Moyen Age dans la pensée historique en France: XVIe–XIXe siècle', in *Revue d'histoire moderne et contemporaine* 24 (1977), 321–340, which is a French summary of the conclusion to his *Das Mittelalter im historischen Denken Frankreichs. Untersuchungen zur Geschichte des Mittelalterbegriffes und der Mittelalterbewerung von der zweiten Hälfte des 16. bis zur Mitte des 19. Jahrhunderts* (Munich: W. Fink Verlag, 1972); but see the detailed criticism by Jean-Michel Dufays, '*Medium tempus* et ses équivalents: aux origines d'une terminologie de l'âge intermédiare', *Pensiero Politico*, 21 (1998), 237–249. Fred Robinson reminds us that '*medievalis* is neither classical nor medieval in origin, but Neo Latin' (Robinson, 747, n. 1).

[22] As a parallel argument on another of the terms which built the agreed picture of the middle ages, see John C. Moore,

Very briefly, then, the development of ideas of middle ages – because I must continually emphasize their plurality – have been traced back in history by slightly redefining a concept (a period in a middle) which already existed, but existed within the context of beliefs in seven ages, four ages and three ages: that is, seven of history, four of man and the world, three of time.[23] These inheritances from the ancient world and the first centuries of Christianity, from Orosius and Augustine (whose ideas seem to have been more of an interim than a middle), include the increasingly doubtful, but always to be resuscitated, idea of a last age, or at least a next-to-last age. These ideas – not systems – sit uneasily together and, given the ways they permeate the textual culture of Europe, remain legitimate for reference. That is, one has to be in a position to look back over a terrain which has at least three divisions in it, not two: the lost period, the period of losing, early recovery (dawn), now, hereafter, which may be the end. Between the Incarnation and the end of time, Augustine was never willing to say when that end might come. The interims are ours.

The idea of the Middle Ages, like that of the novel, is something which comes to look clear in retrospect, but which emerges slowly over a long time, and with many variations. Brian Stock's witty formulation works from a paradigm so familiar as to be invisible. As the novel grows from the romance, so a middle ages gives birth to a renaissance. And as the romance was rediscovered by Warton and the eighteenth century, so one of the ways we know that 'the middle ages' has established itself is when scholars, assuming its existence, begin to revalorize it. One might accept the apparent designation, but appropriate it as a positive rather than a negative evaluation: no longer the Gothic barbaric, but the romantic genius – and, it must be said, one cradle of the national. Perhaps, then, Garrick is 'Pre-Romantic' when he calls Shakespeare 'the bard', 'recognizing' the (aristocratic) singer at the hypothesized medieval court. Just one indication will give a sense of the rhythm of the story: the 'romances' of the author of *Waverley*.[24] One extra complexity is that the story of the story is a case of scholars look-

ing for their own period concerns, their ancestors, what I have already called a genealogy of aristocratic descent (like Warton's attempt to establish an origin of national genius in a mediaeval phase of English poetry).

In 1904 W. P. Ker was still using 'middle age', and the scholarly coinages 'mediaeval', 'médiévale', 'moyen-ageux' are relatively recent. The spelling ligature 'ae' is significant in this context, and has aroused passions similar to Holofernes' assaults on the monster Ignorance, or those over the orthography of the name of the author of the

---

'Courtly Love: a problem of terminology', *Journal of the History of Ideas*, 40 (1979), 621–32.

[23] J. A. Burrow, *The Ages of Man: A Study in Medieval Writing and Thought* (Oxford, 1986) is the exemplary discussion of this subject, and, as he points out, in the life of a man (which we would now recognize as gendered masculine) 'middle age' had a positive connotation (pp. 8–11).

[24] The missing link is Sir Walter Scott. Historians, who also quote each others' references, trace the first use of 'the wars of the roses' to *Anne of Geierstein* (1829): 'the civil discords so dreadfully prosecuted in the wars of the White and Red Roses' (ch. 7), and not to Shakespeare, who only shows the roses plucked as emblems. See, e.g., Robin Storey, *The End of the House of Lancaster* (London, 1966) and S. B. Chrimes, *Lancastrians, Yorkists, and Henry VII* (London, 1964), p. xii. Scott's influence on historians as well as novelists cannot be overestimated. Scott, of course, concocted a kind of medievalizing English for his characters. In *Anne of Geierstein*, Scott's memory of Shakespeare's language and characters (Rosalind and Beatrice for Anne's maid) thickens at certain moments in the narrative, even when, perhaps especially when, his own interpretation of Margaret of Anjou is directly opposed to Shakespeare's. For a suggestive essay on Scott, see now Diana E. Henderson, 'Othello Redux?: Scott's Kenilworth and the Trickiness of "Race" on the Nineteenth-Century Stage', in *Victorian Shakespeare, Volume 2: Literature and Culture*, eds. Gail Marshall and Adrian Poole (Houndsmills, Basingstoke, 2003), pp. 14–29. A fuller analysis would consider how Scott's and his contemporaries' interpretations of Shakespeare were in turn re-emphasized through Scott's historiography, which appeared authorized by his learned notes; how that historiography, in those historical novels, offered a genealogy to continental historical novelists (Dumas and Hugo pre-eminently, but also Michelet); which in turn contributed to anachronistic, yet persuasive, and periodizing historical accounts. I am grateful to Dr Rosemary Horrox for the reference to the historians' references to *Anne of Gierstein*.

Aeneid.[25] If we are looking for Dark Ages we will find them. Their slow retreat is part of this story, too.

The Dark Ages and the Middle Ages – or the Middle Age – used to be the same; two names for the same period. But they have come to be distinguished, and the Dark Ages are now no more than the first part of the Middle Age, while the term mediaeval is often restricted to the later centuries, about 1100 to 1500, the age of chivalry, the time between the first Crusade and the Renaissance.[26]

'Between the first Crusade [i.e. the well-known religion of the Middle Ages] and the Renaissance' – here is the piece that was missing in this picture. An extreme view might argue that there was no dark age, no middle age, no Christian age, no chivalry – except as fantasies of retrospect. As evaluative descriptive words go, 'renaissance' has had a long run of praise, just as barbarism has remained its shadow opposition. But this pairing forgets that there is a story about 'renaissance' too, as a mid-nineteenth-century neologism. A last digression is necessary here. 'Renaissance' is usually traced to writing about art, beginning perhaps with T. A. Trollope's *Summer in Brittany* (1840), becoming current in Ruskin's *Stones of Venice* (1851), normalizing in Arnold's *Culture and Anarchy* (1861) and Pater's almost contemporary *Renaissance* (1873). Arnold's comment on his change of spelling, 'I have ventured to give to the foreign word *Renaissance* an English form' is itself quoted by the *OED* (s.v. 'renaissance'). If we press on this preference for the loan-word, we discover that it replaced the pre-existing English habit of reference to 'the revival of learning' which survives here and there, for example in J. E. Sandys's magisterial *History of Classical Scholarship*.[27] I do not think that there was anything ideological in the shift, unless it was a by-product of a more general campaign by aesthetes to shove their Philistine contemporaries toward Art Appreciation. My point here is that the historical trend toward 'rebirth' reoriented arguments that had been Protestant and national, which were once obvious (if dead) metaphors of resuscitation. But

I do not think this was part of an overt intellectual programme – or 'project'. Thus the master-word of the semantic field is 'restore' ('restoration' makes it more obvious), within a much larger but equally genealogical narrative of Protestant triumphalism. It presupposes something rather different from the idea of rebirth, which may itself allude to a dead metaphor of baptism, of something rather more, if I may put it this way, Christian in the sense of new dispensation. That is, it is the *English* (=language) usage which distinguishes itself from re-birth, a metaphor which Sandys traces back to what we would call the Carolingian Renaissance.[28] If there was a programme, it was one in which periodization is at the service of God's Englishmen (=place) and their national and confessional superiority to the still-Catholic continent.

The Middle Ages are thus an idea which begins as a blank, an interval, an 'interim', but which take on a presumed substance as what we parlously call

---

25 The fulminations against 'rackers of orthography' in *Love's Labour's Lost* (e.g. 5.1) give us a sense of what the astute might mock, but one does not, after all, mock a dead letter. How funny the scenes must have been is clear in Shakespeare's recycling them for Rosalind, for Benedick and for Dogberry, and, perhaps most startlingly, for Hamlet.

26 This is the once well-known opening of W. P. Ker's *The Dark Ages* (London, 1904), in the series 'Periods of European Literature'.

27 The second volume is subtitled *From the Revival of Learning to the End of the Eighteenth Century (in Italy, France, England, and the Netherlands)* (Cambridge, 1908). As early as William Roscoe's *The Life and Pontificate of Leo the Tenth* (Liverpool, 1805, and frequently reprinted) we find the concatenation 'restoration'/'revival'/'reformation', e.g. vol. II, 253, 279, vol. III, 135, 146, 192, 222, 257. He attributes to Warton the orientation of his historical 'story'. I am grateful to Professor Gareth Stedman-Jones for the suggestion that I look at Roscoe, and to Professor Richard Tuck for the reference to Sandys.

28 'Aurea Roma iterum renovata renascitur orbi', from Modoin on Charles' innovations in learning, and he traces 'renaissance' to a translation from Italian 'rinascimento', first remarked in Antoine Furetière's *Dictionnaire universel françois et latin* (The Hague, 1708), *History of Classical Scholarship*, vol. II, pp. 2–3.

the Renaissance establishes itself – and is even, in some sense, over. More importantly, neither 'period' has agreed duration, but *from our perspective* attitudes to problems such as twelfth-century renaissances, high or low middle ages, have been taken as problems to be solved rather than themselves evidence of changes in ideas about time and periodization. Only with the development of a historical sense which is itself dateable, that is, certainly after Vico, perhaps only as late as nineteenth-century historicism, can we begin to think of systems of periods. An article asking whether women had a middle ages would cast an interesting light on the famous title of whether they had a renaissance.[29] Our current shift from renaissance to early modern in English literary studies is testimony to many things, one of which is an intriguing repetition, a polemic which attaches them to us as the locus of our antiquity, and severs us from all medieval history, including literature and art. It is an emulative, competitive attempt at devaluing and erasure, an alibi for ignorance. From a seventeenth-century perspective, in Latin, in French and in English, ideas of middle ages are just coming to be, descriptions which fit different aspects of the past at different times and in different ways. Shakespeare himself, after the dynastic re-storation, comes to belong much more to that repudiated 'middle' than we always allow, an exceptional light in a rude and barbaric age.

WHOSE MIDDLE AGES?

We will not find a systematic approach to the past; there cannot be, as there was not yet systematic history. Even if there had been, what system could have dealt with the dynastic and religious ruptures which it was public business to re-write, to explain away? So, have we arrived at an impasse, from which we cannot emerge because we cannot employ the terms around which the debate itself is launched? From our perspective there is no reason to avoid using 'the middle ages', for Shakespeare read Chaucer and Gower, perhaps Malory,

certainly a series of Italian authors we may (but may not) wish to categorize as medieval. It is, in any case, impossible. Medievalists themselves enjoy their own shifting frontiers; when they discuss Dante, Petrarch, Boccaccio, it may only be the middle poet who is fully renaissance (given Boccaccio's conservative Latin compositions), while C. S. Lewis famously argued that what Chaucer really did was remedievalize the story of Troilus, like Shakespeare's Italy inside his Rome. But then, of course, medievalists are always contending with the prejudice that the renaissance is a sign of progress, and therefore A Good Thing. This article has been inflected by a medievalist's Cassandrism, the historian's fear of forgetting. Nothing more elegaic, perhaps, than that. If it has a moral, it lies in the injunction to resist synthesis.

If we continue to insist on erecting one great 'early modern' divide, we shall occlude and elide matters of language and literature. We cannot afford to refer to early modern law or history if they merely replace an ill-defined renaissance, however inviting the dynastic changes which open and close Shakespeare's English history plays. Present-mindedness is always with us. The economics of retrospectively nascent capitalism or the demographics of plague brought crises, but never one gulf. Change was slow, and not steady as revival passed to reform, to theology's divisions of the Kingdom of Heaven. On the continent the sixteenth century saw civil wars, terror and uneasy peaces, but the vocabulary the participants used is not ours.[30] Shakespeare's tact, his ambiguities and

---

[29] And that is precisely what we find in David Herlihy's 'Did Women Have a Renaissance?: a Reconsideration', *Medievalia et Humanistica*, 13 (1985), 1–22, where, in practice, he surveys changes in legal and social status from about the eighth century to 1500. The *locus classicus* is Joan Kelly-Gadol, 'Did Women have a Renaissance?' in *Becoming Visible: Women in European History*, ed. Renate Bridenthal and Claudia Koontz (Boston, 1977).

[30] As Judith Maltby puts it (p.c.), there is no conversion moment, as may be seen from the arguments of John Jewel in 1587, *An Apology for the Church of England*, ed. John Booty (Washington, 1963). Rather, contemporary

evasions, are so remarkable that they leave room for scholars to reopen debates over his own beliefs. But even in *All is True/King Henry VIII* Wolsey is a man (if a bold bad one [2.2.42]), as Cranmer is a man, and neither is an allegory. Time passes, and Shakespeare writes about its passage, but he did not, because he could not, share our concept of 'the middle ages'.

---

arguments themselves revolved around the question of continuity/discontinuity.

WHO WROTE WILLIAM BASSE'S 'ELEGY ON SHAKESPEARE'?: REDISCOVERING A POEM LOST FROM THE DONNE CANON

BRANDON S. CENTERWALL

The first known poem to be composed in response to Shakespeare's death is an elegy attributed to William Basse (1583?–1653?) that was widely copied into commonplace books of the era under various titles and printed in several seventeenth-century editions. (See Appendix for a list of sigla for the textual witnesses.) The elegy reads as follows in a single-sheet manuscript broadside (siglum C) written and signed by Basse himself (illustration 10):

> On Mʳ William Shakespeare
> who dyed in Aprill 1616.
>
> Renowned Spenser, lye a thought more nye
> To learned Chaucer, and rare Beaumont lye
> A little neerer Spencer, to make roome
> For Shakespeare in your threefold fowerfold tombe.
> To lodge all fower in one bedd make a shift   5
> Untill Doomesday; for hardly will a fift
> Betwixt this day and that, by fate be slaine
> For whome your Curtaines may be drawne againe.
> If your precedency in Death doth barr
> A fourth place in your sacred Sepulchre   10
> Under this carved marble of thyne owne
> Sleep rare Tragædian, Shakespeare sleep alone
> Thy unmolested Peace, unshared Cave
> Possesse as Lord, not Tennant of thy grave.
> That unto us and others it may bee   15
> Honor heereafter to be laid by Thee.
>   Mr Willm Basse.[1]

The poem has a specific agenda. After Spenser was buried next to Chaucer in Westminster Abbey in 1599, it became the practice to honour England's most celebrated poets with burial in what is now called Poets' Corner in Westminster Abbey, W. H. Auden being a recent case in point. The playwright Francis Beaumont was interred there in 1616 and it is the poem's proposal that Shakespeare should be as well (lines 1–8). However, this would entail disinterring Shakespeare's remains from his grave in Stratford and transferring them to Westminster for reburial, an audacious proposition that would require the consent of all concerned. In lines 9–16 of the elegy, the poet concedes that Shakespeare may remain buried in Stratford after all – and he diplomatically gives his assent in advance should that prove to be the case (although it is clearly his second choice).

Since Shakespeare remains buried in Stratford, it is manifest that the proposal failed. To judge from the large number of surviving manuscript copies of the elegy, it failed in a very public manner. In his own elegy upon Shakespeare prefixed to the 1623 First Folio, Ben Jonson satirizes the poem and its agenda, playing off of the first four lines of the earlier piece:

> My Shakespeare, rise; I will not lodge thee by
> Chaucer, or Spenser, or bid Beaumont lye
> A little further, to make thee a roome:
> Thou art a Moniment, without a tombe . . .
>   (lines 19–22)

The allusion indicates that Jonson expects the poem in question to be well known to such

---

[1] Chetham's Library, Manchester, MS Halliwell-Phillips 2757ʳ. Transcript of text provided by permission of Chetham's Library. I have expanded contractions.

10 A single-sheet manuscript broadside of the elegy on Shakespeare, written and signed by William Basse (*c.* 1626). Chetham's Library, Manchester, Halliwell-Phillips MS 2757ʳ (siglum C).

individuals as were likely to be interested in purchasing a Folio edition of Shakespeare's plays – and that they, too, should find it risible.

The ultimate cause of the project's failure is obvious enough. If the poet finally approached the Stratford authorities and Shakespeare's next of kin for their permission to proceed, they could only point to the inscription on Shakespeare's grave:

GOOD FREND FOR IESVS SAKE FORBEARE
TO DIGG THE DVST ENCLOASED HEARE:
BLESE BE Yᴱ MAN Y⁽ᵀ⁾ SPARES THES STONES
AND CVRST BE HE Yᵀ MOVES MY BONES.

How embarrassing! Having failed to do his homework properly, the poet now stood to look very foolish indeed.

Such were the circumstances of this elegy upon Shakespeare, and there would be little more to say

Poems.   149

An Epitaph upon Shakespeare.

R Enowned *Chaucer* lie a thought more nigh
   To rare *Beaumond;* and learned *Beaumond* lie
A little nearer *Spencer*, to make roome
For *Shakespeare* in your threefold fourefold tombe.
To lie all *foure* in one bed make a shift,
For, untill doomesday hardly will a sift
Betwixt this day and that be slaine,
For whom your curtaines need be drawne againe;
But, if precedency of death doth barre
A fourth place in your sacred sepulchre,
Under this curled marble of thine owne
Sleepe rare Tragedian *Shakespeare*, sleepe alone,
That, unto *Vs* and others it may bee
Honor, hereafter to be laid by thee.

Y 3   *Sapho*

11 The elegy on Shakespeare in John Donne's *Poems* (London, 1633), sig. Y3^r (siglum JDP).

about it if it were not for two circumstances. For one thing, Basse was a third-tier poet – competent but uninspiring – whose works, apart from the elegy, have long been sunk in unsurprising obscurity.[2] Yet the elegy is not a third-tier poem. On the contrary, it easily surpasses anything else attributed to Basse. For another, the poem was first published in the 1633 first edition of the *Poems* of John Donne (1572–1631) wherein it is attributed to Donne (illustration 11).[3] The text in Donne's *Poems* (siglum JDP) differs substantially from C:[4]

An Epitaph upon Shakespeare.
Renowned Chaucer lie a thought more nigh
To rare Beaumond; and learned Beaumond lie
A little nearer Spencer, to make roome
For Shakespeare in your threefold fourefold tombe.
To lie all foure in one bed make a shift,   5
For, untill doomesday hardly will a sift
Betwixt this day and that [by fate] be slaine,
For whom your curtaines need be drawne againe;
But, if precedency of death doth barre

A fourth place in your sacred sepulchre,   10
Under this curled marble of thine owne
Sleepe rare Tragedian Shakespeare, sleepe alone,
That, unto Vs and others it may bee
Honor, hereafter to be laid by thee.

(sig. Y3^r)

If, under hypothesis, Donne wrote the poem in question, once the proposal to transfer Shakespeare's remains to Westminster had deteriorated into a fiasco there would be ample motivation for Donne, then Dean of St. Paul's Cathedral, to

---

[2] William Basse, *The Poetical Works of William Basse*, ed. R. Warwick Bond (London, 1893).

[3] John Donne, *Poems* (London, 1633), sig. Y3^r. The page is misnumbered 149, *recte* 165.

[4] In line 7 I have inserted brackets to indicate the omission of the phrase 'by fate' in JDP. The omission results in the loss of a metrical foot in line 7, something that can hardly be attributed to the poet. For this reason, I regard the omission as accidental, most likely the result of eyeskip by the compositor.

abandon any claim of authorship and for Basse to step forward on Donne's behalf to claim both the authorship of the piece as well as general responsibility for the unfortunate turn of events.

In the first part of this chapter I will review the critical conversation regarding the authorship of the poem, from which will emerge an implication for a connection between the elegy and the Stratford monument. In the second part I will present evidence, internal and external, that Donne was indeed the author of the elegy on Shakespeare. In the third part I will argue that Donne's elegy on Shakespeare was integral to the creation of the Stratford monument and that he himself composed its inscription. Lastly, I will attempt to restore the wording of the elegy on Shakespeare to reflect Donne's original intention.

I

Although a version of the elegy (JDP) appears in the 1633 first edition of Donne's *Poems*, it does not appear in the 1635 second edition nor in any edition of Donne's *Poems* thereafter. In fact, the 'Epitaph upon Shakespeare' is the only poem appearing in the 1633 *Poems* to be omitted from the 1635 edition. In all, of thirty-nine textual witnesses, fourteen attribute the elegy to Basse (B4, C, F1, F7, F10, M, N, O3, O5, O6, R1, R2, Y1, SP) as compared to three attributions to Donne (F9b, O1; JDP); the remaining twenty-two witnesses contain no attribution of authorship (see Appendix). The issue of attribution was recognized early on: the seventeenth-century manuscript F9b, which is a transcription from JDP, is headed 'An Epitaph upon Shakespeare / by J Donne', but a different, contemporary hand has added 'not by Donne but by Basse'.

Edmond Malone, in his 1790 edition of *The Plays and Poems of William Shakspeare*, addresses the authorship question in the course of preparing a critical edition of the elegy through a collation of three manuscripts (B5, O5, O7) and two printed texts (JDP and SP):[5]

[These verses] were erroneously attributed to Dr. Donne, in a Quarto edition of his poems printed in 1633; but

his son Dr. John Donne, a Civilian, published a more correct edition of his father's poems in 1735 [*recte* 1635], and rejected the verses on Shakspeare, knowing, without doubt, that they were written by another.

(p. 197)

Malone shows altogether too much confidence in John Donne *fils*. As a matter of fact, the junior John Donne remained uninvolved with the publication of his father's poems until the 1650 fifth edition,[6] so the decision to drop the 'Epitaph upon Shakespeare' from the 1635 second edition of the *Poems* was made by some unknown person, someone who cannot be assumed *a priori* to have had knowledge 'without doubt' regarding the authorship of the elegy. Even after the start of his involvement with the *Poems* in 1650, John Donne the younger never demonstrated the slightest interest or determination to prepare 'a more correct edition of his father's poems', leaving intact and uncorrected the numerous errors he inherited from prior editions of the *Poems* – so his presumed inside knowledge cannot be brought to bear upon the issue.

In 1879 C. M. Ingleby prepared a Shakespeare allusion-book in which he considered the authorship question upon review of ten manuscripts and five printed editions of the elegy.[7] After reviewing the attributional evidence, Ingleby chose to remain agnostic as to whether the poem was written by Donne or Basse.[8] However, he made several observations cogent to the present discussion. In particular, he argued the textual significance of the absence of lines 13–14 (as they appear in C) from the JDP text:

The original was certainly a sonnet, of the usual number of lines; to which two lines (now standing as the

---

[5] Edmond Malone, ed., *The Plays and Poems of William Shakspeare* (London, 1790), vol. 1, pt. 1, pp. 197–8.

[6] Ernest W. Sullivan II, '*Poems, by J.D.*: Donne's Corpus and His Bawdy, Too', *John Donne Journal*, 19 (2000), pp. 299–309.

[7] C. M. Ingleby and Lucy Toulmin Smith, eds., *Shakespeare's Centurie of Prayse* (London, 1879), pp. 136–9. Ingleby's original essays are supplemented with additional comments supplied by Smith.

[8] Ingleby and Smith, *Shakespeare's Centurie*, p. 138.

13th and 14th) were subsequently added. . . . The couplet . . . introduced an absurdity, which the lines in Donne's *Poems* do not contain: for, first, Shakespeare's peace would not be unmolested simply because his grave was unshared; and secondly, it would not be unmolested at all, if others were in after time to be laid by him.

(p. 137)

In her remarks appended to Ingleby's essay, Lucy Toulmin Smith feels that Ingleby has overstated the 'absurdity' introduced by lines 13–14, stating that 'they seem to me quite consistent' with the rest of the poem.[9] I agree with Smith in that while a close reading will reveal the incongruities which distress Ingleby, they do not create such a degree of 'absurdity' as would trouble, or even be noted by, most readers. Rather, the textual problem can be reformulated from a different direction. If the reader should delete lines 13–14 from C, the result is a perfectly designed fourteen-line sonnet in seven rhyming couplets. Now, any competent poet can add two lines to a fourteen-line sonnet in such a way that the result works reasonably well, but the probability that the accidental deletion of two lines from a sixteen-line poem – presumably through the error of a scribe or a compositor – will result in a perfect fourteen-line sonnet is a probability too remote to bear serious consideration. For this reason, I agree with Ingleby against Smith that the elegy on Shakespeare was originally written as a fourteen-line sonnet with the additional couplet added later.

The fourteen-line version of the elegy is limited to JDP and those manuscript witnesses that derive from it (B7, F9a, F9b, and O2). Therefore, JDP is the sole independent witness for an earlier version of the elegy than that being circulated by Basse or as a poem attributed to Basse. The import of the additional couplet relates directly back to the injunction on Shakespeare's grave. Whereas the original fourteen-line composition advocates the disinterment of Shakespeare's relics, the added couplet explicitly affirms that Shakespeare's remains shall not be disturbed (at the cost of introducing those contradictions into the text already noted). It can be inferred, then, that lines 13–14 were added after the nature and scale of the debacle had become apparent.

This implies the possibility that JDP, the version attributed to Donne in the 1633 *Poems*, has the nature of an early, rough draft of the elegy, a draft such as might be found among an author's papers after his death. Several of the readings in JDP are inferior to C in a manner consistent with its hypothesized rough-draft status. In JDP there is an infelicitous duplication of *Beaumond* in the second line and a similarly infelicitous repetition of *lie*, which occurs three times in the first five lines. Both problems are elegantly resolved in C.

More problematic is the reading *curled marble* in line 11, which appears as *carved marble* in C. Ingleby regarded *curled marble* – a reading unique to JDP and those manuscript witnesses deriving from it – as a 'singular blunder' on the part of the copyist behind JDP, only to be understood as a scribal error.[10] In her appended comments, Smith tacitly agrees with Ingleby on this, and then adds the following: 'It seems to me that "Under this carved marble" [as in C] has . . . a possible reference to Shakespere's tomb at Stratford.'[11] She is referring to the plain slab over Shakespeare's grave, carved with the injunction already noted.

Now, *curled marble* cannot refer to the slab over Shakespeare's grave; there is nothing curled about it (illustration 12). But it could well refer to the Stratford monument, ornamented as it is with curled Corinthian capitals carved from marble, to say nothing of curled festoons surrounding the coat-of-arms above (illustration 13). From this perspective, *curled marble* is not an error but a *lectio difficilior*, alluding with exact, poetic precision to what is now referred to as the Stratford monument but which monument, it would appear, was originally intended by the poet to be erected in Westminster Abbey. Under this hypothesis, *curled marble* was the original reading, subsequently revised to *carved marble* once it became clear that Shakespeare would

---

[9] Ingleby and Smith, p. 137.
[10] Ingleby and Smith, p. 137.
[11] Ingleby and Smith, p. 138.

12 Shakespeare's grave and inscription in Holy Trinity Church, Stratford-upon-Avon.

not be exhumed. In that case, *carved marble* alludes to the stone marking Shakespeare's grave, as suggested by Smith – but at a cost. The phrase *carved marble* flattens the tone of the elegy with its pedestrian imprecision. When you come to think of it, all funerary marble is carved.

In 1893 R. Warwick Bond published *The Poetical Works of William Basse*, among which, as editor, he was more than happy to place the elegy on Shakespeare.[12] As he acknowledges, his discussion of the textual issues largely follows that of Ingleby and Smith. He sees no reason to doubt Basse's authorship of the piece:

That [the elegy] should have been first printed amongst Donne's Poems without any acknowledgment [of Basse's authorship] was a literary accident which possibly arose from Donne's possessing a manuscript copy. As it was omitted in all editions of Donne subsequent to the first, perhaps Basse asserted his claim to the authorship.

(p. 114)

Bond goes on to suggest that the reading *curled marble* in JDP was a miscopy from manuscript O1, where the adjective can be easily read as *curved* due to a failure of the O1 scribe to properly close the *a* in *carved* (p. 116). This suggestion fails on the face

of it, since O1 was written *c*. 1638,[13] years after JDP appeared in the 1633 *Poems* of John Donne.

Once the elegy was securely contained within *The Poetical Works of William Basse* that appears to have settled the matter. No further consideration has been given to the authorship question since then. When, in 1987, Stanley Wells and Gary Taylor compiled an edition of the elegy from a collation of thirty-three witnesses (twenty-seven manuscripts and six printed texts), they regarded the authorship question as already closed in favor of Basse.[14] The present chapter expands the collation to thirty-nine witnesses (see Appendix) while re-opening the authorship issue for the first time in over a century.

---

[12] Basse, *Poetical Works*, pp. 113–7.

[13] George Chapman, *The Poems of George Chapman*, ed. Phyllis Brooks Bartlett (London, 1941), p. 476.

[14] For their text of the elegy, see William Shakespeare, *William Shakespeare: The Complete Works*, eds. Stanley Wells and Gary Taylor (Oxford, 1986), p. xlii. For their collation of textual variants, see their *William Shakespeare: A Textual Companion* (Oxford, 1987), pp. 163–4. It should be noted that their text is eclectic and does not correspond to any specific textual witness.

13 Shakespeare's monument and inscription in Holy Trinity Church, Stratford-upon-Avon.

II

Much has been made, quite appropriately, of the observation that JDP appears in the 1633 first edition of Donne's *Poems*, but was dropped from the 1635 second edition. To gauge the significance of this observation, it is necessary to estimate the ability and judgement of the editors involved.

The editor of the 1633 *Poems*, whomever he was, collected together 150 poems for publication as Donne's, including the 'Epitaph upon Shakespeare'. Not counting the poem in question, of the remaining 149 it is now accepted that only one is not by Donne, the metrical *Psalme 137*.[15] This gives us one error out of 149 poems attributed to Donne, for an error rate of $1/149 = 0.7$ per cent. In contrast, although the editor of the 1635 edition, apparently a different person from the first editor, added an additional twenty-seven poems (as well as dropping the 'Epitaph upon Shakespeare'), only fourteen of these twenty-seven are today regarded as canonical,[16] giving thirteen errors out of twenty-seven poems attributed to Donne, for an error rate of $13/27 = 48$ per cent. In other words, the

---

[15] Sullivan, '*Poems, by J.D.*', pp. 301, 308*n*.
[16] Sullivan, pp. 304–5.

273

editor of the 1635 edition of Donne's *Poems* was over seventy times more likely to make an error of attribution than was the editor of the 1633 edition. In summary, the editor of the 1633 edition had excellent judgement as regards what was a poem by Donne and what was not, whereas the editor of the 1635 edition had abysmal judgement in this regard, even by the loose standards of the day. The question is, for a start, whose judgement we are to trust – the editor with demonstrably excellent judgement who chose to include the 'Epitaph upon Shakespeare' among Donne's poems, or the editor with demonstrably poor judgement who chose to exclude it.

But these were not the only editors judging the authorship of the poem, for there was a third – namely, William Basse himself. Subsequent to Shakespeare's death, Basse eventually compiled two anthologies of what he presumably regarded as his best work – the *Polyhymnia* (in two versions that together comprised eighteen poems[17]) and *The Pastorals and other workes* (a collection of three poems).[18] Although the elegy on Shakespeare is agreed to be Basse's finest poem – assuming it is indeed by Basse – it appears in neither the *Polyhymnia* nor *The Pastorals and other workes*, evidently by Basse's choice.

Apart from general statements regarding the superior quality of the elegy as compared to the rest of Basse's work, are there any specific features that might point to Donne as the author? For a start, the poet bids Spenser and Beaumont to move closer to Chaucer

> . . . to make roome
> For Shakespeare in your threefold fourefold tombe.
> (JDP, lines 3–4)

Epanorthosis, the rhetorical figure of 'addition by correction',[19] is here deployed to brilliant effect. As long as Spenser, Beaumont and Chaucer are its sole occupants, the tomb is 'threefold'. But if Shakespeare is buried next to them it will then be a 'fourfold' tomb. So is the tomb 'threefold' or 'fourfold'? It is both and neither. It depends upon whether Shakespeare's remains are transferred to Westminster Abbey or not. The description of that

final resting place as 'your threefold fourfold tomb' sets up the rhetorical tension that drives the rest of the poem.

Epanorthosis is employed nowhere else in the works of Basse. In contrast, it occurs with considerable frequency in Donne's poems:[20]

> But truly keepes his first, last, everlasting day.
> ('The Anniversarie', p. 24, line 10)

> Oft fed with true oaths, and with sweet salt
> teares . . .
> ('The Anniversarie', p. 24, line 15)

> But get a winter-seeming summers night.
> ('Loves Alchymie', p. 39, line 12)

> But now I have drunke thy sweet salt teares . . .
> ('Witchcraft by a picture', p. 46, line 8)

> This must, my Soule, thy long-short Progresse
> bee . . .
> ('The second Anniversarie', p. 257, line 219)

> And we her sad glad friends all beare a part . . .
> ('Elegie. Death.', p. 286, line 61)

> This living buried man, this quiet mandrake, rest.
> ('The Progresse of the Soule', p. 301, line 160)

> All changing unchang'd Antient of dayes . . .
> ('La Corona.', p. 318, line 4)

> The first last end, now zealously possest . . .
> ('La Corona.', p. 318, line 11)

As for the Donnean wording of the elegy, consider the last four lines of C:

---

[17] The two texts of the *Polyhymnia* manuscript have disappeared since they were described in the eighteenth and nineteenth centuries, but their contents were published before the manuscripts went missing. See Basse, *Poetical Works*, pp. 139–48.

[18] *The Pastorals and other workes of William Basse*, in Basse's holograph, is among the holdings of the Folger Shakespeare Library, shelfmark v.b.235. For a published edition, see Basse, *Poetical Works*, pp. 163–343.

[19] Arthur Quinn, *Figures of Speech* (Davis, 1993 [1982]), pp. 68–70. The *oxymoron* is a type of epanorthosis.

[20] All quotations from Donne's poems are from John Donne, *The Poems of John Donne*, ed. Herbert J. C. Grierson (London, 1912), vol. I.

Thy unmolested Peace, unshared Cave
Possesse as Lord, not Tennant of thy grave.
That unto us and others it may bee
Honor heereafter to be laid by Thee.

(C, lines 13–16)

Compare these with the following lines from Donne's verse letter 'To the Countesse of Salisbury. August. 1614.':

In a darke Cave, yea in a Grave doe lie;
For as your fellow Angells, so you doe
Illustrate them who come to study you.

(p. 226, lines 72–4)

Since the verse letter 'To the Countesse of Salisbury. August. 1614' was not published until 1633, it is unlikely that anyone much had access to it before then except for the Countess of Salisbury, John Donne and the author of the elegy on Shakespeare.

Consider the last two lines of the elegy:

That, unto Vs and others it may bee
Honor, hereafter to be laid by thee.

(JDP, lines 13–14)

The author of the elegy has no doubt that he, too, deserves to be laid at rest in the Poets' Corner at Westminster, or to be laid by Shakespeare, wherever the playwright's body might be interred. For Basse to have entertained such a notion would have been absurd. Indeed, one of the few poets in England worthy of such an honour was John Donne – and Donne knew his own worth. The incongruity between the poem's claim and the actual standing of its purported author must have struck Basse as well as quite a few of the readership. No fewer than ten of the manuscript witnesses substitute a more modest 'us or others' for the original 'us and others' of the JDP- and C-type texts. Even more telling, however, are four manuscript witnesses (F1, N, O4, R1) to a revised version of the elegy which concludes

That unto *others* it may counted bee,
Honour hereafter to bee laid by Thee.

(N, lines 15–16; emphasis added)

That certainly fixes the problem.

Then there is Basse's own transcript of the elegy (illustration 10). It is puzzling that he should make an error in the very first line, first writing 'near' before correcting to 'nye', an error that destroys the rhyme. But that would be assuming, of course, that Basse actually did compose the elegy on Shakespeare.

More importantly, Donne was a proficient stylist whereas Basse rarely, if ever, went beyond conventional rhetorical strategies. The 'Epitaph upon Shakespeare' is a small masterpiece of aesthetic simplification. It follows the usual internal structure of a fourteen-line sonnet (thesis in the octave, antithesis in the following four lines, synthesis in the final couplet), but its creator sweeps away all the artifice of a complex rhyme scheme by means of a seemingly unprecedented manoeuvre – composing the sonnet entirely in rhyming couplets. Less is more. The poem's bold simplicity of form shifts the focus of the reader away from the poem itself and toward the poem's true subject, Shakespeare. There is nothing else in the Basse canon that even begins to approach this capacity for innovation.

A note can be added regarding a source for the poem. Following Spenser's burial next to Chaucer's tomb in 1599, it became a poetical commonplace to allegorize the physical proximity of their resting places as reflecting the proximity of their reputations as poets. There were many such poems,[21] but only one in the form of a fourteen-line sonnet beginning with the words *Renowned Spenser*.[22]

Spencers Fayrie Queene.

Renowmed Spencer, whose heavenlie sprite
ecclipseth the sonne of former poetrie,
in whome the muses harbor with delighte,
gracinge thy verse with Immortalitie,
Crowning thy fayrie Queene with deitie,
the famous Chaucer yealds his Lawrell crowne
vnto thy sugred penn, for thy renowne.

---

[21] For a comprehensive listing, see William Wells, comp., *Spenser Allusions In the Sixteenth and Seventeenth Centuries* (Chapel Hill, 1972).

[22] I have taken the text of the sonnet from Francis Thynne, *Emblemes and Epigrames*, ed. F. J. Furnivall (London, 1876), vol. 64, p. 71. See also Wells, *Spenser Allusions*, pp. 80–1.

Noe cankred envie cann thy fame deface,
nor eatinge tyme consume thy sacred vayne;
no carpinge zoilus cann thy verse disgrace,
nor scoffinge Momus taunt the with disdaine,
since thy rare worke eternall praise doth gayne;
then live thou still, for still thy verse shall live,
to vnborne poets, which light and life will give.

Composed by the minor poet Francis Thynne, this sonnet has but a single witness, in the manuscript collection he made of his *Emblemes and Epigrames* in 1600, now Huntington MS Ellesmere 34/B/12 (fol. 53ᵛ). The manuscript survives because, in a quest for patronage, Thynne presented the collection as a gift in 1600 to the Lord Keeper, Sir Thomas Egerton, among whose archives it was thereafter preserved. As it was never published, and no other manuscript copies are known, one of the few persons likely to have ever read this sonnet was Egerton's secretary at the time, John Donne.[23]

In conclusion, the evidence suggests that William Basse's elegy on Shakespeare was in actuality composed by John Donne. The c text, given above, embodies the author's final draft, with the understanding that lines 13–14 were not integral to the poet's original intent, being added as a matter of political necessity. Once the proposed business of exhuming Shakespeare for transfer to Westminster had turned into a fiasco, Basse apparently agreed to claim authorship of the poem – indeed, ownership of the entire proposal – thereby relieving Donne from the public humiliation of a worthy project gone sour.

III

Earlier in this essay it was suggested that the description of the tomb in JDP as *curled marble* implies that the Stratford monument is the very sepulchre alluded to in the elegy on Shakespeare, the monument being originally intended for erection in Westminster (until negotiations broke down over disinterring Shakespeare). The external evidence supports this by way of the monument's inscription (illustration 13):[24]

IVDICIO PYLIVM, GENIO SOCRATEM, ARTE MARONEM,
TERRA TEGIT, POPVLVS MÆRET, OLYMPVS HABET.
STAY PASSENGER, WHY GOEST THOV BY SO FAST?
READ IF THOV CANST, WHOM ENVIOVS DEATH HATH PLAST,
WITH IN THIS MONVMENT SHAKSPEARE: WITH WHOME,
QVICK NATVRE DIDE: WHOSE NAME DOTH DECK Yˢ TOMBE,
FAR MORE THEN COST: SI[T]H ALL, Yᵀ HE HATH WRITT,
LEAVES LIVING ART, BVT PAGE, TO SERVE HIS WITT.

OBIIT AÑO DO[1] 1616
ÆTATIS 53 DIE 23 APᴿ

The first two lines, in Latin, can be translated as follows:[25]

In judgement a Nestor, in intellect a Socrates, in art a Virgil,
The earth encloses, the populace mourns, Olympus holds.

The poet who composed this inscription identifies the deceased solely by his surname, Shakespeare. In Poets' Corner at Westminster Abbey, 'Shakespeare' alone would be entirely sufficient. Who else named Shakespeare would be buried there? In contrast, 'Shakespeare' was a reasonably common last name in Warwickshire and in Stratford especially so. It would be imperative for any monument erected in Stratford to specify the deceased by both his given and surname, William Shakespeare. The poet clearly was not composing the inscription with this common-sense consideration in mind.

Notably, the inscription lauds Shakespeare solely for his literary achievements. It was customary for

---

[23] Donne was Sir Thomas Egerton's secretary from 1597–98 through 1602. See R. C. Bald, *John Donne: A Life* (Oxford, 1970), pp. 93–139.

[24] The text for the inscription is taken from B. Roland Lewis, *The Shakespeare Documents: Facsimiles, Transliterations, Translations, and Commentary* (Stanford, 1941), vol. 2., p. 543.

[25] I have modified Lewis's translation as given in *The Shakespeare Documents*, vol. 2, p. 542.

inscriptions on monuments and tombs to provide a précis of the deceased – achievements and honours, names of worthy ancestors, names of grieving heirs, etc. As Price has noted, the inscription appears truncated, as though 'such commemorative information was originally planned to appear somewhere else nearby.'[26] Indeed, even Shakespeare's date of death is in small letters compressed to fit within the lower margin of the inscription, as though inserted there for lack of a better space.

The inscription states that Shakespeare's 'name doth deck this tomb' (line 6). However, the Stratford monument can in no manner be described as a tomb. This might be dismissed as mere carelessness by the poet except that the inscription also states that Shakespeare is 'placed within this monument' (lines 4–5). This cannot literally be true. However, *tomb* and *monument* each can serve as a synecdoche for a memorial – provided the memorial consists of a tomb surmounted by a monument, 'a two-tiered sepulchre'.[27] In such case, the tomb (the lower tier of the memorial) would provide space for continuing and concluding the epitaph begun on the monument (the upper tier). Price has published an illustration of just such a memorial from Sir William Dugdale's 1656 *The Antiquities of Warwickshire Illustrated* (illustration 14)[28] to which I am now able to add a second from the same source (illustration 15).[29] As can be seen, the upper tier of each memorial corresponds to the Stratford monument, complete with epitaph, whereas the lower tier is the tomb whereon the epitaph is completed – or would have been completed if the Stratford monument were properly mounted upon a tomb.

By implication, a Shakespeare memorial was designed for placement in Westminster, but the project was abruptly broken off sometime after the monument was completed but before the tomb itself was executed. The monument alone then was taken to Stratford and mounted on a wall in Holy Trinity Church, where it remains to this day. An early reference to the monument occurs in the commendatory verses of Leonard Digges, prefixed to the First Folio, wherein he alludes to 'thy Stratford Moniment'. However, a more pungent allusion has already been quoted, wherein Ben Jonson apostrophizes the bust of Shakespeare in *his* commendatory verses, 'To the memory of my beloved, The Author Mr William Shakespeare: And what he hath left us':

> My Shakespeare, rise; I will not lodge thee by
> Chaucer, or Spenser, or bid Beaumont lye
> A little further, to make thee a roome:
> *Thou art a Moniment, without a tombe . . .*
> (lines 19–22; emphasis added)

Herein, Jonson makes it entirely explicit that the elegy on Shakespeare was composed conjoint with the creation of the Stratford monument. The end result was this absurdity of a 'Monument without a tomb'.

As a matter of parsimony, it is a reasonable assumption that the poet who promoted the transfer of Shakespeare's remains to Westminster was also the poet who composed the monument's inscription. If Donne composed the elegy, he probably composed the epitaph as well. Basse is not known to have ever written a funerary epitaph.[30] In contrast, Donne composed epitaphs for the tomb of Elizabeth Drury (d. 1610); for the tomb of her parents Sir Robert Drury (d. 1615) and Anna (d. 1624); for his wife Anne's tomb (d. 1617); and for his own (d. 1631).[31] The text of Anne Donne's epitaph survives in John Donne's holograph and we have Izaak Walton's testimony that Donne composed his own epitaph.[32] The Drury

---

26 Diana Price, 'Reconsidering Shakespeare's Monument', *Review of English Studies*, 48 (1997), p. 181.

27 Price, 'Reconsidering Shakespeare's Monument', p. 182.

28 Price, fig. 7, p. 182. From William Dugdale, *The Antiquities of Warwickshire Illustrated* (London, 1656), vol. 1, p. 383.

29 Dugdale, *Antiquities of Warwickshire*, vol. 1, facing p. 382.

30 I am drawing a distinction between funerary epitaphs, which were to be engraved upon the deceased's tombstone or sepulchre, and literary epitaphs, which were meant to be circulated in manuscript or printed in books. The two are distinct genres.

31 See John Donne, *The Epithalamions, Anniversaries and Epicedes*, ed. W. Milgate (Oxford, 1978), pp. 76–80, 211–19; and John Donne, *The Variorum Edition of the Poetry of John Donne*, ed. Gary A. Stringer (Bloomington, 1995), vol. 8, pp. 174–200, 427–45.

32 Izaak Walton, *The Life of John Donne* (London, 1658), p. 113.

14 A two-tiered sepulchre with the epitaph begun on the monument above and continued on the tomb below. From William Dugdale's *The Antiquities of Warwickshire* (London, 1656), vol. 1, p. 383.

epitaphs are attributed to Donne because of his intimate relations with the Drury family as well as some idiosyncratic resemblances between their epitaphs and the epitaphs Donne composed for his wife and himself.

The epitaphs are entirely in Latin. This hinders comparisons between the Stratford epitaph and those composed by Donne, but not as much as one might think. I will work through the correspondences, some commonplace, some not.

The first line of Elizabeth Drury's epitaph reads as follows: QVO PERGAS, VIATOR, NON HABES:

'Thou knowest not, wayfarer, whither thou goest.'[33]

Compare the third line in the Stratford epitaph:

STAY PASSENGER, WHY GOEST THOV BY SO FAST?

In his own epitaph, Donne personifies Death as envious of our accomplishments and honours, for which reason he strips us of them in the end:

. . . DECANATV
HVIVS ECCLESÆ INDVTVS 27°
NOVEMB: 1621 EXVTVS MORTE
VLTIMO DIE MARTII A° 1631.

---

[33] English translation by Milgate, ed., *Epithalamions*, p. 212.

278

15 Another two-tiered sepulchre with the epitaph begun on the monument above and continued on the tomb below. From William Dugdale's *The Antiquities of Warwickshire* (London, 1656), vol. 1, facing p. 382.

'Having been invested with the Deanery of this Church, November 27, 1621,

he was stripped of it by Death on the last day of March, 1631:'[34]

Compare lines 4–5 of the Stratford epitaph:

READ IF THOV CANST, WHOM ENVIOVS
  DEATH HATH PLAST,

WITH IN THIS MONVMENT SHAKSPEARE...

Even in those poems he composed following his ordination, Donne could not resist indulging in wordplays and puns, especially in the final lines – most famously in his conclusion to 'A Hymne to God the Father' where he addresses God, 'And, having done that, Thou haste done, / I feare no more.' In the final line of his own epitaph, Donne engages in a complex pun that defies translation and can only be explicated:

---

34 English translation by Francis Wrangham. Quoted by Milgate, ed., *Epithalamions*, p. 219.

ASPICIT EVM CVIVC NOMEN EST ORIENS
'[Donne] beholdeth Him Whose name is the
Rising.'[35]

In the Vulgate translation of Zechariah 6.12 (and
nowhere else) occurs the line '*Oriens nomen eius*',
i.e., '*The East* is one of the names of Christ Jesus.'[36]
With its complex, cryptic allusions to the Son/Sun
of God rising in the East as a token of the Resurrection, this was a favorite passage of Donne's,
one he refers to in one of his sermons.[37] Indeed,
it is the basis of one of Donne's most famous
poems, 'Goodfriday, 1613. Riding Westward.' Not
so impressive, but still complex, is the wordplay in
the last two lines of the Stratford epitaph:

...ALL, Y^T HE HATH WRITT,
LEAVES LIVING ART, BVT PAGE, TO SERVE HIS
WITT.

As a page is to his master, as a page is to its Folio,
so is the 'living art' of true poets to the supreme art
of Shakespeare.

The most idiosyncratic feature of the Stratford
inscription has yet to be discussed. As Latinists have
noted, the poet is violating the quantity of *Socratem*
in the first line. As Ingleby puts it, 'Assuredly one
who had scholarship enough to compose the verses
could hardly have believed that the o in [*Socratem*]
had a common quantity.'[38] This is echoed by E. K.
Chambers: 'It was no very accurate scholar who
shortened the first vowel of "Socratem".'[39]

As it happens, although a supremely gifted poet
(or perhaps because of it), Donne was quite prepared to sacrifice quantity for other ends. In what
was probably his last literary creation, in the weeks
before his death Donne composed a one-line Latin
epigraph for his posthumously published sermon
Deaths Dvell (1632):[40]

Corporis hæc Animæ sit Syndon, Syndon Iesu
Amen.
'May this shroud of the body typify the shroud of the
soul: the shroud of Jesus.
Amen.'[41]

As Gardner observed, Donne introduces a false
quantity into the *o* in the second *Syndon* as well
as requiring the *I* in *Iesu* to be vocalized. She fur-

ther observed that a similar false quantity occurs
in *Catechismus* in line 18 of Donne's letter in Latin
verse, 'To Mr George Herbert, with one of my
Seals, of the Anchor and Christ':[42]

. . . [S]*igillum*
Non tam dicendum hoc quam Catechismus erit.
'This Seal's a Catechism, not a Seal alone.'[43]

Nor were Donne's violations of decorum limited
to Latin. In 1619 Ben Jonson advised William
Drummond 'that Done for not keeping of accent
deserved hanging.'[44]

In summary, the inscription on the Stratford
monument corresponds in every important respect
with elements to be found in those funerary epitaphs composed by Donne. To cap it, however, the
wilful violation of quantity by a talented poet virtually serves as John Donne's signature. It is concluded, therefore, that the inscription on the Stratford monument was indeed composed by Donne
and that the elegy on Shakespeare was designed to
promote the placement of the monument in Westminster Abbey (before things went wrong).

As long as Donne was a rector, he was in
no position either politically or financially to be
pursuing any personal project as daring as the transfer of Shakespeare's remains to Westminster Abbey.
That changed when he was appointed Dean of St

---

35 English translation by Francis Wrangham. Quoted by Milgate,
ed., *Epithalamions*, p. 219.
36 Stringer, ed., *Variorum Edition*, vol. 8, p. 444.
37 John Donne, *The Sermons of John Donne*, ed. George R. Potter
and Evelyn M. Simpson (Berkeley, 1953–62), vol. 6, p. 59.
38 Ingleby and Smith, *Shakespeare's Centurie*, p. 125.
39 E. K. Chambers, *William Shakespeare: A Study of Facts and
Problems* (Oxford, 1930), vol. 2, p. 182.
40 John Donne, *Deaths Dvell* (London, 1632). The epigraph
is engraved beneath the frontispiece engraving of Donne's
portrait.
41 English trans. by Helen Gardner. See John Donne, *The Divine
Poems*, ed. Helen Gardner (Oxford, 1952), p. 113.
42 Gardner, ed., *Divine Poems*, p. 112.
43 Trans. by John Donne. Donne, *The Poems of John Donne*,
vol. 1, pp. 398–400.
44 *Conversations with Drummond*, lines 48–9. See Ben Jonson, *Ben
Jonson*, ed. C. H. Herford and Percy Simpson (Oxford, 1925–
52), vol. 1, p. 133.

Paul's in November 1621. He had moved his family into the deanery by early 1622[45] and now all manner of things became possible. It follows that the writing of the elegy on Shakespeare and the commissioning of the sepulchre took place sometime in 1622–3. When – given the curse on Shakespeare's grave – the whole enterprise began to look dangerously sacrilegious, Donne knew someone who, on his behalf, would be willing to take full public responsibility for the affair, William Basse.

IV

Once Basse's folly had receded from public view, the excellence of the elegy on Shakespeare took hold. As we have seen, it became enormously popular as it circulated among the commonplace books of the period. It has not been previously noted, however, that the elegy also went on to inspire John Milton's first published poem in English. Composed in 1630, his response to the elegy first appeared anonymously among the commendatory verses prefacing the Second Folio (1632):[46]

An Epitaph on the admirable Dramaticke
Poet, W. Shakespeare.

What neede my Shakespeare for his honour'd bones,
The labour of an Age, in piled stones
Or that his hallow'd Reliques should be hid
Vnder a starre-ypointing Pyramid?
Deare Sonne of Memory, great Heire of Fame,   5
What needst thou such dull witnesse of thy Name?
Thou in our wonder and astonishment
Hast built thy selfe a lasting Monument:
For whil'st to th'shame of slow-endevouring Art
Thy easie numbers flow, and that each part,   10
Hath from the leaves of thy unvalued[47] Booke,
Those Delphicke Lines with deepe Impression
    tooke
Then thou our fancy of her selfe bereaving,
Dost make us Marble with too much conceiving,
And so Sepulcher'd in such pompe dost lie   15
That Kings for such a Tombe would wish to die.
(sig. πA5)

As with the C-type text of Donne's elegy on Shakespeare, Milton's poem consists of eight rhyming couplets composed in iambic pentameter. Milton's elegy serves as a response to the earlier composition. Donne's poem looks forward to the possibility that Shakespeare's remains might be laid to rest in Poets' Corner in Westminster Abbey; Milton's poem looks back at what might have been (but is no longer possible). Indeed, what need Shakespeare be buried within '[t]he labour of an Age, in piled stones . . . a starre-ypointing Pyramid', that is, Westminster Abbey? In Milton's view we have the Folios and that is enough.

As the last goal of this essay, I shall attempt to restore the text of Donne's elegy on Shakespeare to reflect his final intentions (if matters had not gone badly). As noted, JDP represents Donne's rough draft whereas C represents his final draft, including both his improvements upon JDP and those changes he made to bring the elegy back into a state of acceptability. Dividing the substantive changes in C into these two categories, the goal is to retain the improvements in C while restoring from JDP those original readings that had been earlier set to one side in the light of political considerations.

I will begin with the improvements, which are perhaps easier to see and appreciate. As previously discussed, lines 1–2 of JDP were substantially rewritten to eliminate the infelicitous duplication of *Beaumond* in the second line, to excellent effect. Similarly, substituting *lodge* for *lie* in line 5 effectively dispelled the awkwardness of *lie* appearing three times in the first five lines of the verse.

As for those changes made for political reasons, the insertion of lines 13–14 in C and the substitution of C's *carved marble* for JDP's *curled marble* have already been discussed. To soften the poem's tone, the somewhat peremptory *need* in line 8 of JDP was replaced by the more placating *may* of C, with a consequent weakening of the line.

---

[45] Bald, *John Donne*, p. 382.

[46] See William B. Todd, 'The Issues and States of the Second Folio and Milton's Epitaph on Shakespeare', *Studies in Bibliography*, 5 (1952–53), 81–108.

[47] 'Not estimated or fixed in value; extremely great or valuable.' *OED*.

A more peculiar change occurs in lines 9–10. In JDP these lines read as follows:

> But, if precedency of death doth barre
> A fourth place in your sacred sepulchre . . .

In c they appear as –

> *If your precedency in* Death doth barr
> A fourth place in your sacred Sepulchre. . . .
> (emphasis added)

It has been understood by all editors that 'your precedency in death' refers to the earlier deaths of Chaucer, Spenser and Beaumont. (The sense is, in effect, 'If the three of you being buried first in the Poets' Corner for some reason precludes the burial of a fourth . . .') However, in the earlier (JDP) version the reading permits an ambiguity: it fails to specify whose death is being invoked. It could even refer to Donne's own death, for Donne's sudden and very premature demise would certainly bring to a halt any plan for transferring Shakespeare's relics to Westminster Abbey. Or, for that matter, it could refer to the death of anyone necessary for the success of the project. This would not have been Donne's intended meaning, of course, but the curse on Shakespeare's grave might well have cast his original lines into an ominous light. The revision eliminates this sinister ambiguity – but at a cost. In JDP lines 5–14 form a single sentence whereas the revision of line 9 in c breaks that sentence into two shorter sentences, thereby impairing its gathering power and momentum. With the benefit of history, however, we know that Donne did not come to an untimely end. Therefore, the original reading in JDP can be restored.

This leaves the matter of the title. A rough draft of a poem need not have a title at all. JDP's title, 'An Epitaph upon Shakespeare', appears purely descriptive, a title that might be added by an editor to an untitled draft found among Donne's papers. In contrast, the title of c, 'On Mr William Shakespeare who died in April 1616', has a sharp specificity: first name, last name, social rank and date of death – the last for those unaware of when the great dramatist had died or, in some cases, for those unaware even that he *had* died. It is a call for a redress of honors.

Some of the titles of Donne's poems have a similar specificity – 'Eclogue. 1613. December 26', 'To the Countesse of Salisbury. August. 1614', and, most famously, 'Goodfriday, 1613. Riding Westward.'

In summary, for a postulated 'best' text of the elegy, the title and lines 1–7 are identical with c. The *may* in c's line 8 is replaced by JDP's *need*. c's line 9 is replaced by line 9 of JDP. The *carved* in c's line 11 is replaced by JDP's *curled*. Lines 13 and 14 in c are deleted altogether.[48] In conclusion, and with some trepidation, I put forward a 'best' text for Donne's restored elegy on Shakespeare, with modernized spelling:

On Mr William Shakespeare
who died in April 1616.

> Renowned Spenser, lie a thought more nigh
> To learned Chaucer, and rare Beaumont lie
> A little nearer Spenser, to make room
> For Shakespeare in your threefold fourfold tomb.
> To lodge all four in one bed make a shift   5
> Until Doomsday, for hardly will a fifth
> Betwixt this day and that by fate be slain
> For whom your curtains need be drawn again;
> But if precedency of death doth bar
> A fourth place in your sacred sepulchre,   10
> Under this curled marble of thine own
> Sleep rare Tragedian Shakespeare, sleep alone,
> That unto us and others it may be
> Honour hereafter to be laid by thee.
>
> Donne

APPENDIX

TEXTUAL WITNESSES TO THE ELEGY
ON SHAKESPEARE

In their 1987 *William Shakespeare: A Textual Companion*, Wells and Taylor provide sigla for those witnesses of the elegy known to them, thirty-three in all, twenty-seven manuscripts and six

---

[48] However, since lines 13–14 in c –

> Thy unmolested peace, unshared cave
> Possess as Lord, not tenant, of thy grave;

– are also by Donne, they should be given in a footnote, as here.

seventeenth-century printed texts.[49] The present study employs the Wells and Taylor sigla while adding seven additional manuscripts (B6, B7, C, F9a, F9b, F10, M) and one additional seventeenth-century printed text (WW). In their 1879 *Shakespeare's Centurie of Prayse*,[50] Ingleby and Smith comment upon ten manuscripts and five seventeenth-century printed texts of the elegy. Their correspondences to the present sigla are as follows, in numerical order: for the manuscripts, I = B4, 2 = F1, 3 = C, 4 = O5, 5 = O7, 6 = O6, 7 = B5, 8 = R1, 9 = O1, 10 = B7; for the printed texts, I = JDP, II = SP, III = WR (1640 ed.), IV = WR (1641 ed.), V = FBP.

SIGLA

B1   British Library, London, Add. MS 10309, fol. 119^v

B2   British Library, London, Add. MS 15227, fol. 77^r

B3   British Library, London, Harleian MS 791, fol. 63^v

B4   British Library, London, Lansdowne MS 777, fol. 67^v

B5   British Library, London, Sloane MS 1792, fol. 114^r

B6   British Library, London, Stowe MS 962, fols. 78^v–79^r

B7   British Library, London, Harleian MS 1749, fol. 289^v

C   Chetham's Library, Manchester, Halliwell-Phillips MS 2757^r
(Wells and Taylor siglum HP2 is an 1851 facsimile of C. HP2 is not included here as being redundant with C.)

F1   Folger Library, Washington DC, MS v.a.103, Pt. I, fol. 3^v

F2   Folger Library, Washington DC, MS v.a.125, Pt. II, fol. 8^{r-v}

F3   Folger Library, Washington DC, MS v.a.232, pp. 62–3

F4   Folger Library, Washington DC, MS v.a.262, pp. 57–8

F5   Folger Library, Washington DC, MS v.a.275, p. 174

F6   Folger Library, Washington DC, MS v.a.319, fol. 6^r

F7   Folger Library, Washington DC, MS v.a.322, pp. 189–90

F8   Folger Library, Washington DC, MS v.a.345, p. 74

F9a   Folger Library, Washington DC, MS v.b.35, no. 70
(Transcript of JDP.)

F9b   Folger Library, Washington DC, MS v.b.35, no. 31
(Transcript of JDP.)

F10   Folger Library, Washington DC, MS y.d.338

FBP   Francis Beaumont, *Poems* (1653), sig. M1^r
(Transcript of WR, 1650 ed. A further edition of FBP in 1660 made use of pages remaindered from the 1653 edition. Therefore, the text in the 1653 and 1660 editions of FBP are literally identical.)

JDP   John Donne, *Poems* (1633), sig. Y3^r
(The page is misnumbered as 149 *recte* 165. The text does not appear in editions of Donne's *Poems* subsequent to 1633.)

M   Morgan Library, New York, MS MA 1058, p. 200

N   Hallward Library, University of Nottingham, Nottingham, MS Pw v 37, p. 5

O1   Bodleian Library, Oxford, Ashmole MS 38, p. 203

O2   Corpus Christi College Library, Oxford, MS CCC 328, fol. 59^r

O3   Bodleian Library, Oxford, MS Eng.poet.c.50, fols. 59^v–60^r

O4   Bodleian Library, Oxford, MS Eng.poet.e.14, fol. 98^v

O5   Bodleian Library, Oxford, MS Malone 19, fol. 40^r

O6   Bodleian Library, Oxford, MS Rawlinson poet.117, fol. 16^v

---

[49] Wells and Taylor, *William Shakespeare: A Textual Companion*, pp. 163–4.

[50] Ingleby and Smith, *Shakespeare's Centurie*, pp. 138–9.

o7   Bodleian Library, Oxford, MS Rawlinson poet.160, fol. 13^v

o8   Bodleian Library, Oxford, MS Rawlinson poet.199, p. 54

R1   Rosenbach Library, Philadelphia, MS 239/22, fol. 19^v
(Wells and Taylor siglum HP1 is an 1846 transcript of R1. HP1 is not included here as being redundant with R1.)

R2   Rosenbach Library, Philadelphia, MS 239/23, p. 187

R3   Rosenbach Library, Philadelphia, MS 1083/17, p. 7

SP   William Shakespeare, *Poems* (1640), sig. K8^v

WR   *Wits Recreations* (1640), sig. AA2^r
(Further editions in 1641, 1645, 1650, 1654, 1663, 1665, 1667 and 1683. Editions subsequent to 1641 are entitled *Recreation for ingenious head-peeces.*)

WW   William Winstanley, *England's Worthies* (1684), pp. 346–7.
(Transcript of WR, 1667 edition)

Y1   Yale University Library, New Haven, MS Osborn b.197, p. 48

Y2   Yale University Library, New Haven, MS Osborn fb 143, p. 20
(Transcript of WR, 1683 edition)

'SOMETIME A PARADOX': SHAKESPEARE, DIDEROT AND THE PROBLEM OF CHARACTER

JONATHAN HOLMES

With characteristic flair for paradox, the Argentine writer Jorge Luis Borges describes the protagonist of his parable *Everything and Nothing* in almost entirely negative terms:

There was no one in him; behind his face (which even through the bad paintings of those times resembles no other) and his words, which were copious, fantastic and stormy, there was only a bit of coldness, a dream dreamt by no-one.[1]

Part of the joy of reading this extremely short text comes from the skilled and gradual way in which Borges allows the reader to fill in these instances of lack, these gaps, counterbalancing negative with positive terms, juxtaposing pieces of evidence to the point at which an identity can be surmised. When, in the final sentence, none other than the voice of God confirms the suspicions that have become a certainty, we also feel able to address the protagonist, intimately, as 'my Shakespeare'.

Borges places the reader in a proprietary position that is also one of authorship. The efficacy of the parable relies on the prior knowledge of the reader of such clues as 'small Latin and less Greek', depends, in fact, on her ability to guess the solution before she is told it, creating the identity of the subject herself and coming to own it through the possessive pronoun 'my'. The reader authors, and owns, Shakespeare, a Shakespeare, moreover, who is in the last sentence explicitly connected to the divine in a phrase that also recalls the title, as God tells him, 'you, like myself, are many and no one'. Shakespeare is sacred and omnipresent, yet 'empty' and non-existent, his paradoxical selfhood existing only in his work. Intriguingly, for Borges this work is not principally that of poetry or literature:

Instinctively he had already become proficient in the habit of simulating that he was someone, so that others would not discover his condition as no one; in London he found the profession to which he was predestined, that of the actor, who on a stage plays at being another before a gathering of people who play at taking him for that other person.[2]

Performing is the principal means of the character's self-construction, and the playwriting that follows is merely an extension of this act.

Borges therefore establishes a series of rhetorical operations that play upon both the microscopic act of reading and the macroscopic operations of cultural signification. The reader in turn both participates in the creation of this brief fable and also in the production of the larger Shakespearian myth.[3] In both cases an appropriative move is made in response to the force of this larger authority. And the locus of all these strategies is an actor, who himself is appropriated within the tale by the divine Word.

The connection with performance is underscored by the title of the parable, which is taken

---

[1] Jorge Luis Borges, 'Everything and Nothing' in *Labyrinths*, ed. Donald Yates and James Irby (Harmondsworth, 1964), p. 284.

[2] Borges, 'Everything and Nothing', p. 284.

[3] Much work remains to be done in the remarkably undertheorised area of audience response. See Susan Bennett, *Theatre Audiences: A Theory of Production and Reception* (London, 1990), and Keir Elam, *The Semiotics of Theatre and Drama* (London, 1988).

from Diderot's quasi-Socratic dialogue, *The Paradox of the Actor*:

SECOND SPEAKER If you're to be believed, the great actor is everything and nothing.

FIRST SPEAKER And perhaps it is because he's nothing that he's everything to perfection, since his particular form never stands in the way of the alien forms he has to assume.[4]

Borges therefore identifies Shakespeare before all else as an actor, appropriating Diderot's criteria of totality and invisibility as features also of divinity. It is the complete identification of Shakespeare with the role of actor that deifies him; the consummate actor is God himself. Diderot continues, in what reads almost as an explication of Borges:

It's been said that actors have no character because playing them all makes them lose the one that nature gave them . . . I think people have taken the cause for the effect, and that they're only fitted to play all characters because they haven't got one of their own.[5]

Actors, and Shakespeare as the paradigm of acting, are so proficient at projecting an illusion of complete subjectivity because of the absence of such a quality within themselves. Shakespeare's universality stems from his anonymity, a presence made from absence. As Philippe Lacou-Labarthe, in his analysis of Diderot's text, writes:

The paradox lies, then, in the following: in order to do everything, to imitate everything . . . one must oneself be nothing, have nothing proper to oneself except an "equal aptitude" for all sorts of things; roles, characters, functions and so on. The paradox states a law of impropriety, which is also the very law of mimesis: only the 'man without qualities', the being without properties or specificity, the subjectless subject, is able to present or produce in general.[6]

Within Borges's fable, therefore, lies another paradox – that of ownership. In his state of everything and nothing, the protagonist cannot possess, nor can his divine mimetic model. 'My' Shakespeare is an impossibility, as it presupposes a stable, fixed subject to perform the act of ownership. As Lacou-Labarthe remarks, the paradox is one of 'impropriety and appropriation'. The actor does not own, but for a time appropriates, 'dressed in a little brief

authority',[7] the name of an Other. As Borges illustrates, this is also the condition of Shakespearian authorship, the consequence of an attempt to stand as if he were 'author of himself/And knew no other kin'.[8]

In his Preface to the 1883 edition of *The Paradox of the Actor*, translated by his friend Walter Herries Pollock, Henry Irving wrote that: 'The mind [of an actor] should have, as it were, a double consciousness, in which all the emotions proper to the occasion may have full sway, while the actor is all the time on the alert for every detail of his method.'[9] Irving is deliberately reviving a controversy that flourished in the mid-eighteenth century and focussed on the 'sensibility' of actors – the extent to which they experience the emotion they play. Diderot's *Paradox* was a contribution to this debate, which very much centred on the performances of David Garrick.

Irving's articulation in his Preface of a 'double consciousness', focussing on the character and on the actor, connects to Borges' concept of the parallel production of selfhood with the theatrical work. The actor is always aware of his position in relation to the work as well as his position within it. Irving continues: 'Perhaps it will always be an open question how far these things . . . can be fused in the same mind. Every actor has his secret. He

---

[4] Diderot, *The Paradox of the Actor*, in *Selected Writings on Art and Literature*, ed. and trans. Geoffrey Bremner (Harmondsworth, 1994), p. 129. The *Paradox* was never published in Diderot's lifetime (though a protoype article, *Observations*, appeared in 1779), and was only fully available in English in the early nineteenth century. Diderot did, however, send a manuscript copy to Garrick.

[5] Diderot, *Paradox*, p. 135.

[6] Philippe Lacou-Labarthe, 'Paradox and Mimesis', in *Typography*, trans. Christopher Fynsk (Stanford, 1998, originally published in French in 1979), p. 258.

[7] Shakespeare, *Measure for Measure*, in Stanley Wells and Gary Taylor, eds., *The Complete Works of William Shakespeare* (Oxford, 1988), 2.2.121. All references to the plays of Shakespeare are to this edition unless otherwise stated.

[8] Shakespeare, *Coriolanus*, 5.3.36–7.

[9] Irving, Preface to *The Paradox of the Actor*, reprinted in Diderot/Archer, *The Paradox of Acting/Masks or Faces?* (New York, 1957), p. 8.

might write volumes of explanation, and the matter would still remain a paradox to many.'[10] In an attempt to resolve this paradox, Irving entered into a lengthy and public print debate with the French actor Constant Coquelin. Despite their disagreements, and Coquelin's frequent disparagements of Irving's performances, the pair frequently came close to articulating the same position. In 1887 Coquelin wrote,

The actor must have a double personality. He has his first self, which is the player, and his second self, which is the instrument . . . the first self sees the person such as he was formed by the author . . . and the being that he sees is represented by the second.[11]

Appropriate to its place in a longstanding debate, this notion of dual personalities is first expressed as such by the friend of Garrick, James Boswell, who over a century earlier had written that,

My conjecture is that he [the actor] must have a kind of double feeling. He must assume to a strong degree the character he represents, while he at the same time retains the consciousness of his own character.[12]

Such duality is connected by Coquelin to the division of mind and body, and in turn is derived strongly from the latter's reading of Enlightenment *philosophes* (including Diderot): 'the part of us which sees should rule as absolutely as possible the part of us which executes. Though this is always true, it is especially true of the moment of representation'.[13] Indeed, the very act of representation itself, of mimesis, depends upon this duality. William Archer's famous response to Irving (and to the re-publication of Diderot's text), *Masks and Faces*, concludes that 'mimetic emotion is not, as some people argue, a state of mere vague unspecialised excitement, but is closely analogous to the emotion of real life'.[14] Archer is concerned in his text to effect a reconciliation to the debate on sensibility that had passed to and fro across the English Channel for the previous century and a half by recasting the terms of the argument; for him 'acting is imitative, or it is nothing'. The whole debate on sensibility is missing the point. Actors may feel or they may not feel emotions connected to their

part; what is of issue is the nature of their selfhood and its relationship to their performance personae.

Interestingly, Archer is identifying (though he does not explicitly state this) the nub of the difference between French and English language positions on the argument. The French, from Diderot through Coquelin and up to Lacoue-Labarthe, are discussing consciousness and selfhood (this is also Borges's entry point), while the English, from John Hill's *The Actor*, which started the argument in 1750, through to Irving (and nominally including Lee Strasberg in the twentieth century, who wrote a preface to Irving's introduction of Archer's reply to Pollock's translation of Diderot), focus simply on the subjective experience of performing. (Appropriately enough, given this distinction, the eighteenth-century debate was initiated in fact by English plagiarism of a French text, as we shall see).

In support of his position that actors do not undergo the emotions they portray and effect a dual consciousness, Diderot points to the example of Garrick, who, he claims, was notorious for the artificiality of a method that produced startlingly realistic results. As Joseph Roach in particular has demonstrated, the debt of Diderot to the 'English Roscius' was enormous. Familiar to the *philosophes* from his Paris performances of 1764,[15] comprised principally of monologues from Shakespeare, Garrick 'became the central exhibit in their taxonomy of genius, a natural phenomenon to be studied for clues to the general workings of nature'.[16] Ironically, the text that had galvanised Diderot's

---

[10] Irving, *Preface*, p. 10.

[11] Coquelin, 'Acting and Actors', *Harper's Magazine*, May 1887.

[12] Boswell, 'On the Profession of a Player', *London Magazine*, August 1770.

[13] Coquelin, 'Acting and Actors'.

[14] Archer, *Masks and Faces*, p. 200.

[15] Diderot saw Garrick perform several times and, along with D'Alembert, met him at a reception hosted by the English Ambassador in May 1764.

[16] Joseph Roach, *The Player's Passion: Studies in the Science of Acting* (London, 1985), p. 127. Roach's book is a thoughtful and incisive account of the relationship between acting and the sciences, and an invaluable reconstruction of performance theories and methodologies over four centuries.

repudiation, Hill's *The Actor*, also used Garrick as the exemplar of precisely the opposing view. In it, he writes that 'the performer who does not himself feel the several emotions he is to express to the audience will give but a lifeless and insipid representation',[17] and goes on to describe Garrick's deeply felt characterizations. Garrick himself does not illuminate the matter greatly, writing that:

Would the painter produce a perfect piece to the world, let him copy from the life, let nature herself sit to the artist: would a player perform equally well in his profession, let him be introduced into the world, be conversant with humours of every kind, digest them in his mind, let them be cherished by the general warmth of his conception, transplanted into the fair garden of his judgement, there let them ripen to perfection and become his own.[18]

Garrick's tactful lack of explicit commitment to either position seems deliberate and artful. It is easy to see how he could be co-opted for either side of the argument, and indeed continues to be so to this day.[19]

In Garrick was to be found the collision of two performance traditions, one technical, the other historical. He shared with Diderot a broadly Cartesian understanding of the body as a machine activated by spirit (though Diderot sporadically quibbled with this principle), a similarity of basic medical understanding that had been applied to acting for over a century and which attained a certain fashionable status in this connection in the mid eighteenth century. He also, however, located himself strongly in a genealogy of performing Shakespeare, and it was to this end that his disquisitions upon the art of acting were directed.[20] If 'Diderot thought he had found a perfect acting machine',[21] it was a machine inspired by and devoted to traditions of performing Shakespeare.

In short, Diderot's text and the surrounding debate are based upon a model which itself owed much to the Shakespearian theatre, and as such becomes a kind of reading of Shakespearian performance. The absent presence of Shakespeare, a ghost within the Enlightenment machine, can therefore be recalled in a way that finds the actor to have been elided within a superordinate discourse.

This sense of theatrical tradition underlying aesthetic theory is evident in the polemic that originated the whole debate on sensibility – not Hill's 1750 *The Actor*, but the work he plagiarised to produce his own text; Remond Sainte-Albine's 1747 *Le Comedien*. Sainte-Albine's argument is the dual primacy of 'understanding and sensibility' in the actor, most specifically, the comic actor:

In considering to what set of actors this general sensibility is most necessary, we shall find comedy most demands it . . . all that can affect the human heart comes within [the comedien's] business.[22]

Sainte-Albine's purpose is broadly to assert the superiority of the French tradition of comedy to the English reliance on tragedy, Moliere over Shakespeare. In borrowing his text almost word for word but then eliminating the sections on comedy, Hill manages paradoxically to achieve the reverse. A text designed to promote French traditions of comedy is co-opted to advocate English traditions of performing Shakespearian tragedy. Ironically, the publication of *Le Comedien* seems to have gone almost entirely unnoticed in France, whereas Hill's plagiarised version was an instant success. When the actor Antonio Sticcotti, apparently unaware of Sainte-Albine's original, translated Hill's book into French shortly after its publication (at which point Diderot seems to have become aware of the argument), a generic shift had unknowingly occurred. The argument initiated by Hill's moment of opportunism, which was to run for the better part of two centuries and which preoccupied most of the celebrated practitioners and commentators of both

---

17 John Hill, *The Actor* (London, 1750).
18 *Essay on Acting: In which will be considered the Mimical Behaviour of a Certain Fashionable Faulty Actor, to which will be added a Short Criticism of His acting Macbeth* (London, 1744) p. 13.
19 Jean Benedetti's recent book on Garrick, *David Garrick and the Birth of Modern Theatre* (Methuen, 2001) does just this, co-opting Garrick as prototype Stanislavskian.
20 See in particular his *Essay on Acting*.
21 Roach, *Player's Passion*, p. 152.
22 Sainte-Albine, *Le Comedien*, p. 66.

countries, cemented the association of sensibility pre-eminently with tragedy, and arguably helped assert its dominance in the canons of Romantic taste.

Connectedly, the ongoing debate about sensibility and selfhood gave momentum to a decisive shift in the conception of acting, away from a broadly rhetorical approach and towards one that was increasingly based on a form of introspection and on rudimentary notions of psychology. This shift can be observed by once again looking at Sainte-Albine:

It has been said that whatever passion we would raise by our discourse in others, we must first feel ourselves. This was the art by which the Greek orator bore down all things before him.[23]

Despite the reference to the 'Greek' orator, Sainte-Albine probably has in mind the maxim of Horace, 'if you would have me weep, you must yourself suffer pain'.[24] Yet it is the location of his perspective in the art of rhetoric that is of interest – by the time the text has been plagiarized, translated and re-translated (in other words, by the time Diderot lays hands on it), this emphasis has gone, to be replaced by an analysis of what Garrick does with character and with personality.

The school of rhetorical thought to which Sainte-Albine is elliptically referring originates with Plato, in the *Phaedrus*. In this dialogue, Socrates is at pains to demonstrate the necessity for the rhetorician of both knowing accurately and firmly believing in the truth of any statement. Rhetoric has an ethical responsibility to be truthful, but just as importantly it won't be as effective if it is founded upon lies: As Socrates states, 'there is not nor ever shall be a genuine art of speaking which is divorced from grasp of truth'.[25] A grasp of truth is defined by an awareness of resemblance: 'a man . . . must have an exact knowledge of the likenesses and unlikenesses between things [to know their true nature]'.[26] Truth, in the *Phaedrus*, depends not just on the layers of mimesis which, when stripped away, eventually reveal the Form, but also on degrees of resemblance *between* Forms, and therefore also between

their everyday representations. This in turn correlates with Plato's famous refutation of mimesis in Book III of *The Republic*, where the intrusion of yet another layer of representation – performance – distances those involved in it still further from the truth. Performance is insubstantial and distracting; everything, in Diderot's phrase, and yet nothing. Rhetoric, which does not involve the adoption of a persona and should not involve deception or dissimulation (this is the argument of the *Phaedrus*), is the correct, purely diegetic, vehicle for truth, whereas poetry and performing are mimetic falsehoods. Importantly, this taxonomy of similitude extends also to Platonic ethics, based on the principle of emulation of the Form of the Good. The closer resemblances can be discerned in every aspect of the world, the more the philosopher sees the connections that underlie everything. Oliver Goldsmith famously wrote of his friend Garrick in 1774:

On the stage he was natural, simple, affecting;
'Twas only that when he was off, he was acting.[27]

Garrick's success rested on a performance of mimesis that was not restricted to the stage, but overflowed into conventional life also. He blurred conventional distinctions, creating a persona that was able to adopt any variation of identity without remaining fixed to an unfailing self. In Borgesian fashion he was everything and yet nothing. In his analysis of Diderot, Lacou-Labarthe identifies the paradox of 'everything and nothing' as a founding principle of mimesis as described by Plato: the mimetic act is only possible if identity is simultaneously negated and pluralized, whether this be through fragmentation or multiplication,

---

[23] Sainte Albine, p. 49.

[24] Horace, *Ars Poetica* , in C.O.Brink, *Horace on Poetry* (Cambridge, 1971), vol. 2, 83.

[25] Plato, *Phaedrus*, in Walter Hamilton, ed., *Phaedrus and letters VII and VIII* (Harmondsworth, 1973) p. 73.

[26] Plato, p. 75.

[27] Oliver Goldsmith, *Retaliation*, in Arthur Friedman, ed., *The Collected Works of Oliver Goldsmith*, 5 vols.(Oxford, 1966), 4: 352–62 (357, lines 101–2).

while remaining unfixed and impermanent. Plenitude is a result of absence.

Such an equal aptitude for so many things was
characterized by Plato as dangerous and to be
excluded in case it provoked dissent or, worse, madness. The principle of truth exists in recognition
of the principle of mimetic connection – not in
the adoption (at best potentially criminal, at worst
insane) of the various mimetic roles and categories
themselves. Diderot, in the *Paradox*, is also aware of
this possibility: 'In the great comedy, the comedy
of the world, the one to which I always return, all
the hot-blooded people are on the stage; all the
men of genius are in the pit. The first are called
madmen, the second are called wise men.'[28] The
mimetic act is insane, precisely because it forecloses
one identity in order to open up a proliferation
of other selves. The paradox of being everything
and nothing is sufficiently disruptive as to constitute a condition of insanity. Such a condition also
begins to blur the distinctions between 'stage' and
'pit', as the boundaries between sane and mad are
transgressed.[29]

In the approach to character itself, Coquelin also
is under no illusions as to the insanity of trying to
'be' a character: 'it is false and ridiculous to think
that it is a proof of the highest art for the actor to
forget that he is before the public . . . you have
ceased to be an actor: you are a madman'. In short,
'art is, I repeat, not identification but representation'.[30] For Coquelin the comedic actor, control is
everything: 'the part of us which sees should rule
as absolutely as possible the part of us that executes.
Though this is always true, it is especially true of
the moment of representation. In other words, the
actor should remain master of himself.'[31]

This dichotomy between 'representing' – a safe,
sane, rhetorical act, most conducive to creating art,
and 'becoming' – a dangerous, deceitful and even
psychotic act unconnected to art – is prefigured in
the distinction between Platonic and Aristotelian
mimesis. In the *Poetics*, Aristotle amends Plato's definition of mimesis in one crucial respect; instead of
imitating personality, the poet or the actor imitates
action. For Aristotle, an engagement with personality or character, with *ethos*, is not required; instead

action, *praxis*, is the subject of the mimetic act. Crucially, this removes ethical content from the process
of mimesis itself and places it on the action that is
the subject of this process: 'imitation is differentiated – by the means, by the objects, and by the
manner of presentation'.[32] Therefore, whether or
not mimesis is ethical depends on what is being
imitated. The process itself is neutral, a rhetorical
act rather than a moral one, whereas in Plato artistic
mimesis itself is intrinsically unethical.

Aristotle enhances his ethical rehabilitation of
mimesis further by introducing the notion of
catharsis. In complete contradistinction to Plato,
not only are playgoers not damaged by their experiences, they can actually experience psychological benefits from them. Aristotelian mimesis, of
course, relocates the sensibility debate entirely –
what is important is not the response of the actors,
but of those, in Borges' memorable phrase, 'who
play at taking him for that other person'; the audience, who may well experience some purgative
emotional response to those events. This model is
one of which both Coquelin and his hero Diderot
would have approved.

The eighteenth-century debate on sensibility is
in fact a confused extension of two, distinct prior
arguments: one about the moral contamination
of spectators, the other concerning the nature of
mimesis itself. In its superficial concern with the
authentic experience of emotion by either or both
performers and spectators the debate is heir to a
long tradition of anti-theatricalist polemic and pro-
theatrical folklore. For example, in 1579 Stephen
Gosson railed against the new theatres, claiming
in no uncertain terms that 'if you go to theatres
to drive away fancies, it is as good physicke as for
the ache of your head to knock out your brains'.[33]

---

[28] Diderot, *Paradox*, p. 106.

[29] See the work of Michel Foucault, especially *Madness and Civil-
isation*, trans. R. Howard (New York, 1965).

[30] Coquelin, 'Acting and Actors'.

[31] Coquelin, 'Acting and Actors'.

[32] Aristotle, *Poetics*, trans. James Hutton (New York and London,
1982), p. 47.

[33] Gosson, *The School of Abuse* (London, 1841), p. 50.

Theatre polemicists for the next half-century argued similarly for the invidious influence of the stage upon the spectator's mental state. Plays will make you mad, or at the very least provoke a kind of histrionic hypnosis, under the influence of which almost anything can happen. Famously this view-point reached its logical conclusion in various anec-dotes (designed to promote a positive image of the theatre) describing the spontaneous confession of a guilty party upon seeing a re-enactment of their crime on stage, the popularity of which is evi-denced in the motivation for Hamlet's directorial debut: 'The play's the thing,/Wherein I'll catch the conscience of the King.'[34] The diarist John Evelyn continued this theme of theatre and madness sev-eral years later, remarking after a visit to the famous Bethlehem Hospital for the insane, or Bedlam, in 1657, that 'I stepped into Bedlam, where I saw several poor miserable creatures in chains; one of them was mad with making verses.'[35] The link here is clearly with Hamlet; madness produces an excess of words, words, words, but words that are stifled, quashed and suppressed. This suppression is carried out on behalf of the general populace, preventing a dangerous 'contagion' of madness, though this did not prevent Bedlam becoming a tourist attrac-tion – somewhere to go when there was nothing on at the theatre. As Evelyn was aware, there is a link between the site of madness and the site of performance.

Such excess, such plurality, at once plenitude and absence as Lacoue-Labarthe states, is most elo-quently expressed in the most famous play about madness and acting, *Hamlet*. In seeking to pluck the heart from Hamlet's mystery, Polonius, that soul of wit, defines 'true madness' as 'to be nothing else but mad'.[36] In Polonius's taxonomy, insanity is exclu-sive, incomparable and incompatible with any other state. It is a figure dissimilar from any other trope, famously 'unlike' itself. Hamlet himself later takes this further, characterising madness as an exclusion of identity, an abdication of self:

Was't Hamlet wronged Laertes? Never Hamlet.
If Hamlet from himself be ta'en away,
And when he's not himself does wrong Laertes,

Then Hamlet does it not, Hamlet denies it.
Who does it then? His madness. If't be so,
Hamlet is of the faction that is wronged,
His madness is poor Hamlet's enemy.[37]

The proliferation of Hamlets in this speech conceals the fundamental absence of any interior selfhood that is able to take responsibility for Laertes's wrong. The insanity he claims makes an ethical judgement inapplicable. Hamlet's subjectivity is both decen-tred and plural, everything and nothing.

As can be seen in *Hamlet*, the debate on sensi-bility disguises a more profound concern with rep-resentation – with mimesis – with the connections between exterior and interior selves. It is a debate that in the theatre, until the Shakespearian perfor-mances of David Garrick, had been concerned as much with the impact of performances upon the spectator as with their construction by the actor. The immense fame and admiration that greeted Garrick's career moved the philosophical emphasis firmly onto the experience of performers and their relationship to character, thus effecting a signifi-cant shift in the notion of mimesis itself in acting, away from a post-Aristotelian paradigm of imita-tion of action and *praxis*, and towards a Platonic understanding of theatrical mimesis as a becoming. The repercussions of this shift are significant. As Shearer West, Edward Burns and others have noted, Garrick's performances influenced theorisation and consequent practice in both fine art and the emerg-ing new form of the novel.[38] And Theodor Adorno has discussed at length the consequences that a shift from imitation of action and movement towards one of personality and verisimilitude had for music and its relation to mimesis.[39]

---

[34] *Hamlet*, ed. Wells and Taylor (Oxford, 1987), 2.2. 606–7. All references to Shakespeare are to this edition.

[35] John Evelyn, *Diaries*, April 21, 1657.

[36] *Hamlet*, 2.2.94–5.

[37] *Hamlet*, 5.2.179–85.

[38] See Shearer West, *The Image of the Actor: Verbal and Visual Rep-resentation in the age of Garrick and Kemble* (London, 1991), and Edward Burns, *Character, Actor and Being on the Early Modern Stage* (London, 1990).

[39] See Theodor Adorno, *Aesthetic Theory*, ed. and trans. Robert Hullot-Kentor (London, 1997).

Of course, Garrick himself was indebted to a constantly evolving acting tradition (in his case, probably most of all to the performances of Charles Macklin, particularly his Shylock) for his performance style. But this tradition was almost exclusively a tradition of performing Shakespeare, and it was Garrick's position as the first great international celebrity of his profession that placed this tradition – encapsulated in Garrick's own Shakespearian performances – at the forefront of contemporary European discourse on the arts. While Jean Benedetti's recent appropriation of Garrick as a prototype Stanislavski is tendentious, it is perhaps not stretching a point too far to see the mid-eighteenth-century intellectual controversy surrounding him as the beginning of a shift in the understanding of acting that would culminate a century and a half later in the work of the Moscow Art Theatre. By the time of Diderot's *Paradox* the debates about mimesis in the performing arts had settled into a constellation of recurring concerns that are very much still with us – psychology and neurosis, character and consistency, catharsis and sensibility, and above all the ethical position of mimesis itself. These issues, the central points of contention for debates on acting for centuries, came to a head in a particular series of performances of *Hamlet* towards the end of the twentieth century.

In 1989 The Royal Shakespeare Company performed *Hamlet*, in tandem with *Romeo and Juliet*, at Broadmoor, a secure psychiatric hospital for the criminally insane just outside London. It is one of the most well-known (and often sensationalized) examples of its kind in Europe, and houses some of the most notorious serial killers, rapists and disturbed criminals in Britain. This performance was as site-specific and as audience-specific as theatre can get, as every individual present was known not only by name but by history – the actors by their programme biographies and performance histories, the audience by their criminal records and psychiatric profiles.

The performance was subject to certain logistical restrictions – each member of the audience was vetted before being allowed to take part, and the cast were understandably concerned about taking swords and other weapons into the venue, just in case any guilty creatures were inspired to take action against their own sea of troubles. The venue itself was the central assembly hall of the building, an actual panopticon.

The event was subsequently documented by the organizer, psychotherapist Murray Cox, in his book *Shakespeare Comes to Broadmoor*. This fascinating text is constructed as a sequence of testimonies, in which editor, actors, director, nurses, administrators, patients, dramatherapists and other featured players recall and record the encounter between the Shakespearian text and the hospital.[40] The structure of the book itself, then, can be seen as mimicking a series of analytic interviews, annotated by the constant editorial presence of Cox, placing the Shakespearian text firmly appropriately in a clinical environment. The Chaplain of the institution, Trevor Walt, remarked:

If all the world is a stage and Broadmoor part of it, then those principal players, the patients, who enter centre stage, are those who may have played leading parts in previous tragedies.[41]

And Mark Rylance, playing Hamlet, commented that 'there was no gap between their attention and ours – I felt they were as much players as we were', an impression reinforced by his feeling that 'I wasn't sure that someone wasn't going to jump up and say something or shout out, that the bonds between fantasy and reality wouldn't go totally'[42], echoing another (unnamed) actor:

[I thought] that the whole thing was going to erupt in psychological flames, and real psychosis would take place in the interaction between a very violent play about insanity and violent insecure minds.[43]

---

40 Murry Cox, ed. *Shakespeare Comes to Broadmoor* (London, 1992). The book focuses on the performance of four plays at Broadmoor over three years; *Hamlet*, *Romeo and Juliet*, *King Lear* and *Measure for Measure*. Reasons of space dictate that this paper concern itself principally with the first of these to take place – *Hamlet*.

41 Cox, *Shakespeare Comes to Broadmoor*, p. 19.

42 Cox, p. 36.

43 Cox, p. 146.

The spirit of the Elizabethan polemicists lives on. Georgia Slowe, playing Juliet in a parallel Broadmoor performance, supplements these remarks:

The difference at Broadmoor was that we were performing the play in front of an audience which probably had been through situations as violent, as traumatic and as emotionally fraught as those in the play, and knew what those situations felt like and looked like in real life. The anxiety was that they would know instantly whether we were faking, they were able to judge us on a much higher level of truth.[44]

Here, the process of acting itself is cast in doubt, the emotional truth implicit in post-Stanislavskian approaches to character is negated by the much 'higher level of truth' evidenced by those who have undergone actual experience. Unconsciously echoing Plato, Slowe characterizes dramatic mimesis as a lie, a forgery. The attempt to engage in the sensibility of the part, to feel the portrayed emotion, is revealed as unethical. Feeling becomes subordinate to action, or in Aristotelian terms, *ethos* is supplanted by *praxis*. In Diderot's paradoxical terms, the actor can only avoid lying by also avoiding any overt attempt to find a truth.

Such an interpretation is developed by Clare Higgins, playing Gertrude, who recalled a moment in which Rylance, as Hamlet, for the first time pulled a knife on her in the closet scene, unconsciously mimicking a situation in which Higgins had been threatened in such a fashion in real life:

Here in Broadmoor it seemed that all those worlds came together and fused. I thought: I'm doing this, reliving something that happened to me, within Shakespeare, within the discipline of this production, taking this risk in front of people who know about this, who may have done this, who may have had it done to them.[45]

A kind of vertigo sets in, a state of mind in which staged pretence could have real results, as in Kyd's *The Spanish Tragedy* or, more recently, the abymal world of Peter Greenaway's *The Baby of Macon* or Peter Weiss's *Marat/Sade*. Or, of course, as in the final staged play within *Hamlet* – the fencing match. In Borgesian fashion, the world of the play is a mere extension of the world around it. This extreme metatheatricality of action had surprising consequences for the processes of constructing character, so implicated did the actors' own identities become in the proceedings. Higgins continues:

Gertrude/I sat on stage being watched by therapists watching patients watching the King and Queen watching actors playing actors playing the King and Queen. There was a moment when the distinctions were so complex that they almost disappeared.[46]

Paradoxically, it is the sense that the divisions between reality and fiction were dissolving that prompted Higgins's understanding that an attempt to become the character would be false, and even morally wrong. What created this sense of *mise en abyme* was not a conflation of character but a consonance of action. It was the act of playing, of watching a play, of depicting murder and madness that led to the impression, voiced by all the actors interviewed, that boundaries had collapsed. In Aristotelian fashion, mimesis of *praxis* is what counts and, vitally, what works, both practically and ethically. The dissolution of a fourth wall division in the minds of the performers also undermined their carefully constructed characterisations. The hermetically constructed personalities previously thought to be so three-dimensional and truthful were revealed to be shallow, inadequate and even immoral in front of an audience of individuals who had actual experience of the events depicted in the play.

So novel was the experience of seeing theatre in that space for this audience that the processes became as important as the play – perhaps even more so. One patient recalled:

On two occasions now I have watched the performances brought to us and each time I have been left wondering how it is that these people can allow such personal spaces to be invaded.[47]

---

[44] Cox, p. 49.
[45] Cox, p. 66.
[46] Cox, p. 67–8.
[47] Cox, p. 140.

And another commented that: 'it's really strange for you to bring a play about madness to Broadmoor – we are so protected from it here'.[48] The cathartic intention of bringing the productions to Broadmoor seems to have been justified, with patients recounting, in comments that reflect those of the actors, the uncanny nature of seeing the events of this play depicted with such intensity. It is precisely in this intensity that the differences between the performances and the actual nature of the patients' experiences lay. This distinction is described by the psychiatrist Rob Ferris in terms of inverting the relationship between doer and deed, actor and action. In this way the performer, who hasn't killed, paradoxically identifies with the killing, whereas a patient may have killed but 'fails to identify with the act of killing or is unable to identify with their own act of killing'.[49]

This constitutes a diagnosis of psychosis that brings us back to Hamlet's dissociation of self and act. The director of this production of *Hamlet*, Ron Daniels, draws a parallel between the procedure of the actor and that of the analyst:

An actor who is assembling a character will do precisely what [the therapist] does with patients. He [sic] will put together the case history of the character, so that when you are talking about Hamlet, the character, usually in front of your eyes, goes on this huge emotional journey.[50]

Daniels is being disingenuous, as the end result of the actor's process is finally to remove the distinction and to affiliate herself with the character, rather than to remain objective and separate, as a therapist would. The psychoanalysis of literary character, pioneered by an appropriation of Freud's references to Hamlet in *The Interpretation of Dreams*, and the quasi-analysis of dramatic character, instituted largely by Stanislavski's notes on *Othello*, merge into a model of investigation of neurotic and, in this instance, psychotic disorders. The relationship between actor and character as that of analyst and patient, in contrast, must maintain the equivalent level of detachment. It is in fact the model suggested by both Irving and Coquelin; the dual consciousness. There is no thought of 'becoming';

rather the actor once again relies on building up a case history and then engaging with action, not personality.

For Clare Higgins, the experience of playing Broadmoor began to question the notion of engaging with personality, and to emphasise the importance of action, which she understands as experience:

It is sad to realise that we drag on an enormous bundle of stuff, build it up into a little edifice and then present it for approval . . . playing 'normal' audiences is all about going out and giving them a show. In Broadmoor it is all about the importance of experience.[51]

This experience removes boundaries and brings audience and actor into direct confrontation with the character. A consequence for Higgins was an increased focus on the silences of Gertrude, the gaps in her speech in which she came to locate her character. It is the textual absences that paradoxically offer an opportunity for character to be present, as in these moments the emphasis is exclusively on the performer's physicality. The feelings of fakery experienced so strongly by both Higgins and Slowe are momentarily suspended due to the authority of the actor's body. If forgery is ultimately the substitution of the other for the self, absence masquerading as presence, then this categorical identity with the processes of character-based performance will, in the context of the Broadmoor event, substantially undermine an actor's conviction. The default option is therefore a reliance on the body. If the dominant twentieth century processes of constructing character are seen as congruent with those of therapeutic analysis, the realisation, when confronted by an actual clinical space, is that the subject of this theatrical analysis is absent. The performer has no 'right' to pathologize their character (as several of the actors in this *Hamlet* acknowledged).

Julia Kristeva, herself a psychoanalyst, has famously critiqued the linear, patriarchal nature

---

48 Cox, p. 148.
49 Cox, p. 85.
50 Cox, p. 85.
51 Cox, p. 70.

of language within the literary text. The dramatic text in performance, however, remains dominated by notions of such linear, patriarchal, post-Stanislavskian psychological consistency. By focusing on the moments of disjunction, the silences within the text that can speak volumes in performance, the actresses in this *Hamlet* cease looking, Polonius-like, for neat formulations, bubbles of character, instead beginning to search out the madness itself. They begin to unconsciously adopt a mode of playing closer to that of the Renaissance stage, with an emphasis on physicality and *praxis*, and a minimum of attention to psychology. In a sense, they also begin to agree with Plato's diagnosis of mimetic identity as unethical, though they do not repeat his rationale. In Broadmoor, the ethics of representation depend on a simpler understanding: that the presentation of psychosis is impossible without a personal experience of it, and that the presentation of that experience, were it possible, would be exploitative and immoral. The dramatherapist Alice Thielgaard writes that

Dramatic space is both intrapsychic, inter-personal and corporate. The Broadmoor audience was linked with all other *Hamlet* audiences. The actors connected with their present peers and predecessors. The patients were caught up in the attentive act by what they saw on the stage and its association with their previous life-experience.[52]

Thielgaard here begins to describe clinically the metatheatricality of the moment and its impact on the participants – a major part of the actors' responses was conditioned by their previous playing experiences. Deborah Warner, who at the instigation of Clare Higgins (playing Regan) later brought her *King Lear* to Broadmoor, commented that much of the intensity was provided simply by the difference in playing a smaller, more intimate space. Like the players within the play who present dangerous material to the guilty creatures sitting watching, the actors here become more concerned with their roles as actors, rather than their acting roles. There is a danger that this fictive dislocation will reverse the conventional mimetic order, with the audience coming centre stage and the gap

between the place on the stage and the place of the stage removed. Elsinore becomes Broadmoor.

In short, the experience for the actors is that of inhabiting several simultaneous roles – actor, character, character-as-roleplayer etc – all of which acquire additional signification in this particular place. As Melinda Meyer comments: 'roles do not emerge from the self, but the self may emerge from roles'.[53] Everything emerges from nothing and, as Borges wrote, a simulation of self emerges from the plurality of roles played. Or, in Diderot's terms, it is because selfhood is in itself fictive that other fictive selves can be so readily adopted – though none of this should be confused with reality. By becoming so aware of their multiple roles the actors find a strong sense of identity from the experience, whereas the characters themselves become fragmented. As Mark Rylance recalled: 'you have different aspects of a single psyche, so that when you play the conscious one, it is you who are the spokesperson to the audience'.[54] This is a view shared by Bert States, who has written that 'to confront character properly we must keep one eye on the group and one eye on the individual, who is in a sense always a metonymic extension of the group itself'.[55] Character is constructed and deconstructed as it goes along, in States's words 'character drifts and is known by the company it keeps' and the principle of coherence becomes the linking signifier of the actor's body. This signifier, so taken for granted in conventional theatre, became exceptionally present for the Broadmoor actors who played within yards of convicted murderers and rapists. The actors' discomfort with their own 'fakery' is a response to this perceived overpowering physical authority. The focus on the psychologically absent, the fictional, the presence made of absence, becomes unbearable under the scrutiny of such extraordinary veracity. Clare Higgins comments that Gertrude's silences

---

52 Cox, p. 76.
53 Cox, p. 205.
54 Cox, p. 30–1.
55 Bert O. States, *Hamlet and the Concept of Character* (Baltimore, Md., 1992), p. xx.

in Broadmoor became 'more profound . . . as important to me as words', and highlighted more 'mirror images' within the experience. Gertrude's 'silence . . . prevents her confronting reality. I see my silence reflected back, particularly by Ophelia.'[56] The women are imprisoned in this increasingly stifling silence, which Higgins began to experience 'palpably', remarking that 'a bolt of energy hit me in the stomach' during the closet scene, 'and I suddenly felt united with the energy of the people in the room'.

Members of the audience echoed the increased attention given to the body and to silence. One patient commented, addressing Mark Rylance and unwittingly echoing Higgins's imagery:

When you picked up the skull it really got to me; hit me right in the stomach. I've killed a person and I've done a lot of work on how the relatives must feel, I've played the role of the relatives; but it never crossed my mind until now that there is a corpse somewhere of the person I killed. I have never thought about the corpse before.[57]

The final authority is the body, and it is the physicality of the action that produced catharsis for this spectator. The experience of playing psychology, both clinically and theatrically, is one of presenting a series of roles rather than attempting the illusion (or delusion) of continuous coherence.

Character construction here becomes in modern dramatic terms disconnected and incoherent, but as suggested earlier in Renaissance terms it becomes infinitely more readable. As Katherine Eisaman Maus has argued, 'English Renaissance theatrical method is . . . one of radical synecdoche, endlessly referring the spectators to events, objects, situations, landscapes that cannot be shown them.'[58] The dominant trope of Renaissance performance is metonymy, 'that within which passeth show'. Such fragmentation is linked in psychoanalytic discourse with psychosis. Because Renaissance dramaturgy privileges action over interiority, *praxis* over *ethos*, it renders its characters, in modern parlance, insane. Like the inhabitants of Broadmoor, they act without the need for identification with their actions, their selfhood defined by interaction with the other bodies onstage and in the auditorium. In psychoanalytic terms, they are subject to a succession of 'controlling identities' – son, brother, lover, revenger – which are distinct from each other and which provoke crisis when they come into conflict. Thus Coriolanus's despairing, and unattainable, plea: 'Rather say I play / The man I am'.[59]

One of the implications of this mode of social characterisation for the Jacobean spectator became the necessity of watching plays paradoxically, aware that what he or she was seeing might not be the truth, 'against the grain', to use the phrase coined in Act 3, Scene 2 of *Coriolanus*. From this paradox came the soliloquy, with its emphasis not on truth but on the revelation of intention. Only the imposition of a quasi-fourth wall technique, in which it is assumed that the character is unaware of the spectator, requires the soliloquy to be inward-looking and confessional. No such restriction existed on the Renaissance stage, where both actor and character were fully aware of the audience. As Rylance commented, 'I didn't feel that I had played the part at all. I felt they played it. Something collective came through me, through the words.'[60] Rylance's performance became defined by his exceptional audience, just as the cast of *The Murder of Gonzago* are defined by the roles played by their audience. Self is abdicated by the performer and constructed by the spectator; the actors make no attempt to forge within themselves a sense of completion.

In this sense, then, to play a Shakespearian character is always to play madness, to inhabit a world excluded by conventional modern discourses of the sane. In Broadmoor, these tensions came together and encouraged the actors to assemble their performances differently, no longer constrained by masculine, linear and logocentric preoccupations of psychological consistency. As Clare Higgins concluded, 'for a few hours in Elsinore/Broadmoor

---

[56] Cox, p. 73.

[57] Cox, p. 148.

[58] Katherine Eisaman Maus, *Inwardness and Theatre in the English Renaissance* (London, 1995), p. 32.

[59] *Coriolanus*, 3.2.14.

[60] Cox, p. 30.

we too crossed the line and created a new space within it, one I have never been in before'.[61] This became a space in which the physical became paramount, in which the codes of the body in action, and not the interior self in reflection, were the principal transmitters of meaning. What Higgins, Rylance and others began to realize is that the post-Stanislavskian, and perhaps post-Garrickian, emphasis on introspective, psychologized characterisation is no more truthful than the most 'artificial' of commedia methods. As Gilles Deleuze has written:

Why does theatre remain representative each time it focuses on conflicts? It is because conflicts are already normalized, codified and institutionalised. They are 'products'. They are already a representation that can be represented so much the better on stage.[62]

By adopting such techniques performers are simply signing up for the commodification of experience that is an indelible part of capitalist economics. It is the confrontation of this system with those excluded from this purview – the insane – that reveals its mechanisms for what they are: packaged, prepared and, in this context, unethical. Introspective, linear performance characterization is, paradoxically, neither more truthful nor more real – simply more faithful to the apparatuses of control that surround this and every other mimetic discourse.

The English language contributions to the eighteenth-century sensibility debate were concerned subliminally to establish a strong and coherent theorisation of the national tradition of acting. The contributions of Hill, Boswell, Goldsmith and Garrick himself ran parallel to Johnson's attempt to stabilize the English language, and shared with this project a desire for fixity and intellectual consonance that was part also of a consolidation of English national identity. To secure this, it was necessary to co-opt the poet of the nation as propagandist for the nation: neither the first nor certainly the last time this would occur in English history. The marriage of these various theatrical, ideological, intellectual and even medical projects was to be found in the rhetoric surrounding Garrick's celebrity.

Coincidentally, at the point at which this project of cultural nationalism began seriously to collapse in 1989, the experience of playing Broadmoor for one group of actors reasserted and independently validated Diderot's paradigm of a roleplaying personality as at once everything and nothing, non-linear, inconsistent, and based on *praxis* and pragmatism. The attempt to rely on the creation of a spurious sense of coherent personality, rather than the portrayal of event and action, came to appear a deeply troubled ethical enterprise, potentially exploitative and disrespectful to the experience of others (not unlike cultural nationalism). It is both fitting and suitably paradoxical that the hollowness of a naturalism of personality should be illustrated so starkly in the company of the insane – of those excluded from society and from any nationalist agenda. The ethics of mimesis were found to rest finally on a fidelity to action and the relinquishing of attachment to a fabricated psychology of tendentious selfhood.

The paradox of this necessity to be nothing in order to represent everything was not, I would have thought, lost on Garrick himself, nor on his professional predecessors and successors, who are so influential in our understanding of the relationship of theatre to the world, and who are most in a position to talk, with Borges, of 'my Shakespeare'.

---

61 Cox, p. 75.
62 Gilles Deleuze, 'One Less Manifesto', in Timothy Murray, ed., *Mimesis, Masochism and Mime: The Politics of Theatricality in Contemporary French Thought* (Ann Arbor, 1997), pp. 239–58, 252.

SHAKESPEARE PERFORMANCES IN ENGLAND, 2005

MICHAEL DOBSON

The last instalment of this chronicle of Shakespeare's fortunes on the contemporary English stage closed with the pious hope that the RSC's projected 2005 main-house season of four comedies, the sequel to 2004's uneven batch of tragedies, might restore the company's sometime reputation as an organization committed above all to exploring the canon's continuing relevance to and engagement with contemporary society. This hope, alas, was doomed to disappointment: apart from a very flamboyant and inventive *A Midsummer Night's Dream*, directed by Gregory Doran as if to provide a reckless and affectionate farewell party for the cavernous interior of the Royal Shakespeare Theatre, 'The Comedies' produced little that might not have appeared there just as readily at any time over the last two or even three decades, and the company's collective mind in any case seemed already to have moved on to a larger project before the 2005 season had even opened. Between April 2006 and April 2007 the RSC, at first taking advantage of the simultaneous existence of both the RST as it is and the temporary Courtyard Theatre erected in the Other Place car park to replace it while its interior is completely rebuilt, and throughout deploying the Swan and a range of newly co-opted venues around Stratford (including Holy Trinity Church), will either stage or host productions of every single one of the Complete Works. The artistic reasons behind this massive undertaking have yet to be explained – the strenuous publicity so far ('The Greatest Dramatist – The Essential Year') suggests something between the spirit of the Guinness Book of World Records and whatever it is that moti-vates those cloying continuous marathon chronological play-throughs of the entire Bach canon mounted by North American campus radio stations – and the economics remain puzzling too. It isn't as if the potential local audience for classical theatre in Stratford-upon-Avon were exactly starved of Shakespeare in any given year as it is, and for outsiders the town's grasping determination that all relevant timetables should cunningly be restricted to ensure that no one wanting to get to an evening show by public transport can possibly escape without spending a night in a local bed-and-breakfast establishment mean that even *Shakespeare Survey* will find it adequately taxing to get to every Work on the programme (especially if any other company in the realm stages any Shakespeare in 2006–7 as well, as seems very likely). Those whose theatre-going lives centre on Stratford alone will doubtless find it refreshing to see Shakespeare staged by some non-RSC practitioners for a change alongside the usual suspects, especially given the impressive list of international companies and directors who have signed up to supplement the efforts of the home team (Yukio Ninagawa, Peter Stein, Barbara Gaines, Michael Kahn, Janet Suzman and Luk Perceval, among others), but those who have noticed that the cultural life of this country continues obstinately to focus on its capital are more concerned that the RSC should have committed so many resources to this abrupt twelve-month *Two-Gentlemen*-to-*Two-Noble-Kinsmen* blitzkrieg in Warwickshire without first re-establishing any proper London base at which to present its work to the metropolis.

The arrangement by which the company hired space from the Ambassadors group in the West End for the short-term transfer of the 2004 main house and Swan seasons has been extended for another five years, but this offers nothing like the sense of a London presence provided by the Barbican or the Aldwych in earlier times, and in 2005 the RSC's slightly orphaned-looking London visits attracted far less attention than did the live Shakespeare offered in the capital by rival brands, whether at Wyndham's, the National, the Old Vic or the Almeida. Certainly the scale of the publicity stunt by which the RSC hopes to re-identify the Complete Works as their very own in the public mind in 2006 – not only on stage but in print, as they lend their imprimatur for the first time to a tie-in complete edition, edited by Jonathan Bate and Eric Rasmussen – sits oddly with the company's continuing unconditional surrender of the London summer tourist audience to the Globe. But meanwhile, despite the uncertain profile of the country's largest and most famous classical theatre company, 2005 was a particularly rich year for Shakespeare on the English stage, with notable productions in all the Folio's generic categories and in every corner of the country: a fine *Comedy of Errors* and a moving *Much Ado About Nothing* in Sheffield; a convincing *Twelfth Night* in Plymouth and a superb *Winter's Tale* near Newbury; star turns by Kevin Spacey as Richard II and by Michael Gambon as Falstaff in London, together with Deborah Warner's return to directing Shakespeare with a high-profile *Julius Caesar*; an energetic *Romeo and Juliet* in Manchester; and a searingly articulate and moving *King Lear* in Chichester.

COMEDIES

The RSC's spring and summer batch of comedies was unpromisingly heralded by Fiona Buffini's *Two Gentlemen of Verona* in the Swan, which began touring, along with David Farr's *Julius Caesar*, in September 2004, and loitered in Stratford from November 2004 through February 2005. This was at best a lacklustre show and at worst a derivative and vulgar one. The design, by Liz Ascroft, was meant to suggest inter-war America (inter-polated tableaux of Milan street scenes suggested Depression-era New York, complete with mandatory winsome newspaper vendors, in this instance offering headlines such as 'Latest Outrage In Forest'), but this mise-en-scène fitted neither the cast's complete absence of American pronunciation nor the text's complete lack of interest in situating the play's relationships in any particular place at all, while Conor Linehan's pastiched Cole Porter music seemed little more than a faint echo from David Thacker's much more successful production of this play a decade ago. In this unhelpful setting the cast mainly underplayed, with sporadic inappropriate lunges towards broader and often wildly inappropriate comic effects: not content with rubbing pieces of paper together, for example, Vanessa Ackerman's otherwise genteel Julia threw Proteus's reconstituted letter aside, lay down on the drawing-room carpet and was clearly about to masturbate on 'Now kiss, embrace, contend, do what you will' (1.2.130), before she was mercifully interrupted by the return of Lucetta. Unfortunately the last scene of the play didn't achieve a climax either, with Alex Avery's Valentine throwing away 'All that was mine in Silvia I give thee' (5.4.83) so hastily and indistinctly that it was a wonder Julia even knew what she was fainting about.

The early comedy which did best in 2005 was instead *The Comedy of Errors*, which during the first six months of the year proliferated even more disconcertingly than Antipholi and Dromios appear to do in its action. No sooner had Creation Theatre's production closed in the Midlands than the play re-entered in Northern Broadsides' touring version in the North, which had itself barely exited from Salford before the play had turned up again at the Crucible, and this latter production had no sooner closed in Sheffield in June than it was time for the RSC's to open in the Royal Shakespeare Theatre in July, past thought of human reason.

Of this litter of multiple births, the most intent reading of the text and the most alert to the range of its emotional possibilities was certainly Jonathan Munby's at the Crucible, though Barrie Rutter's Northern Broadsides version, played on a platform resembling an octagonal bandstand, was highly competent (late 1950s clothes, with the Antipholi in Gilbert and George spectacles, and lots of brassy jazz accompaniment for the slapstick), and both Charlotte Conquest's production for Creation in Oxford and Nancy Meckler's for the RSC in Stratford were consistently and vigorously funny throughout. Conquest had the advantage of a venue that might have been purpose-built for this play, the Mirror Tent, an elaborate structure of canvas and timber made before the First World War with the proper wooden doors and windows which apparently enabled it to be used legally as a beer-tent at Central European fairs. (It has since enjoyed a chequered and vagrant career including, in better days, a brief residency by the young Marlene Dietrich.) In this unlikely and fantastical pavilion, sat incongruously down in the car-park outside the BMW plant in Cowley, the audience, surrounded by original decor somewhere between rococo and Art Nouveau and dominated by the ornate mirrored panels which covered most of the walls, found themselves placed at café tables grouped around three sides of a central stage, as if they and their multiple reflections had just been cast in *Cabaret* or perhaps in Trevor Nunn's 1977 Greek café-society *Comedy of Errors*. As the pace of the already convivial evening picked up – accelerating centrifugally from a comparatively stately rendition of Egeon's narrative in 1.1 illustrated by puppets and a memorable toy shipwreck centre-stage to a spendidly literal-minded set-piece in 4.4 in which Dr Pinch was the sort of 'conjuror' who produces implausibly large pieces of frightening medical equipment from a very small black bag – more and more of the action whirled around the perimeter of the room, the characters and their reflections chasing one another perilously past spindly chairs and the vendors of wine and coffee, before the second entry of the Abbess (at 5.1.331) called the proceedings back to the centre, back to order, and into a lightweight sort of harmony.

Meckler's show in the RST was performed in a similar spirit, if on a much bigger scale and with a much larger cast. Here if the playhouse proper didn't belong to an old-time fairground the stage often did, splendidly designed by Katrina Lindsay

to resemble, after a prefatory blast of a foghorn and a brief misty impression of white sails and a lighthouse, an imaginary drawing by Cruikshank of some populously Dickensian Bartholomew Fair. As the improbably-coiffed extras began to bustle elaborately about, we witnessed a little silent tableau of Egeon's arrest in the midst of the fair, from which he was led into what presently materialized as a barber's shop to explain himself to a Duke currently undergoing his morning shave. This Egeon, too, had his narrative illustrated by puppets (there really are a lot of them about in the English theatre just now), their operators dropping into the barber's from the fairground outside, and if all this is beginning to sound an extraordinarily busy and crowded and props-laden way of mounting 1.1, it was: but the saving grace of this scene and indeed of this whole show was that the intricately-detailed business and the costumes and the bizarre 1830s hairstyles had been devised with the same superabundant wit and good humour that characterized the performances, so that the cast and the machinery never seemed in one another's way. This was very much a *Comedy of Errors* seen from the perspective of Antipholus of Syracuse, played with serene, happy-go-lucky warmth and self-confidence by Joe Dixon; his intermittent fears that Ephesus was a place of danger and illusion were played almost entirely for laughs, and the potential emotional costs of the play's events were correspondingly underemphasized, with Suzanne Burden's griefs as Adriana rendered as comic period histrionics in the manner of Mrs Mantolini. As Dromio of Syracuse, Jonathan Slinger resembled an older and thinner Fat Boy from *The Pickwick Papers*, and as Dromio of Ephesus Forbes Masson resembled Dromio of Syracuse. Both got as much mileage as could reasonably or unreasonably be had from some finely got-up slapstick routines (like Conquest's in Oxford, Meckler's Dromios ill-advisedly fetched ice-cream cones onto the stage at vulnerable moments, while Forbes Masson found himself used as a battering ram when his master was locked out of doors in 3.1), without the production ever distracting us from the laughs by suggesting that their slavery could be anything but a sort of cartoon convention. Christopher Colquhoun's Antipholus of Ephesus never seemed to get the chance to insist that his sufferings should be taken seriously either, and at the play's conclusion he surrendered to the general merriment with barely a struggle. Surprisingly, in this production the Dromios were less pleased to be reunited than were their masters, but only to the extent of concluding their performances not with the egalitarian wisdom of the play's last couplet but with yet another gag appended to it, as each simultaneously tried to put his tongue out behind his newly-met brother's back as they exited. This was an immensely enjoyable evening, but all pitched rather monotonously in the same major key: as the interpolated songs-and-dances by fairground extras during the transitions between scenes suggested, it was less a close look at *The Comedy of Errors* than a large jolly show that just happened to have been spun around its text like so much deluxe candyfloss, a sort of twin-infested *Nicholas Nickleby Lite*.

Jonathan Munby's production at the Crucible, the last show mounted there under Michael Grandage's very successful artistic directorship, ought on the face of things to have been just as limited in tonal range and considerably more gimmicky, set as it was in popular culture's current bizarre coding for what the 1970s are supposed to have been like, and in Southern California at that. After a lost-looking Antipholus and Dromio of Syracuse had made an unscripted passage across a swirlingly blue-lit stage, to the sounds of the sea, the word 'Ephesus' was revealed at the back of the set, written in slightly-descending white capitals on a green background in an imitation of the famous sign that labels the Hollywood Hills for the geographically challenged. As Antipholus's blue satin waistcoat had already promised, the design throughout gestured energetically in the direction of *Hollywood Wives* and *Boogie Nights*: Solinus addressed Egeon from a microphone-bearing perspex podium that wouldn't have disgraced the Gubernator himself, the Officer was a fat motorcycle cop out of *Easy Rider*, and the fashions favoured on the streets of Ephesus were a raging disco inferno of flared velvet, white suits, chiffon, silk

cravats, Ray-Bans, rampant sideburns and droopy pimp moustaches. The odd thing, though, is that all this surface camp somehow channelled off the cheaper laughs and left the cast free to play the text as though it were in earnest, the dramatic situations potentially grim and humiliating enough, despite the avowed ludicrousness of the characters' clothes, to be well worth making into comedy. Munby's choice of setting made sense, too, in ways beyond its potential for extraneous kitsch. At home at the Phoenix, Rebecca Johnson's excellent, authoritative Adriana, for example, casually fondled an Oscar statuette that adorned her table as she lamented her husband's absence in 2.1, and the paparazzi who clustered eagerly about Antipholus of Syracuse before sweeping delightedly off with their smiling portraits of him before 'There's not a man I meet but doth salute me / As if I were their well-acquainted friend' (4.3.1–2) confirmed that Antipholus of Ephesus was by trade a Tinseltown celebrity actor – someone even better professionally qualified than a Hellenic nobleman to fear the theft of his identity and public image, and even more likely to respond to speculation about marital difficulties with lavish public gifts of jewellery.

As this tarnished star of an Antipholus, the less obviously sympathetic of the twins, Martin Hutson made a superb job of his descent into paranoia and rage, not just angered by his misadventures but bristling with affront that they should be happening to a man of his supposedly unique calibre. (Like most Antipholi of Ephesus nowadays, incidentally, he was definitely cuckolded by his twin brother during that fateful lunch hour: this year only Northern Broadsides were innocently faithful enough to the text – despite the potential pun in Antipholus of Syracuse's resolve to entertain the offered fallacy, 2.2.189 – to have the arriving twin interested exclusively in Luciana from the first). In Act 4 he was horrified not only that his wife should try to have him declared mad but that she should have gone far enough downmarket to resort to calling in Hilton McRae's Dr Pinch for this purpose, the latter delightfully played, much more aptly than as the mere shrink who

16 *The Comedy of Errors*, directed by Jonathan Munby, Crucible Theatre, Sheffield. Rebecca Johnson as Adriana.

sometimes materializes in modern-dress productions of this play, as a disreputable Texan televan-
gelist who staged a full-scale attempted exorcism
to the strains of an energetic offstage Hammond
organ and cries of 'Hallelujah' from his assistants, so
that his little speech, 'I charge thee, Satan, housed
within this man . . .' (4.4.55–8), became a mock
gospel number in the mode of *The Blues Brothers*.
(Unlike Meckler, Munby added musical numbers
without the need to commission Lionel Bart-like
new lyrics: elsewhere, Dromio of Syracuse's set-
piece about the continual physical abuse inflicted
by his master, 'When I am cold, he heats me
with beating', 4.4.33–40, became a soulful R'n'B
number intoned into a magically-appearing show-
biz microphone to a backing reminiscent of 'The
Great Pretender'.) The prickly, would-be swaggering assertion of dignity by which Antipholus at first

responded here looked like a more violent re-run
of his splendidly petty attempt to save face in front
of his male friends by taking them to dine with
Kirsty Bushell's blaxploitation Courtesan instead of
at home when locked out of the Phoenix, and the
same mixture of the cocky and the small-minded
earned Hutson one of the best laughs of the evening
at the close of his callous and increasingly peeved
disavowal of any knowledge of Egeon in 5.1. He
abruptly denied the old man's first pleas as if merely
offended that anyone should dare add another insult
to the day's accumulated injuries by suggesting he
could conceivably be acquainted with such an obvious loser, but then listened in unexpected silence
and stillness to Egeon's long, moving speech of
entreaty ('Not know my voice . . .?', 5.1.309–
20), pausing afterwards for just long enough to let
the audience wonder whether he too might have

been moved, by compassion if not by recognition, before flatly declaring 'I never saw my father in my life' (5.1.321) as if it constituted an indignant boast, thereby committing a gaffe worthy of Alan Partridge at his most crassly self-incriminating.

The funniest sequence of the production, however, and equally well-rooted in the text, was probably Munby's ingenious treatment of the locking-out itself (the culmination of the first half of the show), during which the white panel at the back of Mike Britton's beautifully economical set, already labelled for the first part of 3.1 with a green neon sign stage left reading 'The Phoenix', acquired a second green neon sign stage right that was an exact mirror image of the first, under which Michael Matus as Dromio of Syracuse arrived to deliver his lines from 'within the Phoenix' (from line 32 onwards). A panel towards the left-hand end of the flat could thus become the inside of the imaginary front door of the house while another towards the right served as its exterior, and, wonderfully, the front door had a letter box, into which John Marquez's Dromio of Ephesus, enraged, briefly thrust his hand in a vain bid to seize the impostor barring his entrance – at which the hand of an unseen double emerged from the corresponding letter box stage right. Dromio of Syracuse retaliated by ramming a broom handle out through the letter box stage right, at which Dromio of Ephesus collapsed clutching his groin from the impact of the corresponding broom handle that came poking savagely out stage left, and the exchange concluded (after much else) with a beautifully developed sight gag by which the twin servants kept almost but not quite looking through the letter box at the same moment, one or the other prevented by the intervention of Luce or Antipholus of Ephesus or Adriana from prematurely making the discovery that would have ended the play before the interval. This sounds a simple and puerile enough piece of pantomime, but it was so tightly rehearsed that it was mildly uncanny to watch as well as surreally funny, allowing the audience to share the sense dimly intuited by the onstage twins that somewhere just out of sight but exerting a definite pressure on the situation there was one body too many.

The ending of the play, as the whole cast at last began to assemble in their different states of physical and emotional disarray, was every bit as precisely choreographed and played as this, right down to the last canned angelic chord to which Carol Macready's massively wimpled Abbess always emerged from her little white stucco abbey. It is much to Rebecca Johnson's credit that she was the only Adriana this year who played her answer to Luciana's question as to why she had been temporarily silenced by the Abbess's reproaches, 'She did betray me to my own reproof' (5.1.91), with the stress on 'betray' rather than on 'my own', so that instead of appearing to confess that the Abbess had only stated what her own wifely conscience had been telling her all along (as too many Adrianas do) she instead agreed that she had only been tricked into rebuking herself, only fleetingly blocked (as the ensuing dialogue confirms) from the relentless pursuit of her own interests in the promising custody dispute between wife and as-yet-unrecognized mother-in-law that this scene initiates over the possession of Antipholus of Ephesus. Nor was this the only piece of familial disharmony likely to outlive the 'gossips' feast' promised by the Abbess at 5.1.408. After all that had happened, the Antipholi were unable to meet one another's eyes after their reunited parents had left the stage, and Antipholus of Syracuse only turned to wish the Dromios well at 5.1.416 ('Embrace thy brother there; rejoice with him') because his own brother had now sulked off after enduring the final humiliation of having had to have this newly discovered rival doppelganger of a brother explain to him which Dromio was which. (There really isn't very much in the way of dialogue from which to make a happy ending of the reunion between the Antipholi, however much directors such as Meckler may desire one: here Antipholus of Syracuse's clarifying 'He speaks to me', the only remark he addresses to his brother after the eclaircissement, might just have developed into a first tentative conversation, but Antipholus of Ephesus was still far too sore to stand even that, and simply winced at his own mistake before turning angrily away.) Left alone, the Dromios made a better stab at fraternal love, however, so that the production could close on the last of its kitsch jokes, with the set parting to reveal a lurid orange-and-purple Technicolour sunset projected onto the cyclorama beyond, into which the two walked off hand in hand as the play's last line specifies, to the strains of wonderfully over-the-top cinematic music. It was a happy ending to the extent that the family had been reunited; and it was a convincing family (and a more convincingly Shakespearian one than any brought together with the more Disneyesque orgies of smiles and embraces that ornamented this scene elsewhere this year) to the extent that it was impossible to imagine that this reunion was going to be an unmixed blessing for any of its members.

Of the three productions of *A Midsummer Night's Dream* I saw in 2005, one was performed in a toy theatre at home and one by the lower forms of a girls' school, and it is enormously to the credit of their sole professional rival, Gregory Doran's production in Stratford (the first and easily best of the RSC's 'Comedies' season), that it had something of the freshness, the oddity, the unforced seriousness and the sheer verve of both. This production was nothing if not eclectic from the outset: Paul Englishby, in charge of the incidental music, even let us hear the opening bars of Mendelssohn's score as the house lights dimmed, though the show had a number of other worlds in mind beyond the nineteenth-century fairy-realms which those chords always call to mind. The visual image onto which the stage lights came up was in fact one that appeared instead to come from the last act of *Troilus and Cressida* – a pair of Homeric-helmeted warriors duelling vigorously centre stage – but this was another short-lived bluff, since when one of the duellists surrendered, overcome, the victorious warrior, instead of killing him or demanding a ransom, laughingly removed her helmet and turned out to be Hippolyta, sparring playfully with a Theseus who had presumably only won her with his sword because she had been slightly off-form the previous season. This was a *Dream*, unusually for current practice, in which Theseus and Hippolyta did not double Oberon and Titania, and it is remarkable what a difference this made:

without the cover-story of really being king of the fairies underneath his smart Victorian-looking tunic, Miles Richardson, as Theseus, could bring out the slightly prissy, rationalistic, Civil Service note in the Duke's voice, here making polite conversation about how to spend the rest of their engagement and reminding Hippolyta who had won on the real battlefield as if diplomatically restoring his proper precedence despite having just been floored by his fiancée. (There was a comparable moment in Act 4 when Hippolyta's praise of Hercules and Cadmus's hounds spurred him to a slightly hurt, grave insistence that his dogs were of course just as good and just as important as theirs, 4.1.111–26). Richardson's Theseus, if latently pompous and clearly inadequate in his support for Egeus' views on how to deal with Hermia (even in Hippolyta's eyes, who committed a grave breach of protocol by stalking off at 1.1.123 in obvious displeasure), was a fair-minded enough sort of Duke within his limitations, but you never doubted the existence of the limitations (limitations apparently denied when the same actor is liable to reappear at any moment in a chest wig brandishing a big magic wand), and the joke of his continuing not to believe in fairies in the last act when the audience and most of the other characters have spent the last two hours in their company here seemed far less knowing than usual and more carefully slanted at the expense of the ducal version of worldly power.

If the separation of Theseus from Oberon helped to cut the Duke down to size in the first and last movements of the play, it also helped to enlarge Oberon during the central scenes in the wood, neither his magic nor his malice contained by his customary identification with the daylight governor of Athens. The designer Stephen Brimson Lewis had decided that this was to be a place of large and dazzling effects, and Joe Dixon, in torso-baring outfits that ingeniously combined russet with sparkle and wouldn't have been entirely out of place in Munby's Ephesus, was more than happy to compere and cue them. Behind the stage, partly animated silhouettes of a pair of dragonfly-winged Victorian fairies were projected onto a huge screen

17 *A Midsummer Night's Dream*, directed by Gregory Doran, RSC, Royal Shakespeare Theatre. Amanda Harris as Titania, Malcolm Storry as Bottom, and fairies.

to introduce the woodland scenes (among yellow drifting shapes like those of a lava lamp), and above it dangled a large orange sphere as a moon. Titania's bower was an equally outsized hammock, in which Amanda Harris's elegant Fairy Queen – wearing a costume that, small as it was, seemed to be at least 75 percent wide-meshed netting, and which must surely have vastly improved the take-up rate on the opera glasses available in the balcony for the deposit of a £1 coin in a slot – was hoisted high above the stage during the lullaby at the start of 2.2. Even higher, though, was the huge, sinister silhouette of Oberon which loomed grandly above and behind her sleeping form for 'What thou seest when thou dost wake' (2.2.33–40), dropping the shadows of petals onto her face, and the climax of the enchantment was just as striking. At the end of 3.1 a tableau

of Titania and Bottom was held behind an enormous flexible disc of transparent plastic, held up by Puck to produce the effect of his having somehow trapped them inside a bubble – while he, mockingly, gestured to the puppet Indian Boy (an articulated toddler whom we had already met, operated by fairies, in the confrontation scene), now securely in his custody. (Despite the unaccustomed presence of a puppet as the object of the fairy monarchs' dispute, provided by the same Little Angel team who worked on Doran's *Venus and Adonis* the previous season, the confrontation scene itself was most remarkable for the grace and poise with which Amanda Harris delivered 'These are the forgeries of jealousy' (2.1.81–117), by which she held the theatre captivated while standing entirely still throughout: her performance provided the

seriousness and stillness at the centre of this production, against which its hysterical and fantastical
comedy were highlit). The removal of the enchantment, then, needed to be another equally arresting
moment, and it was: Oberon pointed at the moon
at the start of 'Be as thou wast wont to be' (4.1.70–
3), at which a speeded-up film of an orchid blos-
soming was projected onto it for the duration of
the spell and a shower of glitter fell onto Titania's
eyes at its culmination. This Oberon was in every
sense a king of shadows, the production determined
to use every unwieldy square inch of the old RST
stage and proscenium while it still had them to play
with.

Such effects produced genuine gasps of pleasure
from the audience when I saw this *Dream*, a sound
which hasn't been heard regularly in the English
theatre since the days when pantomimes still had
proper transformation scenes, but not everything
in this version of the wood was anything like as
deliberately pretty. Perhaps showing the influence
of Lucy Bailey's production at the Royal Exchange
in 2002 (see *Survey 56*), a stylized pile of miscellaneous scrap metal towered over the back of the
stage during acts 2 to 4, apparently fly-tipped on
a grand scale by affluent Athenians – old prams,
bicycles, gramophones, chairs, intermittently lit by
strings of fairy lights – and Titania and her fairies
trundled Bottom onto the stage at the start of
4.1 in a supermarket shopping trolley. This provided, at one level, a jokey note of prosaic realism
(sadly, you are nowadays just as likely to find an
abandoned supermarket shopping trolley in a Warwickshire wood as sweet musk-roses and eglan-
tine), but the rubbish dump also usefully identified the forest as a place not so much of fertility
as of the cast-away, the residual, the disowned, a
flowers-in-the-dustbin zone which could welcome
the Edwardian fairy wings on the cyclorama but
also a slobbish, lower-lip-drooping, urban Puck by
Jonathan Slinger, whose dyed-red hair deliberately
resembled that of a quite different leftover from earlier phases of popular culture, John Lydon. (Puck,
the dump and the bricolage of popular culture
came together nicely as the mechanicals were dispersed in panic in 3.1, when he arranged for Snout

to be chased offstage by a flying bicycle magically
animated as in *ET*). The other fairies nicely combined nostalgic prettiness and urban tat in about
equal measure: heavily choreographed to person-
ify the woods in the lovers' scenes even when not
called for by the text, their performers held out and
manipulated little winged dolls in front of themselves, which would have been painfully cute had
the dolls not had outsized, charmless plastic heads
deliberately reminiscent of Chucky. (Mustardseed's
head, more disconcertingly still, came right off during his dialogue with Bottom). Poltergeist activities were well within their range, especially at the
expense of Sinéad Keenan's stocky, harsh-voiced
Hermia: they waited giggling and predatory for
her to fall asleep in 2.2 so that they could steal
and rifle the case she had brought with her for
her elopement, producing with its contents a little
forest of lingerie dangled from coathangers; they
mockingly and distortingly echoed her calls for
help at 2.2.157; and, to memorable effect, they
kept lifting her from the ground as she tried to
stamp across the stage in 3.3 and carrying her a
few yards obliviously backwards towards the wings
before putting her down again, like children playing with a beetle, so that her baffled 'My legs can
keep no pace with my desires' (3.3.33) got a huge
laugh.

Anchoring all this in something more familiar,
in terms of acting style as well as of appearance,
were the mechanicals, expertly played in modern
working clothes – donkey jackets, safety helmets,
overalls – and in what at times verged on carica-
tures of Birmingham accents. The revelation at the
core of these scenes was something which I had
never previously suspected in years of seeing his
work both in Stratford and elsewhere, namely that
Malcolm Storry, cast against type as Bottom, has a
sense of humour. Given the lugubriousness of his
work in tragedy, you would think that putting him
into an ass's head would just produce Eeyore, but
far from it. In the early scenes his was a big, loping,
eager weaver who never quite seemed in full control of his arms when rehearsing with his peers but
whose body-language as himself was so eloquent
that the furry transformation of his noll made him

more expressive rather than less so. His oblivion downstage as the awakening Titania came partly into view in her hammock, lifting one perfect outstretched leg at a time over its edge just before 'What angel wakes me from my flow'ry bed?' (2.2.122), and his full-body double-take on then turning and seeing this mid-air erotic vision, could hardly have been improved. If anything marred the mechanicals' scenes as a whole, and indeed that of the squabble between all four lovers, it was a customary problem with these scenes, an over-indulgence in business. During 3.2, for example, Doran threw away 'Is all the counsel that we two have shared . . .?' (3.2.199–220) not just by having Caitlin Mottram's Helena gabble it at indistinguishable speed but by allowing Demetrius and Lysander to upstage it throughout, at first lying prone on the stage behind her listening in rapture but then contending with each other as to who could get closest first, crawling at ever-increasing velocity on their elbows. The culminating performance of 'Pyramus and Thisbe' similarly threatened to vanish under the many layers of visual running gags invented around it. As Wall, David Rogers' Snout rather implausibly arrived bare-legged with his arms completely concealed in the white rectangular piece of wattle and daub he wore as his sole outer garment, as if straitjacketed in an old-fashioned Lloyd Loom laundry basket, and at 'And this the cranny is' (5.1.162) he feigned to be unable to release and extricate one arm as he had planned, so that he found himself dismayingly incapable of making the chink with his fingers. Undeterred, however, he decided to remedy the situation by hitching the simulated wall upwards, exposing his bright orange briefs, in order to allow Pyramus and Thisbe to whisper between his legs instead, and . . . well, you can probably imagine how the gags would multiply from there once the scene had got into this particular mode. It should be acknowledged, however, that this was an extremely funny 'Pyramus and Thisbe', and that Doran didn't make any such mistakes with the epilogue. Convincingly sulky and ungracious Slinger's Puck might have been, but he spoke his rhymes beautifully, and the sluggish reluctance he had earlier displayed when ordered

about by Oberon prepared one all the better for the laugh he obtained with his initial recitation's slatternly last couplet, 'I am sent with broom before / To sweep the dust behind the door' (5.2.19–20). Nor did Doran spoil 'If we shadows have offended' by following it with an elaborate curtain call to music: all was closed down, and the solitary Puck asked for applause, and he got it, and the rest of the shadows simply gathered to take their rightful shares. There was plenty to go around, too. I saw this show on a Friday night, among a capacity crowd many of whom had clearly driven down from Birmingham in quest of a good night out, and it was hard to believe in the delighted crush in the foyer afterwards that there really are people who think Shakespeare isn't popular and needs to have his plays paraphrased into short television dramas if anyone is still going to pay them any attention.

That fate, however, befell not only *A Midsummer Night's Dream* but *Much Ado About Nothing* in 2005 (together with *The Taming of the Shrew* and *Macbeth*) during the BBC's 'Shakespeare ReTold' season, even though *Much Ado* seemed to be no less alive and well in the provincial theatre. In the summer Peter Hall directed it at the Theatre Royal in Bath, in a straightforward production reportedly notable for its *Pride and Prejudice* costuming, its eloquent Leonato (Philip Voss) and its interest in Don Pedro's sexuality (in the year in which same-sex civil partnerships became legal in Britain, paradoxically, he seemed to have definitively joined the Antonio of *The Merchant of Venice* in the closet). In the autumn Josie O'Rourke directed it at the Crucible in Sheffield, inaugurating the new artistic directorship of its Benedick, Sam West. O'Rourke's production was the more adventurous of the two, at least in so far as it was prepared to alter the text to suit its own vision of *Much Ado About Nothing*. Wanting to re-adjust the balance in the war of the sexes the play dramatizes, O'Rourke imported more women into the cast, having all the watch except Hugh Oatcake played by actresses and regendering Antonio, Leonato's brother, as 'Innogen', his sister. In this version of the social set-up at Messina (with Leonato's house prettily realized by Giles Candle

18 *Much Ado About Nothing*, directed by Josie O'Rourke, Crucible Theatre, Sheffield. 'Kill Claudio':
Claire Price as Beatrice and Sam West as Benedick.

as a nineteenth-century Italian villa with a veranda and a garden at the front), it wasn't that Hero, Beatrice and their two waiting-gentlewomen were already vulnerably isolated in an all-male household before Don Pedro's demobilized army even arrived. In fact the soldiers who arrived in O'Rourke's 1.1 stood some risk of being outnumbered by women and at first even outranked by them. Laundresses had been singing while folding sheets for several minutes before the action even got under way, and the first member of the army we saw arrive, before any dialogue began, was a drummer boy, embraced with joy by the laundrywoman who was clearly his mother.

If O'Rourke's experiment achieved nothing else, it highlighted how right Shakespeare was to abandon the idea of having Hero's mother in the story after at first writing her name, Innogen, into the opening stage directions of the first two acts. With any senior woman in the picture to fill the role of Mother of the Bride during the rapid courtship and wedding preparations to which we are made privy, whether an actual mother or just an aunt, the Claudio–Hero plot as written would stand very little chance of happening (let alone to such a mature and self-reliant Hero as was Georgina Rich), and the inadequacy and inappropriateness of Antonio's lines to the relations any such woman would have with Hero at such a time were already clear long before Frances Cuka's Aunt Innogen started threatening to fight with Claudio and Don Pedro (incongruously, and to merely comic effect) in 5.1. Given how clear the play already is about the consequences of sexual stereotyping, O'Rourke only seemed to be muting its argument by muddying the distinction between those pushed towards being obedient brides and those pushed towards being obedient soldiers (a muddying which she seemed to compensate for by overstressing the distinction elsewhere, such as by starting 2.1's masked ball with a game in which the soldiers burst onto the dance floor to seize partners from among a group of impractically blindfolded women). Equally, while one could at times see the point of making the Watch predominantly female – by which Leonato's fatal refusal to take the time to hear Dogberry out before the wedding in 3.5 became another instance of men failing to listen to women, and by which the eventual rectification of this mistake became a female achievement in the face of male crime and male self-importance – their actual scenes were completely sabotaged by it. Dialogue imagined for ignorant volunteer village constables just won't work when reassigned to what here became a brisk and mainly middle-class Salvation Army band. Dogberry's best proto-Malapropisms simply disappeared in the flood of Julia Dearden's generalized sent-up earnestness, which wasn't nearly as funny, and someone really ought to have noticed that actions premised on the illiteracy of certain characters (such as the interrogation scene) aren't really compatible with those characters habitually carrying Bibles suspended by chains from their clothing. It wasn't at all clear what Hugh Oatcake was still doing in their midst, and even he had to be provided with a firearm for the arrest of Conrade and Borachio to look remotely likely.

With the Hero–Claudio plot severely handicapped and the Dogberry sub-plot largely spoiled, this *Much Ado About Nothing* was always going to rely even more heavily than usual on its Beatrice and Benedick. Fortunately Claire Price and Sam West both gave as powerful, nuanced and intelligent performances as I have seen in these roles, and the conviction and subtlety of their responses to what happened between Hero and Claudio went a long way towards sustaining their scenes too. Over the time I have been reviewing her work in Shakespeare – since her Rosalind in 2000 – Price has developed an impressive knack of rendering whatever emotion her character is experiencing on the stage irresistibly contagious to her audience without appearing visibly to try to do anything, and her performance as Beatrice was the most sympathetic – in the full eighteenth-century sense of the term – that I have yet seen her give. It would have been as difficult not to smile as she ignored Benedick's proferred arm on her exit from 1.1, happily retaining Hero's instead as the two friends swept out, as it was hard not to sigh at her sadness and discomfiture on being dismissed from the stage by Leonato after the betrothal of Hero and Claudio. On 'Niece, will you look to those things I told you of?' (2.1.316–17) she was momentarily brought up short, casting one regretful look at her oblivious cousin before, her sudden irrelevance to the situation realized, she hurried off, concealing her distress. It was, furthermore, quite impossible not to find oneself crying when she and Benedick were left alone after the broken nuptials, as that old Shakespearian trick of having a character mention tears at a moment of extreme emotional stress or release in the action (and how cunning that here it is Benedick who does so, 'Lady Beatrice, have you wept all this while?', 4.1.258) worked to prompt the audience's tear ducts once again. There was nothing arch or catty or intermittently self-pitying about this Beatrice: she unhesitatingly cried out 'Kill Claudio' with a fierce exhilaration that had no premeditation or self-regard in it. What made her so powerful was that, having evidently given up on the possibility of much happiness for herself, she was transparently much more concerned about her cousin's welfare and feelings than she was about her own.

The miracle in this *Much Ado About Nothing* was that this attitude, too, turned out to be contagious, transforming someone who at first sight was one of the least promising potential romantic partners in the recent stage history of this play. West's Benedick appeared initially to be a constrained, fussy exercise in character acting: in a uniform whose tunic collar would clearly soon be too tight for an incipiently thickening neck, he arrived in 1.1 like something from a Viennese operetta, goading Beatrice in a fat plummy voice placed well back in his throat as though he were permanently carrying a milieu of cigars and brandy in the officers' mess (where he would clearly repeat the highlights of his repartee later). He squeaked in momentary affected alarm on realizing that his young protégé Claudio was serious about Hero, pausing for long enough to sound genuinely taken aback before confirming the worst ('But I hope you have no intent to turn husband – *have* you?', 1.1.182–3), but he had soon resumed his accustomed unappealing smugness, treating his joke about sheep-guts haling souls out of men's bodies (2.3.57–8) less as a witty intellectual speculation than as a piece of suave self-congratulation on his superiority to the less tone-deaf. Even while crouching behind a wheelbarrow to eavesdrop on Leonato, Don Pedro and Claudio, this was a Benedick who was proud to be prematurely middle-aged, almost relieved to be visibly ossifying into the crusty social persona which still succeeded so gratifyingly in irritating the likes of Beatrice. The revelation that she allegedly loved him at first did not so much alter his sense of himself as an established officer as simply redefine his duties – he drew himself almost to attention for 'The world must be peopled' (2.3.229–30), like

a pompous general ostentatiously shouldering the cares of command at a press conference – but when he reappeared in the next scene not just stripped of his *Chocolate Soldier* moustache but out of uniform (in a stripey waistcoat and orange straw hat), something was clearly beginning to happen, and 'Gallants, I am not as I have been' (3.2.14) demonstrated its own truth by sounding almost unaffected, the voice light, puzzled and vulnerable as well as warily defensive. The breakthrough came, as it should, in 4.1, when Benedick found himself setting his own response to the debacle at the altar aside in the face of his overwhelming, compassionate response to the weeping Beatrice: when he suddenly blurted out 'I do love nothing in the world so well as you. Is that not strange?' (4.1.269–70), surprised at his own nearly tearful intensity, he sounded not like a retired major but like a teenager nervously excited in the company of his first real girlfriend. From here onwards he was saved, and so was she, and the whole trajectory of their comedy appeared to enact a wonderful defiance of time, as Beatrice and Benedick moved from their separate versions of ageing in isolation – hers resigned, his stuffy – into a rediscovered youth together. It made an extraordinarily moving spectacle, far beyond the usual amusing picture of a laughing cavalier farcically duped into matrimony, and the laughter in the last scene (not least at West's beautifully mock-grudging, offhand delivery of 'Come, I *will* have thee', 5.4.92) was of a completely different order to that occasioned by any other comedy this year. For all its miscalculations, this was a genuinely joyous production of *Much Ado About Nothing*.

Neither of the year's major revivals of *As You Like It* achieved anything like this level of emotional engagement, though selected parts from both might have been combined to produce a single more than satisfactory production. At Wyndham's in the West End, David Lan's *As You Like It* in the summer attracted the most celebrity-crowded and photographer-haunted press-night I have yet attended for this journal, largely because its cast included two comedians well known from television (Sean Hughes as Touchstone, and Reece

19 *As You Like It*, directed by David Lan, Wyndham's Theatre, London. Sienna Miller as Celia and
Helen McCrory as Rosalind.

Shearsmith of *The League of Gentlemen* as Jaques, both of them embarrassingly out of their depth here to the extent that the 'Lie Direct' set-piece was cut and 'All the world's a stage' might as well have been), along with, more magnetic still, the film starlet Sienna Miller, whose offstage romantic complications during the play's run drew a good deal more press attention than did her onstage activities as a well-drilled, photogenic but completely uninteresting Celia. Lan's production started from a promising idea, that of for once taking seriously the play's claims to be set in France. Hence in the first scene Andrew Woodall's Oliver arrived in his orchard for the confrontation with Orlando as if returning from an excursion to Paris, in rumpled evening dress, smoking a Gauloise,

311

clutching a half-empty champagne bottle and towing not one but two demi-mondaines (ah, these French!), while in the following scene Rosalind and Celia, in Dioresque late 1940s outfits, had their first conversation at a pavement café. This setting might have worked very well (a soi-disant existentialist Jaques in the Forest of Ardennes, for instance, could have been both apt and funny), but much of the middle of the production was unrecognisable as France or as anywhere else, swamped instead by music. Even Denise Gough's bizarre, toothy Welsh Audrey combined herding goats – played by other cast-members, holding umbrellas against their heads as horns in a manner which may have been funny in rehearsal – with playing the cello. Clive Rowe's Duke Senior was a tenor enthusiastic enough to sing 'Under the Greenwood Tree' himself instead of leaving it to Amiens, and he had insisted on bringing a piano with him into the woods, apparently modelling his court-in-exile less on Robin Hood's merry men than on a glee club. Tim Sutton's elaborate close-harmony settings of the songs were presumably intended to sound like Les Compagnons de la Chanson, but in English the result was merely a lamentably accurate impression of the King's Singers. Thankfully, Lan had secured the services of Helen McCrory to play Rosalind, and it was her performance which kept this show alive and at times even exciting. Slightly reminiscent of Victoria Hamilton's in 2000 (see *Survey 52*), McCrory's Rosalind was nervily vulnerable in her own person, touchingly anxious not to risk losing the first great love of her life despite the peculiar and difficult circumstances under which she was experiencing it, so that she burst into overwrought tears on 'O coz, coz, coz, my pretty little coz, that thou didst know how many fathom deep I am in love' (4.1.195–6), and, though she almost mustered the courage to unbutton her male clothes and deal openly with Orlando at 'I will weary you then no longer with idle talking' (5.2.49), she deferred her self-revelation until she had secured his promise to accept Rosalind regardless, improvising the set-piece of the following day in a lifelike attack of cold feet. (Unlike anyone else in this cast, McCrory excelled at reg-

istering when her character was bluffing, when she was ad-libbing, when she was sending herself up, when she was being sent up, able expressively to change tone in a moment.) This Rosalind compensated for occasional failures of resolve as herself by posing as a marvellously coquettish, husky-voiced Ganymede, indiscriminately attractive to either sex in an outfit of dark pinstripe suit, black pumps, white open shirt, waistcoat, fedora and *film noir* cigarette that wouldn't have disgraced any Montmartre cabaret. At 'But come, now I will be your Rosalind in a more coming-on disposition' (4.1.104–6), down which her voice sidled sinuously in a descending cadence of about three octaves, she turned her back on Orlando and slowly, very slowly, slipped her jacket from her shoulders and then dropped it emphatically and negligently to the ground from the fingers of one hand. This was a performance which made for a far better and more teasing epilogue than most of this production deserved, and it's a pity it couldn't have been combined with some of the more solid work provided in supporting roles in Dominic Cooke's simultaneous main-house production in Stratford. In the RST, for example, Amanda Harris played a bespectacled former school goody-goody of a Celia (miraculously dumpy and endearingly awkward in movement compared to her Titania) who actually took the trouble to remain in responsive close-focus centre-stage during Rosalind's love-prates with Orlando, her reactions showing exactly how far Rosalind's behaviour was transgressing the norms to which she was accustomed. McCrory can be thankful, however, that unlike Cooke's cast she wasn't required to share the stage all night with a single tree so enormous that Jonathan Newth's sappy Duke Senior could barely hug it (perhaps someone needs to remind the designer Rae Smith that the text says 'Under the Greenwood Tree', not 'Under the Redwood Tree'), and that she wasn't obliged to rehearse one of those hateful, endless line-dancing RSC comedy curtain calls, a further extension of what had already been some fairly saccharine choreography in the final scene. This particular specimen seemed to go on forever, after a production that had already been allowed to run

20 *As You Like It*, directed by Dominic Cooke, RSC, Royal Shakespeare Theatre. Amanda Harris as
Celia and Lia Williams as Rosalind.

a good forty minutes longer than it should have
done. At the centre of this show, Lia Williams
made an acceptable but unsurprising Rosalind of
the blonde and English variety – not so much excitingly hermaphrodite as Ganymede as comfortably
neuter – and the reinforced normality of it all was
underlined by the presence of Barnaby Kay's dot-
ing Orlando at her feet during the epilogue, keep-

ing Rosalind/Ganymede/Williams to one gender
position despite the bisexual flirtatiousness of the
text.

Twelfth Night too came in both RSC and non-
subsidized variants in 2005, and here the commercial sector definitely had the edge. To be fair,
Michael Boyd's production in the RST was hampered by so much ill-luck that it might as well

have been a *Macbeth*. Lia Williams withdrew from the role of Viola before rehearsals even began after being bereaved by the 2004 tsunami, only for her substitute Kananu Kirimi to be overcome with stage-fright shortly into the production, so that the lead part instead went to an inexperienced understudy, Sally Tatum. Nicky Henson, meanwhile, reportedly an exceptionally good Sir Toby in the previews, fell seriously ill and had to be replaced by Clive Wood, who wasn't nearly so well-cast as a posh degenerate (his Sir Toby resembled not a gone-to-seed knight but a formerly athletic estate agent liable to get aggressive after bibulous rugby club dinners), but possibly no cast could have prevented Boyd from missing the point of the play as thoroughly as he seems to have done. Bafflingly, this Illyria seemed to be peopled entirely by extroverts, with neither a secret nor a hint of introspection between them: even Richard Cordery's Malvolio was a bluff, muscular fellow who wore motorcycle leathers and practised strenuous martial arts moves in Olivia's garden. As ever with Boyd, there was a great deal of Tom Piper's woodwork in evidence, from an immense slatted portrait of Olivia's eyes behind Orsino's court to the rowing boat in which Sebastian and Antonio made a novel entrance in 2.1, lowered vertically downwards prow-first from the flies while they clung trickily in place feigning to row as though we were looking at them from directly overhead. Piper's design was symptomatically allowed even to upstage the moment of recognition between the twins at 5.1.224, when a garden burst into bloom behind them in colours which tastefully reiterated those of the bouquets which characters had been offering one another all evening. All this left the main plot lost and unaffecting, and there were very few laughs to be had either, even from the play's professional clown. Forbes Masson was a Feste of the melancholy school, in checked suit and whiteface, who accompanied his songs on keyboard rather than with a lute and shunned the tabor too (producing a curious emendation at the start of 3.1, 'Dost thou live by thy piano?'), and he seemed sorrowfully jealous of Maria's burgeoning interest in Sir Toby. Maria was otherwise notable principally for making

one incomprehensibly customary piece of business in this role even less plausible than usual: showing how unimpressed she was with Sir Andrew's efforts to accost her at Sir Toby's prompting, Meg Fraser's Scottish waiting-gentlewoman not only placed his hand on her breast at 'I pray you, bring your hand to th' buttery-bar, and let it drink' (1.3.66–8), as many Marias do, but took the advantage of her décolletage to stuff his fingers right down inside her bra.

This seems a very unlikely way of demonstrating a contemptuous lack of sexual interest in someone, and, refreshingly, Anita Booth's Maria, in Patrick Mason's touring production for the Theatre Royal, Plymouth, wasn't having even the U-certificate version of this gesture. Mason's was a cleaner, sharper piece of work all round, with another elegant and simple design by Mike Britton – a white stage, often lit in blue, scattered with a few red leaves, with vertical white bands of curtain across the rear and down the sides, the inside of a dome above it, and furniture restricted to a few clear perspex chairs sufficiently inconspicuous when not in use to render any felonious black-gloved stagehands between scenes unnecessary. This was put to the service of delineating an Illyria that was suitably part-fantastical and part-modern. The performance began with a tableau of Olivia's household processing in black under umbrellas to mourn briefly at her brother's grave – followed at a distance by Hilton McRae's apprehensive, observant Feste – before these so-far silent mourners dispersed, and Bob Cryer's Orsino arrived with his entourage to listen to 1.1's music, in Ruritanian tailcoat and red sash. This was an Illyria in which social distinctions were much more readily legible than they were in Boyd's, but one in which ceremony and the fairytale co-existed easily with the quotidian. Christopher Benjamin's excellent navyblazered Sir Toby read *The Racing Post*, and the seacaptain and Viola were attended to on the beach in 1.2 by reflective-coated rescue workers who draped them in red blankets and offered them mugs of hot soup. There was adequate social context, then, for Matthew Kelly's tall, overbearing Malvolio to work with, and he did so well: already visibly above

21 *Twelfth Night*, directed by Patrick Mason, Theatre Royal, Plymouth. 'Husband?' Bob Cryer as
Orsino, Honeysuckle Weeks as Viola.

himself in Olivia's ménage, he tut-tutted audibly
when Maria reported that it was Sir Toby who was
dealing with the messenger from Orsino at 1.5.101,
and he wheezed with resentful self-importance as
a further rebuke to Viola when accosting her with
the ring in 2.2, allowing her 'Even now, sir, on
a *moderate* pace, I have since arrived but hither'

(2.2.3–4) to become the offhandedly taunting
riposte of an aristocrat to an over-familiar under-
ling. Making his pitiful social ambitions even more
painfully visible than usual, his yellow stockings
formed part of a golfing outfit, revealed beneath
a pair of plus-fours. His final 'I'll be revenged on
the whole pack of you' raked the audience as well

315

as the remainder of the cast with hatred, to disturbing effect, and this well-cast and well-judged performance was matched by Honeysuckle Weeks's Viola. Like McCrory as Rosalind, Weeks managed, crucially, to be equally sexy as a girl and as a boy. Shorn of 1.2's bedraggled long hair, she simulated a sort of arts undergraduate cockiness in male disguise (when she remembered to do so, as she hastily did, for instance, hands abruptly thrust into trouser pockets, to get a quick laugh after the pathos of 'patience on a monument', at 'We men may say more, swear more', 2.4.114), and this persona perfectly suited the white tie in which Orsino's court was uniformed. The effect was of a just-not-quite-spoiled youth unaware of the beauty which nonetheless underpinned his apparently invulnerable insouciance, a Cesario who made the ideal object of fascination and thwarted curiosity for Rebecca Egan's voluptuously Junoesque Olivia; clearly just the sort of privileged fair-haired boy to be mad about. The showiest performance in this production, though, was Hilton McRae's as Feste, endlessly full of comic tricks from which the jester-cum-troubadour himself seemed jadedly detached. He turned up in drag for the catch scene, veiled so that he could at first be mistaken for Maria, treated Orsino to a mock-New Age blessing, hand on forehead, at 'Now the melancholy god protect thee' (2.5.72ff), impersonated Billy Connolly as Sir Topas, sang his songs hauntingly to guitar accompaniment (still no tabor – this time Viola asked 'Dost thou live by thy music?'), and produced a fine wordless aside as of a mind indecently boggling when Viola told him that she was almost sick for a beard, though she would not have it grow on her chin (3.1.45–6 – where *did* this boy hope to grow his beard, then??). It was only when Feste then took her hand while begging a Cressida to his Troilus that he realized her real sex, kissing her fingers in sarcastic courtliness. If I have any reservations about this production, they are with the liberties it was prepared to take in the interests of clarifying Shakespeare's text. The play was well cut (the economical deletion of Fabian seemed fair enough, for example, and allowed Sir Toby for once to have that nice gag about the Dutchman's beard, while Curio got

to read Malvolio's letter aloud in the last scene), but Mason seemed over-eager to replace its less familiar vocabulary, qualifying the sometimes desirably exotic strangeness of Shakespeare's idiom in quest of a readily accessible plainness which wasn't his style even in 1601. Sebastian's destined voyage was mere 'wandering' rather than extravagancy; a 'veil' hid Olivia's heart rather than a cypress; daylight and 'countryside' rather than champaign discovered not more to Malvolio, who thought 'God' was to be thanked rather than Jove (this, admittedly, might be justified on the grounds that Shakespeare's printed text was only euphemizing under compulsion anyway, but I suspect that isn't what this alteration had in mind); Sir Toby called Maria his generic 'Amazon Queen' rather than Penthesilea in particular, and, most oddly of all, he claimed that his lady was a 'Chinaman' – though how this makes more immediately intelligible sense than calling her a Cathayan I don't quite see. Thankfully, the director and cast had retired baffled in the face of Pigrogromitus and the Vapians passing the equinoctial of Queubus, who, spared this creeping 'Shakespeare ReTold' treatment, were left intact to adorn what was otherwise a very satisfying *Twelfth Night*.

The year's most striking performance of a comedy, though, was Propeller's all-male production of *The Winter's Tale* (initially at the Watermill near Newbury, but subsequently on national and international tour), directed by Edward Hall. I have had enough qualms about Propeller's policy of denying work to women in the past, despite the admitted excellence of their *Dream* in 2003, to have approached this undertaking with considerable scepticism, but I found myself completely won over by a highly intelligent and consistently engaging treatment of a difficult text. The cross-gender casting not only helped to hold this play's avowed artifice at exactly the right distance from any inappropriate efforts to read it as wholly realist, but permitted some resonant doubling otherwise impossible since the disappearance of the boy-player. On a stage otherwise chequered like a chessboard, Mamillius – played by an adult actor, Tam Williams – amused himself with doll-like figurines in a sandpit as the audience assembled, more sand

22 *The Winter's Tale*, directed by Edward Hall, Propeller, Watermill Theatre, Newbury. Richard Clothier as Leontes.

pouring down into it as he did so as if he were playing inside an enormous hour-glass. As the houselights dimmed, he initiated the play proper by lighting a candle. Over the course of the first half of the play we grew accustomed to his intermittently watchful, pyjama-clad presence at the back of the stage even in scenes in which he had no scripted role. Except when engaged in those strange, damaged simulations of conversation by his father in 1.2 and playing off his mother and her gentlewomen against one another in 2.1, it became clear, Mamillius was not quite in the same time-frame as the rest of the characters: after his reported offstage death, he administered Antigonus's dream (holding up a female figurine to represent the ghost of Hermione and speaking her imputed lines), and even presided over Antigonus's death, acting the sinking of a toy ship and holding up his teddy bear to menace and kill a male figurine as Perdita's

reluctant exposer fled the stage. At the start of the second half, Mamillius even played Time, moving among the assembled, motionless remainder of the cast whitening the relevant beards as he explained about the sixteen-year gap we were negotiating. Only then did Williams change out of the pyjamas, to reappear, simply enough, in a yellow cotton dress decorated with flowers – as Perdita. This piece of doubling may sound merely sentimental – as though the son lost in the first half of the play was unproblematically regained as the daughter in the second – but that isn't how it worked in practice at all: what happened instead was that the rediscovered daughter was always and also the marker of the unrestored son, simultaneously comic heroine and tragic ghost. (Hence Perdita's discarded garlands from Act 4 became flowers on Hermione and Mamillius's grave – the sandpit – over which Leontes was found grieving at the start of act 5).

317

Mamillius made one explicit return as himself (or his ghost), too, at the end of the statue scene. As the other principals were hastily led away, Williams returned in his pyjamas, and was even seen by Leontes, who stretched his arms yearningly towards him – but Mamillius blew out the candle (which Paulina had re-lit as the visitors filed into her chapel), and left only darkness.

Around this foreceful central conceit, Hall's company performed with their usual inventiveness and ensemble brio. Richard Clothier, Vince Leigh, Bob Barrett and Adam Levy, as Leontes, Polixenes, Camillo and Paulina respectively, were the only players to attempt only one role each, and they more than earned the distinction; Simon Scardifield as Hermione, the woman caught between two men, returned in act 4 as Dorcas, one of the two maids wooing a man. Dugald Bruce Lockhart followed his solid Antigonus by returning as a swaggering, untrustworthy Florizel who seemed only to wind up actually marrying Perdita under the provocation of his father's opposition, and who sounded wonderfully shifty when lying to Leontes about his nuptial voyage to Libya, petering lamely and bathetically out on 'Here – where we are' (5.1.167). Tony Bell, an officer in the first half, returned, in a tremendous rousing full-cast rendition of 'When daffodils begin to peer', as an Autolycus skilled enough to strip James Tucker's Young Shepherd of almost every stitch of clothing in 4.3. Polixenes disguised himself as a monocled duck-hunter for his appearance at the sheep-shearing, complete with a ludicrous pheasant feather in his William Tell hat, while his accomplice Camillo sported a butterfly net. The scene of the opening of the fardel and consequent recognition of Perdita, surprisingly, was staged as a not-exactly dumb show, the lines describing it shared non-naturalistically among the principals, before they froze for the postponed entrance of Autolycus and the three gentlemen, who then gave only a truncated version of the last section of their interchange (before the Old and Young Shepherds arrived to forgive Autolycus as ever) as behind them the kings and princes regrouped ready for the statue scene. ('Who would be thence, that has the benefit of access?'

was here a pointed reminder to Autolycus that he wasn't invited.) The statue scene was conducted with tremendous skill and sleight of hand without a curtain: it was impossible to notice Scardifield's Hermione joining the group of actors looking around Paulina's chapel until suddenly Paulina indicated her, and there she was, immobile until reluctantly responsive to the clock-chiming music by which her friend called her back to a life preserved only to see Perdita – precisely that Perdita who was and was not the unmentioned Mamillius. This was a real coup of a production: I have never seen a *Winter's Tale* succeed in playing out the same argument while maintaining the same momentum across both halves of the play as did this.

The year's other production of the play, one of a series of romances at the Globe which marked the end of Mark Rylance's reign as artistic director, need detain us only briefly. Directed by John Dove with palpable under-confidence – he kept inventing exits and re-entrances within scenes for anyone not currently engaged in a conversation – this was one of those mixed-sex, recreated-clothing-of-the-period Globe shows, and if you've seen any of them to date you will be able to imagine this one: the Jacobean hats and romper-like breeches now impossible to take seriously (as Leontes, Paul Jesson was perpetually looking for an excuse to take his hat off and get some proper attention), the folksy animation of the sheep-shearing, punctuated by plenty of business involving Autolycus helping himself to the groundlings' water-bottles. You might even be able to anticipate that the stately jig at the end of Act 5 would modulate into country dance as, sentimentally, Mopsa and Dorcas suddenly arrived in Sicilia (having hitch-hiked on dolphins?) to join the party. Kathryn Hunter's *Pericles* was much more entertaining, but was based on such a daft reading of the play that it deserved to be less so. According to this production, the play is all about Pericles' coming to terms with his complicity in Antiochus's incest, with an elder Pericles (played, until rescued by a heart attack, by Corin Redgrave, who was then replaced by John McEnery) being therapeutically shown his youthful adventures (enacted by the

23 *The Winter's Tale*, directed by Edward Hall, Propeller, Watermill Theatre, Newbury. Florizel (Dugald Bruce Lockhart) about to assume Autolycus's clothes, with Perdita (Tam Williams) and Camillo (Bob Barrett).

much more Slovakian-sounding Robert Lucskay) by a shamanesque and intrusive Gower/Cerimon licensed to add all sorts of interpretative interjections to Shakespeare and Wilkins' text. ('Could you have saved her?', he repeatedly asked the sorrowful elder Pericles, as Antiochus' white-underwear-clad daughter made yet another late reappearance in his staged fantasies, and 'Relive the next stage of your story!'). In between and around the action, dancers sought to enact, often swinging on ropes, the different cultures and mindsets supposedly represented by the play's different Mediterranean locations (producing a sort of *Around the World in Eighty States of Being*), and it was only when the elder Pericles inexplicably took over his story in person, from Act 4 onwards, that the play resumed anything at all of its *faux-naif* charm and power: the recognition scene, unmolested, was like a sudden brief quotation from a better production, altogether elsewhere. In the best tradition of the actor-manager, Rylance chose the role of Prospero for his farewell to the Globe, but, less predictably, he chose to play a substantial proportion of the other roles in *The Tempest* too, having Tim Carroll direct it with a cast of only three actors, supplemented by three dancers. The results were moderately interesting and at times could almost have been followed by audiences otherwise unfamiliar with the play (though the opening scene, with Rylance staging the storm by wobbling a chessboard about and speaking all the characters' lines while holding up a different piece for each, baffled most), but despite the warmth with which Rylance's final prayer to be set free was answered at this production's sold-out last performance, it seemed a sadly if characteristically perverse note on which to leave an enterprise to which Rylance has brought so much energy and commitment over the last decade. Along with these full-scale productions, it should be recorded, the Globe briefly staged one more Shakespeare play this summer, which since its Quarto called it a comedy may as well be mentioned here. This was a *Troilus and Cressida* directed by Giles Block and played, like a few of last year's performances of *Romeo and Juliet*, in what was billed as Original Pronunciation. Sadly the direction and the acting were so poor (is it really possible in this day and age to charge real money, however little, for audiences to see a young woman give a performance as Nestor consisting solely of a stuck-on grey beard, a stoop and a perpetually shaking walking stick?) that despite the potential interest of hearing about Truylus, the Grex, Tharrsitays and so on for a change, this particular experiment in antiquarian phonetics is probably best summed up by the single word 'unspeakable'.

HISTORIES

Along with the year's notable London *Richard II* and *Henry IV*, one real curiosity stands out in this category, namely Robert Delamere's RSC production of *Sir Thomas More*, 'by Anthony Munday, William Shakespeare and others', in the Swan. Staged in grey and brown more-or-less modern dress (and thereby avoiding looking like a poor memorial reconstruction of *A Man for All Seasons*), this show provided a welcome opportunity to see a work of which only the probably Shakespearian speech by which More quells the 'Ill May Day' riot is usually ever performed, though it has to be said that this fine piece of humanitarian rhetoric isn't much helped when seen in context by the play's earlier depiction of the foreigners against whom the riot is directed as every bit as criminal a bunch of thieves and rapists as the mob claim them to be. Nigel Cooke did his amiable best as More, but over the full length of the play – short as it is – the writers' determination that we should admire him throughout proved entirely counterproductive, the Elizabethan prohibition against explaining what exactly it was that he was not prepared to sign at the offstage king's behest producing what looks like the hagiographic portrait of a man who insists on getting himself executed purely to show up his wife as a worldling and to prove how stoically well he can do it.

That said, Richard II gets himself deposed for what can look like comparably narcissistic reasons, though at the Old Vic in the autumn Kevin Spacey's performance as a man who comes to fancy himself as the tragic sacrificial type better than he fancies political and personal survival was a good deal more compelling than anything on offer in *Sir Thomas More*. It was said that Trevor Nunn only persuaded Spacey to play Richard II rather than Richard III (a part to which Spacey's cinematic performances as ambivalently glossy psychopaths might have appeared to prepare him better) because he had directed *Richard III* before and wanted instead to try a history which his long and crowded career in Shakespeare had so far left untouched. Certainly this wasn't the most obvious piece of casting on the face of things, requiring Spacey to be supplied with a wig to make him look younger even though the text's many references to the king's age were either deleted or changed. (York's shunned advice to Gaunt, for example, 'The King is come. Deal mildly with his youth', 2.1.69–70, dwindled into the inane 'The King is come, and with him is the Queen.') Nunn's chosen setting for the play, moreover, which left it about as English as it could have been, obliged Spacey to moderate

24 *Richard II*, directed by Trevor Nunn, Old Vic, London. The deposition scene: Kevin Spacey as Richard,
Ben Miles as Bolingbroke.

his native American pronunciation into something more closely resembling that of an otherwise
entirely native cast (though Genevieve O'Reilly
repeated the mistake Imogen Stubbs made in Stratford in 1986 by giving the Queen a distracting and
unhelpful French accent). He was spared the necessity of adopting medieval dress, however, by Nunn's
decision to set the play visually not in the fourteenth century but in a version or refraction of
present-day England.

The result was a production which sometimes
seemed like a hybrid between Stephen Pimlott's

modern-dress *Richard II* at the RSC in 2000 and
Nicholas Hytner's 2003 *Henry V* at the National,
adopting something of the look of the former
(though Hildegard Bechtler's designs were much
more straightforwardly representational than Pimlott's white box, providing, among much else, a
solidly oak-panelled presence chamber) and using
the same technique as the latter of showing certain
speeches being videotaped as sound-bites during
scenes and then repeating them as video clips on
large onstage screens thereafter. The show began
with a single spotlight illuminating the royal regalia

as they lay in a glass case downstage front, to be removed by white-gloved officials to the strains of 'Zadok the Priest' as the onstage screens played a montage of film clips of real royal processions (incuding footage from the 1953 coronation) inter-cut with shots of the cast filing solemnly through corridors in a deliberate pastiche of BBC televi-sion coverage of the state opening of Parliament. Eventually, once the royal party had arrived in person on the stage, Spacey ascended his throne on a dais centre-rear, the orb and sceptre were placed reverently into his hands and the crown set upon his head, and his lords sat in their places. Pin-striped, ermine-trimmed and formal, Boling-broke and Mowbray confronted one another across a table from ranked benches on either side of the king, their rapid and aggressive movements for-ward from their seats to lean across and make their speeches at one another deliberately resembling the behaviour of a Prime Minister and a Leader of the Opposition facing off at the despatch box, and indeed wherever in the play Nunn could find the occasion for some such immediate contempo-rary analogy he exploited it. As 1.3 broke up we saw Bolingbroke, suddenly as if at a railway sta-tion, telling television journalists 'Where'er I wan-der, boast of this I can: / Though banished, yet a trueborn Englishman' (1.3.271–2), a sound-bite which would haunt Richard between scenes for the next movement of the play, while Richard's coterie met to discuss their next move in 1.4 in a night-club to which Aumerle had some difficulty gaining access past the security guards in order to describe his cousin's departure. John of Gaunt, splendidly played by Julian Glover, was not speaking pri-vately to York in 2.1 but giving an organized press conference, calling the camera crew and lighting technicians forwards towards his wheelchair before embarking on 'Methinks I am a prophet new-inspired' (2.1.31ff), but then going well beyond his brief, forcing himself to his feet at 'Is now leased out' (2.1.59) and shocking all present with the inflammatory rage of his rhetoric. Northum-berland, Ross and Willoughby had repaired to a small panelled room apparently somewhere in the Palace of Westminster for their conspiratorial dis-

cussions at the end of the scene, while in the next the Queen was found discussing her anxieties with Bushy while undergoing a photo-shoot in a glam-orous ball dress, speaking sotto voce in between the ministrations of hairstylists and makeup artists. In 5.2, the Yorks' country house boasted a huge black leather sofa and a large framed photograph of Aumerle in an academic robe, apparently gradu-ating from Cambridge. This directorial approach inevitably left the audience looking for topical applications in the play's content (in the manner of Hytner's allusions to the dodgy Iraq dossier dur-ing the Salic Law scene of his *Henry V*), but by and large they were disappointed. Nunn's cuts to the script removed a good deal of the medieval polit-ical background – 1.2 was gone entirely, so that the extent of Richard's responsibility for the mur-der of the Duke of Gloucester was more obscured than ever – but the relevance of what was left to anything currently happening in British public life was never obvious. Updating the look of *Richard II* in this manner produced what looked as though it ought to be a play about contemporary politics, but it was a play whose cast, apart from the monarch, all resembled Tory grandees, and even the Conser-vative party is no longer controlled or even fronted by Tory grandees. (It's true that Ben Miles's Boling-broke would have made a much more convincing Leader of the Opposition than either of the real-life candidates for the post who were competing for it during this production's run, but that's by the by.) One of the newspaper critics mentioned the reform of the House of Lords, botched early in the Blair years but largely forgotten as a burning constitutional issue since, but otherwise most con-centrated on the personal rivalry at the core of the play as though politics was merely the medium that happened to give it expression.

Perhaps it was indeed the extra-political dimen-sion of this struggle which Nunn wanted to focus on by placing the play's events in a more imme-diately familiar external world: certainly the con-tention between Miles's tight-lipped Bolingbroke and Spacey's wilful king made for a fascinating show, not least because both performers seemed to understand their characters as two men driven to behave as unreadably as possible, strategically with-holding their real motives from inspection as far as they could. Miles usually behaved as if perpet-ually making a public statement at a time of cri-sis, stoically embodying resolve and the necessity for national firmness, so that on the few occasions when he did visibly falter or look puzzled the effect was of inner devastation: at the end of 3.3, the Flint Castle scene, when Richard anticipated his command to set on towards London, he paused a long time before agreeing 'Yes, my good lord' (3.3.207), looking suddenly bewildered and pan-icky to have lost the initiative. Being king, unfor-tunately, seemed to be the state of having lost the initiative, as his wearily ironic response to Aumerle's repented treason suggested, and his inquiries after his son at the start of 5.3 sounded oddly nostal-gic, as though he were looking back to a different world before his coronation when he could still leave the palace and give his attention to his fam-ily. Richard, needless to say, was more histrionic, but Spacey's outbursts no less than Miles's impas-sive patrician mask seemed like ways of avoiding scrutiny, lordly refusals to be answerable. 'For God's sake, let us sit upon the ground' (3.2.151ff) was a perverse riposte to his more utilitarian followers rather than an exercise in maudlin self-pity, and it was only at 'What must the King do now?' in the following scene (3.3.142) that Richard seemed to have given himself over to unrestrained emotion. In the deposition scene – played out in the same panelled presence chamber as 1.1, so that Richard at first walked automatically up to the dais and had to be prevented by a servant from mounting the throne – he was teasingly and stubbornly unread-able, trying to surrender power while surrendering as little of himself as possible with it. He seemed to be keeping Bolingbroke and all of us guessing as far as he could as to what exactly he was playing at, and he had evidently realized by now that his best weapon against this inhibited, dignified opponent was embarrassment. Deliberately rather than petu-lantly making a scene, he flabbergasted an atten-dant with his demand for the crown at 4.1.172, and his game of commanding Bolingbroke to come and get it and then making an emblematic tableau

of their posture as Bolingbroke sourly and reluc-tantly played along, eyes averted, was maliciously quizzical rather than teasing, a wry strategic par-ody of flirtation. Just when Bolingbroke finally thought that the worst of this irregular specta-cle was over, Richard took the crown back, and to general social dismay he insisted on ascending the dais and crowning himself, to stunned silence, before at last renouncing the throne at 'Now mark me how I will undo myself' (4.1.193ff). Only in prison did this Richard crack and play for pure pathos, finding himself without any onstage audi-ence but his own thoughts for the first time at 'I have been studying how I may compare . . .' (5.5.1–66), and the ensuing death scene was the more shocking and intense as a result. Spacey is every bit as charismatically oblique an actor on stage as on film, and those who only came to this pro-duction to see a star performance were perfectly satisfied.

There was plenty of star acting on view at the National, too, in Nicholas Hytner's production of both parts of *Henry IV*, which filled the Olivier during the summer. Like *Henry V* in 2003, this pro-duction was sponsored by Travelex, so that almost every seat in the house was sold for only £10, but either the scale of the subsidy had dropped or this was a more expensive cast, as the costuming and mise-en-scene looked distinctly low-budget. A steeply raked stage negotiated a no-man's land of dead trees, while above it three long horizontal screens showed different emblematic photographs according to the location of the scene (a mon-tage of half-timbered buildings for Gloucestershire, for example): the effect was slightly as if peering out through the slits in some enormous concrete bunker, into a social world that was never realized any more specifically on the stage than it was in the slides. *Part 1* began, puzzlingly enough, on a battlefield, with scavenging and bereaved women picking among corpses as a group of nondescript men in dark clothes approached slowly down the rake. They wore a melange of dull-coloured clothes drawn from any or no period – thick sweaters, broad leather belts, canvas tunics – and it was only when one of them, a bent figure with a grey beard,

25 *Henry IV Part 1*, directed by Nicholas Hytner, National Theatre (Olivier auditorium). Michael Gambon as Falstaff, Matthew MacFadyen as Prince Hal.

began to speak that one noticed that he was also wearing a crown. 'So shaken as we are, so wan with care, / Find we a time for frighted peace to pant . . .' (1.1.1–2). Even for those already familiar with the text, this seemed a strange choice of setting for the first scene of the play – which battle had this king just won or lost? was he holding some sort of council meeting, and if so why was he doing it while walking around out here? which century were we ostensibly in? – and it wasn't helped by Bradley's monotonously rueful delivery, which rarely distinguished between public and private speech throughout both parts but droned through both in a sort of generalized grumbling dismay. With much of the first scene's exposition lost as the audience tried and largely failed to orient themselves, it was a relief to get to 1.2, even if we were kept waiting for the dialogue to get under way while Matthew MacFadyen's Hal

and Michael Gambon's Falstaff relieved themselves first – stumbling down the rake, turning their backs to the audience and spraying a tree each for what seemed a good deal longer than the gag really warranted. They then settled at a little greasy-spoon café table and were presently being served mugs of coffee and a large fried breakfast, evidently after spending the entire night in sleepless dissipation, so that if their clothes gave little away about the historical setting or the social context – Hal wore a mottled, orange-toned jacket and silk scarf, while Falstaff favoured disreputable burgundy velvet trousers, a long black cardigan and a little plumed toque hat that wouldn't have looked out of place on a down-at-heel nineteenth-century Russian nobleman – it was at least perfectly obvious what time it was. So after setting a scene that begins with a discussion of peace on a battlefield, Hytner had moved on to setting a scene that begins with the question 'Now, Hal, what time of day is it, lad?' at a breakfast table.

This was not a directorial opening that inspired confidence, though the acting in 1.2 was a good deal more encouraging. Gambon might as well have been auditioning for the role of Falstaff for much of the last twenty years, playing a whole succession of intransigent and often debauched old bullies redeemed only by a reckless charm: at the end of this scene, he seized up both his own and Hal's unfinished fried eggs and bacon and crammed them providently and nimbly into his pocket, checking that Hal was suitably appalled and fascinated as he did so. Gambon's performance was unpredictable over the course of the run (not least because he never quite remembered the lines in precisely the same way every night; even on his best behaviour at the press night, Part 2's resolution 'I will turn diseases to commodity', 1.2.249–50, became something that sounded more like 'There's nothing. . worthful. . but commodities'), but it was always characterized by a shrewd and potentially quite hostile sense of Falstaff as a predatory fraud, forever adjusting his often squalid behaviour to secure Hal's attention. (This squalid behaviour reached its apogee as the lights faded at the close of part 1, when Falstaff was to be seen among the scavengers once more picking over corpses on the stage's reiterated battlefield.) Hence Gambon's pronunciation veered wildly between and within scenes, encompassing the most bizarre affectations of Cockney, aristocratic, Irish and on some vowels hints of Australian, according to his addressee or pose at any given moment, with this protean linguistic performance safely anchored, as Falstaff recognizes, in the undisguisable bulk of his stomach. His natural embonpoint enhanced by padding, Gambon's ability apparently to abolish his own spinal column at will, so as to flow shapelessly onto the stage like a male sea elephant, was displayed to splendid effect across both Part 1 and Part 2, and Mark Thompson's otherwise clumsy decision to have the tavern scenes entered from a trapdoor gave Gambon the opportunity to make a whole running-gag out of the different ways he devised over the course of the two shows of arriving with difficulty at the top of an imaginary flight of stairs – sometimes tottering, sometimes overshooting, sometimes briefly pirouetting uncontrollably around the post at the top of the stair-rail. In the midst of all this comic self-invention, however, Gambon's Falstaff always had one wary eye on Hal, towards whom he was physically affectionate as with no-one else: from the first scene onwards, he repeatedly used a little pleading gesture of raising his right forearm to reach a hand towards Hal's sleeve, a gesture left desolately unanswered and unfinished at Hal's final exit after 'I know thee not, old man' in Part 2.

This was a Falstaff who had a good deal to be insecure about, too, since MacFadyen's Hal was a curiously disengaged prince throughout, his heart and even his whole attention never quite given over either to revelry or to the prospect of government. His characteristic pose was one of absent preoccupation, eyes half-embarrassedly downcast, but when you are Prince of Wales, it turns out, this can be a position of great strength. During the confrontations with his father, 3.2 of Part 1 and 4.3 of Part 2, MacFadyen simply sat through the King's tirades as if waiting him out, mildly impatient that his father couldn't seem to grasp that all these rebukes were unfair because Hal hadn't even *started* yet. Nor had he: MacFadyen's performance was essentially the performance of a performance withheld, an impersonation of a young man who went outwardly along with things but who would eventually be crowned as King before he had really quite got round even to being Prince of Wales. 'I know you all', at the end of 1.2, didn't sound like a manifesto statement for a policy he was already pursuing but more like one more irresolute and short-lived attempt at a rationalization, the postponement of a decision rather than the revelation of one already made. Underneath, you wondered whether he wasn't completely indifferent. Partly as a result of this detachment of the protagonist from main and subplot alike, most of the momentum in *Henry IV Part 1* came from the rebels, particularly David Harewood's likeable Hotspur, slightly too old for the behaviour the part requires and as a result appearing almost paternal in his patronizing

26 *Henry IV Part 2*, directed by Nicholas Hytner, National Theatre (Olivier auditorium). Michael Gambon as Falstaff, John Wood as Justice Shallow.

dealings with the nonetheless clearly cherished Kate, but the only performer on the stage to show half the energy of Gambon's Falstaff.

As a whole, Part 1 remained an aimless, unfocused piece of work, an anthology of performances which somehow failed to add up to a production. It was this very desultory quality, though, which came into its own in Part 2, a play that anyway consists almost entirely of miscellaneous people sitting about waiting for something to happen, though the dowdy vagueness of the setting continued to rob the performances of social specificity or resonance. It's true that the whole point of Falstaff's capture of Sir John Coleville was completely lost –

Falstaff was here able to take him prisoner in 4.2 not because he had an inflated impression of Falstaff's valour but because he was already severely wounded, which took away the worrying effect of what looks like a stage practical joke having a real fatal consequence when the unsmiling Prince John then arrives to condemn Coleville to death – but otherwise Hytner's touch seemed to have returned. The scene between Hal and Poins, 2.2, as the Prince wearily just about deigned to notice an increasingly irate and offended Poins (a clenched performance by Adrian Scarborough, who less satisfactorily doubled a Henry Crun-like Silence later on), was MacFadyen's best in the whole production (disappointingly, he was still almost as remote for the renunciation of Falstaff three acts later). Falstaff, meanwhile, was granted a new and much livelier foil in the person of John Wood's Justice Shallow. This was a baroque, virtuoso piece of work, from Wood's first entrance onwards. Although a single entrance is marked for both justices at the start of 3.2, Shallow had got so far ahead of the hobbling Silence that he arrived down the rake a good twenty seconds before Silence became visible at the back of the stage, and a good minute and a half before he caught up: in between, Wood's 'Come on, come on, come on!', the calls separated by long pauses illuminated by a tremendous range of facial expressions, ran a whole gamut of the possible emotions one fussy old man might have towards another under such circumstances: condescending benignity (the first beaming, encouraging 'Come on'), rueful fellow-feeling, impatience, a sighing philosophical resignation to a common fate, more impatience (a tetchier 'Come on'), inner disavowal that one could ever be thus afflicted oneself, yet more impatience, horror at the sight of this *memento mori* as Silence comes inexorably closer into view, resentful hostility towards him, and yet more impatience that he *still* hasn't quite caught up (the final, exasperated 'Come *on*!'). The ensuing dialogue about mutual acquaintances living and dead teetered over an abyss of panic at the banal inevitability of death and the impossibility of acknowledging it except in platitudes, and was hilarious, familiar and desolate by turns, incontrovertible evidence that the author of *The Merry Wives of Windsor* could also take on Beckett or Pinter at their own games. Wood's rapidity at shifting tones of voice and registers of feeling further enlivened a blissfully leisurely and uncut rendition of 5.1 and 5.3 – with selfless and expert support from Gambon – where Shallow displayed a skittish and excited recurrent interest in Falstaff's page, whom he greeted with an odd frisk and a sudden plummeting of his voice at 'And welcome, my tall fellow' (5.1.51–2). If Hytner's production almost refused to interpret *Henry IV* in any very sustained or consistent way, this show at least provided the vehicle for some impressive and sometimes wonderfully elaborated character acting: but for such a large-scale undertaking to find so little to say to or about the nation whose history it supposedly dramatized, especially given that the press night in early May fell on the eve of a general election, seemed a surprisingly missed opportunity. However well non-particularized settings can sometimes work in tragedy, removing history plays from any recognisable history at all seems like a mistake.

TRAGEDIES

To judge from the classical repertory in 2005, the RSC's concerted binge on tragedy during the previous year had completely failed to assuage the theatregoing public's thirst for blood. Among the specimens of this genre revived this year, one really outstanding production stands out – Stephen Pimlott's *King Lear* at the Minerva in Chichester during the summer – but six other shows deserve less extended comment. Jacob Murray produced an exciting, fresh, youthful *Romeo and Juliet* at the Royal Exchange in Manchester in the autumn – which is to say, a satisfactory one, since any *Romeo and Juliet* which isn't all three of these things has clearly got something drastically wrong somewhere – but Murray's production, though otherwise well-designed by Ellen Cairns (*La Dolce Vita* suits, a Vespa for Mercutio, a cigarette holder for Pooky Quesnel's elegant Lady Capulet filled, the programme hastened to reassure us, only with NTB Herbal Cigarettes), was notable chiefly for providing an object lesson in why 2.1 has usually been treated as the 'balcony' scene since the early eighteenth century. In the round as ever in this venue, Murray decided that his balcony scene could do without even the 'window' mentioned in the text, treating one of the four entrances into the acting area as though Juliet's bedroom were on the ground floor and this was a French door opening into the garden. Hence Gugu Mbatha-Raw's Juliet strayed out into the moonlight to sigh 'Ay me' (2.1.67), and came close to tripping over Andrew Garfield's lurking Romeo. I have seen a *Romeo* in the round that did without a balcony once before, but there the lighting kept up a pretence that there was still some physical barrier between them: here the two were simply out in the garden together, unchaperoned and with nothing to keep them out of one another's arms. This sadly unPetrarchan state of affairs had two unwelcome effects: it failed to hold Juliet still at the centre of the stage-picture, so that her authority in deciding on the next day's marriage was much dissipated as she and Romeo moved restlessly around the garden showing themselves efficiently to all sides of the audience; and, at a simpler level, it made their behaviour for much of the scene inexplicable. Why, after kissing so eagerly during their sonnet a few minutes earlier, did they now waste so much time speaking poetry to one another? When they finally kissed, at length, on Juliet's first 'Goodnight' (2.1.199), you couldn't understand why they hadn't started doing so long earlier, and when they finally stopped doing so you couldn't understand why they did that either. Mbatha-Raw and Garfield were otherwise so good at simulating frenetic adolescent desire (the wedding night completely failed to sate this Juliet, who even straight after it at 3.5.80–102 could hardly make her punning remarks to her mother about wanting Romeo to suffer at her hands alone audible, so busily was she writhing on her bed clutching herself in frustration) that one felt that they ought really to have needed the balcony if only as a contraceptive measure. Surprisingly, after refusing the balcony Cairns got very literal-minded about the tomb, trundling a full-scale fake stone structure into the middle of the stage that creaked unfortunately as the lovers perished on it, but this was otherwise a well-paced, absorbing production, with a particularly good, pragmatic Nurse from Maggie McCarthy.

Julius Caesar, rarely anything like such a favourite on the modern English stage, was produced twice in 2005, once by the current RSC – in David Farr's touring production, which visited the Swan along with *Two Gentlemen of Verona* from November to February – and once by what amounted to a reunion of the RSC of the 1980s: Deborah Warner's production at the Barbican brought together Anton Lesser, John Shrapnel, Ralph Fiennes, Fiona Shaw and Simon Russell Beale,

names last seen together in *Shakespeare Survey* some time around volume 39. Both shows were in modern dress, with the proscription lists in 4.1 displayed on laptop computers, but otherwise they differed greatly in both style and scale. Farr's production, on a warehouse-like set featuring flags, a large video screen held up on raw scaffolding and all sorts of trailing electrical flexes, seemed to be nostalgic for a fringe venue from the early 1970s. The opening dialogue among the plebeians – who wore sunglasses and T-shirts and all laughed robotically in unison in a manner that once looked like radical chic but now looks like a television commercial for the Gap – was lit in fizzling plain neon light, but this stylized manner with the crowds sat uneasily with a more naturalistic style of acting among the principals. Certainly there was nothing mannered or remote about Zubin Varla's perpetually overwrought Brutus, who was tense enough to pull a machine pistol on the poor would-be comic poet who showed up in drag during 4.2. It's true, however, that there was something inadvertently automatic-looking about Rachel Pickup's Portia, who combed one hand through her hair during the orchard scene some eight times, and the very fact that I was counting by then may suggest how blurred and uninvolving this noisy, fidgety production was. Despite a strong Caesar by Christopher Saul, the show's expressionistic muddle of live action with videotaped political images and pre-recorded speeches lacked focus, especially since, unlike in Nunn's *Richard II*, there was no clear indication here as to who within the world of the play was in control of all this media activity at any given moment. A bizarre inserted song-and-dance number (a leadenly flippant piece of cod-Russian kitsch called the War Song, placed just before the fourth act), didn't help either.

Warner's more straightforwardly cinematic production ought by rights to have been far more impressive, and generally it was, though given the amount of proven talent in the cast it was still disappointing. With the assistance of the Young Vic, Warner had secured the services of a 40-strong team of professional and semi-professional bit-part actors for the crowd scenes, so that her version of the Forum was bette staffed with friends, Romans and countrymen than any that has been seen in this country for a hundred years, and this certainly made the play's central scenes as exciting as I have ever seen them. The opening, before any dialogue had been spoken, perfectly captured the mood at the end of a long day of public demonstrations – metal barriers near the wide steps of some public building, a lone skateboarder watched by anxious security men, a drunken girl in a cheap fur coat with a balloon walking unsteadily homewards, noises off of walkie-talkies and distant sirens – and the acting by the crowd, when it gathered to hear the tribunes and later in far greater force to welcome Caesar at the Lupercal, was electric throughout. John Shrapnel, in a power-suit and surrounded by the customary modern entourage of security guards and secretaries, paraded up to the barriers and pressed the flesh, striking photo-opportunity poses with his athletic PR specialist, Ralph Fiennes's Mark Antony, all to rapturous applause; a little ritual with champagne toasts and two girls chosen from the crowd accompanied Antony's despatch to run a course which looked rather like a more hysterical and popular version of the London Marathon. Caesar handled the soothsayer with easy familiarity (he looked like a version of the late Screaming Lord Sutch, a plummy-voiced drunken eccentric who on his second appearance held up a cardboard scythe on the line 'Ay, Caesar, but not gone', 3.1.3), and the way in which he fed on the adulation of the crowd was closely and intelligently observed. The source of difficulty and discontent in this energetically popular regime, however, was already visible. Among the fellow members of the elite looking on, one short, rotund figure was wearing not a CIA-like grey suit and tailored mac but a floppy jacket and a cardigan. As Cassius, Simon Russell Beale certainly knew how to look like a disaffected stage academic, even if he is so far from having a lean and hungry look that the line itself, 1.2.195, had to be made into a little joke on Caesar's part (with the stress falling heavily on 'look': 'Yon Cassius has a lean and hungry *look* [however pudgy the rest of him may be]').

It was when this unlikely Cassius and Anton Lesser's more obviously lean and hungry Brutus were left alone together that the production began to run into difficulties. Both already looked so jittery and discontented that it was hard to imagine anyone else in Caesar's entourage trusting them for a moment, and indeed Cassius was clearly driven by such a neurotic set of personal grudges that the conspiracy which he and Brutus rather cattily set in intermittent motion never looked like an affair of political principle at all. The momentum in this production seemed rather to be on Caesar's side, though it's true that the plain-clothes security personnel and uniformed police who had seemed to have the Roman public order situation so thoroughly under control under his dictatorship turned out to be both ineffective and disloyal when the crunch came, mysteriously absent at the crucial moment of the assassination and then as inexplicably willing to defend Brutus from the crowd as he prepared to make his funeral oration as they had been earlier to protect Caesar. The production only regained its full power with the return of Fiennes's Antony, certainly the best piece of work he has done in Shakespeare since the days of his Henry VI: both 'O pardon me, thou bleeding piece of earth' (3.1.257–78) and 'Friends, Romans, countrymen' (3.2.74–225) were overwhelming, the latter much helped by the sheer force of forty supernumerary throats shouting their gradually-won assent. The clarity with which Fiennes delineated not just Antony's cynical rhetorical dissimulation but the genuine anger and loyalty to his dead boss which motivated it was exemplary. By comparison the relationship between Cassius and Brutus looked altogether shallower and less secure, and while 4.2 is sometimes referred to as the tent scene it can never have invited being rechristened the camp scene as irresistibly as it did here. Excitingly crowded before the interval, Warner's production had collapsed into a depopulated desert after it, with the stage suddenly stripped bare to the wings and the back wall, so that Brutus and Cassius appeared to be bitching in the middle of a disused hangar rather than quarrelling in a tent. The forty extras, surprisingly, were completely absent from this second half of the play, so that this was a *Julius Caesar* with an unusually persuasive mob but absurdly tiny armies. Russell Beale seemed especially ill at ease in this military setting: he still wore a civilian suit and a red tie for the quarrel scene although his colleagues had by now adopted army fatigues, and on the battlefield itself he sounded about as little like a soldier as can well be imagined, confiding in the audience that 'This day I breathèd first' (5.3.23) with a little coy simper as though excitedly awaiting a pile of gift-wrapped bijoux. A desultory affair of runnings-about with replica weapons and a few loud bangs, this Philippi made a suitably anticlimactic ending to a *Julius Caesar* which despite a terrific Antony and an estimable mob never quite had the conspiracy its imperialists deserved. It's a sad thing that at the moment the English theatre seems to find it easier to picture successful totalitarian regimes than to remember what effective political opposition ever looked like.

The play's sequel enjoyed only one revival in 2005, and this too was at best a qualified success. Braham Murray's handsomely Roman-looking *Antony and Cleopatra* at the Royal Exchange in Manchester in the spring, blessed with a magnificent Cleopatra in the person of Josette Bushell-Mingo, tried to scale the play down to provide a clearer focus on its principals, as though it were a psychological tragedy in close-up throughout rather than a play as interested in world history as it is in the narrowly personal. Pompey had vanished from the script, as had Ventidius and the Parthians and much else and, while the last act, as the play closes itself down towards a single tableau in a single monument, worked as beautifully as ever under this treatment, the earlier phases of the play – which seem designed to provide a series of glimpses of a more glamorous era passing away as much as sustained personal case histories – seemed thin and ill-paced. It didn't help that Murray's sole venture into the emblematic – an unscripted tableau of Antony on the battlefield being enfeebled by the presence of Cleopatra – was bafflingly placed around 4.5, during the only sequence in the script when we see Antony winning; nor that Tom Mannion's Antony in any case occasioned that sense, so familiar with

revivals of this play, that the audience were forever wondering what she saw in him; nor that Bushell-Mingo's Cleopatra seemed as earnest in the dissimulating, playful, strategic early acts as in the elegiac fifth. But this is always a difficult play to pull off, and hence Murray's production deserves far less criticism than does Stephen Unwin's *Hamlet* for the English Touring Theatre, a competently-spoken affair played in monochromatic Elizabethan dress which somehow gave the impression that the main thing on the cast's minds was not getting the costumes dirty or crumpled. Scene after scene passed without the remotest sense of urgency and without any clue as to why this particular play was being revived by this particular company at this particular time, unless the whole enterprise had really been motivated solely by the opportunity to cast the son of the author of *Rosencrantz and Guildenstern Are Dead* in the title role. Ed Stoppard looks fine in doublet and hose, but it's really no good staging *Hamlet* at all if you don't have some sort of idea why it matters.

John Caird's *Macbeth* at the Almeida in January was a far more intellectually interesting show than this, if equally remote from what is usually thought of as the mainspring of this play. Rather than being a short, fast-moving, suspenseful political thriller, this production was a long, slow psychological meditation: played inside a circle faintly marked with a pentagram and surrounded by lights shining upwards through varying thicknesses of smoke, so that the stage resembled a round raft adrift in Hell, it was throughout more securely located within its protagonist's consciousness than in any recognizable polis. (The predominantly Jacobean-dressed production's main gestures towards mimesis came in the form of some surprisingly literal-minded sound cues: a canned owl to prompt Lady Macbeth's reference to it after the murder of Duncan, the sound of the grooms praying offstage, barking dogs to usher in the murderers.) Macbeth's consciousness, however, was delineated with enough quirky intelligence and ingenuity to sustain this show despite the fact that its first half – with the interval withheld until after 4.2, the killing of Macduff's family – seemed almost as long as the whole

27 *Macbeth*, directed by John Caird, Almeida Theatre. Richard Stacey as Seyton, Simon Russell Beale as Macbeth.

of Murray's *Antony and Cleopatra* and Unwin's *Hamlet* put together. Miscast Simon Russell Beale as Cassius, it turns out, and you just get a *Julius Caesar* with an incidentally ill-fitting Cassius; miscast him as Macbeth and you get a production centred broodingly and intently on his very incongruity in the part, a production less about a warrior-thane who finds himself turning into a murderer than one about a relatively normal citizen who finds himself turning into a poet. Overseen by genteel, mature witches whose governess-like cut-glass accents made their meetings sound like Cheltenham Ladies' College old girls' reunions (especially as they gathered around Macbeth's bed after the banquet in 4.1 as if to provide him with the child-apparitions in his dreams), this production

331

was always and almost exclusively about the protagonist whose progress into evil they blandly
supervised and encouraged. Beale's Macbeth
appeared with Banquo in the very first scene of
the play while they spoke of him, and he remained
visible, immobile and unlit, during 1.2. Even scenes
during which he did not appear were dominated,
unusually, by his very absence, as was the case with
1.6, which found Lady Macbeth awkwardly making conversation with Duncan while both waited
in vain for Macbeth to welcome the king himself (until Duncan gave up at 'Give me your hand.
/Conduct me to mine host', 1.6.28–9). Our speculations as to whether Macbeth could not yet bring
himself to face the man he was now planning to
murder were thus allowed to upstage the performance Lady Macbeth was giving before our eyes
as Duncan's eager hostess; and indeed throughout
the play Emma Fielding was conspicuously sidelined in favour of Beale. Caird had her play 'They
met me in the day of success' (1.5.1–30) as though
she were not reading Macbeth's letter for the first
or even third time but were hastily whispering it
to herself for the last time to check that she had
succeed in memorizing its contents before burning
the incriminating paper with the candle that would
reappear in the sleepwalking scene and, while this
directorial choice certainly highlighted the fear of
being convicted of treason in Duncan's Scotland, it
denied Fielding much chance of establishing what
sort of person her Lady Macbeth was and what she
actually made of the letter's contents. In her dialogues with Macbeth, she was often quietened by
him – the emotion she began to show too audibly at 'Was the hope drunk . . .?', 1.7.35–45, was
hushed with a 'Prithee, peace' that gestured towards
a servant just about to pass across the stage – and
like the witches she too was reduced to mother-
ing Macbeth, hugging him soothingly, for example, while he sobbed at 'But screw your courage
to the sticking place' (1.7.60–1). Their off-centred
marriage seemed to fracture unusually early, too: he
did not meet her eye or even seem to notice her as
he asked to be left 'Till supper time alone' at 3.1.45,
and all their subsequent conversations were dominated solely by mutual recrimination: 'O, full of

scorpions is my mind, dear wife!' (3.2.37), instead
of confiding in her and seeking comfort, became
an outburst in soliloquy which he seemed to regret
that she had even heard: 'O full of scorpions is
my mind!' [turns, looks at her aghast face, bit-
terly reflects that she doesn't understand, resorts to
sarcasm] '– dear wife'. Even Fielding's business in
the very fast-paced sleepwalking scene seemed to
be dictated by Beale's performance rather than her
own: surrounded by the witches (one of whom
took the lines of her attendant lady), she left her
candle on the stage instead of carrying it off to
bed, to bed, to bed, so that he would be able to use
it at 'Out, out, brief candle' two scenes later.

This was a Macbeth sufficiently interested in
himself, however, for the fact that to all intents and
purposes this production barely noticed its Lady
Macbeth to matter very little. The chief effect in
which it was interested was that of a Macbeth who
was forever watching himself, looking surprised to
hear himself say things, registering change in himself, often during long mid-line pauses: at 1.3.138,
'My thought, whose murder [shocked to find the
word in his mind, thinks for a long time about
it, then tries to sound dismissively provisional] yet
is but fantastical'; at 1.7.21, 'And pity,' [cradles
imaginary or remembered baby, hugging himself
hunched as he does so] 'like a naked new-born
babe' [holds this gesture so that 'I have no spur/To
prick the sides of my intent' at 1.7.25–6 means
'I have no potential dynasty to royalize by this
murder'] – this was a Macbeth more visibly interested in children than was his wife, to whom the
messages of impending disaster during Act 5 were
brought by the actors who had played Macduff's
children; at 3.1.138–9, '[Fleance] must embrace
the fate/Of that' [pause while he cannot quite use
the word 'murder'] 'dark hour'; at 5.5.9, 'I have'
[long pause, intense mental self-inspection] 'almost
forgot the taste of fears.' It was almost as if this
Macbeth were surprised to find himself speaking
at all, registering his sheer puzzlement at suddenly
being sufficiently out of kilter with his place in
the world to have fallen into perpetual soliloquy,
a puzzlement he displayed much more thoroughly
than any moral disapprobation of his own actions.

Most weirdly of all, he actually insisted on being present at the killing of Macduff's family, suddenly entering to look closely into the screaming Lady Macduff's eyes as she died at the end of the first half of the play, as though the whole massacre were some sort of solemn experiment on his own consciousness.

Needless to say, Beale being the actor he is, the novel, minute readings were often comic or self-deprecating too. 'My dull brain was wrought / With things forgotten' (1.3.147–8) was delivered in a wonderfully unconvincing tone of dismissal, with a comic scratching of the nose; at 'under him / My genius is rebuked as, it is said, / Mark Antony's was by Caesar' (3.1.56–8) the reference to Antony adopted a self-consciously lofty tone and was followed by a firm nod to the audience, as if Macbeth were an ex-grammar-school boy ponderously congratulating himself on having become a better class of tyrant; the disdainful tone of his congratulation to the murderers, 'Your spirits shine through you' (3.1.129), made him sound like a pantomime dame registering a nose-wrinkling astonishment to find himself working with such dingy co-stars. Most remarkably, this was a Macbeth who actually died laughing, tricking Macduff into stabbing him as they prepared to duel with bayonets: 'And damned be him that first cries 'Hold' [lunges as if to attack, then opens his arms to Macduff's reflex retaliatory blow, guides the blade home with his hands; laughs to discover that the wound is as mortal as he had hoped] 'enough' (5.10.34). Nothing appeared to have changed, however, for those Home Counties witches were still securely in control: after Malcolm had summed up, it was they who blew out the candle to mark the end of the performance. The overall effect was of a production seeking to make up in wilful ingenuity what it lacked in physical excitement or conviction, and if it didn't exactly move its audiences, it certainly kept them thinking.

Call me old-fashioned, but I much prefer productions of Shakespeare's tragedies which are willing and able to be moving and thought-provoking at once, and in this respect Stephen Pimlott's *King Lear*, at the Minerva in Chichester in the summer, excelled every other revival of a tragedy this year.

This was a blindingly clear production throughout, with the 300-strong audience seated around three sides of a perfectly square, white acting area, with an inner square raised by just an inch or two above the surrounding floor. Here the use of non-specific, more-or-less modern clothes and props amply justified itself, perfectly serving this play's own carefully-maintained sense of keeping us guessing as to exactly where or when we are (beyond the fact that we are in the same universe as Dover, and don't know where the centre of power is any more): the designer Alison Chitty had even found a nicely economical way of just adequately defamiliarizing one otherwise clichéd Shakespearian dress code by having some of the cast, including Lear at the start of the storm, wear the usual black leather greatcoats but turned inside out to show the stitching. In Chitty's plain cube of a space, the sixteen-strong cast played a streamlined Folio-based text as if interested above all else in telling psychological detail, but if anything the rootedness in the text of the business they had developed to illustrate different details of their characters' personal stories served the better to explore the tragedy's public dimension too.

Before the action started, for example, the map of the kingdom was already lying at the centre of the stage, and before Kent and Gloucester entered there was Edmond standing over it, his eyes hungrily devouring its every line before he noticed his father's approach and hastily averted his gaze. (Productions which forget that *King Lear* comes within an ace of being the story of how Edmond becomes king do so at their peril, and this one, with Stephen Noonan wearing the customary black leather jacket with ability and dash, never did: he had even taken the trouble to corrupt Curran, buying his information with a discreet bribe at the start of 2.1). The love-test itself, when it came, was both psychologically and politically convincing. The full court assembled, with David Warner's tall, white-robed and white-bearded king taking the sole chair as his throne – bravely, with his back to the central section of the audience – and his explanation of the ceremony that was about to take place was didactic and careful rather than capricious. With

28 *King Lear*, directed by Stephen Pimlott, Minerva Theatre, Chichester. David Warner as King Lear, John Ramm as the Fool.

deliberation he removed his crown as he spoke of his intention to 'Unburdened crawl toward death' (1.1.41), and as he undertook to declare his political will and testament by making public his daughters' respective dowries he leaned forward and caught each child's eye firmly, explaining that his main purpose was 'that future strife / May be prevented – now' (1.1.44–5). The attention this king commanded was respectful, and by now anxious, but by no means terrified or quasi-religious – clearly this was no Ivan the Terrible liable to have the unenthusiastic executed at a moment's notice, nor a father who had habitually devised intolerable public tests for his children before this genuinely well-intentioned but disastrous morning's work – and his response to Cordelia's refusal was at first simply one of incomprehension rather than tyrannical rage. At 'Nothing, my lord' Warner's spine appeared to stiffen and his shoulders to freeze, and

his voice expressed a profound bafflement at 'How, how, Cordelia?' (1.1.94) which would characterize much of his behaviour in the first movement of the play. Suddenly, it became apparent, he found himself in a world he no longer quite recognized; nobody had ever contradicted him in public like this before, and the anger that then overcame him was a baffled lashing-out that always hoped things could somehow be got back to normal if only the immediate obstacles could be repudiated with sufficient vehemence. At 'I loved her most' (1.1.123–4) Lear embraced Cordelia, as though momentarily overcome with nostalgia for his own lost vision of how this scene had been supposed to turn out, but that way madness lay: after 'Hence, and avoid my sight!' (1.1.124) he distracted himself with the improvised administrative business of dividing her third between Cornwall and Albany, trying not to look at Cordelia's face as he snatched off her circlet to throw it to Albany at 'This coronet part between you' (1.1.139). Kent still had sufficient faith in what we inferred was the king's accustomed reasonableness to make his appeal against Cordelia's disinheritance with confidence, but to no avail: Lear motioned to him to kneel at 'on thine allegiance hear me' (1.1.166), gesturing for his crown, which he then placed on his head again in order to pronounce Kent's banishment. The ensuing business with France and Burgundy was particularly striking: in this production Burgundy had clearly enjoyed much fuller access to Cordelia than had France, since the princess and the duke appeared to have a genuine personal relationship which Burgundy now renounced only with painful regret (perhaps Lear had hitherto favoured Burgundy's suit because he had seen that Cordelia did). Kay Curram's Cordelia expressed sorrow and a measure of compassion at 'Peace be with Burgundy' (1.1.247–8) rather than a bitter moral superiority, and her dismissal with the comparative stranger who was France was the more distressing for it. Left alone, Gonerill and Regan were only beginning to realize the impossibility of the situation into which their father had placed them, just as he was, with Zoe Waites's Regan – a beautifully observed study in deference turned sour, initially the most reluctant of the sisters to show any disrespect towards Lear – so far uncertain how to respond to Gonerill's proposed alliance.

Blissfully free of symbols, furs, menhirs, invented pagan rituals or gimmicky it's-only-fairytale props, this account of the first scene had launched the play with a minimum of fuss or condescension, and the momentum never slackened hereafter, helped in this respect by Pimlott's shrewd audience-friendly re-punctuation of the play which gave it two intervals instead of just one (a trick repeated from his 2001 RSC *Hamlet*). The first came as early as the end of the first act – after 'O, let me not be mad, not mad, sweet heaven!' (1.5.45) – then the second at the end of Act 3, immediately after the blinding of Gloucester, so that the play was helpfully divided into the opening, the storm, and the endgame. Or, from the point of view of Edgar, the incrimination by Edmond, the performance as Poor Tom, and

the attempt to look after Gloucester; unusually, Jo Stone-Fewings excelled in each of these capacities, pitifully pleased to see his enjoyably naughty half-brother Edmond at their first meeting in 1.2, touchingly excited in 2.2 by his own idea of playing Poor Tom (as though part of his mind still reflected ruefully what a good notion this would have been, under happier circumstances, for an undergraduate drama festival), and horrified at what he found himself having to do in the last two acts of the play, shocked, for example, to have killed Oswald (the text here denied his speech of retrospective self-justification, 'I know thee well', 4.5.250–3) and in part dismayed to have to kill Edmond in the last scene. The other great supporting role in this play, the Fool, was in equally capable hands: John Ramm, who raced Lear to his throne in their first scene together, 1.4, but was increasingly prone to despair thereafter, was an accordion-playing clown who for once wasn't a music hall veteran. Instead his songs (by Adam Cork) had a rhythmic, melancholy, Slavic edge to them, and the accordion had other uses too: hauntingly, we last saw this Fool at the end of the joint-stool scene, watching heartbroken as the mad king had Kent draw an imaginary curtain around him as he lay down to sleep, and then playing his accordion and weeping, finally ceasing to play notes on the instrument but only making it wheeze in an imitation of the dying man we took the Fool by now to be.

In the end, though, any *King Lear* depends on its Lear, and Warner's was a wonder, full of intricate and witty touches which never distracted from a convincing trajectory from bafflement to rage to a sudden awareness of the physical sufferings of others (the turn to the Fool in a storm which, thanks to the size of the venue, never had to strain for effect, was immensely moving), and beyond that to the contemplation of Poor Tom and the rejection of all authority as illegitimate that overflows through the dialogue with Gloucester in 4.5. A very few examples will have to suffice: a metal bowl, called for to wash Lear's face in after the hunt in 1.4 and peremptorily banged with a riding-crop to become an impromptu gong at 'Let me not stay a jot for DINNER' (1.4.8); an eye-bath administered with the contents of a hip-flask after his arrival in 2.2, emblematic and helpfully explaining his initial failure to notice Kent in the stocks; a little extra softening of the voice on the word 'Sweetheart' in 'Tray, Blanch, and Sweetheart' (13.57), irresistibly reminiscent of the tone in which he had remembered his preference for Cordelia in the first scene; the subtle gradual deepening of the stoop and weakening of the face, so that the retirement-age king of the first scene really did seem to age to fourscore years and upwards before our eyes; the picking of one of the single clump of poppies by which Chitty suggested the South Downs and holding it up to his temples at 'I am cut to th'brains' (4.5.189); above all the brilliance by which the recognition scene with Cordelia, 4.6, had the courage to avoid generalized sentiment by putting one simple prop to exquisitely prosaic and witty use, importing in the most Shakespearian manner a humanizing, familiarizing touch of humour at one of the most moving moments in all the canon. Wheeled on in a metal hospital bed, Lear woke to find the Doctor soon offering him, at Cordelia's behest, some wine as a tonic, initially misrecognized:

LEAR Do not laugh at me,
    For as I am a man, I think this lady
    To be my child, Cordelia.
CORDELIA And so I am, I am [*trying to conceal her tears, gesturing to the doctor to pass a metal cup to Lear for him to drink*]
LEAR Be your tears wet? [*touches her cheek*] Yes, faith. I pray, weep not.
[*notices doctor offering cup*] If you have poison for me, I will drink it.
    I know you do not love me; for your sisters
    Have, as I do remember, done me wrong.
    You have some cause; they have not. [*Rapidly gulps from the cup, as though he does think it is poison; then his face changes, puzzled and then pleased*]
CORDELIA No cause, no cause.
LEAR [*looking upward out front into middle distance, concentrating, moving his mouth slightly; begins almost to smile; suddenly sounding revived and almost ready to reassume command*] Am I in France?

As for the end of the play, Lear had by now regained sufficient strength to carry Cordelia on in the classic manner, clad in a nightshirt-like white robe, and lay her in the centre of the middle square of the stage, all but oblivious to his interlocutors. Shown the dead bodies of Gonerill and Regan, he merely walked absently around the stage, picking small tokens of jewellery from their clothes as if looting just two more corpses on another battlefield – did he half-recognize these objects as his own former gifts too? – but always restlessly focused with part of his mind on Cordelia's body. Albany cried out 'O see, see!' (5.3.280) because Lear had returned to the centre of the stage to kneel over Cordelia, looking like some shockingly revised Pietà in which a dying God cradled a dead Virgin Mary. More movingly still, he asked Kent to undo his button at 5.3.285 so that he could take off his robe and lay it on her body like a coverlet on a sleeping child, as if appalled to find Cordelia's hand so cold: it was a heartbreaking recapitulation of his simple physical compassion for the Fool in the storm and his subsequent self-stripping when confronted by Poor Tom. The old body, exposed, looked genuinely feeble now, for the first time. Warner now broke up 'Look, her lips' (5.3.286) into 'Look' (looking forwards, out front) and 'her lips' (looking down at Cordelia, convinced she was speaking, bending down to listen, his ear to her mouth, as if she were asking him to pick her up, to carry her somewhere), and then at the end of Lear's last speech 'Look there, look there' (5.3.287) was directed not at her but out forwards. To the last, Warner's Lear couldn't believe that this world was as universally comfortless as he had found it, convinced that there was still somewhere just off stage where everything might yet be put to rights, where Cordelia might still live. So he tried to carry her there. Still kneeling, he forced his arms under her body; he strained every sinew to lift her; he failed; he gathered breath, slowly, painfully, and tried again; but the only slight movement he achieved was a fleeting semblance of the crawl towards death he had envisaged in the first scene, as this second attempt brought on a heart attack.

Slowly the lanky pale body collapsed, stiffening, on top of hers, and there was nothing adequate left for any of the survivors to say. Before giving this performance, Warner had not acted on stage, save in one New York production of Shaw's *Major Barbara* four years ago, for thirty-four years: to have left live Shakespeare soon after a brilliant Hamlet and then to return, at the very top of his game, with an equally brilliant Lear must be an achievement with few parallels in the annals of stage history. However many run-of-the-mill or half-cooked or wilfully odd productions of Shakespeare continue to be mounted, it is always worth coming back for more, because out of every twenty-five or so shows there is the chance that one of them will be an absolute miracle. This was one of those miracles, and it would alone have marked out 2005 as a remarkable year in the English Shakespearian theatre.

PROFESSIONAL SHAKESPEARE PRODUCTIONS IN THE BRITISH ISLES, JANUARY–DECEMBER 2004

JAMES SHAW

Most of the productions listed are by professional companies, but some amateur productions are included. The information is taken from *Touchstone* (www.touchstone.bham.ac.uk), a Shakespeare website maintained by the Shakespeare Institute Library. *Touchstone* includes a monthly list of current and forthcoming UK Shakespeare productions from listings information. *The Traffic of the Stage* database, also available on *Touchstone*, archives UK Shakespeare production information since January 1993, correlating information from listings and reviews held in the Shakespeare Institute Library. The websites provided for theatre companies were accurate at the time of going to press.

AS YOU LIKE IT

Forkbeard Fantasy, Theatre Royal Bath Young People's Theatre, Ustinov Studio, Bath, 12–13 March.
www.forkbeardfantasy.co.uk
Director: Katherine Lazare
Rosalind: Sophie Andrews
Part of the Bath Shakespeare Festival

Mad Dogs and Englishmen, Tour 17 June – 1 August.
www.mad-dogs.org.uk

Groundlings Theatre Company, Tour 2 July – 29 August.
www.groundlings.co.uk

Centurion Theatre Company, Courtyard Theatre, London, 28 October – 21 November.

Director: Michael Sargent
Rosalind: Charlotte Endacott

Peter Hall Company, Rose of Kingston Theatre, 3–18 December.
members.aol.com/dramaddict/petrhall.htm
Director: Peter Hall
Rosalind: Rebecca Hall

THE COMEDY OF ERRORS

Oxford Stage Company, Lincoln's Inn, London, 3 August–3 September.
www.oxfordstage.co.uk
Director: Chris Pickles
Antipholus: Henry Everett
Dromio: Cory English

Heartbreak Productions, Tour 9 June – 15 July.
www.heartbreakproductions.co.uk
Director: Maddy Kerr

CYMBELINE

Ludlow Shakespeare Festival, Ludlow Castle, Ludlow, 26 June – 9 July.
www.ludlowfestival.co.uk
Director: Michael Bogdanov
Cymbeline: John Labanowski
Imogen: Nia Roberts

HAMLET

Old Vic Productions, Old Vic, London, 27 April – 31 July.
www.oldvictheatre.com
Director: Trevor Nunn

Hamlet: Ben Whishaw
Ophelia: Samantha Whittaker
Gertrude: Imogen Stubbs
Claudius: Tom Mannion

Miracle Theatre Company, Outdoor tour, 1 July
– 15 September.
www.miracletheatre.co.uk

Royal Shakespeare Company, Royal Shake-
speare Theatre, Stratford-upon-Avon, 21 July
– 16 October, Albery Theatre, 23 November
– 11 December.
www.rsc.org.uk
Director: Michael Boyd
Hamlet: Toby Stephens
Ophelia: Meg Fraser
Gertrude: Sian Thomas
Claudius: Clive Wood

Spilt Milk Theatre Company, Rosemary Branch
Theatre, London, 27 October – 14 Novem-
ber.
Director and Adaptor: Helen Tennison

Thelma Holt Productions and Theatre Royal
Plymouth, Barbican Theatre, London, 10–27
November.
www.theatreroyal.com
Director: Yukio Ninagawa
Hamlet: Michael Maloney

ADAPTATION

The Al-Hamlet Summit
Sulayman Al-Bassam Theatre Company, River-
side Studios, London, 8–14 March.
Director and Adaptor: Sulayman Al-Bassam
Set in Middle East. In Arabic with simultaneous
English translation.

Hamlet in Mind
Poetic Justice Productions Ltd, New Wimble-
don Theatre, London, 17 February – 7 March.

Humble Boy
Library Theatre, Manchester, 2 April – 2 May.
www.librarytheatre.com
Playwright: Charlotte Jones

Marowitz Hamlet
British Touring Shakespeare Company with
Strange Bedfellows, Wickham Theatre,
Bristol, 12–13 March.
www.britishtouringshakespeare.co.uk
Adaptor: Charles Marowitz.

HENRY IV PART 1

New Shakespeare Company, Open Air Theatre,
Regent's Park, London, 7 June – 11 Septem-
ber.
http://openairtheatre.org
Director: Alan Strachan
Henry IV: Christopher Godwin
Prince Henry: Jordan Frieda
Falstaff: Christopher Benjamin

JULIUS CAESAR

Cannon's Mouth Theatre Company, Menier
Chocolate Factory, Southwark, 1–27 March.
Director: Ben Naylor
Brutus: James Tovell
Mark Antony: Richard Simons
Caesar: Edmund Kingsley

Royal Shakespeare Company, UK and interna-
tional tours and Stratford residency.
www.rsc.org.uk
Director: David Farr
Mark Antony: Gary Oliver
Caesar: Christopher Saul

Hull Truck Theatre Company, 22 October – 12
November.
www.hulltruck.co.uk
Director: John Godber
Ninety-minute version with a cast of six.

KING LEAR

Galleon Theatre Company, Greenwich Playhouse, 22 January – 15 February.
www.galleontheatre.co.uk
Director: Bruce Jamieson

Lear: Oliver Bradshaw
Modern dress production.

Royal Shakespeare Company, Royal Shake-
speare Theatre, Stratford-upon-Avon, 30 June
– 29 September.
www.rsc.org.uk
Director: Bill Alexander
King Lear: Corin Redgrave
Cordelia: Sian Brooke
Lear's Fool: John Normington

LOVE'S LABOUR'S LOST

Rain or Shine Theatre Company, Outdoor tour,
June–August.

ADAPTATION

The Big Life
Theatre Royal, Stratford East, London, Feb–12
March and Apollo Theatre, London, 11 May –
1 October.
www.stratfordeast.com
Composer: Paul Joseph
Lyrics: Paul Sirett
Ska version.

MACBETH

En Masse Theatre, Union Theatre, London, 19
February – 6 March.
www.enmassetheatre.co.uk
Director: William Oldroyd
Macbeth: Bertie Carvel
Lady Macbeth: Kate Miles

Kitchen Sink Theatre Company, Oxford House,
London, 26 February – 14 March.
Director: Laura Dunton Clarke
Macbeth: David Vaughan Knight
Lady Macbeth: Naomi Robinson

Royal Shakespeare Company, Royal Shakespeare Theatre, Stratford-upon-Avon, 18
March – 9 October.
www.rsc.org.uk
Director: Dominic Cooke

Macbeth: Greg Hicks
Lady Macbeth: Sian Thomas

Mercury Theatre Company, Mercury Theatre,
Colchester, 18 March – 3 April.
www.mercurytheatre.co.uk
Director: Craig Bacon
Macbeth: Victor Gardener
Lady Macbeth: Katy Stephens

Shakespeare at the Tobacco Factory, Tobacco
Factory, Bristol, 13–22 April, revived at The
Pit, Barbican, 23 September – 23 October.
www.shakespeareatthetobaccofactory.co.uk
Director: Andrew Hilton
Macbeth: Gyuri Sarossy
Lady Macbeth: Zoe Aldrich
Lady Macbeth and Lady Macduff doubled as
witches.

Heartbreak Productions, Tour June – August.
www.heartbreakproductions.co.uk
Director: Peter Mimmack

Glasgow Repertory Company, Glasgow Botanic
Gardens, Glasgow, 15–24 July.
www.glasgowrep.org
Director: Andrew McKinnon
Macbeth: David Ireland
Lady Macbeth: Jennifer Dick
Bard In The Botanics Season.

Theatre Babel, Gateway Theatre, Edinburgh
Fringe Festival, August.
Director: Graham McLaren

Dundee Repertory Theatre, 8–25 September.
www.dundeereptheatre.co.uk
Director: Dominic Hill
Macbeth: Paul Blair
Lady Macbeth: Irene MacDougall

Out of Joint, touring production.
www.outofjoint.co.uk
Director: Max Stafford-Clark
Macbeth: Danny Sapani
Lady Macbeth: Monica Dolan
The Macduffs doubled as witches. Set in con-
temporary, lawless Africa.

ADAPTATION

Macbeth
Shakespeare4Kidz, Schools tour, 19 January – 2
April.
www.shakespeare4kidz.com
Adaptor and Director: Julian Cheney and Matt
Gimblett

Macbeth
3hird Wheel, Tour.
www.3hirdwheel.co.uk
75-minute, 3-man show

OPERA

Lady Macbeth of Mtsensk
English National Opera, Tour.
www.eno.org
Composer: Shostakovich

MEASURE FOR MEASURE

National Theatre Company and Theatre de
Complicite, Olivier Theatre, London, 27
May – 31 July.
www.nt-online.org
Director: Simon McBurney
Angelo: Paul Rhys
Isabella: Naomi Frederick
Duke: David Troughton

Shakespeare's Globe Company, London, 30
June – 24 September, Hampton Court 6–11
July.
www.shakespeares-globe.org
Director: Jonathan Dove
Angelo: Liam Brennan
Isabella: Sophie Thompson
Duke: Mark Rylance

THE MERCHANT OF VENICE

Northern Broadsides, Viaduct, Halifax, 18–21
February and on tour.
www.northern-broadsides.co.uk
Director: Barrie Rutter

Shylock: Barrie Rutter
Portia: Clare Calbraith

ADAPTATION

Shylock
UK Tour.
Performer and Adaptor: Gareth Armstrong
One-man show.

THE MERRY WIVES OF WINDSOR

Theatre Set-up, Tour 4 July – 22 August.
www.ts-u.co.uk

OPERA

Falstaff
English National Opera, Coliseum Theatre,
London, 15 October – 19 November.
www.eno.org
Composer: Verdi

A MIDSUMMER NIGHT'S DREAM

Chichester Festival Theatre, Chichester, 20
May – 23 September.
www.cft.org.uk
Director: Gale Edwards
Theseus/Oberon: Jeffery Kissoon
Hippolyta/Titania: Noma Dumezweni
Bottom: Graham Turner

The New Shakespeare Company, Open Air
Theatre, Regent's Park, London. 11 June –
8 September.
http://openairtheatre.org
Director: Ian Talbot
Bottom: Russ Abbott

Derby Playhouse, Derby, 3 June – 3 July.
www.derbyplayhouse.co.uk
Director: Karen Louise Hebden
Theseus/Oberon: Alexi Kay Campbell
Hippolyta/Titania: Juliette Caton
Bottom: Conor Moloney

Heartbreak Productions, Tour July–September.
www.heartbreakproductions.co.uk
Director: Peter Mimmack

Glasgow Repertory Company, Botanic Gardens,
   Glasgow, 23–6 June, 29 June–3 July.
www.glasgowrep.org
Director: Gordon Barr
Theseus/Oberon: Stephen Docherty
Hippolyta/Titania: Lois Creasy
Bottom: Michelle Wiggins
Revival of 2003 production set in 1920s. Bard In
   The Botanics Season.

Melmoth Productions, Greenwich Playhouse,
   London, 26 October – 21 November.
Director: Stuart Draper

ADAPTATION

Release The Beat
Arcola Theatre, London, August.
www.arcolatheatre.com
Director: Mehmet Ergen
Book: Judith Johnson
Music and Lyrics: Karl Lewkowicz
Simone: Rosalind James
Book/musical loosely based on MND using
   show tunes, hip-hop and house.

A Midsummer Night's Dream
Shakespeare4Kidz, Schools tour, 19 January – 2
   April.
www.shakespeare4kidz.com
Adaptor and Director: Julian Cheney and Matt
   Gimblett

BALLET

A Midsummer Night's Dream
Northern Ballet Theatre, Tour, March – May.
www.northernballettheatre.co.uk
Choreographer: David Nixon

OPERA

Pyramus and Thisbe
Helikon Opera, Peacock Theatre, London, May.

www.helikon.ru
Composer: John Frederick Lampe

A Midsummer Night's Dream
English Touring Opera, Tour, March – June.
www.englishtouringopera.org.uk
Composer: Benjamin Britten

A Midsummer Night's Dream
English National Opera, Coliseum, London, 25
   June – 8 July.
www.eno.org
Composer: Benjamin Britten

MUCH ADO ABOUT NOTHING

Byre Theatre, St Andrews, 27 February – 13
   March.
www.byretheatre.com
Director: Steve Little
Beatrice: Amanda Beveridge
Benedick: Jimmy Chisholm

Bremer Shakespeare Company, Theatre Royal,
   Bath, 3–6 March.
www.shakespeare-company.com
Director: Peter Luchinger
Benedick: Ian Shaw
Beatrice/Claudio: Annette Ziellenbach
Beatrice and Claudio doubled.

Shakespeare's Globe Theatre, London, 2 June –
   25 September.
www.shakespeares-globe.org
Director: Tamara Harvey
Beatrice: Yolanda Vazquez
Benedick: Josie Lawrence
All-female cast.

West Country Theatre Company, Tour, June –
   July.
www.westcountry-theatre-company.co.uk

Creation Theatre Company, Headington Hill
   Park, Oxford, 4 June – 24 July.
www.creationtheatre.co.uk
Director: Charlotte Conquest

British Touring Shakespeare Company, Tour, June.
www.britishtouringshakespeare.co.uk
Director: Miles Gregory

R. J. Williamson Company, Cannizaro Park, London, 6–8 August, Holland Park, London, 12–14 August.
http://britishshakespearecompany.co.uk
Directors: Robert J. Williamson and Frank Jarvis
Beatrice: Penelope Woodman
Benedick: Robert J. Williamson

Salisbury Playhouse, 3–25 September.
www.salisburyplayhouse.com
Director: David Rintoul
Beatrice: Tanya Moodie
Benedick: Mark Bonnar

OTHELLO

Royal Shakespeare Company, Swan Theatre, Stratford-upon-Avon, 18 February – 3 April and Trafalgar Studios, London 3 June – 3 July.
www.rsc.org.uk
Director: Gregory Doran
Othello: Sello Maake ka Ncube
Iago: Antony Sher

Good Company Shakespeare Productions Ltd, Tour, February – March.
Director: Sue Pomeroy

Royal Lyceum Theatre, Edinburgh, 23 October – 20 November.
www.lyceum.org.uk
Director: Mark Thomson
Othello: Wil Johnson
Iago: Liam Brennan

Cheek by Jowl, Tour, including Riverside Studios, London, 15 November 2004 – 4 January 2005.
www.cheekbyjowl.com
Director: Declan Donnellan
Othello: Nonso Anozie
Iago: Jonny Phillips

ADAPTATION

Othellophobia
Explosive Acts Company, Blue Elephant Theatre, London, 24 March – 10 April, plus tour.
Director: Rob Conkie
Othello: Olu Taiwo
Desdemona: Jo Blake
Incorporating martial arts and billed as Shakespeare meets *The Matrix*.

Perfect Blackman – Othello
Blue Mountain Theatre Company, Tour, April – May.

RICHARD II

Playbox Theatre Company, Generator Ensemble, Tour April–May.
www.playboxtheatre.com
Director: Stewart McGill

RICHARD III

Glasgow Repertory Company. Glasgow Botanic Gardens, Glasgow, 30 June – 3 July, 6–10 July.
www.glasgowrep.org
Director: Scott Palmer
Richard III: Kirk Bage
Bard In The Botanics Season

La Panta Theatre, Haymarket Theatre, Basingstoke, 6–8 November.
Director: Guy Delamotte
Richard III: Jerome Bidaux
Performed in French.

ADAPTATION

Bloomsbury Theatre, London, 12–14 February.
www.thebloomsbury.com
Playwright: Bobby Fishkin
Director: Harry Brunges, Bobby Fishkin
A historical play, not based directly on Shakespeare's text, offering a revisionist portrayal of Richard.

ROMEO AND JULIET

Prime Productions, Tour 30 January – 13 March.
Director: Benjamin Twist

Southwark Playhouse, 15–31 January.
www.southwark-playhouse.co.uk
Director: Thomas Hescott

Royal Shakespeare Company, Royal Shakespeare Theatre, Stratford-upon-Avon, 7 April – September, Albery Theatre, London 21 December.
www.rsc.org.uk
Director: Peter Gill
Romeo: Matthew Rhys
Juliet: Sian Brooke

Shakespeare's Globe, London, 19 May – 26 September.
www.shakespeares-globe.org
Director: Tim Carroll
Romeo: Tom Burke
Juliet: Kananu Kirimi

Creation Theatre Company, Headington Hill Park, Oxford, 3 August – 11 September.
www.creationtheatre.co.uk
Director: Abigail Anderson

Vesturport Theatre Company, Playhouse Theatre, London, November.
www.borgarleikhus.is
Director: Gisli Orn Gardarsson
Circus-based production from Icelandic theatre company.

ADAPTATIONS

Cut to the Chase, Queen's Theatre, Hornchurch. 15 March – 3 April.
www.queens-theatre.co.uk
Director: Bob Carlton
Romeo: Ifan Meredith
Juliet: Maria Lawson

Juliet and Romeo
Monkey Productions, Etcetera Theatre, London, 8–27 June.
Directors: Justine De Mere, Andrew St John

Shakespeare's R & J
Splinter Group Company, Tour March – May.
Adaptor and Director: Joe Calarco
Four schoolboys discover and perform *Romeo and Juliet*.

BALLET

Romeo and Juliet
Royal Ballet, Royal Opera House, London, April.
www.royalopera.org
Choreographer: Kenneth MacMillan
Composer: Prokofiev

New Zealand Ballet Company, Tour 21 April – 29 May.
www.nzballet.org.nz
Choreographer: Christopher Hampson

Bolshoi Ballet, Royal Opera House, London, July.
www.bolshoi.ru
Director: Declan Donnellan
Choreographer: Radu Poklitaru

Independent Ballet of Wales, Tour June–July.
Choreographer: Darius James

TAMING OF THE SHREW

Royal Shakespeare Company, Queen's Theatre, London, 15 January – 6 March.
www.rsc.org.uk
Director: Gregory Doran
Katharine: Alexandra Gilbreath
Petruchio: Jasper Britton
Revival of 1993 Royal Shakespeare Theatre production.

Glasgow Repertory Company, Glasgow Botanic Gardens, Glasgow, 14–18 July, 20–24 July.
www.glasgowrep.org
Director: Gordon Barr
Katharine: Candice Edmunds
Petruchio: Kirk Bage
Bard In The Botanics Season.

ADAPTATION

The Tamer Tamed
Royal Shakespeare Company, Queen's Theatre,
  London, 21 January – 6 March.
www.rsc.org.uk
Director: Gregory Doran
Maria: Alexandra Gilbreath
Petruchio: Jasper Britton
Revival of 1993 Swan Theatre production.

TEMPEST

Nottingham Playhouse, 2–20 November.
Director: Richard Baron
Prospero: Clive Francis
www.nottinghamplayhouse.co.uk

ADAPTATION

Prospero's Island
Midland Actors Theatre Company, Tour February – March.
www.midlandactorstheatre.co.uk
Playwright: David Calcutt

OPERA

The Tempest
Covent Garden, February.
Composer: Thomas Adès
Prospero: Simon Keenlyside

DANCE

Before the Tempest, After the Storm
Linbury Studio Theatre, Royal Opera House,
  London, February.
www.royalopera.org
Choreography: Cathy Marston

TWELFTH NIGHT

Ludlow Shakespeare Festival, Ludlow Castle,
  Ludlow, 26 June – 10 July.
www.ludlowfestival.co.uk
Director: Michael Bogdanov

Malvolio: Paul Greenwood
Viola: Heledd Baskerville
Olivia: Eleanor Howell

R. J. Williamson Company, Cannizaro Park,
  London, 3–5 August 2004 and Holland Park,
  London, 10–15 August 2004.
http://britishshakespearecompany.co.uk
Director: Robert J. Williamson and Joyce
  Branagh
Malvolio: Wayne Cater
Viola: Siwan Morris
Olivia: Penelope Woodman
Feste: Wayne Sleep

Albery Theatre, London, August.
Director: Stephen Beresford
Malvolio: Paul Bhattacharjee
Viola: Shereen Martineau
Indian-based modern dress production.

English Touring Theatre, Touring production.
www.englishtouringtheatre.co.uk
Director: Stephen Unwin
Malvolio: Des McAleer
Viola: Georgina Rich

Octagon Theatre, Bolton, 24 September – 16
  October.
www.octagonbolton.co.uk
Director: Mark Babych
Malvolio: Michael Mears
Viola: Kelly Williams

Bristol Old Vic, 26 October – 20 November.
www.bristol-old-vic.co.uk
Director: David Farr
Malvolio: Mark Lockyer
Viola: Nikki Amuka Bird

THE TWO GENTLEMEN OF VERONA

Melmoth Productions, Greenwich Playhouse,
  20 April–16 May.
www.melmothproductions.co.uk
Director: Stuart Draper
Valentine: Azeem Nathoo
Proteus: Luke Leeves

Royal Shakespeare Company, UK. International tour and Stratford residency 20 October 2004 – 7 May 2005.
www.rsc.org.uk
Director: Fiona Buffini
Valentine: Alex Avery
Proteus: Laurence Mitchell

THE WINTER'S TALE

Creation Theatre Company, Spiegeltent, BMW Group Plant, Oxford. 11 February – 3 April.
www.creationtheatre.co.uk
Director: Justin Butcher

POEMS

Venus and Adonis
Royal Shakespeare Company, Little Angel Theatre, 18 October – 15 November; The Other Place, Stratford-upon-Avon, 16 November – 18 December.

www.rsc.org.uk
Director: Gregory Doran
Adaptation incorporating Bunraku puppet techniques.

Venus and Adonis
BBC Radio 3, May.
www.bbc.co.uk/radio3
Adonis: Chris Moran
Venus: Clare Skinner

GENERAL ADAPTATIONS

Shooting Shakespeare
Forkbeard Fantasy, Touring production, including Hackney Empire, 19–23 October.
www.forkbeardfantasy.co.uk
Director: Andy Hay
Playwrights: Chris Britton, Tim Britton, Penny Saunders Set in the early days of cinema and the recording of silent Shakespeare.

THE YEAR'S CONTRIBUTIONS TO SHAKESPEARE STUDIES

1. CRITICAL STUDIES
reviewed by MICHAEL TAYLOR

SHAKESPEARE AND THE NEW

I thought of calling this section something like 'Extravagant Imaginative Dimensions' in order to convey my sense of Shakespeare criticism's often tortuous desire these days for originality. Shakespeare's critics, like his lunatics, lovers and poets, often seem to be of imagination all compact. To take Theseus's dim view of the workings of the imagination, however, hardly does justice to a deeply imaginative book that seems at first blush to set itself apart from any desire for originality. Yet it is, of course, completely original and I deal with it at the beginning of these reviews to remind us why we should bother to wrack our imaginations on Shakespeare in the first place. Alexander Leggatt's *Shakespeare's Tragedies: Violation and Identity* is a set of meditations on seven of Shakespeare's tragedies that has been a long time gestating, the interim end-product of an on-going conversation about them with friends and students. Leggatt prises the term 'thick readings' away from the company it usually keeps in anthropological and cultural circles in order to describe his 'close engagement with the plays themselves' in his attempt to 'keep them free to do their own thinking', although the thinking in question is in fact the creatively synthetic thinking of the critic himself.

Leggatt gives us seven bracing chapters on *Titus Andronicus, Romeo and Juliet, Hamlet, Troilus and Cressida, Othello, King Lear* and *Macbeth*. They are valuably interconnected. He opens the second chapter, for instance, the one on *Romeo and Juliet*, with the remark that 'Romeo's first meeting with Juliet seems designed not only to begin the love story of *Romeo and Juliet* but to heal the wounds of Lavinia in *Titus Andronicus.*' His concluding chapter begins: 'We began with Lavinia dehumanised by violence; we end with the death of Macbeth and Lady Macbeth, the perpetrators of violence, humanised.' As long as Shakespeare wrote tragedy, Leggatt claims, he 'could never get Lavinia out of his mind, could never heal those wounds or silence that silence'. Leggatt never allows Lavinia to get out of our minds either, nor, for that matter, most of the other major characters from the other plays he deals with. By the time we come to the end of the book we realize how inexhaustibly fruitful his cumulative method is. In between those insightful linked framing sentences Leggatt has written a book that seems designed to prove the wisdom of Eliot's dictum that we need to know all of Shakespeare to know any one part of him. Throughout the book 'one play ricochets against another'. And the conclusion of Leggatt's Conclusion is as open-ended as his own readings: 'It is characteristic that Shakespeare's last treatment of the intertwined themes of violation and identity [in *The Tempest*] provides not a final answer, a summing-up, but new and disturbing questions.'

Each chapter is divided into sections with headings such as 'Questioning Lavinia' or 'Unsettling

347

the Ending' or 'Reading the Women' or 'Unmaking Lear'; and, as if to emphasize the coherence of the work, the unsettled ending title and the unmaking title occur more than once. Leggatt shows us that Shakespeare's endings are indeed unsettled; *Troilus and Cressida*, for instance, 'seems to have as many endings as a Sibelius Symphony', and the ending of *King Lear* is Shakespeare's most troubled. The book is unabashedly psychological in approach. The characters' motives and feelings are scrutinized as though they really had them. And we are convinced that they do by the pertinacity of Leggatt's observations about them. At times the writer is aware that he is treading on dangerous ground; in his discussion, for instance, of that old Bradleyan conundrum about Lady Macbeth's fertility he writes: 'we may think that Shakespeare's art has trapped us once again into taking his characters as real and prying into their private lives'. But it is one thing to be trapped by Shakespeare, another to be trapped by A. C. Bradley, and Leggatt's book shows us how well he knows the difference.

Lisa Hopkins's *Beginning Shakespeare* has other fish to fry. She asks students to begin their reading of Shakespeare in as theoretically sophisticated and up-to-date manner as possible. After a short section sprinting over three hundred years of the earlier criticism, she spends the rest of the book on the stuff that really matters, a Shakespeare criticism heavily inflected by psychoanalysis, new historicism, cultural materialism, new factualisms (as she somewhat oddly calls them), gender studies and queer theory, postcolonial criticism and Shakespeare in performance. For her, Shakespeare criticism really got going in 1985 with the publication of *Political Shakespeare*, a collection of essays by Jonathan Dollimore and Alan Sinfield, that was 'a combination of historical context, theoretical method, political commitment and textual analysis'. Despite the short shrift she gives to liberal humanism as a way of thinking about Shakespeare, she very much wants students to think for themselves about him (as long as, presumably, they don't think about him in a liberal humanist way). To that end, she has a section called 'Stop and Think' that crops up every few pages in which she asks the reader to respond to questions that she sets on the previous text. Sportingly enough, she then gives her own responses to those questions, in which she often uses words like 'feelings' and 'personally', which helps to humanize what she has to say, though I suppose not necessarily in a liberal humanist way.

The book seems to me a very good introduction to recent critical trends on Shakespeare. Her chapter on New Historicism is particularly interesting; she reminds us of the extent to which Shakespeare is a product of his culture, one voice among many. In one of her Stop and Think passages here she pauses to criticize the work of Stephen Greenblatt, the architect of the New Historicism, who 'can often sound alarmingly old-fashioned' not to say like a liberal humanist at times. He is 'interesting, elegant, but not convincing'. His notion that power is only ever partially and temporarily evaded by the human subject fails to take into account, among other things, the way in which the repeated performances of the plays constantly reminds its audiences of human possibility. Hence, for example, although nearly everybody from the working class dies in *Henry V* they come alive again with every performance. She also reminds us usefully that genre matters in any critical performance. It is therefore a simple factualism that the romances are more responsive to psychoanalytic criticism than to a criticism with its roots in cultural materialism.

The New Factualism that most interests her is the biographical one, especially the recently renewed interest in the possibility of Shakespeare's Catholicism. Although she herself seems to be agnostic on the subject she makes the important observation that '[o]ne may well feel . . . that it smacks of special pleading to suggest the more anti-Catholic something appears to be, the closer to Catholicism it must therefore really be'. It's a remark that we should bear in mind when reading elsewhere in this year's crop of books on Shakespeare.

Judith Weil's *Service and Dependency in Shakespeare's Plays* is an original, imaginative, and unusual book, unusually well written. She looks at Shakespeare's characters as 'potencies' rather than 'identities', as 'moving intersections of relationships'. She

treats Shakespeare's plays 'as if they were entertaining, provocative hypotheses, ways of thinking
about relationships through actions'. She thinks
that a good title for her study would have
been 'slippery people' – a good title perhaps for
any work on Shakespeare's characters, including
Leggatt's.

The slippery people in the relationship most rigorously examined in this book are to be found in
the networks of service and dependency so important in the society of the sixteenth and seventeenth centuries, in a relationship 'not necessarily
archaic and oppressive'. The book entertainingly
and impressively negotiates the terrain between the
plays and their circumambient culture on the unar-
guable principle that '[s]ocial practice and dramatic
form are mutually illuminating'. Hence the importance for this book of social historians and of other
works from Shakespeare's time, so that Cordelia,
for example, 'becomes even more probable if we
take into consideration social histories, sources and
analogues, parallels with other plays and revisions
of *King Lear* by feminist writers'.

What makes Weil's chosen relationship so
rewarding for investigation is its lively instability
during this period. The boundaries between servant, friend, family, were porous in the extreme:
servants could be friends (with a 'dynamic influence'), members of the family could be servants,
especially wives. Weil argues that it is therefore
unnecessarily restrictive to see the relationship only
in terms of exploitation. In fact, as she provocatively states, 'I'm going to proceed by questioning a cherished belief among many modern lib-
ertarians and democrats: that being in or under
the will of another person, a condition often used
to define servants, is incompatible with freedom.'
Although this remark – one that Lisa Hopkins
might well find interesting – appears in her full-
length chapter on *Macbeth* it should be borne in
mind when reading the rest of her book. She
is, however, well aware of darker social realities:
when servants are mediators, for example, they are
'acutely vulnerable to dismemberment'; the fusions
of service with friendship can have 'deadly consequences'.

Doing Shakespeare, to employ Simon Palfrey's
title about his own book, means, simply, reading
him (as Leggatt so persuasively does) without the
interference of other intermediaries. It's an aggressive locution, obviously, and intended to be so, as
Palfrey, like a good protestant critic, scorns the critical priesthood. He doesn't want anything coming
between him and his imagination and the Good
Book (Shakespeare's Works); let's do Shakespeare,
not let him do us or others do him for us. So his is
a back-to-brass-tacks book in which we (meaning
he) must let 'language mean what it says . . . take
his [Shakespeare's] metaphors literally' – hence, no
footnotes and no references to speak of to other
critics except in a List of Further Reading. All
you need really is a 'curious mind and a playtext'.
Dr Johnson would no doubt approve.

Palfrey's book is divided into two main sections, Words and Characters, and each has chapters with questions as their titles, and they often
sound exasperated: 'Why all of these metaphors?',
'What are these speaking things?' Each of the chapters begins with a précis in italics of what is to
follow even though the chapters are short and
not particularly convoluted. If we take his first
question – why all of these metaphors? – as a
representative one, the answer seems to be that
Shakespeare's 'simple surplus of meaning' is created simply to give the reader's imagination a field
day, making Palfrey's paradoxical claim that 'there
is not a word in Shakespeare that is not doing just
what he wanted' seem comically self-serving. In
Palfrey's case the language means what Palfrey says
it does, the brass tacks are phantasmagorical, taking Shakespeare's metaphors literally means taking
them phantasmagorically. Most of the time, it seems
to me, the spectacle of Palfrey chasing down 'the
most awesomely shadowing implication' of Shakespeare's language is not an edifying one. He's particularly wayward on 'bolster' and 'bear' in *Macbeth*,
'a dew' and 'waves' in *Hamlet*, the 'snorting citizens' in *Othello*, 'pelting' in *King Lear*. At moments
like these Palfrey seems to be doing Shakespeare in
rather than doing him.

He has some good things to say, however, on
Shakespeare's use of the high style when he says,

for example, how easy it is 'to miss how layered and indeed witty Shakespeare's long-winded
public rhetoric can be', on Shakespeare's use of
rhyme, on the soliloquy, on figures of speech like
hendiadys through which 'we get access to motives
or compulsions that the character would wish to
keep a lid upon'. But much of what he says about
Shakespeare's words and characters seems to me
manically far-fetched. He might well be talking
about his own style when he says that the language
of Shakespeare's characters 'has a quality almost of
metastasis', or when he asks us to see Mercutio's
part as 'an experiment in pushing puns beyond their
normal possibilities'.

With Gail Kern Paster's *Humoring the Body: Emotions and the Shakespearian Stage*, an exhilarating
exercise in 'historical phenomenology', we move
from the passions of the contemporary critic to
those of our seventeenth-century forebears, though
Paster's own passion for her subject is plainly evident throughout the book in the changes she rings
on her 'I want to insist' phrasing that opens many
of her sentences. She is interested in exploring
'the possibility of historical differences in modes
of emotional self-experience', and she focuses her
attention on the language of the emotions in Shakespeare's plays. It is difficult in a short review to do
justice to the richness and complexity of her argument, but its essence is that the emotions in Shakespeare's time need to be seen in ecological terms,
in a 'psychophysiological reciprocity between the
experiencing subject and his or her relation to
the world'. In this reciprocity the theory of the
humours looms large. Thinking ecologically about
the passions is something that should not be too
difficult for the modern reader, and at times her
discussion of early modern thinking about them
sounds remarkably familiar, as her footnote on
modern research into the emotions as neurochem-
ical events acknowledges.

Her method is to investigate 'discrete moments
and locutions in the play texts' where the language
Shakespeare uses about the emotions stresses the
permeation of self and world; and so, to take *Hamlet* as an example, we get fascinating discussions of
the 'ecological' ontology of 'roasted in wrath and

fire', 'I'm pregnant of my cause', 'I'll tent him to the
quick', drinking hot blood. Of particular interest,
in the light of Judith Weil's book, is Paster's discussion of the early modern assessment of women on
the ecological chain of being, particularly the disastrous consequences for them of Galen's belief that
the 'Minds inclination follows the Bodies Temperature'. Women may at times demonstrate hot passions, according to this sexist theory, but not with
'the laudable, steady heat' that men have. In the
course of her discussion of women, both in society and in Shakespeare's plays, Paster takes issue, as
Judith Weil does, with the argument that women
invariably lose freedom in marriage. She instances
Desdemona's growing warmth in becoming 'a bold
and confident wife' until 'traduced by Iago' and
finds similar examples elsewhere in Shakespeare,
though her assessment of *The Taming of the Shrew*
as a 'humoral comedy' involving 'lessons of emotional subordination' doesn't allow for the play of
its well-known ambiguities especially the one conveyed in its last line where a sceptical Lucentio is
surely anticipating a rise in Katherine's emotional
temperature: ''Tis a wonder, by your leave, she will
be tamed so.'

Galen looms large in Douglas Trevor's *The Poetics of Melancholy in Early Modern England*, a study,
in this case, that focuses on one early modern
human emotion – if it may so be called – that of
melancholy. Ecumenical in temper, Trevor's book,
with help from Lacan and early modern theories
of the passions, ranges over heterogeneous works
and writers in the belief that 'scholarly and literary methods of analysis and argumentation nurture
rather than oppose one another' (a belief that is very
much part of the mandate of the series in which this
book appears, Cambridge Studies in Renaissance
Literature and Culture). Embedded in illuminating discussions of the inspirational function of the
melancholic mood in the work of Spenser, Donne,
Burton and Milton is a chapter on *Hamlet*, Shakespeare's notorious contribution to the literature of
melancholy.

Trevor's thesis is that melancholy changes in
character over the course of the early seventeenth century. For the Elizabethan, Spenser

representatively, melancholy was a 'holy kind of sadness', neoplatonic, Ficinian, possibly curable (by love for instance), often caused by 'object-loss'. By the time of Donne and Burton, melancholy is no longer a genial influence, but Galenic, dispositionally rooted, a 'self-fuelling depression', linked with a permanent tendency to a destructive scepticism. (For Donne, to live is to study and write and suffer.) The wind shifts a little with Burton and more so with Milton. Melancholy is still basically humoral, but now there is talk of social ills as its contributing causes: the unfair English patronage system, for instance, and too many students looking for too few places. (In this respect we should compare *The Anatomy of Melancholy* with Hobbes's *Leviathan*.) For the solitary Milton, sturdily independent, melancholy stretches beyond the humoral; it's a scholarly melancholy, 'liberating and enriching', Spenserian then as much as Galenic.

And *Hamlet*? Turn-of-the-century Shakespeare is more in Galen's camp, so Trevor believes, than in Spenser's. In the plays after *Romeo and Juliet* and *Love's Labour's Lost* there is an evasion of 'clear objectal explanation': hence Antonio in *The Merchant of Venice* and Jacques in *As You Like It*, in both of whom melancholy can only be explained by a preponderance of Galenic black bile. Likewise with Hamlet himself and the so-called 'nonreferentiality of the Prince's sadness and grief'. Here, I would suggest that *Hamlet* lives up to its reputation as a complicator of tidy critical theses. Gertrude's o'er hasty marriage to Hamlet's uncle, Hamlet's prophetic soul, the stir and bustle in Denmark, Claudius's carousals, are all surely, however mysteriously, part of an 'objectal' explanation for Hamlet's melancholy. And why, for that matter, and along the same lines, shouldn't Hamlet come to question the reliability of the Ghost? The play itself forces us to qualify Trevor's proposition that Hamlet's 'scepticism is grounded . . . on the unqualified acceptance of a humorally based determinism'.

Rounding off this renewed interest in early modern emotion is a collection of essays edited by Gail Kern Paster, Katherine Rowe and Mary Floyd-Wilson, *Reading the Early Modern Passions: Essays in the Cultural History of Emotion*. The essays that deal with or touch on Shakespeare are particularly distinguished, beginning with Richard Strier's forceful affirmation of the underestimated strength of the belief in the primacy of passion in the early modern period, 'Against the Rule of Reason: Praise of Passion from Petrarch to Luther to Shakespeare to Herbert'. In Shakespeare's case, as we might imagine, *King Lear* offers the most devastating critique of a reliance on the workings of a dispassionate reason. In Part II, 'Historical Phenomenology', Mary Floyd-Wilson and Bruce Smith come at their subjects from odd and illuminating vantage points. In 'English Mettle' Floyd-Wilson rejects 'geohumoralism' as an adequate explanation for the mettle of Henry V's English soldiers (as opposed to his Scottish, Welsh or Irish soldiers and of course the 'hyper-civilized' French ones). What distinguishes English mettle is its slow arousal and subsequent staying power: 'England's valorous heat is a painstaking process'. It's an entertaining and insightful essay and so too is Bruce Smith's elegant and amusing exercise in applied synaesthesia, 'Hearing Green'.

We should not be put off by the vague and rather unhelpful title of Yu Jin Ko's book, *Mutability and Division on Shakespeare's Stage*, although I suspect its vagueness may be in response to the lack of any clear-cut thematic connection between Ko's six chapters. Nonetheless (to use one of Ko's favourite words) it's an intriguing, entertaining, and sometimes profound work on Shakespeare, marrying theoretical concerns, literary criticism and criticism of performance. Like a number of books on Shakespeare this year it's death-haunted as it attempts to come to grips with the fractured consciousness of Shakespeare's characters in the face of 'life's finitude'. Hamlet most obviously springs to mind and his turn to the transcendental at the end of his play and his life, in conflict with the pride he takes in his own rough hewing of events, is Ko's 'initial model for exploring how individual and collective ways of answering life's finitude come into entangled conflict between the private and public spheres'.

Ko's treatment of *Hamlet* loops back to his Introduction as Shakespeare's commentary on Ko's theoretical consideration of the conflict between the private and public spheres in criticism and poetry. Unfashionably, Ko follows Harold Bloom's belief in the anti-public primacy of the 'intoxicatingly inventive' artist and critic, though Ko thinks that Richard Rorty's book *Contingency, Irony, and Solidarity* (1989) best examines 'the vexed relation between the private and the public'. Rorty believes that the two spheres should be kept separate; we should not expect art to have a public therapeutic function, just as in Shakespeare we should not hope to be able to align Falstaff with 'the ethos of community'. As Ko wittily puts it, Falstaff cannot in fact ever become the hangman. Nonetheless (once again) the situation in life and art is messier than Rorty imagines and Ko's book goes on to explore fruitfully the ways in which Shakespeare's plays 'dramatize the abiding human need for both perspectives'.

For a book that resolutely refuses to keep the public and the private separate we need to read Julia Reinhard Lupton's *Citizen-Saints: Shakespeare and Political Theology*. Densely, imaginatively written it offers chapters on *The Merchant of Venice*, *Othello*, *Measure for Measure* and *The Tempest* in the illuminating company of 'neo-exegetical' discussions of works by St Paul, Sophocles, Marlowe and Milton. The term 'neo-exegetical' itself is one of many indications in her book that Lupton is aware of the invigorating demands her work makes on the reader's own imaginative co-operation: the constitutional themes of Greek tragedy are 'in a half-remembered key'; things work 'on a deeper level', 'not directly or explicitly', or 'by extension'; something is 'not unlike' something else. Everywhere in the book there are 'allusive' linkages, 'metaphorical lateralizations'; readings are often 'auxiliary'; discourses 'can be joined, adoptedly' or 'distantly and through adoption'; the moves she makes are 'only apparently phantasmatic'.

It says much for the potency and cogency of her argument that her metaphorical lateralizations are indeed rarely phantasmatic. (One such perhaps is her maze-like discussion of the resemblance between Portia and Shylock where Portia's discourse differs from Shylock's, in conclusion 'rendering the rhythmic periodicity of history as the engine of its own ironization'.) At times indeed the book's metaphorical renderings are deeply pleasurable for the reader, as when, in her fine chapter on Marlowe's *The Jew of Malta*, she talks of Barabas's hidden stash of wealth under the floorboards as 'depositing the chance of Jewish survival in the crawl space of Christian history', or when, in her equally fine chapter on *The Tempest*, she parses Caliban's physical amorphousness as 'this inchoate muddiness at the heart of Caliban's oddly faceless and featureless being, caught at the perpetually flooded border between metamorphic mud and mere life, without the solidifying breath of an instilled form'.

In the course of history, the book argues, the saint (or any other exceptional individual) has to make way for the citizen: the Greek aristocratic house has to make way for the polis; the hubris of Creon and Antigone gives way to the collective voice of the Chorus; mediocrity replaces dangerous excellence; the tragic hero has to be ostracized or sacrificed; 'a theology of exceptionalism' gives way to 'a politics of the norm'. And Shakespeare is much more a part of this process than are, say, Marlowe and Milton. His plays 'stage the sacramental marriage, civil divorce, and dangerous liaisons between politics and religion in the West'. Citizen-saints (among whom Shakespeare is one) are Caliban figures, bridging phenomena, hybrids, whose prototype is Saint Paul with whose legacy Shakespeare has an 'inventive engagement'. Thus in her chapter on *The Merchant of Venice* a complex argument sees the play as conscripting its citizen-saint, Shylock, into citizenship, the civic state, demonstrating the sacrifice that liberalism demands of its newly fledged citizens, who may have to embrace what Lupton calls a 'discontented contentment'.

Thomas Betteridge's *Shakespearian Fantasy and Politics*, a 'theoretical engagement with Shakespeare's work', strides forward confidently into the phantasmatic. Why should we read Shakespeare today, Betteridge asks, as though it were self-evident that reading him in the manner of an Alexander Leggatt were no longer viable, perhaps not even possible, certainly not desirable. Somewhat surprisingly, from a work on the cutting-edge of theory, we need to read Shakespeare for the way in which his work is 'a linguistic arena for the production of truths', but these truths can only be excavated with the heavy machinery of twentieth-century theory, especially the work of Slavoj Žižek, the dialectical philosopher and psychoanalyst. Although no doubt Betteridge intends his identification of Shakespeare and his characters with contemporary theorists as good-humoured exaggerations, there is something both bizarre and banal in his telling us that Shakespeare is 'a sophisticated Lacanian', Iago 'appears to have read Derrida' (and also Judith Butler), Paulina 'has read Badiou', or we need to 'embrace the world with Imogen and Žižek'.

Betteridge's book is full of imaginative leaps and bounds. The runaway horse of his imagination gallops through his chosen plays pulling up now and then in a shower of declarative sentences. It's Shakespeare without hesitations. And so in *Twelfth Night*, for instance, 'William Shakespeare explores the ethics of his art' (we might note that portentous 'William'), *The Winter's Tale* is 'a lesson in ethics', while *Othello* 'is Shakespeare's angry, violent repudiation of his drama,' and so on throughout the book. Equally confidently stated are more mysterious dicta. To take just two instances of many: Joan Pucelle in the first part of *Henry VI* 'unlike Henry V and his ilk [his ilk?], floats in the space of history. She is not swallowed up by its lack of fixity, its fluidity, but is instead empowered by its boundless liquidity.' On the other hand, coming back on land for *A Midsummer Night's Dream*, 'the dust that Puck sweeps behind the door ["I am sent with broom before / To sweep the dust behind the door"], which he hides but does not destroy, is the original deadlock that the narrative of the play works around and through without ever actually addressing' (i.e. the materialism of the entrance fee paid by the theatre audience!). Mostly for the wrong reasons, the book is a treasure-trove of quotability. (I don't mean to imply that Puck's lines aren't worth

investigating – see Douglas Bruster's discussion of them, for instance, in *Shakespeare and the Question of Culture: Early Modern Literature and the Cultural Turn* [2003].)

Despite Betteridge's claim to be writing a work of literary criticism, concerned above all with the aesthetic dimension (something that, he says, New Historicism fails fatally to do), he has very little to say about the numerous quotations from Shakespeare in his chapters. When he does descend on Shakespeare's text he does so with a comic ponderousness, talking of Iago's 'ha' in 'Ha, I like not that', for example, as representing 'in Lacanian terms language's point of extimacy – the mark of Other at the center of language'. And despite his confident boldness in the truth claims he makes for Shakespeare's work his book betrays at times a certain (justifiable) hesitation, worrying about 'perverse readings' and other unlikelihoods. (He has sentences that frequently begin 'It is as though' or 'It is as if'.) And despite the arcane flamboyance of his style, the book strikes me as being basically rather old-fashioned in its truth-seeking ambition matched by its strangely old-fashioned form of internal documentation.

Routledge has added *Antony and Cleopatra* and *Julius Caesar* to its list of collections of New Critical Essays on individual Shakespeare plays (the others are on *Hamlet, Othello* and *The Merchant of Venice*). At twenty-one essays *Julius Caesar* bulks larger than *Antony* with fourteen, primarily because Sara Munson Deats's 'Shakespeare's Anamorphic Drama: A Survey of *Antony and Cleopatra* in Criticism, on Stage, and on Screen' takes up over ninety pages. This lengthy survey might have been cut back somewhat to make room for more of what the General Editor, Philip C. Kolin, in a General Introduction (which for some reason only appears in the *Caesar* volume) describes as 'cutting edge essays' providing us with 'the most significant and original contemporary interpretations of Shakespeare's works'. These are self-consciously new critical essays. In Deats's introductory essay she talks of the 'discandying' process in the recent criticism of *Antony and Cleopatra* (and the phrase could be stretched to apply to the recent work on both plays) whereby, for instance, the lovers' passion has been sidelined as a topic of critical interest and with it neat classificatory distinctions including generic ones. Like Antony's crocodile the play may be shaped only like itself.

Certainly, many of the most interesting essays in both collections tend to come at the plays anamorphically and are often discandying exercises. Thus Peter A. Parolin's pleasurable essay '"Cloyless Sauce": The Pleasurable Politics of Food in *Antony and Cleopatra*' revalues feasting in the play noticing that food is not antithetical to the serious business of politics; indeed Antony 'is at his most political when he is eating', and the play ends with Cleopatra's political refusal to eat with Caesar. In similar hedonistic vein, Linda Woodbridge's obliquely slanted piece on gambling in the play, '"He beats thee 'gainst the odds": Gambling, Risk Management, and *Antony and Cleopatra*' – an essay worth the price of admission into the collection – argues that gambling also is not antithetical to the serious business of politics either in the play or in Shakespeare's society where it was linked with a budding capitalism's generation of national wealth. We should thus see Cleopatra as 'a bold international gambler' who lives to 'mock / The luck of Caesar' (5.2.276–7). And James Hirsh in 'Rome and Egypt in *Antony and Cleopatra* and in Criticism of the Play' joins his Erasmian colleagues by praising Egyptian facetiousness. Cleopatra's suicide, from this perspective, 'is a kind of practical joke on Octavius'. Hardly surprisingly, Hirsh denounces critical neutrality: 'my own perspective on the play and commentary remains Egyptian'. Capping this particular strain of anamorphic distortion, Lisa Starks's essay '"Immortal Longings": The Erotics of Death in *Antony and Cleopatra*' sets Antony in the narrative tradition of male masochism in Western mythology, literature, and art, where he can be viewed as an exemplary anti-hero hero. With him we move from 'the death of desire into the ecstatic *desire of death*'. In terms of myth, we should think of the lovers against the story of Acteon and Diana and we should think of Cleopatra becoming 'more white English than black Egyptian in the course of the play'.

Why we should think about *Antony and Cleopatra* (or any other play by Shakespeare) in these unconventional terms – anamorphically so to speak – gets a kind of justification from the collection's flagship essay, Leeds Barroll's 'The Allusive Tissue of *Antony and Cleopatra*'. The spidery fragility of Barroll's 'tissue' (as opposed to more robust terms like intertextuality, sources, influences, or traces) reaches out to take in his notion of a playbook coming to the actors hedged in with culture. Inevitably, 'certain images . . . evoke multiple associations with sites outside the text'. Barroll explores some of these in absorbing discussions, for instance, of Cleopatra's asp and Antony as Hercules. He freely admits that his allusive tissue is difficult to 'incorporate fully in conjectures about performance'; we have to continue to do what critics have been doing for centuries, and what he does so well in this essay, that is, 'stop the action' and read with a readerly eye.

There is more for the readerly eye in *Julius Caesar*, the sister volume in this series, but the essays here on the whole seem to me to be less gripping than those on *Antony*. Unlike the *Antony* volume this one is divided into sections – Introduction, Central Aspects, Current Debates, *Julius Caesar* on Stage – but there is something rather artificial in the distinction between the two largest sections, Central Aspects and Current Debates. As with so much criticism on the play that came before them, most of these fifteen essays at the heart of the book attempt to throw new light on the deliberately injected provocative ambiguity – so it is alleged – at the centre of the play's meaning. And so Vivian Thomas in 'Shakespeare's Sources: Translations, Transformations, and Intertextuality in *Julius Caesar*', is unambiguous in his conviction that '[h]ere is a play about uncertainty'. Audiences have to be on their toes as the play's sources are 'active constituents': Shakespeare is confusingly 'heir to a multiplicity of views'. *Julius Caesar* thus 'generates a sense of the uncertainty attaching to historical events . . . it celebrates intertextuality'.

The intertextuality explored by Clifford Ronan's 'Caesar On and Off the Renaissance English Stage' is that of the other plays on the life of Caesar in the period. There were maybe two dozen Caesar plays in the century before 1642 and they and their historical sources have 'many deeply mixed, complex, and paradoxical versions' of Caesar. Naomi Conn Liebler's essay, 'Buying and Selling So(u)les: Marketing Strategies and the Politics of Performance in *Julius Caesar*', expands on the ambivalent treatment of Caesar to include those by Augustus, Plutarch, Appian and Tacitus. She points out that the liminal place of the theatre in London was perfect for such an evasively minded play: '*Julius Caesar* offers a case study not only *for* but also *in* interpretation, construction, and misconstruction.' Dennis Kezar's timely piece, '*Julius Caesar*'s Analogue Clock and the Accents of History', expands on Liebler's marketing strategies approach to argue that one of the ways to make a work of art transcendent and timeless is to make it infinitely appropriable for opposing viewpoints (as is the case so clearly with *Julius Caesar*). Opposing viewpoints are taken up once again by David Willburn in 'Constructing Caesar: A Psychoanalytic Reading' which talks both of 'the structural ambivalence underlying and fracturing this play' and those 'contradictory images, ideas, and attitudes about Caesar'. It's a play, this essay argues, conspicuously about men: 'Shakespeare's last dramatic investigation of a relatively unalloyed society of men, after the history plays, before the suppressed maternal matter erupts into the tragedies.'

Where we ambivalently are now is pursued by two other useful essays: Martin Jehne's 'History's Alternative Caesars: *Julius Caesar* and Current Historiography', and David Hawkes's 'Shakespeare's *Julius Caesar*: Marxist and Post-Marxist Approaches'. Today's historians, Jehne argues, by and large agree that the Republic would have collapsed had there been no crisis over Caesar, but recently this view is being challenged again. The great thing about literature, however, as Jehne notes, is that it 'can create connections even where the historian has to helplessly face loose ends'. In similar revisionist fashion, Hawkes notes that post-Marxist criticism of the play has returned to its Marxist roots in re-stressing an economic deter-minism, hence his analysis of the play's economic metaphors stressing 'a "homology" between different levels of semiosis'.

SHAKESPEARE AT HOME AND ABROAD

Patrick Cheney's *Shakespeare, National Poet-Playwright* should be read in tandem (if possible) with Robert Crawford's amusing essay 'The Bard: Ossian, Burns, and the shaping of Shakespeare', in a collection later to be reviewed, *Shakespeare and Scotland*. Crawford traces the rise of Shakespeare as the spokes-poet of the sceptered isle – England that is – until achieving full bardic status alongside Ossian and Burns. It's hardly surprising, Crawford argues, that Shakespeare should attain this eminence given his 'deeply hierarchical imagination' and his self-appointed task as adviser to (English) kings. Cheney delves into the depths of this hierarchical imagination from a somewhat different angle and with larger considerations in mind. He constructs a Shakespeare as self-consciously Bloomian as any other harassed major poet, obsessively aware of the achievements of his immediate predecessors, Marlowe and Spenser, and anxious to surpass them. It would seem that we have to take the sentiments of Sonnet 29 very seriously. In this poet-eat-poet world we have to imagine a similar anxious rivalry between Marlowe and Spenser whereby, for instance, 'Marlowe translates Lucan to counter Spenser's cultural authority.' In what Cheney calls a typology of intertextuality, Shakespeare imitates texts 'from a preceding literary system in order to veil and target his rivalry with colleagues from his own literary system'. So Shakespeare imitates Virgil and Ovid at, as it were, Spenser's and Marlowe's expense, for Marlowe is England's Ovid and Spenser England's Virgil. All three are vying for the (unofficial) bardic post of national poet which Shakespeare achieves by trumping both Spenser and Marlowe by the ingenious strategy of writing Ovidian poems and plays 'along the Virgilian path'.

Given this imaginative theory it's no wonder that Cheney thinks that in, say, *The Rape of Lucrece*, the author is also 'processing his own (afflicted) standing as an emergent English poet-playwright' or that *The Phoenix and the Turtle* is 'a work about the politics of authorship itself' (the phoenix rising from the ashes is Shakespeare's tragic art) or that, as Edmond Malone originally contended, in *A Lover's Complaint* Shakespeare is breaking a lance with Spenser. It is, of course, easier to apply this biographical speculation about Shakespeare to the poems, although Cheney ropes in the plays as well, describing, for instance, how the romances, in their staging of Ovid, reveal a Spenserian dynamic. For Cheney, then, the poems (in particular) are the key to Shakespeare's angst-ridden heart, but the door is only half open; the best the book has managed, Cheney admits, is 'to get the author to pause, turn around, and show his face, before he slips around the next corner'.

In the process of catching a glimpse of the real Shakespeare's face Cheney makes important claims for the significance of Shakespeare as poet-playwright rather than as just a dramatist who also wrote poetry or as a dramatist who happened to write plays in poetry. The poems are poetry and the plays poetry, and it is a shame that the 1623 Folio omitted the poetry thus establishing Shakespeare for his readers as a dramatist rather than as a poet. Cheney's conclusion is that Shakespeare's poems should come first in any Complete Works to emphasize his 'original stature as national poet-playwright'. Most of us would have little quarrel with this act of restitution and redistribution, but we may be less certain as to just how much Shakespeare has shown his face to Cheney in the picture Cheney paints of him as a writer so entirely desperate for this man's art and that man's scope.

After this rather dour presentation of Shakespeare as a self-conscious contender in the national poetry stakes, it's something of a relief to turn to a book that celebrates a quite different Shakespeare with a face that, were it discernible, might well be wreathed in smiles. Jeffrey Knapp's award-winning work, *Shakespeare's Tribe: Church, Nation, and Theater in Renaissance England*, argues that for too long the vehemence of the puritan attack on the theatre has obscured the simple fact that much

Renaissance drama is not only not antagonistic to religion, is not merely at best an expression of the 'secular sublime', but 'may have been intended and received as contributions to the cause of true religion'. He is well aware that 'true religion' contains a multitude of permutations and brackets the vexed (and usually unrewarding) question of Shakespeare's precise denominational loyalties. But, taking the history plays and the comedies as his chief textual resource, he argues that Shakespeare's plays should be read as offering serious spiritual guidance for their receptive audiences. It's not just a question, as the New Historicists would have us believe, that, with the decline in the popularity of the preacher, the theatre provided the people with replacement symbolic forms, compensating for the loss of Catholicism. *Pace* Greenblatt and Montrose, the theatre offered its audiences a kind of ministry; the plays may not be sermons but they are religious.

In this quasi-pedagogic endeavour Shakespeare is not, of course, alone. In an entertaining and persuasive history of theatrical religious activism, Knapp places Shakespeare in an Erasmian tradition of good fellowship, the star member of a 'tribe' of 'good fellows' that includes Nashe, Greene, Dekker and Jonson who, from the religious point of view, were accommodationist, inclusive, moderate, anti-factional and doctrinally low-key. And, of course, hugely entertaining, with a 'robust conception of communion', seizing upon moderate Protestantism's desire to entertain its congregations into virtue. And in the mix there is the promotion of a kind of nationalism in the theatre in its celebration of a rogue communality based on the popularity of the vagabond rogue world of Greene and Dekker. But really, Knapp believes, the spirit of these plays, Shakespeare's especially, transcends nationalism, rogue or not, as though Shakespeare and his colleagues were speaking directly to their theatrical audiences over the heads of the official spokesmen for king and church on behalf of an ecumenical Christianity, tolerant, good-humoured, ideologically flexible, supra-nationalist, irenic and internationalist. In this respect, Knapp argues, we should notice

Shakespeare's presentation of churchmen; throughout his work he dramatizes 'the dark comedy of Episcopal militarism'. In *Henry V*, for instance, Shakespeare silently contrasts a 'violent "fellowship" of warriors financed by a corrupt Catholic church to the peaceful communion of an audience in active remembrance of blood spilt', and *King John* dramatizes Shakespeare's hope that religious corruption in Protestant England and Catholic Christendom 'might ultimately lead to a reformation of Christianity in fact'.

This provocative and entertaining book complicates our understanding of Shakespeare as a religious and political thinker. If we at times find it a little hard to swallow, Knapp is very understanding: 'it generally takes some strain to uncover [the dramatists'] purpose, and still more strain to credit it'.

Strain is one of the words that spring to mind in reading Richard Wilson's *Secret Shakespeare: Studies in Theatre, Religion and Resistance*. Its twelve chapters are serviced by over a thousand footnotes, and many of these have branches and offshoots. (Even the five-page Epilogue requires twenty-nine of them, and the six-page Introduction thirty-five.) So much information, ferreted out from the nooks and crannies of social history, bespeaks an immense scholarly effort, and it is not the least of the book's ironies that such industry is in the service of 'a book about what Shakespeare did not write'. What he didn't write was anything revelatory about religion, his or anybody else's; he totally effaced 'the religious politics of his age' (which might come as a surprise to Knapp and Lupton). Like Cheney's book, Wilson's attempts to get Shakespeare to stand still for a moment before slipping round that next corner, to break through his plays' 'strategic opacity', their 'evasive slipperiness'. But there is something to my mind evasive and slippery about *Secret Shakespeare* itself, for although Shakespeare, Wilson argues, is not necessarily a Roman Catholic, or an Anglo-Catholic or a Catholic loyalist, the need to 'historicize Shakespearian secrecy' is *necessarily* to see it in relation to Catholic persecution, and Wilson doesn't leave a stone unturned – not a pebble – to demonstrate, with an extraordinary

circumstantiality, Shakespeare's 'Catholic set of mind'.

I can't really speak to the accuracy or even the fairness of the application of such a mass of historical circumstance to Shakespeare's religious biography. At times, anecdote and gossip about Shakespeare's family, his friends and acquaintances (or possible acquaintances), his mentors and protectors, take on a New Historicist life of their own and can be read as enjoyable contributions to our understanding of the life of the times. Such is the case, for instance, with Wilson's energetic re-telling of the Throckmorton Conspiracy that occupies the first twelve pages of his chapter on *As You Like It*, making new news out of old news, to adapt the chapter's title. At other times, the Catholic context in which Wilson places his readings of Shakespeare's plays is genuinely helpful and enlightening, as in his discussion of Iago's 'self-glorifying' defiance within the conventions of Jesuit martyrdom.

What I might speak to is the sense I get from the book's overall style and method of the difficulties Wilson must have faced in trying to break through what he reads as an intractable, willed determination on Shakespeare's part to disguise his real feelings: his 'legendary inaccessibility', his 'mysterious vacuousness'. In a particularly desperate ploy, Wilson fills his book with quotations from Shakespeare, embedding them in his argument in such a way as to give them a duplicitous evidentiary role. And there is exasperation, it seems to me, in the number of times in the book Wilson has to resort to disclaimers of coincidence: 'it cannot be by accident' or, more hesitantly, 'it may not be coincidental' he says, over and over again. The book is full of probablies, and maybes, and sentences beginning with if. The optative and the imperative mood prevail: something either may or must be the case. 'Tellingly' is the typical arm-twisting adverb. The less Shakespeare mentions something or avoids something the more important it is: what is not mentioned is 'highly suggestive', Wilson maintains, akin to Heidegger's 'notorious silence about the Jews'. In one of Wilson's many striking phrases, all of Shakespeare's silences 'take place in a culture of paranoid circumspection'. On the other hand, the more something is derided, condemned and satirized the more it really isn't, the more, that is, it's really the opposite of what it seems to be, as with those 'scenes of Jesuitical parody' in the plays.

One can't help but feel that these rhetorical strategies, combined with the torrent of reference and citation, are an attempt to bully the reader into agreement. But they may well indicate the sad fact that in terms of his private beliefs Shakespeare will remain permanently hidden somewhere around the next corner.

Although Ros King's book, Cymbeline: *Constructions of Britain*, is much less sweeping than Wilson's, focusing on only one of Shakespeare's plays, it too attempts to shed light on Shakespeare's work 'by reference to the social and political contexts of its time of writing'. A perfectly laudable ambition, of course, and, on the face of it, one that seems particularly appropriate for a play so edgily and mysteriously connected to the culture of Britain in the seventeenth century. At the same time, *Cymbeline* is also, perhaps above all, a play that demands from its audiences 'a peculiarly high level of active, imaginative engagement'. So King's first chapter, 'Poetic Forms: Constructing Meanings', seems at first to be a straightforward exercise in literary criticism to aid us in understanding the 'bemused voicings of half-perceived thoughts' so characteristic of the play's style. One senses, though, a certain half-heartedness with this project as King makes it clear that she believes that the play's abundant 'syntactical complexity' works in the theatre, demonstrating the 'triumph of theatrical practice over rather too literary theory' [*sic*]. The chapter then shifts its attention (as does the rest of the book until the discussions of the history of performances at the end) away from the play itself to the historical circumstances of Shakespeare's time, in this case a detailed description of the building of The Prince Royal, a British battleship built in 1609. And this leads us into a chapter called '*Great* Britain' largely devoted to a discussion of the entertainments written to celebrate the investiture in 1610 of Henry, Prince of Wales, described in detail in order for us to be able to take, if we so wish, 'a rather harder look at the propaganda of power' that we find in *Cymbeline*.

The material on The Prince Royal, the chapter on Great Britain, and the one on 'Empire' that follow, do not seem to me to be wedded sufficiently pertinently to the play itself. And perhaps her own unease with her method is conveyed in sentences such as 'what I'm about to describe may seem initially like an extraordinary and bizarre leap' or in the kind of excessive detail she provides, for example, from the Sermon on the Mount which is, she believes, 'worth quoting extensively at this point'. The penultimate chapter on religion in *Cymbeline* strikes me as being the most valuable one in its presentation of the play as 'ecumenical and humanist in spirit, not sectarian'.

The first part of Scott McCrea's *The Case for Shakespeare: the End of the Authorship Question*, 'The Man who Wrote the Plays', so trenchantly establishes the case for Shakespeare being the Shakespeare who wrote Shakespeare's works that it hardly seems necessary to write the second part, 'The Men who Didn't', unless you're particularly interested in the history of lunatic attribution (the father of Oxfordianism we recall was J. Thomas Looney). We need go no further, McCrea concludes, than the basic, irrefutable evidence provided by the 1623 Folio which gives us for the authorized version of the writer a name, a face, the town of origin, and a profession, not to mention the guarded adulation of Ben Jonson, Shakespeare's friend and chief rival. It says a lot for McCrea's stamina that he not only goes on to demolish the arguments against Shakespeare (the chief of which is the snobbish and wrong one that he was working class and ill-educated, and the even more snobbish extension of it that no one other than a peer of the realm could be so articulate), but wades through the nonsense and special pleading supporting any of the fifty-six other unlikely candidates entails.

McCrea's last chapter is called 'All Conspiracy Theories Are Alike', and ends by pleading for sanity in a mixed metaphor that unintentionally conveys the unlikelihood that sweet reason will ever prevail: 'It's time for every conspiracy theorist to step off the intellectual carousel and become, in the words of an alderman's son, from Stratford, "as one new-risen from a dream."' (That the plea continues to be unheard by those dreamy carousel riders is indicated by the advance publicity for *The Truth Will Out*: *Unmasking the Real Shakespeare* which will claim that newly discovered seventeenth-century documents prove Shakespeare not to be 'the true author of the world's greatest plays'. Stay tuned.)

The Bard, as Daniel Korstein says – somewhat ominously – 'belongs most of all to the educated amateur, and we need more amateurs'. Perhaps so. In the book that follows, this practising lawyer investigates thirteen of Shakespeare's plays to see how Shakespeare's dramatization of specific legal situations or quasi-legal situations – two-thirds of his plays have trial scenes – sheds light on current legal practices and problems. Thus *The Merchant of Venice* 'becomes a dramatic representation of the commonsense wisdom of the equal protection requirement of the Fourteenth Amendment'. Korstein doesn't find it surprising that Shakespeare has so much to say to today's practising lawyers, for Shakespeare was 'a lawyer's dream, a walking litigation factory'. Much of what Korstein has to say about the plays is commonplace. But the book comes to life when he applies Shakespeare to specific cases: *Measure for Measure* to Bowers versus Hardwick; *Romeo and Juliet* to Browning-Ferris Industries versus Kelso Disposal; *Richard II* to Burdick versus United States, and so on.

No doubt the authors of *Shakespeare's Sonnets*, Paul Edmondson and Stanley Wells, would have few problems with Patrick Cheney's assessment of Shakespeare as a poet first and foremost. The sonnets, in their view, are 'central to an understanding of Shakespeare's work as a poet and poetic dramatist'. In this lively, frank and helpful contribution to the Oxford Shakespeare Topics series, myths are dispelled, assumptions queried, difficulties embraced. It is not entirely obvious, for instance, that the opening sonnets are necessarily addressed to a man; to look for a 'tidy pattern' in these 'loosely connected poems' is to try to 'tidy the inevitable mess and freedom that love itself creates'; the sonnets are dauntingly 'complex, elusive, and enigmatic' in nature and should be allowed to be

so (they are hospitable as a result to a 'wide variety of editorial treatment and to a multitude of critical approaches'). Passionate they clearly are, but they are above all sophisticated literary artefacts working in a sophisticated literary tradition: Shakespeare didn't merely look into his heart and write. Is the 'I' then of these sonnets the poet or a shifting persona? Did Shakespeare stop writing them early or late? (He was probably writing them up until 1609 say Edmondson and Wells.) What, above all, is their relationship to the plays? (Intensely familial is the writers' answer and it might help our understanding of the sonnets, they suggest, if we thought of them as dramatic monologues.)

For a short book a lot of ground is covered, from a history of the sonnet form through a delicate assessment of the artistry and concerns of Shakespeare's sonnets and their connection with 'A Lover's Complaint' to their later critical reception and a brief account, interestingly, of them in performance, set to music, for example, by Johnny Dankworth, a jazz composer, and by Dmitri Shostakovich. This book certainly helps us to see why Shakespeare's sonnets 'take their place among the abiding monuments of Western civilization'.

Catherine M. S. Alexander has put together a collection of essays, *Shakespeare and Language*, taken from the pages of *Shakespeare Survey* (1964 to 1997). Their re-publication in a book devoted entirely to their topic gives them a new lease on life. And so Terence Hawkes's well-travelled piece, 'Shakespeare's talking animals' – which argues that Shakespeare's 'true immortality' resides more in 'the apparent ephemerality of speech, less in the apparent permanence of writing' – gets new energy from appearing in the congenial company of Muriel St Clare Byrne's 'The foundations of Elizabethan language', which uses the Lisle letters (1533–40) to pursue Florio's contention that the language is 'so written as it is spoken and such upon the paper as it is in the mouth'. On the other hand, it's challenged stimulatingly by Jill L. Levenson's 'Shakespeare's *Romeo and Juliet*: the places of invention' where her analysis of the play's rhetoric suggests a literary language running amok in its use

of such rhetorical devices as prosopopoeia, polyp-
toton, antimetabole, diacope, asteismus, epizeuxis,
and antanaclasis. Hard to imagine examples of these
tripping off the tongue in daily conversation. But
that's the case with *Romeo and Juliet*. *Macbeth*, on the
other hand, may be a different matter. In another
stimulating essay, 'Household words: *Macbeth* and
the failure of spectacle', Lisa Hopkins notes how
at certain crucial moments the Macbeths 'favour a
low-key, occasionally almost bathetic vocabulary'
in keeping with 'the element of familiarity and
domesticity'.

The moral may well be that Shakespeare's language is plot-driven: the play fits the language, and
the language the play. Russ McDonald's expressive
piece, 'Late Shakespeare: style and the sexes', charts
the malleability of the language in the last plays from
the 'grammatically asyndetic' style of *Coriolanus*
to the Ciceronianism of the romances suggesting in
the case of the latter 'a new devotion to the principles of fabulation'. In her fine essay, '*Hamlet* and
the power of words', Inga-Stina Ewbank focuses
on the difficulty of 'translating' not only Hamlet's
whirling words but the complicated social language
of the Danish court as a whole. Ewbank's own
acknowledgement of the power of words can be
seen in her graceful use of quotations from Henry
James and George Eliot: she asks us to consider, for
instance, in the light of Shakespeare's play, James's
judgement of the importance of 'the way we say a
thing, or fail to say it, fail to learn to say it'. For
Ewbank the greatness of *Hamlet* lies 'in its power
to express so much and yet also to call a halt on the
edge of the inexpressible'. Stephen Booth questions
where that edge is to be found (if anywhere). In
'Shakespeare's language and the language of Shakespeare's time', the collection's most vivacious performance, he expands upon the outrageous suggestion of his opening sentence that 'Shakespeare
is our most underrated poet' in a series of witty and
acute paradoxes. Shakespeare is underrated because
his harmonies are so dense, so 'beyond comfortable
calculation'. It's a density that's often fascinatingly
irrelevant; there's a 'complex, deeply uninteresting patterning'; there are 'substantively insignificant relational harmonies'; passages pulsate with a
'substantively irrelevant energy'; there is 'careless,
submerged play'. And yet, despite all this paradoxical insouciance, we never get the sense that Booth
is doing Booth rather than doing Shakespeare
despite the temptation implicit in the notion that
Shakespeare's harmonies are beyond comfortable
calculation. We might consider, for instance, his
comment – well within our comfort zone – on
the line 'Together with that pale, that white-
faced shore' (*King John* 2.1.23): 'If . . . the phrase
"that white-faced shore" did not intervene to gloss
"pale" and insist that it be understood as an adjective akin in its sense to "white", "pale" would
remain a noun meaning "fence"'.

ABROAD

We don't have to go far to be in foreign territory,
as the collection of essays, *Shakespeare and Scotland*,
makes quite clear. But as David Baker's meditation
'"Stands Scotland where it did?" Shakespeare on
the march' also makes clear, the border between the
two countries, both geographical and cultural, is
uneasily porous and indistinct, separating and at the
same time not separating those 'intimately related,
geographically interpenetrating domains'. Just how
interpenetrating the domains are is the burden (in
more than one sense) of most of the essays in
this book, located as it is on that other border
'between Shakespeare studies and Scottish studies'.
Mark Burnett's thoughtful essay, for instance, 'Local
Macbeth / global Shakespeare: Scotland's screen des-
tiny', shows us how recent performances of *Macbeth*
(one in the theatre, two on television) reflect the
larger cultural movement of our times whereby in
a process theorists have called 'glocalization' 'the
individual and the general co-exist and intersect'.
In these productions Scotland at first disappears
only to reappear in the form of history or of a supplement, aping globalization's 'characteristic movement' between 'a pessimism which involves a loss
of local identity, and an optimism which agitates
for its reclamation and celebration'.

As one might expect the play most frequently
considered in this collection is *Macbeth*, though
there is an interesting essay on *Hamlet* by Andrew

Hadfield, '*Hamlet*'s country matters: the "Scottish play" within the play', that argues that the play is 'saturated with suppressed and disguised references to Scottish history, all designed to express the anxiety felt by English subjects at the prospect of a Scotsman inheriting their throne' (Hadfield admits the argument is a bit forced). The most challenging essay on *Macbeth* is by Elizabeth Fowler called '*Macbeth* and the rhetoric of political forms'. This densely argued piece, already in circulation in a festschrift for Barbara Lewalski, places *Macbeth* in the context of a series of social topoi – military service, the progress and counsel – and the fitness or unfitness of the human beings in the play who practice them or fail to practice them or practice them badly. Christopher Highley's essay on *Macbeth*, 'The place of Scots in the Scottish play: *Macbeth* and the politics of language', notes that English is to Scots in this play what English is to French in the history plays (as argued by Deanne Williams): 'Malcolm and his new regime are insistently Anglicized and hence legitimized, Macbeth's isolation and descent into tyranny is presented as a process of Gaelicization'.

Shakespeare and Renaissance Europe takes us farther afield. This is a collection of eight original essays by different authors designed to be read as chapters of a book (as is the case with *Shakespeare and the Classics*). Although each chapter makes reference to numerous Shakespeare plays, the book as a whole explores the background of Shakespeare's connection to the continent: hence such chapter topics as 'English Contact with Europe', 'The Politics of Renaissance Europe', 'Contemporary Europe in Elizabethan and Early Stuart Drama' and – a fascinating one this – 'Europe's Mediterranean Frontier: the Moor'. Unlike the collection of essays on Shakespeare and Scotland no single play by Shakespeare is singled out for intense scrutiny; but then no single play is to Europe what *Macbeth* is to Scotland. Hardly surprising really as Europe for Shakespeare is so often an imaginary place as François Laroque's essay 'Shakespeare's Imaginary Geography' maintains. Shakespeare's European geography, he tells us, is often vague and should remain so. Something similar might be said of Shakespeare's use of

Italian stage techniques which Richard Andrews explores in 'Shakespeare and Italian Comedy' for he admits that Lyly is more important 'than any Italian derivation'. Like Moliere Shakespeare takes 'total possession' of his borrowings.

Of the essays more directly concerned with Shakespeare, Stuart Gillespie's 'Shakespeare's Reading of Modern European Literature' reinforces the sense outlined above of Shakespeare's total possession of his material; in this case, given his working knowledge of French and Italian, the way in which his translations are uniquely his. In any case, Gillespie believes that the most important European influence on Shakespeare comes not so much from specific plots or storylines of Italian plays or novellas but from what he calls the 'texts of ideas', hence the humanist echoes in Shakespeare's plays of Erasmus, Montaigne and Machiavelli. Along similar lines Nabil Matar and Rudolph Stoeckel's essay, 'Europe's Mediterranean Frontier: the Moor', points out that Shakespeare was not sure whether Europe was a 'geographic, religious or cultural unity'.

The general becomes more particular and more circumscribing in a collection of essays on *Shakespeare, Italy, and Intertextuality*, though the fashionable term intertextuality has the virtue (and the vice) of being more general than particular. Robert S. Miola's 'Seven types of intertextuality' explores the implications of what Michele Marrapodi's 'Introduction: intertextualizing Shakespeare's text' calls the Renaissance principle of 'creative intertextuality' whereby the term, as Miola says, covers 'the widest possible range of textual interactions including those of sources and influences'. A useful word, then, but, as Miola goes on to warn us, ripe for abuse, encouraging 'rampant and irresponsible association, facile cultural generalization, and anecdotal, impressionistic historicizing' (demonstrated to some extent in this volume by Anthony G. Barthelemy's '"What news on the Rialto": luxury, sodomy, and miscegenation in *The Merchant of Venice*'). Keir Elam takes up this notion of intertextuality's elasticity in 'Afterword: Italy as intertext' (an Afterword that might have been better deployed as a Foreword) which traces the use of 'Intertextuality' back to its original formulation by Julia Kristeva in the 1960s (inspired by Bakhtin) and on a par in importance with the coeval concern for textuality in which 'every mode of cultural production' becomes 'a textual event'. And so Italy may be conceived as 'a sort of generative machine producing powerful models'.

There is no question in the minds of these essayists that Shakespeare was dependent on many things Italian – nothing much imaginary here – which, as Marropodi argues, should not be surprising in a culture so heavily indebted to the notion of *imitatio* as the basis of human experience and demonstrating (perhaps) an 'absence of domestic cultural self-confidence'. Italy was 'a treasure trove of intertextual, and indeed interdiscursive, confrontation between texts and cultures'. The many layers of these intertextual and interdiscursive confrontations are explored in a number of these essays of which the most thought-provoking are Charlotte Pressler's 'Intertextual transformations: the *novella* as mediator between Italian and English Renaissance drama', Alessandro Serpieri's 'Shakespeare and Plutarch: intertextuality in action', and Jason Lawrence's '"The story is extant, and writ in very choice Italian": Shakespeare's dramatizations of Cinthio' (which contends that Shakespeare used translation and original at one and the same time). Special mention should be made of Michael J. Redmond's essay 'The politics of plot: *Measure for Measure* and the Italianate disguised duke play' which blames the play's intertextual background for the messiness of its final solution, an 'unstable amalgam of the traditional ransom story, the disguised duke plot, and romantic comedy'.

Jill Line's *Shakespeare and the Fire of Love* is a handsomely produced book with thirteen illustrations and a cover design by Andrew Candy based on George Romney's painting 'King Lear in the Tempest'. It purports to demonstrate the manner in which Shakespeare's works are suffused with neoplatonism especially that of the Italian writer, Marsilio Ficino. The claims the book makes are not inconsiderable: with Ficino's neoplatonism as our interpretative key 'the whole inner meaning of Shakespeare's plays and poems began to fall into

place'. Ficino's assistance, while crucial, is not invasive or difficult to apply: after all in Shakespeare '[t]he meaning is there, in his words, his themes and his poetry'. Such unbounded confidence produces insights such as the following: 'the beauty of Juliet stems from the splendour of God himself'; cross-dressing is really a matter of hiding 'the greater beauty within'; in mastering Kate Petruchio is mastering himself; Romeo's frenzy is Shakespeare the poet's; 'the imagination of all Shakespeare's tragic heroes is well developed'; Octavia is not Antony's 'true soul-mate', and so on. We look in vain, by the way, for just a modest sprinkling of the maybes and perhapses that suffuse Wilson's book.

It should come as no surprise that Line mentions no Shakespeare critics after the 1960s except Ted Hughes and Stephen Orgel. Nor should it come as any surprise that her greatest indebtednesses (after the one to Ficino) are to John Vyvyan and Frances Yates. She quotes at exorbitant length from Shakespeare's works (Sonnet 53 is quoted twice in full in different chapters) but she does very little with the quotations once she has them on the page. If nothing else this handsomely produced book is a testament to the extraordinary variety in the kind and quality of today's writings on Shakespeare, but one wonders how it ever got by the publisher's readers. It was published by Shepheard Walwyn in a series they call 'Our Love of Wisdom' (another is called 'Our Beautifully Written Book Collection') who seem to be attempting to corner the market in up-market self-help books. In the 'Our Love of Wisdom' series, for instance, they have published the work of Marsilio Ficino whose wisdom provides, in their words, 'answers to problems still troubling people's minds today'.

If Knapp's *Shakespeare's Tribe* argues that English Renaissance drama, notably Shakespeare's, catches the conscience of king and commoner alike on behalf of an ameliorative Christianity, then Barbara Parker's *Plato's* Republic *and Shakespeare's Rome: A Political Study of the Roman Works* argues that Shakespeare's Roman plays are dedicated to catching kings' consciences on behalf of the idea of a constitutional monarchy derived from Plato's *Republic*. Two sides of the same coin, perhaps, as Parker intimates when she talks of 'the fusion of pol-itics and religion brought by the war between Protestantism and Rome'. Catching consciences on the English stage was an aspect of the Renaissance use of history 'to gloss contemporary polit-ical issues', encouraged by the recovery of ancient texts fostering the notion of history as 'ameliorative and non-linear' and by the emergence of territo-rial and national states. Shakespeare's Elizabethan Roman poem and plays (*The Rape of Lucrece, Julius Caesar, Titus Andronicus*) are concerned, in their conscience-catching capacity, with the question of the royal succession; his Jacobean (*Coriolanus, Antony and Cleopatra*) with 'court depravity, licen-tiousness and corruption'. This argument, supple-mented by a discussion of Plato's theory of consti-tutional monarchy, can be found in Parker's strong introductory chapter which provides the back-ground to her discussions of Shakespeare's Roman works that follow.

The application of Parker's thesis to Shakespeare has mixed results, however. It is at its most forced, it seems to me, in her treatment of *The Rape of Lucrece* where the political significance of the poem loses its Platonic moorings and becomes instead a rather unconvincing allegory of Queen Elizabeth's relationship with Essex. When Parker argues that it doesn't matter that '*Lucrece* antedates Essex's actions by roughly five years', that this discrepancy 'need not negate its allegorical viability', I don't under-stand how this can possibly be the case, especially as she spends so much time detailing Essex's entry into Elizabeth's bedchamber, presumably because it resembles somehow Tarquin's into Lucrece's. And I think it would then have been more persua-sive if she had gone on to deal with *Julius Cae-sar* or *Titus Andronicus* (the other two Elizabethan Roman plays) instead of *Coriolanus* (a Jacobean Roman play), despite her contention that *The Rape of Lucrece, Coriolanus, Julius Caesar* and *Antony and Cleopatra* amount to a tetralogy that 'collectively traces a continuous span of history coupled with a progressive constitutional decline'. If Plato is a ghostly presence in her chapter on *Lucrece* then he seems to be a no-show in her chapter on *Coriolanus*, replaced in large part by a retelling of the plot. The

book is at its most persuasive in the chapters on *Antony and Cleopatra* and *Titus Andronicus*.

As for the connections with Plato's *Republic*, there is a repeated acknowledgement on Parker's part that it was hardly necessary for Shakespeare to have read Plato directly, he could simply have read Platonic theorists, such as Cicero, Erasmus, Elyot or Plutarch. Indeed, the frequency with which Parker also has to acknowledge that Shakespeare's political concepts were Renaissance commonplaces suggests the dismaying possibility that he could have man-aged without even these intermediaries, at least for his political philosophy if not for his plots.

In *Shakespeare and the French Poet* John Naughton has translated and brought together seven of the prefaces to translations into French of Shake-speare's plays by the French poet and translator Yves Bonnefoy. These are followed by Bonnefoy's remarks on the difficulties of translating Shake-speare into French and an interview. In his Intro-duction Naughton warns us that Bonnefoy writes very much in the tradition of the French poet as grand seigneur, and that his thought is 'pitched at a very high level' in sentences that are Proustian in length and complexity. Whereas English poetry is mimetic, so Naughton – and Bonnefoy – argues, French tends to be Platonic, holding up a crys-tal sphere rather than a mirror to nature, and the language of Bonnefoy's criticism has itself all the drawbacks (and some of the virtues) of a crystalline sphericity as we try to grasp what he means by a world of presence in Shakespeare (as opposed to image) in the context of finitude (a formulation which crops up time and again in the course of his musings). Trying to get a purchase on some of Bonnefoy's critical judgements is like trying to cling onto a crystal sphere: Ferdinand's language, for instance, in *The Tempest*, is 'but glimmerings, reflections, stirrings of a water lost in pools of shadow', while Florizel and Perdita's 'foam of illu-sion is dispelled in the cosmic wave of their mutual trust'. Bonnefoy is fond of pools and seas. In *Oth-ello*, we're told, 'Shakespeare's observatory dives very deep, like a bathyscaph in the swirls of what well may be called the soul since it is a medium more mobile and more conductive than reason.'

What well may be called the soul is Bonnefoy's chief interest, as it is Jill Line's, especially its 'most secret region'. He's fascinated by 'the unfathomable depths of what he or she is, the place where awareness of one's self is rooted beyond the mind's reach'; for him 'the role of the theater . . . [is] to probe into the obscure dialectics of the self'. Fortunately, we can, in the mimetic English manner, apply a reality check to the kind of selves that Bonnefoy finds remarkable in Shakespeare. Questions abound. Is Macbeth, for example, 'never more than a brutal warrior'? Does Mercutio represent Shakespeare? Does Hamlet have 'a very real love for Ophelia'? Is Cordelia's 'a somewhat cool and arid virtuousness'? Are Perdita's views of art Shakespeare's? Is there no value in Polixenes's arguments? Does Leontes have no motivation? Is Antony Shakespeare with 'a series of superb lines that rise straight from the depths of his writing, from his soul'? Does Desdemona listen to Iago's jokes 'in troubled amazement at his hateful words'? Are Rosencrantz and Guildenstern 'those pompous German university students'?

This is a book that tells you more about Bonnefoy than Shakespeare; we cannot help but hear the voice of the modern French poet rather than that of the English Renaissance dramatist. We respond to remarks such as this one about Brutus's speech in *Julius Caesar* – 'the multidirectional space of its monumental prose . . . through symmetries and symmetries within symmetries' – respectfully acknowledging the power of the sensibility that produced it, but aware, as with so much else in the book, that it holds a sphere up to Shakespeare rather than a mirror.

The difficulty I have with Deanne Williams's *The French Fetish from Chaucer to Shakespeare* lies in her use of the word 'fetish'. Neither the dictionary definitions of the term nor its use by the many theorists Williams cites, from Marx and Freud through Aimé Césaire, Homi Bhabha, Jacques Lacan and Michel Foucault (among others) seem to me illuminatingly applicable to the book's argument. It's an obfuscatory term rather than an heuristic one, in this case, and may have been used to give a factitious theoretical underpinning to her discussion of the history of the 'unresolvable relationship . . .

between the rejection of French power and the French past [by the English] and the embracement of it'. She traces this ambivalent cultural legacy of the Norman Conquest from Chaucer to Shakespeare. On the way she discusses (in the main) the Corpus Christi Plays, Caxton, Hawes and Skelton. In Shakespeare's case she concentrates on the history plays and *The Merry Wives of Windsor*.

We don't have to look further than Chaucer to see the fundamental elements of the attraction/repulsion relationship that the English have had with French culture and the French language. On the one hand, for example, Chaucer's *The Book of the Duchess* (written in the 1370s) memorializes John of Gaunt's wife, Blanche, and her aristocratic French culture, but the conflict in the poem between the Man in Black and the Dreamer (the former speaking nothing but French poetry, the latter fluctuating between French and English) produces 'a fascinating and conflicted set of negotiations and disentanglements, from which Chaucer defines the terms for poetic expression in the English vernacular'.

In the fifteenth century there was a growing awareness in England of French as the Other; nonetheless, as in the case of nineteenth-century Russia, speaking and writing French continued to be the hallmark of the sophisticated courtier and intellectual. We can see clearly from Williams's interesting discussion of the career of Caxton, in its Man in Black and Dreamer manifestations, the essential pattern. Caxton moves from an idolization of the French language (a third of his output – twenty-seven books – was French translation) through the 1482 printing of *The Canterbury Tales* and that of *Troilus and Criseyde* in 1484 to the 1490 *Eneydos* whose preface by him celebrates the triumph of English. (As much as anything else, given the increasing popularity of English, the change in direction was a commercial move on Caxton's part.)

Williams's discussion of Shakespeare may well be the richest section of the book. By and large the Histories celebrate the triumph of English culture and language; so, while the civilizing capacity of French is acknowledged in *Richard II*, the play also suggests it's a self-indulgent fantasy. It's a question of throwing off the Norman yoke and channelling English barbarism. A somewhat unexpected but fruitful move at the end of the book sees *The Merry Wives of Windsor* as a sequel to *Henry V*: 'The play . . . seeks to dramatize, in amorous and erotic terms, the relationship between England and France that its historical predecessor sought to establish in military and political terms.'

What are we to make of Adrian A. Husain's *Politics and Genre in 'Hamlet'*? It's the size of a lengthy journal essay, yet it comes in the form of a 34-page hardbound book (fifty-four with notes, bibliography and encomia) from a prestigious university press with an admiring foreword by John Bayley and even more admiring reviews on the back cover by other senior scholars. In his Acknowledgements, Husain tells us that the book 'has been in the offing for at least thirty years' (which works out at approximately one page a year). Surely we must be dealing with something momentous here. (If we are, its proof-readers didn't seem to have noticed as there is a surprising number of minor and not so minor errors, particularly noticeable in a book of this length – beginning, perhaps not inappropriately, with two *to be*'s in Bayley's Foreword. Occasionally, too, the book's English idioms are off-key.)

I deal with the book in this section of the reviews because it is so implacably European in its historicist approach. Husain reads *Hamlet* as poised in the seventeenth century between the thought of Aristotle and Machiavelli, on the one hand, and Plato and Castiglione on the other (Pico della Mirandola and, later, Cassirer and Foucault are also significant). Machiavelli is the most important of these because of his work on the problem of identity, but there is no 'final or definitive resolution'. Husain's most interesting contribution to the vast literature on the enigma of *Hamlet* is to suggest that the play itself, coming as it does at a 'transgeneric moment' in theatrical history, mirrors the European crisis of identity in showcasing its own generic instability. Hamlet himself is a product of *The Book of the Courtier* fertilized by *The Prince*; he's caught between the selfhoods of Old Hamlet from the old

humanist tradition and Fortinbras from the *realpolitik*, materialist new; he is at 'the point where two genres meet'. At this juncture he seems to be a character in a new genre 'where the mysterious rites of pure being are duly performed' – the name of this genre is '*sprezzatura* or aristocratic lassitude'. [Can this be a genre?] Hamlet is 'uniquely displaced or, a precursor of modern Sartrian man, impossibly free'.

These are suggestive, imaginative speculations. Whether they deserve the privileged treatment accorded them by this extraordinary form of publication is open to question.

Emily R. Wilson's *Mocked With Death: Tragic Overliving from Sophocles to Milton* includes discussions of *King Lear* and *Macbeth* though its focus is on the literature of the classical world. By the time of Shakespeare and Milton, part of Wilson's thesis runs, the tragic sense of having lived too long – a 'kind of living death' – is made more unbearable by the possibility of immortality. Between the Greeks and the seventeenth century comes the stern promise of Christianity where what could be a living death stretches into eternity. As a consequence the sense of the living body 'as a burden that can never be cast away is much greater in Shakespeare and Milton than in the classical poets'. Tragic overliving is fundamentally the human condition, Wilson argues; it is not just Shakespeare's and Milton's tragic figures who live too long, it is we ourselves. So Lear's overliving and Macbeth's are both exceptional *and* universal, encouraging in us 'feelings of despair and longing for death that are never completely eliminated'.

The book is at its most powerful, it seems to me, in its discussion of Milton's *Samson Agonistes* and *Paradise Lost*. In the Book of Judges, Samson's end is not as obscure as in Milton. Milton's tragedy is 'all middle'. Only those of its readers who 'suppress all emotions and all questions can avoid the sense of overliving'. Similarly, Adam and Eve end opaquely though '[h]uman despair dominates the last books of the poem' as it dominated Milton after the failure of the republic. Books 11 and 12 'imply that most of the lives of Adam's descendants will entail unmitigated suffering, corruption, and slavery' until the final distant revenge against Satan. Old age will be Struldbruggian; postlapsarian man will feel he has lived too long.

These judgements ring true to me, but I am less certain about Wilson's application of tragic over-living to Shakespeare's two plays. For one thing we're dealing here with works for the public theatre. Characters jostle for our attention; a univocal voice is difficult to hear. Is it true, for instance, – or is it the only truth – that Lear has lived too long? He thinks he has, of course, and so does Kent, but the play as a whole also suggests that he hasn't lived long enough, that Cordelia of course has not lived long enough, and that it is Goneril, Regan and Edmund who have lived too long. From its reason-not-the-need perspective, *King Lear* is as much about the value of old age as it is about the tragedy of it.

Shakespeare and the Classics is a model collection of essays. With a first-rate Introduction by Colin Burrow it covers the Roman and Greek classical worlds, followed by two thoughtful essays on the later reception of Shakespeare's classicism. In '"The English Homer": Shakespeare, Longinus, and English "neo-classicism"' David Hopkins explores the late seventeenth and early eighteenth-century reception of Shakespeare 'in the light of that period's preoccupation with classical literature and literary criticism'. As much as anything else, this essay turns out to be a well argued attack on the notion that Dryden's and Pope's times were the dark ages of Shakespeare criticism. Their misappropriations of him were not for neo-classical reasons but were the result of practical negotiations by men of the theatre responding to contemporary demands. Above all, they dealt with Shakespeare because of his sublimity; they thought of him as the English Homer. Sarah Annes Brown's engaging essay, '"There is no end but addition": the later reception of Shakespeare's classicism', plays with the notion that while what Shakespeare made of the classics was Shakespearian, what we make of them is also at least in part Shakespearian. We read them through him and his take on them. We read them through him anyway, whether or not he's talking specifically about them. Or we read them through him and establish by so doing

our own take on them. And so do other writers. Milton for instance (among many) or T. S. Eliot. Eliot is 'a collagist of flagged fragments'; 'Shakespeare's classicism is reinvented as an Eliotic classicism.'

Colin Burrow's 'Shakespeare and humanistic culture', however, reminds us that the word 'classics' was not recorded before the eighteenth century; it wasn't Shakespeare's word nor was it his way of thinking: 'Shakespeare read, remembered, misremembered and hybridized the works we call the "classics"'. Burrow then goes on to explore how such a way of reading was a product of the Tudor classroom. On a regular basis, Shakespeare and his fellow pupils had to translate out of Latin into English and then back again into Latin. An intimidating and liberating experience which encouraged inadvertently the creative importance of misremembering and mishearing. Shakespeare's education indeed made the 'classics almost invisible in his work'. Almost, but not quite, of course, as most of the essays in this book are at pains to insist. The 'almost' or 'not quite' is given an amusing workout in A. D. Nuttall's 'Action at a Distance: Shakespeare and the Greeks', which argues first that the 'bleak truth' of the matter is that Shakespeare was cut off from Greek poetry and drama, then, in a 'not quite' move on Nuttall's part, goes on to suggest that Shakespeare was such a 'penetrative reader' of English Renaissance Greek translation (Chapman, say) that he had 'a faculty for driving through the available un-Greek transmitting text to whatever lay on the other side'. Because of this extraordinary faculty Shakespeare at times 'out Homers Homer' (without ever having read him in the original); he senses 'Greek forms behind Plautus, Terence and Seneca'. By the end of Nuttall's essay the 'not quite' of Shakespeare's 'Greek eyes' has become something altogether more substantial: maybe, Nuttall concludes – probably tongue-in-cheek – 'Shakespeare did hack his way through some of Homer's Greek.'

We in turn should hack our way through Greek novels, so Stuart Gillespie believes in 'Shakespeare and Greek romance: "Like an old tale still"', for their 'diffuse echoes' were an important element in 'that mackerel-crowded sea of translated, retold, recycled, summarized, excerpted tales that formed a pan-European storehouse for poets and dramatists'. And even Greek tragedy, so Michael Silk proposes in his 'against all odds' essay, 'Shakespeare and Greek tragedy: strange relationship', has 'a real affinity' with Shakespearian tragedy. Echoing Nuttall's action at a distance, the affinity comes 'in the shape of a common inner logic, between the two forms'.

The echoes are not so diffuse, the action not so distant, of course, when it comes to the Latin poets. Shakespeare's favorite poet, Ovid, has three essays devoted to him, the first of which – Vanda Zajko's 'Petruchio is "Kated": *The Taming of the Shrew* and Ovid' – asks two important questions about Ovid in *The Taming of the Shrew* that obviously have a more general application: (1) how do the allusions to Ovid in this play 'add to its interest or enliven our engagement with it?', and (2) what kind of Ovid did Shakespeare create? (The second of these applied more generally is an important concern in this collection.) The answer to both questions is at least partly contained in Zajko's observation that Shakespeare is interested in following Ovid in *Shrew* in order to dramatize 'the dynamics of sexual power in which neither male nor female is automatically in control'. In A. B. Taylor's 'Ovid's myths and the unsmooth course of love in *A Midsummer Night's Dream*', Shakespeare, 'this most gifted and responsive reader of Ovid', rewrites Ovid with the indispensable aid of Arthur Golding's translation of the *Metamorphoses*. Golding strongly echoes Ovid's prefatory moralizing as refracted through his own 'intense and rather narrow Calvinism'. And both writers' moralizing stance fits well with 'the fact that the dramatist is in a conformist mood as he writes his marriage play for the nobility'. The third essay is an interesting one by Heather James called 'Shakespeare's learned heroines in Ovid's schoolroom', which argues that it was Ovid's audacity that attracted Shakespeare and inspired in particular the characterizations of his unconventional comic heroines. They 'reach for their Ovid to think through and resist arbitrary protocols or even laws', as James notes, alerting us to Bianca's bold speech

in *The Taming of the Shrew* and the overall presentation of Portia in *The Merchant of Venice* whose 'bold eloquence makes her a peer of Ovid and Orpheus'.

Virgil, Plautus, Terence and Seneca are the other Roman writers canvassed by this book. Charles Martindale in 'Shakespeare and Virgil' thinks that Shakespeare is not a profoundly Virgilian poet, but that there is something recognizably Virgilian in, say, *Titus Andronicus* with its 'combination of an intense lyrical beauty with extreme violence', and then, of course, there is *The Tempest*. Martindale strikes a familiar note in this collection when he compares Shakespeare's use of Virgil with his classicism generally: it's 'a matter of complex, fragmentary refraction more than a fully organised, head-on response in Jonson's manner'. Wolfgang Riehle, on the other hand, in 'Shakespeare's reception of Plautus reconsidered', thinks that Plautus has as much influence on aspects of Shakespeare as anything in the English native tradition. 'Much of what so far has been attributed to a native English popular and "oral" tradition of performing vitality must now be seen to have been transmitted through a "literary" reception of the printed texts of the Plautine comedies, as they had preserved a very old Italian popular dramatic energy in *written* form.' We can better come to grips with Iago, say, through these texts, and it should no longer be possible to understand *The Comedy of Errors* solely 'in terms of the native medieval and Christian tradition'.

If there is a moral to be gleaned from this year's collection of critical works on Shakespeare it is an extension of Riehle's: namely, the impossibility of understanding anything written by Shakespeare solely in terms of a single, exclusive tradition. To adapt Leggatt's words from the book reviewed at the opening of this article, the books and articles I have discussed have ricocheted against each other, opening up new and disturbing questions which no doubt will be pursued in some form or other in next year's crop of critical work on Shakespeare. And there will be, of course, unanticipated lines of enquiry, all contributing to what E. K. Chambers, talking of the Shakespeare criticism of the late nineteenth century, described as 'a ripe harvest gathered into the barns'.

WORKS REVIEWED

Alexander, Catherine M. S., ed. *Shakespeare and Language* (Cambridge, 2004).

Betteridge, Thomas, *Shakespearean Fantasy and Politics* (Hatfield, Hertfordshire, 2005).

Bonnefoy, Yves, *Shakespeare and the French Poet*, ed. and with an introduction by John Naughton (Chicago and London, 2004).

Cheney, Patrick, *Shakespeare, National Poet-Playwright* (Cambridge, 2004).

Deats, Sara Munson, ed. Antony and Cleopatra: *New Critical Essays* (New York and London, 2005).

Edmondson, Paul and Stanley Wells, *Shakespeare's Sonnets*. Oxford Shakespeare Topics. (Oxford, 2004).

Hadfield, Andrew and Paul Hammond, eds., *Shakespeare and Renaissance Europe*. The Arden Critical Commentaries (2004).

Hopkins, Lisa, *Beginning Shakespeare* (Manchester, 2005).

Husain, Adrian A., *Politics and Genre in* Hamlet (Oxford, 2004).

King, Ros, Cymbeline: *Constructions of Britain* (2005).

Knapp, Jeffrey, *Shakespeare's Tribe: Church, Nation, and Theater in Renaissance England* (Chicago and London, 2002).

Ko, Yu Jin, *Mutability and Division on Shakespeare's Stage* (Newark, NJ, 2004).

Kornstein, Daniel J., *Kill All the Lawyers? Shakespeare's Legal Appeal* (Lincoln and London, 2005).

Leggatt, Alexander, *Shakespeare's Tragedies: Violation and Identity* (Cambridge, 2005).

Line, Jill, *Shakespeare and the Fire of Love* (2004).

Lupton, Julia Reinhardt, *Citizen-Saints: Shakespeare and Political Theology* (Chicago, 2005).

Maley, Willy and Andrew Murphy, eds., *Shakespeare and Scotland* (Manchester, 2004).

Marrapodi, Michele, ed., *Shakespeare, Italy, and Intertexuality* (Manchester and New York, 2004).

Martindale, Charles and A. B. Taylor, eds., *Shakespeare and the Classics* (Cambridge, 2004).

McCrea, Scott, *The Case for Shakespeare: The End of the Authorship Question* (Westport, CT, 2005).

Palfrey, Simon, *Doing Shakespeare*. The Arden Shakespeare (2005).

Parker, Barbara L., *Plato's* Republic and *Shakespeare's Rome: A Political Study of the Roman Works* (Newark, NJ, 2004).

Paster, Gail Kern, *Humoring the Body: Emotions and the Shakespearean Stage* (Chicago and London, 2004).

Paster, Gail Kern, Katherine Rowe and Mary Floyd-Wilson, eds., *Reading the Early Modern Passions: Essays in the Cultural History of Emotion* (Philadelphia, 2004).

Trevor, Douglas, *The Poetics of Melancholy in Early Modern England* (Cambridge, 2004).

Weil, Judith, *Service and Dependency in Shakespeare's Plays* (Cambridge, 2005).

Williams, Deanne, *The French Fetish from Chaucer to Shakespeare* (Cambridge, 2004).

Wilson, Emily R., *Mocked with Death: Tragic Overliving from Sophocles to Milton* (Baltimore and London, 2002).

Wilson, Richard, *Secret Shakespeare: Studies in Theatre, Religion and Resistance* (Manchester, 2004).

Zander, Horst, ed., Julius Caesar: *New Critical Essays* (New York and London, 2005).

2. SHAKESPEARE IN PERFORMANCE
reviewed by EMMA SMITH

Writing in the *Guardian* (13 July 2005) of the Royal Shakespeare's plans for an international line-up of productions as its 'Complete Works' series in 2006, Gary Taylor resists any automatic rejoicing at Shakespeare's geographical reach, observing mordantly that 'Oxfam is an international organization, but so is BP'. Whether an internationalist Shakespeare is the benign partner or the corporate exploiter (yes, I recognize the caveats which should be attached to both these characterizations) is an implicit question within and between a number of books on Shakespearian productions within and without the UK/US. The negative connotations of 'globalization' have taken over in recent years from the saccharine concept of the 'global village': can a worldwide Shakespeare be exonerated from those familiar but necessary charges of cultural imperialism? How far has performed Shakespeare around the globe been, as the marketers would put it, indigenized – and how far is an international McShakespeare merely a global theatrical franchise?

Sonia Massai's collection *World-Wide Shakespeares: Local Appropriations in Film and Performance* is a timely intervention into this contested discussion. Her important, theoretically acute introduction begins with the subheading 'local Shakespeares in a global context', sounding like – and self-conscious about being – the tagline for a multi-national proud of its hegemonic ability superficially to adapt itself to a particular culture. Massai works intelligently with the problematic of interculturalism via Pierre Bourdieu's notion of the 'cultural field', which substitutes for the author 'the sum of critical and creative responses to his work'. Contributors to the volume assess a number of interactions between Shakespeare and local cultures – although largely from the institutional distance of European/American universities, and it begins firmly in the United States. Suzanne Gossett describes the audience's movement, directed by Gower, between seven small stages for the Washington Shakespeare Company's production of *Pericles* in 1998 as a programme note guides them through a historical journey of 1960s American idealism to 1990s disillusionment. She deftly turns her analysis of the production to comment on historicist readings of *Pericles*, the recusant appropriation of the play during a Yorkshire Christmas in 1609–10, and the difficulties of explicitly politicized Shakespearian direction. Her essay concludes with a clever recognition of the relative currency of the essence, spirit or intention of the play in reviews as opposed to much academic criticism. Other essays take on productions which have had little recognition beyond their immediate region: an adaptation of *The Merchant of Venice* in New Mexico which highlighted unexpected contemporary Chicano concerns over crypto-Jews in their community; a challenging Indian *Macbeth* in which Macbeth and Lady Macbeth were played by the same actor and an undifferentiated chorus of actors took on all the other roles; and a Chinese *Romeo and Juliet* that was 'neither traditionally Chinese nor too close to Western cultural influences', in an explicit formulation of the inbetweenness which characterises many of the productions discussed elsewhere. Collectively, the productions offer some insight into different intercultural moments, although sometimes the short essays are burdened with explaining both the context and the productions to an alien readership as the examples flit rapidly around the world.

Thomas Carlyle's famous preference for sacrificing British India over Shakespeare is countered by the title of Poonam Trivedi and Dennis Bartholomeusz's collection *India's Shakespeare: Translation, Interpretation, and Performance*, in which Shakespeare and India are inseparable. Trivedi identifies three strands of post-independence Shakespearian performance: 'conscious universalization', without what Trivedi calls 'Indianization', by which the colonial mastertext is recuperated in Homi Bhabha's influential concept of 'mimickry'; secondly, a Shakespeare assimilated into traditional Indian performance and philosophical contexts; and finally, a playful, deconstructed postcolonial Shakespeare critiqued through rewriting. For the most part, the contributors to the volume are concerned with versions of the second process in what Trivedi calls *desi* or 'folk' Shakespeare, beginning with a mid nineteenth-century Surat adaptation of *The Taming of the Shrew* as 'A Bad Firangi [foreign, non-Indian] Woman Brought to Sense'. Bringing the discussion up to date, Shormishtha Panja discusses 'Oh Shakespeare, thou art translated!' in the National School of Drama's 1997 *Bagro Basant Hai – A Midsummer Night's Dream* – which drew heavily on classical Sanskrit theatre praxis. There is an intriguing photograph from the production of the Indian boy being sung a lullaby by the fairies, but no extended discussion of his role. Panja argues that in fact racial differences were flattened out in this production which gave no space for critique. Ananda Lal discusses another university production, of *The Merchant of Venice*, with a number of roles, including Antonio and Shylock, recast, largely for practical reasons, as female parts. Lal's defence of performance 'gimmicks' – allusions to corruption as 'a way of life in India' and, in the forced conversion of Shylock, to contemporary religious intolerance – is refreshingly honest: 'Shakespeare's texts merely

delivered produce a dreary effect of monotony, elo-
cution, and long speeches that alienate the audience.' Dennis Bartholomeusz's essay on the play in
the Indian theatre begins with Lal's production, and
takes as a synecdoche for the process of indigeniza-
tion Shylock's Islamic kaftan and gold shoes with
turned up Mughal toes.

The model of mixed East–West influences is a
repeated one, creating some suggestive juxtaposi-
tions. Utpal Dutt's significant 1954 Bengali *Macbeth*,
for example, drew on Dutt's classical Shakespearian apprenticeship in Geoffrey *Shakespeare-Wallah*
Kendal's travelling troupe and on the robust, physical *jatra* style of indigenous theatre. B. V. Karanth's
Hindi version of the play as *Barnam Vana* (*Birnam
Wood*) (1979) took on the wood as an image of the
jungle ambition that ensnares Macbeth; the witches
wrapped themselves in the handheld curtain of *yakshagana* performance dividing fair from foul. Laxmi
Chandrashekar discusses another *yakshagana Macbeth*, with a performance style mingling traditional
forms with the rhythms and gestures of Charlie
Chaplin. The Southern Indian form *kathakali* has
been discussed elsewhere: here versions of *Othello* and the different resonances of racial typing
in a region of dark-skinned people with a pan-
theon of deities and demons who are also predominantly black are expertly described. Many of the
essays are conscious of a nineteenth-century history
of Shakespeare in India. Sarottama Majumdar discusses productions in Calcutta from 1775 to 1930,
many under the direct or indirect patronage of the
East India Company. Rajiva Verma's 'Shakespeare
in Hindi Cinema' is revelatory, discussing a number
of adaptations and allusions to *The Comedy of Errors*.
He finds two films which interrogate notions of
cultural authority vested in Shakespeare: *Kaliyattam*
(Jayaraaj, 1998), an adaptation of *Othello*, frustrat-
ingly unavailable on DVD or video, and *Shatranj Ke
Khilari* (Satjayit Ray, 1978) which employs aspects
of the abdication scene from *Richard II*. A number
of Western critics – perhaps sentimentally – have
seen in the non-illusionistic popular native theatrical traditions of India something akin to our ideas of
the Elizabethan stage, suggesting a kind of historical
authenticity about apparently distantly transformed

Shakespearian texts. This enables the return of the
economic metaphor: citing John Russell Brown's
New Sites for Shakespeare in which he sees Asian
theatres as a more fruitful location for Shakespeare's
recuperation than the new Globe, (but apparently
innocent of any allusion to *The Merchant of Venice*,
with or without gold shoes) Trivedi asks: 'may the
loan of Shakespeare to India by England now be
returned with interest?'

Whereas contributors to *India's Shakespeare* are
generally unconcerned with 'fidelity' to the Shakespearian text, for *Shakespeare in Japan* by Tetsuo Kishi and Graham Bradshaw this is a more
pressing criterion. An adaptation of *Julius Caesar* is praised for being 'fundamentally faithful' to
Shakespeare's play; Ninagawa Yukio is chastized
in a comparison with Kurosawa Akira: 'Kurosawa is not flirting with his Japanese material in
the manner of a Ninagawa, and then presenting a
kind of Japanese-Shakespearian cocktail that fails
to take either tradition seriously.' The hyphenated 'Japanese-Shakespearian', the associations of
'cocktail', and the charge of frivolous cultural pick-
and-mix, all resonate in a sober study conscious
of the proprieties of both traditions. In fact, cultural distinctness rather than hybridity seems to
be a keynote of the curious popularity of Shakespeare in Japan: the authors note that Japanese
Shakespeare is 'always foreign', even – especially –
when brought into creative collision with the forms
of Japanese theatrical tradition. Ninagawa is an
interesting and controversial border-crossing figure. Kishi and Bradshaw describe compellingly
his 1980 production of *Macbeth*, conceptualized
as a play-within-a-play set in a Buddhist altar or
Butsudan, covered with cherry blossom, a symbol of ephemerality and using traditional Japanese-
style sliding doors covered with ricepaper. They
observe, wryly, that this production was exported
to England to rave reviews, as was the same
director's *The Tempest*: when, however, Ninagawa
was employed by the Royal Shakespeare Company to direct Nigel Hawthorne in *King Lear*
in 1999, the critics panned it. What particular
orientalist compulsion made reviewers praise the
versions they couldn't understand, and then turn

sneeringly on the English production, is left unstated, but Kishi and Bradshaw are alert to the ways in which Japanese cultural productions for an international audience occupy a mobius strip of prejudice and national stereotypes, shaped by Japanese assumptions of Western assumptions of what is authentically 'Japanese'. Thus, they argue convincingly that the high status of Kurosawa's *Throne of Blood* – and relative neglect of *The Bad Sleep Well* – is due to the unconscious overlaying of the film with non-Japanese assumptions about Shakespeare, about samurai, and about Noh drama.

If the encounter between West and East is at the point of reception in these studies of Asian Shakespeares, in *Othello* this porous and problematic boundary is the theme of the play itself. Julie Hankey has updated her *Shakespeare in Production: Othello* volume for Cambridge University Press's stage history series, and the second edition shows how much has changed in the play's reception since the first, in 1987. At its simplest, *Othello* is a more explicitly politically racialized play than it was, and Desdemona, too, is a more complex figure than previously imagined. Hugh Quarshie's quietly angry 'Second Thoughts about Othello' (1999), in which he argues that black actors should not authenticate Shakespeare's portrayal of blackness by acting the part of Othello, has been highly significant in reactivating questions about colour-blind casting, about blackface and about the new pieties of black actors playing the tragic Moor. Hankey quotes from it alongside productions which experiment with racial casting: the famous 'photo-negative' production in Washington DC with a white Othello amid an otherwise black cast; Charles Marowitz's uneven but provocative *An Othello*, with a black Iago and Othello; two South Africans, Antony Sher and Sello Maake ka Ncube, as Iago and Othello in the most recent RSC production. Although Janet Suzman's production at the Market Theatre, Johannesburg provides a striking cover image, with a bare-chested John Kani, face contorted in agony, bearing the limp body of Desdemona, all white skin and white night-dress and flowing light hair, Hankey has enough to contend with confining her focus to British

or significant US productions. She also includes recent films although not, regrettably, the underrated high school *O*. In the same series, Frances A. Shirley does an excellent job with *Troilus and Cressida*, a play for which critical and theatrical rehabilitation during the twentieth century went hand in hand, with revivals after two centuries of neglect, in England in 1907 and in the United States in 1916. Shirley points out that *Troilus and Cressida* is more of an ensemble piece than many Shakespeare plays, and this usefully allows directorial concept to predominate over individual performances in her analysis. Since the play's stage history is less familiar than many, the introduction is full of surprises. A great photograph of a flapper Coral Browne as Helen in Tyrone Guthrie's 1957 production, sitting on a white grand piano drinking a cocktail, evening gown parted to reveal cross ribboned silk pumps lacing up her legs, conjures up the sleazy decadence and seedy glamour of Shakespeare's Troy. Wars, from Korea and Vietnam to Iraq, feature prominently as graphic intertexts for changing understandings of the play's ironies. For a number of the productions stretching back over four decades, Shirley references her own playgoer's notes.

Although Shirley cites British television versions of *Troilus and Cressida* from 1955 and 1966, as well as Jonathan Miller's version for the BBC Shakespeare in 1981, her history is perforce particularly tied to the stage: Shakespeare's warriors and lovers have escaped the recent spate of big-screen adaptations, with *Troy* (dir. Wolfgang Peterson, 2004) only a distant cousin. For the series *Shakespeare on Screen*, Sarah Hatchuel and Nathalie Vienne-Guerrin have gathered a series of papers on *Richard III*, ranging from silent adaptations in 1911 to Al Pacino's docuadaptation *Looking for Richard* (1996) and Richard Loncraine's fascistic version starring Ian McKellen. As usual the conjunction Shakespeare *and* or *on* or *in* film bridges a sometimes adversarial relation. Dominique Goy-Blanquet argues briskly that 'the first problem [suggesting there are legion] of a film director aiming to disanoint Shakespeare is the text: it is all talk, far more than a film can take, and much of it beyond today's average understanding'. Her argument flips from an attempt to identify what can be done on film that cannot be done onstage to an apologia for the relative freedom of the theatrical experience. Most of the contributions take on a few widely available versions, in particular Jane Howell's BBC Shakespeare television film and those by Olivier and Loncraine. Pacino's film is also prominent, although none of the scholars in a book dedicated 'to the joys of research' directly addresses that text's explicit antagonism towards academics and their analysis: I don't think it's just institutional piety that makes me wince at and for Professor Emrys Jones's sudden and inexplicable bob out of the 'talking head' frame to tie up his shoelace while seated. Mark Thornton Burnett's account of 'Parodying with Richard' takes in some unexpected texts, including *The Goodbye Girl* and *The Street King* in which the play is cited parodically; 'Now is the winter of our discontent', those opening lines already famous in the Cambridge University play *Return from Parnassus* (*c.* 1602) are traced by Mariangela Tempera in *Twin Peaks* and *Being John Malkovitch*. As ever, the discussions after the papers – polite, articulate, self-contained – are exemplary. Hatchuel and Vienne-Guerrin either have a talent for editing these sections or are blessed in their conference delegates, whose humorous ability to interact with the papers without hobbyhorsing is admirable. From this volume I particularly enjoyed the discussion over whether Queen Elizabeth II calls the royal family 'the Firm': reminded by Michael Hattaway that Diana did, Kevin de Ornellas observes that 'what Diana says and what the Queen says are two very different things'. José Ramón Díaz Fernández has done one of his trademark bibliographies – surely he must be in for a medal for this scholarly service? – covering an extensive range of critical responses to the films under discussion.

The discussion format of the *Shakespeare on Screen* volumes is, substantially, the mode of *Shakespeare, Language and the Stage* edited by Lynette Hunter and Peter Lichtenfels for Arden's 'Shakespeare and Language' series. The volume is based on a workshop held at the Globe, designed as an opportunity to break down a so-called 'fifth wall' – an invisible barrier between theatre practitioners and critics. Again, a language of border-crossing is appropriate: should we aim to dissolve this 'fifth wall', or to patrol it more effectively, or to regroove it by agreeing its position? Topics covered ranged from the different meanings each camp attached to apparently shared concepts such as 'character', questions of editing, particularly around the use of stage directions and punctuation, and the broader question of whether our increased critical recognition of the primacy of performance – historically and contemporaneously – should mean that scholarship is authenticated by its use-value in theatrical exploration and production. My own interest in this is clear: I was fortunate to be a participant in these dialogues, and even more fortunate to have Martin White converting staccato email and in-person discussions into a chapter called 'Purposeful Playing? Purposeful Criticism?' (Despite his best efforts, I still sound a bit waspish: arguing that the working model of 'academic' in the discussions tended towards the 'not leading to a decision, unpractical, theoretical, formal or conventional' rather than acknowledging specific professional expertise, and banging on about print as a rival medium for the plays.) My – admittedly schematic – recollection of the discussions is that academics are more interested in, even deferential towards, theatre practitioners than *vice versa* – although Bridget Escolme makes an important disciplinary intervention when she argues for the differently situated academic in an English Literature or in a Drama or a Theatre Studies department. Many of the traditional Eng. Lit. academics seemed to enjoy touching on a different discourse: Margo Hendricks, best known for trenchantly argued and urgent research on racial identities in the Renaissance and now, is here able to work within the physical theatre described by Theatre de Complicite's Annabel Arden radically to dissociate race from the physical body, suggesting that skin colour – in *Titus Andronicus* – might be conceptualized gesturally. It is an important, and complicated, manoeuvre, but an exciting one: reading Lynette Hunter's careful, enabling synthesis of the discussion it is still difficult quite to follow, as if the rhetorical and argumentative patterns are allusive and suggestive, rather than ratiocinatory. I'm described in the editors' endpiece (me, me, me) as 'unmoved' by the arguments: reading the ways in which they have emerged into print – smoothed out in every case by academics, rather than practitioners, so we do have something distinctive to offer the process! – I *am* moved by the commitment of all those involved to listen and to stage their thoughts-in-progress in the particular dramatic form of the joint papers. Hunter and Lichtenfels's visionary book augurs well for this Arden series, instituting provocation rather than overview as one of its signal aims.

Escolme's reflective commentary in *Shakespeare, Language and the Stage* is echoed in her own monograph *Talking to the Audience: Shakespeare, Performance, Self*. Her focus is the ways in which a recent stage history of direct address to the audience from the stage can illuminate or interrogate assumptions about Elizabethan stage practice, and her study begins with a challenge to the method acting assumption of psychological plausibility in Antony Sher's preparations for and performance of Leontes at the RSC. In place of this over-researched modern subjectivity, she argues that the meta-theatrical and self-conscious interaction between character and audience is productive of different kinds of dramatic selfhood – as well as a different, less divided concept of the stage still often bifurcated along Weimann's *locus* and *platea* lines. Using Brecht's notion of 'partial illusion' Escolme's introduction carefully reclaims notions of illusionism alongside a materialist analysis; eschewing sentimental attachment to the figure of the actor, she is good on the shifting personal boundaries between audience member and character, where empathy, recognition, repugnance and bewilderment can fight it out from moment to moment. On *Troilus and Cressida* on the stage she engages with the self-histrionicism built into the play's ironically iterative characterisation by discussing Michael Boyd's production – in which set and concept 'support coherence of character' in a nostalgically Kottian reading of Troilus's tragedy – compared with that of Trevor Nunn at the National Theatre. Further chapters take on *Richard II* and *Hamlet*, with a stimulat-

ing focus on the textual decisions and how these impact on Hamlet's own subjectivity: describing Mark Rylance's performance at the Globe Escolme identifies that 'his is a subjectivity produced in the moment of communication with the audience', echoing Hamlet's own concern with the externalized show of grief in his black clothes. This is a significant book to return to: a real attempt to interrogate theatre praxis alongside sophisticatedly historicized models of subjectivity and a genuine understanding of the willing and willed contracts between performer and playgoer. It's highly recommended as the pick of this year's publications in the field.

Lighter – one is tempted to say, fleet of foot – is John Russell Brown's *Shakespeare Dancing: A Theatrical Study of the Plays*. For Brown, Shakespeare has 'imagined the leading persons of his plays as complete human beings' engaged in the dance of the passions; performance gives body to these personages. His chapters begin by considering comedies and tragedies, and then move on to discuss silence, space, the actor's task, and the evocation of the everyday. The book invokes different performance possibilities rather than specific productions: Brown asks simple but important questions about, for example, Beatrice's 'O God, that I were a man!' – how fast is it? how loud? does she look at Benedick? is she conscious she is in a church? how does it relate to the injunction 'Kill Claudio'? Often the examples are familiar: Gertrude's silence, the parodic play of Pyramus and Thisbe, Macbeth's fatal fight with Macduff, but Brown handles them with wit and affection, and without assuming much prior knowledge other than curiosity. More mechanical in exposition is S. Viswanathan's *Exploring Shakespeare: The Dynamics of Playmaking*, which doesn't quite escape its genesis as a series of articles, although it has some sustained commentary on the inset-play motif and the ways it reflects on Shakespeare's dramatic technique in the play proper. Viswanathan is attentive to the 'wright' in playwright, stressing Shakespeare's technical work as well as more interpretative issues.

If geography has been a more immediate critical axis than history in this year's books, two studies shift that focus. Douglas Bruster and Robert Weimann's *Prologues to Shakespeare's Theatre: Performance and Liminality in Early Modern Drama* sees the performed prologue – as text, performance and actor – as a kind of threshold between the everyday world and that of the play. Here, then, the permeable boundary is representational rather than national or cultural. Bruster and Weimann establish the privileged discourse of prologues as a self-conscious poetics of theatrical art, and discuss their fluctuating popularity through statistical analysis by decade (the majority of extant plays from 1580–9 have prologues; the majority from 1590–9 do not; the proportion of prologues rises steadily during subsequent decades to the 1630s). Shakespeare's *Henry V*, then, employs the form when it is decidedly past its prime, just as he is apparently slow to catch the sonnet boom or the vogue for revenge tragedy. Different chapters consider Marlowe, Peele and Lyly: the final chapter on Shakespeare brings out 'the strange symbiosis of historiography and theatricality in the chorus' to *Henry V* as the rousing speeches are seen to raise epistemological and ontological questions about the nature of stage representation.

Finally, and inexplicably omitted by me last year, is the first volume of Gail Marshall and Adrian Poole's invaluable edited collection *Victorian Shakespeare*, focusing on 'Theatre, Drama and Performance'. The combination of strangeness and recognizability that has structured all my reading for this review is here the encounter with the past. As Victorian practitioners in textual studies and in performance – Macready, Kean, Irving, Furnivall – sought to restore the text of Shakespeare to the stage, so too Shakespeare's redactors were increasingly influenced by European theatrical texts and performers: the metaphor of translation – as Jane Moody points out, always 'at the heart of representation' – has much work to do in the essays collected in the volume. Sara Jan considers Ibsen in London; Inga-Stina Ewbank writes engagingly on the performance of Shakespeare's comedies in continental Europe. Katharine Newey examines the fracas between the Surrey and Coburg theatres over playbills in the early Victorian period, as Shakespeare was apparently co-opted to reformist politics largely for commercial reasons. Dramatic regulation is the subject of Julia Swindells's article on the 1832 Select Committee. She quotes Thomas Morton's representation which argues that the Chorus to *Henry V* is the author's 'command upon his countrymen that his pieces should be produced only in the noblest temples of the Muses'. Lisa Merrill discusses contested forms of masculinity in American performances of *Hamlet* by Edwin Booth and Edwin Forrest; Peter Holland's contribution is on illustration in nineteenth-century Shakespeare editions and its relation to the contemporary stage, arguing that John Gilbert's subtly sympathetic illustrations – he completed a staggering 831 during his career – succeed in 'performing Shakespeare on the page'. The range of Shakespearian emanations discussed in the volume is an extraordinary testament to the forms and contradictions of Arnold's semi-divine Shakespeare in the age of the Victorian crisis of faith.

Moody's own contribution, on immigrant actors including Bernhardt, Salvini and Rossi, interrogates the notion of an English Shakespeare, substituting the nineteenth-century's internationalization of the works, viewed negatively by contemporaries as cultural invasion or usurpation. The idea that Shakespeare has always been in some sense foreign, alien, and that the reception of the plays is inextricably linked with ideas of intercultural exchange, works pleasingly to connect the globalized and the domestic Shakespeare: perhaps it is that fiction of 'home' – variously claimed as Stratford, London, the Elizabethan theatre, historicism, England, the English speaking world – that proves ultimately unnecessary in considering this extravagant and wheeling phenomenon of Shakespeare in performance.

WORKS REVIEWED

Brown, John Russell, *Shakespeare Dancing: A Theatrical Study of the Plays* (Basingstoke, 2005).

Bruster, Douglas and Robert Weimann, *Prologues to Shakespeare's Theatre: Performance and Liminality in Early Modern Drama* (London, 2004).

Escolme, Bridget, *Talking to the Audience: Shakespeare, Performance, Self* (London, 2005).

Hankey, Julie, *Shakespeare in Production: Othello* (2nd edn, Cambridge, 2005).

Hatchuel, Sarah and Nathalie Vienne-Guerrin, eds., *Shakespeare on Screen: Richard III* (Rouen, 2005).

Hunter, Lynette and Peter Lichtenfels, *Shakespeare, Language and the Stage* (London, 2005).

Kishi, Tetsuo and Graham Bradshaw, *Shakespeare in Japan* (London, 2005).

Marshall, Gail and Adrian Poole, eds., *Victorian Shakespeare, Volume 1: Theatre, Drama and Performance* (Basingstoke, 2003).

Massai, Sonia, ed., *World-Wide Shakespeares: Local Appropriations in Film and Performance* (London, 2005).

Shirley, Frances A., *Shakespeare in Production: Troilus and Cressida* (Cambridge, 2005).

Trivedi, Poonam and Dennis Bartholomeusz, eds., *India's Shakespeare: Translation, Interpretation, and Performance* (Newark, 2005).

Viswanathan, S., *Exploring Shakespeare: The Dynamics of Playmaking* (New Delhi, 2005).

3. EDITIONS AND TEXTUAL STUDIES
reviewed by ERIC RASMUSSEN

EDITIONS

Nearly two decades ago, Gary Taylor concluded the revolutionary Oxford Shakespeare on a note of philosophic calm: 'with our own task now behind us', he wrote, speaking for himself and his colleagues, 'we look forward to our future obsolescence'.[1] The publication this year of a second edition, however, suggests that the editors are not yet ready to go gentle into that good night.

The Oxford Shakespeare *Complete Works* (1986) was an undisputed landmark in Shakespearian editing. It may rank as the best-selling edition in history, having sold somewhere in the neighbourhood of 600,000 copies to date, and it was certainly the most influential edition of the twentieth century. Although some of the Oxford innovations never got much traction – no subsequent edition of *Henry IV* has featured 'Sir John Oldcastle', nor have the alternative titles *The First Part of the Contention* or *Richard Duke of York* been embraced by any later edition of *King Henry VI Parts 2 and 3* (not even those in the Oxford single-play series) – the decision to include both Quarto and Folio *Lear* was of major significance, inspiring numerous two-text editions of that play and launching discussions of version-based editing that have reshaped every branch of editorial theory and practice.

But if the Oxford Shakespeare was once a youthful iconoclast, it has now become a middle-aged member of the establishment. Whereas the rhetorical insistence upon groundbreaking uniqueness may have been appropriate in the first edition, that same rhetoric now seems out of place. A new 'User's Guide' to the second edition claims that 'because this edition represents a radical rethinking of the text, it departs from tradition more than most' and lists among its 'most radical departures' the abandonment of 'the tradition of conflation'. It goes on to assert that 'most drastically, we present separately edited texts of both authoritative early editions of *King Lear*'. Obviously, the radical break occurred twenty years ago when the tradition of conflation came to an end and the Oxford Shakespeare ushered in a period of version-based editing. In the late 1990s, however, important conflated editions of two-text plays began to reappear, such as R. A. Foakes's Arden3 *Lear* (1997). More tellingly, the decision to re-conflate *Lear* for the *Norton Shakespeare* (1997), despite the fact that it was supposed to be 'based upon the Oxford edition', must have irritated the Oxford editors. Although they may be implicitly reasserting the status of the *Lear* texts as separate-but-equal in the face of this growing return to conflation, the focus on their original radicalism neglects the potentially more interesting topic of the recursive impact that the

---

With thanks to my editor of twenty years, Arthur Evenchik.
[1] *William Shakespeare: A Textual Companion* (Oxford, 1987), p. 62.

second edition may have on the editorial tradition that has evolved since the publication of the first.

Published on the heels of the publicity surrounding Taylor's attribution of 'Shall I Die?', the first edition was at the vanguard of canon expansion, and the second edition continues this trend by including a new category of texts: plays in which Shakespeare may have contributed a scene or two. The full text of *Sir Thomas More* is now included, rather than just Shakespeare's scenes, as well as the full *Edward III*. Although *Edward III* has featured in other recent editions of Shakespeare, this is the first collected works to include the complete *Sir Thomas More*. (Given the two decades' lapse between the first and second editions, Oxford never found itself in the position of David Bevington's *Complete Works of Shakespeare*, which, having added the supposedly Shakespearian 'A Funeral Elegy for Master William Peter' to its fourth edition [1997], had to remove it from the fifth [2003] after Brian Vickers established that the poem is Ford's.)

Although the act/scene/line numbers of the first edition have been preserved to facilitate citation references, this is truly a new edition, not simply a reprint: Stanley Wells's pithy introductions to each play as well as the general introduction have been revised;[2] errors in the text have been corrected (although at least one mistake that was pointed out in a prominent review many years ago remains);[3] David Crystal has contributed a new essay on 'The Language of Shakespeare' that should prove extremely useful for students; a new alphabetical list of contents makes the second edition easier to navigate for those unfamiliar with the chronological order in which the plays appear.

Critics have long assailed the Oxford Shakespeare for its lack of commentary notes, and the second edition does nothing to fill this void. Curiously, though, the absence of notes turns out to be a selling-point for students in the UK, where some institutions allow texts to be brought into exams provided that they have no scholarly glosses. The fact that the Oxford *Textual Companion* (1987) was not published at the same time as the first edition was a source of frustration for some early

users – and history has repeated itself with the second edition: neither *Edward III* nor *Sir Thomas More* has any textual notes. I understand that the possibility of bringing out a revised edition of the *Textual Companion* has been discussed. But this idea may be scuttled, since textual notes will sooner or later be available in the critical editions of both plays that the editors plan to publish (*Edward III*, edited by William Montgomery and Gary Taylor, in the Oxford Shakespeare series; *Sir Thomas More*, edited by John Jowett, in the Arden3 series).

Given the Oxford editors' proclivity for incorporating new emendations into their edited texts, the lack of textual notes at present creates a bit of a problem for readers, especially those who acquire the second edition specifically because it contains these new texts. One of my doctoral students collated the Oxford *Edward III* against the 1596 Quarto and found two dozen departures from the Quarto that had not been anticipated in any previous edition.[4] The most puzzling of these is at 2.155,

---

[2] The general introduction may have been 'revised in the light of current scholarship' (as the dust-jacket blurb claims) but it continues to identify the Peacham manuscript as a 'contemporary drawing of a scene from a Shakespeare play, illustrating *Titus Andronicus*', with no acknowledgement of the recent scholarly debate over whether the Peacham drawing may in fact depict a sequence from *Eine sehr klagliche Tragaedia von Tito Andronico und der hoffertigen Kayserin* (*A Very Lamentable Tragedy of Titus Andronicus and the Haughty Empress*), a play performed in Germany by English actors which survives, in German, in a volume published in Leipzig in 1620. See June Schlueter, 'Rereading the Peacham Drawing', *Shakespeare Quarterly*, 50 (1999), 171–84; see also Richard Levin, 'The Longleat Manuscript and *Titus Andronicus*', *Shakespeare Quarterly*, 53 (2002), 323–40.

[3] In 1987, David Bevington observed that 'the persons of the play' list for *The True Tragedy of Richard Duke of York* 'assigns several participants to the wrong side in the Wars of the Roses' ('Determining the Indeterminate: The Oxford Shakespeare', *Shakespeare Quarterly*, 38 [1987], 15–16). And yet Lord Stafford – who is clearly on the Yorkist side throughout (see 4.1.127) – still unaccountably appears among those 'of the King's party' in the *dramatis personae* of the second edition.

[4] 'King Phillip' for 'Phillip' (1.6), 'coz' for 'Cosin' (2.84), 'corruptuois stied' for 'corruptions side' (2.155), 'rude' for 'red' (2.182), 'stains' for 'shames' (2.247), 'good my' for 'my'

where Q's 'To spring from ordure, and corruptions side' is rendered 'To spring from ordure and corruptious stied'. In the absence of textual notes, it is impossible to tell whether this is a typographical error or an intentional emendation, so I wrote to ask Bill Montgomery, who graciously supplied me with a draft of his collations. It turns out that 'corruptious' is just a mistake – a typo in which an apparently overturned 'n' splendidly links twenty-first-century printers' devils with those of Shakespeare's time – whereas 'stied' is an emendation, which is (or will be) supported by a note resembling this draft (in which the lemma reads 'stide'):

2.155 stide] *This edition (GT)*; side Q. For the Q reading to be meaningful, *side* must be taken to correspond with *OED* n1, sb.I.1.b: 'Used with reference to generation or birth'. GT's attractive conjecture assumes the substitution of a common word ('side') for a rare one ('stide') where *stied* corresponds to *sty* v1 = 'rise up, ascend' and/or *sty* v2 = 'to confine to or as in a sty' with the concomitant association of a sty with filth.

This elegant defence of the emended reading is, of course, exactly the sort of information that serious students need as they work their way through an edited text. As we await the appearance of textual notes for *Edward III*, in whatever form, it may be useful for readers to know that, 'corruptious' aside, all of the other readings listed in footnote 4 are intentional emendations, some of them inspired, and all unique to the Oxford text.

John Jowett, who would get my vote as one of the greatest living Shakespearian editors, has produced a characteristically first-rate text of *Sir Thomas More* (the only slip I noticed is 'ye' for 'you' at 6.21). In order to give readers a sense of what the introduction rightly characterizes as 'probably the untidiest, most heavily revised dramatic manuscript of the period', Jowett devised some special features of presentation: rules across columns to indicate where the text switches from the original to the revised version, or from one revision to another;

notes in the right margin to specify the section of the manuscript and to identify the hand; a special typeface to highlight annotations in a second hand; and underlining to flag passages marked for deletion in the manuscript. With this extraordinary system, worked out in exacting detail, Jowett's innovative text will no doubt be enormously valuable to students attempting to find their way through the Byzantine complexities of the *Sir Thomas More* manuscript – but it may be somewhat intimidating for more casual readers. A colleague of mine likens Jowett's text to Marshall McLuhan's *Gutenberg Galaxy*, in which the dizzying array of type fonts and highlighting was intended to be daunting and provocative. The analogy is not perfect, because Jowett's intent is to clarify rather than to obfuscate. Yet a reader who finds that eighty-five per cent of the lines in the first scene are underlined (because marked for deletion in the manuscript) may well be put off by the strange look of the page and decide not to persevere.

The current interest in Shakespeare-as-collaborator can be traced back, in large part, to the Oxford first edition, which argued for the collaborative authorship of several plays. The second edition's title-page for *Sir Thomas More* – 'By Anthony Munday and Henry Chettle, with revisions and additions by Thomas Dekker, William Shakespeare and Thomas Heywood' – makes it abundantly clear that we are no longer solely interested in the isolated author. The introduction maintains that Shakespeare's contribution to the play 'shows him as a thoroughgoing professional sharing with colleagues whose work he respected in an essentially collaborative enterprise'. A congenial picture of Shakespeare brainstorming at a table

---

(2.417), 'o'er' for 'on' (2.432), 'Their' for 'Thy' (3.142), 'missed' for 'met' (6.10), 'fell by violence' for 'by violence fell' (8.12), 'him' for 'himselfe' (11.17), a line for the Second Herald to speak, 'I go', that does not appear in Q (12.101), 'pedant ensigns' for 'pendant' (12.26), 'enchased' for 'in choice' (12.136), 'follow it' for 'feare' (12.144), 'indifferent still' for 'indifferent' (12.163), 'utterance' for 'enterance' (13.40), 'thy' for 'the' (13.110, 13.123, 18.193), 'particoloured' for 'pretie-colored' (14.15), and 'and there' for 'and' (18.139). I am grateful to Trey Jansen for assembling this list.

with his fellow dramatists, however, is not really the one that emerges from reading Shakespeare's additional scene in context. As many critics have pointed out, Shakespeare was apparently unaware of the details of both the original version of *Sir Thomas More* and of the revisions made by his collaborators. Indeed, as Taylor observes in the *Textual Companion*, Shakespeare's contribution 'differs from all the others in the degree to which it ignores or contradicts the intentions of the larger work' (p. 461). Shakespeare, like many overcommitted professionals, seems to have 'phoned it in' – supplying a few new passages for a play that he didn't know or care much about – and it may be a mistake to represent his participation in the process as an interactive collaboration.

But no matter how we view the joint venture of Munday, Chettle, Dekker, Shakespeare and Heywood, we have many reasons, and the publication of the second edition now provides the occasion, to celebrate the collaboration of Wells, Taylor, Montgomery and Jowett.

Claire McEachern, whose reputation rests on her work as a literary and cultural critic, was invited to prepare the Arden3 edition of *Much Ado About Nothing* even though she'd had limited experience in textual editing. Anyone who assumes (or secretly hopes) that talented critics will prove to be lousy editors must be humbled by McEachern's achievement. Her text is superb, its sole flaw being an omitted apostrophe (for 'three words conference' read 'three words' conference' at 2.1.247–8); the only errors of substance in the textual notes are confined to a single line (there ought to be a collation note for the emendation of Q's 'about' to 'a bout' at 4.2.28, and the added stage direction in that line is not unique to '*this edn*' but should be credited to Bevington). The other slips in the notes are trivial,[5] and the few errors that creep into the narrative sections of the edition do relatively little harm.[6]

The critical introduction is predictably smart and engaging, exactly the sort of essay one would recommend to students. McEachern is especially good at tracing the arc of the play's dynamic movement (in which Benedick 'goes from being the most articulate source of the play's misogyny to a chivalric defender of woman's honour') and elucidating the inherent pleasure in this structure: 'the fun of this play is the way in which [Benedick and Beatrice] shake off these conventions of misogynist and shrew, and reveal them in the process as inadequate descriptions of human conduct'. There's a rich discussion of 'cuckoldry' from etymological, historical, and cultural perspectives that builds toward an analysis of the 'structural cuckolding' of Beatrice and Benedick, whose 'superior wit' inflames their friends' 'desire to turn them into the butts of others' wits, and so rob them of their preening immunity to the bestial foolery of love'. McEachern calls attention to elements of the play's organic unity, noting how appropriate it is that 'the villain of a play concerned with sexual fidelity is an actual bastard'. She sees the layered action of the multiple plots as 'part of an ongoing enquiry into what constitutes a human being', and notes that 'it may be no coincidence that the word "man" and its cognates occur more frequently, by a substantial margin, in *Much Ado* than in any other work of Shakespeare's'. (One might also suggest that a loose acrostic of '*MAN*' is formed by the first letter of each word in the play's title.)

In a discussion of the play's famous 'ghost' characters, McEachern explains that 'characters are named in entry directions who not only never speak in the scene in question but never appear in the play at all'. I assume that what she means is 'do not appear elsewhere in the play', since, by virtue of having an entrance direction, such characters as

---

[5] In the textual notes, for '*Borachio*' read '*Borachio*' (2.1.192.1), for '*exit.*' read '*exit*' (2.2.52 SD), for '*exit*' read '*exit.*' (2.3.7 SD), for '*Prince*' read '*prince*' (2.3.34.1), for '*45*' read '*40*' (2.3.43.2), for '*and*' read 'And' (2.3.80), for '*Conr.* Masters' read '*Conr* Masters' (3.3.167–8), for 'scene v' read '*SCENE V*' (3.5.0), for '*(exit)*' read '*(exit*' (3.5.52), for 'signior' read 'Signior' (5.1.244, 247).

[6] There's a stray colon after 'humor.:' and 'Com' for 'com' in the quotation from the Stationers' Register on page 126; the 'r' in 'mr' should be superscripted in the quotation on p. 127, and the Greg reference should be '16' rather than '274'; Leonard Digges's dedicatory poem is not in 'the Second Folio' (p. 109) – it appears in Benson's 1640 edition of the *Poems*.

Leonato's wife '*Innogen*' (who enters at 1.1 and 2.1) and '*a kinsman*' (who also enters at 2.1) do, in fact, appear in the play. Given the excellent section of the introduction devoted to early modern notions of the ideal woman – under the rubric '*Chaste, silent and obedient*' – it's surprising that McEachern chooses to delete Innogen, whose silent presence onstage, like that of the silent mother in Bandello's novella, could be said to powerfully represent all of these 'virtues'.

Illustrations in editions of Shakespeare can often seem gratuitous, so McEachern deserves special acknowledgement for putting together a series of illustrations that actually makes a point. Specifically, three eighteenth-century representations of 4.1 (Claudio's repudiation of Hero in the church scene) 'demonstrate an increasing focus upon Leonato's experience'. In the frontispiece to Rowe's edition (1709), Leonato is not differentiated among the group of courtiers; in a later engraving by Jean Pierre Simon of a painting by William Hamilton (1790), Leonato is foregrounded, at the left; in an engraving by Edward Francis Burney (1791), a clearly distraught Leonato occupies a central place in the composition's pyramidal form.

The textual analysis is this edition's weakest link. With its explanations of elementary terms ('Quarto refers to the format of a book made of sheets folded twice . . . a Folio is a book made from sheets folded once') and its statements of the obvious ('at the printer's workshop, it would have been set into type by hand'), this section may strike many Arden readers as unnecessarily dumbed down. Worse still, McEachern relies upon outdated, and largely discredited, textual studies. Quoting Charlton Hinman's introduction to his 1971 facsimile edition of Q1 *Much Ado*, McEachern asserts that the work of Valentine Simmes's Compositor A, who was solely responsible for setting the Quarto, is 'not obviously corrupt, even when it does not follow its original'. She seems unaware of the two subsequent articles by Alan Craven that seriously undermined Hinman's view of Compositor A.[7] As Charles Forker observes in his Arden3 *Richard II*, 'contrary to the assumption of most earlier scholars, evidence from *Richard II* and other plays in which A is believed

to have had a major hand seems to show that this compositor was much given to making substantive alterations of his copy-text' (p. 537). In setting the Q2 *Richard II* reprint, for instance, Compositor A introduced an astonishing 155 substantive changes, including 'smoke' for 'shocke', 'how to compare' for 'how I may compare', and 'the rest of the reuolted' for 'al the rest reuolted'. We also know of at least two instances in which A deliberately omitted lines of text from a Quarto in order to save space. Given the recent work revealing 'the alarming extent of A's general unreliability' (Forker), McEachern's assurance that any departures in Q *Much Ado* from its manuscript copy are 'in all likelihood mainly at the level of insignificant detail' is neither informed nor reassuring.

In a field of critical editions that tend to reprocess existing scholarship without contributing anything new, the originality of Martin Butler's New Cambridge *Cymbeline* is thrice welcome. It is *de rigueur* for editions of this play to begin with Simon Forman's account of the performance he saw in 1611, but Butler provides a fresh transcription of Forman's manuscript and corrects a number of inaccuracies in previously published versions. Butler's is the first edition in history to print the ghosts' verses in 5.3 not as short tetrameters and trimeters but as the fourteeners that metrically they are. Most significantly, Butler's introductory essay, which easily ranks as one of the most astute political readings of *Cymbeline* in recent memory, finely elucidates the play's allegorical relevance in the early years of James's reign. James was hailed as the new Brute of the newly named (by Parliament in 1604) 'Britannia', who would combine the kingdoms of England and Scotland and 'recover the island's ancient geographic identity'. Brute's wife was Innogen, so 'the fact that Shakespeare named his heroine after the mother of the British people makes the attack on her chastity all the more clearly an issue of nationhood'. Then again, Butler

---

7 See Alan E. Craven, 'Simmes' Compositor A and Five Shakespeare Quartos', *Studies in Bibliography*, 26 (1973), 37–60, and 'The Reliability of Simmes's Compositor A', *Studies in Bibliography*, 32 (1979), 186–97.

observes that Shakespeare may be challenging the Brutan myth by having Belarius rename Guiderius as 'Polydore' – a possible allusion to Polydore Vergil, the early Tudor historian who had cast doubt on the Brutus story. Appropriately cautious about analyses that 'telescope the course of future history back into 1610' and 'ignore the sedimented and incomplete union that James's "Britain" was', Butler highlights the fault lines, manifest in *Cymbeline*, between the rhetoric and reality of 'Britain', especially the issue of whether or not Wales is part of Britain in the world of the play.

Butler's reading of the play's perplexing ending, in which Cymbeline resubmits Britain to Rome, is keenly insightful: 'The war is not totally pointless, for though Britain loses autonomy, she remains unconquered . . . Cymbeline's control of the ending and Philarmonus's gloss on it suggest that Britain is the nation to which Rome's historic role will pass, the ultimate beneficiary of the Augustan legacy'. The resolution, then, 'suggests a new account of nationhood, a myth of origin that locates Britain in a chain of political paternity descending to Cymbeline from Augustus and Jupiter'.

That the text of the play in this edition is letter-perfect comes as no surprise: Butler is known to be an extraordinarily meticulous editor. In his capacity as one of the general editors of the forthcoming *Cambridge Works of Ben Jonson*, Butler spotted numerous errors in the text that I had prepared for that edition – a text that I had (hubristically) thought was flawless – for which I am very much in his debt. It appears, however, that Butler's *Cymbeline* may not have received the same level of detailed oversight from the general editors of the New Cambridge Shakespeare. A careful reading reveals a number of errors in the introduction, textual notes, commentary, and stage directions, and one can only regret that these were not caught before publication.

(1) There are several transcriptional inaccuracies in the textual notes and some errors of omission.[8] Moreover, there's a curious shift in the formatting of collations: whereas the first three acts follow the standard practice of quoting parenthet-

ically the exact spelling and case of the F reading (e.g., 1.1.30, 1.1.116, 1.4.21, 1.5.78, 1.6.0, 1.6.61, 2.3.115, 3.1.20, 3.1.35, 3.3.33, 3.4.146, 3.5.69, 3.6.74, 3.7.14), in the final two acts nearly every note of this kind accidentally italicizes the F reading.[9]

(2) There's a slip in the commentary note at 1.4.59 (for 'Malone's insertion of "not" has been generally accepted' read 'Malone's insertion of "but" has been generally accepted'); similarly, in a reference to the same emendation on page 265, for 'I could [not] but believe' read 'I could not [but] believe'.

(3) Ralph Crane did not prepare the copy for 'the first five plays printed in the Shakespeare Folio' (p. 257) – no one has suggested that Crane had anything to do with *The Comedy of Errors*.

(4) The claim that the emendation of F's 'O happy *Leonatus* I may say' to 'O happy Leonatus! I may say' (1.6.156) is unique to '*this edn*' is incorrect.

---

[8] For '*Filorio's*' read '*Filorio's*' (1.1.97), for 'folly' read 'Folly' (1.1.158.1), need to note the lineation change from F's 'Signior . . . it. / Pray . . . 'em' (1.4.140), for 'Think' read 'Thinke' (1.5.85), for 'trust.' read '*trust.*' (1.6.25), for 'numbered' read 'number'd' (1.6.36), need to note the lineation change from F's 'Continues . . . Lord? / His . . . you?' (1.6.56), for 'Leonatus' read '*Leonatus*' (1.6.156), for 'husband' read 'Husband' (2.1.55), for 'make.' read 'make!' (2.1.56 lemma), the citation '2.2.60' should read '2.2.0', for 'then.' read 'then:' (2.2.3), for 'conceited' read 'conceyted' (2.3.14), for 'Music' read '*Music*' (2.3.16), for 'sings' read '*Sings*' (2.3.17), for '149' read '148' (2.4.149), for 'legion' read 'Legion' (2.4.18), for '*Scene*' read '*Scena*' (3.1 heading), for 'and your . . . loue' read '*and your . . . Loue*' (3.2.47–8), for 'us' read 'vs' (3.5.32), for 'Exit' read '*Exit*' (4.2.168), for 'from the cave' read '*from the cave*' (4.2.194.0), for 'Begin.' read 'begin.' (4.2.256), for 'inuries:' read 'iniuries:' (5.3.124–56), need to record the F reading 'operare' (5.4.197), and for 'leo-natus' read '*leo-natus*' (5.4.443).

[9] For '*imperseuerant*' read 'imperseuerant' (4.1.11), for '*Mountainers*' read 'Mountainers' (4.2.71), for '*Companie's*' read 'Companie's' (4.2.100), for '*reake*' read 'reake' (4.2.153), for '*ingenuous*' read 'ingenuous' (4.2.185), for '*easilest*' read 'easilest' (4.2.205), for '*Raddocke*' read 'Raddocke' (4.2.223), for '*wracke*' read 'wracke' (4.2.365), for '*betide*' read 'betide' (4.3.40), for '*geeke*' read 'geeke' (5.3.144), for '*Prunes*' read 'Prunes' (5.3.182), for '*cloyes*' read 'cloyes' (5.3.182), for '*crak'd*' read 'crak'd' (5.4.177), for '*troth*' read 'troth' (5.4.274), and for '*one's*' read 'one's' (5.4.311).

Arden 2, Oxford *Complete Works*, Riverside (and others?) all punctuate the line with an exclamation point following 'Leonatus'. Similarly, I wonder whether the stage direction at 2.4.118, '*Taking back the ring*', is not wrongly identified as unique to '*this edn*'. It's substantially the same as Oxford's '*He takes his ring again*' and Bevington's '*He takes back the ring*'. Is a slight variation in wording sufficient to justify a claim of uniqueness?

(5) Two things are amiss in the collation at 1.4.37: 'not] *Rowe (Durfey)*; not in F'. The word 'not' occurs twice in line 37 ('if I offend not to say it is mended – my quarrel was not altogether') and it's not clear which one is the emended reading. More importantly, a user would assume that F reads 'not in', but this is not the case (as it were): the 'not in' should be italicized, since 'not' was *omitted in* F. Similarly, in the collation at 3.4.94 SD for 'not in' read '*not in*'.

(6) The assertion on page 266 that 'only one' of the Folio press variants is substantive – 'riuete' corrected to 'riueted' (2.2.43) – overlooks the variant at TLN 1482 (3.2.14): 'to go do od seruice' (uncorrected); 'to do good seruice' (corrected).

(7) There's some confusion about the provenance of 'Imogen' in the textual history of the play. Page 36 asserts that 'Folio's "Imogen" is a scribal misreading of an unfamiliar name' – implying that the error originated with Crane, or another scribe, during the copying from a previous manuscript. But page 77 suggests another agent: 'probably *Cym.*'s compositor could not disentangle the minims in his copy and made a guess at an unfamiliar name'. The singular here ('compositor') is a slip, I take it, since two compositors worked on Folio *Cymbeline*. How likely is it that both compositors would have made the same error?

(8) The assertion that Compositor E 'was not usually allowed to handle manuscript copy' (p. 254) and 'was trusted only to set up text from print-copy' until, 'toward the end of the volume, with *Ant.* and *Cym.*, he handled scribal copy' (p. 265) may need to be modified. After all, E seems to have set signature Gg3 of *Timon*, for which the copy was holograph manuscript; he set *Hamlet* pp5 and prob-

ably pp6, also from manuscript; and he set *Othello* ss3v–ss6, tt1–tt3, vv1–vv3, from scribal copy.

(9) Errors of typography include a stray bracket at 5.4.267, accidentally italicized brackets at 3.3.0, non-italicized stage directions at 2.3.48, 3.5.0, and 3.5.41, and roman rather than italic semicolons in the collations for 2.3.104, 2.4.116, 3.3.23, 3.4.88, and 3.4.100.

Among the emerging genre of 'updated editions' in the New Cambridge Shakespeare series, David Bevington's *Anthony and Cleopatra* (1990; 2005) is an exemplary model. The introduction has been seamlessly extended to give an account of recent criticism, in which Bevington devotes a solid paragraph to each of fifteen noteworthy books and articles, and significant performances since 1990. As I've noted in past reviews, updated editions can be pastiches of new material by new editors grafted onto, or even replacing, existing introductions – sometimes weirdly preceded by the original editor's preface but without prefatory words from the new editor; even when the original editor has done the updating (as in Andrew Gurr's *Richard II* and Ann Thompson's *Shrew*), there's often not a new preface. It's a minor detail, to be sure, but the fact that Bevington's preface has been enlarged to acknowledge those who assisted in preparing the update helps to give his edition a sense of unity that has been lacking in some of the previous updated editions.

TEXTUAL STUDIES

A new collection on *Printing and Parenting in Early Modern England*, edited by Douglas A. Brooks, reprints important articles by Margreta de Grazia, Katharine Eisaman Maus, and Ann Thompson and John O. Thompson, and includes some stimulating new work exploring the connections between textual reproduction and procreation. For my money, however, the most interesting essays are those that go off-topic. Stephen Orgel, for example, offers a splendidly illustrated tour of Lady Anne Clifford's heavily annotated copy of *A Mirror for Magistrates*, in which the marginalia are not only in Clifford's hand but also in those of her secretary and one other person to whom she apparently dictated *bon mots* that she wished to have recorded as she read through the book. Orgel finely observes that 'the personae throughout the book shade into each other as Clifford's sense of herself incorporates her servants, and as they ventriloquize her voice'.

Laurie E. Maguire provides a fascinating tribute to Alice Walker, whose contribution is often largely ignored in histories of twentieth-century editing. In an essay that argues, *à la Henry V*, for 'an alternative genealogy' – one that 'comes from McKerrow and that involves the female line' – Walker emerges as a strong figure with the courage of her convictions: she was one of the few contemporaries who dared to criticize Greg, and she requested that Peter Alexander and John Dover Wilson be excluded from the editorial advisory board of the Oxford Shakespeare. Although Walker signed on to edit the Old-Spelling Shakespeare for Oxford University Press, she subsequently developed a distinct preference for modernized spelling, and Maguire attributes Walker's inability to complete the project 'to a loss of belief in what she was doing'. For Maguire, Walker's readable prose style, rich in metaphor, was the precursor of the 'textual rhetoric' employed by Gary Taylor and others. She sees this engaging style as one of the primary reasons for 'the widespread interest in textual studies today', and argues that this may be Walker's most lasting legacy.

The colour plates that accompany Bianca F. C. Calabresi's study of early rubricated printing remind us what is often lost in textual reproduction by xerox, microfilm, and EEBO. Calabresi argues persuasively for the thematic significance of colour, as when she associates the red ink used on the title-page of Dekker's *The Whore of Babylon* (1607) with a line from the text ('We must the surgeon play, and let out blood'): 'If the red ink is read as blood, the bleeding of the body politic then issues forth on the title page.' However, there's at least one extant copy of the 1607 Quarto with the title printed throughout in black, leaving one to wonder if early publishers envisioned two different markets of readers for the play, one that would be attracted by a 'bleeding' title-page and one that might not.

E. A. J. Honigmann has been refining our understanding of Shakespeare's methods of composition for over forty years. His new essay in *The Review of English Studies* focuses on the playwright's 'habit of not deleting cancelled passages'. Honigmann observes that 'when Hand D in *Sir Thomas More* got into a tangle and tried to extricate himself, he left several false starts undeleted'. He suggests that Hemminges and Condell's famous assertion that 'wee haue scarse receiued from him a blot in his papers' may have been literally true: they may have 'misjudged the number of "blots" in the plays because Shakespeare did not always cross out rejected passages'. Honigmann concludes that an awareness of Shakespeare's tendency not to delete cancelled lines 'must affect the balance of probability' when editors are evaluating possible 'undeleted cancellations' in printed texts.

Richard Proudfoot's '"Is there more toyle?": Editing Shakespeare for the Twenty-First Century' offers quite a good overview of the current editorial scene and helpfully suggests specific directions for future work, calling for the full collation of all extant copies of the First Folio and for more detailed attention to the paper used in printing the early texts of Shakespeare's plays. Proudfoot wryly notes that editing Shakespeare can be likened to painting the bridge that spans the estuary of the river Forth north of Edinburgh, the bridge 'which reputedly takes so long to repaint that the job must start again at one end as soon as it is finished at the other'.

In a recent item in *Notes and Queries*, Kathryn Dent points out that whereas Claudius enters '*with two or three*' at the opening of 4.3 in Q2 *Hamlet*, he enters alone in F and thus delivers his eleven-line speech as a soliloquy; she goes on to observe that since Q2's 'Gentleman' does not appear in the F version of 4.5, if Horatio exits to get Ophelia, then Gertrude has a short soliloquy before they re-enter (4.5.17–20), her only one in the play. William Lloyd argues that anomalous stage directions (lacking 'and' or 'with') and similar contractions in Q1 *Richard II* and Q1 *1 Henry IV* perhaps indicate that the same scribe may have produced the manuscript copy behind both texts.

Finally, Edward Pechter's oddly titled 'What's wrong with literature?' in *Textual Practice* is a withering critique of the foundational argument behind much recent textual scholarship and editorial practice. Pechter targets what he terms 'the new theatricalists' – among whom he includes Kathleen O. Irace, Stephen Miller, Scott McMillin, William Carroll, Andrew Gurr, G. B. Shand and Giorgio Melchiori (though it is doubtful these scholars would claim any such affiliation) – all of whom argue, in one form or another, that although a 'bad' (or 'short' or 'early') Quarto may not have the formal complexities of great literature, it should be valued for its immediacy and power as a theatrical text. Pechter has no patience for this 'incoherent and vacuous critical practice', which, he maintains, 'reduces the literary to fancy words and the theatrical to the short, sharp shock of an uninterrupted through line'. In an article much given to wild and whirling words, Pechter concludes powerfully that Shakespearians 'seem to be abandoning *en masse* the long and rich tradition of aesthetic interest, generated out of a sense of interpretative complexity and depth, with which both literature and theatre have until recently been identified'.

WORKS REVIEWED

Brooks, Douglas A., ed., *Printing and Parenting in Early Modern England*, Ashgate's Women and Gender in the Early Modern World Series (Aldershot, 2005).

Calabresi, Bianca F. C., '"Red Incke": Reading the Bleeding on the Early Modern Page', in Brooks, *Printing and Parenting*, pp. 237–66.

de Grazia, Margreta, 'Imprints: Shakespeare, Gutenberg, and Descartes', in Brooks, *Printing and Parenting*, pp. 29–58.

Dent, Kathryn, 'Reading Stage Directions in the Fourth Act of the Second Quarto and First Folio Versions of *Hamlet*', *Notes and Queries*, n.s. 50 (2003), 414–16.

Honigmann, E. A. J., 'Shakespeare's Deletions and False Starts', *Review of English Studies* 56 (2005), 37–48.

Lloyd, William, 'Scribal Copy for Q1 *Richard II*?', *Notes and Queries*, n.s. 51 (2004), 280–3.

Maguire, Laurie E., 'How Many Children Had Alice Walker', in Brooks, *Printing and Parenting*, pp. 327–50.

Maus, Katharine Eisaman, 'A Womb of his Own: Male Renaissance Poets in the Female Body', in Brooks, *Printing and Parenting*, pp. 89–108.

Orgel, Stephen, 'Marginal Maternity: Reading Lady Anne Clifford's *A Mirror for Magistrates*', in Brooks, *Printing and Parenting*, pp. 267–90.

Pechter, Edward, 'What's Wrong with Literature?', *Textual Practice*, 17 (2003), 505–26.

Proudfoot, Richard, '"Is there more toyle?": Editing Shakespeare for the Twenty-First Century', *Shakespeare Studies (Japan)*, 42 (2004), 1–27.

Shakespeare, William, *Antony and Cleopatra*, ed. David Bevington, updated edition, New Cambridge Shakespeare (Cambridge, 2005).

The Complete Works, gen. eds. Stanley Wells and Gary Taylor, ed. John Jowett, William Montgomery, Gary Taylor, and Stanley Wells, second edition, Oxford Shakespeare (Oxford, 2005).

Cymbeline, ed. Martin Butler, New Cambridge Shakespeare (Cambridge, 2005).

Much Ado About Nothing, ed. Claire McEachern, Arden 3 (London, 2006).

Thompson, Ann and John O. Thompson, 'Meaning, "Seeing", Printing', in Brooks, *Printing and Parenting*, pp. 59–88.

INDEX

No book titles or play titles, other than Shakespeare's and anonymous works, are included in this index, but the names of the authors are given. Book titles in review articles are listed, alphabetically by author, at the end of each section.

INDEX

INDEX

INDEX

Malone, Edmond, 30–1, 32n58, 49,
    56–7n20, 57n21, 60, 88, 108, 110,
    111n14, 112n20, 114n28, 114,
    115, 119, 120, 123, 127, 128, 129,
    130, 132–3, 134, 199–200, 214,
    270, 356, 380
Maloney, Michael, 339
Malory, Sir Thomas, 265
Maltby, Judith, 258n10, 265–6n30
Mannion, Tom, 330, 339
Marchitello, Howard, 61n30
Marcus, Leah, 9n37, 17n72, 21
Mariana, Juan de, 250
Marienstras, Richard, 65n6
Mark, Thomas Raymond, 126n9
Marlowe, Christopher, 2, 71, 75, 94, 97,
    98, 184–5, 219, 352, 355
Marotti, Arthur, 118
Marowitz, Charles, 339, 371
Marquez, John, 303
Marrapodi, Michele, 361, 362, 368
Marshall, Gail, 374, 375
Marshall, Herbert, 211
Marston, Cathy, 345
Marston, John, 71, 72, 73, 75, 77, 213,
    214, 216, 219–20, 221–3
Martin, Peter, 30, 30n46, 124n1
Martindale, Charles, 225n1, 366–7,
    368
Martindale, M., 225n1
Martineau, Shereen, 345
Marx, Karl, 150n15, 364
Mason, John, 74
Mason, Patrick, 314–16
Mason, Rev., 122n54
Massai, Sonia, 369, 375
Masson, Forbes, 300, 314
Masten, Jeffrey, 5n16, 213n5, 214n6, 218,
    219n24
Matar, Nabil, 361
Matus, Michael, 303
Maunder, Raymond, 211n58
Maus, Katharine Eisaman, 296, 381,
    383
Maxwell, J. C., 2n5
Mbatha-Raw, Gugu, 327–8
Mears, Michael, 345
Mebane, John, 252n96
Meckler, Nancy, 300–1
Mehl, Dieter, 41
Melchiori, Giorgio, 36, 70, 78, 194n7,
    383
Mendelssohn, Felix , 304
Mendes, Sam, 186
Merchant, W. Moelwyn, 130, 131
Meredith, Ifan, 344
Merrill, Lisa, 374
Messina, Maria Grazia, 130n41,
    131
Methodius, Pseudo-, 241
Meyer, Ann R., 15n65

Meyer, Melinda, 295
Michelet, Jules, 263n24
Middleton, Thomas, 5, 27, 71, 72, 73, 75,
    76, 77, 77n12, 184, 204–6,
    208–10, 213, 214, 217, 220, 222
Miles, Ben, 321, 322–3
Miles, Kate, 340
Milgate, W., 277n31, 278n33
Miller, Jonathan, 198, 371
Miller, Sienna, 311
Miller, Stephen, 383
Mills, David, 247n66
Milns, William, 116
Milton, John, 94, 281, 350, 351, 352,
    365–6
Mimmack, Peter, 340, 342
Miola, Robert S., 250n81, 361
Miskimin, Alice, 259n11
Mitchell, Laurence, 346
Mitchenson, Joe, 211n58
Moloney, Conor, 341
Mommsen, Theodor, 262n20
Mommsen, Tycho, 6
Montaigne, Michel Eyquem de, 257,
    361
Montgomery, William, 69n1, 376–7, 378,
    383
Moodie, Tanya, 343
Moody, Jane, 374
Moore, Harry Thornton, 67–8
Moore, John C., 262–3n22
Moran, Chris, 346
Morgan, Appleton, 157n3
Morgan, Susan, 85
Morosini, Adèle Rossetti, , 103
Morrell, Geoff, 205
Morris, Siwan, 345
Morton, Thomas, 374
Moseley, Humphrey, 23–6, 27
Mottram, Caitlin, 307
Moulton, R. G., 140
Mowat, Barbara, 18, 20, 30n46, 31n53,
    37n87, 51, 89n34, 124n1
Moxon, Joseph, 13
Muir, Kenneth, 41, 42, 44, 47
Munby, Jonathan, 299, 301–4
Munday, Anthony, 5, 71, 72, 74, 77, 78,
    78n15, 377
Murphy, Andrew, 2n4, 51n5, 124n1, 124,
    125, 128, 134, 148n4, 149n6,
    149n7, 151n20, 154n34, 360–1,
    368
Murray, Braham, 330
Murray, Jacob, 327–8

Nagarajan, S., 41
Nashe, Thomas, 1, 2, 42, 356
Nathoo, Azeem, 345
Naughton, John, 363–4, 368
Naylor, Ben, 339
Needham, Paul, 114n27

Neill, Michael, 23n15, 37n87, 48
Nennius, 241
Neville, Sir Thomas, 24n20
New York Herald Tribune, 67
Newey, Katharine, 374
Newth, Jonathan, 312
Newton, Isaac, 228
Nicholas of Cusa, 228, 229
Nichols, John Bowyer, 126, 127, 129
Nicoll, Allardyce, 44
Nietzsche, Friedrich Wilhelm, 35
Ninagawa Yukio, 298, 339, 370–1
Nixon, David, 342
Noonan, Stephen, 333
Normington, John, 340
Northcote, James, 131n47, 132
Nosworthy, J. M., 44
Notary, Julian, 244n38, 246n58
Nunn, Trevor, 190–1, 300, 320–3, 338–9,
    373
Nuttall, A. D., 366

O'Callaghan, Richard, 207
O'Malley, John W., 250n81
O'Reilly, Genevieve, 321
O'Rourke, Josie, 307–10
Oakley, Lucy, 130, 130n36, 130n39,
    130n40, 131n42, 131n45
Oldroyd, William, 340
Oliver, Gary, 339
Oliver, Harold, 47
Olivier, Laurence, 372
Ong, Walter J., 32n57, 91
Opie, John, 131n47, 132
Orchard, Andy, 240n7
Orgel, Stephen, 36, 38n87, 81, 85, 89,
    104n18, 108, 212n63, 362, 381–2,
    383
Orosius, 240, 263
Osborne, Laurie, 62, 199, 204
Ossian, 109–10, 112
Ovid, 249, 355, 356, 367

Pacino, Al, 371, 372
Palfrey, Simon, 349–50
Palmer, Scott, 343
Panja, Shormishtha, 369
Park, Clare, 334
Parker, Barbara L., 362–3, 368
Parker, G. F., 124n1
Paroissien, H. F., 42
Parolin, Peter A., 354
Paster, Gail Kern, 350, 351, 368
Pater, Walter, 264
Patterson, W. B., 250n81, 252n94
Paul, St., 237, 246n53, 352
Pechter, Edward, 32n58, 32n61,
    383
Peckham, Morse, 27n32
Peele, George, 5, 73
Pendleton, Thomas, 161n17

390

INDEX

INDEX